WORLD STUDIES
THIRD EDITION

Dennis Bollinger

bju press®

Greenville, South Carolina

Note: The fact that materials produced by other publishers may be referred to in this volume does not constitute an endorsement of the content or theological position of materials produced by such publishers. Any references and ancillary materials are listed as an aid to the student or the teacher and in an attempt to maintain the accepted academic standards of the publishing industry.

WORLD STUDIES Teacher's Edition
THIRD EDITION

Dennis Bollinger, PhD

Editors
Manda Kalagayan
Grace Zockoll

Bible Integration
Brian Collins
Bryan Smith, PhD

Consultant
Dennis Peterson

Cover Design
Drew Fields
Craig Oesterling

Book Design
Drew Fields

Page Layout
Ealia Padreganda

Project Manager
Dan Berger

Permissions
Sylvia Gass
Holly Nelson
Joyce Landis
Sarah Martin

Photograph credits appear on pages 395–98.

CD-ROM installation instructions are on the last page of this volume.
Produced in cooperation with the Bob Jones University Division of Social Science of the College of Arts and Science.

© 2011 BJU Press
Greenville, South Carolina 29614

First Edition © 1985 BJU Press
Second Edition © 1998, 2000 BJU Press

ISBN: 978-1-59166-977-7 (Teacher's Edition with CD-ROM)

15 14 13 12 11 10 9 8 7 6 5 4 3 2

Activity Icons

Suggested activities are given immediately after the materials list in each chapter. Many of these activities are labeled with icons to help the teacher identify the type of activity without necessarily reading the entire description. If an activity does not have an icon, it is most likely a suggested discussion topic.

The icons are as follows:

 CD

 Bible

 Guest Speaker

 Map

 Video

 Web Site

About National Standards

The five units in the third edition of *World Studies* generally follow the nine eras listed in *National Standards for World History*. More information about how the standards are integrated into the textbook can be found at the end of this volume.

Chapter openers offer a glimpse of major events with a photo or painting and timeline. In addition, the chapter outline lists the major topics that will be covered.

Lessons and Scheduling

The third-edition student text has been completely revised. Therefore, we recommend that you read each chapter before beginning lesson plans.

Each chapter has two to five sections that divide the information into convenient reading assignments. You can combine sections into a single day's lesson or divide them into two or more days, as indicated in the Lesson Plan Chart at the beginning of each chapter. Your students' abilities and interests will determine how you schedule the lessons. The estimated times on the Lesson Plan Chart are only suggestions.

How many chapters should I cover in the first semester?

Most teachers find it convenient to end a semester with a unit break. A natural break occurs at the end of Unit 3 after Chapter 11 (Empires of Eurasia: 1300–1900).

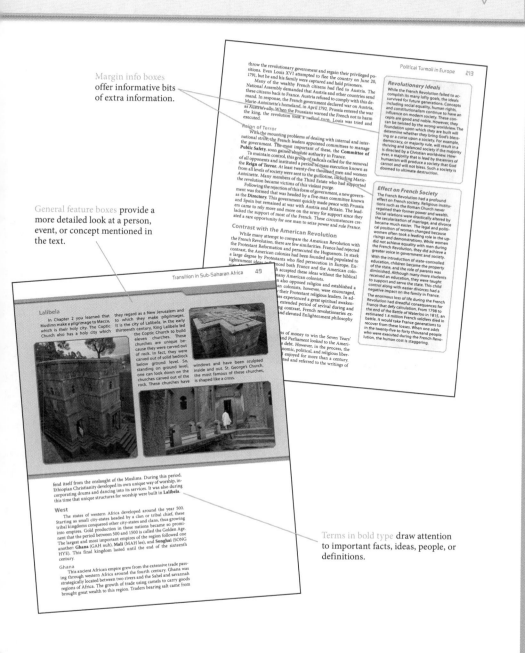

Margin info boxes offer informative bits of extra information.

General feature boxes provide a more detailed look at a person, event, or concept mentioned in the text.

Terms in bold type draw attention to important facts, ideas, people, or definitions.

To the Teacher

The Teacher's Edition of *World Studies* provides a convenient format with suggested teaching schedules, chapter and section objectives, supplemental notes, suggested activities, resources, possible Web links, and answers to review questions. Objectives and annotations are located in the side margins of the Teacher's Edition; activities, suggestions, Web links, and answers are found in the bottom margin.

There are many ways in which a teacher can evaluate students' understanding and mastery of the material taught. For this course, you may use either the prepared tests that are available from BJU Press or build your own tests using the Test Builder program, also available from BJU Press. Whichever test preparation method you use, ensure that you adapt the tests to both the specific needs and abilities of your students and the material that you emphasized in your teaching. Do not fall into the habit of giving only two or three types of questions on all of your tests and quizzes. Rather, vary both your testing methods and question types. In this way, if a student has difficulty understanding and answering a particular type of question, he or she will still have an opportunity to do better on other types of test items. Choose from matching, essay, true/false, multiple choice, and short answer questions.

This Teacher's Edition has been designed to assist the teacher in preparing to teach world studies. It is not a substitute for teacher preparation but a supplement of teaching methods, ideas, and information. Likewise, this manual

How many days do I spend on a chapter?

Once you have skimmed the teacher's edition and determined your end goal for the semester, look at your school calendar and note how many actual teaching days are available. Most chapters will require seven to nine days, which includes a day for review and a day for testing. You can take more or less time per chapter as long as you balance the days to meet your semester goal.

SIDE MARGIN NOTES

Goals and Objectives

The first information in the side margin of a chapter is the student goals for the entire chapter. Those general goals are what you want your students to achieve while studying the chapter. Read them carefully to get an overview of the chapter.

Section Objectives

Each section has specific objectives. They are important facts and principles that your students should learn while studying that section. Those objectives are suggestions. You may make changes to the objectives list as necessary to meet the specific needs of your students.

is not a complete and final authority; it contains only a sample and partial list of suggested sources, methods, background information, and review techniques. It is the teacher's responsibility to select and develop those items that best meet the needs of the students.

Homeschool Ideas

The flexibility inherent in the homeschool schedule allows parents and students to focus on specific topics. Consequently, the home schooling parent will be able to use most of the suggested activities. As much as possible, allow your students to pursue those topics that interest them.

Web Links

Web links are available at www.bjupress.com/resources. Use information from these sites to enhance your lectures and activities. Links have been carefully selected from reputable sites. However, be sure to carefully evaluate all material—especially literature—before you present it to your students or allow them to read from online resources. Also, be aware that links to some sites may become outdated, though efforts are made to keep them updated.

Teacher's Toolkit CD

The CD icon refers to the Teacher's Toolkit CD packaged with this Teacher's Edition. This CD includes photos, maps, and other resources to enhance your lectures and activities.

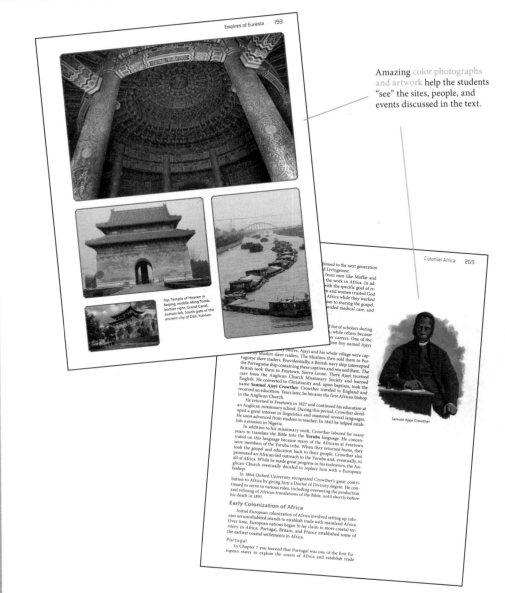

Amazing color photographs and artwork help the students "see" the sites, people, and events discussed in the text.

Additional Information

Information provided in the side margins corresponds to information in the nearby text. It is for the teacher's information and can be shared with the students as the teacher deems fit. Such information is designed for enrichment or further explanation but is not meant to be included in the testing.

BOTTOM MARGIN NOTES

Lesson Plan Chart

As was mentioned, a lesson plan chart is featured at the beginning of every chapter to aid the teacher in scheduling lessons. It is only a *suggested* plan and will vary depending on the teacher's style of teaching, the number of class activities included, and any extracurricular activities that might be included on the school calendar. The chart includes the title of each chapter and section, the main activity in each section, the pages covered by each section, and the suggested time frame for teaching. The time frame includes a day for review and a day for testing.

The Chapter Review asks students to think in terms of higher learning, including understanding, analyzing, evaluating, and creating.

Maps help the students visualize geographic locations.

Section quizzes help the students remember what they have learned so far. In addition, a critical thinking question challenges the students to combine details and demonstrate higher thinking skills.

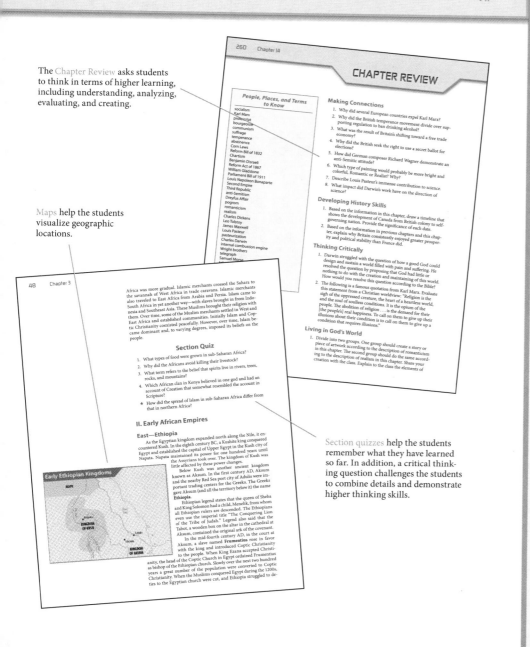

Materials List

Also at the beginning of each chapters is a list of materials for the suggested activities in that section. If you do not have access to certain materials, you might choose to skip those activities or design substitute activities.

Section Review Answers

At the end of each section are the answers to the review questions and the starred question. The starred question is designed to challenge students to engage in critical thinking about that section.

Chapter Review Answers

At the end of each chapter are the answers to the chapter review questions. The "Making Connections" questions are intended to ensure that the students understand the content of the chapter. The "Developing History Skills" questions are designed to develop the students' ability to analyze aspects of the chapter. The "Thinking Critically" questions are intended to help students evaluate elements of the chapter. The "Living in God's World" questions challenge students to respond creatively to the information in the chapter.

PRONUNCIATION GUIDE

Vowels			
symbol	example	symbol	example
a	cat = KAT	aw	all = AWL
a-e	cape = KAPE	o	potion = PO shun
ay	paint = PAYNT	oa	don't = DOANT
e	jet = JET	o-e	groan = GRONE
eh	spend = SPEHND	oh	own = OHN
ee	fiend = FEEND	u	some = SUM
i	swim = SWIM	uh	abet = uh BET
ih	pity = PIH tee	oo	crew = CROO
eye	icy = EYE see	oo	push = POOSH
i-e	might = MITE	ou	loud = LOUD
ah	cot = KAHT	oy	toil = TOYL
ar	car = KAR		

Consonants			
symbol	example	symbol	example
k	cat = KAT	th	thin = THIN
g	get = GET	th	then = THEN
j	gentle = JEN tul	zh	fusion = FYOO zhun

The pronunciation key used in this text is designed to give the reader a self-evident, acceptable pronunciation for a word as he reads it from the page. For more accurate pronunciations, the reader should consult a good dictionary.

Stress: Syllables with primary stress appear in LARGE CAPITAL letters. Syllables with secondary stress and one-syllable words appear in SMALL CAPITAL letters. Unstressed syllables appear in lowercase letters. Where two or more words appear together, hyphens separate the syllables within each word. For example, the pronunciation of Omar Khayyam appears as (OH-mar kie-YAHM).

Project Ideas

As you look through the teacher's edition, you might want to note the suggested student research projects in your planning. Such projects give students an opportunity to use the information they are learning throughout the year. It also gives them an opportunity to demonstrate and develop their creative skills. Ideas include the following:

- Biographical reports
- Papers
- Maps
- Photo collages
- Oral presentations

Give the students a check sheet detailing the requirements of each assignment so that they will have every opportunity for success on their project.

CONTENTS

Objectives for the Book

By the end of the year, students should be able to

1. Explain why humans build cities and trace how cities have changed through the course of history.

2. Trace the growth of Christianity and assess its impact on the cultures of the world.

3. Assess the role of other religions in human cultures, especially Islam, and evaluate each religion studied.

4. Analyze and evaluate how different cultures have viewed the importance of freedom, equality, justice, and citizenship.

5. Analyze the development of trade and explain its impact on human culture and economic growth.

6. Compare and evaluate various economic systems.

7. Explain what roles Christians may play in a global society.

World Studies Lesson Plan Overview

Day(s)	Topic	Pages	Support Materials	Bible Integration
Chapter 1: Turning Points in World History: Creation–476				
1–3	The Beginnings of the Human Race	3–10	Activity 1: The *Epic of Gilgamesh* CD Material	Creation The Fall The Flood Sin's continuation after the Flood Confusion at the Tower of Babel
4–5	The History of Israel	11–14	Activity 3: Comparing Covenants	Abrahamic Covenant Mosaic Covenant Davidic Covenant
6–8	The Coming of the Christ	14–21	Activity 4: *The City of God* CD Material	Coming of Christ "in the fullness of time" Death, burial, and resurrection of Christ The growth and spread of the church Constantine and the church Christian involvement in society
9	Chapter Review		Activity 6: Chapter Review	
10	Chapter Test			
Chapter 2: The Rise of Islam: 622–800				
1–2	The Origin of Islam	25–32	Activity 1: Do Christians and Muslims Worship the Same God? CD Material	Islam and the Trinity Islam and the deity of Christ Islam and salvation Islam and the Bible
3	The Spread of Islam	32–34	Activity 3: Map Study: Expansion of Islam	
4–5	The Culture of Islam	34–36	Activity 4: Abbassid Contributions to Culture CD Material	
6	The Confrontation with Islam	36–38	Activity 5: Chapter Review	
7	Chapter Review			
8	Chapter Test			
Chapter 3: Transition in Sub-Saharan Africa: 1000–1600				
1–2	African Culture	43–48	Activity 1: The Barozvi Creation Narrative CD Material	Creation stories
3	Early African Empires	48–53	Activity 2: The Yoruba Creation Narrative CD Material	Spread of Coptic Christianity to Ethiopia and its role in checking the spread of Islam Creation Mandate: growth of cities The camel—evidence of God's design
4	Growth of Trade in East Africa	53–55	Activity 3: Map Study: Africa CD Material	Creation Mandate: growth of cities
5	Chapter Review		Activity 4: Chapter Review	
6	Chapter Test			

Day(s)	Topic	Pages	Support Materials	Bible Integration
Chapter 4: The Expansion of Asian Cultures: 1000–1600				
1–2	Growth of Cities and Commerce in China	59–65	Activity 1: Marco Polo's Journals CD Material	Creation Mandate: growth of cities Nestorian Christianity spreads across China Chinese religions contrasted with Christianity
3–4	Developments in Japan and Southeast Asia	65–67	Activity 2: Matching Exercise: Japan and Southeast Asia CD Material	
5–6	Rise of the Mongol Empire	67–73	Activity 3: Mongol Invasion of Japan CD Material	Nestorian Christianity and the rise of Islam Mongol religion Limited religious tolerance Persecution of Christianity
7	Chapter Review		Activity 4: Chapter Review	
8			Chapter Test	
Chapter 5: Emergence of European Culture: 500–1300				
1–2	Interval Between the Fall of Rome and Rise of Feudalism	77–82	Activity 1: *The Anglo-Saxon Chronicle* CD Material	Growth of papal power Violation of the Creation Mandate: forbidding priests to marry Christianizing of Europe
3	Decline of Feudalism and Development of States in Europe	82–86	Discussion Activity: Legal Legacy CD Material	
4–5	Expansion of Europe	86–89	Discussion Activity: A Modern-Day Crusade? CD Material	Creation Mandate: growth of cities and nations Decline of political power of the Roman Catholic Church Crusades and the Reformation
6–7	Development of Culture in Europe	89–92	Activity 2: *The Canterbury Tales* CD Material	Christian themes in art
8	Calamities in Europe	92–94	Activity 4: Chapter Review	
9	Chapter Review			
10			Chapter Test	
Chapter 6: Renaissance and Reformation: 1300–1650				
1–2	The Renaissance	97–104	Activity 1: *Utopia* CD Material	Rulers (Romans 13:1–4) Tools of the Reformation—printing press, vernacular literature, and ancient Bible manuscripts
3–4	Discontent with the Church of Rome	104–8	Activity 3: "Why Monks are Shunned"	Development of Roman Catholic doctrine The Inquisition Indulgences
5–6	The Reformation	108–14	Activity 4: Luther's Ninety–five Theses	Forerunners of the Reformation Reformers Results of the Reformation Huguenots
7	Chapter Review		Activity 5: Chapter Review	
8			Chapter Test	

Day(s)	Topic	Pages	Support Materials	Bible Integration
Chapter 7: Age of European Exploration: 1450–1600				
1–2	Native American Civilizations	119–25	Activity 1: Map Study: Indian Civilizations CD Material	Indian religions Indian civilizations and the Creation Mandate
3–4	Origins of European Exploration	125–28	Activity 3: Christopher Columbus	Spreading the gospel through exploration
5–6	Growth of European Exploration	128–32	Discussion Activity: Montezuma	
7–8	Consequences of European Exploration	133–34	Activity 4: Bartolomé de Las Casas	
9	Chapter Review		Activity 5: Chapter Review	
10			Chapter Test	
Chapter 8: Europe Colonizes the Americas: 1600–1800				
1–2	Colonization of Latin America	137–45	Activity 1: Map Study: South America CD Material	John Calvin and missions in South America
3–4	Colonization of North America	145–48	Activity 2: Map Study: Early American Colonization CD Material	Religion and education Pilgrims and Puritans
5–6	Struggle for Independence	148–52	Activity 4: Simón Bolívar CD Material	
7	Chapter Review		Activity 5: Chapter Review	
8			Chapter Test	
Chapter 9: Transformations in European Culture: 1500–1800				
1	The Rising Power of European States	155–59	Activity 1: The English Bill of Rights CD Material	
2–3	The Scientific Revolution	159–65	Activity 2: Galileo's Observations CD Material	Reformation legacy Robert Boyle Attempts to undermine Christianity with science
4–5	The Enlightenment	166–68	Activity 3: Matching Exercise	The Enlightenment's assault on Christianity Corruption of Christianity in culture
6	Chapter Review		Activity 4: Chapter Review	
7			Chapter Test	
Chapter 10: Oceania and Australia: 1600–1900				
1	The Islands of Oceania	171–75	Activity 1: John G. Paton CD Material	Creation Mandate: first inhabitants John Paton and James Chalmers
2	Early European Exploration	175–77	Map Activity: Oceania	
3–4	European Exploration in the 1700s	178–79	Activity 3: James Cook's Journal	The myth of the "noble savage"
5–6	European Settlement in Australia	180–85	Activity 4: Chapter Review CD Material	
7	Chapter Review			
8			Chapter Test	

Day(s)	Topic	Pages	Support Materials	Bible Integration
Chapter 11: Empires of Eurasia: 1300–1900				
1–2	China's Ming and Manchu Dynasties	189–96	Activity 1: Map Study: Ming China CD Material	
3–4	Ottoman Empire	196–99	Discussion Activity: Religious Freedom CD Material	Limited and temporary religious freedom
5	Safavid Empire	200–201	Activity 4: Map Study: Asia Minor CD Material	
6	Mughal Empire	201–03	Activity 5: Chapter Review CD Material	
7	Chapter Review			
8	Chapter Test			
Chapter 12: Political Turmoil in Europe: 1776–1850				
1–2	French Revolution	209–14	Activity 1: Matching Exercise: The Three Estates of France CD Material	Huguenots Contrast: The French Revolution and the American Revolution Reformation heritage
3	Rise and Fall of Napoleon	215–16	Activity 2: The Battle of Waterloo CD Material	Positive and negative aspects of nationalism
4	Revolts Across Europe	216–18	Activity 3: Map Study: Europe	
5–6	German and Italian Unification	218–21	Activity 4: Chapter Review CD Material	
7	Chapter Review			
8	Chapter Test			
Chapter 13: Industrial and Social Revolution: 1700–1900				
1–2	Laying the Foundation for Industry	225–32	Activity 1: Edison, the Inventor CD Material	
3–4	Expansion of Industry and Rise of Social Reform	232–36	Activity 3: "Thoughts upon Slavery"—John Wesley	Rise of the Methodist movement in Britain George Whitefield and the Great Awakening
5–6	End of the Slave Trade	236–40	Activity 4: Letter from John Wesley to William Wilberforce CD Material	William Wilberforce and slavery Jonathan Edwards
7	Chapter Review		Activity 6: Chapter Review	
8	Chapter Test			
Chapter 14: Reform in Western Culture: 1848–1914				
1–3	Reform and Radical Movements	243–49	Activity 1: The Dreyfus Affair CD Material	Karl Marx and religion Temperance movement
4–5	Changes in Culture and Education	249–51	Activity 2: *Hard Times*	
6–7	Progress in Science and Technology	251–55	Activity 3: Charles Darwin	James C. Maxwell Christianity and evolution
8	Changes in Latin America and Canada	255–59	Activity 4: Chapter Review CD Material	
9	Chapter Review			
10	Chapter Test			

Day(s)	Topic	Pages	Support Materials	Bible Integration
Chapter 15: Colonial Africa: 1750–1950				
1–3	Transition from Trading Partner to Possession	263–70	Activity 1: David Livingstone CD Material	Fante Confederation David Livingstone Robert Moffat Samuel Ajayi Crowther
4–5	Partitioning of Africa for Imperialism	270–75	Activity 2: *Through the Dark Continent* CD Material	Missionary activity during colonialism
6	Consequences of Imperialism	276–79	Activity 3: Abuses of Colonialism	
7	Chapter Review		Activity 4: Chapter Review	
8			Chapter Test	
Chapter 16: Spread of Imperialism: 1750–1914				
1	Decline of the Ottoman Empire	283–86	Activity 1: Slaughter of the Armenians CD Material	
2	Changes in Russia	286–90	Discussion Activity: Anarchy	Orthodoxy, autocracy, and nationality in light of Scripture
3–4	Domination of India by Britain	290–93	Activity 2: The Sepoy Mutiny CD Material	Consequences of British rule (for missions)
5–6	Domination of Asia	293–300	Activity 3: The Goforths and the Boxer Rebellion CD Material	The Goforths Missions in the Far East
7–8	Modernization in Meiji Japan	300–301	Activity 4: Perry's Expedition to Japan	
9	Chapter Review		Activity 6: Chapter Review	
10			Chapter Test	
Chapter 17: War, Instability, and Depression: 1914–39				
1	Prelude to World War I	307–10	Activity 1: Alvin York and His Struggle with War	Faith in science and technology
2–3	Course of the War	311–16	Activity 3: World War I Review	
4–5	Instability Following the War	316–21	Discussion Activity: Dictators	Dictators and religion
6	Developments in Science and Art	322–24	Discussion Activity: Media	Disillusionment
7–8	The Great Depression	325–26	Activity 4: "The Only Thing We Have to Fear . . ."	
9	Chapter Review		Activity 5: Chapter Review	
10			Chapter Test	

Day(s)	Topic	Pages	Support Materials	Bible Integration
Chapter 18: World War II: 1939–45				
1–2	Causes of the War	329–35	Activity 1: The Bombing of Rotterdam CD Material	
3–4	Course of the War	335–41	Activity 2: Churchill's Inspiring Words CD Material	Miracle at Dunkirk
5–6	Consequences of the War	341–45	Activity 4: Chapter Review	Consequences of the war Growth of Christianity during and following the war
7	Chapter Review			
8			Chapter Test	
Chapter 19: The Cold War: 1945–91				
1–2	Postwar Reconstruction	349–52	Activity 1: UN Charter	
3–4	Development of the Cold War	353–59	Activity 2: "Ich Bin Ein Berliner . . ." CD Material	
5–6	Transition in the Third World and Middle East	359–63	Discussion Activity: African Independence CD Material	
7–8	Collapse of the Soviet Union	363–67	Activity 4: "Tear Down This Wall!" CD Material	New opportunities for Christians: worship, evangelism, missionary outreach
9	Chapter Review		Activity 5: Chapter Review	
10			Chapter Test	
Chapter 20: The Global Community: 1945–Present				
1–2	Environmental Trends	371–76	Activity 1: European Union CD Material	The Christian and climate change Energy resources from the Creator
3	Global Economy	376–78	Discussion Activity: Product Safety	New opportunities for evangelism through the global economy
4	Technology and Culture	378–80	Activity 2: Stem Cell Research	Christians and technology
5–6	Political and Religious Trends	380–84	Activity 3: Chapter Review CD Material	Growth of Islam and the spread of Christianity Persecution of Christianity
7	Chapter Review			
8			Chapter Test	

Foundations Creation–800

For the Christian, history doesn't begin with a bang. It begins with God laying a foundation when He "created the heavens and the earth." Upon this foundation, God created the human race and all that was required to sustain it. God appointed mankind to build upon His foundation in many ways, including family, civilization, and government.

Following God's judgment of Adam and Eve's sin, God also laid a foundation for salvation in the promise that the Messiah would defeat Satan. God built upon that foundation through the birth and protection of the nation of Israel.

At just the right time, God sent His Son, who fulfilled the Old Testament promises by His virgin birth, sinless life, death on the cross, and resurrection. The risen Christ founded the church and continues to build a living church to the present. During the first three centuries, the church endured the wrath of Rome and triumphed. However, by the seventh century, doctrinal corruption had entered the church in many local assemblies.

During the seventh century, in the deserts of Saudi Arabia, Muhammad founded a new religion that combined elements of existing religions. He rejected polytheism and declared that only Allah should be worshiped. Muhammad united the Arab tribes and conquered Saudi Arabia. His successors quickly conquered lands to the north in the Middle East, to the west across northern Africa, and to the east as far as India.

Islamic forces seemed invincible until the Muslim armies entering France were defeated by a European force in AD 732. Muslim rulers briefly turned from building an empire to building a great culture.

The foundations for Christianity and Islam were laid, and these two religious forces have influenced almost every culture to the present.

Chapter Goals

Students should be able to

1. Explain how the biblical presentation of Creation, the Fall, and God's plan for redeeming this world affects one's view of human culture and civilization.

2. Trace the significant events in the history of Israel and assess the importance of Israel for understanding world history.

3. Defend the incarnation of Christ as the turning point in history and analyze the early development of the Christian church.

4. Evaluate the consequences of the alliance of church and state under Constantine and his successors.

Creation–AD 500

	Birth of Abraham c. 2166 BC		Jacob and family travel to Egypt c. 1876 BC		Exodus from Egypt 1446 BC

2000   1500

Creation   Flood

Chapter 1 Lesson Plan Chart

	Section Title	Main Activity	Pages	Days
I.	The Beginnings of the Human Race	Activity 1: *The Epic of Gilgamesh*	4–10	3 days
II.	The History of Israel	Activity 3: Comparing Covenants	11–14	1–1½ days
III.	The Coming of the Christ	Activity 4: The City of God	14–21	3–3½ days
	TOTAL SUGGESTED DAYS (INCLUDING 1 DAY EACH FOR REVIEW AND TESTING)			9–10 days

Materials List

Section I
- A photo of one of your friends
- A photo of someone playing soccer or having fun with family
- CD: 1A Noah's Ark
- Activities 1 and 2 from the *Student Activities* manual

Section II
- Activity 3 from the *Student Activities* manual

Section III
- CD: 1B Bethlehem Field; 1C Sheep in Bethlehem

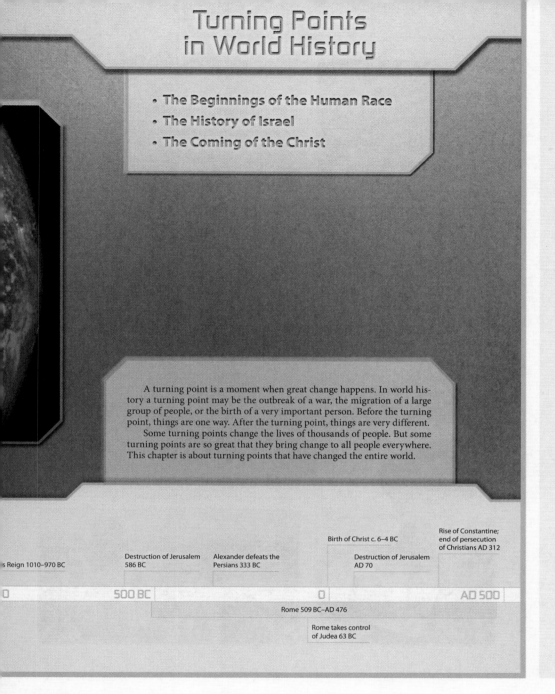

Turning Points in World History

- The Beginnings of the Human Race
- The History of Israel
- The Coming of the Christ

A turning point is a moment when great change happens. In world history a turning point may be the outbreak of a war, the migration of a large group of people, or the birth of a very important person. Before the turning point, things are one way. After the turning point, things are very different.

Some turning points change the lives of thousands of people. But some turning points are so great that they bring change to all people everywhere. This chapter is about turning points that have changed the entire world.

s Reign 1010–970 BC

Destruction of Jerusalem 586 BC

Alexander defeats the Persians 333 BC

Birth of Christ c. 6–4 BC

Destruction of Jerusalem AD 70

Rise of Constantine; end of persecution of Christians AD 312

0   500 BC   0   AD 500

Rome 509 BC–AD 476

Rome takes control of Judea 63 BC

- Activities 4–6 from the *Student Activities* manual
- CD: 1D Spread of Christianity; 1E The Sassanid Persian Empire

Section I

Objectives

Students should be able to

1. Describe God's creation of the universe and affirm His control over human history.
2. Assess the importance of the image of God in humans and the Creation Mandate for understanding human beings and human civilization.
3. Analyze the impact of the Fall on humans, human civilizations, and the natural order.
4. Analyze God's curse on the serpent in Genesis 3:15 and assess its importance for understanding God's plan for redemption in human history.
5. Explain the cause of the Flood and the consequences of this catastrophe for the subsequent development of human civilization.
6. Explain how nations arose in early human history and assess the importance of the rise of nations to the growth of human civilization.

Jehovah or LORD

The student text states that the name of the only true God is Jehovah. The students may find this hard to believe since this name occurs rarely in English versions of the Bible (just seven times in the KJV). The reason for this is that translators through the centuries have tended to translate this name with the English word *lord* rather than transliterating it. But to distinguish this word from other words that mean *lord* in Hebrew, translators have tended to

"God that made the world and all things therein . . . hath made of one blood all nations of men for to dwell on all the face of the earth, and hath determined the times before appointed, and the bounds of their habitation; that they should seek the Lord."
(Acts 17:24, 26–27)

I. The Beginnings of the Human Race

With these words the apostle Paul began preaching a sermon in Athens, one of the most important cities in the ancient world. Much of this sermon was actually a survey of world history. The people of Athens had studied history—Athens was famous for its schools. But Paul knew that they did not understand history. The men of Athens had never done what you are about to do: they had never studied history from the Word of God.

The Creation of the World

"In the beginning God—." The Bible's first four words make a very important point. God (or **Jehovah** [ji HO vuh] as He is often called in the Bible) existed when nothing else did, and all that has come into being was made by Him. For this reason, God owns every galaxy, every planet, and every human. All should honor and obey the One Who has graciously chosen to let them exist.

A Great and Mighty Creator

God created His world simply by speaking. In six days the earth went from being a dark, water-covered planet to a beautiful place that God Himself said was "very good" (Gen. 1:31). God accomplished this amazing work with only a series of commands.

The events of this world's first week teach **divine sovereignty**, God's complete and permanent control over this world. The words of Jehovah are powerful. They determine what is and what will be. Whatever opposition He has faced in history, He has chosen to face it so that He may use it for His own purposes. Jehovah is indeed the Supreme Being, the One Who "worketh all things after the counsel of his own will" (Eph. 1:11).

The Best Part of Creation

God's work of creation came to its climax after He made the animals on the sixth day. Up to that point, God had created by using the impersonal command, "Let there be." But just before His final creation, He said, "Let us make man" (Gen. 1:26).

Knowing God Through Creation

Begin by asking, "From a Christian worldview, what is the first important turning point in history?" (*the creation of the world by Jehovah, recorded in Genesis 1–2*) After having the students read through this passage silently, ask, "What method did God use to create the world?" (*He used speech. "And God said" occurs nine times.*)

Image of God: Human Value

Show the students a photograph of one of your friends, and ask, "Suppose I took scissors and cut this picture into several pieces. What would you likely think about me and my friend?" (*There seems to be something*

wrong with the relationship between you and your friend.) Then say, "But I haven't done anything to my friend. I just cut up some paper. Why do you think there is a problem with me and my friend?" (*Lead the students to understand that when something bears the image of something important, it takes on some of the value of that important thing.*)

Conclude by relating this illustration to the image of God in humans. Humans are made in God's image and are therefore precious and of great value to God. Also, we should highly value each other because we all bear God's image.

Image of God: Human Religion

Hold up a snapshot of someone playing soccer or having fun with family. Then ask, "Suppose I told you that I had never met the person in this picture and that I knew nothing of the circumstances pictured here. Would you trust me if I tried to explain to you what this picture means?" (*no*) "Why?" (*The picture points to a reality beyond it. If you don't know about the reality it represents, you cannot explain it.*)

Lead the students to conclude that humans are the image bearers of God. Just as you cannot understand a picture unless you know about the reality it points to, so humans cannot understand themselves unless

Everyone is made in the image of God to reflect His glory.

Made in God's Image

The reason for this special interest was that humans were to be God's great masterpiece. Unlike the other creatures, humans would be made in God's own image (Gen. 1:27).

The **image of God** in man is a set of qualities possessed by all humans that reflects God's own personality. Because humans are made in God's image, they are like God in many important ways. Like God, they have the ability to think, love, use language, know right and wrong, and enjoy relationships.

Because all humans are made in God's image, all humans are precious in God's sight. They are far more precious than the other creatures. Also, because humans are made in God's image, they are religious beings. They know that they have not made themselves, and they sense that to know themselves, they must know their Creator. This is the reason that all human societies have been religious in some way.

Made to Rule

Jehovah created humans with a job to do. After making the first man and woman, He told them, "Be fruitful, and multiply, and replenish the earth, and subdue it: and have dominion over the fish of the sea, and over the fowl of the air, and over every living thing that moveth upon the earth" (Gen. 1:28). This command, often called the **Creation Mandate**, reveals why God made humans.

The Meaning of the Creation Mandate—The central command of Genesis 1:28 is to "subdue" the earth by having "dominion" over it. Whether that part of God's world is a peanut or the Ganges River, humans are called by God to think of ways to tame the earth and to make it useful.

To exercise this kind of dominion requires all sorts of knowledge and skill—knowledge of science, math, technology, language, and history. The Creation Mandate is not a command about just fish and birds. It is about developing **culture**, the physical and mental environment developed through human thought and labor.

The Creation Mandate and Civilization—Central to the study of world history is the study of civilization. The word **civilization** refers to human culture as it is lived in cities or under the influence of cities. Historically, a **city** is more than a place where many people live. It is a cultural institution in which humans who share certain core values work together to improve their quality of life. They work together by dividing their labor.

Creation Mandate and Culture

Some students may not see the connection between the Creation Mandate and culture. This may be due to a misunderstanding of what *culture* means.

Anthropologists often discuss culture by dividing it into three categories.

1. **Artifacts:** These are the tools that a culture develops in order to get work done, enjoy pleasure, or reflect life and its meaning.

2. **Sociofacts:** These are human relationships and networks of human relationships. A family is a sociofact, but so are schools, churches, and groups of people working at a manufacturing plant.

3. **Mentifacts:** These are the big ideas of a culture. Mentifacts are a culture's attempt to answer the ultimate questions of human existence: Who am I? Where did I come from? Why am I here?

Is there any connection between these three elements and the commands in Genesis 1:28? **Artifacts**—If humans are to make useful objects, they will have to develop tools and use them. **Sociofacts**—The opening commands of the verse suggest the importance of developing networks of human relations for

they know the God who made them in His image.

Conclude by reminding the students that this year they will be studying the history of the human race. To understand the human race, we must know God.

Core Values and Civilization

The following examples show how core values might function in a city:

1. **Freedom:** Specialization frees the citizens to focus on the tasks they enjoy. If a person is skilled at food preparation but not at farming, he may leave farming to someone else while he focuses on running a restaurant.

2. **Justice:** Part of any city is a structure of authority that can settle disputes among the citizens. Without this authority structure, disputes are often settled through violence.

3. **Prosperity:** Specialization enables a person to excel at the particular task he has chosen. His excellence increases the likelihood that he will increase his wealth.

4. **Right relationship with God:** In a city some specialize in religion. If that religion is true, those who work in religion may assist the citizens in knowing God.

Creation

Visit www.bjupress.com/resources for possible links to articles about Creation.

the sake of getting work done. **Mentifacts**—Genesis 1:28 is itself a mentifact answering the question "Why are we here?" It is also one part of a narrative that answers all the ultimate questions faced by any culture.

Creation Mandate and the Environment

Throughout history humans have labored to change their natural environment in order to improve their way of life. Today a movement called environmentalism seeks to significantly limit mankind's attempts at changing the environment.

Since we are called to manage God's world, we should take care not to be wasteful and not to do unnecessary damage to the environment.

However, much of the environmentalist movement is driven by a secular worldview—a view that sees man as a highly evolved animal. A Christian worldview sees mankind as king over creation. God made the earth to be filled with humans and to be ruled by humans. When humans transform a bay into a port or a peninsula into a city, they have done a good thing (provided their work has been responsible and God-honoring).

In a city, individuals specialize in certain tasks necessary for human life. Some specialize in producing food, some in building houses, and some in making tools. The benefit of this division of labor is that individuals no longer need to do everything themselves. Also, because individuals focus on a few tasks, those tasks tend to be done with great skill. The result is progress in science, technology, language, art, and many other things.

The city is not just a human idea. Civilization—the main topic studied in this course—comes from the Creation Mandate. The specialization that makes a city a city is suggested in the first four commands of Genesis 1:28: "Be fruitful, and multiply, and replenish the earth, and subdue it." God recognized that the earth was a huge place. If humans were to have dominion, many humans would need to work together. The Creation Mandate is a command to produce human civilization.

The Fall

The first man was named Adam, and his wife was named Eve. They were part of a wonderful paradise. They were made in the image of God, and because they knew God very well, they understood themselves and their role in this world. Their religion was pure and simple. They loved God, worshiped God, and obeyed God. Their lives were filled with the work of dominion. Their culture—although very limited—was good.

The First Sin

All of this changed in a moment. When God called humans to have dominion over the earth, He also called them to have dominion over themselves. God had prohibited Adam and Eve from eating from the tree of the knowledge of good and evil (Gen. 2:16–17). This divine demand for self-control was taken by Satan, God's enemy, as an opportunity to tempt the first woman.

Satan, appearing as a serpent, told Eve that God had not spoken the truth about the forbidden tree. By saying this, Satan was suggesting that Eve could understand the world by herself without believing what God had said. Eve then doubted the only Person Who is completely trustworthy and trusted the one who cannot be trusted. She then committed the act that changed the world: "She took of the fruit thereof, and did eat, and gave also unto her husband with her; and he did eat" (Gen. 3:6).

The Results of Sin

The consequences of this sin affected both the inner being of Adam and Eve as well as their physical existence. And, as the apostle Paul explained centuries later, the consequences of that choice have been passed on to all humans (Rom. 5:12). The entire history of human civilization has been twisted by sin.

Twisted Love

Since God had made the man and the woman good, they originally loved God with their entire being (Mark 12:30). They also loved each other as much as themselves (v. 31). But when they sinned, their love became twisted. When God asked Adam about what he had done, Adam replied, "The woman whom thou gavest to be with me, she gave me of the tree, and I did eat" (Gen. 3:12). Adam blamed Eve when he should have blamed himself. And in blaming her, he blamed God too.

Fallen Core Values

Discuss ways that the Fall has damaged civilization by twisting core values.

1. **Freedom:** People often understand freedom as a condition in which they can do whatever they want without fear of harm (including sin against God and other humans).

2. **Justice:** Throughout history governmental officials have used their positions to advance their own interests rather than promote justice.

3. **Prosperity:** Individuals often cheat and steal in order to increase their wealth, rather than depending on hard work. Cities have often gone to war in order to claim land and resources that were not rightfully theirs.

4. **Right relationship with God:** In a fallen world, humans use religion to hide from the one true God. Fallen religion gives the participants the feeling that they are right with God when in fact they are worshiping false gods.

This reply from Adam reveals the human race's biggest problem. Humans love themselves more than anything else, and they do not love God or other humans as they should. This moral defect has damaged human civilization. Cities develop when humans who share certain core values work together to improve their quality of life. But in a fallen world, these core values are twisted. This is the reason that the achievements of human cities—achievements in science, art, politics, and philosophy—all bear the tragic marks of selfishness and pride.

Religion too has been damaged. In their religious activities, humans through the centuries have not been seeking for the God Who made them in His image. They have instead been making a god (or gods) in their own image (Rom. 1:23). The fallen human heart cannot love the true God because He is sinless and all-powerful. Humans can, however, love a god made like themselves: sinful and limited.

Frustrated Dominion

God had made humans to subdue the earth. But when humans rebelled against God's rule, God changed the earth so that it rebelled against their rule: "Cursed is the ground for thy sake" (Gen. 3:17). Though humans were to subdue the earth, each human would in the end be subdued by it: "In the sweat of thy face shalt thou eat bread, till thou return unto the ground" (v. 19).

This curse has affected the growth of human civilization. In a civilization, humans work together to improve their quality of life. To do this they work at changing their natural environment. Farmers till the ground, engineers build roads, and carpenters turn trees into houses. But in a fallen world, nature fights against mankind's attempts at dominion. The ground stops producing food, rain floods roads, and tornadoes destroy houses. And one by one every farmer, engineer, and carpenter is taken away by death. Cities are filled with humans busily working to do what cannot be done—improve their quality of life. Their lives may be improved for a time, but before long all will be lost.

God's Plan for Redemption

In the midst of this tragedy, God gave hope to the human race. While pronouncing His curse on Satan, God briefly showed His plan for redeeming this world: "I will put enmity between thee [Satan] and the woman, and between thy seed and her seed; it shall bruise thy head, and thou shalt bruise his heel" (Gen. 3:15). The human race had chosen its own destruction. But only moments after confronting the first sin, God revealed that those made in His image would have the hope of victory.

Genesis 3:15 states very briefly the whole story of human history. Mankind had been called to have dominion over God's world. But now the human race would be divided into the **seed of the serpent** and the **seed of the woman**. God predicted that these two seeds would be in conflict. Each would attempt to exercise dominion according to its own core values. Through the long centuries ahead, Satan's seed (the seed of the serpent) would harm God's people (the seed of the woman) many times. But in the end, God would give victory to His people.

Romans 1:23 says fallen man refused to worship the one true God and worshiped "image[s] made like to corruptible man, and to birds, and fourfooted beasts, and creeping things."

False Religion's Impact on Society

Romans 1:24 states that false religion has a direct impact on the morality of a society. True religion purifies a civilization. False religion denigrates a society. This is because unbelievers are worshiping what is beneath them (images they have made of God's creatures) instead of worshiping what is above them (God, the Creator). God responds by giving them over to their fallenness.

Genesis 3:15

The following passages shed light on the conflict between the two seeds:

1. Matthew 13:38: Here Christ speaks of unbelievers as "the children of the wicked one [Satan]." So it is possible to refer to unbelieving humans as the offspring of Satan.

2. John 8:39–45: Christ states that unbelievers are children of the Devil. In making this claim, Christ alludes to the events of Genesis 3–4.

3. 1 John 3:9–12: This passage indicates that people behave as they do because they are associated with a certain "seed." Cain murdered Abel, and he was born "of that wicked one." But the person who lives a righteous life is "born of God" and cannot live in sin because "[God's] seed remaineth in him."

4. Romans 16:20: Paul indicates that the "feet" under which Satan will be bruised are not only Christ's but also those of all God's people.

5. Genesis 4:25: Here Eve suggests that she views the "seed of the woman" as a line of godly humans.

 ## Understanding False Religion

Romans 1 gives a brief overview of the history of religion in a fallen world. Have the students turn to this passage. Ask them what verse 20 says about mankind. (*The human race is without excuse.*) According to this passage, why are humans in general without excuse before God? (*God has made Himself known to all humans everywhere through nature. Verse 20 states that humans understand that God exists and that He is very powerful.*)

So where does false religion come from? Why have humans throughout history worshiped gods other than Jehovah and bowed down to idols? (*Verses 21 and 23 explain that humans reject the God they know and* choose to worship gods "*made like to corruptible man.*") Why would humans do this? (*Answers will vary. Direct the students to consider that the one true God is intimidating and scary to sinners. It is more comforting to worship a god that is like fallen man.*)

The Ark

In Genesis 6:14 and following, God told Noah to build an ark (box or chest). This floating box was to be 300 cubits long, 50 cubits wide, and 30 cubits high. This translates to a container around 450 feet long, 75 feet wide, and 45 feet high. These proportions are comparable to a modern cargo ship. For more information check out the Answers in Genesis website (enter "ark" in the search engine for several articles).

Where Is the Ark?

People, believers and unbelievers alike, have been fascinated with the possibility of discovering the location of the ark. Periodically, an article will make the news about a recent discovery that may solve this mystery. However, to date, the ark has not been found.

Sin and Judgment

In time, Adam and Eve had two sons, Cain and Abel. The conflict that soon developed in this family was the first clear fulfillment of Genesis 3:15.

Cain and His Seed

Cain grew to be a religious man. He offered to Jehovah a portion of the crops he harvested. But for some reason, Jehovah rejected these offerings. Instead, He accepted Abel's offerings.

God corrected Cain, but he would not submit to this correction. Cain became an angry and bitter man. He could not hurt God, but he could—as Satan did in the garden—harm a person that God loved. One day, while Cain and Abel were working in the field, Cain killed his brother (Gen. 4:8).

Cain then moved to the land of Nod. There he became the father of a group of people who were possibly the first to live in civilization. The first city mentioned in the Bible was built by Cain (Gen. 4:17). The division of labor that is always part of city life was carried on by Cain's descendants. Jabal worked in agriculture as a herdsman. Jubal labored in the arts, making musical instruments. And Tubal-cain worked in industry, producing tools.

Nevertheless, their civilization was not pleasing to God. Their sin was not building a city. Their sin was attempting to live out the Creation Mandate without God. The best statement summarizing Cainite culture is the verse introducing it: "And Cain went out from the presence of the Lord and dwelt in the land of Nod" (Gen. 4:16). Living apart from the will of God was one of the core values that held Cainite civilization together.

Seth and His Seed

God, however, had given Adam and Eve another son. In reflecting on God's promise of a conquering seed (Gen. 3:15), Eve named him Seth ("appointed"). She explained, "God . . . hath appointed me another seed instead of Abel" (Gen. 4:25). For many generations the seed of the woman prospered through the descendants of Seth.

But the Sethites did not remain true to Jehovah. Even righteous people die. Therefore, a godly culture cannot remain godly unless it passes on to each new generation its love for God. At some point in their history, the Sethites allowed their children to marry Cainites (Gen. 6:2). Eventually the Sethites were no different from the Cainites (6:5).

The Great Flood

Grieved by the great sinfulness of the human race, God determined to judge His world. He would cover the whole earth with a great flood. But God chose to show favor to one member of the Sethite line (Gen. 6:8). God instructed Noah to build a massive ark (literally a "box" or a "chest"). Noah was to take his family and representatives of the animal kingdom into the ark, where they would be safe.

God held back His judgment for 120 years (Gen. 6:3). But in the end only Noah, his wife, his three sons, and their wives entered the ark. Then the "fountains of the great deep" were broken up,

The Cause of the Flood

Ask the students what caused the Flood. (*Human sinfulness completely dominated life on earth.*) Because of Genesis 4:26 and all of Genesis 5, we would expect there to be thousands of godly people alive in Noah's day. Why were there so few godly people at the time of Noah? (*Lead your students to consider Genesis 6:1–3. These verses indicate that godliness was nearly completely lost in the human race because of intermarriage with unbelievers.*)

Conclude by emphasizing the importance of Christians marrying Christians (1 Cor. 7:39).

CD: 1A Noah's Ark

An artistic rendering of how Noah's ark may have looked is available on the CD.

Activity 1: *The Epic of Gilgamesh*

This activity contains excerpts from *The Epic of Gilgamesh*, a pagan account of the Flood.

Activity 2: Map Study: Noah's Descendants

This map activity is to help students learn where Noah's descendants settled after the flood.

Space and Earth Science

For more information about the massive geological/climatological changes resulting from the Flood, consult the *Space and Earth Science* textbook (3rd edition) from BJU Press. It is vital for the students to understand that the Flood makes unnecessary the "billions of years" language that students will hear in the media and even when visiting national parks.

The Flood

Visit www.bjupress.com/resources for possible links to articles about the Flood.

and rain fell (7:11). Eventually the entire earth was under water. The Creator had caused the earth to return to its original state: once again it was "without form, and void" (1:2).

Another Beginning

The ark came to rest on the Ararat mountain range. As Noah left the ark, God repeated the Creation Mandate (Gen. 9:1–7). God also emphasized that they were to spread out and fill the earth. The wicked civilizations of the old world were gone. The earth was now populated only by members of the seed of the woman—or so it seemed.

Noah's Prophecy

Noah's three sons were named Shem, Ham, and Japheth. Ham proved to be a wicked man. Noah chose to punish him by placing a curse on Canaan, one of Ham's sons: "Cursed be Canaan; a servant of servants shall he be unto his brethren" (Gen. 9:25).

Shem and Japheth, however, were blessed. Noah said that Shem would have a great future: "Blessed be the Lord God of Shem; and Canaan shall be his servant" (v. 26). Noah was suggesting that Shem's blessing would come from his special relationship to Jehovah. He was also suggesting that God would use Canaan's curse to benefit Shem. Concerning Japheth, Noah promised, "God shall enlarge Japheth, and he shall dwell in the tents of Shem" (v. 27). Japheth would be blessed with wealth and power. He would also somehow share in Shem's blessing.

The Rise and Fall of Babel

As years passed into decades, civilization reemerged. But mankind did not want to spread out and fill the earth as God had demanded in the Creation Mandate (Gen. 1:28; 9:1–7).

The Sin of Babel

At this time all humans spoke the same language. They gathered in the land of Shinar (probably in southeastern Mesopotamia) and began to build the city that would later be called Babel. They planned to build a great tower in the city, which would serve as the religious center. Their reasons for doing this revealed Babel's core values: "Go to, let us build us a city and a tower, whose top may reach unto heaven; and let us make us a name, lest we be scattered abroad upon the face of the whole earth" (Gen. 11:4).

This civilization was trying to enjoy the blessings of the Creation Mandate while disobeying the command to fill the earth. They were also seeking to enter heaven, God's dwelling place. Once again, mankind was trying to become as great as God (see Gen. 3:5–6).

God's Response to Babel

God was not threatened by what was happening at Babel. But He was concerned for the future of mankind. Humans were once again pushing the earth toward judgment.

But rather than pour out His anger on the human race, God chose to restrain mankind's ability to do evil. He confused the people so that they could not talk to each other. Because they could not communicate, they could not work together. Without the ability to divide their labor, the people were forced to abandon this civilization. Thus the complex and confusing differences among human languages began (Gen. 11:9).

Mount Ararat

The Fall of Babel

When the people were divided into nations because of the division of languages, what happened to the believers? While it cannot be proven, it is likely that believers were among each of these nations. God always preserves a remnant of believers who hold to His truth. The remnant among the nations might have been as small as a single family unit, but He provided a way for truth to be preserved.

The Tower of Babel and the Rise of Nations

Have the class give potential reasons for the confusion God brought to the people building the tower. (*Answers could include judgment, separation to form the nations, and building barriers so that man could not rush to embrace the wickedness that led to the Flood.*) Therefore, this confusion also had a redemptive purpose. By being scattered through the earth (unable to pursue a one-world civilization), the people were humbled and kept from thinking of themselves as sufficient to meet all their needs. Paul suggests this in Acts 17:24–26.

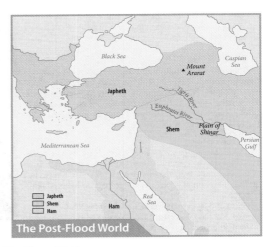

The Post-Flood World

The Rise of Nations

The human race reorganized itself into groups of people who spoke the same language. It was during this period that the first nations developed. A **nation** is a very large group of people (usually including many cities) who share the same language, family history, land area, and culture.

The nations of this ancient time were different from modern nations. Only a few of them became **nation-states**, nations having their own governments, independent of other nations. Most of these early nations were composed of many **city-states**, cities that had their own governments, independent of those of other cities (even those within their own nation).

Genesis 10 is often called the **Table of Nations** because it lists the descendants of Shem, Ham, and Japheth according to the nations that arose from their families. Japheth's descendants developed nations in eastern Europe and modern-day Turkey. Ham's descendants developed nations in eastern Asia and Africa. In particular, Ham's son Canaan settled along the eastern end of the Mediterranean Sea. Shem's descendants formed nations to the east and north of Ham's descendants.

Section Quiz

1. How does God's work of creation show divine sovereignty?
2. Why is the Creation Mandate important for the study of human civilization?
3. What is the human race's biggest problem?
4. Why is Genesis 3:15 important for the study of world history?
5. What caused the Great Flood?
6. What important event led to the rise of nations?
★ Was God's confusing of the people at Babel a judgment, a mercy, or both? Why?

Section Quiz Answers

1. God created the entire world simply by speaking words.
2. The idea of human civilization comes from the Creation Mandate. God's command to "replenish the earth and subdue it" is a command to produce civilization.
3. Because of the Fall, humans love themselves more than anything else, and they do not love God or others as they should.
4. Genesis 3:15 states very briefly the whole story of human history.
5. the great sinfulness of nearly the entire human race
6. God's confusing of human language at Babel
★ Both views could be supported, depending on the reasoning. There is no doubt that God's actions involved judgment. They were also merciful. God prevented the people from continuing in their sinful plan to build the tower.

II. The History of Israel

After the fall of Babel, many nations prospered in Asia, Africa, and Europe. These nations built impressive civilizations, and their accomplishments fill books about ancient history. But all these nations attempted to fulfill the Creation Mandate in a sinful way. God, however, had a plan to set the world right again. A key part of His plan was to raise up a new nation.

God's Covenant with Abraham

Abraham, born around 2166 BC, was a descendant of Shem (Gen. 11:27–32). He grew up in Mesopotamia. Like everyone else in his culture, Abraham initially practiced **polytheism** (PAHL ee thee IZ um), the belief that there are many gods (see Josh. 24:2). But when he was about seventy-five, Jehovah appeared to him and told him to leave all this behind and move to the land of Canaan (the area settled by Ham's cursed son). Abraham became a believer in the one true God.

Important Promises

Following his conversion, about 2091 BC, God made a covenant (a solemn agreement) with Abraham (Gen. 12:1–7). At the core of this covenant were promises of a seed, a land, and a universal blessing. First, Jehovah said He would give Abraham a group of descendants who would become a great nation. This promise shows that God would fulfill Genesis 3:15 through this covenant with Abraham. Second, He said that this nation would possess the land of Canaan. Third, Jehovah promised that Abraham's seed would bring a blessing to all the nations of the earth.

This covenant is often called the **Abrahamic Covenant**. Though very brief, it revealed God's plan to redeem humans, enabling them once again to have dominion as God intended.

Early Fulfillments

In time, Jehovah gave Abraham a son, Isaac, through whom the chosen descendants would come. These descendants continued through Isaac's son Jacob. God later gave Jacob twelve sons. These sons became the fathers of this nation's twelve tribes. Since God had changed Jacob's name to Israel, they became known as the children of Israel or simply Israel.

The Mosaic Covenant

Toward the end of his life, Jacob moved his family to Egypt to escape a famine (c. 1876 BC). The children of Israel remained in Egypt for over four centuries.

Leaving Egypt

During this time Israel became a very numerous people. But a pharaoh (a king in Egypt) came to power who feared this growing nation. To keep them from becoming a threat, he enslaved God's people.

Jehovah, however, raised up Moses to lead Israel out of slavery and into Canaan. In delivering Israel, God worked many miracles. These miracles showed that Israel left Egypt because Jehovah—not man—brought them out. And He brought them out to keep the promises of the Abrahamic Covenant.

Section II

Objectives

Students should be able to

1. Analyze the Abrahamic Covenant and explain how it relates to God's promise of redemption in Genesis 3:15.

2. Describe Israel's exodus from Egypt and its conquest of Canaan as fulfillments of God's promises in the Abrahamic Covenant.

3. Trace the rise and fall of the Israelite monarchy as fulfillments of God's promises in the Abrahamic, Mosaic, and Davidic Covenants.

4. Explain how God's promise of a New Covenant and the Jews' return from exile contributed to God's ongoing work of redemption.

Ishmael

Genesis 16 records the story of Sarai's attempts to fulfill the will of God by having Abraham father a son through Hagar, her handmaiden. From that time to the present, Sarai's decision has had dreadful consequences. However, because Ishmael was indeed the son of Abraham, God graciously preserved him and prophesied to Hagar the nature of Ishmael's descendants (Gen. 16:12).

Activity 3: Comparing Covenants

This chart activity helps the student distinguish the various covenants in Scripture.

Comparing Covenants

Have your students read Genesis 12:1–7 (Abrahamic Covenant), Exodus 19:3–8, 20–22; 20:1–19 (summary of Mosaic Covenant), and Jeremiah 31:31–34 (New Covenant).

Point out that the Mosaic Covenant is different from the other two. It emphasizes the conditions that humans must meet in order to be blessed by God. The other covenants are about what God will do for humans. Ask the students which covenant(s) they enjoyed

reading about. (*Most will say the Abrahamic and New Covenants. They are encouraging. The Mosaic Covenant is scary.*)

Discuss the reasons that the Mosaic Covenant is so troubling. (*The Mosaic Covenant is good, but we are sinful. We don't like it because it is a record of what God expects from us.*) Lead the students to conclude that it is a good covenant because God wrote it. Also, Paul clearly states that the law of Moses is good (Rom. 7:7, 14–16).

Lead the students to consider that the New Covenant solves the problem that the Mosaic Covenant raises: the problem of human sinfulness. The New Covenant states that God will forgive His people of their failure to obey the Mosaic Covenant. He will also

give them new hearts—hearts that will want to obey God's commands. Point out that the New Covenant came into effect when Jesus died on the cross (Luke 22:20). The blessings of the New Covenant are for anyone who will repent and trust Christ.

Conclude by showing students the relationship among these three covenants. The Abrahamic Covenant is a general statement regarding how God will redeem this world to Himself. The Mosaic Covenant reveals the greatest obstacle to the realization of this redemption: human sinfulness. The New Covenant reveals how God will overcome this obstacle: He will forgive His people through the sacrifice of His Son and will give them a desire to love and obey God's commands.

Covenant at Sinai

Israel left Egypt in 1446 BC. But they did not go immediately to Canaan. God directed them to camp at Mount Sinai. There Jehovah offered them a covenant, often called the **Mosaic Covenant**. If they promised to obey all of God's rules, He would make them His own special nation (Exod. 19:5–6). The children of Israel agreed.

At the center of this covenant were the **Ten Commandments** (Exod. 20:1–17), ten laws showing Israel how to love God and other humans. The first of these commands demanded **monotheism** (MAHN uh thee IZ um), the belief in one God. Unlike the other nations, Israel was to worship only one God, Jehovah. From these central commands flowed many other commands about good government and proper behavior.

Comparing Covenants

The Mosaic Covenant was similar in many ways to the Abrahamic Covenant. Since it set up the government of the Israelite nation, it helped fulfill the promise that Abraham's seed would be a great nation. The Mosaic Covenant also gave instructions regarding the conquest of Canaan and the managing of that land. This helped fulfill the land promise of the Abrahamic Covenant. The Mosaic Covenant also helped fulfill the promise of a blessing for all nations. If Israel obeyed God's laws, they would enjoy spiritual and economic prosperity. They would show other nations how to forsake their sin and turn to God.

The Mosaic Covenant was also different from the Abrahamic Covenant. The covenant with Abraham had no conditions. It was

Mount Sinai

a gracious promise to bless Abraham and the whole world. But the covenant through Moses contained a huge condition: Israel must obey God's laws or be cursed (Deut. 27–28).

Rise and Fall of Israel's Kingdom

Repeatedly, Israel disobeyed the covenant they had promised to obey. When Jehovah led them to the edge of Canaan, they refused to enter the land (Num. 14). They feared the Canaanites would defeat them. So God sent them back to the wilderness, where they wandered for forty years. During this time Moses died and was replaced by Joshua. After forty years of suffering, Israel was ready to take the land of Canaan. They invaded and drove out most of the Canaanites, but not all of them.

After Joshua died, Israel gave itself to polytheism (Judg. 2:11–13). They worshiped gods made in the image of the Canaanites instead of the God Who had made them in His own image. So the sin problem that kept other nations from exercising good dominion plagued Israel as well. Then the Canaanites regained their power and began to conquer the Israelites. Israel found itself in a struggle for survival that lasted for centuries. This struggle continued until God raised up David.

The Rise of Israel

David, a descendant of Jacob through his son Judah, was Israel's greatest king. During his reign (1010–970 BC), he defeated Israel's enemies and extended his rule to the Euphrates River. In the middle of this reign, Jehovah made a covenant with David (2 Sam. 7). God promised that his dynasty (a line of rulers from one family) would last forever.

This covenant, called the **Davidic Covenant**, is very important to world history. It revealed that David's descendants would play a key role fulfilling the three promises of the Abrahamic Covenant (as well as the promise of Genesis 3:15). David himself understood this, and he wrote about this covenant in many of his psalms. In some of these psalms, David speaks of a particular descendant who would be great and rule over the entire world (see Pss. 2, 22, 45, 89, 110). The Israelites referred to this great son of David as the **Messiah** ("the anointed one"), the mighty king who would lead humans to exercise dominion just as God had intended from the beginning.

The Decline and Fall of Israel

The Davidic Covenant promised a glorious future for Israel (and for all the world), but it did not remove the curses of the Mosaic Covenant. Those curses were fulfilled in stages as David's descendants disobeyed the law of Moses. God sent prophets, like Isaiah and Jeremiah, to preach against polytheism and sin. But God's people ignored them. The final judgment came in 586 BC. In that year the Babylonians destroyed Jerusalem (the capital city) and took many people captive.

A Hopeful Future

The prophets who predicted the decline and fall of Israel also preached hope. Isaiah promised that God's Servant, the Messiah, would establish justice when he ruled over the world (Isa. 42:1–4). This same Servant would take care of the curses of the Mosaic Covenant for Israel—and for the sins of all the nations—by suffering, dying, and living again (Isa. 52:13–53:12). Through Jeremiah, God

David

The Canaanites

Israel was clearly commanded to destroy the Canaanites. However, the book of Joshua makes it clear that many of the Canaanite tribes were not destroyed. Failure to obey God's command resulted in idolatry, intermarriage of Jews and Canaanites, subjugation, and persecution. Centuries later David finished conquering the Canaanites.

Decline by Stages

After Solomon's reign, the nation of Israel split into ten tribes (Israel) and Judah and Benjamin (Judah). By 722 BC the northern ten tribes had been carried away by Assyrian forces. Judah survived the Assyrian threat but suffered defeat when confronted by the Babylonian forces in the sixth century BC. During this period the Babylonians took control of a large area from the Nile to the Tigris in Mesopotamia.

Section III

Objectives

Students should be able to

1. Describe how the Jewish nation and the Roman world were made ready for the coming of Christ.
2. Explain the life and ministry of Jesus Christ as fulfillments of Old Testament prophecies.
3. Analyze the fundamental teachings of Christianity.
4. Analyze how Christianity spread widely in the Roman Empire, giving special attention to the conversion of Saul and the destruction of Jerusalem in AD 70.
5. Trace the extent and consequences of the growth of the Christian church in Asia, Africa, and Europe to the seventh century.

The World Made Ready

Paul states that Jesus was born when "the fulness of the time was come" (Gal. 4:4). So God had for some time been making the world ready for the coming of His Son.

Roman rule united the Mediterranean world into one political organization. Roman roads made travel relatively easy. The pervasiveness of the Greek language made it possible for a person preaching the gospel to be understood in most places from Spain to India.

Caesar's Decree

Gaius Octavius rose to power in the Roman Republic because of the influence of his uncle, Julius Caesar. When his uncle was murdered, he avenged his death

promised to make a **New Covenant** with His people (Jer. 31:31–34). This covenant would be different from the Mosaic Covenant. It was God's promise to put His rules in the hearts of His people so that they would want to obey. Ezekiel told the people that it would be the gift of the Holy Spirit that would make this possible (Ezek. 36:27). Also in this covenant, Jehovah promised to forgive the sins of His people.

After Israel had spent seventy years in Babylon, God moved the heart of Cyrus, the Persian king who had conquered the Babylonians. He released the captives, and many of God's people returned and began rebuilding Jerusalem. Out of the ashes of God's judgment, a new nation began to emerge.

Section Review

1. What were the three main promises in the Abrahamic Covenant?
2. What do we call the laws at the center of the Mosaic Covenant? What did these laws show?
3. What did God promise in the Davidic Covenant? Why is this promise important to human history?
4. What did God promise to do for His people in the New Covenant?
★ Why do you think that God made a covenant with Abraham even though he had formerly worshiped other gods?

III. The Coming of the Christ

God's people returned to their land at the end of the 500s BC. The next several centuries were filled with upheaval. In 333 BC Alexander the Great defeated the Persians and began to establish the Greek Empire. Then the Romans rose to power. In the 200s BC, they defeated the Greeks, and in 63 BC they took over Judea (one of the names for what had been Israel). The Jews (a name for Israelites living in Judea) longed to be set free.

Jesus of Nazareth

After centuries of predicting the coming of a great Savior, God raised up the Man who would prove to be the most important human who has ever lived, **Jesus of Nazareth**.

Birth

Around 4 BC, God sent the angel Gabriel to Nazareth to speak to a descendant of King David whose name was Mary. He told her that she would give birth to a son and that she should name him Jesus. He also told her that God would give Him the throne of David and that He would reign forever (Luke 1:31–32).

Mary, however, was not married (though she was engaged). So she did not know how she could have a child. Gabriel said that God would cause her to conceive. For this reason, the child would not have a human father. He would be the Son of God.

Because of a Roman decree, Joseph (the man Mary was engaged to) needed to travel to Bethlehem with Mary. It was here that Mary gave birth to Jesus. That night God sent angels to shepherds nearby. They told these shepherds that Jesus was a Savior, Christ, and Lord

Section Quiz Answers

1. the promise of a seed, the promise of a land, and the promise of a universal blessing
2. The Ten Commandments; they showed Israel how to love God and other humans.
3. David's dynasty would last forever; this covenant reveals that David's descendants would play a special role in fulfilling the Abrahamic Covenant. In particular, one great descendant (the Messiah) would rule and would forever restore humanity to the work of dominion.
4. He promised to put His laws in their hearts so that they would want to obey

Him. He also promised to forgive them of their sins.

★ Answers will vary but might include the concept that He wanted to show the world that He was a gracious God.

Pax Romana

Visit www.bjupress.com/resources for possible links to articles on the Roman peace during this period.

(Luke 2:11). By *Lord* they meant that Jesus would fulfill the Davidic Covenant: He would rule as David's greatest son. By **Christ** the angels meant that Jesus was the Messiah (*Christ* is Greek for "anointed one"). By *Savior* they meant that He would save His people from their sad condition.

Teaching

When Jesus was about thirty, He began to travel throughout Judea preaching and healing people. The main point of His preaching was the bold statement, "The kingdom of God is at hand: repent ye, and believe the gospel" (Mark 1:15).

The kingdom of Israel had fallen apart because of sin. But God's own kingdom was at hand because David's great descendant, God's Son, was on earth. As the perfect human, He would one day rule over the earth as Adam and Eve should have. He also would save people from sin and lead them to exercise the right kind of dominion. His many miracles proved He had the power to end God's curse and restore the world to its original state. To become part of this kingdom, people needed to repent; that is, they needed to turn away from their sin. They also needed to believe the gospel—they had to believe that Jesus was the Christ, the One sent by God to save them.

Death

As Jesus continued to teach, He made many enemies. A number of Jews—especially the religious leaders—were offended by His preaching on sin. Even though He had worked many miracles, they refused to believe that He was the Christ.

The religious leaders plotted to have Jesus killed. Around AD 30, they brought Him before the Roman governor, Pontius Pilate. They said that since He claimed to be the Christ, the King of the Jews, He was opposing the Roman authorities. Pilate then sentenced Jesus to die by crucifixion. Just outside Jerusalem on a spring day long ago, the Christ—God's own Son—died a horrible death.

This death, however, was part of God's plan. Jesus told His disciples the night before it happened that the shedding of His blood

Above, the Shepherds' Fields around Bethlehem; *below*, a typical shepherds' field

and became the most powerful man in Rome around 31 BC. The Roman Senate conferred on him the title of "Augustus" (the exalted) in 27 BC. This is the man mentioned in Luke 2 who made a decree about a census that led Joseph and Mary to travel to Bethlehem just in time for the birth of Jesus. It is a wonderful example of the providence of God moving an unsaved political leader to reform a corrupt tax system and, in the process, fulfill the promises of God to the letter.

Crucifixion

Crucifixion is the most painful, humiliating, and agonizing means of execution invented by man. The technique was perfected by the Persians and later practiced by the Romans as an execution reserved for the worst of criminals. The victim was often nailed to the cross beam through the wrists and to the main beam through the ankles. The pain was unbearable. The victim struggled between efforts to breathe and extreme pain that forced him to go limp on the cross. The suffering could go on for days. When the Romans desired to end the process (as mentioned in the Gospels), they would use a club or hammer to break the victim's legs. This would make the victim suffocate and die quickly.

 CD: 1B Bethlehem Field; 1C Sheep in Bethlehem

Photos of Bethlehem field (which is now filled with olive trees) and some sheep in the region are available on the CD.

Answering Skeptics

Many skeptics believe that the disciples of Jesus broke into His tomb, stole His body, and then went around telling people that He was resurrected and had gone back to heaven.

Ask your students how they would respond to such a statement. Allow time for student responses.

Point out the fact that the disciples most likely would not have had the courage to steal the body. They ran away when Jesus was arrested. Also, their commitment to Jesus's cause seems to have been destroyed by the crucifixion. They didn't even help bury Jesus.

Turn the discussion to the behavior of Jesus's disciples as revealed in the Book of Acts. Did they continue to lack courage? (*No. In fact, they stood up to fierce persecution.*) Ask the students why this change in behavior is significant. (*It suggests that Jesus really did rise from the dead. Why would the disciples' lives be changed by a lie—a lie that they had made up?*)

Conclude by emphasizing that the main problem skeptics face is trying to understand history while rejecting the Word of God—the only completely reliable historical account. No person can understand God's world if he refuses to believe God's Word.

There is no way to know whether this is the tomb in which Jesus was buried. This site does, however, fit the description given in the New Testament.

Pentecost and Babel

At Babel God confused human language so that people would not be able to work together in opposition to God's rule. At Pentecost God temporarily removed the effects of the curse of Babel in order to signal that the kingdom of God had arrived and was advancing on the earth.

This parallel reveals the importance of the church and the preaching of the gospel among the nations. The church's work of declaring the gospel is so important to God that when it began, He made it parallel to His work at Babel—a work that triggered the rise of nations.

would mark the beginning of the New Covenant (Luke 22:20). Without the death of Jesus, repenting and believing would be useless. The heel of the woman's seed must be bruised if the serpent—along with all his evil—was to be crushed.

Three days after Jesus' death, His tomb was empty. When His followers had come to the tomb on the third day, they were confronted by an angel who told them good news: "Fear not ye: for I know that ye seek Jesus, which was crucified. He is not here: for he is risen" (Matt. 28:5–6). Over the next forty days, Jesus appeared to His followers, assuring them that He was alive and that they now had much work to do for the kingdom.

Jesus had been sacrificed for the sin of the world, and God had accepted that sacrifice. The death and resurrection of Jesus Christ mark the most important turning point in history. To this point, the nations of the earth were descending deeper and deeper into sin. But now there was hope. God had sent His own Son to live a sinless life, die in the place of sinful humans, and rise again so that death might be defeated. This is the **gospel** in its fullness—that Jesus has died for the sins of humans and has been raised again to save them forever (see 1 Cor. 15:1, 3–4). All who repent and believe this gospel enter God's kingdom; those who reject Jesus will one day be judged by Him.

The Early Spread of Christianity

"All power is given unto me in heaven and in earth. Go ye therefore, and teach all nations" (Matt. 28:18–19). With these words, Jesus told His disciples to tell all nations about the gospel. The kingdom of God was not for Jews only. It was for all peoples. The Christ—the seed of the woman, Abraham's seed, David's great descendant—had conquered sin and death. It was now time to bless all the nations with this good news.

The Holy Spirit and Pentecost

Ten days after Jesus ascended to heaven, during the Jewish Feast of Pentecost, He gave the Holy Spirit to His people, just as was promised in the New Covenant (Acts 2). Through the work of the Spirit, thousands believed the gospel. Once they believed, they too received the Holy Spirit. The Christian church was born.

The Conversion of Saul

As the Christian church grew, so did opposition from **Judaism** (the religion of the Jews, distinct from Christianity). An early leader of this opposition was **Saul of Tarsus**. Saul showed great zeal in attempting to wipe out the church. But one day, while traveling to persecute Christians, he was confronted by Jesus personally (Acts 9:3–6). Saul then believed the gospel and began preaching that Jesus was the Christ.

Saul, later known as Paul, played a leading role in the spread of Christianity. God led him to emphasize two important truths. First,

What Does Christianity Teach?

Have your students suppose that they are being interviewed by a historian who is studying the religions of the world. How would they explain to him the basic teachings of Christianity?

Guide your students in constructing the following outline of three questions and answers.

1. **Who is Jesus of Nazareth?** Jesus is the Son of God. He is also the Messiah, the descendant of David whom God promised to send to fulfill the dominion that Adam failed to fulfill.

2. **What did Jesus do?** He established the kingdom of God by dying for sin and rising again in victory over sin and death. He offers eternal life to all who will repent of sin and believe in what He has done for them.

3. **What are Christians to do?** Christians are those who have entered the kingdom by repenting of their sins and believing the gospel. As members of the kingdom, they seek to live in victory over sin. They obey God's rules—not to become right with God but because God's Spirit is in them and leads them to love God and others.

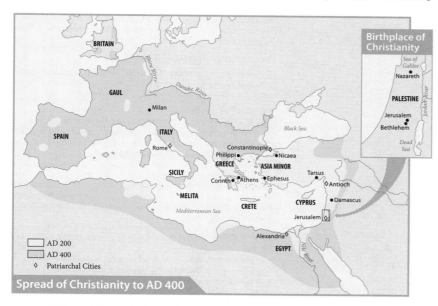

Birthplace of Christianity

Sea of Galilee
Nazareth

PALESTINE

Jerusalem
Bethlehem

Dead Sea

Jordan River

BRITAIN

Rhine River

GAUL

Danube River

Milan

SPAIN

ITALY

Black Sea

Rome

Constantinople
Philippi   Nicaea
GREECE   ASIA MINOR
Corinth Athens Ephesus   Tarsus
SICILY   Antioch

MELITA   CYPRUS
CRETE   Damascus
Mediterranean Sea   Jerusalem

Alexandria

EGYPT

Nile River

☐ AD 200
☐ AD 400
◇ Patriarchal Cities

Spread of Christianity to AD 400

no one could be saved from sin by obeying the conditions of the Mosaic Covenant. The failure of Israel proved this. Salvation came by trusting in Jesus, the only One Who obeyed these conditions. Because of His perfect life and death, all who believe are right with God. Because of the Holy Spirit, believers are made more and more like Jesus (Gal. 2:11–21; 5:14–26).

Second, Paul taught that Jesus was the promised seed of Abraham Who would bring a blessing to all the nations. That blessing was salvation from sin. All who believe the gospel become part of Jesus, and they are therefore part of Abraham's seed. So, Paul concluded, there is no difference between Jews and Gentiles (a name for non-Jews). Both are descendants of Abraham and citizens of the kingdom of God (Gal. 3).

Many Jews were offended by these teachings. But great numbers of Gentiles believed Paul. These Gentiles abandoned their polytheism and became Christians. Paul spread Christianity in Asia Minor, Greece, Rome, and perhaps even Spain. By the time Paul died (c. AD 67), Christianity was well established in many major cities of the Roman Empire.

The Destruction of Jerusalem

The Jewish people had become weary of living under foreign empires. In AD 66 the Jews rebelled against the Romans. Rome sent a large number of troops to stop the rebellion. In AD 70 the Roman soldiers broke through Jerusalem's defenses, destroyed the city, and burned the temple. The Jews were then expelled from Jerusalem and from their homeland.

This tragic event actually helped the spread of Christianity. First, it ended the persecution of Christians from Judaism. This religion

Masada

In AD 66 as the situation in Israel deteriorated and the threat of a Roman invasion seemed more likely, a group of Jewish zealots captured a fortress built by Herod the Great. This massive stone plateau is located near the Dead Sea. From this fortress the zealots attacked their enemies. After the fall of Jerusalem in AD 70, the Romans turned their attention to areas like Masada. The Romans surrounded this walled fortress and bombarded it with great stones using machines that hurled the stones up several hundred feet to the plateau. Using slave labor, the Romans also built a ramp on the western side and eventually destroyed the wooden gate that had prevented entrance. The next day when the Romans entered, they found that all of the people in the fortress had committed suicide rather than surrender to the Romans.

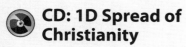

CD: 1D Spread of Christianity

This map from the student text is also available on the CD.

no longer had authority to harm Christians. Second, it drove Christians out of Judea. The church at Jerusalem had become huge. Those believers were now scattered through the empire.

Later Growth in the Roman World

In the years following AD 70, the Christian church experienced amazing growth in and beyond the Roman Empire. This growth occurred even though the church faced opposition.

Roman Persecutions

At first, Roman authorities were not bothered by Christianity. As it grew, however, they worried that the Christian belief that Jesus was Lord was at odds with the Roman state. Roman officials accused Christians of not being loyal to the empire.

The first official Roman persecution of Christianity began under the emperor **Nero** (NEE roh) (r. AD 54–68). He blamed the Christians for a great fire that swept through Rome in AD 64. The Roman historian Tacitus recorded many of the violent ways in which Christians were killed, including dipping them in tar and using them as human torches.

From Nero until AD 250, the persecution of Christians was sporadic and limited to small areas. But beginning in 250, persecution became empire-wide.

The last and most widespread persecution happened during the reign of emperor **Diocletian** (dy uh KLEE shun) (r. 284–305). In decree after decree, he dismissed Christians from the army, ordered the destruction of church buildings, and had copies of the Bible burned. Later it was decreed that all Christians would have to offer sacrifices to pagan gods or be tortured and killed.

The Romans hoped that these persecutions would put an end to Christianity. But Jesus Christ, the Lord of the earth, was on the side of His church. He had given His followers the Holy Spirit to give them strength and wisdom. He had also promised them the same

Many Christians died for their faith in the Coliseum of Rome.

victory over death that He had experienced. Some people did leave the Christian church because of the persecution. But, with few exceptions, the true followers of Jesus remained faithful. Christianity was purified through this opposition, not destroyed.

Roman Acceptance

The situation changed dramatically when, in AD 312, the Roman emperor **Constantine** (KAHN stun teen) (r. AD 306–337) converted to Christianity. The next year, in AD 313, he issued the **Edict of Milan**, which put an end to almost three-hundred years of persecution. Many have questioned whether Constantine's conversion was sincere. What is not questioned, however, is that his acceptance of Christianity changed history. Rome now protected and helped the church. Constantine gave back property that had been taken from Christians. He made Sunday a legal holiday. He gave money for new church buildings, and he encouraged people throughout the empire to become Christians.

The emperor even became involved in controversies within the church. When a church teacher named **Arius** (EHR ee us) claimed that Jesus was not God, Constantine stepped in and organized a council of church leaders. In AD 325 the **Council of Nicaea** (ny SEE uh) met to consider the deity of Christ. The council concluded that Jesus was God. They also affirmed the doctrine of the Trinity—the teaching that there is only one God, but He exists in three distinct persons: the Father, the Son, and the Holy Spirit.

As Constantine and his successors became more involved in supporting churches, Christianity gained more favor and power in the Roman world. At the end of the 300s, the emperor **Theodosius I** (THEE uh DOH shis) (r. 379–395) made it the only recognized religion in the empire. All other religions were considered illegal.

As a result of the freedom and privileges granted by the Roman government, church congregations grew rapidly in numbers. But this favor also led to a swift decline in the purity of many church members. Some people truly believed the gospel. But others simply wanted to enjoy the favor that church membership granted. Such "Christians" brought with them many of their pagan beliefs and practices. For this reason, many churches soon began to look like the pagan religions that had once filled the Roman world.

Christianity and the Decline of the Empire

Christianity continued to grow even as the Roman Empire continued to decline. For years the empire had struggled with political turmoil, high taxes, and problems along its borders. By the time Constantine had come to the throne, the empire was in a crisis. Constantine attempted to bring renewal by moving the capital from Rome to the ancient Greek city of Byzantium. He renamed the city New Rome. The people called it **Constantinople** ("Constantine's City").

The western part of the empire deteriorated as it was invaded by wave after wave of **barbarians** (a Roman name for peoples not part of Greek or Roman culture). In 395 Theodosius I declared that the empire was now two separate empires. The old western portion became known as the Roman Empire, and the old eastern portion became the **Byzantine Empire**.

Cut off from the stronger, more secure Byzantine Empire, the Roman Empire was an easy prey for the barbarians. In 410 the city of Rome was plundered. Though the empire had been in serious decline for more than a century, its citizens—Christians included—

Constantinople (modern Istanbul)

Conversion of Constantine

Ask your students whether the conversion of Constantine was a blessing from God or an attempt by Satan to destroy the church. (*Lead them to consider that it was probably both.*) Paul labored to preach the gospel to those in positions of authority (e.g., Acts 13:7–12; 24:24–25). He also told believers to pray for the salvation of governmental officials so that the church might enjoy peace (1 Tim. 2:1–5). But it seems clear from history that Satan used Constantine's conversion as an opportunity to tempt believers and cause trouble. The church was now overwhelmed with insincere members and false teachers.

Conclude by asking the students what lesson can be gleaned from this event. (*Emphasize that though relief from persecution is a good thing, God's church must work hard at maintaining pure teaching and separation from worldliness during times of cultural acceptance. When the church does not work hard at this, it slips away into error and sin.*)

⊕ Constantinople

Visit www.bjupress.com/resources for possible links to articles about rulers of Constantinople.

Augustine

Augustine lived from the mid-fourth to the mid-fifth centuries (354–430) and witnessed the rapid decline of the Roman Empire. He came to Christ during his adult years and became the bishop of Hippo in northern Africa. As a philosopher and theologian he profoundly influenced Christianity for several centuries. His works, including *The City of God* and *Confessions,* are used by Catholics and Protestants alike. He also wrestled with diverse subjects including original sin and the definition of a "just war." As with any of the writings of the church fathers, Augustine's writings should be evaluated in light of Scripture.

The Coptic Church

The official title of the Egyptian Orthodox Church is The Coptic Orthodox Church of Alexandria. This is the largest Christian church in Egypt and is similar to the Orthodox family of churches (Greek, Russian, etc.). In 451 the Coptic church differed on its understanding of the nature of Christ with the Eastern Orthodox and Western churches. The Coptic church survived the initial invasion of Islam in the seventh century and maintained a viable presence for about six hundred years. By the end of the twelfth century, Islamic conversions had reduced the Coptic church to a minority group in Egypt and Ethiopia.

---

were shocked. As the empire fell apart, many pagans blamed the rise of Christianity for the decline of Rome.

Augustine (354–430), a Christian leader in Hippo, North Africa, responded by writing *The City of God.* In this book he laid out a Christian view of history. He said that history is the story of two cities with two opposing ways of life. The earthly city is the home of sinful men. The heavenly city, however, is the city of God, filled with those who have turned away from evil. These two cities exist side by side in this world, but at the final judgment, God will separate them. Citizens of the heavenly city will enjoy eternal life, while the earthly city will perish. Augustine concluded that Christians should not fear Rome's fall. Empires come and go, but God's city is forever.

Rome's decline continued as barbarian tribes reached deep into the empire. Finally, in 476, a barbarian general claimed the emperor's throne. The Roman Empire had officially ended. But just as the destruction of Jerusalem contributed to the growth of the Christian church, so also the fall of Rome helped spread Christianity. In time, many influential barbarians converted and Christianity continued to spread throughout these new cultures. These cultures became the foundation of Medieval Europe.

Growth beyond the Empire

Christianity spread not only throughout the Roman Empire but also beyond its borders. We will note the growth that took place to the east and west of the empire.

To the East

The Sassanid Persian Empire stretched from Rome's eastern border all the way to what is today Afghanistan. Beginning in the first century, Christians took the gospel to the major Persian cities. Sea trade in the Persian Gulf and Indian Ocean allowed Christianity to spread to the coasts of Arabia and probably to India as well.

Constantine's support enabled Christians in the Roman Empire to practice Christianity without persecution. But Persia, an enemy of Rome, responded by increasing the persecution of Christians under Sassanid rule. Persia did, however, accept Christians who were considered heretics in the Roman Empire. Some of these Christians

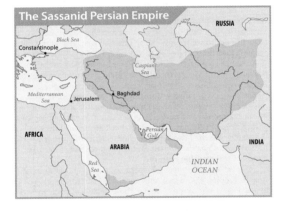

The Sassanid Persian Empire

CD: 1E The Sassanid Persian Empire

This map from the student text is also available on the CD.

Lessons from the Growth of Christianity

Have the students outline the growth of the Christian church. Write for display the events they mention. Try to keep the events listed to about ten.

Ask the students what lessons are to be learned from the early spread of Christianity. (*Emphasize at least these three: [1] God sustains His church by doing for believers what they cannot do for themselves—e.g.,*

Pentecost and Saul's conversion; [2] God uses difficult circumstances and fierce persecution to advance His work in the earth—e.g. the destruction of Jerusalem, Roman persecutions, and the fall of Rome; [3] God's church can be greatly damaged by political and cultural favor.)

Activity 4: *The City of God*

This excerpt from Augustine's *City of God* provides the students with a Christian response to the Roman claims that Christianity was responsible for the fall of Rome.

Activity 5: St. Patrick

This excerpt from Patrick's writings helps the students understand missionary endeavors in the early church.

St. Patrick

Visit www.bjupress.com/resources for possible links to articles about Patrick of Ireland.

taught that Jesus was God but was not really human. The Coptic Church, for example, taught this. Others taught that Jesus was God and human but was not a single person. The **Nestorians**, for example, taught this.

Nestorians and Copts grew to be powerful in the east. By the seventh century, the Nestorians had sent missionaries into China. The Copts, who were most powerful in Egypt, sent missionaries south along the Nile River to establish churches in Nubia and Aksum (Ethiopia). The king of Aksum, Ezana, became a Coptic Christian. The official church of Ethiopia remains today the Coptic church.

To the West

In the far west, Christianity spread beyond the Roman Empire through men such as **Patrick**. Born in Britain in the late 300s, Patrick was captured by pirates and taken to Ireland as a prisoner when he was about sixteen. He later escaped back to Britain, where he became a Christian. Around 432 he returned to Ireland and served there as a missionary. Through his work, thousands converted, and the Christian church not only thrived there but also began sending missionaries to other regions.

Several Irish monks traveled to various parts of Europe during the 500s and 600s. Their goal was to spread Christianity to such groups as the Picts and Franks. Although records are scarce, it seems that Christianity continued to spread beyond the Roman Empire.

With the coming of God's Christ, the doors to the kingdom of God were thrown open to all the peoples of the earth. Millions crowded into this kingdom by repenting of sin and believing the gospel. Nevertheless, there were many problems. Persecutions attacked the church from the outside, and insincere Christians threatened it from the inside. But God would not fail to keep His promise of giving the seed of the woman victory and eternal life. Empires would rise and fall, but Jesus, the King of kings, would never abandon His throne.

Section Review

1. Why did the angels refer to Jesus as a Savior, Christ, and Lord (Luke 2:11)?
2. What is the gospel?
3. Name three causes of the early spread of Christianity.
4. What key event happened in AD 313?
5. What group sent missionaries into China by the seventh century?
★ What did Jesus mean when He said, "The kingdom of God is at hand: repent ye, and believe the gospel" (Mark 1:15)?

Nestorius

Nestorius served as archbishop of Constantinople from 428 to 431. He lost his position as a result of his objection to the common practice of referring to Mary as the "Mother of God." Nestorius preferred to speak of Mary as the "Mother of Christ." He was condemned at the Council of Ephesus for this view. Whether or not he was actually a heretic is the subject of speculation. However, he maintained a strong following in the East, and some of his followers spread his teachings as far as Turkey and China.

Christian Involvement

The whole sweep of world history argues for cultural involvement for the Christian. God made humans to engage in cultural activities and to produce civilization. When humans fell into sin, God did not tell them to abandon culture and civilization but rather to continue in this work. The history of redemption demonstrates that cultural engagement is still important. God raised up Israel to be an instrument of redemption as a cultural institution. When God sent His Son into the world, He sent Him to confront and engage not just individuals but also culture. Jesus came to claim the throne of David. The Christian church has also engaged culture throughout history. The persecution that Christians have faced has resulted from Christianity's influence on the society in which it exists.

Section Quiz Answers

1. *Savior* meant that He would deliver His people from their sinful condition. *Christ* meant that He was the Messiah. *Lord* meant that He would fulfill the Davidic Covenant.

2. the truth that Jesus has died for the sins of humans and has been raised again to save them forever (1 Cor. 15:1, 3–4)

3. the coming of the Holy Spirit at Pentecost; the conversion of Saul of Tarsus; the destruction of Jerusalem in AD 70

4. The Roman emperor Constantine issued the Edict of Milan, which ended nearly three centuries of persecution.

5. Nestorians

★ God's own Son had come to earth. In order to become part of this kingdom, people needed to turn away from their sins. They also needed to believe that Jesus was the Christ, the One sent by God to save them.

Activity 6: Chapter Review

This activity helps the students prepare for the chapter test.

CHAPTER REVIEW

People, Places, and Things to Remember

Jehovah
divine sovereignty
image of God
Creation Mandate
culture
civilization
city
seed of the serpent
seed of the woman
nation
nation-states
city-states
Table of Nations
polytheism
Abrahamic Covenant
Mosaic Covenant
Ten Commandments
monotheism
Davidic Covenant
Messiah
New Covenant
Jesus of Nazareth
Christ
gospel
Judaism
Saul of Tarsus
Nero
Diocletian
Constantine
Edict of Milan
Arius
Council of Nicaea
Theodosius I
Constantinople
barbarians
Byzantine Empire
Augustine
Nestorians
Patrick

Making Connections

1. Why have all human societies been religious in some way?
2. How has the Fall damaged human religion?
3. What were the core values of the city of Babel?
4. How were the Abrahamic and Mosaic Covenants similar? How were they different?
5. Why is Jesus of Nazareth the most important human in world history?
6. What two teachings of Paul helped Christianity spread among the Gentiles?
7. How did the favor of the Roman government change the Christian church?
8. Explain how Genesis 3:15 tells the story of human history.
9. How did Christ fulfill the Creation Mandate in His coming?

Developing History Skills

1. Scan through the chapter, writing on a separate piece of paper each date mentioned. Place these dates on a timeline and label the significance of each date. What does this timeline suggest about the character of Jehovah?
2. In Paul's sermon in Acts 17, he says that God has scattered the nations and set boundaries for them, boundaries of time and place. Paul then states that God has done this so that the nations might "seek the Lord" (v. 27). Review the main events of this chapter. Explain what these boundaries did that could lead people to seek the Lord.

Thinking Critically

1. What do you think was Eve's main mistake, leading her to the first sin?
2. Evaluate this statement: "The Christian church poisons everything it touches. It caused the fall of the Roman Empire. Before the empire embraced Christianity (AD 313), the empire was strong. After this, however, the empire declined and fell."

Living in God's World

1. Study Genesis 6:1–7 in the light of this chapter's presentation of world history. Prepare a brief Sunday school lesson on what these verses teach a Christian about dating and marriage.
2. Use an encyclopedia to study the history and culture of a particular nation. From that study, write a brief report on the core values that have held that nation together throughout its history.

Chapter Review Answers

Making Connections

1. Humans are made in God's image. They know that they have not made themselves, and they sense that to understand themselves they must know their Creator.

2. Instead of seeking to know God, fallen humans seek to produce a god that is made in their own image.

3. build, make a name for themselves, and remain together (Gen. 11:4)

4. By laying out many laws that made it possible for Israel to be a nation-state, the MC helped fulfill the promise in the AC that Abraham's seed would be a great nation. The AC was God's unconditional promise to bless Abraham and all the world through Abraham. The MC was conditional. If Israel did not obey, it would be cursed.

5. He is the One sent by God to fulfill all the major promises in Scripture. He fulfilled Genesis 3:15, the AC, the MC, the DC, and the NC.

6. Jesus fulfilled the conditions of the MC; Jesus is Abraham's seed, so anyone who is united with Jesus is a descendant of Abraham.

7. The church grew even more rapidly than before. However, the purity of the church was damaged.

8. Genesis 3:15 predicts the future of the human race. Sin divided humanity into two groups: the seed of the serpent (those opposed to God) and the seed of the woman (those who follow God).

9. Christ came to restore the dominion lost by mankind in the Garden of Eden. He defeated the two main obstacles to exercising dominion: sin and death.

Developing History Skills

1. Answers will vary. Jehovah is remarkably patient. He will judge sin, and He will accomplish the redemption He has promised. But He may wait centuries to accomplish these works.

3. Suppose the United States were invaded by another nation, and many of your friends were fearful that Christianity will be destroyed. What would you say to reassure your friends?

---

2. Boundaries remind a person that he lacks power and authority. By being constantly reminded of their limitations (e.g., mountains, war, lack of knowledge, and death), humans are led to look for salvation outside of themselves and in the one true God.

Thinking Critically

1. Answers will vary. Students may mention that Eve assumed she could understand the world without believing what God had said.

2. This statement ignores the fact that the Roman Empire was in serious decline before the Edict of Milan in AD 313. Unrest, border troubles, and economic woes had plagued the empire for many years. Christianity brought to the world much more than the fall of Rome took away.

Living in God's World

1. The intermarriage of the Sethites and the Cainite line had devastating consequences, reducing the number of Jehovah's followers from perhaps millions to only eight. Christians should not marry unbelievers. Doing so damages the kingdom of God, instead of helping to build and expand it.

2. Answers will vary. Depending on the nation, the students may note values such as justice, liberty, the right to own property, and economic growth.

3. Answers will vary. Genesis 3:15 states that Satan and his forces will always try to destroy God's people, but God has said they will not prevail. Students may mention Augustine's *City of God* and reason that although nations rise and fall, God's kingdom will last forever. In fact, an invasion of America might be God's way of expanding His work in the earth (as was the case with the fall of Jerusalem and the fall of Rome).

Chapter Goals

Students should be able to

1. Trace the emergence of Islam in the Arabian Peninsula.
2. Trace the spread of Islam in Southwest Asia, North Africa, and Europe.
3. Identify the significance of the Abbasid Caliphate.
4. Describe the response of the Byzantine state to the expanding Islamic Empire.
5. Identify major contributions of the Byzantine state during this period.
6. Discuss the consequences for Europe of Charles Martel's victory over the Muslim army in 732.

500–950

Birth of Muhammad 570

Muhammad receives first revelation 610

Muhammad flees to Medina 622

Muhammad returns to Mecca 630

Muhammad dies 632

Abu Bakr dies 634

Muslim forces take control of Palestine 636

Muslim forces conquer Sassanid Empire 637

Dome of the Rock Completed 691

Muslim forces invade Iberian Peninsula (Spain, Portugal)

500   550   600   650   700

Chapter 2 Lesson Plan Chart

Section Title	Main Activity	Pages	Days
I. The Origin of Islam	Activity 1: Do Christians and Muslims Worship the Same God?	26–32	2 days
II. The Spread of Islam	Activity 3: Map Study: Expansion of Islam	32–34	1–1½ days
III. The Culture of Islam	Activity 4: Abbasid Contributions to Culture	34–36	1–1½ days
IV. The Confrontation with Islam	Activity 5: Chapter Review	36–38	1–2 days
Total Suggested Days (including 1 day each for review and testing)			7–9 days

Materials List

Section I

- CD: 2A Byzantine and Sassanid Empires; 2B Cutaway of the Dome of the Rock; 2C Cutaway of the Ka'bah; 2D Dome of the Rock—Photo 1; 2E Dome of the Rock—Photo 2; 2F Muslim Fountain for Ritual Cleansing

- Activities 1 and 2 from the *Student Activities* manual

- Pictures (or drawings on card stock) of the symbols of the three major religions of the Middle East: the star of David, the cross, and the crescent

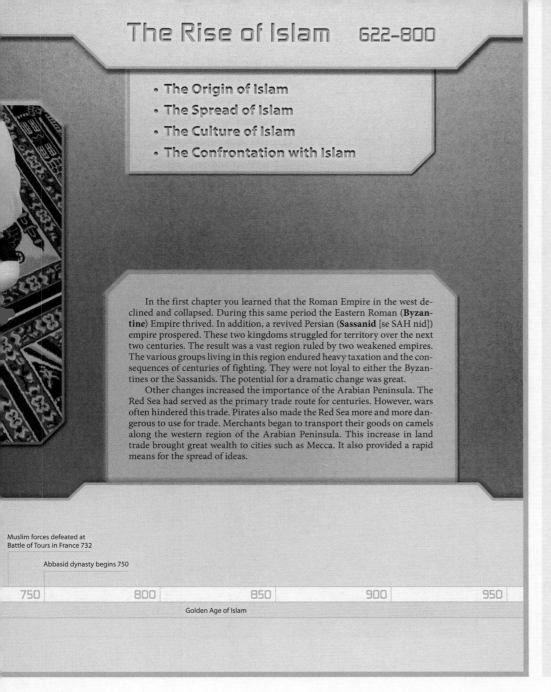

The Rise of Islam 622–800

- The Origin of Islam
- The Spread of Islam
- The Culture of Islam
- The Confrontation with Islam

In the first chapter you learned that the Roman Empire in the west declined and collapsed. During this same period the Eastern Roman (**Byzantine**) Empire thrived. In addition, a revived Persian (**Sassanid** [se SAH nid]) empire prospered. These two kingdoms struggled for territory over the next two centuries. The result was a vast region ruled by two weakened empires. The various groups living in this region endured heavy taxation and the consequences of centuries of fighting. They were not loyal to either the Byzantines or the Sassanids. The potential for a dramatic change was great.

Other changes increased the importance of the Arabian Peninsula. The Red Sea had served as the primary trade route for centuries. However, wars often hindered this trade. Pirates also made the Red Sea more and more dangerous to use for trade. Merchants began to transport their goods on camels along the western region of the Arabian Peninsula. This increase in land trade brought great wealth to cities such as Mecca. It also provided a rapid means for the spread of ideas.

Muslim forces defeated at
Battle of Tours in France 732

Abbasid dynasty begins 750

| 750 | 800 | 850 | 900 | 950 |

Golden Age of Islam

Section II
- A large outline map of the region shown in Activity 3 from the *Student Activities* manual
- Activity 3 from the *Student Activities* manual

Section III
- A copy of the book *The Arabian Nights*
- Activity 4 from the *Student Activities* manual

Section IV
- CD: 2G The Spread of Islam
- Activity 5 from the *Student Activities* manual

Section I

Objectives

Students should be able to

1. Describe the conditions on the Arabian Peninsula prior to Muhammad.
2. Evaluate the influences and events that led Muhammad to found Islam.
3. Analyze the basic teachings of Islam and evaluate them according to Scripture.
4. Explain why the Muslims became divided into Sunnis and Shiites

The Setting

The Byzantine and Sassanid empires had worn each other down in a vain attempt to take one another's territory. This vast region suffered from a power vacuum, and some invading force was going to fill this vacuum. The form of Christianity in the Byzantine Empire and across northern Africa had long since grown ritualistic. Perhaps God allowed Islam to sweep across much of the "Christian" world in order to remove the paganized Christianity that had developed. While we cannot make definitive declarations, God's hand is evident in the rise and rapid spread of Islam.

Translations and Spellings

There is no standard English translation of the Qur'an (Koran) available. Also, translations made by Muslims can vary significantly from translations made by non-Muslims. Some Muslim translators appear to obscure passages that Christian scholars have used to point out the dark side of Islam. This may or may not

Ka'bah

The Ka'bah is a stone building in Mecca that was used for pagan rituals. The original structure existed long before Muhammad's time. The Arabs worshiped hundreds of gods prior to the rise of Islam. Many of these gods were stored in the Ka'bah. Today the Ka'bah is about forty-three feet high with sides measuring thirty-six feet by forty-two feet. A black stone is set in the eastern corner of the structure. (Some people believe this stone is a meteorite.) The outside of the Ka'bah is covered by a black curtain made of silk and embroidered with gold. Muslims are required to walk around this structure seven times as part of their pilgrimage to Mecca.

I. The Origin of Islam

Life of Muhammad

Birth and Early Life

Muhammad (moo HAHM ahd) was born in **Mecca** in 570 as a member of the Quraysh tribe. This tribe was responsible for care of the **Ka'bah** (KAH buh). Muhammad's father died before his birth, and his mother died when he was six years old. His uncle cared for him and took him on commercial trips to Syria. As a young man he became a merchant and led caravans across Arabia in behalf of a wealthy widow. They married and had several children.

His travels brought him into contact with many religions, including Christianity and Judaism. Muhammad used his acquaintance with these religions to form a new faith.

Visions

At the age of 40, during the month of **Ramadan** (rahm uh DAHN), Muhammad claimed to have had a vision in which the angel Gabriel gave him revelations. He memorized the content of this and other visions. During the course of several visions he spoke with God and Satan. Muslim historians teach that the revelations were later written down by his followers in a work known as the **Qur'an** (ku-RAHN) ("recitations"). He rejected polytheism and began to teach that there was only one god (in the first chapter you learned that this practice is known as monotheism). He declared the name of this god to be **Allah** (AL uh), which is an Arabic word meaning "the god." Muhammad began to speak out against the evils practiced by the people of Mecca. He rebuked them for their practice of polythe-

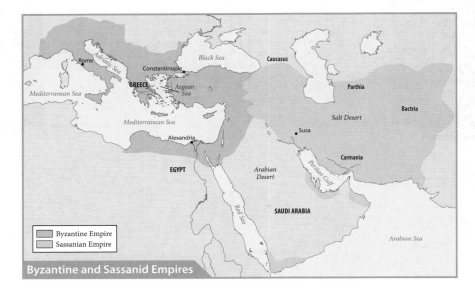

Byzantine and Sassanid Empires

- Byzantine Empire
- Sassanian Empire

CD: 2A Byzantine and Sassanid Empires

This map from the student text is also available on the CD.

Islam

Additional information about the history and doctrines of Islam, including perspectives from the Christian viewpoint, can be found in the following books:

- *Islam Rising* (Books 1 and 2) by Jim Murk
- *The Prophet and the Messiah* by Chawkat Moucarry
- *Cross and Crescent: Responding to the Challenge of Islam* by Colin Chapman

Muhammad Biography

Visit www.bjupress.com/resources for possible links to articles about the life of Muhammad.

ism and other vices. At this time the Ka'bah contained many idols and helped to bring a measure of unity to the Arab tribes. Muhammad's message threatened this unity and the prosperity that resulted from Mecca's religious importance. He gained a small following, but also faced strong opposition from his own tribe (Quraysh) and was forced to flee from Mecca in 622.

Flight to Medina

Muhammad and a small group of followers traveled to a small oasis called **Medina** (mih DEE nuh). This move to Medina became known as the **Hegira** (hih JIE ruh) ("flight"). (This event would later mark the beginning of Islam.) Medina was north of Mecca and was occupied by a group of tribal warriors. Three clans of Jews also lived and grew profitable crops there. The tribal warriors soon accepted Muhammad's teachings and submitted to his leadership. The Jews initially welcomed Muhammad's teaching about monotheism. However, they soon rejected many of his other teachings that contradicted the Old Testament text. Muhammad quickly changed from being friendly toward the Jews to oppressing them. He expanded his influence and increased his following among Arab tribes by raiding passing caravans. Muhammad took the treasures from these caravans and divided them with his growing army. These attacks also served to punish the merchants of Mecca for their rejection of his teachings. During this time he began to develop the beliefs of this new religion that would be called **Islam** (is LAHM) ("submission"). The Five Pillars of Islam comprised the core of these beliefs (see below).

Return to Mecca

The attacks on caravans led the people of Mecca to send a force against Muhammad. His army was outnumbered but prevailed in the **Battle of Badr**. Muhammad saw this victory as divine approval of his religious teachings. By 630 he had gathered an army of 10,000 and had taken control of Mecca with little fighting. He removed the idols from the Ka'bah and established monotheism. Muhammad forced the people of Mecca to accept Islam and submit to his leadership. He continued his conquest of the Arabian Peninsula until his death in 632.

Early Successors and Divisions

When Muhammad died, some **Muslims** (followers of Islam) chose Abu Bakr, one of Muhammad's first converts, to lead the movement. He took the title of **caliph** (KAY lif) (from an Arab word that means "to succeed"). However, many of the Arab tribes decided that their loyalty to Islam ended when Muhammad died. They sought political and religious independence. This breach provoked conflicts that became known as the **Wars of Apostasy**. Abu Bakr's forces defeated all who sought independence. He maintained political and religious unity by military force. Bakr and his successors also sent Arab forces to attack areas of the Sassanid Empire to distract the Muslim soldiers from possible rebellion. These attacks revealed the weakness of the Sassanids and led to a rapid conquest of their territories.

Uthmann, the third caliph, was killed by his own troops in 656 during a dispute. His army chose Ali, a cousin of Muhammad, as the next caliph. This led to a split that resulted in the two major groups in Islam: **Shiite** and **Sunni**. The Shiites believe that Muhammad intended Ali, his cousin (and son-in-law), to be his successor. They insist that he retained Muhammad's political and spiritual authority.

be intentional, but it complicates the task of accurately representing what is taught in the Qur'an. In addition, there are various spellings of words like Qur'an (Koran), Muhammad (Mohammed), and Muslim (Moslem). The authors have attempted to consistently use the most current spellings of these and other words related to Islam.

Animosity Toward the Jews

In *Islam Rising: The Never Ending Jihad Against the Jews and Israel*, Jim Murk describes Muhammad's initially positive relationship with Jews in Medina that quickly turned to oppression and ultimately violence when they rejected his teachings. Modern hatred of Jews by Muslims can be traced back to Muhammad and the beginnings of Islam.

Dangerous Job?

After Abu Bakr's death in 634, Umar became the second caliph to rule the rapidly growing Muslim Empire. He was assassinated in 644, and Uthmann succeeded him as the third caliph. However, a dispute with soldiers led to his murder in 656. The soldiers selected Ali (cousin and son-in-law of Muhammad) to be the next leader. Not surprisingly, he was assassinated in 661! Being chosen as a leader of Islam seemed to make a person more likely to be murdered.

Sunni and Shiite

Those who chose Ali as the successor of Muhammad unwittingly created a division in the Muslim world between Shiites and Sunnis. The Shiites teach that Muhammad intended Ali, a relative, to succeed him upon his death. Modern Shiites believe that only a member of

Wars of Apostasy

Take a few moments to define the term **apostasy** (abandonment of one's beliefs, including a religion or a cause) and give the students examples. Ask them to come up with other examples. Ask the students whether or not these wars were truly over apostasy. (*No. The various tribes wanted to regain their independence and practice Islam as they understood it.*)

Muhammad's tribe qualifies to become leader. In addition, the Shiites believe religious and political authority resides in one leader. The Sunnis believe that any worthy Muslim may become caliph. They also divide religious and political authority between an imam and caliph respectively. Sunnis make up around 85% of the Muslim world, and Shiites represent around 10–15%. Much of the Muslim-against-Muslim violence occurs between Sunni and Shia Muslims.

The Place of Women

While many Muslim men treat their wives with love and respect, women in Islam are relegated to a second-class role at best. The following examples from the Qur'an justify male domination over or mistreatment of women:

(1) Allah has made men superior to women. (Sura 4:34)

(2) Wife beating is allowed when the husband deems it necessary. (Sura 4:34)

(3) A Muslim woman's testimony in court is worth half as much as a man's. (Sura 2:282)

(4) Muslim men may take up to four wives. (Sura 4:3)

(5) A woman's key to Paradise is gratitude to her husband (implied in Hadith 1:28).

To learn more, see John Ankerberg's work, *Fast Facts on Islam* (pp. 53–60).

Divorce

Islam restricts the right to divorce to the man (Sura 65). While Muhammad made provision for divorced wives in the Qur'an, the practical application has left

Adding to Scripture

When you discuss the development of Islam (especially the Qur'an), ask students to give names of other religions that accept parts of the Bible but add their own "final revelations" or "holy books" to the Bible. (*Examples include Jehovah's Witnesses, Mormons, and Roman Catholics.*)

The "Unlettered Prophet"

He said, "My chastisement shall fall on whom I will, and my mercy embraceth all things, and I write it down for those who shall fear me, and pay the alms, and believe in our signs, [and] who shall follow the Apostle, the unlettered Prophet—whom they shall find described with them in the Law and [Gospel]." (Sura 7:156–157)

Dome of the Rock with cleansing fountain in the foreground

Muslims throw seven stones at Satan during their pilgrimage.

The Shiites refer to their leader as **imam** (ih MAHM) rather than caliph. The Sunnis believe that Muhammad did not appoint a successor. Instead, they believe that any worthy Muslim could be selected to lead Islam. The Sunnis refer to their political leader as caliph and their spiritual leader as imam.

Teachings of Islam

The Qur'an

Muslim scholars use Sura 7:157 to prove that Muhammad could neither read nor write. They claim that his teachings had been recited and memorized by his closest supporters. Muslim historians credit Abu Bakr and other early Muslim leaders with collecting these oral teachings and composing the Qur'an. Whether these claims are accurate or not cannot be proven. However, several versions of the Qur'an did appear among the Arab tribes. Some contained significant differences. Uthmann became caliph in 644 and collected the different versions of the Qur'an. He then produced an edited version that would become the official text of Muhammad's recitations. All other versions were burned. Shia Muslims believed that Uthmann's text excluded some of their teachings. This may have played a part in his death.

The Holy Books

Islam places the Qur'an and the **Hadith** (huh DEETH) at the top of a list of holy books that includes the writings of Moses, David (Psalms), and the "Gospel given to Jesus." The Hadith contains a description of Muhammad's life, including what he said, what he did, and what he approved. A key goal for Muslims is to follow the example of Muhammad's life.

There are many positive references to the Bible and its teachings in the Qur'an (Sura 5:44, 46, 68; 10:94; 29:46). However, Muslims believe many things that contradict the teachings of the Bible. They explain these differences by saying that the Bible was very different when the Qur'an was written. Muslims teach that the Bible contains false teaching or has been corrupted over the centuries. They claim that the Qur'an contains the final revelation from God and has been preserved from any error.

The Five Pillars

While still living in Medina, Muhammad developed the five requirements that are called the **Five Pillars** of Islam. The first pillar is repeating the creed, "There is no God but Allah, and Muhammad is the prophet of Allah." The second pillar is the daily practice of prayer. Rather than an informal prayer, it is more of a recitation. Before Muslims pray, they engage in a thorough ritual cleansing. The third pillar is almsgiving. Muslims are required to give a percentage of their wealth to those in need. The fourth pillar is fasting (going without food or drink) during the month of Ramadan (the holy month to Muslims). This fast extends from sunrise to sunset. After sunset, Muslims are allowed to resume normal eating and drinking. The fifth pillar is a pilgrimage or trip to Mecca at least once in a lifetime. Each Muslim must make this journey if he is able to do so. While at Mecca Muslims are expected to perform several rituals, including throwing seven stones at stone pillars that represent the devil.

Islamic Law

Sharia (shah REE uh) law developed early in the history of Islam. It is based on the teachings of Muhammad and those who have interpreted his teachings. Sharia can be defined as a system of divine law, belief, or practice that shapes all of life. There is no separation between religion and the state in Islam. Therefore, Muslim teachings have dominated the development of law. There are a variety of interpretations, but throughout the history of Islam, Sharia law has often resulted in harsh punishments.

Jihad

The Qur'an contains over one hundred verses that command Muslims to practice **jihad** (zhi HAHD). Jihad comes from an Arab word that means "to strive hard." Some Muslims view this as a mental struggle for each believer to become a good Muslim. However, the Qur'an uses this term in the context of a "holy war" against non-Muslims. From the beginning of Islam, Muhammad commanded his followers to kill or subdue all unbelievers. (Sura 9 contains many such references.) In Sura 47:4, Muhammad said, "When ye encounter the infidels, strike off their heads till ye have made a great slaughter among them, and of the rest [bind them tightly]." The Hadith also contains several references to this kind of jihad (Hadith 4:55, 125, 161; 9:45). Therefore, Muslims are commanded to continually be at war with all who do not submit to Islam.

Evaluation of the Teachings of Islam in Light of the Bible

The Trinity

The Qur'an denies the doctrine of the Trinity. But in rejecting this Christian teaching, it refers to the Trinity as the Father, Jesus, and Mary (Sura 5:116). The Bible nowhere teaches that Mary, the mother of Jesus, is God. And even though many through the centuries have honored—even worshiped—Mary, Christians have never claimed that she was part of the Trinity. If the Qur'an was given to Muhammad by Gabriel (who spoke for Allah), how could the beliefs of Christians be so misrepresented?

The Bible, however, teaches that God is Triune. There is only one God (Isaiah 44:6). But God exists in three Persons. The Father is called God (1 Corinthians 8:6), Jesus Christ is called God (John 1:1), and the Holy Spirit is referred to as God (Acts 5:3–4). Because God is Triune, Christians are instructed to baptize new believers in the name of the Father, the Son, and the Holy Spirit (Matthew 28:19).

Jesus Christ

Islam teaches that Jesus was a prophet and that he taught with authority. However, they deny His deity and death by crucifixion. The Qur'an (in Sura 4:171) declares that it is offensive to say that Jesus is God. However, the Bible is clear in such passages as John 10:30, Matthew 14:33, and Mark 2:5–10 that Jesus is God and has the authority to forgive sins. Muslims also deny Christ's death on the cross. They do not believe that any great prophet of God would die such a shameful death (Sura 4:157–159). Yet each of the Gospels details the crucifixion of Jesus (Matthew 27, Mark 15, Luke 23, and John 19). And the New Testament contains many references to the crucifixion of Christ as a historical event.

> #### Islam and the Trinity
> O ye people of the Book! overstep not bounds in your religion; and of God, speak only truth. The Messiah, Jesus, son of Mary, is only an apostle of God, and his Word which he conveyed into Mary, and a Spirit proceeding from himself. Believe therefore in God and his apostles, and say not, "Three:" (there is a Trinity)—Forbear—it will be better for you. God is only one God! Far be it from His glory that He should have a son! . . . whatever is in the Heavens, and . . . the Earth [is His]! And God is a sufficient Guardian. (Sura 4:171)

> #### Islam and Jesus
> And when God shall say—"O Jesus, Son of Mary: hast thou said unto mankind—'Take me and my mother as two Gods, beside God?'" He shall say—"Glory be unto Thee! it is not for me to say that which I know to be not the truth; had I said that, verily thou wouldest have known it: Thou knowest what is in me, but I know not what is in Thee; for Thou well knowest things unseen! I spake not to them aught but that which thou didst bid me—'Worship God, my Lord and your Lord.'" (Sura 5:114)

Muslim women powerless and subject to the whims of a husband who merely needs to declare "I divorce you" to make the divorce effectively final.

Sixth Pillar?

Since there are over 100 verses in the Qur'an that command Muslims to participate in holy war, many Muslim leaders (beginning with Muhammad) have established warfare against non-Muslims as a core principal of Islam. Violence in the name of Islam is nothing new. It would be dishonest to relegate this violence to a radical wing of Islam. While many Muslims do not follow this practice, it remains a central teaching in the Islamic faith.

Sharia

Islamic law developed under Muhammad to bring various groups together and bring them under submission of Islam. Islam is not just a religion but a way of life. Hence *sharia* (from an Arabic word that means "prescribed" or "ordained" [of God]) evolved to enforce submission to Islam in every area of life. All Muslims are subject to sharia. This law has many interpretations, and enforcement has varied greatly from one culture to another. However, it has often been used to inflict severe punishment. For example, sharia is used to punish Muslim women whose only crime is to report that they have been assaulted. By one estimate, about 75% of women imprisoned in Pakistan are there because they reported being assaulted. Under sharia, they are assumed to be guilty of committing adultery, a punishable offense. (See Kerby Anderson's work, *A Biblical Point of View on Islam*, pp. 87–88.)

Islam and Sin

Muslims deny the concept of original sin (inherited from Adam) and human sinfulness. They teach that Adam and Eve sinned and were removed from Paradise to the earth (Sura 2:35–37). At this point God forgave them. Therefore, Muslims reject the concept that men have a sinful nature. They deny the Fall and see no need for a Savior to pay for sin.

The Bible teaches that Adam is the representative human for the whole human race. As a result when Adam sinned, all humans were considered guilty of sin, and all humans are born with a sinful nature.

Have your students compare Muslim teaching in Sura 6:164; 17:15; 35:18; 39:7; and 53:38 with Genesis 3, Romans 5:12–19, and 1 Corinthians 15:21–22.

The Five Pillars of Islam

Portion of Saudi flag, which includes the Shahadah in Arabic

①

Shahadah
Recitation of the creed

"There is no God but Allah, and Muhammad is the prophet of Allah."

Salat
Daily practice of prayer

Muslims are called to prayer five times a day. Before they recite the *Fatiha* (Sura 1), they wash their hands, forearms, face, and feet. The also rinse their mouths and clean their nostrils. Their prayers are composed of recitations from the Qur'an.

"In the Name of God, the Compassionate, the Merciful PRAISE be to God, Lord of the worlds! The compassionate, the merciful! King on the day of reckoning! Thee only do we worship, and to Thee do we cry for help. Guide Thou us on the straight path, The path of those to whom Thou hast been gracious;— with whom thou art not angry, and who go not astray." (Sura 1)

Muslims must pray toward Mecca.

②

Poor Indonesian Muslims wait to receive a donation. Muslims are required to give at least two and one-half percent of their income to the needy.

Zakat
Almsgiving

③

Visuals

Bring in pictures of (or make from cardstock) the symbols of the three major religions of the Middle East—the "star of David" (Judaism), the cross (Christianity), and the crescent (Islam)—and discuss the importance of symbols to religions (particularly these three religions), what each symbol means, and where one might expect to see them (e.g., in cemeteries).

Activity 1: Do Christians and Muslims Worship the Same God?

This activity will help your students discern the differences between Islam and Christianity.

Activity 2: Shiite Versus Sunni

Use this activity to help the students understand the differences between these two main versions of Islam.

Escape From Darkness

Visit www.bjupress.com/resources for possible links to articles about former Muslims who have become Christians.

Pilgrims traveling to Mina to throw seven stones at pillars representing Satan

Date merchant where Muslims would shop

Sawm

Fasting during the month of Ramadan

Hajj

Pilgrimage to Mecca at least once in a lifetime

Only Muslims are permitted to enter Mecca. This is the holiest city in Islam for at least two reasons. Muhammad was born there. Also, the Ka'bah is located there.

The participants in this pilgrimage perform several rituals.

1. They circle the Ka'bah seven times.

2. They run seven times between the two hills of Mecca.

3. They travel about thirteen miles to the place where Muhammad is believed to have preached his last sermon.

4. They travel to a village to throw seven stones at pillars said to represent Satan.

Then they repeat 2 and 1.

The rituals of the *Hajj* actually predate Islam. They were practiced by Arabs long before the birth of Muhammad. He merely incorporated them into Islam.

Salvation

Islam teaches that salvation is earned by doing good works. Muslims are required to perform the Five Pillars of Islam and model their lives after that of Muhammad. However, even then there is no guarantee of salvation. Islam speaks of a day of judgment and each man's works being weighed on a great scale. The good works must outweigh the bad in order to have any chance to enter Paradise. But they are also taught that Allah predestines them to Paradise or Hell as he pleases. Therefore no Muslim can have assurance of entering Paradise and escaping Hell. However, God's Word declares that one who trusts in Christ as Savior is saved by God's grace alone (Ephesians 2:8–9, Titus 3:5). In addition, believers in Christ have assurance of eternal life in heaven (John 6:40, 47; 10:28).

The Bible

Muslim teaching about the Bible is inconsistent and contradictory. Muhammad taught that Allah had sent many prophets (including Moses and Jesus) to remind man of Allah's teaching (Sura 3:3; 5:44–48). However, he also taught that the teachings of these prophets had been lost or corrupted (Sura 2:75, 144–146; 3:65–67, 71, 78, 187; 4:46; 5:13, 15, 41; 6:91). It is worth noting that Muslims do not prove that the Bible has been corrupted. They simply quote verses in the Qur'an that make this claim. Even so, the Bible declares its contents to be inspired of God in passages such as 2 Timothy 3:16 and 2 Peter 1:19–21.

Muslims believe that Muhammad was the final spokesman for God. However, the Bible reserves this unique role for Jesus Christ. Passages such as John 1:1–3 and Hebrews 1:1–5 speak of Christ as the Word of God and the ultimate revealer of God. While Islam professes to exalt Jesus as a prophet and representative of God, it rejects Him as the Son of God. Muslims refuse to acknowledge the Christ who is clearly revealed in the Bible.

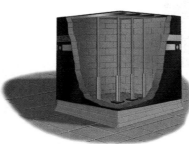
Muslims circling the Ka'bah in Mecca

Illustrations of the silk-covered Ka'bah

Cutaway of the Ka'bah

Section II

Objectives

1. Explain how Muslim forces overthrew the Byzantine and Sassanid forces.
2. Analyze how Islam spread north of the Arabian Peninsula and west to the Mediterranean region.
3. Analyze Arab Muslim success in founding an empire stretching from western Europe to India.

Section Quiz

1. What term describes the worship of many gods?
2. What book is based on the teachings of Muhammad and means "recitations"?
3. What does the term *Islam* mean?
4. What are the two main groups within Islam?
5. According to Muslims, how is one saved? Does this agree with the Bible? Cite a Bible verse to support your answer.
★ Evaluate the Muslim claims that the Bible is God's Word and yet has been corrupted.

II. The Spread of Islam

Conquest of the Arabian Peninsula

Following the Wars of Apostasy when Abu Bakr consolidated his control over Muhammad's followers, the Islamic armies quickly swept over the Arabian Peninsula and claimed it for Islam. This military campaign was a practical move for Bakr and his successors because it kept the various Arab tribes fighting the **infidels**

CD: 2B Cutaway of the Dome of the Rock

See the CD for artwork showing a cutaway of the Dome of the Rock.

CD: 2C Cutaway of the Ka'bah

See the CD for artwork showing a cutaway of the Ka'bah.

CD: 2D and 2E Dome of the Rock Photos

See the CD for photos of the Dome of the Rock.

CD: 2F Muslim Fountain for Ritual Cleansing

See the CD for a photo of a Muslim fountain used for cleansing near the Dome of the Rock.

The Ka'bah

Visit www.bjupress.com/resources for possible articles about the Ka'bah located in Mecca.

Section Quiz Answers

1. polytheism
2. Qur'an
3. submission
4. Sunni and Shiite
5. by works; no; Ephesians 2:8–9 and others
★ Answers should include the fact that the Muslim claims are inconsistent and contradictory. Muslims also fail to provide evidence to support their claims.

(unbelievers) rather than opposing the caliph or fighting with each other. In addition, it proved to be a strategic move because the Muslim forces encountered little resistance. They were able to seize large areas and greatly expand the region under Islamic control.

Expansion of Islamic Forces

Conquest of Sassanid and Byzantine Territories

The Islamic armies advanced north and west. They quickly absorbed Egypt, Syria, Palestine, and Iraq. In 637 the Arabs defeated the Sassanid forces. They were able to topple the Sassanid Empire. They also took large sections of the Byzantine Empire. Muslim forces were able to do this for several reasons. The Sassanid and Byzantine empires had fought over land for almost two hundred years. This had drained both empires of financial and military resources. They also taxed the people heavily. These empires combined many ethnic groups (including Arabs) and tribes with little in common. Many of the people living in these regions were open to change. The Muslim forces appeared to many as liberators. The caliphs also quickly gained support by lowering taxes.

Spread of Islam into Southwest Asia and the Mediterranean Region

From 661 to 750 the Muslim Empire continued to gain control of territory. This expansion began after internal conflict led to a new Muslim dynasty known as the **Umayyad** (oo MI ad) Caliphate (kal i FATE). This dynasty moved the capital of the Muslim Empire to **Damascus**. By 732 the Muslims had expanded west across northern Africa and into Europe through modern Spain. By 750 they had conquered additional territory in Southwest Asia to the western border of India.

Islamic Conversions

Conversion to Islam evolved between initial conquest and crises that occurred around the fourteenth century. During the early years, Muslim leaders were often content to allow Christians and other non-Muslims to worship freely. Non-Muslims paid a tax that

Umayyad Mosque in Damascus

The Dome of the Rock was built in Jerusalem on or near the Jewish temple site. Construction was completed in 691.

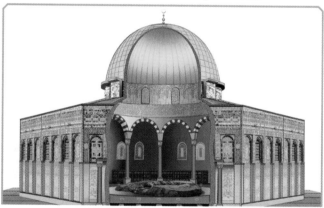
Cutaway of the Dome of the Rock

Façade Empires

A façade is "an artificial or deceptive front." By the seventh century the Sassanid and Byzantine empires only appeared to be vast and impressive. However, behind their façade lay tired and poorly managed kingdoms that lacked strong central authority and had decimated armies. Two centuries of fighting had left both empires financially and militarily vulnerable. In addition, the people who occupied these territories were a mix of many cultures, languages, and religions with little in common. Heavy taxation, compulsory military draft, and periodic religious persecution made the people resentful toward their distant rulers and willing to accept anyone who would promise them a better life.

Expansion of Islam

On paper or card stock, make a large map outline of the region shown in Activity 3 of the *Student Activities* manual. Have students take turns tracing the expansion of Islam from the Arabian Peninsula to the west and north. You could also make a similar outline on regular paper and have each student do this exercise as each conquest is mentioned in class. This will help the students visualize the tremendous expansion of Islam and will sharpen their geography skills.

Activity 3: Map Study: Expansion of Islam

This activity requires the students to practice their map skills and reinforces their knowledge of the region's geography.

Section III

Objectives

Students should be able to

1. Evaluate Abbasid contributions to mathematics, science, medicine, literature, and the preservation of Greek learning.

2. Assess how Islam won converts among culturally diverse peoples across wide areas of Africa, Europe, and Asia.

Ink versus Blood

Following the statement in the Qur'an that "the ink of scientists is more holy than the blood of martyrs," the Abbasid leaders set about to make Baghdad the "House of Wisdom." Muslim and non-Muslim scholars worked together to collect and translate all available works into Arabic. Many works of antiquity would have been lost without this great undertaking. Works gleaned from the Roman, Chinese, Indian, Persian, Egyptian, North African, Greek, and Byzantine civilizations were preserved by these Muslim scholars.

Muslim Contributions

Math

The name of the Persian scientist who developed algebra is very long and difficult to pronounce. But the term "algebra" came from the title of his work which includes the phrase *al-Jabr wa.*

---

became a great source of income for the Muslim rulers. Some Islamic rulers even sought to reserve Islam for Arabs. For various reasons, they discouraged others from converting to Islam.

Pressure to convert to Islam developed over time due to various causes. The Crusades provide one example. These campaigns by Europeans to free the Holy Land often led to forced conversion to Islam of religious groups. Other threats to Islam often led to popular demand for conversion to Islam.

In addition, under Islam, conversion became a one-way process. Those who converted to Islam were not allowed to return to their previous faith. Also, Muslims were not allowed to convert to Christianity or any other religion. To do so meant abandonment by family and friends, and it often meant death. According to Islamic teaching, those who reject Islam and those who convert to another religion from Islam are condemned to hell. Restoration is not possible (Sura 3:32).

Section Quiz

1. What term did the Muslims use to describe those who did not accept Islam?
2. Name the two large empires that lost territory or were destroyed by a Muslim invasion.
3. What Muslim dynasty moved the capital of the Muslim Empire to Damascus?
4. Were non-Muslims initially required to convert to Islam? What circumstances led to forced conversions?
★ Explain why the Muslim armies were able to defeat the Sassanid and Byzantine forces so quickly.

III. The Culture of Islam

In 750 the Islamic Empire came under new leadership with the defeat of the Umayyads. This dynasty became known as the **Abbassid** (ah BASS id) Caliphate. The capital was moved to **Baghdad** in Iraq. This move reflected a growing influence by Persians on the Muslim Empire. The emphasis of this dynasty changed from conquest to learning and culture.

Beginning in the eighth century, Islam achieved a golden age. Many non-Muslim scholars who lived under Islamic rule preserved knowledge from earlier civilizations, including Egypt, Rome, and Greece. In addition, they worked with Muslim scholars to develop important advances in science, math, and medicine. Much of this knowledge had been lost in Europe. Baghdad became the intellectual center, and many works of antiquity were initially translated into Arabic. Muslim scholarship became a storehouse from which Western scholars would later recover vital information.

Math

Nestorian and other Christian groups shared with Muslim scholars knowledge of ancient mathematical learning such as geometry (developed centuries earlier by Euclid). In addition, a Persian mathematician developed algebra during this period. Syriac Christians introduced "Arabic" numbers (1, 2, 3) to the Muslim world.

Section Quiz Answers

1. infidel
2. Byzantine and Sassanid
3. Umayyad
4. no; Crusades and other threats to Islam
★ Answers should include the fact that two centuries of fighting had left these empires weak and vulnerable.

Science

Scientific Method

Alhazen (al HA zen) developed an early scientific method based on experiments (empirical method) to prove or disprove a scientific theory. He is also regarded as the Father of Optics for his research on the theory of light. He recorded his findings in his *Book of Optics*.

Medicine

Muslim physicians took the information passed on by Nestorian scholars and made great advances in medicine during this period. Over eight hundred doctors worked in Baghdad, and they discovered important information about anatomy and diseases. One of the best-known doctors during this time was the Persian scientist Avicenna (a vi SEE na). He is regarded as the Father of Modern Medicine for works such as *The Canon of Medicine* and *The Book of Healing*.

Astronomy

Islamic scientists made corrections to the geocentric (JEE o sen trik) model (the earth is the center of our solar system) that Copernicus later used to develop his heliocentric (HEE lee o SEN trik) theory (the sun is the center of our solar system). They also made improvements on a Greek invention, the astrolabe (AS troh lab) (a tool used for solving problems relating to time and the position of the sun and stars). This instrument was later taken to Europe. It was used for such functions as computing the time during the day and night.

Chemistry

Muslim scientists laid the foundation of modern chemistry with their experiments and writings. Men like Roger Bacon and Isaac Newton read the works of Arab scientists and were greatly influenced by these works. Muslim scientists discovered chemical processes that included refining of liquids and production of chemicals such as alcohol.

Literature

While Muslim writers composed much literature during this period, the work that is best remembered is *The Book of One Thousand and One Nights* or *Arabian Nights*. This work is a collection of many folk tales told over several centuries. Characters such as Aladdin, Sinbad, and Ali Baba remain popular to this day.

Among their many works, the Persians composed a poetic romance filled with tragedy and eternal love. This work is similar to Shakespeare's *Romeo and Juliet*.

Philosophy

Islamic philosophy was not limited to religious issues. It was also not restricted to Muslims. Rather, it could be described as a type of philosophy that occurred in the Muslim Empire. The Muslims gained access to the teachings of men such as Aristotle and Plato

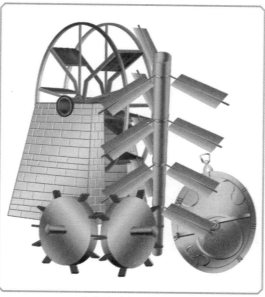

Early Islamic inventions: water turbine, crank shaft, vertical windmill, and astrolabe

Medicine

The superiority of Islamic medicine compared to that available in Europe was demonstrated when Crusaders insisted on using Muslim physicians rather than European ones. The Muslim physicians would often treat in such a way as to enable the wounds to heal. The European doctors generally amputated the injured limb but could do little else.

Chemistry

Geber (Jabir ibn Hayyan) is considered the Father of Chemistry. His works and the works of other Muslim chemists were read and utilized by European chemists in succeeding generations.

Advances

Have a volunteer research the various scientific and technological advances made during the Abbasid Caliphate and present a short report to the class.

Arabian Nights

Read aloud (or have one or two students read aloud) a story about Aladdin and other characters from the book *Arabian Nights*.

Activity 4: Abbasid Contributions to Culture

This activity will help students review the cultural advances during this period.

Technology

Muslims took many discoveries from other cultures, including China, and made improvements. They produced a number of products (including paper, glass, medicines, chemicals, and steel) in factories powered by other discoveries such as watermills, steam power, and energy from tides. They also developed crankshafts and turbines in combination with gears to mechanize their plants.

Section IV

Objectives

Students should be able to

1. Explain how the Byzantine state withstood Muslim attacks between the 7th and 10th centuries.

2. Evaluate the Byzantine role in preserving and transmitting ancient Greek learning.

3. Analyze the expansion of Greek Orthodox Christianity into Russia between the 9th and 11th centuries.

4. Evaluate the importance of Charles Martel's defeat of Muslim forces at the Battle of Tours in 732.

Section Quiz Answers

1. astrolabe

2. Avicenna

3. irrigation

4. water, steam, air, oil

★ Umayyad—primarily military expansion; Abbassid—primarily culture and scholarship

from groups such as the Nestorians and Byzantines during this period. The works of these philosophers were debated and interpreted. Perhaps the key Muslim contribution to philosophy was helping to preserve the writings of these Greek philosophers and other Greek manuscripts.

Technology

Papermaking and Other Chinese Technologies

Muslims learned from the Chinese how to make paper. They improved the process by inventing mills to make the paper. Several centuries would pass before Europe would learn of this process.

Muslim contact with China also led to knowledge of gunpowder. Muslim scientists refined the mixture and developed a much more powerful form of gunpowder.

Farming

The Muslim world made great improvements in farming by effective use of irrigation. They also developed the windmill to pump water out of the ground. This invention led to the increased production of crops such as almonds, sugar cane, and citrus fruit. These goods were later exported to Europe and brought great wealth to the empire.

Engineering

Muslim engineers learned how to use water, wind, steam, and oil to produce power. They used this energy to power such devices as paper mills, saw mills, and steel mills. They also developed crank shafts and water turbines to provide power to factories.

Industry

Many industries were developed in the Muslim Empire during this period. As new discoveries were made, factories were often built to produce new products. Some examples include glass, medicines, silk, and various chemicals. Many of these processes were later taken to Europe.

Section Quiz

1. What Greek invention that aided naval travel did the Muslims improve?

2. What Muslim scholar is regarded as the Father of Modern Medicine?

3. What farming improvement did the Muslims make to increase productivity?

4. What natural resources did the Muslims harness to produce power?

★ Contrast the Umayyad dynasty with the Abbassid dynasty.

IV. The Confrontation with Islam

Byzantine

Obstacle to the Spread of Islam

The expansion of Islam into Asia Minor was delayed for centuries by the stubborn resistance of the Byzantine Empire. While

The Confrontation with Islam

Ask the students what the heading "The Confrontation with Islam" says about the response of Constantinople and Europe to the continued expansion of Islam. (*The Byzantines and Franks fought fiercely to remain free of Islamic domination.*)

the Muslim armies conquered all the Byzantine lands in the Middle East, they could not overpower **Constantinople** (kon STAN teh NO pul), the capital of the Byzantine Empire. This large city was located on an easily defended point. It was surrounded on two sides by water and rugged terrain. The city's walls were also thick and extensive. In addition, the Byzantines had a secret weapon known as **Greek fire**. This chemical mixture burned upon impact and spread when doused with water. The Byzantine Empire gained and lost ground over the next four centuries but effectively halted the spread of Islam in this region.

Byzantine ships launching Greek fire to destroy enemy ships

During the eleventh century, Seljuk Turks took control of the Muslim Empire. In 1071 they destroyed the Byzantine army and threatened Constantinople. A small remnant of the Byzantine Empire survived for another four hundred years before a final Muslim victory.

Contributions

With the fall of the Western Roman Empire, the Byzantine Empire became the preserver of knowledge from previous generations in the West. The Greek language and important Greek manuscripts were carefully stored and copied. In addition, Greek Orthodox Christianity spread from the Byzantine Empire to the north into the Balkans and beyond. In 988 Vladimir I established Orthodox Christianity as the approved religion in Russia. The Orthodox Church had a great impact on Russia, including the development of a Slavic (SLAH vik) alphabet based on the Greek alphabet. This script made possible the translating of Greek works into the Slavic language. Russian literature prospered as a result. In addition, the Russians copied the Byzantine style of construction for their cathedrals.

European

Under the Umayyad dynasty, Islam rapidly spread across northern Africa. Soon Muslim forces were within striking distance of Europe. They crossed a narrow strait from western Africa into Europe and quickly conquered the Germanic tribes on the Iberian Peninsula.

Greek Fire

The Byzantine Empire developed a most effective weapon by combining ingredients that possibly included some of the following: petroleum, niter, sulphur, naphtha, quicklime, phosphorus, and saltpeter. Initially they launched it at ships or approaching armies with catapults. Later, they developed ways of discharging it from their ships onto enemy ships, which were quickly destroyed. The formula for this chemical mixture was such a closely guarded secret that the exact combination of chemicals is still the subject of speculation.

Thinking Critically

Islam has had a mixed history. At times Islam advanced at the point of a sword. Other times Islam advanced gradually with little coercion. Ask your students if they can think of any peaceful means used by Muslims today to attain their goal of world conquest. (*Examples might include getting Islam taught in public schools and universities, claiming rights to practice Islam under laws that prohibit discrimination, and even having large families.*) None of these are violent, and most occur without drawing public attention. It is important that your students understand the goal of Muslim conquest, but they should also be comforted by the knowledge that God and His people will ultimately triumph. Rather than hate Muslims, Christians must love them and seek to win them to Christ.

Charles Martel

Charles was born in present-day Belgium under less than royal circumstances. He rose to power, becoming the Mayor of the Palace and ruler of the Franks. Contemporaries described him as a very large man who was surprisingly agile for his stature. He was said to be a brilliant commander and the creator of heavy cavalry in the West. He laid the foundation for the Carolingian Empire (named after him), which would play a leading role in Europe during the Middle Ages.

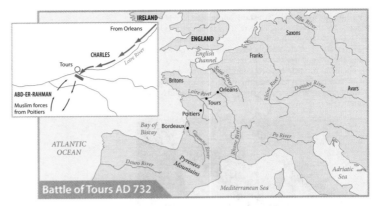

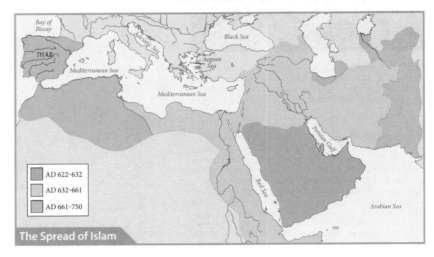

Battle of Tours AD 732

Charles, ruler of the Franks (French), led an army to stop the advance of the Muslim forces in Europe. At the Battle of Tours in 732, Charles decisively defeated the Muslim army. He effectively used heavy cavalry and wise military tactics to stop the Muslim advance. This victory earned him the name **Charles Martel** ("the Hammer") and ended the Muslim threat.

The Spread of Islam

AD 622–632
AD 632–661
AD 661–750

Section Quiz

1. What empire stopped the Muslim advance into Asia Minor?
2. Why were the Muslims unable to conquer Constantinople?
3. What title did Charles, ruler of the Franks, receive after defeating the Muslim forces? What does this title mean?

CD: 2G The Spread of Islam

This map from the student text is also available on the CD.

Charles Martel

Visit www.bjupress.com/resources for possible links about Charles Martel and his defeat of advancing Muslim armies.

Section Quiz Answers

1. Byzantine
2. Constantinople had a defensible position and thick walls, and the Byzantines had Greek fire.
3. Charles Martel; "the Hammer"

Activity 5: Chapter Review

This activity will help students review the material from the chapter.

Chapter Review

Making Connections

1. How did Muhammad and his followers gain wealth while in Medina?

2. How did Abu Bakr maintain political and religious unity?

3. How did Uthmann resolve the problem of various versions of the Qur'an?

4. Which biblical writings do the Muslims include in their list of holy books?

5. In carrying out jihad, what did Muhammad command his followers to do?

6. What does the Qur'an teach about the doctrine of the Trinity?

7. What does the Qur'an teach about the deity of Christ?

8. Why were Islamic forces easily able to conquer Sassanid and Byzantine territories?

Developing History Skills

1. Based on the information in this chapter, construct a timeline for Islam.

2. What reason do Muslims give for claiming that the Bible cannot be trusted?

Thinking Critically

1. What are some ways in which biblical Christianity is different from Islam?

2. What devices or concepts did Muslims invent/develop that still benefit us today? What was occurring in Europe during this same time period?

Living in God's World

1. With several of your classmates, write a tract that shows the differences between Islam and Christianity. Use verses mentioned in this chapter to support your work.

2. Look for articles in newspapers and magazines that deal with Islam. Bring them to class and discuss them. Ask questions such as "Is the author writing from the point of supporting Islam, or is the author opposed to Islam?" and "Is the author objective, or does the author have an agenda?"

People, Places, and Things to Remember

Byzantine
Sassanid
Mecca
Ka'bah
Ramadan
Qur'an
Allah
Medina   *Russia Tours*
Hegira
Islam
Battle of Badr
Muslims
caliph
Wars of Apostasy   *Hajj*
Shiite
Sunni
imam
Hadith
Five Pillars
Sharia
jihad
infidels
Umayyad
Damascus
Abbassid
Baghdad
Constantinople
Greek fire
Charles Martel

---

destroy Byzantine army and threaten Constantinople

2. They claim the Bible has become corrupted over the centuries.

Thinking Critically

1. Answers may vary but should include most of the following. Islam teaches a works salvation; Christianity teaches salvation by grace alone. Islam claims the Qur'an is God's final revelation through Muhammad; Christianity teaches that the Bible is the preserved Word of God. Muslims are commanded to kill or subdue all non-believers; Christians are commanded to love their enemies.

2. Answers may vary but should include several of the following: distillation, algebra, steam power, saw mills, wind mills, crankshafts, and water turbines. The so-called "Dark Ages" was a period of very limited literacy in Europe.

Living in God's World

1. Students should develop a tract showing the differences between Islam and Christianity. Refer to the chapter for this information.

2. Using the articles that students bring in, help them learn to discern between objective journalism and propaganda.

Chapter Review Answers
Making Connections

1. by raiding passing caravans

2. by military force

3. He chose one and ordered the others to be destroyed.

4. writings of Moses, David (Psalms), and the "Gospel given to Jesus"

5. to kill or subdue all unbelievers

6. The Qur'an denies it.

7. The Qur'an denies it and declares it to be offensive.

8. Those territories had fought for two centuries and had drained their financial and military sources.

Developing History Skills

1. 570—birth of Muhammad; 610—Muhammad's first "vision"; 622—flight to Medina; 630—Muhammad conquers Mecca; 632—death of Muhammad; 637—Arabs defeat Sassanid forces; 656—Uthmann, third caliph, killed by his own troops; 691—Dome of the Rock completed in Jerusalem; 732—Muslims complete conquest of Northern Africa and enter Europe; Battle of Tours; 750—conquest of Southwest Asia to the border of India; Umayyad dynasty replaced by the Abbassid Caliphate; Islamic capital moved to Baghdad; 1071—Seljuk Turks

Changes and Development in the Cultures of the World 1000–1650

This unit will examine the great contrasts between the East and the West during a six-hundred-year period. During the first half of this period, sub-Saharan Africa and Asia enjoyed great advances and strong economies. During this same era, Europe endured the Middle Ages and survived feudalism by trading goods and services. Cities in Africa and Asia flourished and experienced great access to learning. At the same time, cities were almost nonexistent in Europe and learning was limited to monks in monasteries.

However, change came to each region during the second half of this era. China endured the Mongols for a century before reclaiming their independence and expelling the Mongols by military force. African empires faded into a shadow of their former glory due to changes of trade routes and other factors that remain a mystery. Europe emerged from the Middle Ages and experienced dramatic expansion during the Renaissance and the Reformation.

Chapter Goals

Students should be able to

1. Explain key elements of African culture.
2. Analyze the significance of states in Ethiopia and West Africa.
3. Discuss the consequences of the rise of towns and the development of a maritime trade in East and South Africa.

CHAPTER 3

0–AD 1600

Greeks trade with Aksum (Ethiopia) 1st century AD				Frumentius introduces Coptic Christianity to Egypt 4th century		Rise of kingdom of Ghana in West Africa c. 500		
0	100	200	300	400	500	600	700	

Chapter 3 Lesson Plan Chart

Section Title	Main Activity	Pages	Days
I. African Culture	Activity 1: The Barozvi Creation Narrative	44–48	1–2 days
II. Early African Empires	Activity 2: The Yoruba Creation Narrative	48–53	1–1½ days
III. Growth of Trade in East Africa	Activity 3: Map Study: Africa	53–55	1–1½ days
TOTAL SUGGESTED DAYS (INCLUDING 1 DAY EACH FOR REVIEW AND TESTING)			5–7 days

Materials List

Section I

- *Cultural Geography,* 3rd edition (BJU Press)
- CD: 3A Sub-Saharan Africa; 3B Ankole-Watusi Cattle
- Activity 1 from the *Student Activities* manual

Section II

- CD: 3C Early Ethiopian Kingdoms; 3D Lalibela Churches; 3E West Africa; 3F Songhai Empire
- Activity 2 from the *Student Activities* manual

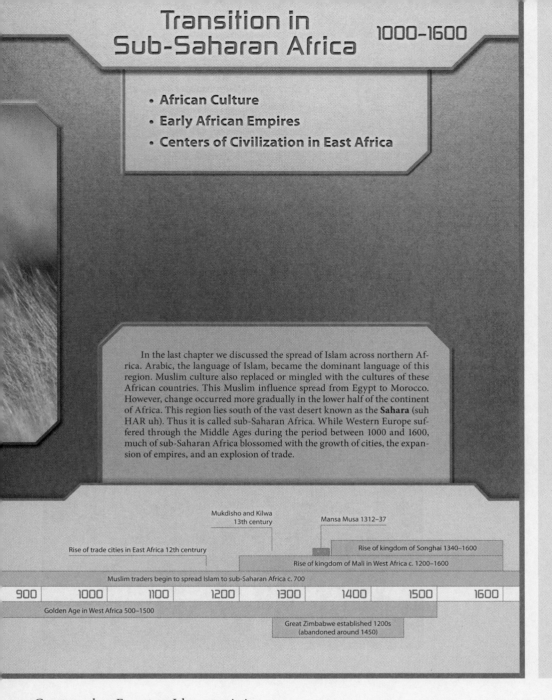

Transition in Sub-Saharan Africa 1000–1600

- African Culture
- Early African Empires
- Centers of Civilization in East Africa

In the last chapter we discussed the spread of Islam across northern Africa. Arabic, the language of Islam, became the dominant language of this region. Muslim culture also replaced or mingled with the cultures of these African countries. This Muslim influence spread from Egypt to Morocco. However, change occurred more gradually in the lower half of the continent of Africa. This region lies south of the vast desert known as the **Sahara** (suh HAR uh). Thus it is called sub-Saharan Africa. While Western Europe suffered through the Middle Ages during the period between 1000 and 1600, much of sub-Saharan Africa blossomed with the growth of cities, the expansion of empires, and an explosion of trade.

Mukdisho and Kilwa
13th century

Mansa Musa 1312–37

Rise of trade cities in East Africa 12th centrury

Rise of kingdom of Songhai 1340–1600

Rise of kingdom of Mali in West Africa c. 1200–1600

Muslim traders begin to spread Islam to sub-Saharan Africa c. 700

| 900 | 1000 | 1100 | 1200 | 1300 | 1400 | 1500 | 1600 |

Golden Age in West Africa 500–1500

Great Zimbabwe established 1200s
(abandoned around 1450)

What About North Africa?

The Sahara was (and still is) a dividing line separating northern Africans from southern Africans. Communication took place over this divide, but distinct cultures developed that differentiated the north from the south. The north, because of its proximity to the rest of the known civilized world, became involved in world affairs and lifestyles, whereas the south developed differently. North Africa is considered to be a distinct culture from the rest of Africa and so is not discussed in this chapter. Portions of northern Africa will be discussed in later chapters.

Sahara

The name "Sahara" means "desert," and it is the world's largest. This desert is roughly the same size as the United States, and it spans the width of the African continent. Annual rainfall varies from one to five inches. The average temperature is around 90°F, but it often soars above 120°F. Despite these extremes, the Sahara has served as a vital trade route for thousands of years.

- Guest speaker: Expert on Islam or missionary to a Muslim country (see p. 52)

Section III
- Activities 3 and 4 from the *Student Activities* manual
- CD: 3G East Africa; 3H Great Enclosure

Section I

Objectives

Students should be able to

1. Evaluate the importance of agriculture and iron-working for the continued development of civilization in Africa.
2. Explain the importance of extended family groups to African society.
3. Analyze the indigenous religions of Africa.
4. Describe the various geographical regions of sub-Saharan Africa and the impact of geography on African societies.

I. African Culture

Continued Development of Civilization

Agriculture

Just like other people around the world, Africans adapted to changing conditions and lived on the natural resources around them.

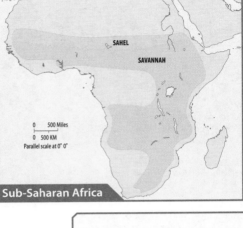

Some were able to blend growing crops with raising livestock to meet their dietary needs. Others learned to thrive on either crops or livestock depending on the available resources.

Over time, the soil became less productive or the food for livestock decreased. The people often had to move in order to survive. In time, the depleted soil would again become able to support crops and sustain life. However, as the Africans found better ways to fertilize the soil, more permanent dwellings were built and groups were able to build cities.

Improved efficiency resulted in greater yields. As more food was produced than was needed, the excess provided opportunity for trade. Increased trade and permanent settlements helped the continued development of civilization.

Crops

Depending on the region, crops such as roots or various grains were harvested. In the rain forests, inhabitants gathered roots such as yams. On the **savannah** (suh VAN uh) (flat grasslands), the people developed grain crops such as millet, sorghum, and maize (corn). Other crops such as cotton and watermelon began to appear in West Africa and in the

Sub-Saharan Africa

 Savannah

Sahara

Ask the students to name other major deserts of the world. *(Answers might include Gobi, Sonoran, Chihuahuan, Atacama, Patagonia, Kara Kum, and Arabian deserts.)* Refer to *Cultural Geography*, 3rd edition, page 380 for more information about the Sahara.

Europe in This Time Period

Have a volunteer do some research on Europe during this same period (1000–1500). *(very little trade, minimal travel, very low literacy rate, no access to spices, almost no access to the outside world, barter economy, and so on)* As you study this chapter, you may want to point out the contrast between

advances in African culture during this time and the stagnation in European culture.

CD: 3A Sub-Saharan Africa

This map from the student text is also available on the CD.

Sahel

Flaxseed and millet that will be ground into flour

Sahel (sah HAYL) (a narrow strip of land between the Sahara and the savannah). Crops such as finger millet, peas, and flax took hold in Ethiopia.

Livestock

Africans raised a variety of animals, including sheep, goats, and cattle. However, they prized these animals and seldom killed them. The animals provided milk and other benefits (such as wool)

Ankole-Watusi cattle are native to Africa.

Sahel and Savannah

Refer to *Cultural Geography,* 3rd edition, for more information about the Sahel and the savannah.

 ### CD: 3B Ankole-Watusi Cattle

Another photo of Ankole-Watusi cattle is available on the CD.

Iron

A group that learned how to process iron ore would have many advantages over a group which did not yet have this technology. The advantages include better tools, more productive agriculture and industry, superior weapons, and potential military superiority.

Dwellings

Africans used the materials available to them for construction of their dwellings. Note similar examples in early American history: logs or bark for longhouses of Eastern Indians, logs for American frontiersmen, adobe for Indians of the American Southwest, animal skins for tepees of the Plains Indians.

Extended Families

Other cultures have also placed great importance on the extended family, including the Orient.

The Dowry

Arranged marriages and a dowry have been a common tradition in many civilizations, including those in Africa and the Middle East. The dowry was the money, goods, or land a daughter brought to her new husband. It not only assured the daughter a husband but also provided the daughter with financial independence should anything bad happen in the family. The dowry was not the property of the husband. It remained the wife's throughout the marriage. In theory, it helped to ensure that the husband would remain true to the wife because if the wife returned to her family, she took her dowry with her.

for their masters. Cattle especially were considered a sign of wealth. Therefore, to kill an animal meant the loss of one's wealth. Rather than kill their livestock, the Africans added to their diets by hunting or fishing.

Ironworking

No one can say with certainty where the processing of iron ore began. Many think that it was first developed in modern Turkey or the Middle East. However, processing of iron may have developed separately in sub-Saharan Africa as early as 1,000 B.C. Even though few details are known, processing of iron seems to have appeared very early across this region. Iron proved to be valuable because it is more durable than stone, wood, or bone. In addition, it can be bent into various shapes when heated. African craftsmen forged the iron into tools, weapons, and other devices. Items made from iron also could be traded for food or other commodities. Bars of iron even served as a form of money in countries such as Ethiopia.

Importance of Extended Families

The family was the most important element of traditional African culture. An African's family affected every area of his life. The family provided a person not only with a history and traditions but also with guidance throughout his life. The family leader decided where its members lived and how they earned their living. Family leaders also told them how to behave and what to believe. Often, Africans evaluated a person according to his position in a family rather than as an individual.

The Africans believed that children were important. A man would often have several wives to rear many children. As was true in many ancient cultures, love was rarely the motivation for marriage. The parents of the children arranged the marriage for money and political benefit. In these cultures love was expected to follow marriage rather than precede it. In addition, one of the primary reasons for marriage was the rearing of children. This would make possible the survival of family traditions. Marriage and large families also led to increased family honor and wealth.

A man with several wives had children who were either brothers and sisters or half brothers and half sisters. Sometimes rivalry to gain the father's favor occurred among the wives and their children. Keeping peace at home was a difficult job for the husband. Usually each wife had a dwelling in the family compound. Daughters and sons lived in separate dwellings as well. This arrangement helped to prevent many quarrels.

The typical African family had other members besides parents and children. African families often included grandparents, uncles, aunts, and cousins. When a young woman married, she left her family group to join her husband's family group. These groups tended to live together. Sometimes a whole community consisted of people belonging to the same family.

The extended family was very important to the African culture for several reasons. It provided security for the family members. The extended family also provided a pool of wisdom and skills. Older members of the family could pass on life experience and provide a connection to the past. The extended family was a building block for African civilization.

The largest family group in Africa was the **clan**. A clan included everyone who could trace his ancestry to a common relative. The clan

> ### Dwellings
> What materials were used to build the house where you live? Africans used the materials that were available to them to house their families. Existing materials varied from region to region. Where stone was plentiful, they built their houses of stone. In other areas wood was available in sufficient supply to construct their houses. Some regions had a plentiful supply of clay, and the people baked bricks to use in building. Where no other resources were available, the inhabitants used a combination of sticks, leaves, grass, and clay to build their homes.

Extended Families

Have the students compare and contrast the role of extended families in Africa and the United States. Ask the students to suggest factors that have weakened the influence of the extended family in the United States. *(lack of respect for elders, distance between family members, diminished influence of extended family members such as aunts and uncles)*

gave the individual his history and culture. In Africa, single families belonged to clans and lived under the authority of the clan elder or chief. The clan, not families and individuals, often owned and controlled the land used by the clan members. The chief decided where the clan lived, divided the land, and determined its use. A small clan might live together in a single community, while larger clans lived in several communities. On important occasions the whole clan met together to celebrate.

African society continued one level beyond families and clans: **tribes**. A tribe consisted of two or more clans that shared the same language, beliefs, and customs. Some tribes were small, while others had thousands of members. Africa's traditional clans and tribes formed the basis for later African states and kingdoms.

Indigenous Religions

Almost all Africans believed in a Supreme Being or High God. In addition, some African accounts of Creation often bore an amazing resemblance to the biblical account in Genesis. Some believed that the High God was a spiritual being who walked with man until something caused him to separate himself from the people. The Dinka tribe of Ghana told the story that the High God walked with man until a selfish woman made him angry and he left man's company. The Sudanese told the story that a woman was so noisy that the High God went into heaven to get away from her. Africans saw the High God as kind but generally unconcerned with the affairs of men.

In addition to a Supreme Being, many Africans also believed in lesser gods who had certain areas of authority. In many ways African deities loosely resembled the gods of the Greeks and Romans. However, African clans like the **Kikuyu** did not worship many gods, but believed in one god, Ngai.

The family also played a key role in traditional African religion. Knowing that the High God was a spirit, Africans also believed that those who left this life continued to live in spirit. Thus the family included not only living members but also those dead and unborn. Like the Chinese, Africans believed that their dead ancestors influenced their present lives. They also believed that their actions affected their yet unborn children.

Many Africans believed that when the High God left, he left both spirits and humans in the world to run its affairs. This belief resulted in most Africans living in fear of vengeful spirits. These many spirits, not the Creator God, became the object of African worship. Many Africans believed that some spirits lived in trees, rocks, rivers, or mountains, while others simply lived in the air. This belief is called **animism**. By praying and sacrificing to these spirits, the Africans hoped to receive blessings. They treated the spirits of ancestors the same as these other spirits. They believed that all spirits had power to affect a person's life.

Islam

In Chapter 2 you saw the origins and spread of Islam across northern Africa. Less than a century after the death of Muhammad, Islam controlled this region north of the Sahara. The spread of Islam to regions of sub-Saharan

> ### Tribes
> The use of this term tends to cause the reader to picture people living in a primitive culture. However, in reference to Africa, the term is simply meant to describe groups that are united by a common ethnic background.

> ### Creation Stories
> The Kikuyu story of creation includes the creation of a male (Kikuyu) by the god Ngai. Kikuyu was given a wife (Mumbi), and they had nine daughters. When the daughters were old enough to marry, they met nine young men from a distant land. Their descendants became the Kikuyu clan in modern Kenya.

Egyptian mosque

Activity 1: The Barozvi Creation Narrative

The Barozvi creation narrative is an African account of Creation. You may want to lead a class discussion that highlights the similarities and differences between this account and the Genesis account.

Some similarities:

- Man is distinguished from the animals.
- Man, after killing, is sent into another land.
- Man is given a garden to keep.
- Humans try to build a tower to heaven.

Some differences:

- The god seems to be little different from the man.
- The god needs to seek advice.

Reasons for similarities and differences

The similarities probably exist because these peoples' traditions retained a memory of what really happened as recorded in Genesis. The differences exist because fallen man suppresses the truth and creates gods out of the creation (Romans 1).

Section II

Objectives

1. Explain the expansion of the Christian Ethiopian kingdom and its role in checking Islam.

2. Analyze the importance of agriculture, gold production, and the trans-Saharan caravan trade in the growth of the Ghana, Mali, and Songhai empires.

3. Explain how Islam expanded in West Africa and assess its importance in the political and cultural life of Mali and Songhai.

The Coptic Church

The Coptic Church, centered in Alexandria, claims to be the fulfillment of Isaiah 19:19. The Coptic Church is very formal and values outward, beautiful rituals. St. Mark's Cathedral in Alexandria is one of the religion's most important buildings, and the Hanging Church in Cairo is one of the religion's oldest churches. The current structure of the Hanging Church dates back to the seventh century and features the typical twin-tower façade (front), central nave, and side aisles. Coptic Church interiors feature icons, which are paintings and images of saints and apostles. The church also encourages monastic living. Near Cairo stands the oldest functioning monastery, the Monastery of St. Anthony, which dates back to AD 356.

Africa was more gradual. Islamic merchants crossed the Sahara to the savannah of West Africa in trade caravans. Islamic merchants also traveled to East Africa from Arabia and Persia. Islam came to South Africa in yet another way—with slaves brought in from Indonesia and Southeast Asia. These Muslims brought their religion with them. Over time, some of the Muslim merchants settled in West and East Africa and established communities. Initially Islam and Coptic Christianity coexisted peacefully. However, over time, Islam became dominant and, to varying degrees, imposed its beliefs on the people.

Section Quiz

1. What types of food were grown in sub-Saharan Africa?

2. Why did the Africans avoid killing their livestock?

3. What term refers to the belief that spirits live in rivers, trees, rocks, and mountains?

4. Which African clan in Kenya believed in one god and had an account of Creation that somewhat resembled the account in Scripture?

★ How did the spread of Islam in sub-Saharan Africa differ from that in northern Africa?

II. Early African Empires

East—Ethiopia

As the Egyptian kingdom expanded north along the Nile, it encountered Kush. In the eighth century BC, a Kushite king conquered Egypt and established the capital of Upper Egypt in the Kush city of Napata. Napata maintained its power for one hundred years until the Assyrians took over. The kingdom of Kush was little affected by these power changes.

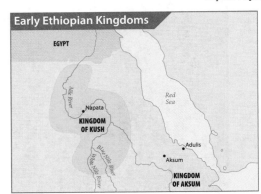

Early Ethiopian Kingdoms

Below Kush was another ancient kingdom known as Aksum. In the first century AD, Aksum and the nearby Red Sea port city of Adulis were important trading centers for the Greeks. The Greeks gave Aksum (and all the territory below it) the name **Ethiopia**.

Ethiopian legend states that the queen of Sheba and King Solomon had a child, Menelik, from whom all Ethiopian rulers are descended. The Ethiopians even use the imperial title "The Conquering Lion of the Tribe of Judah." Legend also said that the Tabot, a wooden box on the altar in the cathedral at Aksum, contained the original ark of the covenant.

In the mid-fourth century AD, in the court at Aksum, a slave named **Frumentius** rose in favor with the king and introduced Coptic Christianity to the people. When King Ezana accepted Christianity, the head of the Coptic Church in Egypt ordained Frumentius as bishop of the Ethiopian church. Slowly over the next two hundred years a great number of the population were converted to Coptic Christianity. When the Muslims conquered Egypt during the 1200s, ties to the Egyptian church were cut, and Ethiopia struggled to de-

---

Section Quiz Answers

1. grains, watermelon, peas, and roots (yams)

2. They were considered a sign of wealth, so people used them for milk and other products.

3. animism

4. Kikuyu

★ The spread of Islam in sub-Saharan Africa followed trade routes. It was gradual and generally nonviolent. The spread of Islam in northern Africa resulted from rapid military conquest.

🔘 CD: 3C Early Ethiopian Kingdoms

This map from the student text is also available on the CD.

🔘 Ancient African Empires

Visit www.bjupress.com/resources for possible links to articles about ancient African empires.

🔘 The Coptic Church

Visit www.bjupress.com/resources for possible links to articles about the Coptic Church.

Lalibela

In Chapter 2 you learned that Muslims make a pilgrimage to Mecca, which is their holy city. The Coptic Church also has a holy city which they regard as a New Jerusalem and to which they make pilgrimages. It is the city of Lalibela. In the early thirteenth century, King Lalibela led the Coptic Church to build eleven churches. These churches are unique because they were carved out of rock. In fact, they were carved out of solid bedrock below ground level. So, standing on ground level, one can look down on the churches carved out of the rock. These churches have windows and have been sculpted inside and out. St. George's Church, the most famous of these churches, is shaped like a cross.

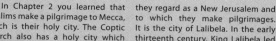

fend itself from the onslaught of the Muslims. During this period, Ethiopian Christianity developed its own unique way of worship, incorporating drums and dancing into its services. It was also during this time that unique structures for worship were built in **Lalibela**.

West

The states of western Africa developed around the year 500. Starting as small city-states headed by a clan or tribal chief, these tribal kingdoms conquered other city-states and clans, thus growing into empires. Gold production in these nations became so prominent that the period between 500 and 1500 is called the Golden Age. The largest and most important empires of the region followed one another: **Ghana** (GAH nuh), **Mali** (MAH lee), and **Songhai** (SONG HYE). This final kingdom lasted until the end of the sixteenth century.

Ghana

This ancient African empire grew from the extensive trade passing through western Africa around the fourth century. Ghana was strategically located between two rivers and the Sahel and savannah regions of Africa. The growth of trade using camels to carry goods brought great wealth to this region. Traders bearing salt came from

Salt

Salt seems to be such an insignificant item today. Of course, salt is in almost every processed food that we buy and is essential to many foods (yeast breads, for one), but as far as value is concerned, a 26-ounce container of salt can be purchased for a few cents an ounce.

However, at one time salt was an important trade item. Everyone needed salt. Salt was a crucial item for preserving foods. It continued as an important preserving item until refrigeration became available in the early 1900s. Salt was considered so valuable that gold-producing regions, such as Ghana, would trade gold in exchange for salt.

CD: 3D Lalibela Churches

Photos of the Lalibela churches are available on the CD.

Activity 2: The Yoruba Creation Narrative

This activity contains an excerpt from the Yoruba creation narrative. The Yoruba were a people group in western Africa.

Salt

For more information about salt, consult Mark Kurlansky's book *Salt: A World History*.

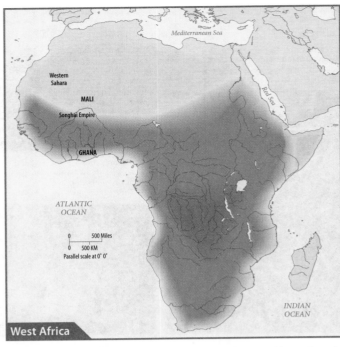

West Africa

Timbuktu

This city is located in western Africa near the Niger River at the southern edge of the great Sahara. (See map on p. 51.) Around the year 1100 Timbuktu became a leading city of the African kingdom of Mali. Trade caravans crossed the desert to buy and sell goods in Timbuktu. Merchants from as far away as Egypt and Italy traded fabrics, salt, ivory, spices, ostrich feathers, and, most importantly, gold and slaves.

The great Mali ruler Mansa Musa (1312–37) transformed the city into a center for the arts and learning as well. He built a great Islamic mosque and encouraged the founding of schools and libraries. So many scholars came to Timbuktu that books soon became an item of trade almost as important as gold and slaves. At its height, Timbuktu had over twenty-five thousand inhabitants, a large number for medieval times. (By comparison, Rome at that time had a population of seventeen thousand.) A merchant from Florence, Italy, Benedetto Dei, visited in 1470 and found a prosperous city with ornate mosques and the rich and the poor dwelling together. In the sixteenth century, Leo Africanus, a Moor (a Muslim of North African and Berber descent), told of a splendid city with many scholars and a dazzling court life. Such prosperity did not last, however. Warfare disrupted trade and stopped the flow of wealth into the city. By 1828 French explorers found the city in ruins.

the north, and traders bearing gold came from the south. The people of Ghana profited from this trade. With the expansion of Islam after the seventh century, Ghanaians (gah NAY ans) began to trade with Muslim merchants. By the eleventh century Ghana's rulers had converted to Islam.

The Soninke people formed the main ethnic group in this region. The Soninke ruler demanded gold nuggets as a form of taxation for the traders to pass through Ghana. This tax provided great wealth and growth for the empire. However, by the beginning of the thirteenth century, Ghana's military might had faded. Leaders of another kingdom absorbed this territory into what became known as Mali.

Mali

During the early thirteenth century, a new power arose in western Africa. Under the leadership of King Sunjata, the forces of Mali defeated the current rulers. Sunjata then built a much larger empire and absorbed territories south and west to the Atlantic Ocean. In addition, the empire controlled land east across the savannah. Mali retained influence

CD: 3E West Africa
This map from the student text is also available on the CD.

Timbuktu
Visit www.bjupress.com/resources for possible links to articles about Timbuktu.

over this great region because of its ability to raise a large army and control trade, especially gold. Since the rulers were able to provide a secure environment, trade flourished and great wealth poured into this empire.

Eventually the rulers of Mali converted to Islam. The most famous *mansa* (MAHN sa), "ruler", was **Musa** (MOO sa) (Mansa Musa). In 1324 he made a pilgrimage to Mecca. Musa brought along a great number of slaves, camels, and much gold. His trip and great display of wealth brought Mali to the attention of the medieval world. According to tradition, Musa gave away so much gold that he reduced the value of gold in that region for several years.

Songhai

As Mali's influence declined, a new empire developed that replaced it. The Songhai Empire lay farther to the east toward the Niger River. It was founded by Sunni Ali. He ruled during the last half of the fifteenth century. Ali conquered land along the Niger River and westward to the remnants of the Mali Empire. He struggled to maintain a smooth relationship with the general population and key Muslim merchants in newly conquered cities, especially **Timbuktu** (tim buk TOO). This empire collapsed in 1591 when overrun by Moroccan forces with muzzle-loading firearms.

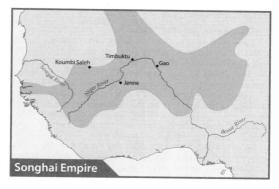

Songhai Empire

Commerce

Agriculture

West Africa is located on the savannah and Sahel regions that lie between the Sahara and tropical forests. As previously mentioned, crops ranged from grains and roots to cotton. However, this region became one of the first to combine a farm-based economy with a trade-based economy. West Africans developed iron production and turned this ore into many useful products. They also learned to work with **camels** and soon became involved in trade across the Sahara. In addition to cultivating food, the West Africans produced valuable trading items such as iron, cotton cloth, and gold.

Gold Production

Following the decline of Mali and Songhai, some of the West Africans (known as Akan) thrived through a combination of farming and mining for gold. They traded with tribes from the Sahel and the

Gold nuggets

CD: 3F Songhai Empire

This map from the student text is also available on the CD.

Mansa Musa

Visit www.bjupress.com/resources for possible links to articles about Mansa Musa.

More about Camels

If camels are used early in the morning or on moonlit nights (the preferred times for crossing the desert), they can cover 30 km (19 mi) in a day. Also, camel milk is the principal source of nourishment for desert nomads.

Camel in Egypt near Giza

Ships of the Desert

Many people believe that camels store water in their humps. However, they store water in their body fluids. This enables them to go for days without having access to water. Camels can also lose up to thirty percent of the water in their bodies with no ill effect (most mammals would die after losing up to fifteen percent). When they do drink, camels can take in twenty-six to forty gallons in about ten minutes! They also draw moisture from green plants that they eat to meet some of their moisture needs.

The camel is able to eat plants that most other animals could not. Its lips and mouth are tough to allow it to eat thorns and branches. Its teeth are sharp and enable the camel to feed on many things, including skin and bones. In addition, the camel swallows food after brief chewing, like a cow, and regurgitates and chews the food as a cud later.

God designed camels in such a way that men could use them to travel across deserts. This creature is one example of how God has enabled man to carry out the Creation Mandate to subdue the earth, even in the hostile environment of the Sahara.

Ivory Coast. Their diligent labor produced wealth and power as they gained control of trade. The Akan also exchanged gold for products from distant lands through the Portuguese traders at coastal settlements. The abundance of gold mined in this region led Europeans to refer to it as the **Gold Coast.**

Trans-Saharan Caravan Trade

Caravans traveled from oasis to oasis in order to survive the hazardous journey across the Sahara. Often the distance between oases took several days to travel. As was previously mentioned, West Africans were among the first to use camels to travel across the Sahara. They were one of the few animals that could survive these journeys.

Camels are uniquely suited for this harsh, sand-covered terrain for many reasons. They are able to store energy-rich fat in their humps, which provides nourishment as needed. In addition, camels can store enough liquid to survive five to seven days without water. They also have long eyelashes and nostrils that can be closed during sandstorms. Finally, these animals are able to withstand the extreme temperature changes found in the desert.

Camels were used to carry many goods on trade routes through this desolate and arid region since they are able to carry loads over long distances where water is very scarce. This made them a vital tool in hauling goods. Trade across the Sahara would have been greatly reduced, if not impossible, without the use of camels.

Expansion of Islam

The expansion of Islam to western Africa by way of Muslim traders led to an increased Islamic influence on African culture. Over time, the number of Muslims in this region increased to the point where Islam became the most influential religion. There would often be a great effort to convert rulers to Islam. Their conversion would ensure the security and influence of this religion. However, the conversion of a ruler seldom led to the conversion of average citizens. The people were generally free to practice whatever religion they desired. Some blended Islam and an ancient religion, praying to Allah and offering sacrifices to their gods.

In addition to their beliefs, the Muslims brought a written language. Islamic scholars traveling in Africa taught the people to read

Gold

Have the class develop a list of the many uses of gold. Students might immediately think of jewelry, coins, or even dental work. Help them to expand their list with lesser known technological applications of gold, such as thread for embroidery, reflector material used in satellites and space suits, and photo development. Gold wire was also used in some of the experiments during the Manhattan Project, which developed the first atomic bomb during World War II.

Camels

Have a student volunteer to research and report to the class on various kinds of camels and where they are found. Ask one student to do a report on how the U.S. Army once tried to use camels in the deserts of the American Southwest.

👤 Guest Speaker

Invite a Christian who is an authority on Islam (or a missionary to a Muslim nation) to discuss the problems, challenges, and opportunities of working and ministering in a Muslim country.

and write Arabic. The same scholars recorded what they saw in Africa and gave us the first written history of the continent. Slowly the ability to read and write changed the culture of Africa, which had known only oral recording of history and tradition.

Section Quiz

1. What name did the Greeks give to Aksum and all territories below it?
2. What was the name of the slave who introduced Coptic Christianity to Ethiopia?
3. List the three early empires of West Africa in chronological order.
4. What famous city was located near the Niger River?
5. The abundance of gold in West Africa led Europeans to refer to this region as the _____.
★ Why was the camel essential for trans-Saharan trade?
★ Why did Christianity decline while Islam expanded in West Africa?

III. Growth of Trade in East Africa

Trading cities grew up along the coast, where Africans from the interior brought gold, ivory, and precious stones. Many of these goods arrived at the coastal cities on the heads of porters who had walked hundreds of miles across the continent. Merchants from Arabia, India, and even China sailed to these cities to trade. Eventually these goods from Africa went to markets throughout Asia. The language of these cities reflects the meeting of many cultures. The people spoke a common trade language known as Swahili (see below).

East African Cities

Rise of Commercial Cities

Around the twelfth century, the development of trade along the coast of East Africa resulted in the formation of many cities. These cities became points of exchange between goods produced or mined in the interior and those offered by foreign traders. Cities such as Mapungubwe, Manda, and Shanga thrived on the trade of products such as gold, slaves, and ivory. However, within a century, these cities declined in importance as other cities arose to take their place. Cities like Mukdisho (modern Mogadishu on the Somali coast) and Kilwa rose in prominence during the thirteenth century. (More about the city of Kilwa will be discussed below.)

Traders came to cities along the East African coast by July to have their goods loaded on ships bound for Asia. The summer monsoon winds carried the ships east. Then the goods would be exchanged for Asian products. In October the winds reversed direction and carried the ships back to the ports in Africa. As long as this trade was protected, commercial prosperity was ensured. Empires developed, in part, to protect this profitable trade.

Significance of Swahili

Swahili is a trade language built upon the Bantu language. This language has served as the native tongue of various groups living

Section III

Objectives

Students should be able to

1. Explain the rise of commercial towns on the East African coast and the significance of Swahili as a language of trade.
2. Assess the importance of Islam, Arab settlement, and maritime trade in the economic and cultural life of Kilwa and other East African coastal cities.
3. Analyze the importance of Great Zimbabwe as a state and commercial center with links to the Indian Ocean trade.

Somalia

Mukdisho (modern Mogadishu) was a vital coastal city involved in African trade during this period. Today this city and the country of Somalia are known only for violence, revolution, and piracy. Somali pirates often make the news for their daring attacks on vessels passing through the Gulf of Aden at the southern tip of the Red Sea.

Section Quiz Answers

1. Ethiopia
2. Frumentius
3. Ghana, Mali, Songhai
4. Timbuktu
5. Gold Coast
★ Answers may vary. The camel could store its food and water and travel for five to seven days without water. The camel could withstand the extreme temperatures of the desert climate.
★ Islam came to West Africa with Muslim traders. Continued Muslim migration to West Africa led to a dominance of Islam and conversion of African rulers to Islam.

 Activity 3: Map Study: Africa

This map activity will reinforce the students' knowledge about the location of regions and other features found in Africa.

Swahili

Ask the students to suggest reasons that trading centers developed along the coasts of Africa and why the use of a common language such as Swahili was essential to the development of trade. Explain why English has become the language of trade and diplomacy (e.g., the British Empire; American involvement around the world since the late 19th century).

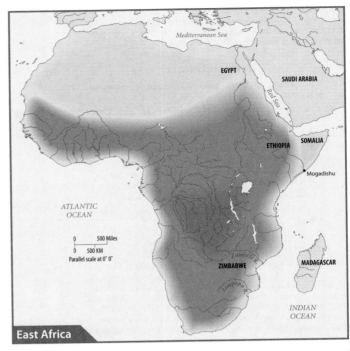

East Africa

along the southeast African coastline. About thirty-five percent of the Swahili words are Arabic in origin. This Arab influence resulted from centuries of contact between Arab traders and many different Bantu-speaking peoples living along Africa's Indian Ocean coast. Swahili also uses words from many other languages, including English. This foreign influence was caused by the migration of many nationalities to this region and by contact through trade with different groups of people.

This common language enabled many tribes and nationalities to carry on trade. It made large-scale trade possible and resulted in goods traveling from Africa to places as far away as Cathay (China) and Cambay (a city in India). In addition, goods from distant countries made their way to East Africa.

Zimbabwe

In the mid 1200s Mapungubwe was abandoned, and the city of Great **Zimbabwe** (zim BAHB weh) was established on the Zimbabwe Plateau near the Sabi River. This city grew to a population of 15,000 to 20,000 citizens in the 1300s. The empire that developed was located in southeastern Africa between the Limpopo and Zambezi rivers. Zimbabwe thrived on raising cattle and exporting gold, slaves, and ivory to the coast. Trade from India and China also passed through this empire.

Great House of Stone

Zimbabwe means "great house of stone" or "place of stone houses." This city-state grew into a great empire over two centuries. The ruins cover 1,800 acres and include an area more than one hundred miles in diameter. In addition, bone fragments show that thousands of cattle were killed for meat. The vast eating of beef indicates a large wealthy class who could afford such luxury.

CD: 3G East Africa
This map from the student text is also available on the CD.

For at least two hundred years Zimbabwe expanded and built massive stone buildings and enclosures. The most famous structure is the Great Enclosure, which still stands thirty-five feet high with a base about fifteen feet thick. Perhaps even more impressive is that these great buildings were built without mortar. The stones were carefully cut and fitted together with precision. Many of the structures have survived for over seven hundred years.

This empire lay about two hundred miles from the East African coast. Therefore, it relied on coastal cities to receive and transport trade. **Kilwa** became a key port through which Zimbabwe's gold was transported north.

For reasons unknown, this empire fell into rapid decline during the early fifteenth century. By the 1450s Great Zimbabwe was abandoned by most of its occupants.

> ### Kilwa
> Muslim explorer Ibn Battuta wrote about his visit to this city in 1331. He described Kulwa (Kilwa) as "one of the finest and most substantially built towns; all the buildings are of wood and the houses are roofed with *dis* reeds. The rains there are frequent. Its people engage in *jihad*, because they are on a common mainland with the heathen Zinj people and contiguous [next to] them, and they [citizens of Kilwa] are for the most part religious and upright, and Shafiites in rite."

Ruins of the Great Enclosure

African Culture and European Bias

For many years Europeans denied that Africans could have built such structures as the Great Enclosure and other lasting architectural works. They found it inconvenient to have their subjects being the descendants of great cultures and empires. Instead, they attributed these works to the lost tribe of Israel, the Queen of Sheba, the Phoenicians, or even King Solomon's mines. Since European colonization of Africa was often justified as a means of bringing civilization to this continent, the facts of pre-existing civilization had to be explained away.

Section Quiz

1. List three products traded in East Africa.
2. What trade language developed from the Bantu dialect?
3. Goods traveled from East Africa to what distant lands?
4. What was the name of the city where the Great Enclosure was built?
5. What city became a key coastal port for the empire of Zimbabwe?
6. What do the remains of thousands of cattle bones indicate about the city of Great Zimbabwe?
★ What religion did Ibn Battuta find in Kilwa?
★ Why did the people of Kilwa engage in *jihad*?

CD: 3H Great Enclosure
Photos of the Great Enclosure are available on the CD.

Kilwa Kisiwani
Visit www.bjupress.com/resources for possible links to articles about Kilwa.

Section Quiz Answers
1. Answers will vary but could include gold, ivory, and precious stones.
2. Swahili
3. Answers should include India and China.
4. Great Zimbabwe
5. Kilwa
6. A large number of very wealthy people lived there who could afford the luxury of eating beef.
★ Islam
★ because they considered the non-Muslims to be "heathen"

Activity 4: Chapter Review
This activity will help students review the material covered in the chapter.

CHAPTER REVIEW

People, Places, and Things to Know

Sahara
savannah
Sahel
clan
tribe
Kikuyu
animism
Ethiopia
Frumentius
Lalibela
Ghana
Mali
Songhai
Musa
Timbuktu
camel
Gold Coast
Swahili
Zimbabwe
Kilwa

Making Connections

1. Why did early African tribes need to migrate?
2. How did Islam spread to sub-Saharan Africa?
3. How did Ghana grow into an empire?
4. What led to the decline of Timbuktu?
5. Why was the west coast of Africa referred to as the Gold Coast?
6. Why was the camel called the "ship of the desert"?
7. How did the development of Swahili enhance trade?
8. Why did Zimbabwe's empire decline?

Developing History Skills

1. Talk with your parents and grandparents and construct a family tree based on what you can learn from them. This is a form of oral history that was used in many cultures, including Africa. Graph your findings on a sheet of paper and share them with your class.
2. Contrast the level of trade and learning in Europe and in sub-Saharan Africa during this period. You may need to refer to the World History textbook or other sources to learn more about Europe during the Middle Ages in order to complete this assignment.

Thinking Critically

1. Empires are formed when one country takes control of other countries. What are the benefits of an empire? What are the problems with an empire?
2. When Europeans discovered Great Zimbabwe, they said Africans could not have built this structure. Evaluate this position biblically. (Use verses such as Genesis 4:17 and 11:1–4 for ideas.)
3. Read the Barozvi creation myth (available in the Student Activities Manual in Chapter 3, Activity 1) and write a brief paragraph explaining why there are similarities to the Genesis account. Then write a brief paragraph explaining why there are differences from the Genesis account.

Living in God's World

1. Write an editorial on why maintaining strong trade relations with others nations in the world is important for your country. Use the history of Ghana, Mali, and Songhai as evidence to develop your argument.

Chapter Review Answers

Making Connections

1. The soil became less productive, and the food for livestock decreased.
2. gradually through Muslim merchants
3. through extensive trade that passed across western Africa
4. warfare that disrupted trade and stopped the flow of wealth into the city
5. the abundance of gold mined in this region
6. Camels are uniquely suited for this harsh region. They can store energy-rich fat and store enough liquid to survive for five to seven days.
7. This common language enabled many tribes and nationalities to carry on trade.
8. No one knows why Zimbabwe declined.

Developing History Skills

1. Answers will vary.
2. Answers will vary. Europe was largely restricted to local trade or living off the resources available on the manor. Learning was also limited to a tiny percentage of the European population, mostly those living in monasteries. Trade in much of Africa included many precious commodities through contact with distant nations by land and by sea. Learning was much more widespread, and sprawling empires developed.

Thinking Critically

1. Answers will vary. Economic benefits would include extensive trade and protected trade routes, which would lead to greater wealth; an empire might also lead to a common language and a common currency. Problems might include the question "Is it right for one group to take over another group by force?" Also, empires lead to a concentration of wealth, which often leads to corruption.
2. Cain built a city shortly after Creation. The descendants of Noah built a great city and a tower shortly after the Flood.

2. Keep a journal about how you have evaluated people for the past week (don't use real names). At the end of the week, review your evaluations in light of African values noted in the extended families section. How would your evaluations be different? Compare both sets of evaluation with what you know the Bible says about how you should think of others.

God has gifted man so that building structures seems to be a natural instinct. The denial of African achievement was at best misguided and at worst racism.

3. Similarities exist because generations passed down accounts of Creation and some details remained very similar to the Genesis account. Differences exist because men are sinners and they altered the actual story of Creation to fashion gods like themselves. They also tended to place the blame for the Fall and all of its consequences on their gods rather than on themselves.

Living in God's World

1. Answers will vary.
2. Answers will vary.

Chapter Goals

Students should be able to

1. Explain why China experienced growth of cities and commerce during the 10th through 16th centuries.

2. Analyze the developments in Japanese and Southeast Asian civilizations during the 10th through 16th centuries.

3. Evaluate the consequences of the Mongol invasions and the Mongols' demise during the 11th through 17th cen-turies.

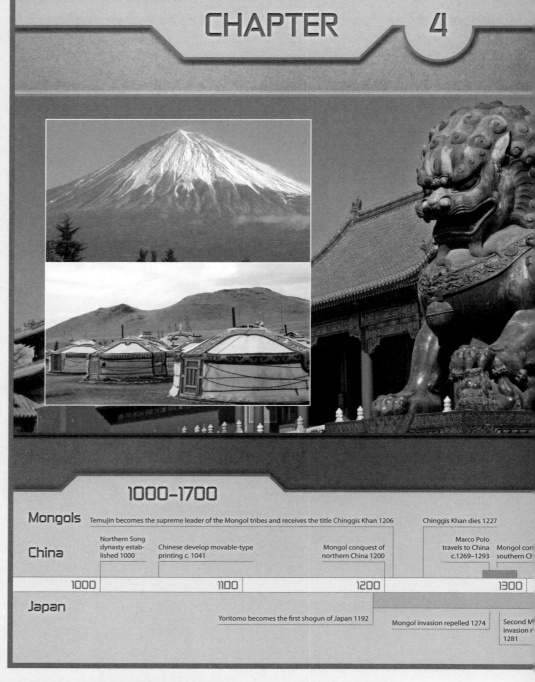

1000–1700

Mongols	Temujin becomes the supreme leader of the Mongol tribes and receives the title Chinggis Khan 1206		Chinggis Khan dies 1227	
China	Northern Song dynasty established 1000 — Chinese develop movable-type printing c. 1041	Mongol conquest of northern China 1200	Marco Polo travels to China c.1269–1293 — Mongol con[...] southern Ch[...]	
	1000 1100 1200 1300			
Japan	Yoritomo becomes the first shogun of Japan 1192	Mongol invasion repelled 1274	Second M[...] invasion r[...] 1281	

Chapter 4 Lesson Plan Chart

Section Title	Main Activity	Pages	Days
I. Growth of Cities and Commerce in China	Activity 1: Marco Polo's Journals	60–64	1–2 days
II. Developments in Japan and Southeast Asia	Activity 2: Matching Exercise: Japan and Southeast Asia	65–67	1–1½ days
III. Rise of the Mongol Empire	Activity 3: Mongol Invasion of Japan	67–73	2–2½ days
TOTAL SUGGESTED DAYS (INCLUDING 1 DAY EACH FOR REVIEW AND TESTING)			6–8 days

Materials List

Section I

- CD: 4A Asia and Surrounding Countries; 4B Early Chinese Coins
- A teabag
- Activity 1 from the *Student Activities* manual

Section II

- Activity 2 from the *Student Activities* manual
- Guest speaker: someone from the Far East or Southeast Asia (or a missionary)
- CD: 4C Japan; 4D Vietnam Prior to 1471

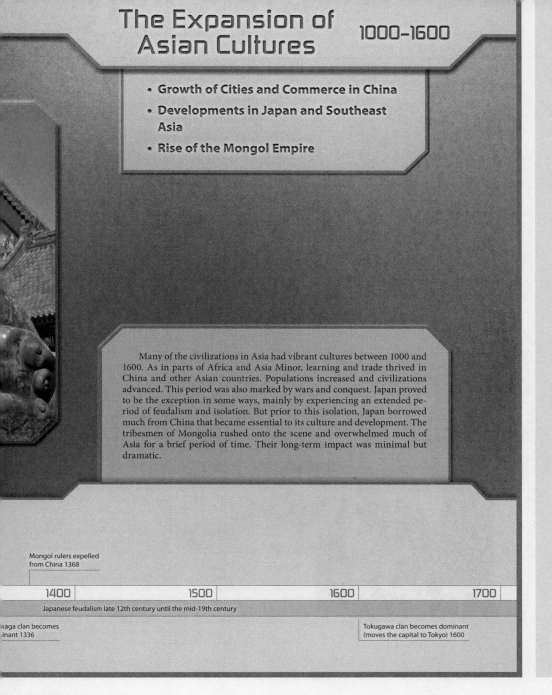

The Expansion of Asian Cultures 1000–1600

- **Growth of Cities and Commerce in China**
- **Developments in Japan and Southeast Asia**
- **Rise of the Mongol Empire**

Many of the civilizations in Asia had vibrant cultures between 1000 and 1600. As in parts of Africa and Asia Minor, learning and trade thrived in China and other Asian countries. Populations increased and civilizations advanced. This period was also marked by wars and conquest. Japan proved to be the exception in some ways, mainly by experiencing an extended period of feudalism and isolation. But prior to this isolation, Japan borrowed much from China that became essential to its culture and development. The tribesmen of Mongolia rushed onto the scene and overwhelmed much of Asia for a brief period of time. Their long-term impact was minimal but dramatic.

Mongol rulers expelled
from China 1368

| 1400 | 1500 | 1600 | 1700 |

Japanese feudalism late 12th century until the mid-19th century

kaga clan becomes
inant 1336

Tokugawa clan becomes dominant
(moves the capital to Tokyo) 1600

Section III
- CD: 4E Mongol Empire 1279
- Activities 3 and 4 from the *Student Activities* manual

Section I

Objectives

Students should be able to

1. Understand the transitions in leadership and expansion in agriculture, population, and commerce in China.
2. Explain the importance of Chinese inventions and technology for all cultures and nations.
3. Analyze why the merchant class were historically minimized and had to struggle for recognition.
4. Analyze the religions of China.

Dynasty

This term is used to refer to a progression of leaders from the same family. When a family or group with a common ancestor rules for several generations, this group is known as a dynasty. Often the dynasty is named after its most famous member. At other times a dynasty is named after the city that serves as its capital or center of power.

Census in China

Population numbers varied greatly for several reasons. Some counts were based only on tax lists. Women and children, among others, did not pay taxes and were not included in those census counts. At other times the dynasty in power was in decline and could not produce an accurate count. Tragically, wars also lowered the census counts due to deaths ranging from thousands to millions of people. For example, when the Ming dynasty fell to the Manchus in the

Asia & Surrounding Countries

Chinese Government

During the T'ang dynasty, the emperors developed a strong centralized government. To staff the government, civil service tests were given, and only the best and brightest scholars were selected. As long as the process was strictly monitored, the most capable men were appointed to government positions. Over time, however, bribery and corruption entered the process, and government positions were sold to the highest bidders. China suffered the consequences of a corrupt government.

Samples of sorghum grain

I. Growth of Cities and Commerce in China

Transitions in Leadership

China's history can be traced back to a very early period. In fact, China's first dynasty began about the same time that Moses was commanded to lead Israel out of Egyptian captivity. For the first two thousand years of China's dynastic history, five dynasties ruled in China, beginning with the **Shang** around 1500 BC and ending with the T'ang in the seventh century AD. After the fall of the T'ang dynasty, strong central power did not exist for three centuries. By the tenth century, China remained divided into northern and southern kingdoms. By 1000 the northern kingdom became known as the **Song** or Northern Song dynasty. This kingdom experienced strong economic growth. During the early 1200s, this region fell to the invading Mongols. The southern kingdom or Southern Song dynasty came under the control of the Mongols in 1279.

For nearly a century, the Mongol Empire, known as the Yuan dynasty, ruled China. However, by 1368 the Mongol rulers had been driven out of China and pushed back into Mongolia. A new Chinese dynasty was established that sought to restore Chinese influence and prestige.

Expansion

Improvements in Agriculture

China is a land of great geographical diversity. Its landscape varies from mountains to hills and from plains to river basins. China also has a variety of climates. Crops grown on the plains often differ from those grown in the hills or mountains. River basins provide growing options that vary from the plateau regions. Crops include rice, barley, sorghum, millet, soybeans, and wheat.

The Chinese developed ways to irrigate their crops and used iron farm implements to make farming more effective and to make more land available for farming. They produced larger harvests and made it possible to support a growing population. Chinese merchants also turned excess food into increased trade.

Increase of Population

Providing accurate population numbers in early China is difficult, if not impossible. The earliest count considered reliable by some historians was made in 2 BC. The numbers ranged from 57 to 59 million. In AD 754 the count showed a population of 52.8 million. However, by the beginning of the twelfth century, the population is believed to have risen to about 100 million. This doubling of the population occurred just prior to and during the Song dynasty in

---

🔘 CD: 4A Asia and Surrounding Countries

This map from the student text is also available on the CD.

🕸 Song Dynasty

Visit www.bjupress.com/resources for possible links to articles about the Song dynasty.

northern China. The great increase in population was sustained by increased production of rice, wheat, and other crops in central and southern China.

Growth of Cities

Another development in China during the twelfth century was the growth of large cities. Several cities in China increased to populations of over one million people. Movement of the people to the cities reflected a change from employment on farms to labor in cities. As in many cultures, population growth and an increasing food supply combined with the growth of industry resulted in growing cities.

In addition to at least ten large cities, towns developed where people met for trade. These smaller cities developed as centers of commerce where a variety of products were exchanged. The growth of trade led to the development of an urban society in China.

Expansion of Commerce

From the earliest days of civilization in China, the people carried on trade with their neighbors. Tin was imported from the southwest regions of China to make bronze. Cowry and turtle shells came from the coast of the South China Sea. Since China had an abundance of iron ore, the sale of iron products developed into a major commercial enterprise. Silk was also a major product developed by the Chinese and became a major item for export (see p. 62).

> **Cities and the Creation Mandate**
>
> How did the growth of cities in China play a role in carrying out the Creation Mandate?

Early Chinese paper money

Cowry shells were valued by the Chinese and other cultures.

Early Chinese merchants used a variety of items as money, including bolts of silk, jade, pearls, pieces of metal, and leather. Even dogs and horses could be used as a form of money. Over time, the Chinese looked for more portable and standardized items to serve as money. By 500 BC they were casting bronze into various shapes to serve as money. Bronze coins in the shape of tiny spades or knives appeared early in China. During the Ch'in dynasty, the Chinese used small, round bronze or copper coins with a square hole in the middle as currency. These coins would be strung together, and a certain number of them would equal a bushel of grain or a bolt of silk. The Chinese even developed the first known paper money as a form of currency.

Early Chinese coins

Innovations

Scientific

The Chinese made many scientific discoveries. For example, they discovered how to process iron ore and how to make such things as paper, gunpowder, and the compass. They also invented methods for

1600s, an estimated twenty-five million people died during this struggle.

Paper Money

The Chinese are believed to be the first civilization to print paper money. This was done to make funds more portable in some cases or at other times because of a shortage of metal to make coins. Chinese merchants found that carrying the strings of coins became difficult, and early paper money was merely a record of coins deposited with a trustworthy person. The paper record could be redeemed for the coins as needed. Kublai Khan was the first ruler in China to issue paper money in quantity. By the beginning of the Ming dynasty, so much paper money had been printed that hyperinflation resulted. The money was worthless. The rulers of the Ming dynasty ended the use of paper money.

CD: 4B Early Chinese Coins

The drawing of early Chinese coins is available on the CD.

Class Discussion

Use the information in the side margin note above as a springboard to a discussion of inflation. Mention any examples from history (or from the present day) that come to mind. What will happen to the value of our paper money if the government just keeps printing it?

Silk

Perhaps as long ago as 2000 BC, the Chinese discovered that silk moth caterpillars that are fed mulberry leaves produce strands of silk. For a time the emperors reserved the use of silk fabric for themselves and diligently tried to keep the technique for producing silk a state secret. However, it soon became a highly prized commodity and one of China's most significant exports.

The silk moths lay eggs. When the eggs hatch, the caterpillars are fed mulberry leaves. About 35 days later the silkworm caterpillars weigh 10,000 times their original weight. Then they spin a cocoon. Two glands in the silkworms produce liquid silk that turns into a solid when it comes into contact with the air. Within two or three days the silkworm caterpillar has spun about one mile of silk fiber and has built a cocoon around itself. The caterpillars are then killed by heat, and the silk is unwound from the cocoon.

Silk

Fabric created from silk moth cocoons was first developed in ancient China. It was initially reserved for Chinese rulers but soon spread throughout China. Chinese emperors tried to keep the knowledge of how to develop silk a secret, but the technique was eventually smuggled into other lands.

Silk moth cocoons are spun into thread to weave silk fabric.

printing. These and many more discoveries, such as the development of silk fabric, became the basis for a long list of technological developments. We will briefly examine a few of these discoveries.

Technological

Technology, simply defined, is putting knowledge to effective use. Technology can be a concept (idea) or a technique (process). For example, when the proper ingredients were mixed to form paper, a recipe (concept) was developed. Over time, factories were built to make quantities of paper, and the procedure was used over and over as the paper was produced.

Technology contributes to culture. The development of culture is a natural outgrowth of the Creation Mandate that you read about in Chapter 1. God created mankind to "subdue" the earth and to "have dominion" over it. As the Chinese discovered new uses for God's creation, they were maximizing the usefulness of their resources. Even though the Chinese did not worship the Creator, they were demonstrating the truth of God's Word (Genesis 1:28).

Paper

China developed the earliest known **paper**, perhaps as early as a few years before the birth of Christ. They formed paper by combining fibers and rags with water. The mixture was pressed and then allowed to dry. The Chinese used paper for wrapping, padding, and writing. By the sixth century, the Chinese developed toilet paper. Later they folded and sewed paper into bags to protect the flavor of tea. During the Song dynasty, the Chinese issued the first known paper money for general use.

Compass

Lodestone, a magnetic mineral, aligns itself with the earth's magnetic field. The Chinese were among the first people to discover

Silk

Ask for a volunteer to research and report to the class on silk and how it is taken from worm to clothing.

Teabags

Show your students a typical teabag and demonstrate how tea can be brewed without getting tea leaves in the beverage. Remind them that this was a Chinese invention.

this. However, the Chinese probably first used the **compass** to align buildings. Records indicate that during the Song dynasty the Chinese learned to use compasses for finding direction.

Gunpowder

For centuries the Chinese mixed ingredients with **saltpeter** to make items such as medicines. In the ninth century the Chinese discovered **gunpowder** by accident. They were trying to create a substance that would give them eternal life. The Chinese quickly developed many weapons with gunpowder, including flamethrowers, rockets, and crude bombs. They had developed guns or firearms around the time of the Ming dynasty in the fourteenth century.

Printing

During the third century, the Chinese became the first to develop woodblock **printing**. They carved images into a block of wood and then applied ink or paint. The woodblock was then pressed against paper or cloth. A reversed image of the carving would be imprinted on the material.

The Chinese also developed a method of printing that uses movable characters. This method, known as movable-type printing, was first developed in China around 1041. The characters were made out of ceramic. Although the Chinese invented this technology, they made little use of it. The Chinese language is very complicated, and printing with this method involved a great amount of labor. Johannes Gutenberg, around 1450, was the first-known person to use movable type with great success. However, he was German, not Chinese.

Iron

Iron smelting industries developed, and these industries employed many workers. The Chinese were also among the first to develop **cast iron**. This process would not be used in Europe for

Saltpeter

This is another name for a mixture of sulfur, charcoal, and potassium nitrate. It is commonly referred to as gunpowder. It burns rapidly and produces hot solids and gases. These gases can be used to propel a bullet or to launch and create beautiful fireworks displays.

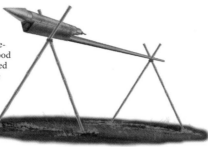

Early Chinese rocket

Cast iron

Cast iron is formed when iron ore and a small amount of carbon and silicon are heated to about 1200°C. At this temperature the iron becomes a liquid and can be poured into a mold. Iron in this form has several advantages, including increased hardness, durability, a lower melting point (about 300°C lower than pure iron), and the ability to be cast into almost any shape. Cast iron has been used to make bridges, columns for buildings, machine parts, weapons, cooking utensils, and many other products. Archaeologists have found hundreds of molds for casting iron in China.

Levels of Chinese Society

Traditionally, officeholders (i.e., scholars) were ranked highest in Chinese society, followed by farmers, artisans, and then merchants. Another important group included the "salt-producing" families. As in Africa, salt was a valuable commodity.

Nestorian Christianity

(See TE margin note about Nestorius on p. 21.)

Christianity probably traveled to the East during the first generation of Christianity from some of the converts listed in Acts 2 (Parthians, Medes, and dwellers in Mesopotamia). In addition, the apostle Thomas was recorded to have traveled to the East and been martyred in India. However, the Church of the East adopted the teaching of Nestorius in the fifth century AD.

This group spread east and endured two Persian empires and the Mongols. Nestorian missionaries carried their beliefs to China and endured until the tenth century. A fragment of Nestorians remained and enjoyed a period of renewal during the Yuan dynasty in the thirteenth and fourteenth centuries. After this, they disappeared from history.

The Art of War

Sun Tzu is believed by many to be the author of a Chinese book on war. *The Art of War*, also known as the *Sun Tzu*, became an influential book on military strategy. This work has had a profound effect on Chinese and Asian military strategy and remains influential for military leaders. Its influence extends to Western cultures. Remarkably, it is

another thousand years. The sale of iron products brought great wealth to the rising merchant class in China.

Trade with Southeast Asia and Other Lands

In Chapter 2 you learned that merchants brought gold, ivory, and other products from Africa to China. Camel caravans also carried silk across Central Asia from China to Europe. In addition, ships carried goods between nations in Southeast Asia and along the Indian Ocean. These ships worked out of ports in southern China. Chinese merchants served as an important link to foreign markets.

Growth of the Merchant Class

Various groups served as the elite members of Chinese society, including rulers and scholars. However, merchants were regarded as the lowest members of society for over two thousand years. No "honorable family" would even engage in trade. In addition, Confucianism condemned the practice of making a profit. Merchants were considered undesirable, in part because they were mobile and wealthy. These traits were thought to be dangerous. Therefore, merchants were not allowed to own property or serve in government.

Circumstances for the merchant class improved when the Song dynasty came to power in the eleventh century. The merchant class quickly took advantage of new freedoms. Members of their families took examinations to enter civil service. The merchants now had friends in government to help protect their business interests. They worked to become respected and influential members of Chinese society.

The growth of the merchant class provided many benefits to the Chinese people. As merchants bought and sold goods, they produced wealth. Factories were built to produce goods made from materials such as iron, paper, and silk. Many Chinese were employed to produce these goods. Some areas concentrated on making weapons, while others produced various products that merchants sold at home and abroad. Towns arose around trading centers, and cities multiplied to meet the needs of the growing population. Products previously reserved for the Chinese rulers became available to many of the people. Their standard of living improved, and many new products were available for them to purchase.

Religion in China

A great variety of religions developed in China or were brought to China. **Ancestor worship** has been an important religious practice throughout the history of China. In the fifth century BC, the teachings of the Chinese teacher **Confucius** began as a philosophy based on relationships. Later it was combined with **Buddhism**, which developed in India, and became an influential religion in China. **Taoism** (DOU iz um) developed in China from the teachings of **Lao-tzu** (LOU dzuh). He encouraged people to live in harmony with nature. This religion promoted the mystical and superstitious elements found in Chinese society.

By the seventh century, Nestorian missionaries had traveled to China. They were influential for several centuries and established many churches in China. Some Mongol rulers even converted to Nestorian Christianity. However, with the growth of Islam during the period of Mongol rule, Nestorians were persecuted to near extinction.

Chinese Religions

Ancestor worship – The family is very important in Chinese culture. The cult of ancestor worship became the leading religion early in Chinese history. Almost every home in China contained an altar where the Chinese burned incense to honor their dead. They hoped this would cause their ancestors to bless and guide them.

Confucianism – At the core of Confucius's teaching is ethical behavior within the five human relationships: father and son, elder and younger brothers, husband and wife, friend and friend, and ruler and subjects.

Buddhism – Buddhism is founded on Four Noble Truths: (1) Suffering is part of all existence. (2) Suffering has a cause—selfish desires. (3) Suffering can be overcome by destroying selfish desires. (4) If man follows the Eightfold Path, he will destroy selfish desires and end suffering. (The Eightfold Path includes right beliefs, intentions, speech, conduct, labor, effort, thoughts, and meditations.)

Taoism – Lao-tzu founded this religion and claimed that peace and harmony can be found by living in harmony with nature. This is a very passive religion that rejects striving after power, wealth, and learning.

Activity 1: Marco Polo's Journals

This activity contains an excerpt from Marco Polo's journals. This primary source enables the student to read an author who lived during this period.

Class Discussion

Discuss possible reasons that merchants ranked so low in Chinese culture. How are merchants ranked today in Chinese society (as well as in America)? Do we tend to rank people by their occupational classes today? If so, how?

Discussion of Chinese Religions

Lead the class in a discussion contrasting the Chinese religions mentioned in this chapter with Christianity.

Buddhism

Visit www.bjupress.com/resources for possible links to articles about Buddhism.

Lao-tzu

Visit www.bjupress.com/resources for possible links to articles about Lao-tzu.

Section Quiz

1. What was the name of the first Chinese dynasty?
2. Under which Chinese dynasty did the population double?
3. What product developed by the Chinese became a major item for export?
4. List four of the most important discoveries/inventions made by the Chinese.
5. Which group in Chinese society was considered the lowest class?
★ What contributions did merchants make that led to the development of cities?

II. Developments in Japan and Southeast Asia

Japan

Japan borrowed much from China. Chinese contributions included a written language, concepts of a central government, and various forms of Buddhism. However, the Japanese did more than just imitate China. The Japanese modified each of these contributions until it became thoroughly Japanese in nature.

Government

Japan's earliest known history reveals government by clans or extended families. During the eighth century, the Fujiwara (fu jee WAR ah) clan became dominant in Japan. In AD 794 Kyoto became Japan's capital, and a Chinese-style government was formed. This transition is known as the Taika (tie EE kuh) ("Great Change") Reform. In theory, Japan became a centralized government led by the emperor. However, authority resided in the powerful families. They continued to control important government offices.

Over time, the Fujiwara rulers neglected the needs of the people. The decline of a central government caused Japan to pass into an extended period of **feudalism**. Japan's period of feudalism extended from late in the twelfth century until the middle of the nineteenth century.

In 1192 the Fujiwara clan lost power and Yoritomo (yor ih TOH moh), a leader of another clan, took control. He received the title of **shogun** (SHO gun) ("great general") and began to change Japan into a warrior state. Yoritomo ruled from Kamakura; therefore, this period of Japanese feudalism is called the Kamakura period.

The fighting among the clans ceased for a time during the thirteenth century while Japan fought off foreign invaders. (Later in this chapter you will read about these invaders, the Mongols.) Once the foreign threat had ended, struggle for control of Japan continued under various clans. The Ashikaga clan became dominant in 1336, and the second period of Japanese feudalism is named after them.

By 1600 the Tokugawa clan became dominant and moved the capital to Edo (Tokyo) in 1603. The final period of Japanese feudalism is called the Tokugawa period. Strife between the clans continued until the nineteenth century.

Japan

Feudalism

Feudalism resulted when local rulers replaced a central power and the loyalties of the people were confined to that local ruler. Land formed the basis of wealth and power. Those lands were controlled by lords or warriors (the samurai in Japan). The families who worked the land owed their allegiance to the lord. They paid the lord with labor or produce in order to live on the land. Some, such as blacksmiths, were skilled craftsmen and had a measure of independence. However, most were bound to the lord and had little or no freedom. Contact with areas beyond their local region was limited, and change occurred very gradually if at all.

---

considered to be a primary example of Taoist strategy.

Section II

Objectives

Students should be able to:

1. Describe early Japanese government and the rise of feudalism in Japan.
2. Analyze the rise of the warrior class and its role in feudalism.
3. Explain the development of Shintoism and the distinctive forms of Japanese Buddhism.

Section Quiz Answers

1. Shang
2. Song
3. silk
4. (any four) paper, compass, gunpowder, printing, cast iron
5. merchants
★ Answers will vary but should include some of the following: They bought and sold goods. This produced a need for labor and provided jobs for more people. Cities grew out of centers of trade. This led to economic development. Economic development led to greater prosperity for more Chinese people.

Activity 2: Matching Exercise

This activity will help the student distinguish and review various terms that appear in this chapter.

CD: 4C Japan

This map from the student text is also available on the CD.

History of Japan

Visit www.bjupress.com/resources for possible links to articles about the history of Japan.

Minamoto no Yoritomo

Visit www.bjupress.com/resources for possible links to articles about Yoritomo.

Bushido

The concept of the warrior class remained vibrant long after Japan had opened its doors to Western culture. In fact, this mindset resulted in strong resistance by the Japanese during WWII when the Allies began to retake islands captured by the Japanese. When the Allies were finally able to take control of an island, many of the Japanese chose to commit suicide rather than surrender to Allied forces.

Rise of the Warrior Class

With the rise of the office of shogun, warriors became the leaders of Japanese society. The Japanese warrior was called a **samurai** (SAM uh reye) or *bushi*. Almost from birth, the samurai were trained in all methods of fighting, on foot and on horseback.

The samurai were also trained in history, literature, and writing. They needed to know about history in order to appreciate the culture they were fighting to protect and to understand how previous wars were won or lost. The samurai were taught literature to help them appreciate the less tangible aspects of culture and to broaden their understanding of abstract thought. Writing was an essential tool for communication. At the very least, writing instructions for battle plans or important information about troop movements could mean the difference between victory and defeat for the samurai.

The samurai lived by an unwritten military code known as the **Bushido** (BOOSH ih doh) ("the way of the warrior"). This code required the warrior to display traits such as loyalty, honor, duty, and courage. It also required the warrior to commit suicide, known as *hara-kiri* (HAR ih KEER ee), rather than be captured or prove disloyal to his master. The loyalty of these warriors to their masters led to the endurance of feudalism until the 1870s.

Religion in Japan

Shintoism is an ancient form of Japanese religion. It was originally a form of nature worship. The Japanese believed that everything in nature that was unusual, such as fire, a waterfall, or a high mountain, possessed deity. Shintoism also viewed the sun as a goddess and the emperor as a descendant of the sun goddess. Shintoism inspires devotion to the homeland and worship of the emperor as a god. It became Japan's national religion and was used to further promote patriotism and loyalty to the emperor.

Zen Buddhism came to Japan from China near the end of the twelfth century. As you have already read, Buddhism emphasized suffering and meditation. Remarkably, this version of Buddhism had a great impact on the military class of Japan. Zen required its followers to develop intense mental concentration. This enabled the samurai to endure the hardships of battle. Zen also stressed self-control and concentration of energy. These qualities made the difference between success or failure on the battlefield.

Southeast Asia

Vietnam

Lying south of China and forming the western border of the South China Sea is the land of Vietnam. Much of its early history is unknown. However, there is evidence of two kingdoms living in this region during this period. The kingdom to the north was called Dai Viet. The kingdom called Champa occupied the central and southern regions of modern Vietnam. Champa traded with and was influenced by India and China.

By the ninth and tenth centuries, the kingdom of Champa had developed into a thriving civilization. However, during the next five centuries, the Dai Viet exerted increasing pressure on Champa. In 1471 troops from Dai Viet invaded and destroyed the capital of Champa. The Dai Viet came to be known as the Vietnam-

Vietnam Prior to 1471

Comparing Cultures

Ask the students to name other cultures in history that have highly regarded military leaders and developed a warlike or militaristic national attitude. *(Answers might include Prussia, later Germany, and a few American Indian tribes such as the Comanches and Apaches.)*

Guest Speaker

Invite someone who is familiar with Japan, Cambodia, Korea, or Vietnam to come and speak to your class. A missionary to one of these countries could be very informative.

CD: 4D Vietnam Prior to 1471

This map from the student text is also available on the CD.

ese. They gained complete control of remaining Cham territories in 1832.

Angkor Wat

Angkor (Cambodia)

Cambodia has a long history that may be traced back as far as 1000 BC. During the third century AD and beyond, Cambodia was influenced by India and China. An empire known as the Khmer (kuh MEHR) developed in this region between the ninth and the thirteenth centuries. Angkor served as the Khmer's center of power. Many capitals were constructed in this area during the empire's peak. In addition, over one thousand temples, including **Angkor Wat**, were built in this area.

Over time, the Khmer engaged in a failed series of wars with its neighbors and steadily declined in power. In 1432 Angkor was pillaged by the Thai and later abandoned. Over the next four centuries, the Cambodians were ruled by the Thai and Vietnamese.

Section Quiz

1. Japan borrowed its written language from what country?
2. Yoritomo was the first Japanese leader to receive what title?
3. What kingdom was eventually overtaken by the Dai Viet kingdom?
4. Vietnam developed from what two kingdoms?
5. What modern country developed from Angkor?
★ Certain characteristics of Zen Buddhism easily applied to the military class in Japan. Explain what they were and how they applied.

III. Rise of the Mongol Empire

The Mongols were nomads who lived in tribes on the Mongolian plateau north of China. As nomads, the Mongols traveled across the

Section III

Objectives

Students should be able to

1. Explain the world-historical significance of the Mongol Empire.
2. Assess the importance of Mongol rule in China.
3. Analyze Mongol religions.
4. Explain how the Mongol domination came to an end.

Section Quiz Answers

1. China
2. shogun
3. Champa
4. Dai Viet and Champa
5. Cambodia
★ intense mental concentration, which enabled the warrior to endure hardships of battle; self-control and concentration of energy, which proved vital for success on the battlefield

Angkor Wat

Visit www.bjupress.com/resources for possible links to articles about Angkor Wat.

Yurts

The Mongols were called the "People of the Felt Tents" because they lived in round tents called yurts. The round shape kept the yurt standing in the strong winds of the open plains. The Mongols made their yurts with frames of light wood covered with layers of heavy felt. The Mongols used the fur and wool of their animals to make the heavy felt, which they waterproofed by greasing. The outer layer of felt on the yurt was whitened with a coat of lime. This helped to reflect the hot summer sun and keep the tents cool inside.

The doorway of the yurt was draped with heavy felt. The women painted or embroidered designs of birds, animals, vines, and trees across the felt. These designs made each tent unique.

Regardless of their size, all the yurts were movable. When it was time to move, the Mongols took down the smaller tents and transported them on carts. The larger yurts (up to thirty feet wide) were not taken apart but were put directly on carts. Sometimes as many as twenty oxen were needed to pull these carts.

plains of Mongolia in search of grazing land for their large herds of horses. Their lifestyle demanded homes that could be moved with them. The Mongols built **yurts** to provide shelter and a place to live. The yurts were designed so that they could be packed up and transported when the Mongols moved.

These tribes often fought among themselves over grazing lands. However, two factors led these tribes to combine and become a great empire. First, the climate cooled over a vast region. This cooling included Mongolia and resulted in less food for the vast herds of Mongol horses. The Mongols began to look for better grazing lands in northern China. The second factor was the birth of a gifted Mongol boy during the twelfth century. He proved to be one of the world's greatest military commanders.

Founding of the Mongol Empire

Chinggis Khan

Temujin (TEM yuh jihn), the son of a Mongolian tribal chieftan, was born around 1162. When he was a boy, his father was killed and he had to flee for his life. After wandering for a few years, he returned to his tribe and avenged his father's murder. He then spent several years gaining power and influence and forming alliances with other tribes. In 1206 he became the supreme leader over all the Mongol tribes. All the tribes acknowledged his position and gave him the title of **Chinggis Khan** (CHING-gihs KAHN) ("Great Ruler").

Mongol Unification

Chinggis unified the Mongols using several means. Some of these means included developing a government, common law, and an organized military.

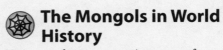

The Mongols in World History

Visit www.bjupress.com/resources for possible links to articles about Mongol history.

Chinggis organized Mongol government by dividing the people into groups of tens, hundreds, thousands, and ten thousands. He also chose trusted followers to lead these groups. Working through these leaders, he led the people in times of battle and peace. In this form of government, a person's loyalty to his leader was supreme. Chinggis placed great value on loyalty. He believed it was one of the greatest character qualities a person could have.

Chinggis also saw the importance of law. He wrote a law code called the **Great Yasa**, which dealt with every area of life. This law provided military rules, criminal punishments, tax regulations, court procedures, and moral standards. The punishment for many crimes was death. Less severe punishments included beatings and fines. Every Mongol, including the khan, was subject to the law. Chinggis used this code to govern his people and prepare them for military conquest.

Mongol Conquest

The Mongols were trained to be warriors from an early age. Warfare was the Mongol way of life. Chinggis used this lifestyle to organize his men into a strong, disciplined army.

The success of the Mongol army demonstrated the military genius of Chinggis Khan. He took full advantage of the Mongols' horsemanship skills in building a well-trained army. Taught to be the ultimate fighting cavalry, the Mongols quickly overran northern China, then turned west to conquer all of Central Asia.

Fast, ruthless, and deadly, the Mongol forces overwhelmed city after city. All who resisted were killed or used for human shields in future battles. The Mongol archer was skilled in battle. Trained to ride at a very young age, the archer learned to string his bow while riding and shoot his arrows when all the horse's hooves were off the ground. This ensured that his arrows would strike their target. The Mongols attacked their enemies with great speed on their horses and used arrows, lances, and swords.

Chinggis had to develop new fighting methods when his armies began to attack towns instead of other nomads. Many towns were surrounded by moats (trenches filled with water) and thick stone walls. These seemed to be unconquerable barriers at first. However, Chinggis used several methods to overcome these barriers. One effective method was **siege warfare**, in which Mongol soldiers fired arrows and flaming objects into the cities for weeks. They also kept food from going into the city until the people were starving. The Mongols borrowed rocket technology from the Chinese and fired gunpowder-filled bamboo rockets into the towns. These were not accurate but must have terrified those inside the towns.

Another effective tactic used by Chinggis and his forces was known as the **pretend retreat**. The Mongol soldiers would pretend to be beaten and appear to leave their camp empty. When the townspeople came out to plunder the Mongol camp, the Mongols would suddenly reappear. The startled people were unprepared to defend themselves, and the Mongol forces would destroy them. When everything of value had been removed from the town, it too would be destroyed.

The Mongols were ruthless. They killed and destroyed wherever they went. As stories of Mongol cruelty spread, the very name *Mongol* struck fear in the hearts of their enemies. The Mongols took advantage of this fear and captured towns without a fight as people chose to surrender rather than face certain destruction. The

---

Specialization and Organization

Were the methods of organization used by Chinggis Khan to unify the Mongol tribes good or bad? Why?

Mongol Army

The army was organized into units of tens, hundreds, and thousands. Ten thousand elite soldiers formed the core of the Mongol army. The entire Mongol army numbered up to 130,000. An additional 130,000 non-Mongols could be used. These forces were made up of various groups who decided to join the Mongols rather than fight them.

The Mongol army was a splendid fighting force. The soldiers lived in the saddle and even slept while riding on a march to the next battle. They endured all types of hardships in their quest to build an empire.

The Mongol horse was well suited for conquest and the extremes of the climate. Soldiers would often change horses several times a day, so vast numbers of them were needed for conquest.

Mongol Armor

To protect themselves, Mongol horsemen wore stiff armor made from animal hides. Chinggis also ordered his soldiers to wear a shirt made of raw silk because arrows could not easily penetrate the silk. Of course, if a man was shot, he was still hurt. But then his fellow soldiers gently pulled the shirt to remove the arrow from the wound. Protected from the arrow tip by the silk, the wound stayed cleaner and usually healed quickly.

Pretend Retreat

This tactic did not originate with Chinggis Khan. In fact, there are several examples of this method being used in the Old Testament. Joshua employed this tactic in Joshua 8 in the second attack on the city of Ai. The children of Israel also employed it against the tribe of Benjamin in Judges 20:28–48.

Arrow Riders

Once he had conquered other lands and peoples, Chinggis needed to keep his empire in order. To keep in touch with every part of this empire, he organized a system of postal riders that crossed the empire. These horsemen were known as "arrow riders" because of their swift travel.

Their bodies bandaged and greased against the weather and the wear of riding, the arrow riders ate and slept on horseback, never stopping until they reached their destination. Bells attached to the horses warned people of the approach of the arrow rider so that no one would get in his way or hinder his progress. Orders, messages, and reports between the khan's headquarters and his leaders and spies traveled through this system.

Division of the Mongol Empire

Chinggis Khan had four sons: Jochi, Chaghatai, Ögödei, and Tolui. He warned them against dividing the empire and counseled them to hold the Mongol Empire together. Then he assigned the richest part of his empire to his third son, Ögödei.

This decision ran counter to Mongol tradition, which gave the major portion of an estate to the youngest son. However, Chinggis believed that Ögödei had a better grasp of human nature. Therefore, Chinggis thought Ögödei would prove to be the best one to rule.

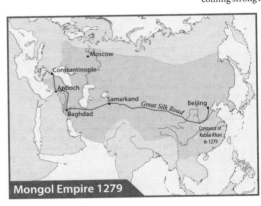

Mongol Empire 1279

Mongols used many men captured in this manner to increase the size of their forces. Women and children were often used as slaves.

Chinggis died in 1227. He had established a Mongol empire that spanned Central Asia from Beijing in northern China to Russia. Upon his death his empire was divided among his sons. However, the Mongol conquests continued as before. Mongol forces marched into Korea in 1231. From Korea they renewed their advance into northern China. In 1252 the Mongols invaded the Dali kingdom. The Mongols seemed invincible.

Mongol Rule in Asia

In the west, Mongol forces took control of Kiev, Russia, in 1240. By 1258 they had overrun Baghdad in Iraq. However, Mongol forces made no attempt to invade western Europe. Some believe it was because there were not enough open plains to supply food for their horses. Whatever the reason, western Europe was spared from conquest.

In 1260 Kublai Khan, one of Chinggis's grandsons, came to power. His first priority was to become the ruler of all China. Overcoming strong resistance, Kublai gained control of the Southern Song empire in 1279. This fulfilled his grandfather's dream of conquering China. Kublai established a new dynasty that he named the Yuan (YOO ahn) ("The Origin") dynasty. The Yuan was China's first foreign dynasty. However, Kublai was not content to stop with China. In 1274 he attempted to invade Japan but failed. In 1281 he assembled a larger force and attacked Japan from China and Korea. This attempt also failed. Despite great efforts, Kublai was unable to expand his empire beyond China.

Kublai tolerated the Chinese but staffed the government mostly with Mongols and other non-Chinese. The Mongols placed their subjects in four categories, with Mongols at the top and most of the Chinese at the bottom. Nevertheless, the Yuan dynasty promoted Chinese culture without trying to change it. In the end, the Mongols brought very little change to China. By 1368 Mongol rule of China had ended.

Japanese Success at Defeating Mongol Invaders

As you have already read, the Japanese endured two invasion attempts by Mongol forces during the thirteenth century. The Japanese had been forged into a military state just prior to these invasions. This arrangement prepared the tiny country for an attack by the undefeated Mongols.

In 1274 Kublai sent a force of up to 30,000 men from Korean ports to invade Japan. However, a storm destroyed the Mongol fleet, and the Japanese drove back those who were able to land.

In 1281 Kublai sent a much greater force numbering 140,000 men to invade Japan. However, the Japanese had built defenses and were prepared for another attack. Every resource was used to protect Japan against the Mongol invasion. Another storm sank the Mongol fleet during the second invasion, and Japanese monks gave credit to a *kamikaze* ("divine wind") for protecting Japan. Over time, these victories led to a myth that the Japanese could not be defeated. Not until World War II would this myth be destroyed.

 ### CD: 4E Mongol Empire 1279

This map from the student text is also available on the CD.

Activity 3: Mongol Invasion of Japan

This activity is an excerpt of Marco Polo's first-hand account of the attempted Mongol invasion of Japan.

Southeast Asian Resistance to Mongol Rule

Kublai Khan also sent forces to conquer Vietnam, Burma, and Java. The people of these countries resisted conquest by the Mongols. As a concession, they agreed to a ritual submission. During this time Kublai Khan also had to contend with another Mongol ruler for control of Mongolia. Kublai was forced to divert his soldiers to ensure his continued rule there. This diversion preserved Southeast Asia from Mongol domination.

The Golden Horde

Batu Khan, another grandson of Chinggis, led Mongol forces into Europe. Between 1237 and 1240 the Mongol forces (known in Europe as **Tartars**) smashed through Russian defenses. Hungary and Poland were also unable to stop the Mongol advance. A combined force of Poles, Czechs, and Germans tried to stop the Mongols at the **Battle of Liegnitz**. Accounts vary, but the Mongol forces seem to have destroyed this army. However, Batu did pull his forces back to the Volga River in Russia. He established an empire in Western Asia known as the **Golden Horde**.

The Mongols had a great influence on the history of Russia. Mongol conquest isolated Russia from western Europe for over two centuries. During this period Russia became greatly influenced by Asian culture. Russian architecture from this period provides an example of this influence.

During this period Moscow also developed from a small town to the capital of Russia. As Moscow became more powerful and influential, the Golden Horde weakened. By 1480 cities like Moscow led Russia in overthrowing Mongol rule.

Religion in the Mongol Empire

Traditional Mongol Religion

You learned in Chapter 1 about the error of polytheism. The Mongols worshiped many gods and believed that good and evil spirits controlled the world. They also believed in a supreme god who ruled all the spirits. They called him **Tengri** (TENG gree), meaning "the great god of heaven." The Mongols lived in fear of the spirits and hoped for blessings from them.

Every yurt had small idols made of felt. The women made these idols at sewing parties. The Mongols believed that these idols protected their families and their animals. Before every meal they spread food and drink on the lips of the idols. They also prayed to them. They believed that these idols had power to bless them.

The Mongols also believed that certain men, called **shamans** (SHAH muhnz), had power over the spirits. The shamans were the priests of the traditional Mongol religion, which is called shamanism (SHAH muh NIZ um). The shamans were medicine men and witch doctors who used a special language when performing their magical rituals. The Mongols often consulted their shamans before making important decisions.

Spread of Nestorian Christianity

In Chapter 1 you learned that Nestorian Christianity spread as far as China by the seventh century. The Nestorians conducted the first mission work in China long before the Mongolian invasions. As

> #### The Golden Horde
> The word *horde* comes from the Mongol word *ordu* which means "camp." The Russians called the Mongols the "Golden Horde" because their greased huts (yurts) shone in the sun.

Russian architecture reflects the influence of the Mongols

Worshiping God

Discuss with your students the fact that the Mongols had a knowledge of a high god. Direct their thoughts to the Flood and the Tower of Babel, referring to chapter one.

Persecution and Growth

Despite severe persecution by brutal rulers such as Tamerlane, Christianity has endured. The early church survived the assaults of Rome, and the Reformation survived repeated assaults by ruthless men and women who were determined to exterminate the truth. Today, Christians thrive in such inhospitable countries as China, Vietnam, and India. The numbers of believers are increasing dramatically despite regular persecution and systematic attempts to eradicate Christianity. Genesis 3:15 reminds us that there will be ongoing assault on God's people by Satan and his followers. However, it also promises that believers will prevail through Christ, Who will ultimately crush the serpent's head.

a witness to their Christian faith, the Nestorians erected a monument in 781. Rediscovered in 1623, part of this monument reads as follows:

> "One Person of our Trinity, the Messiah, who is the Luminous Lord of the Universe, folding up Himself and concealing His true Majesty, appeared upon earth as a man. Angels proclaimed the Glad Tidings. A virgin gave birth to the Holy One. . . . A bright star announced the blessed event. Persians saw the splendour and came forth with their tribute."

When the Italian explorer Marco Polo traveled to China from Europe in the 1300s, he found Nestorian churches all along the route.

Religious Tolerance

The later empire of the Mongols included people of many religions, including Christians and Jews. Members of the family of Chinggis Khan even married Nestorian Christians. However, this liberty would prove to be short-lived.

Rise of Islam

Islam also spread throughout the Mongol Empire. Once Islam became dominant, the Muslims often persecuted other religious groups. Christians and Jews were pressured to convert to Islam.

Muslim rulers made Nestorians wear distinctive clothes, such as a yellow patch, marking them as Christians. They required Christians to wear special haircuts and even ride horses sidesaddle so Muslims could easily identify them. Once a group of Muslims hung a Nestorian bishop upside down, removed his clothes, and filled his mouth with ashes. They then beat him and demanded that he convert to Islam.

The final blow to Christianity under Mongol rule came during the brutal reign of Tamerlane. He persecuted the Nestorians without restraint. Following his vicious assault, Christian populations were reduced to small groups living in remote areas of the Mongol empires.

Trading in the Mongol Empire

The Mongols manufactured nothing beyond what they needed for daily living, such as felt, harnesses, and carts. Because they did not stay in one place for a full growing season, they rarely grew crops. The Mongols resorted to trade to obtain other goods. Even before Chinggis Khan built his empire, the wealthier Mongols traded fur and hides for Chinese silk and cotton.

As the empire grew, trade grew also. When the Mongols conquered all of China in 1279, their empire reached from the Caspian Sea to the Pacific Ocean. They reopened trade along the ancient silk routes, which had been closed for centuries. After nearly a thousand years, the West finally had direct contact with the cultures of the Far East. Between 1100 and the 1200s, the Crusaders were traveling from western Europe to fight the Muslims in the Middle East. During this same period, Mongol traders brought exotic goods from the Far East into Middle Eastern markets. Western merchants and Crusaders carried these goods back to western Europe.

The Mongols quickly developed a desire for the goods they saw. In time the Mongols settled into towns and gave up their nomadic ways. Once settled, the zeal for conquest faded. For example, Kublai

Khan stopped living in a yurt, built a palace, and settled in northern China.

After a century of peaceful trade, the Muslims in the Middle East closed the East-West trade routes and renewed their attacks on what remained of the Byzantine Empire. Europeans, now familiar with the goods of the Far East, still wanted them. With the closing of the land routes, Europeans sought to find other ways to the East. As they searched for new routes, the Age of Exploration began.

Decline and Collapse of the Mongol Empire

Collapse of Mongol Rule in China

Over time, the Mongols' control of China weakened as the Mongol tribes returned to fighting one another. The Chinese encouraged this fighting and viewed it as a way to break free from Mongol rule. By 1368 the Chinese were able to expel the Mongols from China. The **Ming** ("brilliant") dynasty was established, and the Chinese sought to remove all traces of Mongol rule.

Timur (Tamerlane)

During the second half of the fourteenth century, another Mongol leader came to power in central Asia. Timur suffered from an accident during his youth and was lame. He was called Timur the Lame or **Tamerlane** (TAM ur LANE). Despite his physical limitation, Tamerlane became a powerful conqueror. He demonstrated unusual cruelty as he extended his empire from Turkey to India. Tamerlane's forces captured Baghdad and Damascus and defeated the Ottoman Turks. He even invaded southern Russia and weakened the Golden Horde. However, rather than building a well-ruled empire, Tamerlane concentrated on collecting treasures taken in battle. As a result, his empire collapsed shortly after his death.

The last Mongol empire was the small **Mughal** (MOO gul) dynasty in India. The Mughals brought an era of peace and artistic achievement to India. The most famous Mughal ruler was **Akbar** (AHK bar), a wise and generous leader. He extended his empire over most of India. The Mughals were a peaceful people, far different from their Mongol ancestors. Under the Mughals, some of India's greatest architecture was built, including the **Taj Mahal** (TAHZH muh-HAHL). After Akbar's death, the Mughals had few strong leaders. Their empire slowly declined until the British finally took over India in the nineteenth century.

> ### Economics and Trade
> Evaluate Tamerlane's priorities regarding wealth. How might he have built a more lasting empire? Contrast it with the manner in which China established trade and developed a growing economy.

Section Quiz

1. Name the Mongol leader who first united the Mongol tribes.
2. What was the Japanese term for the "divine wind" that prevented Mongol invasions?
3. Name the Mongol leader who invaded Russia.
4. What was the name of the Mongol empire in western Asia?
5. What Chinese dynasty followed the expulsion of the Mongols from China?
6. Name the Mongol leader whose empire extended from Turkey to India.
★ Evaluate Tamerlane's rule in light of other Mongol empires.

Closing of Trade with the West

Have the students discuss how they would be affected if their local grocery store suddenly could no longer stock basic goods such as milk and bread. Help them to understand how the closing of land routes by the Muslims led to an enormous effort to find another route to the East.

Section Quiz Answers

1. Chinggis Khan
2. *kamikaze*
3. Batu Khan
4. Golden Horde
5. Ming
6. Tamerlane
★ Answers may vary but should include: most brutal, lasted the shortest amount of time.

Activity 4: Chapter Review

This activity will help the students review the material in the chapter.

CHAPTER REVIEW

People, Places, and Things to Know

Shang
Song
technology
paper
compass
saltpeter
gunpowder
printing
cast iron
ancestor worship
Confucius
Buddhism
Taoism
Lao-tzu
feudalism
shogun
samurai
Bushido
hara-kiri
Shintoism
Zen Buddhism
Angkor Wat
yurts
Chinggis Khan
Great Yasa
siege warfare
pretend retreat
kamikaze
Batu Khan
Tartars
Battle of Liegnitz
Golden Horde
Tengri
shamans
Ming
Tamerlane
Mughal
Akbar
Taj Mahal

Making Connections

1. Why were merchants prevented from serving in government in China?
2. Why did Japan descend into feudalism?
3. What impact did the invention of the compass from lodestone have on China?
4. Explain the irony of the Chinese discovery of gunpowder in their quest for eternal life.
5. Why was cast iron a great improvement over pure iron?
6. Why were Japanese warriors trained in history, literature, and writing?
7. How did the rise of the warrior class in Japan affect Japanese culture?
8. How did silk shirts minimize the damage to a Mongol soldier from an arrow strike?

Developing History Skills

1. Go to your local library or go on the Internet and discover the various raw materials that have been used to record written information. Organize them in chronological order. Compare your list with others in the class.
2. Construct a timeline that includes early Chinese history through the time of the Mongol invasions and that includes the rise of the Ming Dynasty. (You may need to do outside reading or spend time on the Internet to complete a thorough list. This will be up to your teacher.)

Thinking Critically

1. Evaluate traditional Mongol religion in light of God's Word (using passages such as Exodus 20:4–5 and Romans 1:23).
2. When Islam becomes dominant, as it did in the Mongol empire, how are other religions, especially Christianity, treated?
3. Why did the Mongol Empire collapse? Provide a one or two sentence answer for each of the empires (China, Russia, Asia Minor [Tamerlane], and India).
4. Evaluate the various religions found in China and explain what biblical elements are missing.
5. How can you reconcile the fact that Christianity has been nearly destroyed in many cultures? How does the promise in Genesis 3:15 provide assurance for the believer?

Chapter Review Answers

Making Connections

1. They were mobile and wealthy. The leaders considered them to be a threat.
2. the decline of central government
3. Initially, the impact was minimal because they did not realize how important the compass could be for travel and determining direction.
4. Gunpowder has been used in wars to kill countless people. The use of gunpowder has shortened the lives of many while giving none eternal life.
5. Answers should include the following: cast iron has a lower melting temperature, is able to be cast into many forms, is durable, and will not bend or lose its original shape.
6. Answers should include the following: they needed to know about history in order to appreciate how previous wars were won or lost. They needed to know literature to appreciate the less tangible aspects of culture. Writing was an essential tool for communicating battle plans or information about enemy troop movements.
7. The rise of the warrior class led Japan into a lengthy period of isolation and feudalism. Most people were bound to their feudal lord and had little or no freedom, and they had limited contact beyond their local region. There was little opportunity for the development of civilization (part of the Creation Mandate).
8. Arrows could not easily penetrate raw silk. The shirt protected the wounded soldier from the arrow tip, allowing the wound to heal more quickly.

Developing History Skills

1. Answers should include some of the following: papyrus, animal skins, stone tablets, clay tablets, paper made from rags, and paper made from wood pulp. The organization by chronological order will vary with each student.
2. Answers should include at least some of the following: 1500 BC (Shang), 1000 BC (Chou), 247 BC (Ch'in), AD 618 (T'ang), 1000 (Northern Song), 1200 (Southern Song), c. 1209 (Mongol invasion of northern China), 1279 (Mongol conquest of southern China and establishment of Yuan dynasty), 1368 (expulsion of the Mongols and establishment of the Ming dynasty). Some of these are not in the chapter and would have to be discovered through research.

Thinking Critically

1. Answers should include the fact that the Bible condemns idolatry; the Mongols changed the incorruptible God into an image made like to corruptible man; they did recognize a supreme god, but not the true God; they were supersti-

Living in God's World

1. You go on a summer mission trip to China. You have a lengthy conversation with a Chinese girl your age. She asks you, "If Christianity is the true religion, why didn't it exist in China until just recently?" How could you respond?

2. Christianity did not take root in Asia until the 19ᵗʰ century. Gather into several groups to answer this question: why does a Christian need to know about the history covered in this chapter since very little of it concerns the advance of Christianity? Use Acts 14:15–18 and 17:24–31 in your answer. The groups should report their answers to the class, and the class should discuss which answers are best.

tious and essentially worshiped spirits (demons).

2. They are persecuted, with forced conversions or worse.

3. Answers should include the following: China—Mongols grew soft and weak. They were expelled by the Chinese, who resented their domination. Russia—Mongols grew soft and weak. They were overthrown under the leadership of cities like Moscow, which had grown powerful. Asia Minor—Tamerlane made no plans for a stable government, concentrating instead on brutality and storing up treasures. His empire crumbled after his death.

India—Following the death of Akbar, there were few strong leaders to maintain Mongol rule.

4. Answers should include some of the following: sin, salvation, and a relationship between man and God.

5. The following provides a possible answer: Christians, and before that Old Testament believers back to Abel, have endured the opposition and assaults of Satan and his followers. While many Christians have died for their faith, God's plan and promises cannot be defeated. Often the death of believers has led to the salvation of many others, as in the example of Stephen in Acts 6–7. The promise of Genesis 3:15 includes the attack by Satan as well as his ultimate destruction. Knowing that God and His people will enjoy the ultimate victory gives great assurance to believers.

Living in God's World

1. Even though God has revealed Himself to all people everywhere through His creation (Rom. 1:20), men have consistently rejected God and created idols to worship instead (Rom. 1:21–23). The news of Christianity did spread to China shortly after the death and resurrection of Christ, but the Chinese in large part continued their false worship. Thankfully, in the last several hundred years many Chinese have turned to Christ for salvation.

2. The answers should include the idea that God has been providentially at work in the history of pagan countries. In many ways He has shown them great goodness. Even in "determining the times before appointed and setting the bounds of their habitation," God was acting in ways that should have led these people to repentance. Christians should be able to show people from these countries the providential working of God in their history. Also, by understanding the traditional religions and philosophies of these peoples, Christians are better equipped to evangelize them.

Chapter Goals

Students should be able to

1. Explain the rise of the papacy and the decline into feudalism following the fall of Rome.
2. Analyze the decline of feudalism and the growth of monarchies and city-states in Europe.
3. Explain the expansion of Christian Europe after 1000.
4. Evaluate the patterns of social change and cultural achievement in Europe's emerging civilizations.

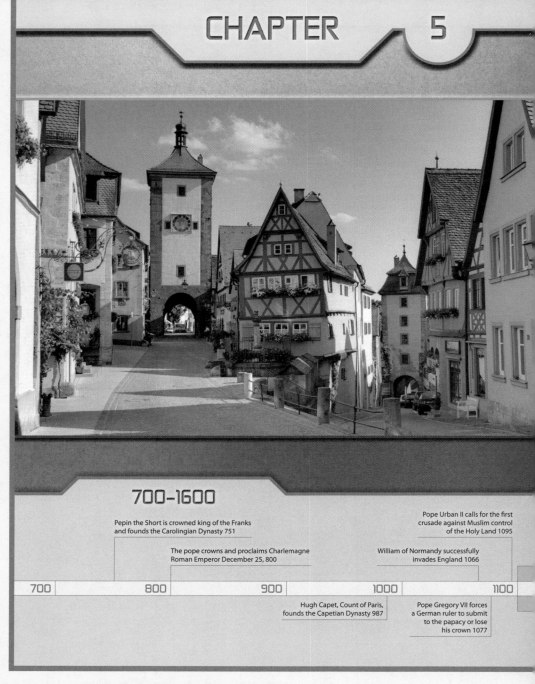

700–1600

Pepin the Short is crowned king of the Franks and founds the Carolingian Dynasty 751

The pope crowns and proclaims Charlemagne Roman Emperor December 25, 800

Pope Urban II calls for the first crusade against Muslim control of the Holy Land 1095

William of Normandy successfully invades England 1066

| 700 | 800 | 900 | 1000 | 1100 |

Hugh Capet, Count of Paris, founds the Capetian Dynasty 987

Pope Gregory VII forces a German ruler to submit to the papacy or lose his crown 1077

Chapter 5 Lesson Plan Chart

	Section Title	Main Activity	Pages	Days
I.	Interval Between the Fall of Rome and the Rise of Feudalism	Activity 1: *The Anglo-Saxon Chronicle*	78–82	1–2 days
II.	Decline of Feudalism and Development of States in Europe	Discussion Activity: Legal Legacy	82–86	1–1½ days
III.	Expansion of Europe	Discussion Activity: A Modern-Day Crusade?	86–89	1–1½ days
IV.	Development of Culture in Europe	Activity 2: *The Canterbury Tales*	89–92	2–2½ days
V.	Calamities in Europe	Activity 4: Chapter Review	92–94	1 day
TOTAL SUGGESTED DAYS (INCLUDING 1 DAY EACH FOR REVIEW AND TESTING)				8–10½ days

Materials List

Section I

- CD: 5A Barbarian Invasions and the Division of the Roman Empire; CD: 5B Charlemagne's Empire
- Activity 1 from the *Student Activities* manual

Section II

- CD: 5C Growth of France from the 11th to the 14th Century; 5D The Magna Carta; 5E Structure of the Venetian Government

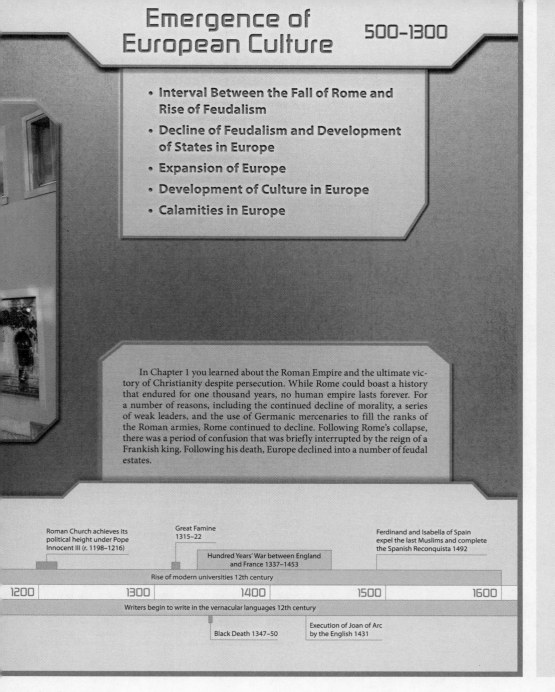

Emergence of European Culture 500-1300

- Interval Between the Fall of Rome and Rise of Feudalism
- Decline of Feudalism and Development of States in Europe
- Expansion of Europe
- Development of Culture in Europe
- Calamities in Europe

In Chapter 1 you learned about the Roman Empire and the ultimate victory of Christianity despite persecution. While Rome could boast a history that endured for one thousand years, no human empire lasts forever. For a number of reasons, including the continued decline of morality, a series of weak leaders, and the use of Germanic mercenaries to fill the ranks of the Roman armies, Rome continued to decline. Following Rome's collapse, there was a period of confusion that was briefly interrupted by the reign of a Frankish king. Following his death, Europe declined into a number of feudal estates.

Roman Church achieves its political height under Pope Innocent III (r. 1198–1216)

Great Famine 1315–22

Ferdinand and Isabella of Spain expel the last Muslims and complete the Spanish Reconquista 1492

Hundred Years' War between England and France 1337–1453

Rise of modern universities 12th century

| 1200 | 1300 | 1400 | 1500 | 1600 |

Writers begin to write in the vernacular languages 12th century

Black Death 1347–50

Execution of Joan of Arc by the English 1431

Section III
- CD: 5F Crusader Fortress in Caesarea; 5G Medieval Weapons; 5H The Iberian Peninsula

Section IV
- Activities 2 and 3 from the *Student Activities* manual

Section V
- Activity 4 from the *Student Activities* manual

Section I

Objectives

Students should be able to

1. Understand the rise of European kingdoms.
2. Analyze why Europe descended into the medieval period.
3. Describe the growth of papal power in Europe and its effects.
4. Evaluate the Christianizing of Europe.

I. Interval Between the Fall of Rome and the Rise of Feudalism

Rise of European Kingdoms

During the fifth century, German tribes began to migrate onto land governed by the Roman Empire. They often fled more aggressive tribes. As the Roman Empire weakened, German tribes increased in power. By 476 the Western Roman Empire had fallen.

While the Roman government collapsed, Christianity thrived and spread throughout the German tribes. These tribes became the foundation of Medieval Europe. For example, the Franks settled in the region of Gaul (France) and formed several powerful kingdoms.

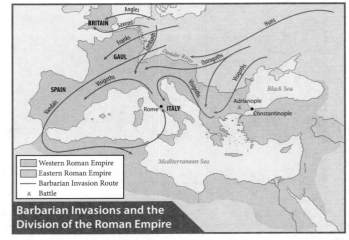

Barbarian Invasions and the Division of the Roman Empire

Merovingian House

Clovis became the leader of one of these Frankish kingdoms in 481. He used military force and other means to combine several kingdoms. During an important battle, he cried out to God for victory and promised to be baptized. He won the battle and fulfilled his promise. Clovis also ordered three thousand of his soldiers to be baptized into the Roman Church. The embracing of this form of Christianity won Clovis the support of the Roman Church. This alliance between the Frankish rulers and the Church of Rome endured for centuries.

When Clovis died, the kingdom was divided among his four sons. This royal line became known as the Merovingians. By the seventh century, this family had lost influence due to careless and immoral living. The **mayor of the palace** (the leading palace official) became the real power in the kingdom.

Carolingian House

Near the end of the seventh century, Pepin II became the mayor of the palace in a strong Frankish territory. He conquered neighboring territories and united them under one rule. Charles Martel (see

Forced Conversions

Discuss with your students the practice of forced conversions. Lead them to understand that the result of such conversions is an empty pretense of Christianity.

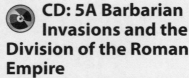 **CD: 5A Barbarian Invasions and the Division of the Roman Empire**

This map from the student text is also available on the CD.

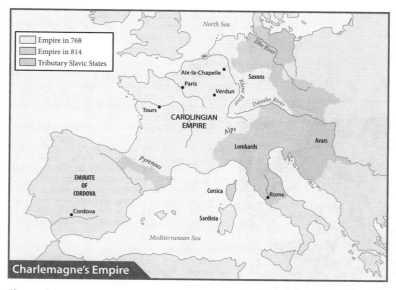

Charlemagne's Empire

Chapter 2) was Pepin's son and expanded this kingdom. Charles's son, Pepin the Short, received permission from the pope to take the title of king in 751. A new family now ruled the Franks. It would be named after its most famous member, Charlemagne.

After Pepin the Short died, his sons Carloman and Charles ruled together. Carloman soon died, and Charles became the sole ruler of the Frankish kingdom. His influence over Europe resulted in his title **Charlemagne** (SHAR luh mane), or "Charles the Great."

Charlemagne demonstrated strong leadership in many ways. He led his army and defeated many other tribes in Europe, including the Lombards and the Saxons. Charlemagne also organized his empire into districts. His government worked to ensure justice and maintain peace throughout his kingdom. (Charlemagne's contribution to education will be discussed later.)

On Christmas Day in 800, another important event occurred. The pope placed a crown on Charlemagne's head and proclaimed him Roman

The interior and exterior of the cathedral in Aachen, where the pope crowned Charlemagne

CD: 5B Charlemagne's Empire

This map from the student text is also available on the CD.

Activity 1: *The Anglo-Saxon Chronicle*

This excerpt from the *Anglo-Saxon Chronicle* describes the invasion of England in 1066.

emperor. While this did not increase Charlemagne's power, it did raise an important question: who is supreme—the state or the church? Later popes would point to this event and claim authority over kings.

Feudal Lordship

Following Charlemagne's death, Europe was divided among his sons. The division of Europe and lack of strong leadership led to the decline of central power. This decentralization resulted in the rise of feudalism. You learned about feudalism when we examined Japan in the last chapter.

While there were differences between feudalism in Japan and feudalism in Europe, there were also many similarities. For example, a few wealthy nobles controlled large tracts of land. A large majority of the people did not own land. Instead, they farmed or performed other duties that were useful to the nobles. In exchange for a portion of the produce or services rendered, the noble would allow the people to live on his land. They were loyal to him and submitted to his authority. In fact, many were little more than slaves. In many situations they were not free to leave the lord's estate.

Typical feudal manor

Manorialism

The estate on which most people lived was known as a **manor.** Over time, the manor became largely self-supporting. The manor would often have its own blacksmith to make and repair iron tools, a mill to process grain, and skilled laborers to meet the needs of those living on the estate. It would also have a church and priest. Since few could read, the people learned about God from the spoken words of the priest. Images in many of the churches were also intended to teach stories from the Bible. Tragically, what was taught in word and picture was often very different from what is found in the Bible.

European Monarchies

Even though Europe descended into a feudal society, there were men who retained the title of king. During this period they often had little real power. The king needed the support of the nobles. He depended on them for financial and military support. Several generations of monarchs worked to strengthen their office and increase their authority. They often used wars and marriage alliances to expand their influence.

Preservation of Learning

You may be surprised that learning survived after the fall of Rome. The Roman Church, through monasteries, preserved much of the Greco-Roman knowledge.

Charlemagne also became a strong supporter of education during his reign. He encouraged the education of the clergy and children of nobility. His reforms stirred an interest in the Bible and writings of classical authors. Charlemagne also encouraged the discovery and copying of many ancient works. His royal court became a place of learning and scholarship.

Under Charlemagne's influence, monasteries became centers of Western knowledge. Monks taught others to read and write. They also preserved Christian learning by storing and copying docu-

Medieval painting showing a king and queen crowned by Christ. Peter and Paul stand behind them. This artwork visualizes the close relationship between church and state.

Medieval English Towns

Visit www.bjupress.com/resources for possible links to articles about medieval English towns.

Feudalism and Medieval Life

Visit www.bjupress.com/resources for possible links to articles about feudalism and medieval life.

ments. Long after Charlemagne's death, monasteries continued to educate and preserve written works. European culture and civilization would be built upon this preserved knowledge.

Growth of Papal Power

As you have already learned, Rome, the empire, declined and collapsed. During this same time the Roman Church began to develop. Gradually, the Church of Rome became a powerful member of medieval society. A brief examination of key popes will help to show this growth of power.

Leo I, bishop of the city of Rome, became the first to receive the title of **pope** ("papa") in the fifth century after he convinced a violent barbarian tribe (the Huns) not to destroy the city of Rome. Gregory I (6th century) was one of the first bishops of Rome to claim supremacy over all other Christians. **Papal** (PAY pul) power increased during the ninth century when Pope Nicholas I claimed that the pope was supreme over the church and state. Gregory VII also confirmed the power of the papacy during his reign. In 1077 Gregory forced a German ruler to submit to him or lose his crown.

The power of the papacy peaked during the beginning of the thirteenth century under Pope **Innocent III**. He took the title "vicar of Christ" and claimed to have supreme authority over all. While others had claimed an increasing level of authority for the papacy, Innocent III succeeded in enforcing absolute authority over clergy and kings. He sent armies and issued papal decrees to force rulers and nation-states to submit to his will.

Along with the growth of the power of the bishop of Rome, other changes slowly took place in the church. For example, the pastors (clergy) were forbidden in 1074 to marry. This decree led to a class of men who were loyal to the pope. However, it also created a terrible problem since it violated the Creation Mandate in Genesis 1–2. God made humans to marry, have children, and exercise dominion over His creation. Forbidding the clergy to marry minimized the marriage bond created by God. In addition, the Roman Church determined that the bread and wine in the Lord's Supper changed into the body and blood of Christ during mass. A church council under Innocent III decreed this in 1215. To believe otherwise was considered heresy (false teaching). Heresy was punishable by torture or death.

The Christianizing of Europe

As we have noted, Christianity spread throughout Europe through missionaries and believers who lived among the German tribes. The bishop of Rome sent monks to areas such as Gaul (France), Spain, and Britain to introduce them to a form of Christianity. He also appointed church leaders who were loyal to him.

Rulers found an alliance with Rome useful. Men such as Clovis and Pepin the Short encouraged or required their people to submit to the Church of Rome. There were certainly genuine conversions throughout this period. However, many people were baptized into a form of Christianity that imitated their pagan worship.

These rising nation-states were considered Christian if the king accepted Christianity as the official religion of his realm. Sadly, however, many of the people in these realms remained ignorant of the Bible's most basic teachings. As a result, medieval European Christianity was very different from biblical Christianity.

The Sacraments

Over several hundred years the Roman Church developed several *sacraments* or ways to earn grace necessary for salvation. Eventually the Church of Rome established seven:

(1) Baptism (to remove original sin)

(2) Confirmation (to receive the Holy Spirit)

(3) Confession/penance (to receive forgiveness from a priest)

(4) Communion/Eucharist (This is the primary sacrament to receive redemption from sin.)

(5) Matrimony (Marriage is controlled by the church, and children are to be educated by the church.)

(6) Holy orders (The priest is considered another Christ; the nun is considered the bride of Christ.)

(7) Last rites (Anointing of the sick brings forgiveness of sin and prepares one for death.)

The Morphing of the Church of Rome

As the Church of Rome rose in prominence and expanded, it spread throughout the Germanic tribes in Europe. Over time the Roman Church accepted baptism and outward conformity as evidences of conversion. Some pagan practices even found their way into Roman worship, such as the prayer beads used by Catholics when reciting the Lord's Prayer and the *Ave Maria* (Hail Mary). The worship of the virgin Mary is an outgrowth of pagan practices that predate Christianity.

Section II

Students should be able to

1. Describe feudal lordship and explain how it provided a foundation for political order in Europe.

2. Analyze how European monarchies expanded their power and consider the limitations of this power.

3. Analyze the developments in medieval English legal practice and their importance for modern democratic thought.

4. Explain the changing political relationship between the Roman church and nation-states.

Medieval Warm Period

Given the current attention global warming receives, it is worth noting that the earth periodically goes through warming and cooling cycles that are natural, recurring, and not related to human activity. The Medieval Warm Period was followed by a cooling period in the fourteenth century. All of this occurred without human-produced carbon emissions and other events often blamed for global warming.

Section Quiz Answers

1. mayor of the palace

2. the pope

3. Charlemagne

4. Innocent III

5. grace necessary for salvation

★ First Corinthians 11 states that communion is a remembrance, not a sacrifice. Hebrews 10 states that Christ "offered one sacrifice for sins for ever." The idea that a priest can transform the bread and wine into Christ's body and blood is unscriptural, as is the idea that Christ's sacrifice is repeated in every celebration of the Eucharist.

Population and Productivity

It is hard to say which came first, population growth or increased productivity. However, each depended on the other. A larger population required additional food. Greater productivity required more laborers. Several factors during the period between the eleventh and fourteenth centuries led to the increase of population and productivity.

During the beginning of the eleventh century, people in Europe began to carve additional farmland out of forests and marshes. (The heavy wheeled plow made it possible to farm this rich, heavy soil.) As the people plowed more land, more crops were grown. With the increased production came larger families. Farmers needed big families to help with the duties of running a farm. The increase of food also enabled others to sustain larger families.

Farmers also learned to increase yield by rotating crops and allowing some fields to lie fallow (to rest) for a season. Rotating crops and allowing fields to lie fallow renewed the soil. These methods enabled the fields to produce crops for many years.

Also, beginning in the eleventh century, there was a warming of the climate in Europe known as the **Medieval Warm Period**. This provided a longer growing season and further enabled the farmers to grow more crops.

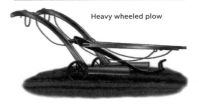

Heavy wheeled plow

Nevertheless, the Bible was accepted by most Europeans as God's Word. Medieval Europeans did not divide their world into the religious and political spheres as later Europeans would. Christianity was understood to have something to say about every aspect of life. The influence of Christianity in the culture paved the way for the Reformation, in which the fullness of the gospel was once again widely proclaimed.

Section Quiz

1. What leading palace official held the true power in the Merovingian dynasty?

2. Who granted Pepin the Short the right to take the title of king?

3. What ruler supported a revival of learning and made monasteries the centers of Western knowledge?

4. Under what pope did the papacy reach its peak?

5. The Roman Church taught that sacraments were means of earning _____.

★ Evaluate the Roman Church's sacrament of Communion/Eucharist in light of 1 Corinthians 11:23–26 and Hebrews 10:11–14.

II. Decline of Feudalism and Development of States in Europe

Decline of Feudalism

Castles had dominated Europe's landscape during the early Middle Ages, but from the beginning of the Crusades to about 1500, a change occurred. Although many people continued to live on lands controlled by nobles, more and more people moved to towns. These new townspeople came from many places for many reasons and started new towns or settled in old ones. Towns began to dominate the land.

One reason for the growth of towns was Europe's population growth. Improved farming methods meant that farmers could produce more and better crops to feed more people. Better methods in crop production meant that the nobles needed fewer people to run the castle lands. Many people, no longer needed by their lord, bought their freedom and moved to towns. Younger children of nobles also moved to the towns, since the firstborn son would inherit the land.

Another reason for the growth of towns was the growth of trade. Along the trade routes reopened by the Crusades came exotic, desirable goods from the East. Places where trade routes or roads intersected became logical locations to build settlements. These settlements grew into towns and became centers of trade for all types of goods.

Towns became places of opportunity. Poor farmers, butchers, bakers, carpenters, and other craftsmen moved to towns and prospered. In time, they would challenge the power of the nobles to govern their lives.

Nobles often owned or controlled the land on which towns developed. Over time, the leading citizens of towns convinced nobles to give their town a charter. The **town charter** was a legal document listing the privileges of the townspeople. This freed the people from many feudal duties. The people still paid taxes to the lord, but they were now allowed to govern themselves. Kings also expanded their power by granting town charters. This redirected the loyalty of the people to the king and the taxes to his coffers. These were significant advances and contributed to the decline of feudalism.

Development of States in Europe

Rise of Strong Monarchies

England

The conquest of England by **William the Conqueror** in 1066 laid the foundations for a strong monarchy in England. He established a new royal dynasty, the Normans. This line was soon replaced by another dynasty through William's grandson, **Henry II**. Henry strengthened English royal authority by expanding the use of royal courts. He developed **circuit courts** with judges who heard cases in a particular province (circuit) of England. This strengthened the power of the king and captured the loyalty of the people.

France

France began as a fragmented piece of Charlemagne's empire. However, by the end of the tenth century, **Hugh Capet** (HYOO KA-pit), the count of Paris, founded a new royal line in France. The Capetian (kuh PEE shun) rulers gained territory by conquest and marriage alliances. They also developed an efficient centralized government. The Capetians supported the claims of the Roman Church and granted rights to towns in exchange for their support. These strategies increased royal power.

Jewish Contributions and Tribulations

Rulers such as Charlemagne and Louis the Pious valued the skills and contributions of their Jewish subjects. Since many Jews had connections to the Middle East and Asia, they became vital to trade. Jewish merchants were able to travel freely in Muslim controlled areas where others were not. They traded in slaves, fur, and other items from the Near East. From China they purchased spices and silk.

In some countries, they served as ambassadors, physicians, or tax collectors. Many Jews developed great skills in manufacturing glass, making jewelry, and processing gold. Others farmed the land, served as merchants, or built ships. Wherever Jews were allowed to live in peace, those countries prospered in a variety of ways.

However, the Crusades drastically changed the way Europeans viewed Jews. Many who answered the call to expel the infidels from the Holy Land also viewed Jews with suspicion. Because the Jews often refused to convert and be baptized, they were viewed as the enemies of "Christian" Europe. Under the banner of the cross, crusaders slaughtered helpless Jews by the thousands.

The hard-working Jews often had great wealth. This made them become even more despised by many in Europe. Rumors about the Jews were spread, and often whole villages of them were murdered. In part, many Europeans killed Jews simply to take their land and wealth. Perhaps the worst lie told about the Jews was that they poisoned wells and rivers. As the plague known as the Black Death spread across Europe, the Jews were often blamed and whole Jewish populations were slaughtered.

Growth of France from the 11th to the 14th Century

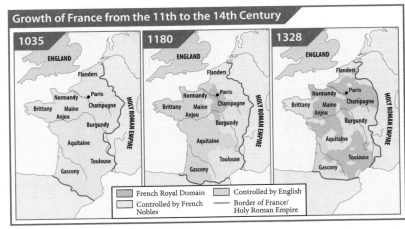

Phillip II continued the thrust to develop a strong monarchy in France. At this time the English controlled large areas of French land. Phillip responded by seizing much of the English-controlled land in France during the reign of King John of England. In addition, he improved the effectiveness of the royal government by sending out royal officials called *baillis* (bah YEE), or bailiffs. These men collected taxes for the king and ensured justice in carrying out laws.

The Capetian family ruled France for over three centuries. During this time each ruler was able to pass the crown to a son. Thus France was spared from revolts and major struggles for power. The resulting stability made possible a strong and powerful monarchy in France.

Developments in English Legal and Constitutional Practices

Before a circuit judge would travel to his province in England, a **jury** (group of local citizens) would make up a list of accusations known as **indictments**. This list was a record of the crimes committed and the people suspected of committing the crimes. The modern grand jury developed out of this procedure. (A grand jury decides if there is enough evidence to bring an accused person to trial.)

Trial by jury had its beginnings in this system of dealing with crime. However, in early English practice, the jury provided evidence to the judge to determine guilt. In modern practice, the jury hears the evidence and renders a verdict of guilty or not guilty.

The justices that Henry II sent out across England developed uniform laws for all of England. These laws overruled local laws that varied from region to region. This **common law** was intended to guarantee justice, and it helped to unify England.

England differed from other countries such as France by setting limits on royal power. The abuses of King John (1199–1216), including demanding excessive taxes and ignoring the will of the nobles, led to a revolt. The victorious nobles forced John to sign the **Magna Carta** ("Great Charter"). Originally, this document only assured rights for the nobility. However, over time, the English people viewed

---

Legal Legacy

Discuss with the students how English legal practices have contributed to America's legal system. Make sure they understand terms such as "circuit courts," "jury," "indictment," and "grand jury."

this document as declaring the principle that the king's power over all citizens was limited.

During the reign of Edward I, **Parliament** developed. It began as a group of advisors to the king. By the fourteenth century, Parliament was composed of two groups. The leading vassals were represented in the prominent group (House of Lords) and the knights and leading citizens were represented in the less prominent group (House of Commons). Over time, the Parliament gained more power by granting or withholding its approval of new taxes. Through this "**power of the purse**," Parliament could limit the king's power.

Changing Political Relationships

The Decline of Political Power of the Roman Catholic Church

You have learned that the political power of the Roman Church grew during the Middle Ages and peaked during the rule of Pope Innocent III (1198–1216). However, within a century, the political influence of Rome had almost disappeared. There were many reasons for this decline, including weak popes and frustration over the abuses by the Roman Church. Kings were quick to take advantage of Rome's loss of political power to increase their own power during this period.

The Rise of Political Power in the Nation-States

At least two obstacles stood in the way of the rise of a central power in the emerging nation-states. Feudal lords and the Roman Church resisted this process. Nobles were naturally reluctant to submit to a king and accept a reduction of their power. The Roman Church had made great claims about its authority over religious and political affairs. Thus Rome opposed the growth of political power in the nation-states. Monarchs used various means to bring the nobles under control and often struggled with the Roman Church to limit its control in their land.

City-States Versus Centralized Monarchies

Another form of government that developed during this period was the city-state. Venice was the most successful and prominent of these city-states. Located on the Adriatic Sea, this city traded extensively with the Byzantine Empire and the Muslim world. To carry

Various scenes from the city of Venice

Legislative Branch

Have the students read about the legislative branch of the United States and then compare and contrast the English Parliament with the U.S. legislative branch. (The *American Government* textbook from BJU Press has a section on the legislative branch in unit four.)

 ### CD: 5E Structure of the Venetian Government

A diagram depicting the structure of government in Venice is available on the CD.

Section III

Objectives

Students should be able to

1. Analyze connections between population growth, increased agricultural production, and technological innovation.
2. Explain urban growth, causes for expansion of trade, and the development of a money economy in Europe.
3. Analyze the success of Christian states in overthrowing Muslim powers in central and southern Iberia.
4. Analyze the consequences of the European Crusades.

Crusades

Definitions of the term *crusade* vary from a military expedition to a vigorous and strenuous movement for a given cause. One crusade that fits the latter definition is the Children's Crusade of 1212. When the pope issued a call for a new crusade, children responded from many countries and joined in a march to the sea. Many people expected the waters to part and allow the children to walk to the Holy Land on dry ground. Instead, many of the children were captured by slave traders. While it had a sad ending, it demonstrates the determination of some children to do what few adults were willing to do.

A Representative Government

The city of Venice was governed by the Great Council, which was made up of members of the wealthy families in Venice. Around two hundred members of the Great Council were selected to form the Senate. From the Senate, the Council of Ten made the day-to-day decisions of government. One member of the Council of Ten was chosen to be the *Doge* (duke) and often held this ceremonial position until death.
(Venice retained its independence until Napoleon conquered the city in 1797.)

out its trade, Venice developed a vast navy of over three thousand ships. These ships could be used to promote trade and defend trade routes against pirates.

The form of government practiced in Venice was similar to the republican form of government in ancient Rome. Power was shared by a senate made up of nobles and a lower body composed of a large number of wealthy citizens. Through the lower body, the citizens had the power to accept or reject the newly elected leader of the ruling council.

Venice, like rising nations, struggled with the demands of the Roman Church. Venetians remained loyal Catholics but refused to persecute their citizens for religious "heresy." Rome responded by placing Venice under the **interdict** (the people were denied access to most of the sacraments) on at least two occasions.

Section Quiz

1. After 1500 many people moved from the manor to _____.
2–3. List two things that contributed to the decline of feudalism.
4. What nobleman conquered England in 1066?
5. What French king took land in France from an English king?
★ How was the government of Venice similar to the government of ancient Rome?

III. Expansion of Europe

The Crusades

For centuries Christians had traveled to the Holy Land to visit holy sites. However, the Seljuk Turks cut off access to Jerusalem and other sites during the eleventh century. In response, Pope Urban II called for a **crusade** to liberate the Holy Land and defeat the infidels. This call was issued in 1095, and several armies traveled to the Middle East over the next two centuries. Only the First Crusade enjoyed a measure of success and gained control of a narrow strip of land for a brief period. Other Crusades failed, and the effort to free the Holy Land ended by the late thirteenth century.

Crusader fortress in Caesarea with vaulted ceilings and a dry moat

---

Section Quiz Answers

1. towns
2–3. Any two of the following: population growth, growth of towns, growth of trade, rise of monarchies
4. William the Conqueror
5. Phillip II
★ Any of the following: republic, representative government, power originating from the citizens.

A Modern-Day Crusade?

Have the students discuss possible reasons that many Muslims were offended when President Bush, early in the war on terrorism, referred to it as a "crusade." Compare and contrast the war on terror and the Crusades.

 CD: 5F Crusader Fortress in Caesarea

These photos from the student text are also available on the CD.

When efforts to free the Holy Land ended, the Roman Church redirected the Crusades. Muslims on the Iberian Peninsula came under attack. Groups in Europe that taught doctrines that differed from those approved by the Church of Rome were also killed by crusading armies.

Motives

Motives for the Crusades differed, depending on which group is being discussed. For the Roman Church, the Crusades created an opportunity to expand its influence. Many of the nobles who led forces in the Crusades saw these wars as an opportunity for gaining wealth and land. Religious fervor and the promise of rewards in the afterlife motivated many. Others saw the Crusades as a great opportunity for travel and adventure. Merchants found the Crusades to be a source of great wealth as they delivered armies and supplies and returned with shiploads of treasures to sell.

Results

The Crusades resulted in the deaths of many thousands of fighters and civilians. Yet, after all of the violence and bloodshed, the Europeans were unable to maintain their hold on the Holy Land. Numerous historians have called these religious wars a mistake and a failure. However, God is not hindered by the failures of fallen man. He enabled many positive results to emerge from the Crusades.

For example, much of the knowledge that had been preserved by the Muslims and the Byzantine Empire found its way back to Europe. Knowledge about science, diseases, astronomy, math, and many other subjects was taken to Europe. Greek and Arabic documents brought to Europe played an important role in the revival of education and the rise of universities in Europe.

Merchants filled their ships with spices, muslin, silk, and furs as they returned from taking crusading forces to the Middle East. These goods found a ready market in Europe and resulted in a great increase in trade. Merchants became very wealthy and formed part of a **middle class**. The middle class was composed of those who lived in towns and included the merchants, bankers, craftsmen, and other skilled laborers.

In addition, manufacturing methods used by the Muslims were copied and taken back to be developed in Europe. These factories provided work for many poor Europeans and contributed to the growth of towns. New products and goods became available, and opportunities to make wealth abounded.

The Development of Cities

God made humans to work together in exercising dominion over the earth (Gen. 1:28). For this reason, cities have always been important to human existence. In almost every period of human history, as culture develops in a region, cities emerge to help the development of that culture. As a people group grows, it becomes highly centralized, its members begin to specialize in particular tasks, and thus a city begins to flourish. Tragically, as time progresses, another nation often invades, and the city is destroyed or goes into decline. Then, eventually, the cycle is repeated.

Following the decline of Rome, the empire splintered and cities fell into decay. Populations declined for various reasons, including war and famine. However, over time, the population began to increase again. Then, once again, cities began to emerge in Europe.

The Crusades and the Protestant Reformation

Important documents also traveled back to Europe with the crusaders. Manuscripts of ancient Greek works and other documents were reintroduced to European scholars. However, none was more important than copies of the New Testament. These were compared with the Latin texts that had been used in Europe for centuries. For the first time, the accuracy of the Latin Vulgate was questioned. In addition, enterprising men such as Erasmus prepared Greek New Testaments for printing on the newly invented movable-type printing press. Access to these Greek texts played a role in the Protestant Reformation during the sixteenth century.

Middle Class

In a society that allows economic and personal freedoms, the number of people who occupy the middle class tends to increase. The economic and social welfare of a society can be measured by the growth or decline of its middle class.

Population Growth

Beginning in the eleventh century, the population continued to grow rapidly for three hundred years. Towns grew into cities as more and more people moved from the feudal estates and the birth rate continued to rise.

Food was plentiful, and workers were needed to produce goods in newly built factories. Trade and the growth of a money economy also created many jobs and great wealth. Cities symbolized the prosperity and liberty that were not available on the feudal estates.

Cities such as Paris and Venice had large populations. It is estimated that the population of Paris may have reached two hundred thousand during this period. The population of Europe may have grown to one hundred million people.

Technological Innovation

Medieval weapons: longbow, crossbow, and trebuchet

Medieval Europe was better known for finding new ways to use technology than for inventing new tools or devices. For example, Europeans used ancient Roman inventions and recently acquired knowledge of Muslim devices to improve their lives. Use of such discoveries as the horse collar, water mills, Arabic numerals, and windmills enabled European civilization to develop. Wind and water were also harnessed to power industry and enable mass production. Use of the compass and stern-mounted rudders made it possible to navigate the oceans. And instruments of war such as the cannon, crossbow, and armor changed the ways wars were waged.

While the Europeans improved many existing devices, they also invented several things themselves. For example, mechanical clocks are believed to have been invented by the Europeans around the thirteenth century. In addition, spectacles (or glasses) were developed in Florence, Italy, near the end of the thirteenth century. The first spectacles used convex lenses, which improves the vision of the far-sighted. Concave lenses (for the near-sighted) were probably not developed until the fifteenth century.

Convex and concave lenses

Continued Growth of Trade

The increase of trade was tremendous. The wealthy had their gold and silver turned into coins in order to buy many of the items that became available. Farmers and others sold their excess produce and other goods for money. Over time, they bought their freedom from the nobles and moved to the towns. The growing towns promised greater opportunity and freedom.

Money Economy

With the increase of trade, a money economy developed. Problems arose, however, because every town had its own kind of money. Merchants traveling from town to town had to use many different kinds of money. To handle these problems, some men became moneychangers. They knew the value of different kinds of coins. At the market they exchanged money from other towns for local coins.

Banks developed as a result of the use of money. The word **bank** comes from the Italian word *banca* (BAHNG kuh), meaning "bench." Moneychangers and early bankers sat on benches, and people referred to doing banking business as "going to the bench."

Muslin

Muslin is fabric made from finely woven cotton threads. Europeans named this material "muslin" after the city in Iraq, Mosul, where they first encountered it.

Money Economy

During this period, "money" was in the form of coins. Various metals were used, and coins made of silver or gold maintained the highest value.

Early versions of paper money were backed by an equivalent value in gold or silver (hard currency). This was true of U.S. paper money until the 1930s.

 ## CD: 5G Medieval Weapons

This artwork from the student text is also available on the CD.

Banks soon became more than just places of exchanging money. As banking grew, bankers began to lend money to merchants for business and trading ventures. With this extra money, a merchant could expand his business. Banks also issued letters of credit to wealthy merchants. To obtain a **letter of credit**, a merchant first left an amount of money with the banker, who gave him a letter that credited the merchant for that amount. Thus, the merchant could travel without having to carry large sums of money. When he arrived at his destination, the banker in that town accepted the other bank's letter of credit and gave the merchant his money.

The Expulsion of Muslim Powers from Iberia

Driving out foreign powers became another way to expand European culture and influence. In Chapter 2 you learned about the Islamic conquest of the Iberian Peninsula (modern Spain and Portugal) in the eighth century. The reconquest (*Reconquista*) of this peninsula began almost immediately. Christian and Muslim forces struggled for control of sections of this peninsula over the next five centuries. By the end of the thirteenth century, non-Muslim forces had regained control of most of this region. Only the Muslim kingdom of Granada remained. In 1492, Ferdinand II of Aragon and Isabella I of Castile took control of Granada, and Muslim rule came to an end.

> #### Letters of Credit and the Crusades
>
> The Knights Templar, a monastic order of knights, formed around 1120 to protect pilgrims who traveled to the Holy Land. Over time, they developed a banking system to aid wealthy pilgrims. A noble would deposit his funds with the Templars in Europe to be managed and protected during his journey. In exchange he would receive a letter of credit that stated the value of his deposit. Upon arriving in the Holy Land, he would submit his letter of credit to the Templars and receive his funds. This arrangement made it much safer for the pilgrims to travel. The fees charged added to the wealth of the Templars.
>
> Before long this concept became common practice in the growing banking industry. The modern version would be a checking account and the writing of checks.

Iberian Peninsula 910

Spain 1400

Section Quiz

1–3. List three motives for the Crusades.

4–5. List two devices invented by Europeans in the Middle Ages.

6. What role did banks play in assisting the growth of trade?

★ How did the growth of cities play an important role in the expansion of Europe? Was this growth a good thing for Europe?

IV. Development of Culture in Europe

In Chapter 1 you learned that culture is the physical and mental environment developed through human thought and labor. The concept of culture and its development began in the Garden of Eden.

Objectives

Students should be able to

1. Analyze ways in which the ideals of chivalry affected feudal society.

2. Describe Jewish contributions to Europe's development.

3. Analyze how the rise of schools and universities in Italy, France, and England contributed to literacy, learning, and scientific advancement.

4. Analyze how major works of art, architecture, and literature shed light on values and attitudes in European society.

CD: 5H The Iberian Peninsula

These maps from the student text are also available on the CD.

Section Quiz Answers

1–3. (any three) to expand the influence of the Roman Church, to gain wealth, to gain land, to prove religious fervor, to travel, to seek adventure, to trade

4–5. mechanical clock and spectacles

6. changing money, making loans to merchants, issuing letters of credit

★ Answers will vary. Cities provided a place for people to live and work. They provided economic opportunities for rich and poor alike. They became the centers of trade and provided a money economy. Yes, the growth was a good thing. Growth is a partial fulfillment of the Creation Mandate.

Although sin forced Adam and Eve from the Garden, it did not nullify the Creation Mandate. Even the unbeliever tends to fulfill aspects of this mandate in one way or another. We will find more and more examples after AD 1000 of men exercising dominion over God's creation through thought and labor.

Chivalry

Knights were trained to live by a strict set of rules called the "code of chivalry." *Chivalry* comes from a French word meaning "horseman." It is also similar to the English word *cavalry*. Knights were expected to be brave in battle and limit their fighting to other armed knights. A group of knights could not attack a single knight. Instead, they were expected to fight him one at a time.

The Roman Church also sought to influence the behavior of knights. They worked to improve the conduct of the knights and to limit the destruction of warfare. The church decree known as the **Peace of God** placed church property out of bounds for fighting. This decree was also intended to protect those not directly involved in the fighting. The **Truce of God** restricted fighting to certain days of the week. For example, combat was not allowed from Wednesday evening until Monday morning. While these decrees were not always followed, an effort was made to improve conditions when fighting occurred.

Rise of Universities

During the Middle Ages education was not available to most Europeans. However, as previously mentioned, education was preserved in monastic and cathedral schools (eleventh century) for a privileged few. Students were trained in the **liberal arts**. These studies were reserved for "free" (*liberei*) men (nobility) rather than "common" men. All subjects were taught in Latin.

The concept of a university became one of the unique contributions of European culture. Universities began to develop in the twelfth century. During the formative years, students would travel to places where well-known teachers instructed, and a university would later develop. Newly acquired Muslim and Byzantine documents about medicine, science, and other subjects also provided a wealth of information for instruction in these universities.

Italy boasted two early universities, and Paris developed one soon thereafter. Over time, the universities became known for particular areas of study. Students traveled to Salerno in Italy to study medicine. Those interested in studying law traveled to Bologna. The university in Paris concentrated on the study of theology.

From the universities of Bologna and Paris, two types of universities developed. The university in Paris was made up of teachers who had earned masters of arts degrees. They regulated the university. The university in Bologna was made up of groups of students who regulated the university and hired their teachers. Nations in Northern Europe tended to follow the Parisian pattern as they established universities. Nations in Southern Europe tended to follow the Bologna pattern.

Students attending these universities often met in rented buildings, and some sat on straw as they listened to their teachers. Since paper was expensive and hard to find, the students often spent hours each day memorizing their lessons. The typical day for a student began at 4 a.m. and ended at bedtime around 9 p.m.

Medieval knight

The University of Bologna

Most students at the University of Bologna (buh LOAN yuh) came from outside Italy. They were forced to organize in order to protect themselves from local citizens, robbers, and teachers who might otherwise fail to give the students a quality education. They elected officials to perform such duties as making sure the bells rang on time, presiding over examinations and graduation, and assembling student committees to report on faculty abuses. If town officials refused to resolve a student's complaint, the students had the right to carry out a university strike to demand justice. Powerful leaders such as Pope Honorius III protected this university and intervened in students' behalf.

While Italy and France were the first countries to develop universities, schools began to appear in England, Spain, and Portugal by the end of the twelfth century. Warfare often made travel difficult or impossible, and countries started their own universities to meet the needs of their students. By the fourteenth century, Germany, Bohemia, and other countries were establishing their own universities as well. More subjects were offered, and universities began to meet in permanent buildings.

Universities served a vital role in increasing literacy and scientific advancement. They produced medical doctors, lawyers, theologians, and many other professionals. This system enriched European culture and spread knowledge throughout Europe. Kings and popes supported universities because they valued the services of graduates to promote their causes.

Works of Art, Architecture, and Literature

Christian religion played a central role in European culture and society. Christian themes were found at the center of European culture during the Middle Ages. These themes are evident by looking at the art, architecture, and literature from this period.

Art

During the Middle Ages, Christian themes and subjects dominated most art. Bible characters such as John the Baptist, Mary, Christ, and various saints appeared in most of the artwork. Halos were often added to emphasize the holiness. Others, like John the Baptist, were shown wearing an animal skin (to represent camel's hair). Art served to visually teach stories from the Bible and the Roman Church.

Painting of the appearance of Christ to the eleven after the Resurrection

Architecture

During this period in Europe, architecture often centered on the construction of **cathedrals**. Growing towns and cities displayed their wealth and prosperity by building these large and impressive churches.

Medieval Art

As the text mentions, religious themes dominated art during the Middle Ages. Often "saints" were the subjects of the works. During this period, the term *saint* was limited to a specially designated person who had done something exceptional by church standards. However, the Bible often refers to living believers as saints and reveals that all who are saved in Christ qualify as saints. (See passages such as 1 Corinthians 1:2 and Ephesians 1:1.)

Purgatory

Dante wrote of traveling through purgatory in his work *Divine Comedy*. There is no reference to this realm in the Bible. The only hint of such a place is found in an apocryphal book called 2 Maccabees. According to the Roman Church, purgatory is a temporary place of suffering where a person who dies "in a state of grace" is purified and prepared for heaven. In contrast, the Bible speaks of being absent from the body and present with the Lord in 2 Corinthians 5:8. Believers are either here in the body awaiting death or absent from the body and in the presence of the Lord. No other location is supported by Scripture.

Section V

Objectives

Students should be able to

1. Explain the characteristics of the famine, plague, and warfare that decimated Europe.

2. Assess ways in which long-term climate change contributed to Europe's economic and population growth beginning in the eleventh century.

3. Analyze major changes in the agrarian and commercial economies in Europe following the drastic population decline.

4. Explain how the Hundred Years' War led to the development of modern France and England.

Notre Dame Cathedral serves as an example of Gothic architecture.

Divine Comedy

It may seem odd to name a 14,000-line poem about hell, purgatory, and heaven a comedy. However, in its historical context, this name makes sense. During the medieval period, writing that had a sad ending was called a tragedy. A work that had a happy ending was called a comedy. A comedy had to be written in the vernacular so the common individual could read it or understand it when it was read to him.

During the early Middle Ages, the architectural style was called **Romanesque** (ROH muh NESK) because it used many elements of Roman style. This style used rounded vaults (made from putting several arches together) for roofs. Thick stone walls were needed to support these heavy roofs. These buildings were dark inside because only small windows could be used. Candles and torches were used to provide some light. But Romanesque churches were dark and cold.

A new style of construction, called **Gothic**, developed during the thirteenth century. Using external supports known as **flying buttresses**, the cathedrals could have higher ceilings and thinner walls. This construction allowed for larger windows and doors. Gothic cathedrals were warmer and brighter. Stained-glass windows added beauty and color to the interior of the churches. These windows often used arranged pieces of colorful glass to picture Bible stories.

Literature

Latin was the language of the Roman Empire. It remained the language used for writing, government, and instruction during the Middle Ages. However, it was not the language spoken by most of the people in Europe. Languages varied by region and included French, German, Italian, Spanish, and English.

During the twelfth century, writers began to compose their work in the **vernacular** (vur NAK yuh lur) (common spoken languages). Writing in the language of the people helped to develop and preserve that language. Use of the vernacular also contributed to the growth of nationalism.

Two of the best known writers from this period are **Dante** and **Chaucer**. Dante, an Italian, wrote the *Divine Comedy*, a poem about an imaginary journey through hell, purgatory, and paradise. His work sheds light on the unrest and skepticism of the late Middle Ages. Chaucer, an English poet, wrote *The Canterbury Tales*, which is about a group of pilgrims traveling to visit the tomb of a famous religious leader in England. He gives the reader a glimpse of English life during this period.

Section Quiz

1. Knights were trained to live by what code?
2. Which church decree limited the days on which fighting could occur?
3. During the Middle Ages, students were taught in what language?
4. Which university was composed of student groups who hired their teachers?
★ What was the significance of writing in the vernacular?

V. Calamities in Europe

A calamity can be defined as an event that causes dreadful loss, enduring suffering, or great misery. Famine, war, and plague are ex-

---

Activity 2: *The Canterbury Tales*

This excerpt from *The Canterbury Tales* provides the student with an example of early vernacular literature.

The Canterbury Tales

Read selected portions of the story to your students. You could also assign a portion as outside reading. The *British Literature* (second edition) textbook from BJU Press has a section on this work in unit one.

Activity 3: Romanesque and Gothic Architecture

This activity reviews the features of Romanesque and Gothic architecture to help the students distinguish them.

Rheims Cathedral, France

Visit www.bjupress.com/resources for possible links to articles about the Rheims cathedral in France.

Section Quiz Answers

1. chivalry
2. Truce of God
3. Latin
4. Bologna
★ This developed and preserved the spoken language of the people. It also contributed to the growth of nationalism.

amples of calamities. Beginning in the fourteenth century, Europe was decimated (great loss of population) by all of these.

Great Famine

The **Great Famine of 1315** was the first calamity to strike large areas of Europe during this period. It began with heavy and frequent rain over much of Europe starting in 1315. The spring and summer remained cool, and the crops rotted in the fields. Food for people and animals became very scarce. Also, salt to preserve meat became scarce. The producers of salt needed dry weather to extract it from salt water through evaporation. So meat spoiled. As a result, the price for food and salt became too expensive for the vast majority of the people.

To survive, people slaughtered their farm animals for food and ate seed grain. Some parents abandoned their children because they could no longer feed them. This calamity even resembled scenes from the Old Testament (2 Kings 6) as some resorted to eating human flesh to survive. The rain continued until 1317, and people were reduced to eating roots, grasses, and even bark from trees to survive.

Many of those who survived the two years of rain and famine had been weakened by pneumonia and other illnesses. In addition, with the destruction of livestock and lack of seed for planting, the recovery was slow. Somewhere between ten and twenty-five percent of the people died of starvation or illness between 1315 and 1322. While other calamities would take more lives, this one lingered for years and caused slow and agonizing deaths.

Hundred Years' War

Between 1337 and 1453, England and France fought a series of battles to settle the issue of English control of land in France. This became known as the **Hundred Years' War**. The French had steadily taken land away from the English for many years. However, the death of the last Capetian king without a male heir led to a crisis.

The English king, **Edward III**, was related to the French royal line through his mother and claimed the right to the French throne. However, the French nobles rejected this claim and selected Philip VI of the house of Valois (val WAH) as king. War was to be expected. However, this series of battles began as a contest between feudal nobles and ended as a rivalry between two emerging nations.

English forces started the war by crossing the English Channel. Although they were outnumbered, the English quickly won several key battles. They defeated the French by using new tactics and weapons. The longbows used by the English destroyed French forces from a safe distance. Thousands of French soldiers were slaughtered in these battles.

Although the English won most of the battles, the drain on English forces and England was great. Over time, the people of England tired of the cost of war, and political unrest resulted. Also, a plague killed many in England. There were simply not enough soldiers to take advantage of English victories.

The French finally rallied to victory under the leadership of a peasant girl named **Joan of Arc**. She believed that she was being directed from heaven to drive out the English. Desperate for a leader, the French followed her and defeated the English. The English were able to capture her and burned her at the stake. However, her example strengthened the French to emerge as victors.

Hundred Years' War

Visit www.bjupress.com/resources for possible links to articles about the Hundred Years' War.

The Black Death

Visit www.bjupress.com/resources for possible links to articles about the Black Death.

Black Death

Historians differ on how the plague known as the **Black Death** originated and was spread. However, there is no doubt that something similar to the bubonic plague killed millions of people throughout the world. Europe suffered a great loss of people as this plague spread from city to city and engulfed whole countries.

The plague may have begun in China and spread by trade ships to Europe by 1347. Rats and their fleas have been blamed for the spread of the fatal bacteria, although opinions vary, and we cannot be certain. What is certain is that millions of people were killed by this disease. Some estimate that up to twenty-five million people in Europe died from the Black Death.

Cities in Europe were especially vulnerable to the spread of the plague for several reasons. Open sewers and improper disposal of trash made the cities unsanitary. Rats and fleas thrived in the cities. Houses were also often close together, and the people lived in crowded settings. These unhealthy conditions provided a breeding ground for disease and its spread.

Besides the obvious reduction of the population in Europe, there were several other consequences. The people quickly turned to the Roman Church for deliverance. Many made trips to Rome and made donations to the Church in hopes of rescue from the plague.

However, the Roman Church proved to be unable to stop the plague. When people saw the priests and nuns dying as quickly as others, they lost faith in the claims of the Roman Church. In addition, many concluded that the plague was sent by God to punish the people for their sins. The Roman Church lost much of the authority that church leaders had built up over the years. People began to look in other places for answers.

The wealthy left the cities and lived on secluded estates in order to avoid contact with the plague. Others gave themselves over to sinful living since they decided that death was imminent anyway. Crime also became a serious problem. As previously mentioned, many blamed Jews for the plague, and thousands of Jews died as the people slaughtered whole Jewish communities for their imagined crime.

By 1350 the Black Death had run its course, but it took many years for Europe to recover. The Church of Rome had lost much of its credibility during this time. On the other hand, the movement toward nationalism continued to gain momentum. The Hundred Years' War, interrupted by the Black Death, resumed and concluded with France and England emerging as nation states.

Section Quiz

1. Which of the three calamities mentioned in this chapter caused the slowest and most agonizing deaths?

2. What English king triggered the start of the Hundred Years' War?

3. Who rallied the French to defeat the English during the Hundred Years' War?

4. What animals have been blamed for spreading the Black Death?

★ Why did the Church of Rome lose influence during the Black Death? What did this do to the faith of the common people in Europe?

Section Quiz Answers

1. the Great Famine of 1315

2. Edward III

3. Joan of Arc

4. rats and their fleas

★ The Church of Rome was unable to stop the plague; priests and other church officials died of the plague just like everyone else. Answers will vary but might include the following: The loss of faith in the teachings of Rome prepared people for the Reformation. It also led some people to reject religion and search for human answers.

Activity 4: Chapter Review

This activity reviews the material covered in the chapter.

Chapter Review Answers

Making Connections

1. German tribes

2. Charlemagne

3. to regain access to the Holy Land and defeat the infidel Muslims

4. trade, wealth, development of a middle class, access to knowledge that had been preserved by the Byzantine Empire

5. unusual rainfall over a two-year period, loss of crops, short supplies of salt to preserve meat, consumption of livestock and seed grain.

6. Answers should include some of the following: granting town charters; developing common law; establishing circuit courts; gaining control of large areas of land; making alliances with the Church of Rome and towns.

7. The English exhausted their resources and suffered from unrest at home. Joan of Arc was able to inspire the French to fight on to victory.

8. Flying buttresses enabled higher ceilings, thinner walls, and larger windows

CHAPTER REVIEW

Making Connections

1. What tribes moved into Roman territory and eventually took over the Roman Empire?

2. After whom was the Carolingian house named?

3. Why did Pope Urban II call for the First Crusade?

4. What resulted from merchants taking crusaders to the Holy Land?

5. What chain of events resulted in the Great Famine of 1315?

6. How did monarchs develop centralized power during this period?

7. Why did the English win most of the battles during the Hundred Years' War and yet lose the war?

8. Why were Gothic cathedrals considered warmer and brighter than Romanesque cathedrals?

Developing History Skills

1. Using this chapter and information found in Chapter 2, compile a list of the kinds of documents that Crusaders would have brought back to Europe. Based on this list, what kinds of cultural changes would have resulted?

2. Construct a timeline by centuries that includes the significant events of political development in France.

Thinking Critically

1. What developments in England limited royal power? Why?

2. How would you respond to the following statement: "An important lesson we learn from the Black Death is that the Christian religion is unable to live up to its claims. It claims that God will take care of those who follow Him. But many Christians in Europe died from this plague."

Living in God's World

1. Divide the class into two groups, one group favoring the Crusades and one opposing them. Have each side discuss its reasons for its position and then choose a spokesman to present its reasons. After both sides have spoken, they should again discuss among themselves how to respond to the opposing side. Then different spokesmen should give each side's responses.

2. Pretend that you are a preacher in England in 1210. The king is claiming that he rules England by divine right; that is, he believes he has complete authority over the realm because God has made him king. Using Scripture, write a speech that disputes the claim of the divine right of kings.

People, Places, and Terms to Know

Clovis
mayor of the palace
Charlemagne
manor
pope
papal
Innocent III
Medieval Warm Period
town charter
William the Conqueror
Henry II
circuit courts
Hugh Capet
Phillip II
baillis
jury
indictments
common law
Magna Carta
Parliament
power of the purse
interdict
crusade
middle class
bank
letter of credit
Reconquista
chivalry
Peace of God
Truce of God
liberal arts
cathedrals
Romanesque
Gothic
flying buttresses
vernacular
Dante
Chaucer
Great Famine of 1315
Hundred Years' War
Edward III
Joan of Arc
Black Death

---

to allow for more light and warmth from the sun.

Developing History Skills

1. From ch. 2—Alhazen's *Book of Optics*, Avicenna's *Canon of Medicine* and *Book of Healing*. From this chapter—New Testament Greek texts and other Greek and Arabic texts. Answers might include the following: improved medical care, broad discussion of ancient Greek and Roman philosophers; discussion and debate about the accuracy of the Latin Vulgate (Latin translation of the Bible).

2. 10th century—Hugh Capet founded the Capetian dynasty; 11th century—Phillip II expanded the Capetian dynasty at the expense of English holdings in France; 14th century—Edward III (of England) and Philip VI (of France) were opponents in the Hundred Years' War; 15th century—Joan of Arc led French forces and turned the tide against English forces near the end of the Hundred Years' War.

Thinking Critically

1. Magna Carta and Parliament; the Magna Carta established limits to royal power, and Parliament exercised the "power of the purse" to limit royal options.

2. Answers might include the following: God does not promise to keep His followers from disease and death. However, He does sustain them whether in this life or by safely taking them into His presence in heaven.

Living in God's World

1. Answers should include some of the following:

   Pro: increased trade; access to ancient learning and documents; resulted in exploration for new trade routes; brought Greek copies of the New Testament back to Europe; resulted in growth of factories and provided jobs.

   Con: Futile effort that led to the deaths of many thousands of civilians and crusaders; resulted in violence against Jews in Europe; ultimately failed to control the Holy Land.

2. Answers may include some of the following:

   (1) Kings have authority from God, but they have authority to do what is good and just, not what is evil and unjust. Romans 13:1–5 and 1 Peter 2:13–14 do say that citizens are to submit to kings, but they also say that God sets up kings to reward the good and punish the evil. Kings who do otherwise are misusing their authority.

   (2) God judges kings who do not do His will (e.g., 2 Chron. 26:16–19; Acts 12:21–23).

   (3) God sometimes gives His people success when they oppose the authority of wicked rulers (e.g., 2 Kings 11).

CHAPTER 6

Chapter Goals

Students should be able to

1. Explain the major causes of the Renaissance.
2. Briefly discuss the major achievements in literature, art, and architecture in Renaissance Europe in contrast to the medieval period.
3. Analyze the disconnect among Europeans with the late medieval church.
4. Explain the three key principles of the Reformation.
5. Contrast the Protestant Reformation with the Counter Reformation.

1200–1700

John Huss burned at the stake (during the Council of Constance) 1415

Brief and failed papacy of Boniface VIII 1294–1303

Life and ministry of John Wycliffe c. 1320–84

Fourth Lateran Council 1215

| 1200 | | 1300 | | 1400 |

Inquisition by the Roman Church 13th through 17th century

Council of Constance — ends the controversy over multiple popes 1414–18

Chapter 6 Lesson Plan Chart			
Section Title	**Main Activity**	**Pages**	**Days**
I. The Renaissance	Activity 1: *Utopia*	98–104	2 days
II. Discontent with the Church of Rome	Activity 3: Why Monks Are Shunned	104–7	1½–2 days
III. The Reformation	Activity 4: Luther's Ninety-five Theses	108–14	1½–2 days
TOTAL SUGGESTED DAYS (INCLUDING 1 DAY EACH FOR REVIEW AND TESTING)			7–8 days

Materials List

Section I

- Library books containing examples of medieval and Renaissance art
- Library book showing sketches from Leonardo da Vinci's notebooks
- A copy of Machiavelli's *The Prince*
- A copy of Erasmus's *In Praise of Folly*
- A copy of Thomas More's *Utopia*
- CD: 6A Sistine Chapel Detail; 6B Ghiberti's Doors
- Activities 1 and 2 from the *Student Activities* manual

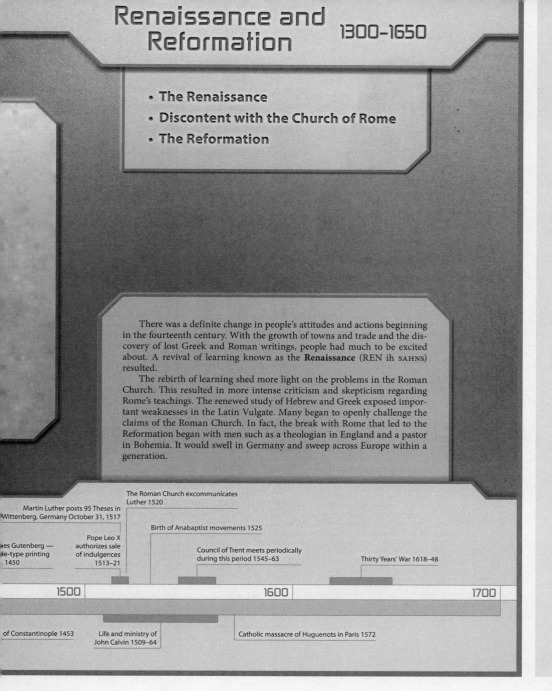

Renaissance and Reformation 1300–1650

- The Renaissance
- Discontent with the Church of Rome
- The Reformation

There was a definite change in people's attitudes and actions beginning in the fourteenth century. With the growth of towns and trade and the discovery of lost Greek and Roman writings, people had much to be excited about. A revival of learning known as the **Renaissance** (REN ih SAHNS) resulted.

The rebirth of learning shed more light on the problems in the Roman Church. This resulted in more intense criticism and skepticism regarding Rome's teachings. The renewed study of Hebrew and Greek exposed important weaknesses in the Latin Vulgate. Many began to openly challenge the claims of the Roman Church. In fact, the break with Rome that led to the Reformation began with men such as a theologian in England and a pastor in Bohemia. It would swell in Germany and sweep across Europe within a generation.

Martin Luther posts 95 Theses in Wittenberg, Germany October 31, 1517

The Roman Church excommunicates Luther 1520

Birth of Anabaptist movements 1525

...es Gutenberg — ...le-type printing ... 1450

Pope Leo X authorizes sale of indulgences 1513–21

Council of Trent meets periodically during this period 1545–63

Thirty Years' War 1618–48

1500   1600   1700

...of Constantinople 1453

Life and ministry of John Calvin 1509–64

Catholic massacre of Huguenots in Paris 1572

Section II
- Activity 3 from the *Student Activities* manual
- *Flame in the Wind* on DVD (available from BJU Press)

Section III
- Activities 4 and 5 from the *Student Activities* manual

Section I

Objectives

Students should be able to

1. Assess the impact of the rediscovery of classical learning on European thought and culture.
2. Explain the patronage of rich merchants and the Roman Church as a financial resource for the Renaissance.
3. Assess the significance of movable-type printing.
4. Analyze the effect of the use of the vernacular in literature.
5. Explain Renaissance art and architecture as a reflection of Renaissance thought.
6. Compare and contrast Renaissance writing in Italy and Northern Europe.
7. Evaluate the significance of major changes in the techniques of painting, sculpture, and architecture.

The Middle Class

Societies that have a growing or established middle class (as was present during the Renaissance) also tend to have the time and education to read literature and support fine arts. However, societies with no (or a declining) middle class must devote most of their time, money, and energy to subsisting.

Reactions to the Printing Press

When the printing press was first developed, politicians and the church denounced it, saying that it would spread

Portrait Bust of Lorenzo de Medici, probably after a model by Andrea del Verrocchio and Orsini Benintendi (painted terracotta) by Italian School Palazzo Medici-Riccardi, Florence, Italy/ The Bridgeman Art Library

Lorenzo de Medici of Florence, Italy, was an early and generous patron (financial supporter) of the Renaissance. He was also an accomplished poet. His poetry is considered to be some of the finest written during the Italian Renaissance.

A careful look at his statue reveals a broken nose. He considered this a blessing because it prevented him from smelling unpleasant odors.

The Printing Press

Europe began to produce paper during the thirteenth century. However, an efficient method of printing was needed in order to turn out a large volume of work at a low cost. You may recall that the Chinese first developed the movable-type press centuries earlier. However, Gutenberg appears to have developed this process on his own in the fifteenth century. While the Chinese did not find much use for a printing press, Europeans found this invention to be revolutionary. The printing press would prove to be an essential tool in spreading Renaissance writings. It would become even more vital for the spread of the Reformation.

I. The Renaissance

The Renaissance began in Italy and spread north into other European countries. The change was gradual. However, the results were profound. The Renaissance affected many areas of life, including art, architecture, and literature.

Transition

In the last chapter you learned about the rise of universities. In addition, you found that there was a rediscovery of classical Greek and Roman learning. Crusaders had brought many documents to Europe from Constantinople that provided scholars with much information. Also, the fall of Constantinople in 1453 caused many scholars from that city to travel to Europe. This flood of information led to a revival of learning.

During the Middle Ages, life was difficult and opportunities for education were very limited. However, with the growth of a middle class and wealth, funds were now available to support this revival of learning. Wealthy merchants and the wealth of the Roman Church paid for paintings, sculptures, and architecture that reflected the new spirit of the Renaissance. Talented writers produced enduring works in the vernacular.

Profound Changes

Tools

As we learned in the last chapter, writers had already begun to write in the vernacular. During the Renaissance, this practice continued and expanded. Works produced in the language of the people allowed Renaissance ideas to spread to many more people. As citizens became more prosperous, they found time to read and discuss these new ideas. The often tedious life of the Middle Ages was being replaced by a period of hope and optimism.

The invention of the movable-type printing press by **Johannes Gutenberg** in the mid-fifteenth century made literary works available to the public at a very low cost. Prior to his invention, books had to be copied by hand. This made them very expensive and available only to the very wealthy. The printing press now made books available quickly and at a cost that many more people could afford.

Art and Architecture

Art

The two paintings at the top of page 99 show the same subject: the Madonna and Child (Mary and Jesus). The first one comes from a medieval Gothic church. The second was painted during the Renaissance. You can see that they differ, but you may not be able to tell why. By taking a closer look, we will find out how the Renaissance artists made their paintings look different.

Perhaps the first thing you notice is that the people in the Renaissance painting look real, whereas the people in the other painting look flat. Renaissance artists had begun to study how bones and muscles work together. The artists learned about **anatomy**—the structure of humans, animals, and plants. Using this information, they could make their subjects appear more real. The change toward realism reflected a change in thinking. During the Middle Ages, people stressed heavenly things. By the Renaissance, people began to realize that nature and humans were important too because they

---

Offensive Odors

As the caption on page 98 states, Lorenzo de Medici's broken nose kept him from smelling offensive odors. Ask the students why offensive odors might have been common in that time period. *(open sewers, livestock, rotting fruits and vegetables, etc.)*

Art

Using library books (and your own discretion), show the students some examples of medieval and Renaissance art. Help them to see the difference between the two periods (anatomy, shading, perspective, color variations, etc.). Also, if possible, show them some of the artists' preliminary sketches of hands, arms, etc., by which the artist practiced and perfected what he wanted to include in the larger painting or sculpture.

Madonna and Child with Saints, Niccolò de Pietro Gerini, Bob Jones University Collection

Madonna and Child with St. John the Baptist and Angels, Ansano di Michele Ciampanti, called the Master of San Filippo, Bob Jones University Collection

were creations of God. Instead of painting flat people who were only symbols of the saints, Renaissance painters painted real people.

The Renaissance artist also added dimension to his figures by **shading**. You can see that some parts of the faces, bodies, and clothes are darker. This shading makes these areas seem farther away. The Renaissance artist painted nearer areas lighter and farther areas darker to make objects and figures appear rounded. The gradually changing colors in the folds of cloth show this technique especially well.

In the Renaissance painting, the background seems to be far away. The Renaissance artist gave depth to his background by painting far-away objects smaller than nearby objects. The ability to give depth to paintings was the result of the new study of **perspective**. The artist could figure out mathematically what size objects should be and at what angle they should be placed to give the appearance of reality. A Renaissance artist had to be a good mathematician as well as a painter.

Two men stand out as Renaissance artists. Both were from Italy. **Leonardo da Vinci** (LEE-uh-NAR-do duh VIN-chee) was truly a Renaissance man in that he developed many skills. His best known paintings are *The Last Supper* and the *Mona Lisa*. The second man,

Mona Lisa, da Vinci's famous painting

The Last Supper, 1495–97 (fresco) (post restoration) by Leonardo da Vinci (1452–1519) Santa Maria della Grazie, Milan, Italy/The Bridgeman Art Library

rebellious ideas. They probably did not realize how prophetic their comments were.

Da Vinci as a Painter

Although we think of Leonardo da Vinci as a Renaissance painter, he actually completed very few painted works. He tried to be innovative and thus experimented with new techniques, often with disastrous results. His famous fresco *The Last Supper* was painted on an experimental surface that began flaking away almost as soon as he was finished painting. The paintings he did complete were imitated for years to come. His use of background elements and pyramid placement revolutionized Renaissance painting.

Michelangelo

Truly a Renaissance man, Michelangelo excelled as a painter, sculptor, architect, poet, and engineer. He had sculpted the *Pieta* and *David* before he turned thirty. In addition to painting key sections of the Sistine Chapel, he also designed the dome of St. Peter's Basilica. So great was his contribution to the Renaissance that he was often called *Il Divino* ("the divine one").

Leonardo da Vinci

If you are able to find a book that shows the sketches from Leonardo's notebooks, students will no doubt enjoy seeing his ideas for inventions, war machines, etc. Students will find his "mirror" writing particularly intriguing.

The Sistine Chapel

Built for Pope Sixtus, the Sistine Chapel was erected and painted in the late 1400s. The first artists painted the side walls with the stories of Moses and Christ. Pope Julius II commissioned Michelangelo to paint the ceiling and later the altar wall of the chapel in 1508. The ceiling contains nine scenes from the Old Testament. Three are about Creation, three are about Adam and Eve, and three are about the Flood. The front of the chapel is painted with a scene that depicts the Final Judgment. Michelangelo sometimes used the faces of people he disliked for bad characters in his paintings.

David

Michelangelo sculpted this seventeen-foot statue of David over a four year period from a single block of marble. This sculpture has become one of the most well-known sculptures from the Renaissance. A careful examination reveals that the head, upper body, and hands are slightly larger than the proportions of the rest of the body. Some suggest that Michelangelo distorted these features in case it was placed on a high pedestal. From the ground the statue would have appeared to be proportional.

The Sistine Chapel

Perhaps the most impressive example of Renaissance sculpture is Michelangelo's *David*. This sculpture highlights the Renaissance's exalted vision of man. In this sculpture, the biblical David is used to portray the ideal man. This reflects the Renaissance ideal of man as the measure and center of all things.

Michelangelo (MY kul AN juh loh), is best known for his painting on the ceiling of the **Sistine** (SIS teen) **Chapel** in Rome. He worked on this project for four years while lying on scaffolding.

Sculpture

The sculptures of the Renaissance resemble the sculpture of the Greeks and Romans. The statues are lifelike, powerful, and stunning. The new knowledge of anatomy helped sculptors in forming human figures. Working with stone or bronze, they tried to make their figures as realistic as possible.

Much medieval sculpture was relief sculpture. That is, it was attached to a flat surface such as the wall of a cathedral or castle. This type of sculpture could not be viewed from all sides. However, many Renaissance sculptors preferred to make freestanding statues. They followed the principles of classical art: balance, harmony, and realism. Yet, even in relief sculpture, Renaissance works differed from medieval sculpture. By rounding the figures, showing anatomy, and following the rules of perspective, the artist brought flat sculpture to life. One of the greatest examples of Renaissance relief sculpture is the doors sculpted by **Ghiberti** for the baptistery of Florence.

Architecture

Renaissance architecture rejected most of the Gothic style. Architects came to believe that pointed arches, tall towers, and flying buttresses were neither graceful nor beautiful. Instead, they wanted to return to the architectural style of the Greeks and Romans. Rounded arches, columns, and domes characterized Renaissance structures. The soaring towers and ornate decoration of the Gothic cathedrals were considered old-fashioned. In contrast, Renaissance churches and palaces sat solidly balanced on the ground.

 CD: 6A Sistine Chapel Detail

Photos of the Sistine Chapel, including one close-up photo showing detail, are available on the CD.

 St. Peter's Basilica

Visit www.bjupress.com/resources for possible links to articles about St. Peter's Basilica.

Around 1401, Ghiberti defeated Brunelleschi in a competition to create the bronze doors to the baptistery of Florence. He labored for about twenty years to complete the twenty-eight panels of these magnificent doors. Each panel depicts a story from the New Testament.

CD: 6B Ghiberti's Doors

Photos of Ghiberti's doors are available on the CD.

Brunelleschi and the Dome

In 1419 a competition was held to design the dome for the Cathedral of Florence. Two men were leading competitors: Brunelleschi and Ghiberti (who won the competition to create the baptistery doors). This time, Brunelleschi won and designed a unique dome that was double-walled and constructed from over four million bricks. This dome weighs about thirty-seven thousand tons. He had to design special machines to lift the heavy larger stones. Brunelleschi even had to develop new methods of laying the bricks to make construction possible.

The Cathedral of Florence, pictured above, is a stunning example of Renaissance architecture. **Brunelleschi** (broo nuh LES key) designed the dome for this huge structure. He solved several architectural problems in order to construct this eight-sided dome. The structure demonstrates Brunelleschi's keen understanding of mathematics. This dome even exceeded the one atop the Roman Parthenon. Men like Brunelleschi demonstrated that the Renaissance man had surpassed the ancient Romans, whose knowledge they had used.

Learning

Knowledge about science, medicine, and many other fields improved at an ever increasing pace. The recovery of ancient knowledge led to more study and new discoveries. An education became more and more important.

To study the world around him, the Renaissance man needed to know how to read, write, and reason. With increased prosperity students could afford to hire private teachers. In addition, many towns started academies where boys could learn Latin and Greek. Girls often had tutors at home. Students spent hours reading classical works. Wealthy men collected and read large libraries of manuscripts.

The subjects taught in the Renaissance differed from those of the Middle Ages. Known as the **humanities**, these subjects covered human interests and experiences. Literature, philosophy, art, history, grammar, and speech were all taught. Renaissance teachers encouraged their students to invent, explore, and discover. They also expected students to appreciate and create beauty through art. The goal of Renaissance education was to make the student a well-rounded person, educated and interested in many fields.

As previously mentioned, Leonardo da Vinci was an excellent example of the Renaissance man. He excelled in sculpture, architecture, painting, music, and poetry. Leonardo also studied subjects that included anatomy, botany, engineering, and mathematics. His notebooks were filled with sketches of inventions, including early versions of a tank, a submarine, a helicopter, and a machine gun.

Variations

An examination of the writings from Italy and Northern Europe reveals two distinct themes.

Italy

Italian writers patterned their writing after the works of ancient Greece and Rome. They studied the ancient writings and imitated their style. They were also concerned with advancing human knowledge and acceptable behavior. Three Italian authors will be briefly examined.

Petrarch was a pioneer of Renaissance humanism and a central figure in Italian literature. He sought out ancient manuscripts and studied them. He also composed poetry in Latin and followed the style of ancient Roman poets. Petrarch spread the ideas of the Renaissance and became known as the **Father of Humanism**.

Castiglione (CAH stil YOH nay) was another Italian author. He wrote a famous book on etiquette (social behavior). Good manners were considered essential to the growing middle class, who were eager to behave in a proper manner. His book, *The Courtier*, described proper conduct for the Renaissance man.

Machiavelli (MAHK ee uh VEL ee) worked for the government in Florence, Italy, and observed political events in Europe. From his observations he wrote an essay called *The Prince*. In previous works on politics, the Greeks held up the virtues that a good prince should possess. These writings along with the Bible were very influential during the Middle Ages. But Machiavelli taught that those who lived by the classical and biblical virtues would not be able to gain or keep power. If a virtue helped a ruler gain power, Machiavelli wrote that the ruler should use it. If not, the ruler should disregard it. In this way Machiavelli represented the Renaissance trend of freeing people from religious tradition. This would allow man to be the measure of all things.

Northern Europe

The writers of Northern Europe tended to emphasize religious issues. They often gave more attention to Christian rather than classical sources. Two authors will be briefly examined.

Erasmus of Rotterdam was one of the most highly regarded and influential scholars of the Renaissance. He mastered Latin and Greek. In the last chapter we learned that he was the first to publish a Greek New Testament that was printed on a movable-type press. This work became an essential tool for the Reformation. Reformers like Luther and Calvin used Erasmus's text to help prepare their own translations of the Bible. Despite having made this contribution to the Reformation, Erasmus refused to leave the Church of Rome.

Sir **Thomas More** was a close friend of Erasmus and served in the court of King Henry VIII in England. His work *Utopia* (which means "nowhere") is a story about an imaginary country based on Christian principles and the philosophy of Plato. In this work More presented his view of an ideal state.

While More was a man of personal piety, he vigorously rejected the principles set forth in the Reformation. More supported the supremacy of the pope and wrote in defense of Rome's teaching on subjects including purgatory and the seven sacraments.

> ### Proper Conduct
> Another book of etiquette, *The Book of Manners*, written by Giovanni Della Casa, provides some useful advice for the Renaissance man.
>
> "When you have blown your nose, you should not open your handkerchief and inspect it, as if pearls or rubies had dropped out of your skull."
>
> "It is bad manners to clean your teeth with your napkin, and still worse to do it with your finger. . . ."

> ### Rulers are Not a Terror
> How does Machiavelli's observation of rulers compare with Paul's description of God's purpose for government in Romans 13:1–4? How should men rule?

> ### In Praise of Folly
> Erasmus wrote this satire to expose many of the abuses in the Roman Church. However, even though he was critical of the failures of the Church, Erasmus supported reform of the Roman Church and opposed separation from it.

Machiavelli

Born in Florence, Italy, and educated in Latin, Machiavelli spent most of his life serving in various political posts on behalf of his city. He began as a clerk and quickly rose to the position of ambassador. Machiavelli represented Florence in France, Spain, and Rome. He witnessed the ruthless methods of rulers like Cesare Borgia (son of Pope Alexander VI).

In 1494 Machiavelli participated in the restoration of the republic when the Medici family was expelled from power in Florence (after ruling for sixty years). He also directed the local militia that defeated an attack from the forces of Pisa, Italy, in 1509. Three years later Machiavelli survived an assault on Florence by the Spanish troops hired by the Medici and Pope Julius II. Machiavelli was deposed from office and tortured as a conspirator. When he denied involvement, he was released. Machiavelli then retired to his estate and wrote several works, including *The Prince*.

Personal Piety vs. True Religion

Sir Thomas More was a pious man who prayed for hours each day. He took his role of father seriously and endeavored to "train up a child in the way he should go." He led his family in personal devotions on a daily basis. More even had his children read Scripture before every meal. Yet he utterly rejected the Reformation and became an outspoken critic of men like Martin Luther. More even helped King Henry VIII write *Defense of the Seven Sacraments*. When confronted by the truth of Scripture, More chose to embrace the errors of Rome. More

The Prince

If desired, read selected excerpts from this work to the students.

In Praise of Folly

If desired, read selected excerpts from this work to the students.

Utopia

If desired, read selected excerpts from this work to the students.

Activity 1: *Utopia*

For this activity, the students will read excerpts from Thomas More's work and then answer questions.

Castiglione

Visit www.bjupress.com/resources for possible links to articles about Castiglione.

Sir Thomas More

Visit www.bjupress.com/resources for possible links to articles about Sir Thomas More.

demonstrates that professed devotion to God and personal piety do not guarantee that a person is truly a Christian.

Portrait of a Young Man, by Agnolo di Cosimo, shows the confidence of Europeans during the Renaissance.

This portrait of Henry VIII demonstrates the renewed emphasis on the individual.

Consequences

Positive

The Renaissance was an age in which many placed their faith in human ability. Yet the Renaissance also led men to inquire and seek the truth. People were no longer content to accept the teachings of Rome without question. For many, this scrutiny led to a return to the clear teachings of Scripture and a Christianity that was free of unbiblical rituals.

The Renaissance also led to a renewed interest in the manuscripts and languages of the Old Testament and first-century Christianity. Copies of the Old and New Testament Scriptures were recovered and studied. Access to these documents resulted in an interest in the study of Greek and Hebrew.

The individual was emphasized in the Renaissance. A brief look at portraits from this period demonstrates this new attitude of the importance of the individual. It was also found in Renaissance education, where the student was encouraged to discover and develop his abilities.

Finally, the development of movable-type printing and widespread education provided lasting benefits to Europe and far beyond. Literature became more available and education became accessible to many more people. Europe began to experience an intellectual renewal.

Negative

The emphasis of the Renaissance was on man rather than God. This emphasis led to the weakening of moral restraints. The Church of Rome should have set an example of righteous living. Instead, many of the Renaissance clergy and popes openly lived in great wealth and immorality. They spent church funds on such luxuries as expensive architecture. To bring in additional funds, they sold church offices to the wealthy and empty promises of forgiveness to the poor. Many noted the failures of the Roman Church and looked elsewhere for the truth.

Section Quiz

1. What does the term *Renaissance* mean?
2–4. List three techniques that resulted in differences between medieval and Renaissance art.
5. What did the change in art reveal about the shift in thinking from the medieval to the Renaissance periods?
★ Evaluate the consequences of the Renaissance.

II. Discontent with the Church of Rome

We have discussed the growing dissatisfaction with some of the practices and doctrines of the Roman Church. We will briefly examine four doctrines with which many disagreed. When men argued against these doctrines, the Roman Church often resorted to persecution. In addition to disagreement over doctrines, many lost faith in the Church of Rome during a period of scandals connected to the papacy. These embarrassing events further eroded faith in the Roman Church.

Section II

Objectives

Students should be able to

1. Evaluate the struggle to limit the power of the papacy by political and religious authorities.
2. Explain how the existence and practices of the Inquisition encouraged discontent with the Roman Church.
3. Describe the scandals of the late medieval Roman Church.
4. Assess the impact of behavior by clergy and popes on the reputation of the Roman Church during the Renaissance.

Activity 2: Erasmus and Access to Scripture

This activity uses Erasmus's own words to reveal his views on access to Scripture.

Consequences of the Renaissance

Have the students list on a sheet of paper the positive and negative consequences of the Renaissance. Then as a class compare the lists and discuss the reasons for the students' conclusions.

Section Quiz Answers

1. rebirth, revival
2–4. knowledge of anatomy, use of shading, study of perspective
5. People of the Renaissance placed greater values on the created world and upon man.
★ Positive: led men to inquire and seek the truth; resulted in discontent with the Roman Church; renewed interest in manuscripts and languages of the Bible; renewed importance of the individual; movable-type printing made Bibles and other literature readily available at more affordable prices. Negative: emphasis on man's ability in contrast to trusting revelation from God; weakened moral restraints; failure of the Church of Rome to provide a moral example to restrain evil

Activity 3: Why Monks Are Shunned

This activity contains an excerpt from the writings of Rabelais.

Doctrine

In the last chapter you learned that the Church of Rome declared that the bread and wine of the Lord's Supper were transformed into the body and blood of Christ. This teaching was made official church doctrine at the Fourth Lateran Council in 1215 and is known as **transubstantiation** (TRAN sub STAN shee AY shun) (the transforming of the substance). According to this teaching, the wine and bread change into the very blood and body of Christ each time the priest recites the Latin phrase *hoc est corpus meum* (this is my body). Those who rejected this dogma (doctrine) were charged with heresy.

Another teaching that had become accepted in the Church of Rome was the necessity of works in addition to faith for salvation. Works varied from being mildly inconvenient to extreme and health threatening. However, no amount of self-inflicted suffering could guarantee anyone acceptance before God. Not even the greatest saint or most pious pope could be sure of going to heaven upon death.

Over the centuries many writings and practices came to be placed on an equal basis with the Scripture. The writings of the early church fathers, anonymous works, and traditions became authoritative in the Roman Church. Even though a careful study reveals that these works often contradicted the Scriptures, the Church of Rome preserved this error.

A fourth error taught by Rome was that believers had to confess their sins to a priest. The Church of Rome taught that the priest was another Christ who was empowered to forgive the guilt of sin. This prevented the repentant sinner from having direct access to God and also forced him to endure sensitive and probing questions from the priest. Many instances of priests abusing their power resulted.

Persecution

By the thirteenth century, more and more people questioned the teachings of Rome. The Roman Church responded by authorizing the **Inquisition** (in kwi ZISH un). The Inquisition was a church court set up to find and punish heretics. New monastic orders such as the Dominicans demonstrated their zeal by leading in the search for heretics. Many people were tried and tortured to confess their heresy. The suspect had no right to counsel, and his accusers could remain unnamed. Suspects were considered guilty and had to prove their innocence, often without even knowing the charge against them. However, what was intended to purge the Roman Church of false doctrine led many to reject the Church of Rome entirely.

Corruption

Beginning in the fourteenth century, several scandals further weakened the influence of the Church of Rome. In the last chapter you learned that the Roman Church lost credibility during the plague known as the Black Death. The behavior of many of the clergy and popes during the Renaissance further reduced respect for the Roman Church. In addition, two events brought the Church's reputation to a new low.

Pope Boniface VIII (1294–1303) tried to strengthen the power of the Roman Church by issuing a decree that everyone, including kings, had to submit to the pope in order to be saved. This was a bold statement, but Boniface did not have the power to enforce this decree. Instead, he was removed from office by an invading French force.

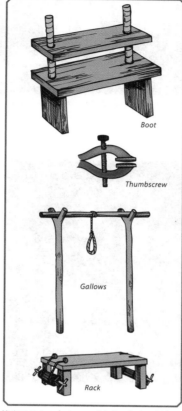

Boot

Thumbscrew

Gallows

Rack

Various torture devices used during the Inquisition

Luther's Trip to Rome

This event occurred in the middle of the Renaissance when corruption in the Catholic Church was commonplace. Luther traveled to Rome on behalf of his monastic order and anticipated a great spiritual experience. However, everywhere he turned he saw greed and vice. When Luther had the opportunity to say the mass in a church, he was urged to hurry through the words in order to let the next priest have a turn. Luther left Rome disillusioned and filled with doubt. The inconsistencies he saw in the church's hierarchy and practices encouraged him to continue in his quest for peace.

Guilty or Innocent

Have students contrast the principle of the Inquisition that the accused was presumed guilty until proven innocent with the premise on which the British and U.S. legal systems are founded: that the accused is innocent until the accuser proves him guilty.

▶ Persecution

Show your class the film *Flame in the Wind* and discuss the reality of persecution of believers during the Reformation. Help the students to understand that persecution of Christians occurs today in India, China, and many Muslim countries.

Indulgences

Technically, the Catholic Church did not "sell" indulgences. The church's position was that the indulgence was the "gift" of replacing penance in return for a "gift" of money. The selling came about with those who offered the indulgences to the people. The indulgence seller who came to Luther's attention was Johann Tetzel. To sell indulgences, he went far beyond a normal sales pitch. Tetzel said that when a coin went into the indulgence bowl, the person's soul for whom the coin was given immediately went to heaven. Though his claims were scandalous, his coffers quickly filled with money to pay for the pope's extravagant building program. The Roman Church gladly took the money and overlooked Tetzel's outlandish claims.

Avignon palace where the kings of France kept a watchful eye on French popes

Pope Leo X

For the next seventy years, the French and Italians struggled for control of the papacy. Beginning in 1378 there was a French pope and an Italian pope at the same time. In a failed effort to resolve this embarrassing problem, a third man was chosen to become pope, but that only resulted in there being three popes. This problem was finally solved at the Council of Constance (1414–18). All three men were convinced to step down, and Martin V became the next pope. However, this struggle left many in the Church shaken and doubting. Faith in the authority of the pope and in the claims of the Church of Rome was further diminished.

In an effort to repair some of the damage, church officials decided to have church councils meet and resolve future issues. This would limit the power of the pope and seek to restore confidence in the Roman Church. However, this movement was short lived because popes resisted this limitation of their authority.

The second event that created a major controversy was the sale of **indulgences** (in DUL jens ez) (a paper that granted pardon from the punishment of sins). Indulgences had been granted for centuries to people in the Roman Church who performed good works and prayers. However, Pope Leo X (1513–21) needed money to finish building St. Peter's Basilica in Rome. So he sent out agents to sell indulgences and raise the needed funds. One monk in particular, Johann Tetzel, sold indulgences near Wittenberg, Germany, where Martin Luther pastored. Many opposed the sale of indulgences, but Luther wrote his views on paper and offered to debate them. The resulting controversy over the sale of indulgences played an important role in the birth of the Reformation.

Dissatisfaction of the People

Individuals often had to express their dissatisfaction with the corruptions of the Roman Church behind closed doors. To speak out publicly might lead to a hearing before an inquisitor. However, broad discontent often found expression in popular works such as writings of men like Erasmus. The following is an excerpt of Erasmus's writings where Pope Julius II finds himself excluded from Heaven by St. Peter:

JULIUS: Hey in there, open this door at once!

Pope Leo X

Visit www.bjupress.com/resources for possible links to articles about Pope Leo X.

Interior of St. Peter's Basilica

ST. PETER: It's a good thing we have adamantine doors; otherwise this man would have broken in. . . . Who are you and what do you want?

JULIUS: As if you could not see for yourself!

ST. PETER: Indeed I see a key silvered all over although it is only one and very different from those keys which Christ as the true pastor of the church once gave over to me. And how should I recognize this proud crown? No barbarian tyrant ever wore such a one, still less anyone who demanded to be admitted here. Nor does this pallium in the least move me who have always despised gold and gems as rubbish.

JULIUS: I am Julius the Ligurian and you will surely recognize the two letters P.M.

ST. PETER: I believe they stand for "Pestis Maxima" [Supreme Plague].

JULIUS: No, "Pontifex Maximus" [Supreme Pontiff].

ST. PETER: If you were three times "Maximus" . . . you would not come in here unless you were also "optimus," this is, holy. . . . What kind of monster are you who, although you wear outside the garments of a priest, underneath bristle and clink with a covering of bloody armor? . . . how savage are your eyes, how stubborn your mouth, how threatening your brow and how haughty and arrogant your glance! It is shameful . . . that you always belch and smell of [drunkenness] and seem to me to have just vomited. . . . I suspect that you are that most pestilential heathen Julius returned from hell to [make fun of] me.

Section III

Objectives

Students should be able to

1. Trace the development of the Protestant Reformation in Germany, Switzerland, and France.

2. Analyze the ideas of the leading reformers in terms of the three common doctrines.

3. Analyze the Counter Reformation and evaluate this movement as a response to the Protestant Reformation.

4. Explain the influence of the Protestant Reformation on European cultural values.

5. Explain why wars based on religion are futile.

John Wycliffe

Wycliffe felt that everyone should have access to the Word of God. He translated the Bible into English and wrote several religious books in the vernacular. The Lord took his teachings to Bohemia through the queen of England, who supported Wycliffe. The queen told her brother, King Wenceslas of Bohemia, and his wife, Sophia, of Wycliffe's writings, which were spreading across the country. As time went on and Wycliffe became more outspoken, he lost the support of the nobility. After his death his books and Bible translation were burned, and his bones were dug up, burned, and thrown into the river. However, Wycliffe's work lived on in his followers, the followers of John Huss, and a later translation of the English Bible authorized by King James.

English reformer and scholar, John Wycliffe

Left, Bohemian reformer, John Huss; *right*, drawing of the execution of John Huss

Section Quiz

1. What Roman Church doctrine declares that the bread and wine are changed into the body and blood of Christ?

2. What is the name of the Church court that was established to discover heresy?

3. Who decreed that everyone must submit to the pope?

4–5. List two practices in the Roman Church that led to discontent among many in Europe.

★ Why was the effort to have church councils meet and resolve church issues doomed to fail?

III. The Reformation

Forerunners

John Wycliffe (c. 1320–84) was a pastor, teacher, and theologian in England. He rejected the authority of the papacy and much of the authority claimed by the Church of Rome. Wycliffe taught that an individual became part of the church of Jesus Christ through an invisible, miraculous work of the Holy Spirit. Once made a part of the body of Christ, a believer could not be excluded by anyone—pope, council, or bishop. He also produced the first Bible in the English language. This translation played a key role in a later English Bible known as the King James Version.

John Huss (c. 1372–1415) was a pastor in Bohemia who was influenced by Wycliffe's teachings. Huss also spoke out against the claims of the papacy and the corruption of the Church of Rome. He was called to defend himself at the Council of Constance and given a promise of safe-conduct. Instead, the Roman Church tried Huss and burned him at the stake for his teachings.

Section Quiz Answers

1. transubstantiation

2. Inquisition

3. Boniface VIII

4-5. (any two) cruelty of the Inquisition, confession to a priest, failure of church councils to reform the Roman Church, sale of indulgences

★ Because the popes resisted this limitation of their authority

Reformation Roots

Have the students name local churches in their area that follow the teachings of reformers mentioned in the text. (*Lutheran, Reformed, Mennonite, Brethren, and others*)

⊕ John Wycliffe

Visit www.bjupress.com/resources for possible links to articles about John Wycliffe.

Reformers

Martin Luther (1483–1546)

Martin Luther lived in Germany and became a monk after a frightening experience during a thunderstorm. He studied the writings of the church fathers and prepared to be a priest. As he continued his studies, he began to read the Scriptures. Luther studied Greek and Hebrew in order to study the Scriptures in their original languages. He struggled with the fact that he was a sinner and often went to his superior in order to make confession. The head of Luther's monastery pointed him to the Scriptures. Soon Luther was appointed to preach at the church in Wittenberg.

When Luther learned of Tetzel and the sale of indulgences to his congregation, he became angry. Luther wanted to debate the value of indulgences and so followed the custom of the day, writing his arguments on a sheet of paper and posting it for debate (October 31, 1517). These ninety-five points of disagreement are commonly called Luther's **Ninety-five Theses**. Although he wrote them in Latin, they were quickly printed in German and read by many citizens.

The Roman Church ignored Luther for a time but finally threatened to dismiss him from the Roman Church in 1520. This action, known as **excommunication** (EKS kah myoo ni KAY shun), denied him the possibility of salvation. By this time Luther had discovered the truth found in Romans 1:17—"The just shall live by faith." He realized that salvation is a gift of God that cannot be earned. (A gift is by nature free, or else it is not truly a gift.) Luther was transformed by this truth as he trusted in Christ's work on the cross rather than his own works for salvation.

At first Luther believed that he could reform the Church of Rome from within by debate. However, he soon learned that church councils and popes were not free from error. When he was ordered to recant (take back what he had written) in 1521 he told the assembly:

> Unless I am convinced by the testimony of the Scriptures or by clear reason . . . I am bound by the Scriptures I have quoted and my conscience is captive to the Word of God. I cannot and I will not retract anything, since it is neither safe nor right to go against conscience. I cannot do otherwise; here I stand, may God help me. Amen.

Luther went on to translate the New Testament and then the whole Bible into German. This work was printed many times, and copies spread throughout Germany. He also wrote many commentaries and an official statement of Lutheran beliefs called the Augsburg Confession.

Luther married a former nun in 1525, and they had six children. (We will look at Luther's family life later in the chapter.) Despite his status as a wanted man, Luther traveled freely through much of Germany and ministered until his death in 1546.

Ulrich Zwingli (1484–1531)

Zwingli was born in the German-speaking area of Switzerland. He became acquainted with Erasmus, who encouraged him to study

Martin Luther Discovering Justification by Faith, Edward Matthew Ward, From the Bob Jones University Museum & Gallery Collection

---

Excerpts from the 95 Theses

81. This unbridled preaching of pardons [indulgences] makes it difficult, even for learned men, to rescue the reverence due to the pope from slander, or even from the shrewd [clever] questions of the laity. [At first, Luther was willing to give the pope the benefit of the doubt. Later he would learn that the pope played a key role in the sale of indulgences.]

82. [They ask] such questions as the following: Why does the pope not empty purgatory, for the sake of holy love and for the sake of desperate souls that are there, if he redeems an infinite number of souls for the sake of miserable money with which to build a church?

Protestants

The people who chose to follow Scripture and leave the Roman Church were called **Protestants**. They received this name when German princes protested the attempt by Roman Catholic princes in Germany to stop the Reformation. The Protestant movement grew as other people learned of God's truth.

John Huss

John Huss (John Hus) heard of Wycliffe's new ideas at a disputation at Charles University. After the disputation a vote was taken to accept or reject the new viewpoint. Huss was in the minority of those who accepted Wycliffe's ideas. Huss, like Wycliffe, came into conflict with the church for preaching against its claims.

The climax of Huss's conflict with the Roman Church came over indulgences. Huss was incensed that indulgences could be said to replace true repentance. Unfortunately for Huss, the Bohemian king received a portion of the indulgence money, so as Huss spoke out more vehemently, the king removed his support. Rather than compromise his convictions, Huss said, "It is better to die well than to live wickedly. One should not sin in order to avoid the punishment of death. Truth conquers all." John Huss was judged a heretic and sentenced by the Council of Constance to burn at the stake.

Luther would later say of Huss's writings, "I could not understand why they burned so great a man, who explained Scripture with so much discernment and wisdom. Inasmuch as the very name of Huss was such an abomination . . . , I shut the book with a sad heart." Soon, Luther himself would take joy in being called the Saxon Huss.

95 Theses (More Excerpts)

81. This unbridled preaching of indulgences makes it difficult for learned men to guard the respect due to the pope against false accusations, or at least from the keen criticisms

---

Activity 4: Luther's Ninety-five Theses

Students will read excerpts from the Theses and answer questions.

Martin Luther

Visit www.bjupress.com/resources for possible links to articles about Martin Luther.

Ulrich Zwingli

Visit www.bjupress.com/resources for possible links to articles about Ulrich Zwingli.

of the laity. [Luther was willing to give the pope the benefit of the doubt. Later he would realize this was not a false accusation.]

82. They ask, e.g.: Why does not the pope liberate everyone from purgatory for the sake of love (a most holy thing) and because of the supreme necessity of their souls? This would be morally the best of all reasons. Meanwhile he redeems innumerable souls for money, a most perishable thing, with which to build St. Peter's church, a very minor purpose.

Luther's Bible

Luther's translation had a profound effect on Germany. Not only did he provide his people with God's Word in the vernacular, but he also captured the German language in print. This also tended to standardize the German language so that those who spoke various German dialects could all read and understand this translation.

John Calvin

John Calvin was born in France in 1509, twenty-five years after Luther's birth. Gerard Calvin, John's father, wanted his son John to become a Roman Catholic priest and educated him for that position. As a young boy, along with sons of other aristocratic families, John was taught by tutors. At age twelve he was awarded several benefices (church endowments). With this income he continued his education and at age fourteen enrolled in college in Paris.

When Calvin was eighteen, his father had a dispute with the church and re-

Swiss reformer, Ulrich Zwingli

the Bible. Zwingli became a priest in the Roman Church but was displeased with the corruption he found there. In 1519 he became the preacher at the largest church in Zurich, an important town in the Swiss city-states.

Zwingli read some of Luther's writings, and he too realized that salvation comes by grace through faith. He began to preach and teach from the Bible and made important changes in his church. Just as Luther had penned his Ninety-Five Theses, Zwingli wrote a document known as his Sixty-seven Conclusions. Along with Luther, Zwingli rejected Roman doctrines such as the mass (bread and wine turned into the body and blood of Christ), celibacy (forbidden to marry) of the clergy, purgatory, and the exalted claims of the pope.

Civil war broke out in Switzerland between the city-states that remained loyal to Rome and those who embraced the Reformation. Zwingli accompanied his companions in 1531 and served as their chaplain. He was killed in battle as he attempted to help a wounded soldier. However, Zwingli's work was carried on by his followers in Zurich.

Anabaptists

There was another group in Switzerland who followed Zwingli in the early days of the Reformation. However, by 1525 they had become impatient with Zwingli's slow reforms that were subject to approval by the magistrates (city rulers). They called themselves the Swiss Brethren, but their rejection of infant baptism soon earned them the name **Anabaptist** (those who baptize again). While many groups received this label, a core group of the Brethren continued to promote their views about a genuine reformation. The Anabaptists spread throughout Switzerland, Germany, and the Netherlands. They fled from country to country and endured suffering and death. Even though they were often persecuted, some of their teachings contributed to the completion of the Reformation.

For example, Anabaptists rejected the idea of Luther, Zwingli, and other reformers that everyone who lived under a Lutheran or Reformed prince should be a member of the state church. These churches had congregations that included godly and ungodly members. Most Anabaptists refused to attend a state church. Instead, they insisted that true believers should be members of local churches that were free of state control.

They were also among the first to support the idea of separation of church and state. Anabaptists did not want the state to interfere in the affairs of the church, and most had no desire to participate in the affairs of the state.

John Calvin (1509–1564)

John Calvin was born in France and became a leading figure in the Reformation. However, he ministered from Geneva, Switzerland, due to the hostility of the French government toward Protestant believers. He taught and influenced many who would help to carry the Reformation to other countries such as England and Scotland. In addition, Calvin wrote the *Institutes of the Christian Religion* as well as commentaries on many books of the Bible. The *Institutes* was originally written as a defense of the Protestant movement to the king of France. However, over time, this work has had a great influence on the development of Protestant theology (the study of God). Calvin's name is often associated with the idea of **predestination** (PREE des teh NAY shun) (God's deciding one's destiny before birth). While

John Calvin

Visit www.bjupress.com/resources for possible links to articles about John Calvin.

there are many opinions about this subject, Calvin's writings and labors demonstrated great concern about spreading the gospel.

Though Calvin could not live in France, he retained a burden for his homeland. Calvin trained and sent ministers to France to give the good news of the gospel to his people. In addition, many of his works were smuggled into France to educate and encourage the Christians who remained despite persecution. Many persecuted Protestants also spent time in Geneva. For instance, John Knox fled to Geneva for a while before returning to his homeland of Scotland to establish Protestantism there.

John Calvin

Central Doctrines

While there were doctrinal and practical differences between Luther, Zwingli, Calvin, and other reformers, there were also central doctrines upon which all agreed. We will briefly examine three of them:

Scripture alone—The reformers pointed out that Scripture and tradition often conflicted. However, God's Word is inspired, while man's traditions are not. Therefore, Scripture is the only reliable authority on anything it speaks of (2 Timothy 3:16).

Faith alone—As each of the reformers read the Bible, he discovered that salvation cannot be earned but is a gift received by faith. The sacraments of the Roman Church had no power to save. The reformers taught that a person is saved by faith in Christ's shed blood alone (Titus 3:5; Ephesians 2:8–9).

Priesthood of the believer—The Renaissance emphasis on the individual prepared people to accept this doctrine. The reformers emphasized that people had to come to God as individuals. Upon receiving salvation through Christ, each person is made a priest (1 Peter 2:9; Revelation 1:6). In other words, each believer has direct access to the saving benefits of Christ without the need of priests and sacraments. The Roman Church had taught that priests stood between individuals and God. However, the reformers pointed to passages such as 1 Timothy 2:5—"For there is one God, and one mediator between God and men, the man Christ Jesus."

Results

The Reformation spread throughout Europe, including countries such as Germany, Switzerland, France, and England. The printing press made possible the rapid publication and spread of Reformation writings and Bibles in the vernacular. Protestants who were persecuted in one region fled to other regions and helped to spread the scriptural truths rediscovered during the Reformation. Despite political and religious opposition, the Reformation could not be contained.

Freedom

The reformers opposed spiritual oppression. This prepared the way for a greater emphasis on freedom in many areas of European life. Limited religious freedom was given to those who lived under a prince who shared their religion. However, the Anabaptists sought full religious freedom—the right to worship according to one's own conscience no matter where one lived.

Citizenship

The reformers emphasized the role of Christians in society. They taught their followers that God desired servants who worked not for

moved his son from further theological studies. John Calvin continued his education in law and literature, including Greek. When his father died in 1531, Calvin again pursued the religious life.

Calvin's conversion was sudden. For a time he stayed in the Roman Catholic Church and tried to reform it from within. Finally, he realized the impossibility of that task and withdrew from the church.

Forced to leave France after an associate published a pamphlet in favor of the Reformation, Calvin settled in Geneva at the urging of a reformer there. He served in a church there for several months, trying to preach reform and improve the moral climate of the city. City leaders resisted Calvin's teachings and discipline and finally forced him out of Geneva. Calvin went to Strasbourg, where he pastored a French-speaking church for several years. Then the government in Geneva changed, and his former congregation asked him to return. Calvin spent the rest of his life laboring in Geneva. During those years he organized the church leadership and outlined church practice, discipline, and instruction.

John Calvin's unwavering stand against sin was often resented by leading citizens and government officials in Geneva. He faced both public insult and physical danger. Still he continued his work and sought no extra protection. He was faithful to the truth of the Scriptures, and he knew that God was faithful to protect him.

their own glory but for God's glory (1 Cor. 10:31). Christians are responsible to God for how they use their talents and abilities. Unlike the Renaissance humanists, the reformers said that a person should dedicate his talents to God, not to himself.

They also encouraged Christians to work hard at their occupations. Any faithful Christian worker, whether shoemaker, carpenter, or farmer, is serving God just as much as a pastor or missionary is serving God. The reformers taught that everything a believer does is to honor God. They encouraged their followers to be a testimony of God's grace as they performed their daily tasks.

Family Life

Besides emphasizing right doctrine, the reformers also emphasized right family relationships. They knew families were a gift from God. For example, while Luther remained single for several years after breaking with Rome, he encouraged other former monks and nuns to marry. In 1525, he was convinced to marry when a former nun, Katherine von Bora, refused to marry any other man but Luther. They had six children and also took in several orphans.

From the Scripture the reformers formed definite ideas about families. A faithful, loving, and obedient wife was a blessing second only to the Word of God for the Christian man. The husband was also to love his wife as Christ loved the church (Eph. 5:25). Parents were to love and discipline their children to teach them to obey authority—whether it be God's, a parent's, or the government's. Bringing up children to honor and serve the Lord is a Christian parent's God-given responsibility. The reformers knew that what a child learned at home greatly influenced his moral and spiritual life.

Education

Many of the reformers were well educated. They often knew Latin, Greek, and Hebrew, and some had read many ancient manuscripts. Therefore, the reformers placed a high priority on teaching everyone to read and to diligently study. Luther, Calvin, Zwingli, and many other reformers established schools and made education a priority.

Following Luther's example, many reformers also translated the Bible into the vernacular. This enabled the people to read God's word in their own language. In addition, books and pamphlets were printed in the common languages, and the people learned about many subjects related to the Reformation.

Reaction

The Church of Rome was slow to react to the initial development of the Reformation. However, as the church leaders realized how quickly the Protestant movement was spreading, the reaction quickened and intensified. Through existing monastic orders and the introduction of new orders, the Roman Church launched an extensive campaign to stop and reverse the spread of the Protestant movement. In addition, the Church of Rome used a revived Inquisition and other means to counteract this challenge to Roman Catholic doctrine.

Catholic Counter Reformation

Sometimes known as the Catholic Reformation, the Counter Reformation differed greatly from the Protestant Reformation. The Protestants had opposed the false doctrine that had slipped into

---

Luther's Example

Luther's family set an example for other Christian families. The Luther home was a happy, busy place. Mealtimes with children and students were usually times of talking. The students so admired their teacher that they often brought paper and pens to the table to take notes. On special occasions, Luther wrote pageants and songs for his household. His children especially enjoyed the Christmas carols he wrote for them.

The Importance of Literacy

The reformers placed a high value on teaching everyone from the prince to the peasant to read. They realized that since every believer is a priest, every person needs to be able to read in order to have access to God's Word. The principle of Scripture alone also commits Christians to work toward universal literacy.

the Church of Rome. However, the Catholic Reformers worked to give the Roman Church a new image by dealing with some of the more obvious moral problems. For the Catholic reformers, doctrinal change was not an option. Four aspects of the Counter Reformation will be briefly discussed.

Society of Jesus

In previous centuries, monasteries had been established for various reasons that included escaping the influences of the world, helping the poor, or satisfying God by practicing denial of self. However, as the Reformation developed, new monastic orders, such as the Society of Jesus, or **Jesuits**, were founded to stop the spread of the Reformation. This order ruthlessly sought to suppress heresy (Protestantism) and zealously promoted Roman Catholic education. The Jesuits used any means necessary to gain converts for Rome and reverse the gains of the Protestants.

Inquisition

The Inquisition was reorganized by Pope Paul III to root out heresy. These church courts assumed that anyone who was accused of heresy was guilty. Many were arrested at night, taken before an inquisitor, and told to confess their errors. The accused weren't even allowed to know the charges or who had brought the accusation. Failure to confess led to torture and being burned at the stake. Other members of one's family could also be arrested and property taken.

Index

When the Roman Church realized the impact that printed materials were having on the spread of the Reformation, the Church of Rome established the **Index of Prohibited Books**. Most versions of the Bible and all Protestant literature were declared heretical. The Roman Church forbad Catholics from reading anything that appeared on this list.

Council of Trent

As the Reformation spread throughout Europe, the supporters of the Roman Church grew more dissatisfied with their church. Many members of the Roman clergy were corrupt and lazy. The Roman Catholics began to demand change. In response to these demands, a meeting of high church officials was called. Known as the **Council of Trent**, it met several times over a twenty-year period.

The council wrote a statement of Roman Catholic beliefs and practices. This was the first written statement that contained all Catholic doctrines. The council members confirmed the authority of both Scripture and tradition. They insisted on faith *and* works as a Roman doctrine. They also preserved the doctrine of a human priesthood that stood between God and the individual. Essentially, the Roman Church made no changes in its doctrines. Instead, the council ordered some of the corrupt practices to stop, removed many of the corrupt clergy, and set stricter standards of discipline. While the visible corruption was reduced, the doctrinal errors remained.

Wars of Religion

Wars erupted in several regions, including France. These wars were motivated by a desire for territory and other typical reasons for war. However, these wars were also fought over religion.

Council of Trent

Society of Jesus

Ignatius Loyola founded this religious order in 1540. Unlike other religious orders, the Jesuits swore an oath of total submission to the pope. Jesuits became a highly educated and skilled group of agents whose goal was the suppression of heresy and the promotion of the Roman Church. They used every possible means to bring people to the Church of Rome. Jesuits developed the concept that it was acceptable to do wrong in order to accomplish a worthy goal. Some even promoted the murder of a king—if that death promoted Catholic purposes.

They were also very active as missionaries to bring people as far away as India, China, and Japan to the Catholic Church. Francis Xavier (1506–52) became the best known of these missionaries. He would convert the leader of a tribe or nation and then stage mass baptisms of its members to bring them to the Church.

Henry of Navarre

Henry was the head of the Bourbon family in France and served as the leader of the Huguenots. In the struggle for the French throne he emerged as the victor. Even though he declared himself king, the majority of the French population were Catholic and would not allow a Protestant king. To resolve this dilemma, he made a nominal conversion to Catholicism. Even though he abandoned his Huguenot heritage for the crown, he tried to ensure them a measure of religious toleration by signing the Edict of Nantes in 1598. This allowed the Huguenots to live in certain fortified cities and gave them other protections. However, this limited toleration was systematically reduced by future rulers and finally abolished under King Louis XIV about a century later.

"Paris Is Well Worth a Mass"

Henry of Navarre is said to have spoken these words when he agreed to convert to Roman Catholicism in order to become king of France. While he did abandon his Huguenot supporters, Henry also guaranteed them limited religious toleration in the **Edict of Nantes** (1598). However, even with this written guarantee, the toleration was gradually reduced. Under a future French king, this edict would be revoked and the Huguenots would be forced to flee France.

Even though rulers in France vigorously supported the Church of Rome, the number of Protestants continued to increase. Known as **Huguenots** (HYOO geh nahts), these French Protestants endured fierce persecution and broken promises of peace. In 1572 twenty thousand Huguenots in Paris were massacred in their homes during a carefully planned attack. Seventeen years of fighting between Catholic and Protestant forces followed. In 1589 the French Protestants received a temporary reprieve (relief) when Henry of Navarre became king of France.

The **Thirty Years' War** (1618–48) began as a revolt by the Bohemians against loss of religious liberty. However, it soon became a major conflict between Catholic and Protestant forces in Europe. While most of the fighting occurred on German soil, many nations joined the battle for one side or the other. Germany was destroyed by these battling forces. Eventually, Catholic France supported the Protestant forces in order to end the war. This move by the French prevented their political enemies in Spain and the Holy Roman Empire from becoming too powerful. This became the last great religious war fought in Europe.

The people of Europe emerged from the medieval period to experience the beauty and wealth of knowledge made available to them in the Renaissance. While the Renaissance failed to address the spiritual needs of men, it did prepare the way for the Reformation by stressing the importance of the individual and providing access to the Bible in the vernacular.

Men like Wycliffe and Huss prepared the way for a break with the Roman Church. Luther and many others built upon their work, and the Reformation brought to light the scriptural principles by which men are saved (by faith alone) and led by God (through Scripture alone).

The Thirty Years' War demonstrated the futility of fighting over religion. Following this three-decade-long struggle, nations became nominally (in name only) either Catholic or Protestant. Nations turned to building empires, and religion became more of a personal matter. Religious competition continued, but it was generally characterized by nonviolent efforts to convert others, including the populations encountered in the Age of Exploration.

Section Quiz

1. Name a forerunner of the Reformation.
2. What action by the Roman Church denies an individual access to salvation?
3. What does the term *Anabaptist* mean?
4–5. List two ways the Roman Church responded to the Reformation.
★ Distinguish the Reformation doctrine of Scripture alone and the teaching of Rome regarding Scripture. Provide a scriptural reference to support the position that most closely reflects your personal view.

Section Quiz Answers

1. One of the following: John Wycliffe, John Huss
2. excommunication
3. to baptize again
4–5. (any two) Society of Jesus, Inquisition, Index of Prohibited Books, Council of Trent
★ The Reformation doctrine of Scripture alone recognizes that Scripture is inspired while church traditions are not (2 Tim. 3:16). Rome teaches that Scripture and church traditions are of equal authority.

Activity 5: Chapter Review

This activity helps students review the chapter content.

Thirty Years' War

Visit www.bjupress.com/resources for possible links to articles about the Thirty Years' War.

CHAPTER REVIEW

Making Connections

1. What contributed to the revival of learning known as the Renaissance?
2. How did Gutenberg's invention contribute to the Renaissance and Reformation?
3. How was Renaissance art different from medieval art?
4. What did Renaissance sculpture resemble?
5. How did the subjects taught in the Renaissance differ from subjects taught in the Middle Ages?
6. Why was Petrarch called the Father of Humanism?
7. Briefly describe the subject of Thomas More's book *Utopia*.
8. What rights did a suspect have when standing before the inquisitor during an inquisition?

Developing History Skills

1. Using the information found in this chapter, compile a list of books that would have been included on the *Index of Prohibited Books*.
2. Construct a timeline that includes the significant events of the Reformation.

Thinking Critically

1. What changes were made to the Roman Church at the Council of Trent? What was the importance of these changes? What was the end result?
2. What impact did the Reformation have on family life?

Living in God's World

1. Pretend that you are a French believer who has had to flee to Geneva. In a letter to your family, state what you believe, why you believe it, and how your beliefs differ from Catholic teaching. Be sure to base your defense in Scripture.
2. Choose a significant person from the Renaissance or the Reformation and research that person. Tell his or her life story in first person. Talk about personal history as well as significant achievements. If you have time, decorate the room and use costumes. A list of people to choose from might include the following: Leonardo da Vinci, Michelangelo, Machiavelli, Erasmus, Thomas More, Henry VIII, John Wycliffe, John Huss, Martin Luther, Ulrich Zwingli, Balthasar Hubmaier, John Calvin, Catherine de Medici.

People, Places, and Terms to Know

Renaissance
Johannes Gutenberg
anatomy
shading
perspective
Leonardo da Vinci
The Last Supper
Mona Lisa
Michelangelo
Sistine Chapel
Ghiberti
Brunelleschi
humanities
Petrarch
Father of Humanism
Castiglione
Machiavelli
Erasmus
Thomas More
transubstantiation
Inquisition
indulgences
John Wycliffe
John Huss
Martin Luther
Ninety-five Theses
excommunication
Protestants
Zwingli
Anabaptist
John Calvin
predestination
Jesuits
Index of Prohibited Books
Council of Trent
Huguenots
Edict of Nantes
Thirty Years' War

Chapter Review Answers

Making Connections

1. rise of universities, discovery of classical Greek and Roman learning, Byzantine documents, Byzantine scholars
2. Rapid printing of books and pamphlets lowered the cost of literature.
3. The people in Renaissance paintings look real; the people in medieval art look flat.
4. the sculpture of the Greeks and Romans
5. During the Renaissance, the humanities were taught, covering human interests and experiences.
6. He was a pioneer of Renaissance humanism and spread the ideas of the Renaissance.
7. a story about an imaginary country based on Christian principles and Greek philosophy; More's view of the ideal state
8. none

Developing History Skills

1. all Bible translations in the vernacular languages, Wycliffe's writings, John Huss's writings, Luther's Ninety-five Theses, The Augsburg Confession, Luther's commentaries and pamphlets, Zwingli's Sixty-seven Conclusions, Calvin's commentaries, *Institutes*
2. John Wycliffe (1320–84), John Huss (1372–1415), Martin Luther (1483–1546), Ninety-five Theses (1517), Luther excommunicated (1521), Luther's marriage (1525), Zwingli (1484–1531), Anabaptists (1525), John Calvin (1509–64), massacre of Huguenots (1572), Edict of Nantes (1598), Thirty Years' War (1618–48)

Thinking Critically

1. No doctrinal changes were made; some corrupt practices were ended; stricter standards of discipline were established. Answers will vary but might include the following: The Council of Trent retained the doctrinal errors that had slipped into the Roman Church and made them the official doctrine of the Church of Rome. Visible corruption was reduced, but error remained
2. Answers should include some of the following: emphasis on family relationships, restored biblical standards for family members, homes where children's character was shaped by the proper application of Scripture, a greater appreciation for marriage.

Living in God's World

1. Answers will vary but should at least include a defense of Scripture alone, faith alone, and the priesthood of the believer.
2. If your students need help understanding this assignment, consider showing portions of the DVD set *Church History in First Person* (available from BJU Press).

UNIT 3

Dominant Powers in Europe and Asia 1450–1750

European states, beginning with Portugal and Spain, began to search for new trade opportunities and routes to the Orient. Soon, other nations joined in this exploration. Some established routes by sailing around Africa, while others traveled west in search of other avenues to access vast wealth. Anyone who could bring spices and other sought-after treasures to Europe would gain an immense profit.

Quite by accident, some of these explorers discovered many lands not previously known to Europeans. The explorers mapped and settled the Americas, Australia, and other remote lands during this period. The raw materials they discovered would soon fuel an accelerated period of industrial growth. In addition, Europe experienced a period of rapid scientific discovery that produced the Scientific Revolution.

Chapter Goals

Students should be able to

1. Describe the development of complex societies in North America and Mesoamerica.

2. Discuss the origins of European overseas expansion in the 15th and 16th centuries.

3. Describe the encounters between Europeans and the peoples of the Americas, sub-Saharan Africa, and Asia in the late 15th and early 16th centuries.

4. Explain some of the consequences of the importation of plants, animals, and diseases to the Americas.

1200–1700

Marco Polo travels to the Far East 1271–95

Aztecs build the city of Tenochtitlán 1347

| 1200 | 1300 | 1400 |

Chapter 7 Lesson Plan Chart

Section Title	Main Activity	Pages	Days
I. Native American Civilizations	Activity 1: Map Study: Indian Civilizations	120–24	2 days
II. Origins of European Exploration	Activity 3 : Christopher Columbus	125–28	1½–2 days
III. Growth of European Exploration	Discussion Activity: Montezuma	128–32	1½–2 days
IV. Consequences of European Exploration	Activity 4 : Bartolomé de Las Casas	133–34	1 day
TOTAL SUGGESTED DAYS (INCLUDING 1 DAY EACH FOR REVIEW AND TESTING)			8–9 days

Materials List

Section I

- CD: 7A Shoshone Tepees; 7B Iroquois Longhouse; 7C Mayan Civilization; 7D Mayan Acropolis; 7E Valley of Mexico; 7F Machu Picchu; 7G Map of the Americas; 7H Alpacas

- Activities 1 and 2 from the *Student Activities* manual

Section II

- A picture of an ancient map of the New World and a current map showing the same area

- Activity 3 from the *Student Activities* manual

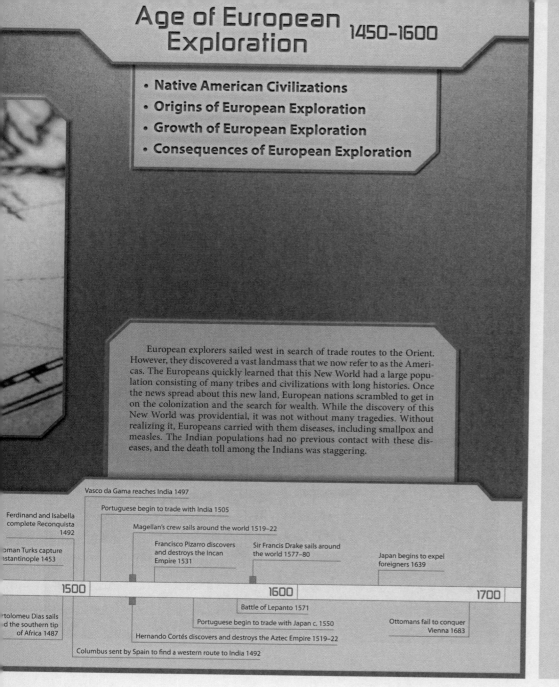

Age of European Exploration 1450–1600

- **Native American Civilizations**
- **Origins of European Exploration**
- **Growth of European Exploration**
- **Consequences of European Exploration**

European explorers sailed west in search of trade routes to the Orient. However, they discovered a vast landmass that we now refer to as the Americas. The Europeans quickly learned that this New World had a large population consisting of many tribes and civilizations with long histories. Once the news spread about this new land, European nations scrambled to get in on the colonization and the search for wealth. While the discovery of this New World was providential, it was not without many tragedies. Without realizing it, Europeans carried with them diseases, including smallpox and measles. The Indian populations had no previous contact with these diseases, and the death toll among the Indians was staggering.

Vasco da Gama reaches India 1497

Portuguese begin to trade with India 1505

Ferdinand and Isabella complete Reconquista 1492

Magellan's crew sails around the world 1519–22

[Ro]man Turks capture [Co]nstantinople 1453

Francisco Pizarro discovers and destroys the Incan Empire 1531

Sir Francis Drake sails around the world 1577–80

Japan begins to expel foreigners 1639

1500   **1600**   **1700**

[Bar]tolomeu Dias sails [aroun]d the southern tip of Africa 1487

Battle of Lepanto 1571

Portuguese begin to trade with Japan c. 1550

Ottomans fail to conquer Vienna 1683

Hernando Cortés discovers and destroys the Aztec Empire 1519–22

Columbus sent by Spain to find a western route to India 1492

Section III

- March/April 2004 issue of *Homeschooling Today* magazine

Section IV

- Activities 4 and 5 from the *Student Activities* manual

Section I

Objectives

Students should be able to

1. Distinguish the varying North American Indian groups and note adaptation to their environment.

2. Explain major aspects of Mayan society, religion, and culture as well as reasons for the civilization's decline.

3. Explain major aspects of Aztec government, society, religion, and culture.

4. Explain Incan social, political, and religious institutions.

Native Americans

Visit www.bjupress.com/resources for possible links to articles about Native American civilizations.

Complex Indian Societies

The Europeans were startled to find highly developed Indian societies with towns and political structure. However, Christians should remember that man was created in the image of God and given dominion over the earth (Genesis 1:26–28). God enabled man to develop complex cultures. Rather than be startled to find complex cultures, we should expect to discover them all over the world.

I. Native American Civilizations

At some point in early history following the Flood, the ancestors of the American Indians came to the American continent. Theories vary about how and when they came. Those explorers fanned out across the continent, moving in all directions. Some settled in the East and some in the West, and others migrated into Central and South America. Most lived in settled villages and cultivated the land. They also developed societies of great complexity. Corn, squash, and beans were common crops among most of the tribes. While few details are available, we will briefly examine some of the civilizations that developed.

North America

Pueblos

Many of the Indians who lived in the Southwest region of North America were known as the **Pueblos**. *Pueblo* means "town." These Indians lived in small villages composed of several family groups or clans. Some of the Pueblo Indians made their homes in caves and became known as cliff dwellers. Others made homes out of adobe (uh DO bee) (dried clay). Each Indian town was independent, and population growth was restricted by limited food and water supplies due to the desert climate in which they lived. Some of the tribes among the Pueblos included the Hopi, Ute, Paiute, Navajo, and Apache.

Pueblo village

Getty Images

Plains Indians

These Indians migrated over the grasslands of the Great Plains and lived in tepees. They hunted buffalo, elk, and antelope. Before the Spanish brought horses to this continent, the Plains Indians traveled and hunted on foot. The Plains Indians included such tribes as the Sioux, Cheyenne, Crow, Blackfeet, and Comanche.

Eastern

Many of the Indians who settled in eastern America built villages and developed structured societies. They farmed, hunted, and fished to provide food for their families. We will look at three of the Indian cultures found in the East: the Mound Builders, the Iroquois, and the Five Civilized Tribes.

Mound Builders

Hundreds of mounds have been found throughout the eastern half of North America. Indians who built these earthen mounds are called the **Mound Builders**. Some mounds were built as grave sites, while others served as temple mounds. The Indians also built another kind of mound called an **effigy mound** (a mound in the shape of an animal or object), such as the Serpent Mound located in southern Ohio.

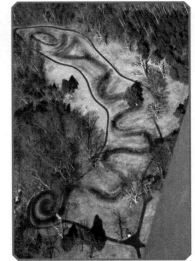

Tepee used by the Plains Indians

Alligator Mound located in central Ohio

Serpent Mound located in southern Ohio

These Indians probably lived in wooden structures made from bent saplings that were covered with animal skins or tree bark. While little is known about them, archaeologists have discovered that the Mound Builders obtained copper from the Great Lakes area, seashells and shark teeth from the Atlantic and Gulf coasts, and quartz and grizzly bear teeth from the Rocky Mountains. By the time the Europeans began to explore North America, the mound-building Indians were dying out.

Eastern Woodlands Indians

Six tribes who spoke the common language of Iroquois formed a league in the early fifteenth century known as the **Iroquois Confederacy**. These tribes lived in what is today northern New York and became one of the most powerful groups in eastern North America. British and French colonists as well as other Indian tribes needed the cooperation of the Iroquois in order to accomplish anything.

Indian Religions

Little is known about the various religions practiced by the various Indian tribes in North America. However, the Plains Indians may serve as an example of what many Indians believed. These Indians had no single religion. However, most, if not all, practiced animism—the belief that all things possess spirits. Many worshiped the Great Spirit. In addition, they believed in good spirits as well as evil spirits. Plains Indians often expressed their worship in prayer, song, and dance. Many tribes also had *shaman* (people with the power to heal, seek spiritual direction, and look into the future). Tragically, their religions did not have a Savior or any way to atone for sin.

CD: 7A Shoshone Tepees

A photo of Shoshone tepees is available on the CD. The Shoshones were a nomadic Plains Indian tribe.

Native American Civilizations

Conduct a little research (or have your students do the research) about the Indians that lived in your area. As time permits devote some time to discussing these local Indians.

Lesson from the Mayans

Of the Indian societies in the Americas, the Mayans were the most advanced. They developed an accurate calendar and made many discoveries in mathematics and astronomy. However, they also developed a religious system that involved the murder of fellow humans to appease their false gods. Modern society too, though technologically advanced, falls short of the standard of godliness. Godliness, not technology, exalts a society in God's eyes. Technology is simply a tool that can be used for good or evil. Societies that use their God-given technological abilities to do evil (for instance, to perform abortions) should not expect to escape judgment.

Iroquois Confederacy

Between 1400 and 1450 an Indian leader convinced several Iroquois tribes to establish a peace treaty known as the Great Law of Peace. Five nations initially joined. By 1570 the confederacy was composed of six Indian nations: Mohawk, Oneida, Seneca, Cayuga, Onondaga, and Tuscarora.

Although the tribes of this confederacy were able to develop complex cultures, the Iroquois, due to their spiritually fallen condition, were also capable of great savagery. They often tortured captured enemies to death. The Iroquois were also known to eat parts of their enemies in order to gain some of the fallen warriors' courage.

Mayan Civilization

The Mayas fulfilled aspects of the Creation Mandate by developing an advanced civilization that included mathematical and astronomical discoveries. However, they also revealed the tragic consequences of the Fall through their idol worship and human sacrifice. How is the Mayan civilization reflected in Romans 1?

Iroquois longhouse

In the Southeast, five tribes formed an alliance similar to the Iroquois Confederacy. The Cherokees, Chickasaws, Choctaws, Creeks, and Seminoles formed what European settlers called the **Five Civilized Tribes**. These tribes were given this name because they maintained peaceful relationships with neighboring tribes and adopted many colonial customs.

Central and South America

The Mayas

The **Mayas** (MAH yuz) lived in what is today a portion of Central America that includes Guatemala and the Yucatán Peninsula. Unlike the Aztecs and Incas, the Mayas did not have one strong central government. Mayan civilization, like that of the ancient Greeks, consisted of many independent city-states. Each city-state had its own ruler and government.

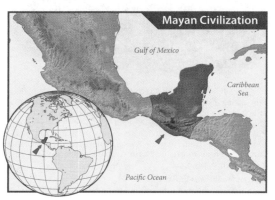

Mayan Civilization
Gulf of Mexico
Caribbean Sea
Pacific Ocean

The height of Mayan culture lasted from AD 300 to 800. Intellectually, the Mayas outshone the Aztecs and Incas. They developed a calendar as accurate as the one we use today. The Mayas also had a form of writing far superior to any other system found in the New

CD: 7B Iroquois Longhouse

The artwork depicting an Iroquois longhouse is also available on the CD.

CD: 7C Mayan Civilization

This map from the student text is also available on the CD.

World. They were accomplished mathematicians and astronomers as well. For example, they predicted eclipses of the sun and moon with impressive accuracy. For easier numbering and counting, the Mayas also understood and used the concept of zero.

The Mayas built large pyramids similar to the ones in Egypt in the middle of many of their cities. The Mayan pyramids, however, were not always burial places for kings. Usually they served as temples. Mayan religion was cruel and involved human sacrifice. Archaeologists have found large graves containing the remains of men and women whom the Mayas slaughtered to please their gods.

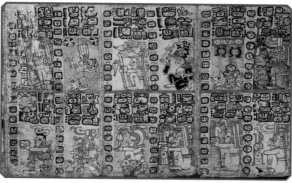

Maya Codex

The different Mayan city-states often fought against one another. As a result, they proved unable to unite in resistance against other enemies, especially the Aztecs, who took many Mayan cities. The Mayas grew weaker and weaker. When the Spanish came in 1450, the remaining Mayas offered no resistance.

The Aztecs

Around 1345 the **Aztecs** built their capital, **Tenochtitlán** (te NOCH tee TLAHN), on an island in the middle of a lake in central Mexico. To build the city there, the Aztecs first made floating islands from mounds of water plants and put them in the middle of the lake. When these had rooted, the Aztecs filled the roots with soil and built on them. The finished city had many islands that the Aztecs accessed by boats and bridges. Several long causeways connected the islands of Tenochtitlán to each other and to the mainland.

Valley of Mexico

Aztec Sun Stone

Maya Codex

The student text has a photo of a portion of the Maya Codex. The Mayas produced bark paper that was around eight inches high and several feet long. They folded the paper like an accordion. Scribes carefully painted images to record astronomical, religious, and agricultural events. They also included information about weather, including rainy seasons and floods.

With their astronomical observations, the Mayas developed an ability to predict eclipses and record alignments of constellations and planets.

Pyramids

Have the students research and discuss with the class the differences and/or similarities between the Egyptian and Mayan pyramids.

CD: 7D Mayan Acropolis

A photo of the Mayan Acropolis, a center of royal power, is available on the CD.

CD: 7E Valley of Mexico

This map from the student text is also available on the CD.

The Mayas

Visit www.bjupress.com/resources for possible links to articles about the Mayas.

Human Sacrifice

Cortés wrote about the Aztec practice of sacrificing humans and described it as "the most terrible and frightful thing they [had] ever witnessed." (Anthony Pagden, tr. and ed., *Hernan Cortes: Letters from Mexico*, p. 35)

However, the Spanish often burned heretics to death during the infamous Spanish Inquisition. In fact, the Spanish conquistadors burned Indians at the stake because they would not accept the teachings of the Church of Rome.

It is ironic that men like Cortés considered one form of human sacrifice to be terrible while practicing another form of human sacrifice in the name of their religion.

Ruins of Machu Picchu, an Inca city built around 1450 high in the mountains of Peru

Aztec society was characterized by war and warriors. Every Aztec man who was able to fight had to serve in the army. The Aztec warriors used ferocity and military skill to conquer many tribes around them. Over time, the Aztecs conquered a large area with five million people who were required to pay them tribute (taxes).

They worshiped many gods and built large temples to honor these gods. Part of their worship included human sacrifice, during which they cut out the hearts from living people and offered them to the gods. Many of those captured in war were sacrificed to appease (satisfy) these gods.

The Aztecs believed that one of their gods, **Quetzalcoatl** (ket SAHL ko AH tul), once lived on the earth and brought prosperity to the people. He was forced to leave, but promised to return in the future. The Aztecs anticipated his return, and this belief made them open to deception by the Spanish conquerors.

The Aztec people were governed by an elected monarchy. The nobles selected four noblemen who chose the monarch from the brothers or nephews of the deceased monarch. Once elected, the monarch lived in great splendor.

The Aztecs also developed a judicial system with a chief judge for each of the major cities. Aztec law was recorded in picture writing. The crimes considered most serious were punishable by death. For example, the punishment for adultery was death by stoning because marriage was recognized as a vital part of Aztec culture.

The Incas

The **Incas** developed their civilization very early and built upon earlier cultures. At its peak, the territory under Incan rule extended three thousand miles in length and up to three hundred and fifty miles in breadth. Located along the western coast of South America, the Incan empire developed in the Andes (AN deez) Mountains. In order to make travel, communication, and trade possible, the people constructed two major highways that ran the length of the empire. To cross the steep valleys and ravines, the Incas built long bridges.

The capital of the Incan empire was **Cuzco** (KOOS ko). Here they built large buildings out of stone with great precision. Without the use of mortar, the Incas constructed buildings with such accuracy that a knife blade cannot fit in between the stones. This city served both as the political and religious capital of the empire. The buildings were said to be covered with sheets of gold to reflect the sun and remind the Incas of their sun god. Tribute poured into the capital city in the form of food, copper, gold, silver, and alpaca wool. Since the Incas did not have a money economy, gold was used to make such items as ornaments, vases, and temple vessels.

While the religion of the Incas was polytheistic, the ruler retained the title of "Inca" and served as the empire's living god. He owned the land, and authority resided in him. The people sacrificed animals during the four great festivals, and there is no record of human sacrifice. The Inca and his officials made all significant decisions for the people. This control produced a society of passive followers. Conquest by a foreign power would be easy in the event that the Inca should be captured or killed.

 CD: 7F Machu Picchu

An additional photo of the ruins of Machu Picchu is available on the CD.

 CD: 7G Map of the Americas

This map on the CD shows the location of the various Indian groups in North, Central, and South America.

 Activity 1: Map Study: Indian Civilizations

This activity requires the students to identify the locations of the various Indian groups.

Activity 2: Letters from Mexico

This activity contains an excerpt from Cortés's first-hand account of the Aztecs and their practice of human sacrifice.

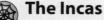 **The Incas**

Visit www.bjupress.com/resources for possible links to articles about the Incas.

Herd of alpacas

Section Quiz

1. Which group of North American Indians migrated?

2–3. List two reasons why Indians built mounds.

4. Which Indian civilization punished adultery by stoning?

5. Who owned the land in the Incan Empire?

★ How did the Iroquois Confederacy impact other Indian tribes and European explorers?

II. Origins of European Exploration

Between the years 1271 and 1295, Italian explorer Marco Polo journeyed to the Far East, a land of mystery to thirteenth-century Europe. His descriptions of the vast wealth of China were recounted in a book. The Europeans were amazed by what they read. Polo spoke of a land of gold, silks, and spices. He referred to their burning of black stones (coal) instead of wood to provide heat. With this knowledge of the existence of foreign lands, Europeans spent the next several centuries finding ways to get there. This period is known as the Age of European Exploration.

Motives

Exploration was driven by many motives. These motives ranged from practical to noble.

Economic

While trade with the East continued after the Crusades, the goods passed through many agents, and the final cost was very high. Therefore, Europeans began to search for new trade routes that bypassed Muslims, local leaders, and the Italian merchants. Many believed that a water route to the East could be discovered.

Adventurers sailed south and west with the confidence that they could find another route to the wealth of the East. Motivated by dreams of shiploads of gold, silver, and spices, many risked their lives by sailing into uncharted waters.

Social

Others explored to experience the thrill of adventure and receive the praise of men. Some were driven by curiosity and others by the quest for glory. Explorers often wrote journals of their exploits, and some sent detailed letters back to their monarchs to document their activities.

Section II
Objectives

Students should be able to

1. Analyze the major social, economic, political, and cultural features of European society, and in particular Spain and Portugal, that stimulated exploration and conquest overseas.

2. Identify major technological developments in shipbuilding, navigation, and naval warfare.

3. Analyze the various motives (including religious), nature, and short-term significance of the major Iberian military and commercial expeditions to Asia and the Americas.

CD: 7H Alpacas
An additional photo of alpacas is available on the CD.

Section Quiz Answers

1. Plains Indians

2–3. (any two) graves, temples, effigies (images)

4. Aztecs

5. the Inca (ruler)

★ They created a powerful alliance to deal with other Indian tribes and European explorers. (Something could also be said about influencing trade.)

Political

Over time, monarchs sponsored exploration in order to accomplish many things in addition to gaining wealth. As news of initial discoveries reached Europe, some rulers authorized exploration in order to lay claim to these foreign lands. When empire building became popular, explorers were sent to establish colonies and discover raw materials needed by the home country.

Religious

The continuing threat of Muslim invasions gave Europeans great concern. With the fall of Constantinople in 1453, the Ottoman Turks swept into what remained of the Byzantine Empire. Muslim forces also posed a serious threat to Italy because the Muslims had made several attempts to invade nearby Austria. Explorers sailed in search of a mythical king, **Prester John**, in Africa who was thought to be a Christian. Europeans hoped to get his help to defeat the Muslims and preserve Christianity.

Some explorers went out with the goal of spreading the gospel to heathen cultures. Since most of the early explorers were followers of the Roman Church, the converts were often won to the Church of Rome and its teachings.

Technology

Technology made exploration possible. The construction of ships that could cross the open seas and tools to navigate those voyages were essential. With each returning ship, mapmakers learned more and produced more accurate maps. As more and more countries built navies and explored, naval warfare depended on technology to improve weapons to protect trade routes.

Shipbuilding

Ships that sailed along the coastlines of the continents were not capable of traveling on long journeys on the open sea. Advances in shipbuilding resulted in the **caravel**. This ship utilized a combination of previous designs. The caravel could travel on the open sea and sail upriver in the shallow coastal waters. This ship had three or four masts and used triangular sails combined with one or more square sails. The triangular sails enabled the caravel to maneuver in port and travel fast over shallow water. The square sail allowed the ship to catch more wind and travel quickly on the open sea.

Ships played a central role in exploration, trade, and defense. Since the Muslims had cut off the land routes to the Orient, water routes were the only other option. The caravel and other ships carried spices, silk, and other treasures back to Europe. Eventually, nations would realize the importance of a navy to trade, to defend trade routes, and to enable the establishment of colonies. Ships would also play a key role in wars between nations.

Caravel

Navigation

As Renaissance scholars learned more about their world, they provided the explorers with new inventions. Other navigational information came to Europe through contact with the Islamic world.

Maps

Maps of the areas familiar to the Europeans became more and more accurate by the fifteenth century. Italians excelled at making maps and improved them with input from traders and fishermen. However, beyond the Mediterranean Sea or the coast of Europe, little

Maps

Find a picture of an ancient map of the New World and have the students point out where the map is different from a current map of the hemisphere.

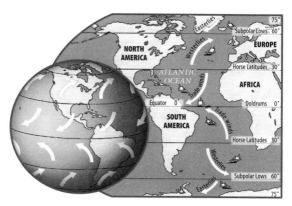

Wind patterns

or no information was available. Those who sailed west in search of trade routes to the Orient traveled in uncharted seas. As they returned from their journeys with new information, the existing maps were updated and improved. The invention of the printing press made rapid reproduction of maps possible and reduced the cost of making them.

Over time, these maps would include valuable information about wind patterns. Winds that were especially important to the early explorers were the **trade winds**, belts of consistent winds that blow from east to west. These fast-moving, favorable winds blew the explorers across the Atlantic Ocean.

Instruments

The sailor's most useful instrument was the **compass**, which allowed him to set a course and follow its direction faithfully. As you learned in Chapter 4, the Chinese developed the first crude compass from a magnetic mineral called lodestone. The European sailors found the compass to be essential for navigating the open sea with no landmarks. By the fifteenth century, an improved compass was composed of a needle spinning on a pin over a base. Several points of direction were marked on this base, making it possible to set and maintain an accurate course.

The **astrolabe** proved to be another helpful instrument. Sailors used it to measure the angle between the sun or a star and the horizon at a specific time of day or night. From this measure the sailor could determine his latitude. However, the astrolabe had serious limitations. For example, measuring the angle on a tossing ship was difficult or impossible. In addition, time was measured by an hourglass, so the captain rarely knew the exact time of his reading. Over time, the astrolabe was replaced by more accurate measuring devices.

Most early seamen navigated by **dead reckoning**. They decided what they thought their location was, estimated their speed, looked at the map, and aimed for a compass heading that they believed would get them to their goal. With the aid of the astrolabe, the sailors were able to improve their accuracy by traveling north or south to get to the desired latitude. Then they would sail east or west on that latitude until they came to land.

Compass Accuracy

If you have ever held a compass in your hand and had difficulty keeping it steady, you will understand how difficult it would be to keep the compass needle steady on the deck of a ship pitching back and forth on a rolling sea.

Navigating by Astrolabe

The astrolabe, developed in ancient Greece, consisted of a disk suspended from a ring. On the side of the disk was a pointer that could be aligned with the sun or the stars. Around the edge of the disk, degree markings helped to determine the angle between the horizon and the celestial body. While the instrument determined latitude, no method for accurately determining longitude existed until the late eighteenth century.

Activity 3: Christopher Columbus

This activity is an excerpt from Columbus's first-hand account of his discovery of the New World.

Christopher Columbus

Visit www.bjupress.com/resources for possible links to articles about Columbus.

Piracy

Piracy (the act of robbing at sea) is probably about as old as trade on early ships. The Roman Empire had to deal with it, as have many nations since then. Piracy was a special problem for the Portuguese and Spanish as they sailed ships filled with treasures across the seas.

During this period, nations such as England used pirates to weaken their enemy—Spain. Sir Henry Morgan was one well-known pirate who was encouraged by the English government and commissioned by the governor of the English colony of Jamaica. He worked for the government but kept the profits. Over time, Morgan stopped working for the government and began openly working for personal profit. He and other pirates soon began attacking any trading vessel, even if it was English.

Conversions

The conquistadors and priests made it very desirable to convert to Roman Catholicism. Conquistadors often gave the Indians the choice of conversion or being burned alive. The priests used a more subtle approach by allowing the Indians to retain many aspects of their native religions in addition to accepting baptism into the Roman Church.

Section III

Objectives

Students should be able to

1. Analyze Portuguese maritime expansion to India and Southeast Asia and interactions between the Portuguese and the peoples of these regions.

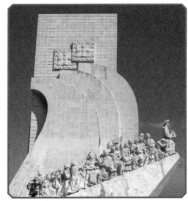

The Monument to the Discoveries in Belém, Portugal

> ### 1492—A Remarkable Year
> Two important events occurred during this year. The nation of Spain had been formed in 1469 when Ferdinand II of Aragon married Isabella of Castile. Together they used their forces to push the remaining Muslim powers out of the Iberian Peninsula. This struggle ended in 1492 with the victory of the Spanish. With all the important decisions to be made, it is significant that one of those decisions involved sending Columbus on a voyage to discover a route to the East. Given the great financial cost and risk of this voyage, it was a remarkable choice.

Prince Henry the Navigator

Naval Warfare

Naval warfare is ancient and can be traced back to battles such as those between the Greeks and the Persians in the fifth century BC. During the Age of European Exploration, a new weapon was attached to ships: the cannon. The Venetians were among the first to use cannon onboard their ships. They used their fleet both to carry on trade and to defend against piracy. Later, the Portuguese developed fighting vessels to escort their ships along their many trade routes. Soon the use of cannon on ships became common as Europeans discovered how to effectively use them at sea and in coastal attacks on their enemies.

Initiation of Exploration

It is remarkable that Columbus sailed in search of a western route to the East in the same year (1492) that the Iberian Peninsula was freed from the last trace of Muslim influence (see margin text box). From this peninsula Portugal and Spain would begin to explore Africa, Asia, and the Americas. These two nations had several advantages that enabled them to take the lead in European exploration.

Spain and Portugal were bordered by the Atlantic Ocean and the Mediterranean Sea. Therefore, they had a long history of shipbuilding and navigating these bodies of water. With access to the Atlantic Ocean, Spain sent explorers west and Portuguese sailors traveled south to find a new water route to the East. These experienced sailors also had the advantage of access to navigational and mapmaking skills that they had acquired from the Moors (Spanish Muslims).

Finally, Spain and Portugal were motivated by a strong crusading spirit that had enabled them to forcibly remove the remnants of Muslim influence in their region. They went out to spread the doctrine of the Roman Church and to continue the struggle against Muslims in other lands. Everywhere they explored and every colony they established had a strong Roman Catholic presence. Every effort was made to convert the natives to Catholicism.

Section Quiz

1–3. List and briefly describe three motives for European exploration.

4–5. List and briefly describe two navigational improvements that made exploration possible.

★ Why were Spain and Portugal among the first European nations to explore?

III. Growth of European Exploration

New Regions and New Routes

To compete with Arab and Italian traders (who controlled the land routes to India and China), countries needed to find a sea route to those lands. Portugal and Spain eagerly set off to accomplish that goal.

Portuguese Exploration

Prince Henry of Portugal sent out sailors and ships to explore the coast of Africa in the fifteenth century. For these explorers the

Section Quiz Answers

1–3. (any three) Economic—seeking wealth from trade with the East; Social—adventure, praise of men, curiosity, seeking glory; Political—seeking to lay claim to foreign lands, searching for raw materials for the home country; Religious—defeating Islam and preserving Christianity, evangelizing the heathen cultures

4–5. (any two) Maps—improved maps allowed for more extensive exploration; Compass—allowed the sailors to set a course and follow it; Astrolabe—enabled the sailors to determine latitude.

★ They had a long history of shipping and navigating the Atlantic and Mediterranean; they had ready access to the Atlantic and Mediterranean; they had access to navigational and mapmaking skills acquired from the Moors; they were motivated by a strong crusading spirit.

sea contained many unknown dangers. They heard stories of sea monsters, deadly heat at the equator, and violent storms. Despite these dangers, some men, supported by their kings, set out to find and explore distant lands.

To prepare his sailors for these dangerous voyages, Prince Henry set up a school for navigation. Portuguese sea captains learned how to use new methods and instruments. For his emphasis on training, Henry became known as Prince Henry the Navigator.

The Portuguese gradually sailed farther and farther south along the western coast of Africa in search of a route to the East. In 1487 the Portuguese explorer **Bartolomeu Dias** (DEE us) finally turned the corner that would open sea trade with India. Caught in a bad storm, Dias's ships rounded the tip of Africa without his realizing it. When Dias did become aware of where he was, he turned back and saw land. He wanted to continue to explore, but his frightened crew insisted on returning to Portugal. The Portuguese had proved that they could reach the East by sailing south around Africa.

Ten years later, in 1497, the first Portuguese ship landed in India. After rounding the **Cape of Good Hope** (southern tip of Africa), **Vasco da Gama** (VAHS-ko duh GAHM-uh) and his crew sailed up the east coast of Africa, stopping at trading cities where they met both African and Arab traders. Landing on the southwest coast of India, da Gama and his men were surprised to find an advanced people.

When they tried to trade, the Portuguese were surprised that the Indians rejected the items they had brought. The Indians were not impressed by the Portuguese goods of cloth, honey, and oil. In addition, Muslim merchants opposed da Gama's efforts to trade with the Indians. Eventually the Portuguese sold enough to buy spices and return to Portugal. The spices that were bought in India were sold to pay for the voyage, and enough money was left over to finance sixty more voyages. This insured that the Portuguese would make many more trips and extend their exploration even farther East.

Portuguese sailors soon made regular voyages to the port cities of East Africa and India. Muslim efforts to block Portuguese trade were easily defeated by the heavily armed Portuguese ships. The Portuguese sent a fleet of twenty-two ships to India in 1505 to establish settlements and to protect their growing trade with India.

Early in the sixteenth century, the Portuguese became the first Europeans (after Marco Polo) to make contact with China. Portuguese traders quickly moved to establish trade directly with the Chinese. This further weakened the Muslim and Italian monopolies on goods from the East and resulted in great wealth for Portugal.

In the mid-sixteenth century, the Portuguese were among the first Europeans to land in Japan. A few years later the Jesuit missionary **Francis Xavier** arrived in Japan and sought to convert the people to Roman Catholicism.

Early Spanish Exploration

While the Portuguese monarchs sent their ships to the East by sailing south, another Portuguese explorer believed he could get to the East by sailing west. However, his ideas were rejected by the Portuguese. So **Christopher Columbus** met with **King Ferdinand** and **Queen Isabella** of Spain and convinced them to finance his exploration. By sailing west, he hoped to discover a shorter route to China and the Indies (the islands near China, now known as Indonesia). In

Vasco da Gama

Vasco da Gama

Da Gama led a fleet of four ships on a one-year journey to India. Instead of following the African coast as others had done in the past, he sailed west and then south in a broad sweep. This maneuver allowed him to take advantage of favorable winds and currents. By the time his ships reached the southern tip of Africa, he had sailed out of sight of land for fourteen weeks. In future explorations, wind-driven ships would often use this maneuver.

One of the men who accompanied da Gama on this voyage was Dias, the explorer who had first discovered the passage around Africa ten years earlier.

Christopher Columbus

2. Compare the success of the Ottoman, Indian, Chinese, Japanese, and Siamese powers restricting European commercial, military, and political incursion.

3. Describe the political and military collision between the Spanish and the Aztec and Inca empires and analyze why these empires collapsed.

Indian Reluctance to Trade

Why did Vasco da Gama have a difficult time trading with the Indians? It is helpful to recall that India had access to goods from many parts of the world, including silk from China. The relatively poor quality of the Portuguese cloth in comparison to what the Indians had readily available must have made the Portuguese products seem almost worthless.

When you add in the fact that Muslim merchants used their significant influence to discourage buying goods from the Portuguese, it is remarkable that the Portuguese were able to sell their goods at all. However, the Portuguese traders' profit was so enormous that they used any means to gain access to this vast wealth.

Scurvy

One of the most serious dangers faced by the explorers was scurvy. Caused by a vitamin C deficiency, scurvy generally appeared among soldiers, sailors, prisoners, and people in famine areas—those whose diets included almost no fresh fruits or vegetables. The disease causes rashes, bleeding gums, brittle bones, internal bleeding, and poor healing of wounds. Scurvy has been a problem

Navigation School

Discuss with the students what types of things might have been taught in Prince Henry's navigation school. If possible, have someone come in and speak to the class about subjects taught in a modern naval academy.

⊛ Latitude

Visit www.bjupress.com/resources for possible links to articles about the concept of latitude and its role in exploration.

since ancient times. The Greek physician Hippocrates described symptoms that were probably caused by scurvy, and the affliction was definitely known among the Crusaders. Later it would trouble pioneers in the American West.

In the fifteenth and sixteenth centuries, with the increase of long sea voyages for trade and exploration, scurvy reached epidemic proportions. In 1497 Vasco da Gama lost 100 of his 160 men to scurvy on his trip around the southern tip of Africa. Although we can easily cure scurvy today, explorers knew little about combating the problem; all they could do was try to recover from it after it had struck. Cape Town, South Africa, was founded by the Dutch as a place for crews from their Far East trading ships to recuperate and obtain fresh produce.

Although the Dutch had begun using citrus in sailors' diets some time before, it was not until 1749 that Dr. James Lind, a Scottish naval surgeon, showed by careful studies that citrus fruit would cure and prevent scurvy. Lind suggested a way to preserve citrus fruit juice so that it could be carried on long voyages.

Columbus and His Ships

The *Niña* and *Pinta* were caravels. The caravel was more maneuverable and could sail upriver in shallow waters. The *Santa Maria* was a larger ship known as a *carrack*. The carrack was a three or four-masted ship that was large enough to be stable in heavy seas and could carry enough supplies for long voyages.

While we tend to think that these ships were paid for by Ferdinand and Isabella, they were privately owned ships. The Spanish monarchs forced the owners to

Ferdinand Magellan

Pacific Ocean

When Magellan rounded the tip of South America, he left the Atlantic and entered a new ocean. This ocean was so calm and peaceful that he named it the *Pacific*, from the Latin word for "peace." Unfortunately for Sir Francis Drake, he did not find this ocean peaceful at all when he encountered it on his voyage.

Sir Francis Drake

August 1492 he set sail with three ships. In October he landed on an island in what he thought were the Indies.

Although Columbus was right about sailing west to get east, he did not sail far enough. Thinking he had landed in the Indies, he called the natives "Indians." However, he had landed in the Caribbean. The nearby mainland was not China but the Americas. Neither the Caribbean islands nor North America yielded the precious metals and spices sought by the explorers. Yet Columbus did discover a new continent that would impact the course of Western civilization in years to come.

In 1519 **Ferdinand Magellan** (FUR-duh-nand muh-JEL-un) sailed west from Spain in an effort to sail around the world. His ships rounded the tip of South America and crossed the Pacific Ocean. Tragically, Magellan was killed in the Philippines. The surviving members of his crew continued the voyage and returned to Spain. This journey lasted three years, but it proved that Columbus's theory was correct: it was possible to reach the East by sailing west.

Early English Exploration

Not to be outdone by the Spanish and Portuguese, **Sir Francis Drake** was sent from England to sail around the world in 1577. Queen Elizabeth sent Drake on this three-year journey. On returning, he published a report of his voyage. Drake told of seeing new lands and peoples and enjoying God's gifts in nature. He also described times of hardship on this expedition. For example, winds, storms, heat, and lack of fresh water plagued the voyage.

Spanish Conquest

Columbus always believed that America was China, a land of gold. America was not China, but later explorers continued to believe that America was a land of gold. Spain sent out several men to find this gold, conquer the people, and convert them to Roman Catholicism. Called **conquistadors** (kon KEES tuh DORZ), Spanish for "conquerors," these men discovered and brutally destroyed Indian civilizations in Central and South America in search of gold.

Central America

In the region of modern Mexico, the conquistador **Hernando Cortés** (er-NAHN-do kor-TEZ) encountered the Aztecs. In 1519 he arrived in the Aztec capital, Tenochtitlán (modern Mexico City). The Aztec ruler, **Montezuma**, greeted Cortés and gladly showed him samples of the Aztec's great wealth. Cortés convinced Montezuma that the king of Spain was the Aztec god Quetzalcoatl and demanded that the Aztecs submit to Cortés as the king's representative. Montezuma submitted to Cortés's demands and urged his people to cooperate.

Despite the honor and gifts he received, Cortés eventually massacred (MAS uh kurd) (to kill a large number of) most of the Aztecs. As the Aztec people began to realize that the Spanish appetite for gold and power knew no bounds, they refused Cortés's leadership. When Montezuma again urged his people to submit to the Spanish, they stoned him to death. However, with guns, armor, and horses, the Spanish had a great advantage over the Aztecs. In 1521, during a four-month siege, Cortés destroyed Tenochtitlán. In its place he built Mexico City. Over the temple of the Aztecs, Cortés built a Roman Catholic cathedral. The Spanish compelled the Indians to outwardly

Models

Allow a student volunteer to make a model of one of Columbus's ships. (The ships are often available at hobby shops.)

Additional Resources

There is a helpful article entitled "Ferdinand Magellan" in the March/April 2004 issue of *Homeschooling Today* magazine.

Montezuma

Does the story of Montezuma welcoming Cortés and showing him the Aztec wealth sound familiar? Read the story of Hezekiah in Isaiah 39 where he welcomed the Babylonians and showed them all of Judah's wealth. Have the students discuss these two historical accounts and compare them.

Ferdinand Magellan

Visit www.bjupress.com/resources for possible links to articles about Ferdinand Magellan.

Hernando Cortés

Visit www.bjupress.com/resources for possible links to articles about Hernando Cortés.

Cathedral built by Cortés using the stones of the Aztec temple

submit to the Church of Rome while allowing them to retain many aspects of their pagan worship.

South America

Francisco Pizarro (pih ZAHR o) proved to be even more brutal than Cortés. He traveled to the new world to find gold, and he used violent methods to seize it at every opportunity. Pizarro heard of an Indian nation in South America—the Incas—that had much wealth. He led a small group of men and sailed from Panama to Peru in 1531. Pizarro and his men worked their way through jungles for six months and attacked villages along the way. When they reached the Inca Empire, they took the Inca, **Atahualpa** (AH tuh WAHL puh), captive. The Inca offered to fill the room in which the Spanish held him prisoner with gold and silver in exchange for his release. Over the next few weeks the Incas delivered about thirteen thousand pounds of gold and almost twenty-six thousand pounds of silver. However, Pizarro brutally murdered Atahualpa anyway and made himself ruler of the Inca Empire.

Pizarro destroyed Cuzco and founded the city of Lima. However, he did not live to enjoy the treasures he had violently taken from the Incas. In 1541 a group of Spaniards stormed Pizarro's palace and brutally killed him.

Efforts to Limit European Access

As the Europeans explored other continents, they interacted and sometimes collided with other civilizations. Responses to European exploration varied from one area to another. We will briefly examine some of these responses.

Ottoman

While Europe ventured out on the seas to explore new lands, the Ottoman Empire continued its expansion. Having conquered Constantinople in 1453, the Ottomans continued to capture land and expand their Muslim empire. A collision with Europe was unavoidable. Clashes between Europe and the Ottomans occurred in several battles. In 1571 an alliance of Roman Catholic nations, led by

Getty Images

Francisco Pizarro

contribute these ships to make the expedition possible.

Columbus's Discovery

On October 12, 1492, Columbus and his crew landed in what he believed was an island near India. We now know that he discovered the Americas. But where did he land? That has been the subject of endless speculation. The evidence points to the Bahamas, but opinions vary as to which island.

Sir Francis Drake

Drake was a man of many talents. In addition to sailing around the world, he served as second in command of the English fleet when it sailed against the Spanish Armada in 1588.

With the blessing of Queen Elizabeth, he also attacked and stole the treasures on many Spanish ships. The Spaniards called Drake *El Draque*, "The Dragon." Philip II, king of Spain, is said to have offered a great reward for the capture of Drake, but to no avail.

Machu Picchu

In 1911 an American named Hiram Bingham made one of the greatest discoveries in Amerindian archaeology. He was exploring Peru in search of Incan ceremonial sites. After searching fruitlessly for many weeks in the Peruvian heat and humidity, Bingham was ready to give up. Then he chanced upon an old man who talked about ruins on a mountain. Eagerly, Bingham climbed to the spot the man had described. His first sight of the city, a stone wall, only hinted at the archeological treasures he and his men would uncover.

Sir Francis Drake
Visit www.bjupress.com/resources for possible links to articles about Sir Francis Drake.

Francisco Pizarro
Visit www.bjupress.com/resources for possible links to articles about Francisco Pizarro.

The city that Bingham discovered was called Machu Picchu, "old peak," after a nearby mountain. (The Incan name was probably *Vilcapampa*.) The site, sixty-seven hundred feet up on the side of a mountain, was a natural spot for a fortress. Although archaeologists do not know exactly when or why the city was built, they believe that Machu Picchu was the last stronghold of the Incas. Pizarro apparently never detected the mountain city, but it was abandoned about the time of the Spanish conquest, possibly because of the death of the last Incan ruler and the collapse of the empire. Until Bingham found it four hundred years later, Machu Picchu lay lost and forgotten under an overgrowth of vegetation.

The five-square-mile site contains buildings and walls of expertly hewn stones that fit together without mortar. (Some walls and roads built by the same Indians are still being used.) It is clear from the ruins that a magnificent temple and citadel once stood there, surrounded by terraced gardens linked by more than three thousand steps.

The Closing of Japan

The Roman Catholic Church had some moderate success in Japan because of Francis Xavier's efforts. However, the samurai warlord Hideyoshi felt that Christianity was just a ploy that the West was using to attempt a political takeover of Japan. He ordered the "pope's generals" out of the land. Later, warlords executed the Catholic converts and began to close the doors of trade in 1639.

Phillip II of Spain, defeated the Ottoman naval fleet at the **Battle of Lepanto**. However, the Ottoman Empire quickly rebuilt its fleet and forced Venice to sign a peace treaty. By 1683 the Ottoman Empire found itself unable to maintain the two armies needed to fight the Austrians in Vienna and a rival Muslim kingdom in Persia. After this time the Ottomans fell behind the Europeans in the areas of military technology and strategy. The Ottoman Empire faded as a threat to Europe and its continued expansion.

Indian

During this period of European exploration, India struggled with internal conflicts and was unable to resist European efforts to establish colonies. Many countries, including Portugal, the Netherlands, France, and Great Britain, set up trading posts that were followed by colonies in India. Soon much of India was under the control of Europeans.

Chinese

The Chinese allowed limited trade with the Europeans during the early period of European exploration. Portuguese traders had only restricted access to China by way of coastal cities such as Canton. While the Chinese government remained strong, European trade remained limited. However, Europeans continued to pressure China to open its borders for more trade and on terms that were favorable to the Europeans.

Japanese

As noted earlier, Jesuit missionaries traveled to Japan during the sixteenth century. For a brief period, commerce and cultural exchange occurred between Japan and Europe. However, by 1639 the Japanese began to expel foreigners and isolate themselves from continued foreign influence. This isolation continued for the next two and one-half centuries.

Siamese

Siam (Thailand) traded with the Europeans beginning with the arrival of the Portuguese in the sixteenth century. However, this country stood alone in Southeast Asia in its ability to avoid European efforts to establish colonies on its soil. Strong leaders and skillful diplomacy protected Siam from European pressures to allow the development of European colonies. The Siamese leaders quickly recognized a tension between French and British powers and used this to their advantage.

Section Quiz

1. What Portuguese prince prepared his sailors for exploration?
2. Name the first Portuguese explorer to land in India.
3. What European country was the first to establish trade with Japan and China?
4. Who was the ruler of the Aztecs when the Spanish conquistadors arrived?
5. What was China's response to European exploration?
★ Why were the Siamese able to avoid European colonization?

Section Quiz Answers

1. Henry the Navigator
2. Vasco da Gama
3. Portugal
4. Montezuma
5. restricted trade and limited access
★ They took advantage of the tension between French and British powers.

IV. Consequences of European Exploration

Spread of Roman Catholicism in Latin America

As previously mentioned, Spanish explorers were sent to the Americas to find gold, to conquer territory, and to convert the natives to Roman Catholicism. History demonstrates that they had great zeal for the first two. However, most of the work of converting the surviving Indians was left to the Catholic clergy. In 1502 a Roman Catholic friar named **Bartolomé de Las Casas** came to the Americas to serve as a missionary to the Indians. Las Casas and others like him spoke out against the cruel treatment of the Indians by their fellow Spaniards. Las Casas spent the rest of his life seeking the passage of laws to protect the Indians from slavery and forced conversion to the Roman Church. He played a key role in improving the treatment of the Indians.

Since the Roman Church became the protector of the Indians, many converted to Roman Catholicism. The Indians developed a strong loyalty to the priests and the Catholic Church. The Roman Church took advantage of this loyalty and brought most of Central and South America under its influence.

Bartolomé de Las Casas

Introduction of Plants, Animals, and Diseases

While the Americas were not barren of food-producing plants before the arrival of the Europeans, the explorers did bring several new crops to the New World. These included fruit trees and grapevines from Europe. However, the plant that had the greatest impact was tobacco. While the Indians already grew tobacco, the English brought tobacco from the West Indies and planted it in America. This variety of tobacco proved to be very profitable, and colonists planted large areas with this plant. Tobacco brought wealth to the settlers, but it also depleted the soil rapidly. Soon more and more land was needed to maintain production and meet the growing demand. Forests were cleared in order to plant more tobacco, and depleted soil was used for grazing growing herds of livestock.

In addition to plants, the explorers also introduced several animals, including cattle, horses, and pigs, to the Americas. The horse proved to be the most beneficial animal to the Indians. Previous to the arrival of horses, all hunting and travel by the Indians was on foot. The horses were a welcome addition for their speed and strength. Horses made it possible for the Indians to hunt the buffalo herds more effectively. In addition, horses made carrying loads and traveling much easier.

Some scholars believe that pigs were the most destructive of the animals brought with the explorers. The pigs often ran wild and tended to eat many of the plants used by Indians for food, including the corn planted by the Indians. Pigs are also carriers of various diseases that may have spread throughout the wildlife and into the food supply of the Indians. Opinions vary about what caused the spread of disease among the Indians and killed many of them, but pigs brought from Europe may have played a role in this tragic loss of life.

Various human-borne diseases may also have killed large numbers of Indians. Smallpox is now believed to have killed many Incas beginning around 1525. It spread rapidly throughout the empire. This plague destroyed many of the Inca leaders about six years

---

How Many Indians Were There?

Estimates vary greatly regarding the number of Indians living in the Americas when the Europeans arrived. Las Casas, an eyewitness of Spanish atrocities, referred to the death of about fifteen million Indians at the hands of the Spaniards (although he provided no documentation). It has become popular in the last few years to speculate that the Indian populations could have totaled over one hundred million. However, others point out that there is no evidence for such inflated numbers. Historians know that many Indians died around the time of European colonization, but no one knows with certainty what killed the Indians and how many died. The truth is that we don't have any evidence that enables us to answer the question of how many Indians there were.

Section IV

Objectives

Students should be able to

1. Trace the early spread of Roman Catholicism in Latin America.

2. Assess how the exchange of plants, animals, and diseases around the world in the late 15th and 16th centuries affected European and American Indian societies.

3. Describe the effects that knowledge of the people of the Americas had on European religious and intellectual life.

Activity 4: Bartolomé de Las Casas

This activity is a first-hand account of the treatment of the Indians by the Spanish.

Bartolomé de Las Casas

Visit www.bjupress.com/resources for possible links to articles about Bartolomé de Las Casas.

Barbarians

The term *barbarian* has had more than one meaning in history. In this chapter the Europeans looked down on the Indian cultures as barbaric because the Europeans considered them to be uncivilized. When the term *barbarian* is used in the New Testament (1 Cor. 14:11; Col. 3:11), it refers to those outside of the Roman world.

before Pizarro and his men arrived. No satisfactory source for this outbreak has been determined, although there are several theories. Other diseases such as typhus and measles were possibly brought with the explorers and settlers. Without realizing it, those who survived the plagues that had reduced populations in Europe may have brought with them the means of transmitting these diseases to the Indians. Diseases that had been spread to Europe from other countries were possibly carried to the Americas with the explorers. Since the Indians had no previous exposure to these diseases, they had not developed immunity to them. For reasons that are not entirely known, the death toll among the Indian populations was great.

Results of Interaction with Other Cultures

European explorers struggled to understand many of the cultures they encountered in foreign lands. Some were surprised to find complex cultures in India, China, and the Americas. Others were horrified at the sight of human sacrifice among the Aztecs in Central America. The Europeans were also appalled by the violent methods of defeating enemies, such as beheading and cannibalism.

While most Europeans looked down on other cultures as being less civilized, some of these cultures challenged the Europeans to consider their own barbarities. If the Europeans and Indians were both barbaric, who could say that one culture was better than the other? This kind of thinking would later prove to be a challenge to Christianity when it confronted pagan religions.

Yet many of the European explorers displayed a disregard for the lives of native populations. Conquistadors like Cortés and Pizarro slaughtered Indians by the thousands and destroyed whole villages. Spanish forces in general were especially brutal in conquering the Indian civilizations and then enslaving the survivors to labor in the mines and fields. Spanish thirst for riches and power could not be quenched, and many died at the hands of fellow Spaniards who shared this thirst.

Section Quiz

1. What Roman Catholic friar traveled to the Americas as a missionary to the Indians?
2. Why did many Indians convert to the Roman Catholic Church?
3–4. Describe the impact of the introduction of horses and pigs to the Americas.
5. What impact did human-borne diseases have on the Indian population?
★ Compare the European response to Indian civilizations with the conduct of the conquistadors.

Section Quiz Answers

1. Bartholomé de Las Casas
2. The Indians viewed the Roman Church as their protector and felt a strong loyalty to the priests and Church.
3–4. Horses became a great asset to the Indians for travel, hunting, and carrying loads; pigs may have spread disease and led to the deaths of many Indians.
5. The Indian populations were drastically reduced by a terrible death toll.
★ Answers will vary. The Europeans were surprised to find complex cultures and were horrified at the sight of human sacrifices and other barbaric methods such as beheading and cannibalism.

The conquistadors demonstrated a barbaric disregard for the Indians and slaughtered them without mercy. They violated promises and displayed greed.

Activity 5: Chapter Review

This activity will help the students review the chapter content.

CHAPTER REVIEW

Making Connections

1. What did the relationship between Europeans and the Iroquois Confederacy reveal about these tribes?

2. How did the Mayan civilization respond when the Spanish conquistadors arrived?

3. How was the city of Tenochtitlán built in the middle of a lake?

4. Why were the Aztecs open to deception by the Spanish conquerors?

5. Why did the Incas cover their buildings with sheets of gold?

6. Why was the caravel better suited for exploration?

7. How did Prince Henry of Portugal contribute to Portuguese exploration?

8. Why were Portuguese sailors willing to endure the risks and difficulties to sail to India?

Developing History Skills

1. Using the information found in this chapter, create a timeline of European exploration.

2. Draw a basic map of Central and South America and label the locations of the empires of the Aztecs, Incas, and Mayas.

Thinking Critically

1. Given the initial advantages of Portugal and Spain, what would you expect their position in relation to other European nations to be?

2. Evaluate the religions of the civilizations in the Americas in light of Romans 1.

Living in God's World

1. Read an excerpt from Michel de Montaigne's essay "On the Cannibals." Compose an essay in response from a Christian perspective. Note both what is correct and what is incorrect with Montaigne's essay.

2. Divide into groups representing counselors to the monarch of an exploring nation. Each group will write a document giving the reasons for an upcoming exploration of the Americas along with guidelines for how to interact with the native peoples. Write as Christian counselors of a Christian king. Upon completion, each group will present its document to the class.

People, Places, and Terms to Know

Pueblos
Mound Builders
effigy mound
Iroquois Confederacy
Five Civilized Tribes
Mayas
Aztecs
Tenochtitlán
Quetzalcoatl
Incas
Cuzco
Prester John
caravel
trade winds
compass
astrolabe
dead reckoning
Prince Henry
Bartolomeu Dias
Cape of Good Hope
Vasco da Gama
Francis Xavier
Christopher Columbus
King Ferdinand
Queen Isabella
Ferdinand Magellan
Sir Francis Drake
conquistadors
Hernando Cortés
Montezuma
Francisco Pizarro
Atahualpa
Battle of Lepanto
Bartolomé de Las Casas

Chapter Review Answers

Making Connections

1. They were powerful enough that the Europeans had to work with them.

2. They offered no resistance.

3. from floating mounds of water plants that were later filled in with soil

4. because of the legend of Quetzalcoatl and his promise to return

5. to reflect the sun and remind them of their sun god

6. multiple masts and a combination of triangle and square sails for added maneuverability and speed

7. He set up a school to teach his sailors new methods of navigation.

8. The spices they purchased were worth up to sixty times the cost of the voyage.

Developing History Skills

1. 1487—Dias rounds the corner of Africa; 1492—Columbus discovers islands near America; 1497—Vasco da Gama lands in India; 1502—Las Casas comes to evangelize the Indians; 1505—Portuguese send fleet to establish settlements in India; (early 1500s)—Portuguese make contact with China; 1519—Magellan begins his journey around the world; 1519—Cortés discovers the Aztecs; 1521—Cortés destroys Tenochtitlán and builds Mexico City; 1531—Pizarro attacks the Inca Indians; (mid 1500s)—Portuguese make contact with Japan; 1571—Phillip II defeats Ottoman navy at Battle of Lepanto; 1577—Francis Drake begins his journey around the world

2. Maps will vary depending on the skills and efforts of the students.

Thinking Critically

1. Answers will vary. Students would likely expect Portugal and Spain to become rich and powerful and to develop large colonies in the New World and the East.

2. Answers should include some of the following: When they knew God they didn't glorify Him. Their hearts and imaginations became vain and darkened. They changed the glory of God into a corruptible image. They changed the truth of God into a lie and worshiped and served the creature more than the Creator. God gave them over to all kinds of wicked conduct.

Living in God's World

1. Answers will vary.

2. Answers will vary.

Chapter Goals

Students should be able to

1. Describe the colonization of Latin America and the difficulties of ruling the colonies from Europe.

2. Discuss the colonization of North America and the differences between French, Spanish, and English colonization.

3. Explain the struggle for independence and the founding of a nation in North America.

4. Explain the struggle for independence in Latin America and the ongoing difficulty of translating freedom into liberty.

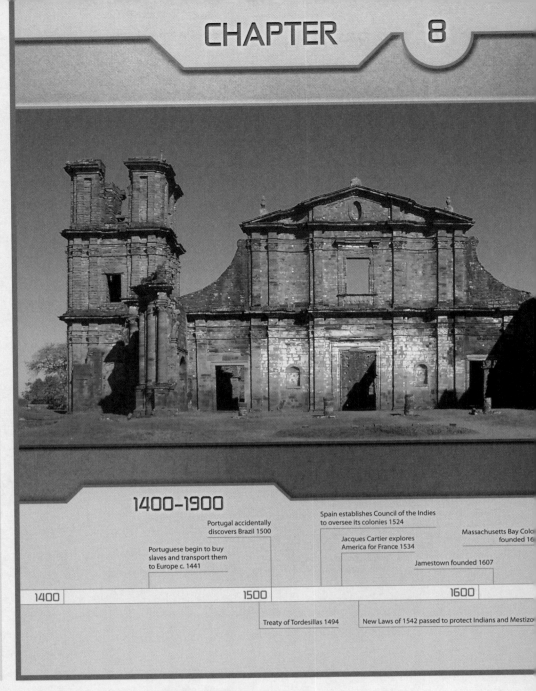

CHAPTER 8

1400–1900

Portugal accidentally discovers Brazil 1500

Portuguese begin to buy slaves and transport them to Europe c. 1441

Spain establishes Council of the Indies to oversee its colonies 1524

Jacques Cartier explores America for France 1534

Massachusetts Bay Colo founded 16

Jamestown founded 1607

| 1400 | 1500 | 1600 |

Treaty of Tordesillas 1494

New Laws of 1542 passed to protect Indians and Mestizo

Chapter 8 Lesson Plan Chart			
Section Title	**Main Activity**	**Pages**	**Days**
I. Colonization of Latin America	Activity 1: Map Study: South America	138–44	2 days
II. Colonization of North America	Activity 3 : Why the Pilgrims Left the Netherlands	145–48	1½–2 days
III. Struggle for Independence	Activity 4: Simón Bolívar	148–52	1½–2 days
TOTAL SUGGESTED DAYS (INCLUDING 1 DAY EACH FOR REVIEW AND TESTING)			7–8 days

Materials List

Section I

- CD: 8A South America; 8B Settlement Areas
- Activity 1 from the *Student Activities* manual

Section II

- CD: 8C Early French Exploration; 8D English Settlements
- Activities 2 and 3 from the *Student Activities* manual

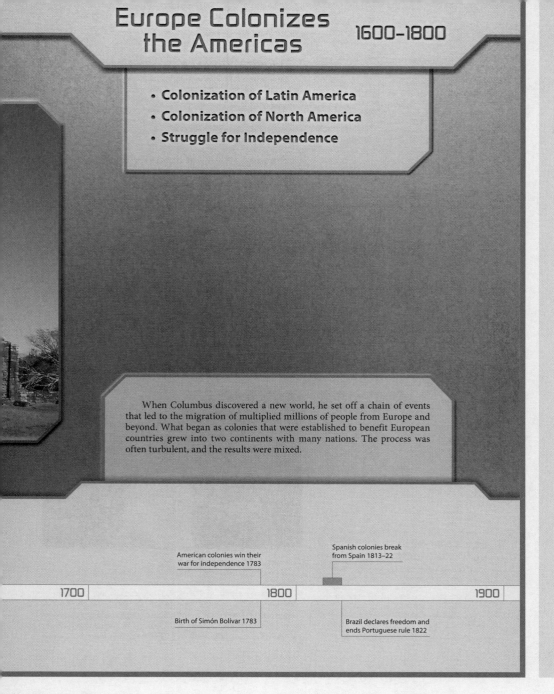

Europe Colonizes the Americas 1600–1800

- **Colonization of Latin America**
- **Colonization of North America**
- **Struggle for Independence**

When Columbus discovered a new world, he set off a chain of events that led to the migration of multiplied millions of people from Europe and beyond. What began as colonies that were established to benefit European countries grew into two continents with many nations. The process was often turbulent, and the results were mixed.

American colonies win their
war for independence 1783

Spanish colonies break
from Spain 1813–22

| 1700 | 1800 | 1900 |

Birth of Simón Bolívar 1783

Brazil declares freedom and
ends Portuguese rule 1822

Section III

- Activities 4 and 5 from the *Student Activities* manual
- CD: 8E Gaucho

Section I

Objectives

Students should be able to

1. Explain the initial attempts to divide the New World between Spain and Portugal.
2. Analyze the response of other European nations to the Line of Demarcation.
3. Evaluate the Portuguese failures to rule and properly manage their colonies.

Dividing the World

It was a huge assumption on the part of the pope and Portugal and Spain that it was even possible to divide the world between two countries for future exploration. There was very little information upon which to base such a momentous decision. Therefore, the pope drew the line 100 leagues west of islands that had already been discovered (the Azores). The length of a "league" was not defined, and a specific island in this cluster of islands wasn't specified. Still, the Portuguese contested the rather arbitrary decision and convinced the pope and the Spanish to move the line farther west. Some believe the Portuguese already knew about the existence of Brazil. Before long, the Line of Demarcation become obsolete as many countries rushed to join the exploration of the New World.

Latin America

South America is often referred to as **Latin America**. The term *Latin* refers to the fact that Spanish and Portuguese are classified as Romance (or Romanic) languages. In other words, they developed out of the Latin language used by their Roman conquerors during the time of the Roman Empire.

South America

Why Would the Pope Divide the World?

Spain and Portugal were the leaders in early exploration. They were also both Roman Catholic nations. It seemed logical to them to appeal to the Vicar (substitute) of Christ to make this monumental decision. Why do you think the other European nations refused to abide by this decision?

I. Colonization of Latin America

South America was settled by people from the Iberian Peninsula in Europe—that is, from Spain and Portugal. Once the boundaries dividing their holdings were set, the Spanish and Portuguese rarely conflicted. Their similar cultures enabled them to establish a single Latin American culture. This development was often accomplished by abusing the native peoples through forced labor and requiring them to adopt European customs.

European Settlement in South America

Settlement

In the previous chapter you learned that the Portuguese led in the race to find a sea route to China. Prince Henry the Navigator had trained his sailors to navigate, and they were charting new waters. Once the Portuguese had traveled around Africa, they quickly established a monopoly (exclusive control) on trade to the East along this route. This monopoly forced the Spanish to seek another route to China. However, instead of finding a way to China, Spanish explorers discovered what they called the New World.

The Spanish rushed to establish a monopoly over the New World just as the Portuguese had over the Eastern trade route. Spain laid claim to lands in North, Central, and South America. To support their claims, the Spanish established colonies as they continued their search for riches. Over time, the Spanish established settlements in Peru, Ecuador, Bolivia, Chile, Argentina, and Venezuela. A quick look at the map of South America shows that the Spanish settled the western portion of South America. A logical question to ask would be why the Spanish didn't settle all of South America. The answer lies in a line drawn by a pope on a map in 1493 and a treaty between Spain and Portugal.

San Ignacio Miní; early Spanish architecture in the New World

The Line of Demarcation

To establish their early claims, Queen Isabella and King Ferdinand of Spain called on Pope Alexander VI, a Spaniard, to decide which country (Spain or Portugal) could explore and lay claim to certain areas. The line the pope decided on was called the **Line of Demarcation.** Everything to the east of the line could be claimed by Portugal; everything to the west, by Spain. The Portuguese were not pleased with this arbitrary division. The route they followed to catch

CD: 8A South America

This map from the student text is also available on the CD.

Activity 1: Map Study: South America

This map activity will help the students learn the locations of various countries in South America.

favorable winds for their voyages around Africa often took them into Spanish waters and put them at risk for conflict.

In a final agreement between Spain and Portugal, the line was moved in 1494 by the **Treaty of Tordesillas** (tord uh SEE yuhs). The new line was moved west about 10° longitude, or about 600 miles west of the original line. If the Spanish had understood what they were giving up, they probably wouldn't have signed this treaty. Without realizing it at the time, the Portuguese were given a vast territory now known as Brazil. The "island of Brazil," as the Portuguese referred to it, was accidentally discovered by the Portuguese in 1500 when one of their ships was blown off course on its way to Africa. Several years later the Portuguese took advantage of this discovery and colonized this region of South America. Hence, Portuguese became the spoken language of Brazil on a continent where Spanish is spoken in most of the countries.

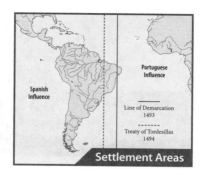

Settlement Areas

Conflicts over Settlements

Although conflict between Spain and Portugal was unusual, it did erupt at times as their claims to territories overlapped. A major area of conflict occurred in present-day Uruguay. The Portuguese claimed the land down to the Uruguay River, but Spanish settlements were established on the Portuguese side of the river. The Spanish agreed to give up these settlements but established other Spanish settlements in disputed lands. The conflict continued until a treaty was signed in 1777.

Other European nations were not willing to allow the New World to be divided between Spain and Portugal. These two nations had to compete with exploration by the French, Dutch, and English. The French explored the Brazilian coast from 1503 to 1509. Their explorations made the Portuguese nervous enough to send a fleet of ships to protect Portuguese claims. However, the Portuguese soon gave up this effort, and in 1604 the French established a settlement in the northern region of South America. This territory later became known as French Guiana.

Guiana seems to have been a popular name for settlements in South America. The Dutch and English also established settlements by this name in the northern region of South America. Oddly enough, in 1581 the Dutch settled what later became British Guiana, and the British settled the area that later became Dutch Guiana. The Dutch lost their original territory to the English after several battles, and the English traded their Guiana to the Dutch for New York. Later, the names of both areas changed. British Guiana became Guyana, and Dutch Guiana became Suriname.

While the Spanish were certainly the most brutal in their treatment of the native populations, other European explorers also tended to take advantage of the natives. Even with the best of intentions, Europeans tended to look down on the Indians and to pressure them to become more civilized, or European. The Europeans often claimed the right to control the land and the development of natural resources without the consent of the natives. At best, the natives were second-class citizens who were expected to perform whatever menial tasks the Europeans were unwilling to do.

Ruling Distant Settlements

The problems Spain and Portugal faced when they tried to rule these distant settlements directly were enormous and similar to the

Early Missionary Efforts in South America

The Reformer John Calvin sent missionaries from Geneva to take advantage of French explorations in South America. This was one of the earliest attempts at Protestant foreign missions.

CD: 8B Settlement Areas

This map from the student text is also available on the CD.

Native Civilizations

Discuss with the students what impact Spanish and Portuguese colonization had on the native populations.

Treaty of Tordesillas

Visit www.bjupress.com/resources for possible links about the Treaty of Tordesillas.

Donatarios vs. Viceroys

The concept of having noblemen manage the territories for Portugal seemed ideal. This enabled the Portuguese to hold large territories in the New World without expending much money or effort. The donatarios provided total care for their region out of their own resources. Therefore, when the Portuguese government wanted to regain control of the territory, it had to purchase it from the nobles to pay back some of their expenditures. This practice continued until 1630. By this time Portugal had regained all of its territory.

In contrast, the Spanish viceroys were all appointed by the king. The viceroy did not purchase the land over which he ruled. In this way Spain maintained control throughout exploration and colonization. However, several other offices were filled by purchase. Over time this worked against Spanish control as more and more creoles grew wealthy enough to purchase offices.

The ocean often proved to be tempestuous for travelers.

dilemmas faced by the Roman and Mongol Empires. The Romans and Mongols made traveling easier with well-planned roads and routes. However, the Spanish and Portuguese were separated from their colonies by hundreds of miles of ocean. To add to the difficulty, the ocean was an ever-changing and often dangerous route for travel.

Attempts at Direct Rule

Early Spanish and Portuguese rule in Latin America was strict. Since the rulers of Spain and Portugal had absolute power in their own countries, they exercised the same level of authority in the new settlements. At first, this method of governing was acceptable, but as the settlement populations increased, more problems needed to be resolved quickly. Waiting for orders from the Spanish or Portuguese ruler proved to be impractical.

The Spanish and Portuguese also made other decisions that doomed their long-term control of these colonies. For example, they ignored the **creoles** (KREE olz) (people of pure Spanish or Portuguese descent born in the Americas). The kings of Spain and Portugal gave all the governing duties to those born in the **mother country** (European country) and did not grant the creoles any rights to rule even though they were direct descendants of noble families from the mother country. This disregard eventually led to revolt.

European management of the production of goods in the colonies also created difficulties. Spain and Portugal determined the price, quantity, and types of goods that could be produced and sold in the colonies. The mother country also placed a high tax on goods being **exported** (taken out of the colonies) and charged high prices on goods being **imported** (brought into the colonies). This practice severely restricted personal as well as colonial economic growth. These policies also contributed to the unrest that finally led to revolt against the mother country.

Portuguese Rule in the New World

The system of government initially used by the Portuguese proved to be very ineffective. Instead of retaining most of the power for itself, Portugal granted great authority to twelve nobles. These nobles received the title of **donatario** (doh nah TAH ree oh), and their rule was to be hereditary (passed on to their children). The Portuguese government gave the donatarios total control of the land, and the donatarios determined how the land would be divided among colonists. They were responsible to colonize, defend, and tax their territory and to send excess funds to Portugal.

The Roman Church provided some checks to the power of the donatarios. Church officials brought the complaints of the colonists before the donatarios. If these complaints were ignored, the officials would send word of the complaints on to authorities in Portugal. This resulted in many bitter disputes between the colonial governors and the Roman Church.

In 1549 King John of Portugal began a process that eventually enabled Portugal to regain control of the colonies in Brazil. Conditions in Brazil improved for a time, but the Portuguese officials also proved unable to govern well. Despite these problems, the tiny country of Portugal was able to maintain control of a colony eighty times its size for three hundred years.

Spanish Authority in the New World

As we stated earlier, all laws and policies for the Spanish colonies came directly from Spain. This included all religious and economic policies. For example, the Roman Church became the official church in all of the Spanish colonies. No other forms of worship, such as Protestantism, were allowed. In addition, Spain took advantage of the economic resources by taking twenty percent of the mined gold and silver from the colonies.

In 1524 Spain established the Council of the Indies to oversee its colonies. The king appointed a **viceroy** (*vice*=in place of; *roy*=king) to rule each colony. Early viceroys appeared to be very powerful when dealing with the problems that affected the colonies; however, the viceroys had to answer to the council. This supervision limited their options when making decisions.

The Council of the Indies tried to direct colonial affairs from Spain. Since the viceroys lived in Mexico, the distance and expanse of land over which the authorities ruled proved too great to allow for effective rule. To solve this problem, the territories were subdivided into several lesser levels, and more government officials were appointed so that there was an official for each village or city. The Spanish allowed only Spaniards born in Spain, *peninsulares*, to hold most government positions. Creoles played only a minor role in government even though some had great wealth and owned much land. However, all people are created in the image of God and therefore desire to be treated equally. For this reason, oppression and injustice often lead to social unrest. Over time, the Creoles and the native peoples would repeatedly rebel against Spanish authority.

Developing the Colonies

At the beginning of exploration, possessing and controlling an area was the goal. The Spanish rulers saw the New World as a vast supply of resources for the mother country. The Portuguese, with their attention directed toward their African and Indian trade routes, at first paid little attention to Brazil other than to ensure its possession. However, the Spanish were driven by the desire for riches. The discovery of gold and silver motivated them to explore farther and farther south along the western region of South America. In the last chapter you read about the discoveries of Cortés and Pizarro. Long-term settlement and development of the colonies proceeded after these early, dramatic discoveries.

Treatment of the Native Population

Officially, the Spanish government never approved of enslaving the native South Americans. They sent the explorers as ambassadors from the Spanish ruler to the Indian empires. The explorers and settlers were given permission to enslave only Indians who were cannibals or who attacked the Spanish. Given these instructions, it was not long before the explorers sent reports back to Spain that most Indian groups were cannibalistic and hostile. Thus, virtually all of the Indians could be enslaved.

The Roman Church gained great influence as the clergy worked with the Indian population. The Church sent friars and priests to the colonies to convert the Indians to Catholicism. While they evangelized, many of the priests also promoted European culture. Thus,

---

Clergy in Government

During this period in the Spanish colonies, many Roman Catholic clergy held positions in government. Do you think this was a good or bad idea? Why?

Why the Spanish Would Not Work

To understand why the conquistadors would not work, one must understand the class system in Spain during the exploration. In Spain there were basically two classes: the rich and the poor. One characteristic of the lower class was that they did all the manual labor. The upper class did not labor in that way. They were the trained and educated overseers.

For the conquistadors to come to the New World and grub in the dirt was unthinkable. They believed they needed laborers. Some were brought with them, but the rest had to be recruited, willingly or unwillingly.

the clergy played a key role in pressuring the native peoples to adapt quickly as the colonies grew.

When the Spanish wanted to reward a conquistador, they awarded him an estate or property that often included an Indian labor force. With this ready-made group of virtual slaves, the former conquistadors were able to farm, mine, or manufacture goods for trade or sale. Unfortunately, many conquistadors were brutal in their treatment of the Indians. Mistreatment, exposure to European illnesses, and harsh responses to Indian uprisings all drastically reduced the Indian population.

The Roman Church often represented the Indians during labor disputes and defended them against ill-treatment. As you learned in the last chapter, Dominican friar Bartolomé de Las Casas spoke out against the terrible treatment of the Indians. Through his efforts, the **New Laws of 1542** were passed. Those laws set up a government system in which courts were established to protect the Indians and **mestizos** (mes TEE zohz) (people with Indian and Spanish parents) from some of the abuses that they suffered. The laws also prohibited the enslaving of the Indians and outlawed the passing on of government-awarded estates to later generations. Sadly, the landowners used their political influence to overturn many of these reforms.

Limiting the Control of the Roman Church

The Roman Church had an increasing influence on and control over the Spanish and Indian population of South America. Because of its protecting power, the Church received more loyalty from the Indians than the Indians gave to the Spanish and Portuguese.

The Jesuits, a powerful arm of the Roman Church, especially fell into disfavor with the Spanish and Portuguese governments. The disfavor resulted largely from the Jesuits' control over trade and their influence over the Indians.

The Jesuits established missions soon after initial settlement in the New World. In those missions the priests worked toward converting the Indians. They learned the Indians' language and taught them to read and write. Over time, Jesuit control over the Indians resembled that of Spanish and Portuguese control over the Indians. While the Jesuits spoke out against abuse of the Indians and supported Indian rights, they often used them as workers at the mission facilities. This apparent contradiction angered the other landowners. Eventually, the Portuguese and Spanish governments acted to correct this problem.

Bringing African Slaves into Latin America

The Portuguese began buying slaves in Africa and taking them to Europe as early as 1441. The number of slaves purchased was small at first but increased with demand. Slaves were common in Portugal and Spain, and some conquistadors even brought their slaves with them when they traveled to the New World.

In Brazil and the Caribbean Islands, the Indian population declined to the point where more workers were needed. Tragically, large numbers of African slaves were brought in to work on the plantations and in the mines. At least nine million Africans were enslaved and brought to the New World. Over three million black slaves were forced to labor in Brazil, and millions more were sent to other Latin American colonies. Eventually, between six and seven hundred thousand blacks were taken as slaves to the colonies in North America.

Expulsion of the Jesuits

Some Jesuits with their Indian helpers eventually controlled large tracts of land and the agricultural production on the land. They operated sugar mills and slaughter houses. Because the Roman Church did not have to pay taxes and also received additional income from tithes, the Church was often able to monopolize an industry. The tradesmen who did not have these advantages could not compete. Jealousy over profits and power led to the expulsion (forced to leave) of the Jesuit order from the New World. The Jesuits were expelled by the Portuguese in 1759 and by the Spanish in 1767.

Slavery in Latin America

Have a volunteer research the slave trade in Latin America and share the findings with the class.

Developing Natural Resources

Refined silver and sugar were the two major exports of colonial Latin America. Slaves were most often used in mines in Peru and on sugar plantations in Brazil and the Caribbean. In the mines, Indians often worked as free laborers. Over time, the Indians were elevated to serve as skilled laborers and to provide supervision. Black slaves performed the general hard labor of digging and loading.

One of the most important resources of South America was the land itself. Development of the land occurred as the immigrant population increased. Overcrowding and lack of available land in Europe made people willing to move to the colonies, where they could make a new life for themselves and their children.

One of the most profitable resources in South America today is coffee. But coffee is not native to South America. Coffee originated in Arabia, and coffee plants were later taken to Indonesia. Eventually, a coffee plant was brought to the Caribbean island of Martinique. Coffee plants flourished in South America and became a major crop.

Coffee beans

Coffee plants

The Dutch and Land Reclamation

Early attempts to settle the inland areas of South America failed due to poor soil. Later, the Dutch discovered the rich soils on the coastline of Dutch Guiana. The Dutch were accustomed to reclaiming land below sea level and used sea walls and dike systems to retrieve land from the sea. They established sugar plantations on this reclaimed land.

Living in the Colonies

The people who came from Spain and Portugal to the New World faced many changes in lifestyle. Although the European world at the time was not extremely advanced by today's standards, the colonists still faced many surprises when they came to a world where there were unusual animals, strange foods, foreign people, and few roads. Those who came adapted quickly to this new situation. Since many of the early settlers came from Spain and Portugal, they brought their Iberian culture and architecture to the New World.

Living in the City

Much of South America's colonial redevelopment took place around cities. The center of the city became the hub of trade and society. The wealthy built their homes and businesses nearby to have ready access to this center of trade.

These homes were easily distinguished from those of the lower classes. Often two-story in design, the houses of the wealthy were set up for business on the first floor while the second floor was reserved for the family. The whole house opened onto an interior courtyard. The kitchen was often a separate building at the back of the house.

If You Can't Stand the Heat . . .

Why would the kitchen be separated from the house? Remember that the climate in Central and South America is often hot and humid. If you add the heat produced by cooking and baking, then it makes the temperature in the house unbearable. The colonists quickly learned to move the kitchen away from the main house to prevent unwanted heating of the home. It may also have been a practical measure to prevent a kitchen fire from burning down the house.

Education and Self-Government

The emphasis on education in the English colonies helped to prepare the people for eventual self-rule. Only people who know how to think can adequately rule themselves. Education is also vitally important to the Christian who seeks to serve God to the best of his ability.

Coffee

Have a volunteer research the process involved in producing coffee and share the findings with the class.

Additional Resources: Coffee

The third edition of *Cultural Geography* (BJU Press) has a feature box on coffee in the student text and a flow chart about coffee on the CD in the teacher's edition.

Homes of wealthy South Americans

Barrios where the poor lived

Not only was the house itself a beautiful structure with decorative moldings and carved shutters, but the furnishings inside were elegant as well. Imported Spanish goods were often intermingled with oriental silk draperies and items made from New World silver.

Beyond the wealth of the central city were the *barrios*, or neighborhoods, of the poor. These were the homes of the free blacks, Indians, and mestizos. Here apartments provided most of the housing. A family often lived in a one-room apartment divided into two rooms by a blanket. While simple and small, these apartments were better than the shacks where the very poor people lived.

Social or economic status played a part in the poor *barrios* just as it did in the wealthy area of the central city. New immigrants from Spain, poorer Spanish people, and Indian craftsmen formed the highest level. On the next level were gardeners, laborers, porters, and merchants. Unskilled or temporary Indian laborers and others often occupied the bottom level.

City life held more opportunity for entertainment than rural life did. In the city, the rich could attend plays, banquets, and concerts. They entertained with lavish parties to display their wealth or show off the latest imports.

The poor in the city also had several diversions. Cock fights, where roosters were made to fight to the death while crowds bet on the outcome, were common. Religious holidays with parades and religious ceremonies also provided a break from work. The poor even enjoyed watching the wealthy parading in their fancy clothes and fine carriages.

Living in the Country

The settlement of the Latin American countryside took a different course from that of North America. Most Latin Americans did not settle on individual family farms because the government did not generally allow immigrants to own land. Instead, a few wealthy men owned most of the land, from which they made large country estates called **haciendas** (HAH see EN duhz). Most of the people remained poor and worked on these estates for low wages. They had little hope of ever owning their own land.

Many of these landowners cared little for developing their own land or those forced to work it. As long as landowners gained wealth from the crops grown on their estates, they were content. This attitude prevented the workers from improving their lives and the land from being developed.

Home on a Latin American hacienda

Dramatic Variations in the Concept of the Home

Have the students compare/contrast homes of the upper and lower classes in South America. As time permits, discuss how homes in your city differ among the upper, middle, and lower classes.

Limited Opportunities

Compared to the North American colonies, opportunities for upward mobility in the Latin American colonies were very limited. Have your students discuss the opportunities for success people have in the United States today if they are willing to work, sacrifice, and save.

Section Quiz

1. What line divided the world between Spain and Portugal?
2. People of pure Spanish descent who were born in America were called _____.
3. What role did the donatarios play in Brazilian society?
4. Spaniards born in Spain who held government positions in the American colonies were called _____.
5. What institution first spoke out against the unjust treatment of the native population but later participated in oppressive practices?
★ How do Genesis 1:27 and Mark 12:30–31 condemn the European treatment of creoles and native peoples?

II. Colonization of North America

If the Americas were the New World for many Europeans, then Europe had become the **Old World**. To many Europeans, the New World was more attractive than the Old. Many of these Europeans became so attracted to the New World that they left Europe for the growing settlements in America. From the early period of American settlement up to 1780, the greatest number of Europeans came from England, France, and Spain.

Patterns of Immigration

Because Spanish exploration began in the Caribbean and Gulf of Mexico, the Spanish tended to establish their settlements in southern North America. Explorers did travel farther north, but the difficulties that they faced there caused them to give up further exploration or settlement inland.

With reports of Spanish successes in the New World, the French and English soon began to send out explorers and establish colonies. They concentrated their efforts in the north. The winters there were treacherous, but the rewards were great.

You learned in Chapter 7 that Europeans left the Old World for the New for several reasons. Some came to discover wealth and become rich. Religion was another motivation for coming to the Americas. Many came to escape the religious persecution they had experienced in Europe.

The French in the Far North

In 1534 the French king sent explorer **Jacques Cartier** (kar TYAY) to find riches in the New World and a water route to China. While he did not find riches or a route to China, Cartier made several trips and discovered the St. Lawrence River. He also made contacts with several Indian tribes with whom the French would later establish trade. Cartier traveled farther into modern Canada and built a settlement in modern Montreal.

Samuel de Champlain was another major French explorer. He discovered two of the Great Lakes (Ontario and Huron) and Lake

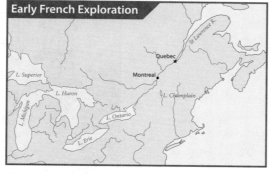

Early French Exploration

St. Lawrence R.
Quebec
Montreal
L. Superior
L. Michigan
L. Huron
L. Champlain
L. Ontario
L. Erie

Section II

Objectives

Students should be able to

1. Identify the differences between French colonization and English colonization.
2. Evaluate the role of religion in the founding of many colonies in America.
3. Evaluate the importance of education in the various New World colonies.

Fur Trade in North America

The fur trade in Canada began as a by-product of the early explorers' search for an all-water route through North America to China. Over a period of years, hats made from beaver skins, with the closely-trimmed fur on the outside, became the fashion in many parts of Europe and created a demand for thousands of beaver pelts. Wildcat, rabbit, fox, wolverine, and otter pelts were also prized for their beauty and warmth.

Fur trappers by the hundreds set out to meet the demand for beaver and other furs. Since the prices were best for the highest-quality pelts, these hardy men trapped in winter. Trappers were willing to face difficult conditions because they could make over a 1,000 percent profit on the furs they took. A trapper might bring back more than sixty canoes loaded with furs and clear almost $40,000 in one trip. In those days, that much money could make the trapper a very rich man.

The fur trade had another source of furs besides the European trappers: barter

---

Section Quiz Answers

1. Line of Demarcation
2. creoles
3. These were Portuguese nobles who were given total control of the land and its distribution. They also defended and taxed their territories.
4. peninsulares
5. the Roman Church
★ Genesis 1:27 states that humans are made in God's image. Thus all humans are precious in the sight of God and should be treated justly. The Portuguese and Spanish, however, oppressed the native peoples and treated the creoles unfairly. Mark 12:30–31 states

that every person should love others as much as he loves himself.

Reasons for Immigrating

Discuss with the students reasons why Old World residents viewed the New World as more desirable than the Old. (This information will be covered in the text, but it will set the tone for the reading of this section.)

CD: 8C Early French Exploration

This map from the student text is also available on the CD.

Activity 2: Map Study: Early American Colonization

This map exercise will help the students locate important sites of the early colonial period.

Jacques Cartier

Visit www.bjupress.com/resources for possible links to articles about Jacques Cartier.

Samuel de Champlain

Visit www.bjupress.com/resources for possible links to articles about Samuel de Champlain.

with the Indians. Indians gave the traders a rich supply of animal pelts in exchange for metal knives, axes, guns, woven blankets, cloth, and trinkets.

The trappers and Indians were so thorough that they almost eradicated the American beaver. Not only were the harvested furs worth fortunes, but the territorial claims based on their fur-seeking expeditions were worth much more. The fur trade itself was so lucrative that claims on fur-trapping areas caused international disputes until the end of the nineteenth century.

Jamestown

The site of the first permanent English settlement was a swampy, mosquito- and fly-infested area. The settlers insisted on wearing their woolen coats and linen shirts even in the extreme heat of the summer. The best thing about the location was that it gave the English claim to all the lands touching the Chesapeake Bay.

Champlain, but Champlain's greatest legacy may have been his love for the French frontier. He was given the title **Father of New France**.

A New World for the English

The English began to settle the New World after the Spanish and French had already claimed regions of it. English nobles and private companies sponsored settlements from the Carolinas to Massachusetts. Early efforts often met with failure, but ships continued to bring colonists to the New World and settlements began to survive. Many of the early settlers were not properly equipped to carve out settlements from the wilderness, and others were not willing to work and help make the venture a success. Strong leadership by men such as **John Smith** and **Sir Thomas Dale** turned the **Jamestown** settlement into a thriving colony.

In addition to fishing and farming, the colonists developed **cash crops** (crops which could be sold for cash or supplies) with the introduction of tobacco in 1614 and indigo, a plant used to make blue dye, in 1744. These crops enabled settlers to pay off their debts in England and develop a thriving economy in the New World.

Another group sailed to the New World in 1620 and landed near modern Plymouth, Massachusetts. Several of those who arrived on this ship came to escape persecution, to establish a place to bring up their children, and to advance missions. They were the **Pilgrims**. Since they landed in a region unclaimed by the Virginia Company in England, they were free to establish the colony according to their religious convictions. They set up a legal system that included trial by jury, and a free market system where prices were set by individuals, not the government.

The Pilgrims had less difficulty with the local Indians than some of the other colonies for two reasons. Just prior to the arrival of the Pilgrims, the Indian tribes had been decimated by a plague. The sur-

English Settlements

The Pilgrims leaving England

Activity 3: Why the Pilgrims Left the Netherlands

This original source account by Bradford explains why the Pilgrims chose to brave danger and hardship rather than remain in the relative safety of the Netherlands.

 CD: 8D English Settlements

This map from the student text is also available on the CD.

viving Indians were too weak to pose a serious threat. In addition, the Pilgrims treated the Indians with respect and shared the gospel with them. When the Indians were willing to do so, the Pilgrims made alliances with them in order to maintain peace.

The English settlements differed from French and Spanish settlements in three important ways. Most of the English colonists came under private investors, not government sponsorship. The English colonists brought their families with them, and most English colonists who came were Protestants. However, the English settlements were similar to the French and Spanish in that they found, instead of Eden, a hostile and unfamiliar environment filled with dangers, challenges, and adventures.

Religion and Education

When Columbus made his voyage to the New World, he asked King Ferdinand and Queen Isabella to set it aside for Roman Catholics alone. But God ordained that people of other faiths would come to the New World. Their religious convictions would affect every area of life in this new land.

Religion in North America

Many people traveled to the New World for religious reasons. Many of the English settlers came in order to establish a society based on biblical principles rather than remain in a society that retained some false practices of the Roman Catholic Church. In addition to the Pilgrims in Plymouth, the **Puritans** settled the **Massachusetts Bay Colony** (1630).

Initially, each English colony had its own **established church**, a church recognized and supported by the colony's government. In many colonies, every colonist was expected to believe the doctrine of this church and live by its teachings. Those who openly refused were often expelled from the colony. As time progressed, however, the role of the church in these colonies changed. Roger Williams, a Baptist preacher, left the Massachusetts Bay Colony because he rejected this colony's religious restrictions. Later he established the colony of Rhode Island. Williams refused to allow an established church in this colony. Soon other colonies were set up that encouraged religious pluralism, which allowed many different religions to be freely practiced in a colony. Pennsylvania was the largest of these colonies. When the colonies joined as united states after the War for Independence, the Bill of Rights prohibited the establishment of a national church. The states all eventually eliminated established churches, and religious pluralism became an American principle.

In the parts of Canada ruled by France and in the Spanish colonies, there was no religious freedom. The Roman Church controlled the religious life of these settlements and did not allow Protestantism in their lands. The Church of Rome was able to prevent other religious practices in these regions because they had the support of the government. The concept of separation of church and state was rejected in Catholic-controlled French and Spanish colonies.

Education in the New World

In the English North American colonies, education was considered important. The settlers in Massachusetts believed that education was necessary for reading Scripture, learning of God, and understanding His will. Initially, parents taught their children at home. Many parents recognized their God-given responsibility to

---

Pilgrims

These English believers had separated from the Church of England because of the worldliness and unscriptural practices in the state church. They were persecuted and forced to flee to the Netherlands, where they were allowed to worship according to their understanding of the Scripture. However, they began to worry that their children might cease to be English and might also adopt the culture and morals of the Dutch. A group of these believers traveled to the New World in 1620 and established the Plymouth colony. William Bradford served as their first governor and wrote a detailed history of the colony.

Bradford wrote of the missionary motivation of the Pilgrims:

"Last and not least, they cherished a great hope and inward zeal of laying good foundations, or at least of making some way towards it, for the propagation and advance of the gospel of the kingdom of Christ in the remote parts of the world, even though they should be but stepping stones to others in the performance of so great a work."
(*Plymouth Plantation*, Vision, 1999, p. 21.)

John Cotton was an early leader in the Massachusetts Bay Colony.

Virginia Company Settlement

As the student text states, English expeditions were privately funded. Few individual men wanted to risk their money alone on a venture, so they formed companies such as the Virginia Company. These ventures combined several people's investments. The profits were then dispersed much like stock dividends.

Failed Attempts at Communal Living

Early English colonies typically tried to practice communal living where everyone shared in the food supply. In every instance food shortages resulted. When the leaders gave land to each person or family and made them responsible to provide for their own food, food shortages ended and abundance resulted. A communal economy is socialism in a nutshell. It always fails. Free enterprise, or capitalism, always succeeds when left unfettered by government control.

Section III
Objectives

Students should be able to

1. Describe the differences in colonial participation in government between French and English colonies.
2. Analyze the reasons for discontentment in Latin American colonies.
3. Describe the roles of Simón Bolívar and José de San Martín in bringing independence to Latin America.
4. Analyze the reasons for the failure of many Latin American countries to develop into stable nations.

Typical one-room school in early settlements

teach their children (Deut. 6:7; Prov. 22:6). As villages and towns developed, one of the first buildings the settlers constructed was a one-room school. The local pastor often taught the students in early colonies. In time, a teacher was hired, and the students learned the basics of reading, writing, speaking, and mathematics. Colleges were founded to promote biblical learning and train preachers to minister to the people. Harvard and Yale were founded during these early years to prepare men for the ministry.

In the colonies where the Roman Church was strong, the colonists placed less emphasis on education. In French Canada, for example, only the wealthy pursued an education. The sons of wealthy families received a basic education in these colonies and often traveled to Europe to study in the universities. Because the Roman Church strongly discouraged Bible reading, there was little motivation to teach the poorer people to read or write. Although the Church established some schools, few people had the time or money to attend.

Section Quiz

1. What region was regarded as the Old World?
2. What religious reasons motivated the English to colonize North America?
3. The French king sent this man to find riches in the New World.
4. This type of crop could be sold or traded for supplies.
5. This group settled Plymouth, Massachusetts.
6. The Puritans settled this colony.
★ What are the benefits of permitting many religions in a country? What are the problems?

III. Struggle for Independence

Given the great distance between the mother countries and the colonies and the desire for self-rule, independence was inevitable. However, the differences between independence in North America and South America were immense.

Despite Britain's military and naval advantages, the British colonists were enabled by God to obtain their independence. The Americans were able to win their freedom through a war that, humanly speaking, was not winnable. The stable nation that emerged resulted in large part from a strong religious influence among its people.

In South America, independence came through a series of revolutions. However, the religious tyranny of the Roman Church had not prepared the people for self-rule, and instability became common for many years to come.

North America

By the mid-1700s, the English colonies between the Atlantic coast and the Appalachian Mountains contained over one million people. In contrast, only about seventy thousand settlers lived in the French territory stretching from Canada down along the Mississippi

Section Quiz Answers

1. Europe
2. to escape persecution and to establish a godly society (some may mention missions)
3. Jacques Cartier
4. cash crop
5. Pilgrims
6. Massachusetts Bay Colony
★ If any religion is tolerated, true religion is tolerated. Since true religion is persecuted in some places, this is a benefit. On the other hand, allowing any religion the right to worship and proselytize allows false teaching to spread. It also can lead to a society where tolerance is prized above truth. It is difficult to evangelize in such a society because that is seen as intolerant of other religions. Also, when all religions are tolerated, religion ceases to play a central role in society. A society cannot take seriously a cultural entity that is not unified and is filled with contradictions.

Additional Resource

Consult the *American Republic* student text for much more information about the colonial period and the War for Independence.

River to Louisiana. Fewer than eight thousand Europeans called the Spanish territories in the West and in Florida home.

Ruling the Colonies

In their new lands, European nations established colonies, which they controlled. The amount and type of control differed from colony to colony. In general, France kept a tighter hold on its colonies, while England gave its colonies more freedom for self-rule. This freedom allowed English colonies to prosper and grow at a greater rate.

William Penn and colonists at conference

Each English colony in the New World had some control over its own government. Every colony had a governor. Some were appointed by the king, but most were elected by the colonists. The governor ruled with the help of the legislature. The citizens of the colony had the right to elect members of the legislature, although citizenship was limited to free, white men who owned some property or paid taxes. The king and governor reluctantly granted more rights and privileges when the colonial legislatures withheld money. The English colonists' heritage of self-rule helped to prepare them for independence.

In contrast to the English colonists, the French colonists had little say in their government. The French king believed he should have absolute rule over his Canadian colonies just as he had over France. He appointed governors who ruled Canada without a legislature. The French Canadians had no opportunity to develop a heritage of self-rule. The king also controlled the colonies' trade and taxation. Canada's wealth supported the king's court in France rather than developing the colonies in Canada.

Independence in the Colonies

Between 1776 and 1867, most of the colonies of North America gained independence from their mother countries. The story of how the thirteen English colonies in North America became the **United States of America** is probably familiar to you. The colonists' success

Simón Bolívar

Following the death of his parents, Bolívar was under the care of his uncle, Carlos Palacio. In 1799 Uncle Carlos sent Bolívar to Spain to complete his education. During this time in Europe, Bolívar assembled several dissidents who gathered in the home of General Francisco de Miranda, a fellow Venezuelan. Miranda thought Bolívar was young and ungovernable, so when Bolívar returned home in 1807, convinced that the South American colonies were ready for independence, General Miranda gave him only a minor military position. Even though ordered not to recruit his own troops, Bolívar disobeyed and with a small army caused much damage to the Spanish forces in Venezuela.

After freeing many colonies in South America, Bolívar became gravely ill with tuberculosis. Despite this he maintained control in Peru, Columbia, and Venezuela. He also wrote constitutions for the emerging nations.

When Bolívar received the news of General Sucre's assassination in June 1830, his health declined even further. Six months later, the man who had helped Bolivia, Colombia, Ecuador, Chile, Peru, and Venezuela achieve independence died at the age of forty-seven.

Cowboys of Argentina

Like the cowboys of the western United States, the gauchos of Argentina have become a symbol of rugged independence.

The early gauchos roamed the Pampas, slaughtering wild cattle and selling the hides on the black market. Even after gaining respectability in the fight

U.S. Constitution

Visit www.bjupress.com/resources for possible links to articles about the U.S. Constitution.

The U.S. Constitution

in the **War for Independence** finally delivered them from English rule in 1783. Following a brief period of trial and error, a constitutional convention produced the **Constitution**. When the states ratified (voted to accept) the Constitution, it became the working document outlining the pattern of government. The Constitution sets down limits of power on both the government and the citizens and guarantees certain rights for the citizens.

The type of government set up by the United States recognized a biblical view of man and attempted to restrain his sinful nature. Both the government and the people are meant to be kept in check by this form of government. No one part of the government—whether it be president, legislature, or court—should have too much power. Each branch of government is designed to check the power of the others. The government then protects the people by passing and enforcing laws. Most important, the people are able to limit government by electing those who run it.

Latin America

Independence came to Latin America through numerous revolutions in the nineteenth century. The creoles had grown to resent their lack of power in the government. They saw an opportunity to gain independence while the Iberian nations fought in Europe.

Discontentment in the Spanish Colonies

Part of the colonies' dissatisfaction with Spanish rule was the control exerted by the mother country. Until the 1700s, the Spanish colonies were allowed to trade only with Spain. They could not even trade with each other. The Spanish did not limit their control to physical goods. They also tried to limit the sharing of new ideas among the colonies. The Spanish government had no desire for their subjects to accept the teachings of English and French philosophers. These teachings eventually helped revolutionary ideas take hold in America and France. The Spanish wanted to keep their colonies isolated from European influence. But that tight control only made the colonists want more information and freedom. Many secretly passed European philosophies and discontentment from person to person. This quiet network of information spread seeds of revolution.

Leaders of the Movement for Independence

The desire for independence grew stronger in Latin America. All that was missing were effective leaders to unite the various classes and defeat the Spanish. Two men are best known for their role in leading the Spanish colonies in their struggle for independence:

Simón Bolívar (boh LEE vahr) and José de San Martín (ho-ZAY day san mahr-TEEN). They are still regarded as great heroes in Latin America today.

Born in 1783 in Caracas, Venezuela, Simón Bolívar was the fourth child of Juan Vicente and Doña María Bolívar. Both his parents had died by the time Bolívar was nine. Bolívar and his brother and sisters were left in the care of an uncle.

As a boy, Bolívar learned Latin, Greek, Spanish, and French from a tutor. His tutor exposed Bolívar to the teachings of several eighteenth-century philosophers. Bolívar came to believe that freedom was the source of men's happiness. This conviction stirred the spirit of independence in his heart.

In 1810 Bolívar was sent to England as an ambassador. Despite his objections to being sent to this country, he gained valuable insight that would help him later when he wrote constitutions for the emerging Latin American nations.

Beginning in 1813, Bolívar led his troops to push the Spaniards out of Venezuela from the south, east, and west. Bolívar's men followed him through plains, deserts, swamps, and rivers. On several occasions Bolívar led his men through the Cordillera Mérida in the Andes, which rises to sixteen thousand feet in some places.

In 1816 the final move toward independence began with Venezuela and then spread to Colombia. Bolívar determined that the only way to free Venezuela was to free the entire continent of foreign rule. His greatest victories came in 1819 at the battle in Boyacá, Colombia, and in 1821 at the battle for Carabobo, Venezuela, with the support of his faithful general Antonio José de Sucre (SOO cray). In 1822 Sucre went on to free Ecuador from Spanish dominion.

While Bolívar was fighting for independence in the north, Buenos Aires, Argentina, declared its independence from Spanish control in 1810. That independence quickly spread across the country. The Argentine government then chose José de San Martín to take independence to Peru.

San Martín was born to a prominent Argentine family in 1778. At age nine he crossed the ocean to study in Spain and went on to serve in the Spanish army. In 1812 San Martín resigned from the army to help in the independence movement in South America.

Cordillera Mérida

to liberate Argentina, the gauchos maintained an independent spirit. They chose whom they worked for and roamed from place to place. In those days the Pampas were unfenced, so the gauchos drove their herds across vast stretches of prairie unhindered.

Much like the traditional American cowboy, the gaucho has a traditional outfit that consists of a wide-brimmed hat, a collared shirt, and baggy pants called *bombachas,* which are tucked into leather boots. A colorful sash or a wide leather belt decorated with silver coins or buckles goes around his waist, and round silver spurs decorate his boots. When working, a gaucho also wears a wide leather apron.

Today the way of the gaucho is fading. Fenced pastures, trucks, roads, and automation are changing the gaucho into a stationary ranch hand and farmer instead of the independent individual of the past. Traditional dress is left for festival days, when sentimental songs remind the gaucho of his glorious past.

The Golden Law of Brazil

A slave-based agricultural system was Brazil's major source of income during the 1800s. Though isolated for many years from the abolitionist movements to the north, the government finally yielded to British pressure and outlawed the slave trade in 1831. However, the wealthy landowners who depended on slave labor wielded great political power, and the slave traffic did not actually cease for over twenty years. In 1871 the parliament finally passed a bill that provided for gradual emancipation; from

Activity 4: Simón Bolívar

This activity allows students to read a source document from this period written by one of the main participants.

Simón Bolívar

Visit www.bjupress.com/resources for possible links to articles on Simón Bolívar.

Contrasting Revolutions

Have the students compare and contrast the South American revolutions and the American War for Independence.

Have the students compare and contrast the American heritage of relatively peaceful government (including transfers of power) and the South American heritage of civil wars and violence.

that time, all children born to slaves would be considered free.

The abolitionists wanted still quicker action, and in 1883 a writer published *O, Abolicionismo,* in which he argued that slavery was corrupting Brazil and would cause its downfall. In response, all slaves over sixty were freed in 1885. Finally in 1888 the parliament passed the "Golden Law of Brazil," granting all slaves their freedom and compensating their owners. Over 700,000 slaves were freed by the law. By alienating the wealthy landowners, the "Golden Law" contributed to the eventual overthrow of the monarchy and establishment of the republic.

Negative Aspects of Culture

[**Note:** Sharing this information with your students may help them answer Chapter Review question 2 under "Living in God's World."]

A powerful example of negative cultural customs that missionaries have encountered and opposed is the practice of *suttee.* This was common when missionaries such as William Carey worked in India. The Hindu widow would either voluntarily or under coercion leap onto her deceased husband's funeral pyre and be burned to death. The practice is now outlawed in India, thanks, in large part, to the efforts of Christian missionaries. However, some would object to this intervention by foreign missionaries.

Gaucho

Independent but Not Free

After obtaining independence, the Spanish colonies faced many problems in governing themselves. The wealthy landowners took over the governments and continued many Spanish policies. The only difference in their rule was that the wealth went to them rather than to Spain. The common people still had no say in government. They were no better off under these leaders than they had been under the Spanish. These weak governments were often overthrown by other strong men, called *caudillos* (kaw DEEL yohs). Most of these men ruled as dictators. Civil wars and revolts became a way of life in many of these new nations.

San Martín chose as his troops the **gauchos** (cowboys in Argentina). Although they were not disciplined, they proved to be faithful fighting companions and fought fiercely for independence. Prior to following San Martín, the gauchos had been little more than outlaws. However, their role in the fight for independence caused the people to respect the gauchos. Many of them began herding cattle for the wealthy landowners.

Unlike Bolívar, who tended to rush into battle, San Martín studied the strategies of great European generals as he made decisions about the best methods to defeat the Spanish. San Martín decided that instead of attacking the Spanish in Peru as ordered, he would cross the Andes Mountains and free Chile first. In 1817 his troops crossed the Andes and forced the Spanish from one city after another. With Chile free, San Martín turned to liberating Peru.

In August of 1820, San Martín packed troops onto ships and set sail for Pisco, Peru. It was there that San Martín received a letter from Bolívar offering his assistance in Peru's struggle for independence. San Martín's forces moved up from the south and Bolívar's troops came down from the north. Through these combined assaults, Peru was liberated from Spanish control.

Independence in Brazil

Brazil gained its independence at the same time as the other Latin American nations, but without violence. There were early stirrings of revolution supported by the upper class. However, the plans were discovered in the early stages, and the leaders were executed.

Oddly, independence came as a result of Portugal's capture by Napoleon of France. In 1807 the Portuguese royalty fled to Brazil and declared it the center of the Portuguese empire. King João (John) then adopted economic reforms to make Brazil a proper environment for the monarchy. He repealed an earlier ban on factories, introduced a trade treaty with England, established a printing press, and declared Brazil to be equal to, instead of a colony of, Portugal. All these things pushed Brazil toward independence.

In 1820 Portugal demanded that King João return. He left his son Pedro as regent of Brazil. In 1822, when Pedro was to return to Portugal, he refused. On September 7, 1822, Pedro shouted "Independence or death!" and tore the symbol of Portugal from his military uniform. He was crowned emperor of an independent Brazil as **Pedro I**.

Section Quiz

1. Which European country had the most colonists in North America by the mid 1700s?
2. What document outlines the pattern of government for the United States?
3. What man liberated Venezuela?
4. What liberator freed Chile from Spanish rule?
5. Who became the first emperor of an independent Brazil?
★ Why did many people in Latin American countries fail to get freedom when they became independent of Spain?

Bolívar and San Martín

Discuss with students the pros and cons of the different methods used by Simón Bolívar and José de San Martín as they conducted the wars for independence (rushing to battle versus studying European generals' methods).

 CD: 8E Gaucho

This photo from the student text is also available on the CD.

Section Quiz Answers

1. England
2. the Constitution
3. Simón Bolívar
4. José de San Martín

5. Pedro I
★ The wealthy landowners took over the governments and continued many Spanish policies. These weak governments were overthrown by caudillos, who ruled as dictators.

Activity 5: Chapter Review

This activity will help the students review the material from the chapter.

Chapter Review Answers
Making Connections

1. They were Roman Catholic nations and viewed the pope as the vicar or representative of Christ.

2. when their claims overlapped
3. great distance and dangerous seas
4. The Church brought complaints of the people to the donatarios and then on to officials in Portugal if the complaints were not resolved.
5. They often used their influence to overturn these reforms.
6. his discovery of several important lakes and his love for the French frontier
7. strong leadership
8. to set up a community based on scriptural principles

CHAPTER REVIEW

Making Connections

1. Why did Spain and Portugal ask the pope to decide where they could explore?
2. When did the Spanish and Portuguese argue over settlements?
3. Why was it difficult for Spain and Portugal to rule their American settlements?
4. How did the Roman Church limit the power of the donatarios?
5. How did landowners respond to reforms that were designed to protect the Indians and mestizos?
6. Why was Samuel de Champlain given the title Father of New France?
7. What did John Smith and Sir Thomas Dale provide to turn Jamestown into a thriving colony?
8. Why did the Puritans establish the Massachusetts Bay Colony?

Developing History Skills

1. Based on the information in this chapter, briefly describe the role of the Constitution of the United States.

Thinking Critically

1. Contrast the emphasis on education in the English colonies with that found in the French or Spanish colonies.
2. Based on his reading of philosophers, Simón Bolívar came to believe that freedom was the source of man's happiness. Is this a biblical conclusion? Why or why not?

Living in God's World

1. If you as a Christian had the authority to change the colonial systems set up by the Spanish and Portuguese, how would you change them in light of Genesis 1:27?
2. Some people claim that modern missions is just as bad as the mistreatment of the Native Americans by the European powers because Christians are encouraging people to abandon their own cultures to adopt a European religion. Pretend that you have been asked to defend the Christian position on a nightly news program. Write a two- to five-minute dialogue between you and a news anchor. These can then be performed in class. Be sure to deal with the following potential objections:
   - Christianity is a European religion.
   - Evangelism implies that you think you are better than those of another religion.
   - Converting people from other cultures to Christianity destroys cultures that Christians should learn to appreciate.
   - Missionaries are intolerant of other viewpoints.

People, Places, and Terms to Know

Latin America
Line of Demarcation
Treaty of Tordesillas
creoles
mother country
exported
imported
donatario
viceroy
peninsulares
New Laws of 1542
mestizos
barrios
haciendas
Old World
Jacques Cartier
Samuel de Champlain
Father of New France
John Smith
Sir Thomas Dale
Jamestown
cash crops
Pilgrims
Puritans
Massachusetts Bay Colony
established church
United States of America
War for Independence
Constitution
Simón Bolívar
José de San Martín
Antonio José de Sucre
gauchos
Pedro I
caudillos

Living in God's World

1. Genesis 1:27 teaches that all people are created in God's image. Thus there should be no discrimination based on birth or lineage. Assuming that the European conquest of the South American empires had already taken place, a Christian would make sure that native-born peoples had the opportunity to fully participate on any level of society. The colonizing country should also make independence an option. If the native peoples choose independence, the European nations could continue trade, but would need to treat the native peoples as equal trade partners. They should not oppress them with their superior military might.

2. Christianity began in Asia, not in Europe. More important, since Christianity was founded by the Son of God and is based on the Word of God, it is the religion for all nations, not just Europe.

   Christianity teaches that all humans are equally sinful and need a Savior. Evangelism is telling people how they can be saved.

   Missionaries often have a better appreciation for other cultures because they leave their own culture and live with and befriend people in another culture. Every culture has negative aspects, however, because every culture is affected by sinful people. Missionaries do hope that by seeing people transformed by Christ, the negative parts of their cultures will be transformed and the positive aspects will be strengthened. All people are intolerant of viewpoints that are clearly abusive and damaging to others. People today are offended by the human sacrifice and cannibalism practiced in the Americas during the sixteenth century. Likewise, missionaries are intolerant of viewpoints that are contrary to the Word of God.

Developing History Skills

1. Answers should include the following: It is the working document outlining the pattern of government. It limits power of both the government and the citizens while guaranteeing certain rights for the citizens. The framers had a biblical view of man and attempted to restrain his sinful nature. The goal of the Constitution is a balance between the legislative, executive, and judicial branches of government.

Thinking Critically

1. Answers should include some of the following: The English considered education important and necessary for reading Scripture, learning about God, and understanding His will. Colleges were first founded to train men for the ministry. In colonies where the Roman Church was strong, there was less emphasis on education and it was often limited to the wealthy. Since it discouraged reading the Bible, the Church was not motivated to teach the poor to read and write.

2. No. The book of Judges teaches that a people can be free (doing whatever is right in their own eyes) and still not be happy. Furthermore, such freedom can lead to political bondage and oppression. Psalm 1 teaches that true happiness comes from living in submission to God and His Word.

Chapter Goals

Students should be able to

1. Describe the rising military and bureaucratic power of some European states between the sixteenth and eighteenth centuries.

2. Explain how the Netherlands and England were exceptions to that trend of rising military and bureaucratic power.

3. Describe several of the accomplishments of the Scientific Revolution.

4. Briefly describe the Enlightenment and its significance in history.

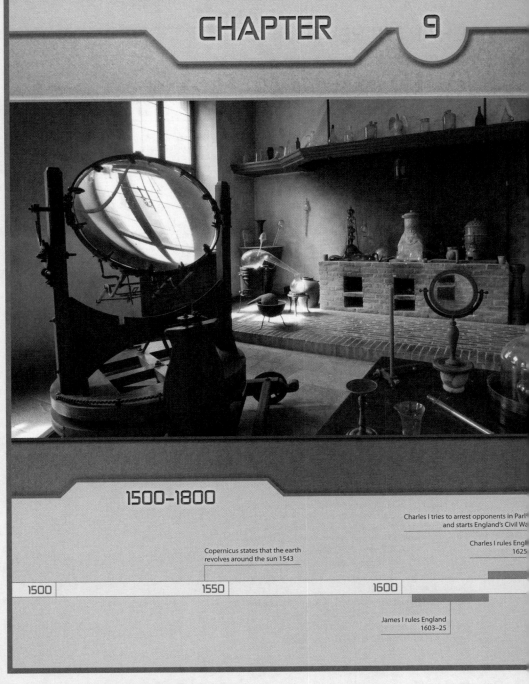

1500–1800

Copernicus states that the earth revolves around the sun 1543

Charles I tries to arrest opponents in Parl▮ and starts England's Civil Wa▮

Charles I rules Engl▮ 1625

James I rules England 1603–25

1500	1550	1600

Chapter 9 Lesson Plan Chart			
Section Title	**Main Activity**	**Pages**	**Days**
I. The Rising Power of European States	Activity 1: The English Bill of Rights	156–59	1½–2 days
II. The Scientific Revolution	Activity 2 : Galileo's Observations	159–65	1½–2 days
III. The Enlightenment	Activity 3: Matching Exercise	166–68	1 –1½ days
TOTAL SUGGESTED DAYS (INCLUDING 1 DAY EACH FOR REVIEW AND TESTING)			6–7½ days

Materials List

Section I

- CD: 9A Western Europe, 1648; 9B The English Bill of Rights

- A copy of the U.S. Declaration of Independence or the Bill of Rights

- Activity 1 from the *Student Activities* manual

Section II

- CD: 9C Antoine Lavoisier and His Wife

- Activity 2 from the *Student Activities* manual

- A copy of the periodic table of elements

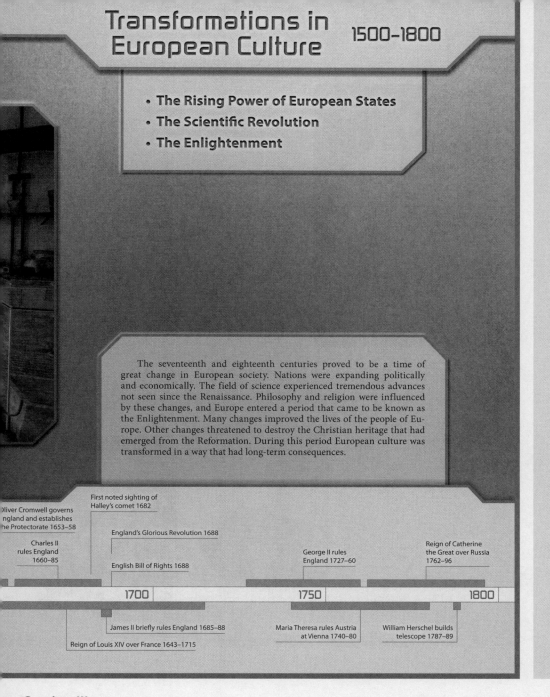

Transformations in European Culture 1500–1800

- **The Rising Power of European States**
- **The Scientific Revolution**
- **The Enlightenment**

The seventeenth and eighteenth centuries proved to be a time of great change in European society. Nations were expanding politically and economically. The field of science experienced tremendous advances not seen since the Renaissance. Philosophy and religion were influenced by these changes, and Europe entered a period that came to be known as the Enlightenment. Many changes improved the lives of the people of Europe. Other changes threatened to destroy the Christian heritage that had emerged from the Reformation. During this period European culture was transformed in a way that had long-term consequences.

Oliver Cromwell governs England and establishes the Protectorate 1653–58

First noted sighting of Halley's comet 1682

Charles II rules England 1660–85

England's Glorious Revolution 1688

English Bill of Rights 1688

George II rules England 1727–60

Reign of Catherine the Great over Russia 1762–96

1700　　**1750**　　**1800**

James II briefly rules England 1685–88

Reign of Louis XIV over France 1643–1715

Maria Theresa rules Austria at Vienna 1740–80

William Herschel builds telescope 1787–89

Section III
- Activities 3 and 4 from the *Student Activities* manual

Section I

Objectives

Students should be able to

1. Evaluate the development of strong bureaucratic monarchies in the sixteenth century.
2. Analyze how the Dutch Republic emerged as a powerful European state.
3. Explain how the English Civil War and the Revolution of 1688 affected government, religion, and society in England.
4. Analyze the impact of the English Revolution on political institutions and attitudes in the North American colonies.

Louis XIV

I. The Rising Power of European States

Countries throughout Europe profited from the growth of trade and the influence of the Renaissance and the Reformation. States such as Spain and Portugal took the lead in exploring and expanding their empires. Other nations followed their example, and European nations extended their influence around the world.

Monarchs continued to strengthen their power and increase their authority over their subjects. During the seventeenth century, rulers began to claim and exercise absolute power. Absolute monarchs sought to make all decisions for their people. This absolutism resulted in less freedom and economic opportunity for many of their citizens. Other nations chose another path and became powerful through economic and representative means. These later nations provided their citizens with greater freedom to build wealth and prosperity.

Growing Wealth and Royal Power

European countries rushed to establish colonies and take advantage of unclaimed lands to enhance the wealth and prestige of the mother country. Trade in such products as furs, fish, precious metals, and tobacco brought great wealth to these countries. At the same time, many European governments were growing in influence and power. Royal control of the colonies and taxation of the wealth from the colonies enhanced royal power.

Of all the rulers who sought to become absolute monarchs in this period, the French king **Louis XIV** (r. 1643–1715) was one of the most successful. As an absolute ruler, he had unlimited power over his people. Louis directed all of the activities in his kingdom, from major state decisions down to everyday details. In return, every activity of his subjects was designed to glorify the king. Other rul-

Powerful Women in Europe

In 1740 **Maria Theresa** (r. 1740–80) became monarch of Austria. During her reign she turned Vienna into an important center for the arts, especially music. She sought absolute power by tightening her hold on the government and by improving conditions for the peasants. Her foreign affairs policies included sending troops to fight in the wars of Europe and taking territory from Poland.

Catherine the Great (r. 1762–96) reigned in Russia and increased the power of the Russian monarchy. She also increased Russian territory, adding land in the west and south, including part of Poland. During Catherine's reign, Russia became a strong power in Europe.

Empress Maria Theresa of Austria, c.1770 by Jean-Etienne Liotard, Kunsthistorisches Museum, Vienna, Austria/The Bridgeman Art Library

Catherine the Great

Louis XIV

Visit www.bjupress.com/resources for possible links to articles about Louis XIV.

Maria Theresa

Visit www.bjupress.com/resources for possible links to articles about Maria Theresa.

ers followed Louis's example and tried to establish absolute rule over their people. Sadly, the financial and social cost of absolute monarchies was great. While these kingdoms seemed to thrive in the short term, the people suffered and these nations declined in power and prosperity.

Western Europe, 1648

Growing Wealth Without Royal Power

During the seventeenth century, the Dutch Republic of the United Provinces stunned everyone by building a vast economic empire. This nation had no centralized monarchy to forge a political or economic plan. Instead, Dutch merchants played a major role in world trade. They sent out a huge fleet of ships to establish a large colonial empire and bring great wealth to the Dutch Republic. For example, their powerful navy enabled the Dutch to end the Portuguese monopoly on trade with India and China. In a spirit of free trade, the Dutch also established a modern stock market to raise funds and finance trade. The Dutch developed a banking system to manage the wealth and enable financial business. Other countries, such as England, were quick to adopt the Dutch banking system, and English economic productivity expanded as a result.

Growing Wealth with Limited Royal Power

While nations such as France, Austria, and Russia were developing governments that gave the ruler more and more power, the English struggled to limit the power of their monarchy. In Chapter 5 you learned that Parliament gained the power to approve taxes. This power of the purse forced the king to work with Parliament in order to raise funds. However, King James I (r. 1603–25) refused to work with Parliament and built up a strong resentment between the king and Parliament.

James's son **Charles I** (r. 1625–49) followed in his father's footsteps. Charles continued to assert the divine right of kings and struggled to defeat Parliament's efforts to deny him absolute power. He also secretly supported the Church of Rome and sought to bring Scotland and England into submission to Rome. The Scots defeated Charles's forces when the English invaded Scotland, trying to force the Scottish church to use the English prayer book, which had a strong Catholic emphasis.

Charles I

Mercantilism

This was the accepted economic theory during this period. Mercantilism advocates that the prosperity of the nation depends on its supply of capital. Economic wealth is measured in quantity of gold, silver, and valuable trade. The goal of mercantilism is to enrich the country by encouraging exports and discouraging imports. For mercantilistic countries, colonies provided an outlet for their exports and income through tariffs for products brought from the colonies.

 CD: 9A Western Europe, 1648

This map from the student text is also available on the CD.

Catholic or Protestant Rulers

Discuss with the students the contrast between the past situation in England when a new king came to power and the situation in modern-day America when a new president comes to power. Whenever a new monarch came to power in England, the people whose religion differed from that of the king feared that they would be persecuted. The religious freedom that America has enjoyed has spared us from this type of fear. U.S.

presidents and other leaders have professed support for religious freedom.

Roundheads and Cavaliers

The troops who followed Charles I were known as the Cavaliers. Those who served in Parliament's army were dubbed Roundheads due to their short haircuts. In addition, Charles enjoyed the support of the Church of Rome and loyal Catholics. Parliament was composed of many Protestants, and many of those who fought in Cromwell's army were Protestants as well. They fought for religious as well as political freedom.

William of Orange

William received his title from a principality called the Country of Orange, which was first part of the Holy Roman Empire. Later it came under the control of the Dutch monarchy and eventually became part of France. In Ireland, a Protestant organization known as the Orange Order was named after William. On St. Patrick's Day members of that order wear orange to honor their Protestant heritage instead of the traditional green that represents Patrick's supposed Roman Catholic heritage.

Oliver Cromwell

Cromwell and the Protectorate

Following the capture and execution of Charles I, England experimented with new forms of government. When Parliament refused to cooperate with Cromwell, he dismissed its members in 1653 and ruled the country until his death in 1658. He called himself the Lord Protector and established the **Protectorate**. To provide some guidelines, he wrote a constitution, *Instruments of Government*. Despite his efforts to introduce a constitutional government to England, the people soon longed for a king and the restoration of the English monarchy.

English Civil War

In January 1642, Charles entered the House of Commons with several hundred soldiers and tried to arrest his opponents. They had already escaped, but this move caused both the king and Parliament to hire soldiers and prepare for battle. The **English Civil War** resulted. After the king's forces won the first battles, Parliament reorganized its forces and appointed **Oliver Cromwell** to lead their army. Cromwell defeated the king's forces and eventually took Charles into custody. Charles was tried and executed in 1649. Cromwell filled the resulting power vacuum and ruled until his death in 1658.

Shortly after Cromwell's death, the English invited **Charles II** (r. 1660–85), son of Charles I, to take the throne. Charles continued the policies of his father and grandfather. However, he was often able to ignore Parliament by raising funds from the French king Louis XIV. In exchange for French support, Charles promised to promote French foreign policy and become a Roman Catholic. When Charles died in 1685, his brother **James II** (r. 1685–88) became king. James was a strong supporter of the Roman Church, but the English tolerated him due to his advanced age. However, when his wife gave birth to a son, the English feared that their country would be ruled by Roman Catholic monarchs for many years to come. They solved the problem by inviting the son-in-law and daughter of James, both Protestants, to come to England and receive the throne.

Revolution of 1688

In June 1688, William of Orange and his wife Mary (daughter of James II) accepted England's invitation and landed in England with a small Dutch army. James found that he had no other option than to flee England. This change of power without resorting to war became known as the **Glorious Revolution**.

In exchange for this generous offer of the throne, Parliament insisted that **William and Mary** sign the **English Bill of Rights**. This

William and Mary

English Civil War

Visit www.bjupress.com/resources for possible links to articles about the English Civil War.

document set limits on royal power, provided the English people with basic civil liberties, and prevented future rulers from being Roman Catholics.

Effect on England

In addition to basic civil liberties and limits on royal power, the English moved toward a more representative government. During the reign of George II (r. 1727–60), a **cabinet** system of government developed. The men who formed the cabinet gradually answered less to the king and more to Parliament. This transferred additional power to Parliament, which had more contact with the people. Eventually, the leader of the cabinet, the prime minister, was elected by the people. These changes made the government more directly answerable to the people and more responsive to their needs.

Influence on American Colonies

The American colonists took note of the Glorious Revolution and the granting of rights to the people. They saw that the king did not have absolute power and that abuses by the king could be resisted. When the king and some members of Parliament decided to impose a number of taxes on the American colonies, the colonists resisted. Most taxes had been collected by colonial legislatures for many years. This intrusion by the king and Parliament threatened the independence of the Americans. The king responded by sending troops to force the colonists into submission and by suspending their freedom. However, the English had declared a standing army during time of peace to be illegal. The quartering of troops in the homes of the colonists was also illegal according to the English Bill of Rights. The colonists responded by insisting on having the same civil liberties as those found in the English Bill of Rights. When British forces invaded the colonies, the colonists fought to preserve their liberty.

Section Quiz

1. Who was the most successful of the absolute monarchs?
2. What nation built an economic empire without a centralized monarchy?
3. Who led Parliament's forces during the English Civil War?
4. What event resulted in the Revolution of 1688 in England?
5. How did the cabinet system of government benefit the English people?
★ How did the English Bill of Rights influence the American colonies?

II. The Scientific Revolution

The seventeenth and eighteenth centuries in Europe are often called the **Age of Reason**. During this period, men learned about many things by studying the world around them. This study was based on reason, the ability to think clearly and logically. The book of Genesis reminds us that God created man with a mind that could reason. However, because of the Fall and man's sinful nature, human reason can lead people into error. For example, during the Age of Reason, many people came to believe that reason could replace faith in the Bible. Although many good things came out of this period,

English Bill of Rights

English Bill of Rights

This document prohibited the king from

"assuming and exercising a power of dispensing with and suspending of laws";

"raising and keeping a standing army within [his] kingdom in time of peace . . . and quartering soldiers contrary to law";

"causing several good subjects being Protestants to be disarmed at the same time when papists [are] both armed and employed contrary to law."

Cabinet Government

George of Hanover (Germany), a descendant of James I, became king of England in 1714. He could speak no English and relied on English advisors to conduct most of the tasks of government. These advisors or ministers later developed into a cabinet (committee) headed by a prime minister. Gradually, many of the powers of the king shifted to the cabinet.

Cabinet Forms of Government

The American and British governments both have cabinets. The American cabinet system is composed of the senior federal officials in the executive branch, who are appointed by the president. The British system is also composed of senior government ministers who are chosen by the prime minister.

A significant difference is that the American cabinet answers to the president and is part of the executive branch of government, while the British cabinet answers to Parliament, which is the legislative branch of government. In addition, members of the British cabinet must be selected from Parliament, while American cabinet members cannot serve in Congress and the cabinet at the same time.

Section II

Objectives

Students should be able to

1. Explain the connections between the Scientific Revolution and previous civilizations and movements.
2. Describe the astronomical discoveries and innovations from Copernicus to Newton.
3. Evaluate the importance of discoveries in medicine, mathematics, and chemstry.
4. Explain the development and significance of scientific methodology.
5. Analyze how the Scientific Revolution diminished the reputation of Christianity in the public square.

CD: 9B The English Bill of Rights

The text of this document is available on the CD.

Activity 1: The English Bill of Rights

This activity requires the students to read an excerpt from the document and then answer questions about it.

Comparing Early American Documents

If you are able to obtain a copy of the Declaration of Independence or the Bill of Rights, have the students look for points of comparison with the English Bill of Rights.

Section Quiz Answers

1. Louis XIV
2. Republic of the United Provinces (the Dutch)
3. Oliver Cromwell
4. the birth of a son to James II
5. This system increased the power of Parliament and made the government more accountable to the people.
★ Answers should include the following: The English document prohibited the suspension of laws by the king, prohibited a standing army and the illegal quartering of soldiers, and protected the right to bear arms. All of these were echoed in foundational American documents.

Eratosthenes

Contrary to popular belief, people long before Columbus knew that the earth was round, not flat. Eratosthenes realized this and calculated the earth's circumference more than two centuries before Christ.

the emphasis on man's ability often turned people away from the Creator.

Contributions from the Past

Man has demonstrated an interest in the world about him since the beginning. One of the descendants of Cain, Tubalcain, is mentioned in Genesis chapter four as working with brass and iron. So the process of extracting and purifying ore to produce metals preceded the Flood. This demonstrates man's God-given ability to take parts of God's creation and press them toward the ideal. In the example from Genesis, Tubalcain took the raw ore that God had created and processed it into useful metals. Man's instinct to fulfill the Creation Mandate appears again and again in civilization. In this section we will review a few examples of this impulse.

Greeks

The Father of Medicine was a Greek physician who lived around 400 BC. **Hippocrates** (hih PAHK ruh TEEZ) rejected the popular notion that disease was a supernatural punishment by the gods. Instead, he taught that every illness has a natural cause. Rejecting magic and superstitious cures, he prescribed rest and a healthy diet as part of a treatment. The oath taken by many modern physicians is named after Hippocrates, although many changes have been made to his original oath.

Euclid (YOO klid) earned the title Father of Geometry. He founded a school of mathematics in Alexandria, Egypt, during the fourth century BC. Euclid also developed many mathematic principles that are known as Euclidean (yoo KLID ee uhn) geometry. His textbook, *Elements*, formed the basis for all geometry textbooks, including those used today.

The early Greek astronomer and geographer **Eratosthenes** (er uh TAHS thuh NEEZ) determined the distance around the earth (circumference) with great accuracy. He used Euclid's geometry to make this calculation. Eratosthenes also devised the lines of latitude and longitude found on maps today.

Muslim Science

In Chapter 2 you learned that Muslims preserved Greek and Roman scientific discoveries. In addition, they expanded knowledge in areas including medicine, optics, and chemistry. This information was passed to the Europeans through various means, including the Byzantine Empire, the Crusades, and a growing trade in Arab documents.

Medieval Science

Much of the knowledge that led to the development of science in Europe resulted from access to Muslim documents. **Albert the Great**, a Dominican friar, played an important role in introducing the documents to medieval universities. Robert Grosseteste, Bishop of London, also proved to be a central character in advancing medieval science. Grosseteste influenced one of his students, **Roger Bacon**, in the area of optics and astronomy. Bacon made significant contributions in the areas of physics, geography, and optics.

Medieval science came to a sudden halt with the appearance of the Black Death. Massive loss of life and the isolation that resulted in order to escape this plague ended the advance of science until the fifteenth century during the Renaissance.

> **Hippocractic Oath (Original)**
>
> I will prescribe regimens for the good of my patients according to my ability and my judgment and never do harm to anyone.
>
> I will not give a lethal drug to anyone if I am asked, nor will I advise such a plan; and similarly I will not give a woman a pessary [device] to cause an abortion.
>
> In every house where I come I will enter only for the good of my patients.
>
> If I keep this oath faithfully, may I enjoy my life and practice my art . . . but if I swerve from it or violate it, may the reverse be my lot.

Roger Bacon

Additional Resources: Euclid

There is an interesting article about Euclid in *Geometry* 2nd ed. (BJU Press) on page 30.

Renaissance Humanism

You learned in Chapter 6 that knowledge expanded rapidly during the Renaissance. Science enjoyed a renewal during this period as well. Traditions were questioned and various sciences developed. The discoveries of many, including Copernicus, Galileo Galilei, and William Harvey, will be discussed in the next sections. These men and others made major contributions to the fields of astronomy, medicine, mathematics, and chemistry. Some made contributions in multiple fields.

Reformation Legacy

The interest in learning about the world continued in the Reformation era. Built on the idea that God is supreme and that all claims must be tested, many new ideas, methods, and inventions were added to the scientific knowledge of this time. People questioned how and why things worked. Tradition was replaced with observation as scientists experimented, recorded findings, and reached conclusions. Several of their methods are similar to those used by scientists today.

Astronomical Discoveries and Innovations

The discoveries in astronomy that occurred during this period changed people's understanding of nature as well as the way people thought about themselves and the world. In 1543 **Copernicus** (koh PUR nuh kus) presented his view that the earth revolved around the sun, not the sun around the earth. He relied on mathematics to

Copernicus

Andreas Cellarius portrayed Copernicus's theory of the universe on a two-dimensional chart

Family Traditions

During the Renaissance, various cultural traditions were challenged. Have the students discuss various family traditions they may have. How did they come about? How were some of them changed by family circumstances (deaths, marriages, etc.)? You could expand this into a discussion of when it is best *not* to eliminate traditions as well as when it is *good* to change traditions.

Copernicus and Galileo

The discovery that the earth revolved around the sun created a theological crisis in the Roman Church. The Church had embraced the geocentric view that the earth was the center of the universe. The discoveries of Copernicus and Galileo demonstrated the error of this position. Because Copernicus (a Catholic cleric) feared persecution, he refused to publish his theory until he was almost seventy. He died shortly after the book was released. However, Galileo published his support for Copernicus's findings and was forced to go before the Inquisition and recant (take back) his findings. He spent the rest of his life under house arrest.

Herschel and Telescopes

William Herschel designed the largest telescope of his day. With it he could see deep into our solar system. Today we have modern observatory telescopes. In addition, the Hubble Space Telescope orbits above the distorting atmosphere and enables us to view distant galaxies with much greater clarity. It can also record events in space across a broad spectrum of light and wavelengths that are otherwise not visible to the human eye.

Galileo Galilei before the Inquisition

develop his theory. Another astronomer, **Galileo Galilei** (GAL-uh-LAY-oh GAL-uh-LAY), used the newly invented telescope for his observations. His results supported Copernicus's ideas.

By the time Galileo made his observations in the early 1600s, a great controversy had arisen over these ideas. People were concerned that if Copernicus and Galileo were right, the Bible must be wrong because the Bible refers, in verses such as Genesis 15:12, to the sun as appearing to move through the heavens. There was also a concern about mankind's place in the universe. If the earth—man's home—is not at the center of the universe, then perhaps man is not important in this world. This idea had great influence on thinkers in Europe in the coming centuries.

Sir Isaac Newton (1643–1727) discovered concepts that have become known as the **laws of gravity and motion**. According to these laws, gravity keeps the planets in their orbits. Among his many other accomplishments, Newton developed an advanced form of calculus (method of calculating) and invented the reflecting telescope. These contributions enabled an improved use of mathematics and more detailed observation of the universe.

English astronomer **Edmond Halley** (1656–1742) recorded the position and motion of hundreds of stars. He also developed a theory about the orbit of comets. Halley accurately predicted that a comet which appeared in 1682 would return to our solar system seventy-six years later. This comet was later named Halley's comet.

Sir William Herschel (1738–1822) spent much of his life contributing to the field of astronomy. He made many discoveries, including the planet now known as Uranus. In 1784 he began to build telescopes to sell, and many wealthy men purchased them. His large

A replica of Isaac Newton's second reflecting telescope of 1672

Activity 2: Galileo's Observations

This activity includes an excerpt from Galileo's writings.

Sir William Herschel

Visit www.bjupress.com/resources for possible links to articles about William Herschel.

telescopes enabled men to look farther out into the universe and view sights that previously could not be seen. Between 1787 and 1789 Herschel built a massive forty-foot-long telescope. With this telescope he could see several of the moons around Saturn.

Discoveries in Other Fields

While some were looking to the heavens to find new worlds, others were looking through newly invented microscopes or expanding ancient knowledge. Advances were made in many areas, including medicine, mathematics, and chemistry.

Medicine

Rejecting superstitious remedies, scientists began to investigate the body and treat its diseases. One scientist, **Paracelsus** (PEHR uh SEL sus), stated that the body is mostly chemicals and should be treated with chemicals. Other scientists studied anatomy. By learning the positions of bones, muscles, and organs, they were able to give better diagnoses and treatment. For example, **Andreas Vesalius** (vi SAY lee us) (1514–64) developed his work on human anatomy by dissecting human bodies. The Englishman **William Harvey** also made important contributions to medicine by discovering that blood is pumped by the heart, travels through the body in blood vessels, and returns to the heart in the circulatory system. Another Englishman, **Edward Jenner** (1749–1823), discovered a way to prevent people from getting a disease known as **smallpox**. This disease killed or terribly scarred many until Jenner found a way to protect against it by developing a **vaccine**, or weakened form of a similar disease known as cowpox. Jenner's research led to the practical elimination of this disease.

Mathematics

The interest in business and science encouraged improvements in mathematics. Three improvements that occurred around the time of the Renaissance were the more common use of Arabic numerals, the decimal point, and mathematical notation. Prior to this time, mathematic equations were written in standard form (every number word written out), making equations enormous and difficult to read.

During this period great advances were made in the theoretical understanding and practical application of mathematics. For example, it was vital to understand mathematics in order to explain the orbit of planets or to predict when asteroids would return to our solar system. As we noted, Sir Isaac Newton used mathematics to develop his theory of gravity.

Chemistry

You learned in Chapter 2 that Muslim scholars laid the foundation of modern chemistry. They introduced careful observation and controlled experimentation.

The Granger Collection, New York

Herschel's telescope

Collection of the University of Michigan Health System, Gift of Pfizer Inc. UMHS.23

Edward Jenner administering a smallpox vaccination (detail)

Inoculations vs. Vaccinations

The practice of inoculation (purposely infecting a person in a controlled environment to develop immunity) was practiced long before vaccinations (exposing a person to a weakened or dead form of the disease) were developed by Jenner. Two notable American Christian leaders supported inoculation to protect against disease in a day when this procedure was misunderstood and very unpopular.

Cotton Mather, a famous Puritan leader in Boston, took a great risk and made many enemies by supporting the use of inoculation to stop the spread of smallpox. Many believed that this procedure poisoned the recipients rather than protected them. Mather's home was set on fire by opponents of inoculation, and he endured much opposition because of his support for this medical procedure.

Jonathan Edwards, the great New England theologian, also supported the principle of inoculation and allowed physicians to inoculate him as an example. Unfortunately, his health was frail, and he died from the smallpox inoculation soon after receiving it.

Medicine

Have a volunteer study the concepts of inoculations and vaccines and report their findings to the class.

🕸 Edward Jenner

Visit www.bjupress.com/resources for possible links to articles about Edward Jenner.

Over time, these scholars discovered many chemicals. Chemistry became important in Europe as a result of repeated plagues. Men labored with various substances to develop medicines that would prevent or cure diseases.

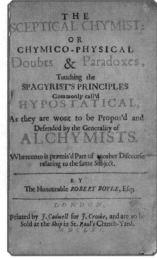

Left, title page of Robert Boyle's work *The Sceptical Chymist*; *right*, Robert Boyle

Robert Boyle (1627–91) contributed to chemistry with his work on gases that produced **Boyle's law**. His book *The Sceptical Chymist* was foundational for modern chemistry. Boyle was also a Christian who lectured in defense of Christianity. He actively opposed the enemies of Christianity who arose during the Enlightenment.

Antoine Lavoisier (luh VWAH zee AY) (1743–94) is known as the Father of Modern Chemistry. His many contributions include naming oxygen and hydrogen and working to develop the metric system. Lavoisier formulated the law of conservation of matter. This law states that matter cannot be created or destroyed. Rather, it can only change form. Lavoisier also assembled the first-known list of elements.

Scientific Methodology

The scientific method refers to a pattern of steps that scientists use to answer questions about the physical world. These steps may vary, and their order may differ depending on the circumstance. However, they are designed to produce accurate and provable answers to the questions that scientists encounter. The steps may include the formation of an initial theory, experimentation to test the theory, collection of information, revision of the theory, and repetition of the experiments to prove the accuracy of the theory.

Antoine Lavoisier and his wife

Periodic Table

Show the students a large copy of the periodic table. Discuss how it is used and how it has changed over the years as scientists have discovered more elements.

 CD: 9C Antoine Lavoisier and His Wife

This photo from the student text is also available on the CD.

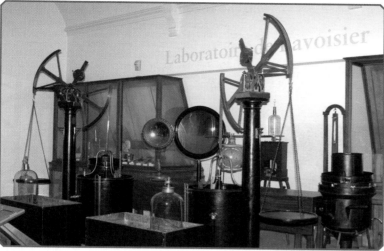
Lavoisier's laboratory

Development

In Chapter 2 you learned about the Muslim scientist known as Alhazen. He was one of the first to develop a scientific methodology in his research on light. He demonstrated this process in his *Book of Optics.* Many of the people already mentioned in this chapter developed their own procedures to answer questions and prove their theories through observation and experimentation.

Significance

Myths and legends were disproved as scientists developed these methods and discovered many workable models to explain creation. Astronomical discoveries were made, and men developed a greater appreciation for the vastness and beauty of God's handiwork. Medicines were developed and diseases were diagnosed and treated. Advances were made in many fields, and the lives of many were extended or improved. At its best, scientific methodology contributed to the advance of learning in many areas. However, the seeds of doubt were planted regarding the truthfulness of God's Word. Europeans were being encouraged to trust human reasoning and observation more than the Bible.

Section Quiz

1. What early example of pressing creation toward the ideal is found in Genesis 4?
2. Who was the Father of Medicine, and what did he reject?
3. Who determined the circumference of the earth?
4. Who first declared that the earth revolves around the sun?
5. Who developed a vaccine for smallpox?
★ Why did the theory of a sun-centered solar system create such alarm?

Section Quiz Answers

1. Tubalcain's work with brass and iron
2. Hippocrates; the notion that disease was a punishment by the gods
3. Eratosthenes
4. Copernicus
5. Edward Jenner
★ It appeared to contradict the Bible and threatened man's position as the center of the universe.

Section III

Objectives

Students should be able to

1. Explain the connections between the Enlightenment and other movements such as the Renaissance, the Protestant Reformation, and the Scientific Revolution.
2. Explain the principal ideas of the Enlightenment (including rationalism, secularism, and empiricism).
3. Assess the impact of Enlightenment ideas on modern institutions.

The Enlightenment

This movement arose as philosophers proposed that—apart from the Bible—human reason, human sensory experience, or both provided a sure guide to truth.

Rationalism

Rationalists propose that most or all knowledge can be discovered through the use of reason alone. They believe that truth is logical and may be revealed through deductive reasoning. Benedict de Spinoza became a leading proponent of rationalism.

Secularism

Secularists believe that entities (including government and education) should not be influenced by religion or religious beliefs. They seek a society that is free from religious rule and teachings.

Empiricism

Empiricists believe that knowledge is gained from evidence gathered through

III. The Enlightenment

The very name *Enlightenment* shows how the philosophers and scientists of this period viewed the previous eras. To them, earlier periods were covered in darkness and urgently needed the new ideas of this new era. Those ideas came from the belief that human reason and careful observation were the only sure ways to know the truth. Freed from devotion to the past, these people re-examined the values and religious beliefs of Europe. This period introduced many political and social changes that were important to democratic societies, but it also undermined the central role of Christianity in the culture of Europe. Europe would never be the same.

Leading Ideas of the Enlightenment

While a student, **René Descartes**, (day KART) (1596–1650) read many of the classics recovered by the Renaissance, but he found them to be as weak as structures built on sand. Descartes noted that philosophy settled nothing. Instead, every philosophical point was debated. And though Descartes professed to be a good Catholic, he realized that the Reformation showed that even theology was a matter of great dispute. Descartes also concluded that man can even be deceived by what he observes through his senses and through experiments. To demonstrate this, Descartes pointed to the foolishness of alchemy and astrology. He decided that only mathematics led to certainty. This belief motivated Descartes to develop a method for knowing truth that was based on mathematics. He proposed doubting everything except basic axioms (statements about which there can be no doubt). Working from the axiom, one should then reason through all the issues until truth is established.

Because Descartes did not trust any path to truth except human reason, his approach is a form of **rationalism.** This approach to truth was very different from the previous thousand years of European history. During most of this time, reason had been a servant to the teachings of the Roman Church. In Reformation churches, philosophies like those of Plato and Aristotle were even less influential because the Reformers stressed the supremacy of Scripture in determining truth.

Descartes insisted that he was not trying to undermine Christianity. But the Dutch philosopher Benedict de Spinoza applied Descartes's approach to the foundation of the Christian faith, the Bible. **Spinoza** doubted that the Bible was any different than any other book. He doubted everything in Scripture that he thought contrary to reason, and Spinoza thought almost everything in Scripture was contrary to reason.

Unlike Descartes, **John Locke** (1632–1704) believed that rationalism was insufficient. He insisted that the ideas Descartes found axiomatic (obvious) were not implanted by God in the human mind (as Descartes had claimed) but were developed through careful observation of the world. Locke argued in favor of **empiricism**, the belief that the best way to find true knowledge was through experience rather than through human reason. Instead of arriving at truth through a sequence of careful reasoning, the empiricist observes the world around him to determine truth. The scientific revolution seemed to strengthen the case for empiricism. For example, close observation of nature resulted in important discoveries like Newton's formulation of the concept of gravity.

René Descartes

Spinoza

Activity 3: Matching Exercise

This activity is designed to help the students learn the names and accomplishments highlighted in the chapter. You might want to use it as a class review.

The Enlightenment

Visit www.bjupress.com/resources for possible links to articles about the Enlightenment.

René Descartes

Visit www.bjupress.com/resources for possible links to articles about René Descartes.

Influence of the Enlightenment

No single enlightenment philosophy gained prominence over another. Other philosophers disputed Locke's arguments for empiricism. Various people responded to Spinoza's atheism and skepticism. The debates raised in the Enlightenment have not, even to this day, been resolved with one side clearly victorious over the other. However, key ideas that are commonly accepted today find their origins in the Enlightenment.

Democratic Thought and Institutions

Despite disagreements about various philosophies, Enlightenment thinkers shared a democratic urge. Before the Enlightenment, people accepted that God had given them rulers and overseers in both the state and the church. Because wrong ideas could condemn souls to eternal punishment, rulers worked with ministers to prohibit books that promoted heretical teaching.

Enlightenment ideas challenged not only Christian orthodoxy but also the very idea that anyone should attempt to regulate the ideas of a nation. Descartes taught that all people have the same reasoning capacity (though some use it better than others). If this is true, then why should some men decide what others may or may not read?

Spinoza argued tirelessly for the toleration of all ideas. He insisted that all men were created with certain rights and that the purpose of the state was actually to protect the citizens' freedom. Spinoza believed that religion limits liberty and does not tolerate contrary views. As a result, he argued it was the responsibility of the state to limit the influence of the church for the sake of liberty. Spinoza especially wanted the state to lessen the influence of Christianity in education. What Spinoza really desired was **secularism**, that is, a society free from religion.

Many Christians were suspicious of secularism. They feared that a government without religious influence would be unjust and evil. Those who cried the loudest for freedom rejected a biblical basis for morality and rejected the Bible's teaching about the sinfulness of man. These same philosophers rejected the core biblical principle of salvation through Jesus Christ. Some were even atheists, denying the existence of God.

Christian support for religious toleration and representative forms of government developed first in the North American colonies. Many of the first-generation colonists had fled some kind of religious persecution. This experience, combined with opposition to the abuses of Great Britain, led many Christians in America to accept the ideas of toleration and religious freedom that had been resisted in Europe.

Corruption of Christianity in Culture

As Enlightenment thought became increasingly accepted, it threatened the dominant place of Christianity in Europe. Rationalists questioned whether miracles were reasonable. Empiricists wondered why miracles were not observed today if they had happened before. Also, science seemed to be able to explain in natural terms events that people had long considered supernatural. By Enlightenment standards, the Bible's claims about a God Who providentially works His will in all things were unreasonable.

Scholars influenced by the Enlightenment—including ministers and professors—began to study the Bible not as Scripture but as any

John Locke

sensory experience. They emphasize the role of experience in determining truth.

Decline of the Roman Church

By the end of the Middle Ages, the Roman Catholic Church suffered from both moral and theological decay. The Renaissance exposed many of its weaknesses. For instance, the Donation of Constantine, on which the church based it claims of temporal power, was shown to be a forgery. The recovery of Greek and Hebrew along with an emphasis on the study of original sources brought about a renewed study of Scripture in the original languages. This study produced the Protestant Reformation. The recovery of right doctrine among believers undermined the authority of Roman Catholicism. No longer would the word of the pope or the council be considered supreme in Europe.

Division in the Reformation

The Reformers argued that the Word of God was supreme. However, Lutherans, Reformed, Ecclesial Anabaptists, and other groups argued over the right interpretation of some aspects of Scripture. When various princes aligned themselves with Protestants or the Catholic Church, wars broke out among them. Though orthodox Protestants could demonstrate that on the core doctrines of Christianity they were united, to outsiders it looked as though neither the Church nor Scripture had the authority or ability to determine truth.

John Locke

Visit www.bjupress.com/resources for possible links to articles about John Locke.

other religious book. They compared it with other religions in the Middle East and looked for evidence of contradictions. These theologians claimed the Bible had been stitched together by men long after the period when the biblical books themselves claimed to have been written. Spinoza pioneered this approach to Scripture. His goal was to convince philosophers to abandon the use of Scripture in philosophy.

Those who wished to defend Christianity often failed to attack the false theories at the root of Enlightenment thought. Instead of rejecting the idea that reason or sense experience are sufficient to determine truth and asserting the necessity of revelation, these defenders tried to reveal the truth of Christianity on the terms set by the Enlightenment. What often resulted was not true Christianity but some form of deism that fell far short of Christianity as revealed in Scripture.

Section Quiz

1. What did Descartes conclude about the philosophy he had studied as a student?
2. According to Descartes, what leads to certainty?
3. Rationalism teaches that _____ _____ provides a path to truth.
4. John Locke rejected rationalism in favor of _____.
5. Spinoza argued for the _____ of all ideas.
★ Why were Christians suspicious of secular pleas for government that was not influenced by religion?

Section Quiz Answers

1. He found it as weak as a structure built on sand.
2. mathematics
3. human reason
4. empiricism
5. toleration
★ The secularists rejected Scripture as a biblical basis for morality, and Christians feared that a secular government would be unjust and evil.

Activity 4: Chapter Review

This activity will help the students review the chapter content.

Chapter Review Answers

Making Connections

1. loss of individual freedom, limited economic opportunities, national decline
2. They raised an army to defend against his forces.
3. He developed a vaccine for smallpox and virtually eliminated this deadly disease.
4. They rejected the Bible as the source of truth and concluded that human reason alone could reveal truth.
5. During most of the previous thousand years, reason had been a servant to the teachings of the Roman Church.
6. through careful observation of the world
7. because all people have the same reasoning capacity
8. Advocates of Enlightenment reasoning questioned the reality of miracles and claimed to explain events that had long been considered supernatural in natural terms. They also considered the Bible's claims about God to be unreasonable.

Developing History Skills

1. 1603—James I; 1625—Charles I; 1653—Oliver Cromwell; 1660—Charles II; 1685—James II; 1688—William and Mary; 1714—George I; 1727—George II

CHAPTER REVIEW

Making Connections

1. What was the long-term effect on a nation ruled by an absolute monarch?

2. How did Parliament respond to threats of arrest by Charles I?

3. How did Edward Jenner's observations and experiments result in the saving of many lives?

4. How did men use science to challenge the authority of Scripture?

5. How did Descartes's approach to truth differ from that of the previous thousand years?

6. According to John Locke, how is truth discovered?

7. Why should the ideas of a nation not be regulated, according to Enlightenment reasoning?

8. Why did Enlightenment thought threaten the dominant place of Christianity in Europe?

Developing History Skills

1. Using the information provided in this chapter, develop a timeline of English rulers.

2. Historians are divided in their appraisal of Cromwell. How should a historian work through this debate?

Thinking Critically

1. Read the excerpts from the Hippocratic oath on page 160 and write down several issues that Hippocrates addressed. Are any of these issues currently being debated in our society?

2. Does the Bible support the divine right of kings? Provide references to support your answer.

3. Why are reason and/or experience not sufficient to judge the truthfulness of Scripture?

Living in God's World

1. Imagine that you are sharing the gospel with someone who protests that the Bible is full of errors. The person notes specifically that Joshua 10:12–13 speaks of the sun's stopping in the sky, which implies that the sun, rather than the earth, is moving. How would you respond? Include Psalm 50:1 in your answer.

2. Individually, or as small groups, research an Enlightenment figure (Descartes, Spinoza, Locke, Newton, Hume, Rousseau, Voltaire, Leibniz). Present a brief report to the class that explains the philosopher's belief along with a Christian response.

People, Places, and Terms to Know

Louis XIV
Maria Theresa
Catherine the Great
Charles I
English Civil War
Oliver Cromwell
Protectorate
Charles II
James II
Glorious Revolution
William and Mary
English Bill of Rights
cabinet
Age of Reason
Hippocrates
Euclid
Eratosthenes
Albert the Great
Roger Bacon
Copernicus
Galileo Galilei
Sir Isaac Newton
laws of gravity and motion
Edmond Halley
Sir William Herschel
Paracelsus
Andreas Vesalius
William Harvey
Edward Jenner
smallpox
vaccine
Robert Boyle
Boyle's law
Antoine Lavoisier
René Descartes
rationalism
Spinoza
John Locke
empiricism
secularism

---

2. Answers might include some of the following: The historian should read widely so he knows both points of view. He should investigate primary sources. He should evaluate Cromwell (and the historians writing about him) according to a biblical worldview.

Thinking Critically

1. Harm no one; do not perform doctor-assisted suicide; do not perform abortion; seek the good of the doctor's patients. Yes, these are current issues.

2. Answers will vary. No, the Bible does not support the divine right of kings. Passages such as Romans 13 and 1 Peter 2 teach Christians to be subject even to wicked kings as long as those kings do not require a violation of God's law. Nonetheless, the Old Testament is clear that kings themselves were subject to the Mosaic Law (Deut. 17:14–20). The Bible would thus support a system in which the king is bound by a constitution. Furthermore, biblical principles such as the depravity of man point toward the wisdom of placing checks on a ruler's power.

3. Answers will vary. Humans do not know all, and thus reason cannot serve as an infallible guide to truth. Because of the Fall, human reason is often distorted to defend error. Debates between philosophers demonstrate this. Both sides use reason, yet at least one must be wrong. Experience is not sufficient because humans cannot observe all things. Furthermore, their senses can deceive them in what they do observe. Reason and experience are tools from God that He has given us to help us make sense of the world, but unless they are guided by a word from the Creator (found in Scripture), they are bound to lead away from and not to the truth.

Living in God's World

1. Explain that the Bible speaks of these events in terms of how they appear. For instance, the Bible also speaks of the sun rising and setting (Psalm 50:1), just as we do today. When people today speak of the sun rising and setting, they are speaking in terms of appearance, not science. This same liberty must be extended to Scripture as well.

2. Reports will vary with each student.

1550–1900

Alvaro de Mendaña discovers the Solomon Islands 1567	Mendaña and Pedro Fernández de Quirós discover the Marquesas Islands 1595	Abel Tasman begins exploration trip for the Dutch 1642

1550	1600	1650	1700

Tasman charts and maps out sections of Australia's western coastline 1644

Chapter 10 Lesson Plan Chart

Section Title	Main Activity	Pages	Days
I. The Islands of Oceania	Activity 1: John G. Paton	172–74	1 day
II. Early Exploration	Map Activity	175–77	1–1½ days
III. European Exploration in the 1700s	Activity 3: James Cook's Journal	178–79	1 day
IV. European Settlements in Australia	Activity 4 : Chapter Review	180–85	2–2½ days
TOTAL SUGGESTED DAYS (INCLUDING **1** DAY EACH FOR REVIEW AND TESTING)			5–6 days

Materials List

Section I
- An outline drawing of Texas (see p. 172)
- CD: 10A *Kon-Tiki*
- Activities 1 and 2 from the *Student Activities* manual.

Section II
- A large world map

Section III
- Activity 3 from the *Student Activities* manual

Oceania and Australia

1600–1900

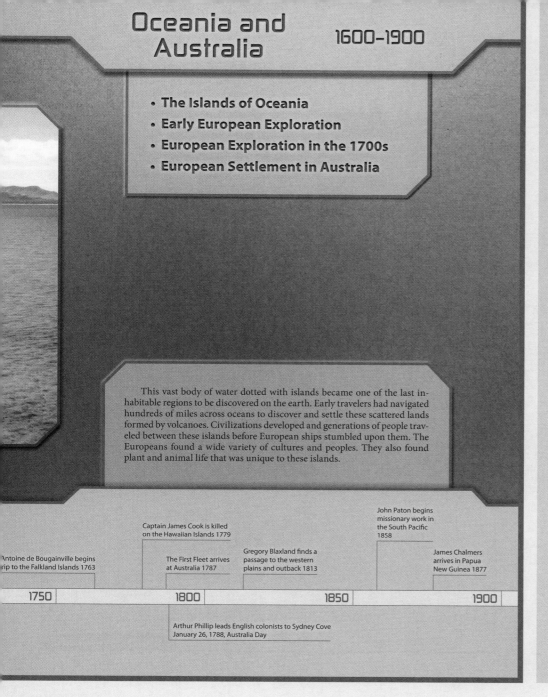

- **The Islands of Oceania**
- **Early European Exploration**
- **European Exploration in the 1700s**
- **European Settlement in Australia**

This vast body of water dotted with islands became one of the last inhabitable regions to be discovered on the earth. Early travelers had navigated hundreds of miles across oceans to discover and settle these scattered lands formed by volcanoes. Civilizations developed and generations of people traveled between these islands before European ships stumbled upon them. The Europeans found a wide variety of cultures and peoples. They also found plant and animal life that was unique to these islands.

Antoine de Bougainville begins trip to the Falkland Islands 1763

Captain James Cook is killed on the Hawaiian Islands 1779

The First Fleet arrives at Australia 1787

Gregory Blaxland finds a passage to the western plains and outback 1813

John Paton begins missionary work in the South Pacific 1858

James Chalmers arrives in Papua New Guinea 1877

| 1750 | 1800 | 1850 | 1900 |

Arthur Phillip leads English colonists to Sydney Cove January 26, 1788, Australia Day

Chapter Goals

Students should be able to

1. Identify the islands of Oceania.
2. Describe the original discovery and colonization of these islands.
3. Survey European exploration of the Pacific islands, including Australia.
4. Provide an overview of discovery, colonization, and impact of European contact with the native peoples.
5. Trace the development of English settlements into the nation of Australia.

Section IV

- CD: 10B Didgeridoos; 10C Eucalyptus Trees; 10D Cabbage Palm Tree; 10E The Outback; 10F Australian History; 10G Australia and New Zealand
- Activity 4 from the *Student Activities* manual

Section I

Objectives

Students should be able to

1. Identify the characteristics of high and low islands.
2. List the three groups of Pacific islands.
3. Evaluate the efforts of John Paton and James Chalmers.

Pacific Water Transportation

Most early canoes in the Pacific were dugouts made from hollowed-out logs. These canoes were used on rivers and streams. However, ocean travel required some adjustments.

The small island trees resulted in narrow canoes that were somewhat unstable. Islanders solved this problem by adding an outrigger (a long, thin float that ran parallel to the canoe). From this basic design Pacific islanders developed their own distinct models. Around Indonesia and the Torres Strait, the people used a double rigger canoe. On New Caledonia and Fiji, the people developed catamarans made from two hulls lashed together. In some parts of New Guinea, the people placed several dugouts next to each other, lashed them together, and placed a flat deck on top. Some added a sail. Some traditional canoes can still be seen in the Pacific islands.

High island

Low island

I. The Islands of Oceania

During the exploration of the Pacific in the 1700s and 1800s, many of the Pacific islands were discovered and claimed by Europeans. The island people of the Pacific had developed interisland trade and navigation many years before the Europeans arrived. The people of these islands saw no need for European discovery and did not want to be claimed by other nations. However, the Europeans used many of these islands to supply their trade ships sailing from the Orient.

Defining the Islands

The islands of Oceania lie east of the Philippines and south of Japan. If all the islands were combined, they would be about the size of the state of Texas. The largest island is New Guinea, and half of it is claimed by Indonesia. Some of the islands have achieved independence, while others are still territories of other countries.

There are two types of islands in the Pacific—**high islands** and **low islands**. The high islands are composed of volcanic mountains and volcanic debris; the low islands are composed of coral remains that developed on submerged volcanoes. The resources of each type of island greatly affect the lifestyle of the inhabitants.

High islands tend to be better for people and agriculture. The high altitude of volcanic mountains allows the islands to capture moisture from the warm ocean breezes. As the air travels across the island, it rises over the mountains, cools, and then releases its moisture in rain or snow. Consistent moisture makes it easier to grow crops, and mountain streams provide plentiful drinking water. High island soil is fertile volcanic soil that makes plants more productive. This steady agricultural supply provides a stable economy for the people. When explorers were sailing around the Pacific, they were much more likely to find needed supplies on high islands.

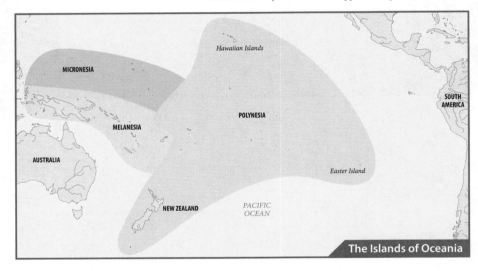
The Islands of Oceania

Pacific Islanders

Discuss possible reasons that the islanders did not desire contact with Europeans. Point out that the islanders found everything they needed on their islands or traded with other islands for needed items. These native peoples had survived for many generations before the Europeans arrived and had no desire to be "discovered" or claimed by the Europeans.

Making Comparisons

Make an outline of Texas the same scale as a map of the Pacific Islands and overlay it on the Pacific map to show comparative sizes.

Historical Fallacy

Have the students offer theories about why European historians originally thought that the islanders could not have traveled to distant islands across the open ocean. (*The Europeans thought the native peoples were not intelligent or sophisticated enough to navigate these great distances.*) What lessons can we learn about making historical assumptions? (*They are often proven to be wrong.*)

Low islands, on the other hand, tend to be drier. The low profile of these islands results in much less rainfall. Coral sand lacks the nutrients needed to grow most crops. Therefore, people living on these islands are more dependent on fishing as a food supply. Low islands also tend to suffer greater damage from tropical storms and high waves.

Another way of defining the Pacific islands is by the geographic groups of **Melanesia**, **Micronesia**, and **Polynesia**. Melanesia is named after the dark-skinned people who live in the region. It includes Papua New Guinea, the Solomon Islands, and Fiji. Micronesia ("small islands") is north of Melanesia and east of the Philippines. Most of Micronesia's more than two thousand islands are small and low. Some are less than one square mile in size. Polynesia ("many islands") lies within the great triangle formed by the Hawaiian Islands, Easter Island, and New Zealand.

Original Discovery and Colonization

Some scientists have theorized that the islands of the Pacific were first colonized from the west. They believe that Indonesians and Asians first made their way to New Guinea and then "island hopped" across the Pacific.

Scientists who support this theory offer at least three observations about these islands. First, the archaeological record (remains of buildings) of New Guinea shows earlier civilizations than the other islands in the Pacific. Second, the languages of the island people are similar to Indonesian and Asian languages. Third, many of the plants and animals on the islands are also found in Indonesia and Asia.

At first, Europeans and others doubted that the islanders could navigate miles of open water. Then scholars found evidence of islanders trading with far-off islands. These modern islanders were able to get to other islands, sometimes crossing as much as five hundred miles of open ocean. This evidence forced the scientists to agree that the Pacific islanders could have traveled as far as Easter Island, which is near South America—a distance of two thousand miles.

Offering a different theory, Norwegian explorer **Thor Heyerdahl** proposed that the first Polynesians came from South America rather than Asia. To substantiate his theory, he constructed a boat from balsa logs and other materials found in Peru. In the *Kon-Tiki*

Thor Heyerdahl's balsa raft

Easter Island

This high volcanic island is located midway between the Polynesian Islands and South America. It is separated from both by a distance of about two thousand miles.

In 1722 a Dutch explorer named the island. He discovered it on Easter Sunday.

Easter Island forms the southeastern point of the triangle that bounds the Polynesian islands. It is also the home of the famous monumental statues shown below. Nearly nine hundred of these statues have been discovered on the island.

Easter Island

Over 1,400 miles from its nearest neighbor, Easter Island is one of the most mysterious places in the world.

The Dutch explorer Jacob Roggeveen first sighted the island in 1722. He arrived on Easter Sunday, thus giving the island its name. During his one-day visit, the Dutchman saw islanders worshiping the sun among huge stone statues.

Researchers have theorized about how the islanders first raised these statues, but they are still unsure of the process. Some of the stones weigh up to 80 tons. One statue, still in the rock quarry, weighs 270 tons; no wonder they left it there! On some of the statues' heads, red stone cylinders were added. Some think these additions were crowns and that the statues were meant to honor ancestors.

The mysteries of Easter Island might be solved by reading the records the people left. Unfortunately, no one has been able to conclusively decipher the rongo-rongo tablets. Only about twenty-one wooden tablets exist, making the job for researchers difficult.

Kon-Tiki

Heyerdahl named his raft *Kon-Tiki* after the Incan sun god. He and five crew members sailed for 101 days across forty-three hundred miles of the Pacific Ocean. The raft crashed onto a reef in the Tuamoto Islands in Polynesia, but the crew reached land and survived. His trip proved the plausibility of his theory. Heyerdahl wrote of his adventure in the book *Kon Tiki: Across the Pacific in a Raft*. A documentary movie, *Kon-Tiki*, was made about this famous expedition.

CD: 10A *Kon-Tiki*

This artist rendering of the *Kon-Tiki* is also available on the CD.

Kon-Tiki

Refer to the book *Kon-Tiki: Across the Pacific in a Raft* or look for the documentary movie *Kon-Tiki* at your local library.

John Paton

James Chalmers

expedition in 1947, Heyerdahl proved that it was possible to travel in a balsa boat from Peru to the island of Tuamoto in the Pacific. While many scientists rejected Heyerdahl's claims, he demonstrated that his theory was a possible answer to the question of where the original inhabitants of the Pacific islands came from.

European Discovery and Impact

Of the many islands claimed by European countries, only a few were heavily colonized. As in other endeavors, colonization brought positive and negative consequences.

The negative consequence that was most obvious was the introduction of diseases that ravaged many of the islands. Not having been exposed to common European diseases, the native peoples had not developed immunity against them. As in the Americas, diseases such as smallpox wiped out large portions of the native populations on some islands.

One change that had both negative and positive consequences was the introduction of European culture. The Europeans brought new clothes, new trade goods, and new customs. Some islanders embraced the new ways, while others longed for the culture that existed before Europeans arrived.

The most important positive impact on the people of the Pacific islands was the arrival of missionaries. We will briefly look at two missionaries to the Pacific and examine their ministries to the native peoples.

John Paton left Scotland with his new bride, Mary Ann, and sailed for the South Pacific in March 1858. They landed on an island in the New Hebrides in November. Their child, Peter Robert, was born three months later. Nineteen days after the birth, Mary Ann died of a tropical fever. A few days later, the baby died as well. Despite these overwhelming losses, John Paton continued his ministry among the hostile natives.

His life was constantly in danger, and the native peoples made many attempts to kill him. Despite these threats, he endured, married again, and developed a thriving ministry on Aniwa Island. Maggie, John's second wife, held classes with the women and taught them to sew, make hats, and read. The Patons built two houses for orphans, a church, and a printing house to produce a printed New Testament in the language of the people. More than thirty years of ministry by the Patons on Aniwa led to the professed conversion of everyone on that island. By 1899 the Aniwa New Testament was printed and missionaries were established on twenty-five of the thirty islands of the New Hebrides.

James Chalmers arrived in Papua New Guinea in 1877 with his wife Jane and worked tirelessly to establish a ministry among the native peoples. Those who accepted Christ were carefully nurtured in the faith. Chalmers was careful to baptize only those who demonstrated a genuine transformation and a growing desire to know the Word of God.

In 1901 Chalmers attempted to contact an isolated tribe that had been especially hostile toward outsiders. He and his assistant, Oliver Tomkins, accompanied some of the natives. Later, the natives returned without Chalmers and Tomkins. British investigators found that the native people had killed and eaten Chalmers and his assistant. Chalmers died as he had lived, striving to meet the spiritual needs of the native peoples of New Guinea.

Activity 1: John G. Paton

This activity includes excerpts from missionary John G. Paton's writings.

Activity 2: James Chalmers

This activity includes excerpts from missionary James Chalmers's writings.

Is Missions Detrimental?

Secularists (those who strive to exclude God from the public square) oppose mission work among native islanders, citing the "detrimental" influence that conversion has on native cultures. Discuss with the students whether this is a valid viewpoint. Point out that missionaries helped to address such issues as tribal warfare and the heathen customs of cannibalism and human sacrifice. They also brought medicine and education to the Pacific islands. They helped to improve the quality of life and the longevity of the native peoples by teaching about sanitation and clean water.

Missionaries and Culture

Have students discuss how missionaries can reach native peoples without causing unnecessary changes to cultural practices that do not present moral or ethical problems.

Have a visiting missionary from one of the Pacific islands speak to the class on his/her work in the mission field and the challenges of dealing with native cultures.

Section Quiz

1. What is the largest island of Oceania?
2. What type of island provides fertile volcanic soil?
3. Which group of Pacific islands is composed of small islands?
4. What expedition did Thor Heyerdahl conduct to prove Polynesians could have migrated from South America?
5. Where did James Chalmers serve as a missionary for twenty-four years?
★ What impact did Europeans have on the Pacific islands?

II. Early European Exploration

The Europeans did not stop exploring when they discovered the New World. Within one hundred years of Columbus's discovery, Europeans began directing their attention to the lands across the Pacific Ocean and the wealth they believed these lands possessed.

Europeans also believed a great land existed at the southern pole of the earth. Mapmakers called this land the unknown southern land. They found support for this idea in the writings of the early Greek astronomer Ptolemy, who proposed that there must be a land in the Southern Hemisphere equal in size or mass to Europe and Asia in order to keep the world from toppling over. The Europeans pictured a huge continent, probably as large as Asia, overflowing with riches and treasures. Believing this wealth existed, each European country sought to be the first to find the mythical southern land.

Spanish Exploration

The Incas told their Spanish conquerors of a great Incan king who had traveled west over the ocean and discovered a land filled with riches. Whether it was true or the Incas just wanted to draw attention away from themselves for a while, Spanish interest was aroused.

In 1567 the viceroy of Peru commissioned an expedition into the Pacific to find this great land. The first expedition, led by **Alvaro de Mendaña**, included two ships. This expedition sailed west for two and one-half months before discovering land. The island at which they arrived appeared fruitful at first, and hopes ran high that they had found the mythical Incan land. They named the island chain the **Solomon Islands** after King Solomon of the Bible since he was famous for his great riches. After an initially friendly welcome and

Alvaro de Mendaña

Beach on Mahe, one of the Solomon Islands

Section II

Objectives

Students should be able to

1. Explain the motivations and patterns of Spanish exploration.
2. Describe the discoveries that resulted from Dutch exploration.

Solomon Islands During World War II

In July 1942, Guadalcanal, the largest island of the Solomons, again saw ships approach its shores. This time they weren't the Spanish, but Japanese transports bringing troops. American forces quickly moved in to recapture the island. Japanese resistance was strong. The vital importance of the island is reflected in a Japanese document that said, "Success or failure in recapturing Guadalcanal . . . is the fork in the road to victory for them or for us." The Japanese reinforced their land forces, but costly naval battles with American forces soon made that difficult. By early 1943, Japanese forces had been evacuated and the campaign ended. On land, 14,800 Japanese troops were killed, as well as 1,600 Americans.

Section Quiz Answers

1. New Guinea
2. high islands
3. Micronesia
4. *Kon-Tiki* expedition
5. Papua New Guinea
★ Answers will vary but should include the following: diseases, new clothes, new trade goods, new customs, and mission work.

Alvaro de Mendaña

Visit www.bjupress.com/resources for possible links to articles about Alvaro de Mendaña.

Santa Cruz

It is noteworthy that the Spanish gave religious names to many of the places they explored. *Santa Cruz* means "holy cross." In the Americas the Spanish also named Los Angeles ("the angels") and San Francisco ("Saint Francis").

Shipworms

Wooden ships like those used during these early voyages were constantly threatened by tiny enemies—shipworms. After attaching themselves to a piece of wood, the worms begin to bore over half an inch per day.

Shipworms are found in many areas. They live in most oceans and seas of the world where water temperatures are warm enough.

Shipworms are not really worms at all, but are small clams with minimal shells. Their shape resembles a worm, and they "worm" their way into wood.

Water Shortages on the Ocean?

On long expeditions the sailors had to be careful to bring along enough water to drink. Although there is an abundance of water on the earth's surface, most of it is salt water. Drinking salt water is dangerous, in part because it actually draws out the water in the body's membranes. This action results in dehydration and the death of cells, leading to seizures, coma, and even death.

a brief time of peace, the Spanish offended their hosts. The Spanish, rather than trying to trade with the islanders, used force to get food. They fired shots and wounded or killed several islanders. The Spanish were no longer welcome on the island.

When a ten-man landing party tried to go ashore after that incident, they were attacked. Only one man escaped to swim back to the ship. The next day reinforcements rowed toward shore to save the missing men. However, they were prevented from landing by angry islanders.

Mendaña wanted to continue exploring for other islands but was forced to return to Peru because the water and food supplies were running low. The Solomon Islands that the Spanish discovered were not visited by other Europeans for another hundred years.

However, Mendaña was not discouraged by this failure, and he led another expedition in 1595 with a young navigator named **Pedro Fernández de Quirós**. This time the expedition had four ships and carried settlers, including women and children. Among the passengers were Mendaña's own wife, Doña Isabel, and her three brothers. They were pampered aristocrats and brought their own supplies of animals, water, oil, and wine for their personal use.

The expedition charted a course for the Solomon Islands but miscalculated. Instead, they came to a new set of islands that they named the **Marquesas** after the viceroy of Peru. The islanders were friendly, and Mendaña invited them aboard. But when the natives began to steal supplies, the Spanish crewmen shot and wounded several people. Sadly, the Spaniards continued to deal brutally with the islanders; they had killed two hundred people by the time the Spaniards resupplied the ship.

Santa Cruz

Mendaña and Quirós continued to search for the Solomon Islands. However, the next island they found was not the intended goal. Mendaña tried to communicate with the native peoples without success. He decided to settle this island that he named **Santa Cruz** (holy cross). Fever soon spread among the settlers and many died, including Mendaña. Quirós took over the command of the ships and rationed supplies in order to survive the voyage. However, Doña Isabel and her brothers still had a large supply of animals, water, oil, and wine.

With his ships wearing out due to shipworms, Quirós headed northwest for the Philippines, where the Spanish already had an established colony. Three months later, the one remaining ship of the expedition arrived at Manila Bay. The Spanish authorities were shocked to find almost one hundred men, women, and children starving to death while two of Doña Isabel's pigs rested on the deck. The authorities ordered the pigs to be slaughtered to feed the starving travelers.

Quirós requested and finally received support for another expedition. During the voyage Quirós became ill, and his navigator took control of the ship. This voyage ended with no significant discoveries and marked the end of Spanish exploration. Spain could not afford to continue sponsoring expeditions that failed to bring home riches.

Dutch Exploration

The Dutch authorities in Batavia, the chief Dutch base of the East Indies, called on one of their best captains, **Abel Tasman**, to

Map Activity

Using a large world map, locate the various places mentioned in this section (e.g., the Solomon Islands, the Marquesas, Santa Cruz). You could also have the students trace the route of Abel Tasman's first voyage (from southern India to Tasmania and then on to New Zealand).

Abel Tasman

Visit www.bjupress.com/resources for possible links to articles about Abel Tasman.

View from the Abel Tasman Coastline trail in New Zealand

search for the mythical unknown southern land. In 1642 Tasman took two ships and began his voyage. He started in southern India and sailed east. This way, Tasman thought, he could not miss the huge landmass that he believed to be the southern land.

Tasman sailed on, vainly looking for the unknown land. He sailed south of Australia and landed on the island now named for him: **Tasmania**. The Dutch sailors found signs of life on the island but could not find the shy native peoples.

Tasman soon realized that this island was not the continent that he sought, so he sailed even farther east. He crossed a large body of water (now called the Tasman Sea) and discovered another set of islands that we now call **New Zealand**. Tasman and his men made contact with the native peoples there and discovered that they were not friendly. The tall, fierce **Maoris** (MOU reez) resisted Dutch attempts to land. As the Dutch sailors explored one of the bays, the native peoples killed four sailors and drove the others back to the main ships. Tasman named this place Murderer's Bay.

On a second expedition in 1644, Tasman mapped out parts of the western coastline of Australia. Even though the west coastline looked uninviting, the Dutch knew that in such a sizeable land there might be better places for settlement. However, the Dutch lacked the manpower and the money to explore and colonize. To avoid drawing attention to the area, the Dutch East India Company suppressed many of Tasman's findings. They claimed the land they found and named it **New Holland**. Tasman retired in 1652, having failed to locate the mythical unknown southern land. However, he had discovered three new and important islands: Australia, Tasmania, and New Zealand.

Section Quiz

1. How did Mendaña treat the native peoples during his visit to the Solomon Islands?

2. Why didn't Doña Isabel and her brothers suffer from starvation like the others on the Spanish ship?

3–5. What islands did the Dutch discover?

★ Why was Quirós forced to sail to the Philippines?

Section Quiz Answers

1. He tried to use force and killed several natives.

2. They brought their own food supplies and didn't share them with the others.

3-5. Australia, Tasmania, and New Zealand

★ The ship was wearing out due to shipworms, and the food was running out.

Section III

Objectives

Students should be able to

1. Describe the discoveries that resulted from French exploration in the Pacific.
2. Assess the impact of English exploration in the Pacific.

Reasons for Cook's Voyage

Captain Cook's voyage from 1768 to 1771 was not solely for the purpose of searching for the "unknown southern land" but also to search the skies. The Royal Society of London commissioned Cook to observe Venus as it passed in front of the sun. This was an event that would not occur again until 1874. Through the observation, astronomers hoped to be able to measure the earth's distance from the sun. This knowledge would help in measuring longitude and aid future exploration.

Mutiny on the *Bounty*

The events surrounding the mutiny on the HMS *Bounty* took place on Pitcairn Island in Tahiti. Have a volunteer research the mutiny and present a report to the class.

Activity 3: James Cook's Journal

This activity includes excerpts from English explorer James Cook's journal.

Louis Antoine de Bougainville

Tahiti

James Cook

III. European Exploration in the 1700s

During the sixteenth and seventeenth centuries, the English and French stayed busy developing territory in the American colonies. However, when circumstances changed in their colonies in the 1700s, the French and British renewed efforts to explore. Several French and British explorers sailed the Pacific during the 1700s, but only one man from each country will be examined.

French Exploration

In the midst of his training to become a lawyer, **Louis Antoine de Bougainville** (BOO gun vil) became bored with his studies and decided to pursue the challenge of a military career. He served with the French in Canada and witnessed the loss of Quebec to the British.

Hoping to regain power and respect for France, Bougainville organized an expedition to settle the Falkland Islands off the coast of Argentina. With thirteen colonists from Nova Scotia, he set sail for the Falklands in the fall of 1763. Due to English and Spanish claims to these islands, Bougainville was ordered to close his settlement. The French then sent him in search of the mythical unknown land to the south.

Two scientists accompanied Bougainville on the voyage. Philibert Commerson, a naturalist, was brought along to describe and classify the animals and plants discovered. Antoine Véron, an astronomer, sought to work out new ways to determine longitude. Their contributions to the voyage were perhaps the most significant. Bougainville's idea of taking a naturalist and an astronomer became the custom for other explorers.

On his journey across the Pacific, Bougainville revisited and claimed for France several islands, including **Tahiti**. These explorers were influenced by the concept of the "noble savage." Contrary to the Bible doctrine of original sin (all humans are born sinners), these thinkers claimed that humans are born good and are then corrupted by civilization. Enlightenment philosophers supported their claims with Bougainville's reports that the Tahitians were good and lived simple lives in harmony with nature. They ignored or were unaware of reports that the Tahitians practiced cannibalism, performed human sacrifices, and engaged in frequent tribal warfare.

English Exploration

English captain **James Cook** became the most famous explorer of the Pacific. His fame is especially amazing since he came from a working-class background and had little formal education. He rose in rank during a time when the wealthy and well-educated were usually the only men put in high-ranking positions such as captain.

Cook was one of the best sailors and explorers of his time. His mission for the British was to discover the truth about the unknown southern land and claim land for England. In three voyages he crisscrossed the Pacific. First, Cook sailed around Australia. Then he sailed north between Alaska and Russia, vainly trying to find a passage above northern Canada. Finally, he sailed south of the Pacific islands until massive icebergs and fierce snowstorms forced him back into more temperate waters. Cook and his crew became the first men to sail completely around Antarctica, although they never actually saw that continent. Information gathered during his voyages proved that there was no great southern land.

Louis Antoine de Bougainville

Visit www.bjupress.com/resources for possible links to articles about Loius Antione de Bougainville.

James Cook

Visit www.bjupress.com/resources for possible links to articles about James Cook.

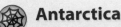
Antarctica

Visit www.bjupress.com/resources for possible links to articles about Antarctica.

During Cook's voyages, danger was often present. Once while sailing along the Great Barrier Reef off the coast of Australia, Cook's ship grounded on a reef. Cook ordered his men to lighten the ship, hoping that the tides would lift it off the reef. When the ship broke free, a large piece of coral broke off as well, plugging the hole until the ship could be repaired.

In his travels, Captain Cook discovered many islands in the Pacific, notably the Hawaiian Islands. He differed from other explorers by treating the native peoples fairly and generously. Cook often noted in his diaries good characteristics and abilities that he observed in the native peoples. He treated the Indians with respect, tried to make friends, and avoided violence whenever possible. Cook became one of the first white men to make peaceful contact with the Maoris of New Zealand.

One way that Captain Cook dealt with problems with the native peoples, however, led to his death. When native peoples stole an item from the English ships or camps, Cook would capture a chief or other important person. Then he would announce that the captive would not be freed until the thief returned the stolen items. This method worked well until he tried it in Hawaii in 1779. Some native peoples stole tools and a canoe. Cook responded by trying to take an old chief hostage. However, a mob of angry native peoples attacked Cook and his men. Cook's men escaped, but he did not. The furious native peoples beat Cook to death with their war clubs.

Getty Images/The Bridgeman Art Library

Captain Cook and Sauerkraut

Captain James Cook was one of the greatest explorers in history, and he owes a small part of his success to sauerkraut.

On long voyages, sailors often suffered from **scurvy,** a deadly disease caused by a lack of vitamin C in their diet. Captain Cook convinced his officers to eat large amounts of sauerkraut (fermented cabbage) and set an example for the crew. His men learned to eat the sauerkraut to meet their vitamin C needs, and few ever came down with scurvy.

Maori chief

Death of James Cook

Section Quiz

1. Why did Bougainville establish a colony on the Falkland Islands?

2. What idea did Bougainville develop that became a custom for other explorers?

3. Who was the most famous explorer of the Pacific?

4. What was Captain Cook's mission?

5. On what chain of islands did Captain Cook die?

★ Why were tropical islands like Tahiti described as proof that man was born unspoiled? Why were these claims inaccurate and unbiblical?

Cook set up an observation point on Tahiti called Fort Venus. Plans were proceeding well until about May 2, a month before Venus's transit on June 3, when some Tahitians took Cook's quadrant. The instrument was vital to the observation, and a search party was organized. The thieves were never found, but the instrument was returned piece by piece. Fortunately, crewman Charles Green of the Royal Observatory in Greenwich was able to repair the quadrant. On June 3, Venus passed in front of the sun and the observation was recorded by Cook and members of several other expeditions. To ensure accuracy, the Royal Society had placed observers in several parts of the world: Tahiti, Hudson Bay (Canada), and the North Cape of Norway.

Section Quiz Answers

1. He hoped to regain power and respect for France.

2. He took a naturalist and an astronomer on his voyages.

3. James Cook

4. to discover the truth about the unknown southern land

5. Hawaiian Islands

★ These islands appeared to be an unspoiled tropical paradise. The explorers assumed the islanders were good because they lived simple lives in apparent harmony with nature. However, the islanders often practiced cannibalism, performed human sacrifices, and engaged in frequent tribal warfare.

Section IV

Objectives

Students should be able to

1. Describe the life and culture of the original Australians.
2. Assess the impact of English immigration on Australia.
3. Describe the expanded colonization of Australia.
4. Describe the development of Australia into a nation.

Olympian Cathy Freeman

Freeman won gold at the 2000 Olympics in the 400-meter run.

X-Ray Painting

X-ray painting is a style of aboriginal art that developed about 2000 BC, and it is still used by some Aborigines today. The artist paints a silhouette of a person or animal that also depicts the bone structure and internal organs.

Aussie Football

Australia has developed a culture all its own, even in sports. One of the most popular team sports in the country is Australian Rules football. During the weekend of the Grand Final, the sport attracts a crowd so large that the host city, Melbourne, literally shuts down.

The game is more like English rugby than American football. Play takes place on an oval field 150–170 yards wide and 150–200 yards long. One oval-shaped ball is carried during play, which consists of four 25-minute quarters. Two teams of eighteen try to break through each other and take the ball down the

Great Barrier Reef

Australia's Great Barrier Reef is a beautiful yet dangerous area. Two of the most serious dangers for swimmers are the great white shark and the jellyfish. Have students research and report on the diverse forms of animal life that inhabit this vast reef, which can even be seen from space.

 CD: 10B Didgeridoos

Photos of didgeridoos are available on the CD.

AFP/Getty Images

Olympic gold medalist Cathy Freeman from Australia

Aboriginal x-ray painting

Didgeridoo

IV. European Settlement in Australia

We may never know which European explorer was the first to see the coast of Australia. The Portuguese may have seen Cape York Peninsula when they passed through the Torres Straits in 1606. The Dutch followed Australia's coastline many times as they explored the region in search of the mythical southern land. Captain Cook and his men landed in Botany Bay on August 23, 1770, and then surveyed the entire eastern coastline. All these countries viewed Australia as a land ready to be claimed and developed by Europeans. However, Australia already had a native population.

When Captain Cook landed in Botany Bay, he met a group of native people who had no name for themselves. The Europeans called these people **Aborigines**. The word *aborigine* comes from a Latin word that means "origin" or "original."

The Original Australians

Life and Culture

The indigenous (in DIJ eh nus) (original) Australians were one of the most isolated groups of people in the world. They were separated not only from other countries but also from each other within Australia. The rugged coastline of the west and north created one barrier. This hostile front helped to prevent earlier European and Asian contact. Australia's rugged and dry terrain also separated groups of Aborigines from each other. In a continent the size of the United States, the small population of the Aborigines was spread far and wide.

The native peoples of Australia followed a lifestyle similar to many hunter-gatherer tribes. The men spent time hunting and worshiping the tribal gods using a variety of rituals. The women gathered food early in the day and spent the rest of the day preparing dinner and caring for the children.

The native peoples developed forms of music as part of their worship. They used pieces of eucalyptus wood that had been hollowed out by termites to make an unusual musical instrument, the **didgeridoo** (DIJ eh ree DOO). While this instrument produces a single note, the person blowing through this tube can add his own vocal sounds to vary the final sound. The length of the didgeridoo determines the pitch of the sound, with longer instruments making a deeper drone.

Another reflection of their religious expression is found in Aboriginal art. Aborigines painted their bodies, rocks, and pieces of bark. The paintings often depicted religious stories, including the Aboriginal accounts of Creation.

Some of the native peoples in western Victoria developed a game called **Marn Grook**. This game has elements of football and soccer and is played with a ball shaped like a football and made out of possum hide. Australian Rules football may have developed from this Aboriginal sport.

Impact of European Immigration

Although the Aborigines were often involved in tribal conflict, they were very rarely hostile to the early settlers. The English settlements became well established and began to push into Aboriginal

:

territory and hunting grounds. When the native population tried to resist, they were no match for the weaponry of the English. Gradually the Aborigines lost more and more of their land and rights.

Perhaps the most lethal things the Europeans brought with them were diseases such as smallpox. In Chapter 7 you learned that many Indians in the Americas died from European diseases. In a similar manner, the Aborigines had not been exposed to or developed immunity to these diseases. The outcome in Australia was tragically similar to that of the Americas. Many Aborigines died from diseases to which the Europeans exposed them.

Left, replica of Captain Cook's ship; *right*, the *Charlotte* from the First Fleet

England Claims New South Wales

The Dutch had claimed an area called New Holland in northern Australia, but that did not mean the Dutch could claim all of Australia. Various European countries claimed land in Australia as they had in North America. Claims were based on a first-come-first-served basis. For example, when the *Endeavour* sailed into the harbor of Botany Bay, Captain Cook claimed the land he saw for England. He called this land **New South Wales**.

When the American colonies declared their independence from England, the prison colony of Georgia was no longer available to Britain. The English decided to rid themselves of many of the occupants of the overflowing British prisons and poorhouses by relocating those people to the land Cook had claimed in Australia. The **First Fleet** left England in May of 1787 and sailed to New South Wales. Of the more than one thousand people on these ships, over eight hundred were convicts.

After traveling for about eight months, the fleet's captain, **Arthur Phillip** (later the colony's first governor), sighted Australia. He had sailed ahead with the intention of preparing a small settlement before the other ships arrived. However, the remaining ships arrived two days after he had sailed into Botany Bay. Phillip soon realized that this bay was too shallow and exposed to the open ocean to provide protection for the fleet. He found a more suitable port a few miles to the north (Port Jackson). This bay had a deep harbor and included many protected coves. Phillip chose to settle in a cove that became known as **Sydney Cove**. This bay had a deep, sand-fringed harbor with a freshwater stream. The Fleet arrived on January 26, 1788. This date is now celebrated as **Australia Day**.

Arthur Phillip

field. Four posts are lined up at the end of both sides of the field and players score points by kicking the ball through (*6 points*) or behind the posts (*1 point*).

Only three players on each team have unlimited movement on the field. All the others guard zones and opponents. Unlike rugby or American football, players are not allowed to throw the ball. They must transfer it by either kicking, punching, or bouncing the ball. Once a player takes possession of the ball, he can travel only ten yards before he has to bounce it on the ground. Until recently, the only place outside Australia where the game was played was Papua New Guinea, a former Australian possession.

The Stolen Generations

Between 1869 and 1970, the Australian government removed many of the native children from their families for various reasons ranging from racism to a desire to protect the children from further population decline due to diseases introduced by European settlers. The Australian government finally issued a formal apology in 2008, led by Prime Minister Kevin Rudd.

Eucalyptus

Although the early English settlers found this tree unsuitable for building homes, the eucalyptus has several medicinal uses. The leaves and oil have been used to heal wounds and fight fungal infections. Eucalyptus oil has strong antibacterial properties, loosens phlegm in the throat, and deodorizes.

Eucalyptus trees

The future of the colony depended on building homes and cultivating the land. However, there were no skilled laborers among the crew or convicts. In addition, the eucalyptus and other gum trees that were in abundant supply were very hard and quickly ruined the axes. When the settlers were finally able to cut down one of these trees, it took up to twelve men a full day to dig out the stump. In order to survive, the settlers resorted to building houses from cabbage trees covered with wattle and daub (sticks and mud plaster).

Another problem soon surfaced. On the long voyage Phillip had kept his crew and the convicts healthy, but much of the transported grain and flour was ruined. Without flour or grain the settlers would have no bread. In addition, many settlers began to show signs of scurvy. In desperation, they resorted to eating plants that they found around them to survive.

Phillip carefully rationed the remaining flour while the settlers waited for the supply ship that was scheduled to arrive within the first year. Unknown to the colonists in Australia and authorities in England, the supply ship struck an iceberg during the voyage and sank. The colonists had to survive for two years before they received any news from England. By that time the colony faced famine.

Governor Phillip had stationed an outpost at Botany Bay to look for ships that would arrive from England since the colonists had first planned to settle there. Finally the news came that an English ship had been sighted, and the settlers were excited when they received this report. However, their excitement soon turned to disappointment when the ship was found to be another transport ship with over two hundred convicts and few supplies. Providentially, a well-stocked supply ship soon arrived. The famine ended, and the colony became firmly established.

Expansion and Establishment

For several years the colonists remained near the coast. The **Great Dividing Range**, with its steep rock faces and giant gorges, effectively confined the colonists to living along the ocean. However, settlements continued to be established. Many convicts finished

Great Dividing Range

Fri002/Flagstaffotos

CD: 10C Eucalyptus Trees

Photos of eucalyptus trees are available on the CD.

CD: 10D Cabbage Palm Tree

A photo of a cabbage palm tree is available on the CD.

serving their prison terms and became profitable members of the colony.

Settlers soon learned how to live entirely off the land. Using crop rotation and fertilizer, more and more farmers established successful farms on land grants from the colonial authorities. In order for the colonists to receive this land, they had to accept convict laborers to work the farms. The greatest problem with this arrangement proved to be thievery by the convict laborers.

The crossing of the Great Dividing Range provided a great opportunity for expansion into the interior of Australia. In May 1813 **Gregory Blaxland** and two companions started out from Blaxland's farm at the foothills of the mountains. After three weeks of exploring, these men looked down from a cliff edge and saw a stream running through the center of a valley. Further exploration revealed a passage to the western plains that enabled the exploration and colonization of the outback (remote, dry region located in the center of the island).

The Outback: Geography

This region contains a mixture of desert regions, plains, and mountains. Agriculture is usually limited to grazing animals in areas where rainfall supports adequate vegetation. Tourists enjoy the beautiful vistas afforded them in many parts of this area. In addition, explorers have discovered vast mineral deposits such as iron, aluminum, diamonds, and gold. As a result, mining has become a major industry in the outback.

Ubirr in the Kakadu National Park

Ayers Rock in the Uluru-Kata Tjuta National Park

Mount Connor

View from the Larapinta Trail in the MacDonnell National Park

CD: 10E The Outback

Additional photos of the Outback are available on the CD.

The Outback: Wildlife

Despite the harsh conditions found in much of the outback, this region has an abundance of wildlife. Animals ranging from camels, kangaroos, and koalas to dingos and wild pigs rest during the day and become active during the cool of the night. Vast flocks of cockatoos and many other birds also add color and noise to the outback.

Left to right, Koala, Dingo, Kangaroo

In 1836 explorers traveled southwest from Sydney around the coast and founded a new colony called **South Australia**. In 1852 sheep farmers in search of more pasture traveled south overland and discovered a river that they named the Murray. South of this river they founded the town of Melbourne and called the colony **Victoria** after Queen Victoria of England.

A New Nation

All the Australian colonies were under the rule of England when gold was discovered in New South Wales, and a gold rush resulted in 1851. Around that time the convict transports to the east coast stopped, and with the rush of gold-hungry immigrants, the percentage of free citizens increased dramatically. About 400,000 people lived in the Australian colonies in 1850. Within ten years the population had increased to over one million.

Australian History

Western Australia 1829

New South Wales 1788

Van Dieman's Land 1825

South Australia 1836

Victoria 1854

Northern Territory part of South Australia 1863-1911

Western Australia

South Australia

Queensland 1859

New South Wales Australian Capitol terr. 1911

Victoria

Tasmania renamed in 1855

 ## CD: 10F Australian History

These maps from the student text are also available on the CD.

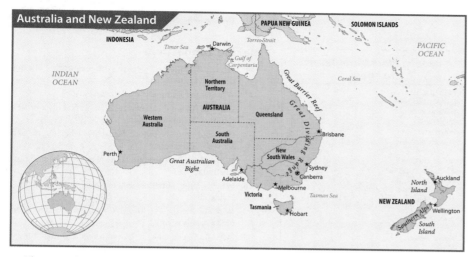

These new colonists wanted more freedom to govern themselves. In 1856 England responded by granting self-government to most of the colonies. However, England still protected the colonies and intervened in foreign affairs.

In 1901, after intense discussions, Australia became the **Commonwealth of Australia**, made up of six states—Queensland, New South Wales, Victoria, Tasmania, South Australia, and Western Australia—and two federal territories. Instead of each colony governing independently, the Commonwealth formed a single federal capital. By 1927 the government buildings in the new capital of **Canberra** were ready for use. Canberra is similar to Washington, D.C., in the United States. It is the seat of government but is not part of any state.

Section Quiz

1. What did Captain Cook call the native peoples that he found in Australia?

2. What musical instrument is made from hollow eucalyptus trees?

3. What did the Europeans bring to Australia that proved lethal to the native population?

4. Who was the first colonial governor of New South Wales?

5. What did the colonies of Australia become in 1901?

★ Why did Australian colonists remain along the coast for several years?

 ## CD: 10G Australia and New Zealand

This map from the student text is also available on the CD.

Activity 4: Chapter Review

This activity helps the students prepare for the chapter test.

Section Quiz Answers

1. Aborigines

2. didgeridoo

3. diseases such as smallpox

4. Arthur Phillip

5. the Commonwealth of Australia

★ Natural barriers such as the Great Dividing Range confined the colonists to coastal areas.

CHAPTER REVIEW

People, Places, and Terms to Know

high islands
low islands
Melanesia
Micronesia
Polynesia
Thor Heyerdahl
John Paton
James Chalmers
Alvaro de Mendaña
Solomon Islands
Pedro Fernández de Quirós
Marquesas
Santa Cruz
Abel Tasman
Tasmania
New Zealand
Maoris
New Holland
Louis Antoine de Bougainville
Tahiti
James Cook
scurvy
Aborigines
didgeridoo
Marn Grook
New South Wales
First Fleet
Arthur Phillip
Sydney Cove
Australia Day
Great Dividing Range
Gregory Blaxland
South Australia
Victoria
Commonwealth of Australia
Canberra

Making Connections

1. What is the difference between the composition of a high island and a low island?
2. Why did the Europeans explore the Pacific?
3. Why did Alvaro de Mendaña name his first discovered island chain the Solomon Islands?
4. What did Spanish authorities discover when Quirós finally arrived at Manila Bay?
5. Why did the Dutch suppress many of Tasman's findings about Australia?
6. Why was Bougainville forced to close his colony in the Falklands?
7. Why was James Cook forced to abandon his exploration south of the Pacific islands?
8. Why did England begin to send convicts to Australia in 1787?
9. Why do scientists believe the islands of the Pacific were first colonized from the west?

Developing History Skills

1. Locate the following on the map below:
   a. Australia
   b. Easter Island
   c. Hawaiian Islands
   d. Melanesia
   e. Micronesia
   f. New Zealand
   g. Polynesia

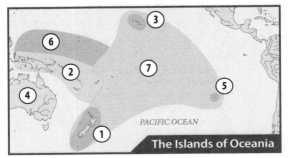
The Islands of Oceania

2. Based on the information in this chapter, write a list of the barriers the explorers found when surveying and exploring Australia. Briefly describe how they overcame these barriers.

Chapter Review Answers

Making Connections

1. High islands are composed of volcanic mountains and volcanic debris. Low islands are composed of coral remains that developed on submerged volcanoes.

2. They were searching for lands with riches and the unknown land believed to be in the Southern Hemisphere.

3. He named them after King Solomon of the Bible because of Solomon's great riches. He thought he had discovered the rich, mythical Incan island.

4. They discovered that most of the people were starving while Doña Isabel and her brothers had ample food supplies.

5. They lacked the manpower and money to explore and colonize this land, and they didn't want other European colonial powers to take conrol of it.

6. because of English and Spanish claims to these islands

7. massive icebergs and fierce snowstorms

8. because the American colonies had declared their independence and the prison colony of Georgia was no longer available to Britain

9. archaeological evidence, language similarities with Indonesians and Asians, and similar plants and animals to those found in Indonesia and Asia

Developing History Skills

1. a. (4)
   b. (5)
   c. (3)
   d. (2)
   e. (6)
   f. (1)
   g. (7)

2. Answers will vary, but should include the following: rugged western coast, Great Dividing Range, desolate Outback. They settled on the eastern side of the island, discovered passes through

Thinking Critically

1. How did the myth of the "noble savage" appear to support the claims of the Enlightenment philosophers? Is the concept of the noble savage biblical in light of Romans 1 and 3:23?

2. Why do you think the Australians wanted more freedom to govern themselves? Was this desire right or wrong?

Living in God's World

1. Divide into groups. Each group should plan a missionary venture to Australia or a Pacific island in the late 19th century. Research the area where you plan to work and detail how you plan to establish and maintain a ministry there.

2. Imagine that you are a native on one of the islands in the Pacific or an Aborigine in Australia. Write an account of your encounter with explorers.

the mountains, and traveled by ships to establish new colonies.

Thinking Critically

1. Supporters of the Enlightenment claimed that humans are born good and later corrupted by civilization. Reports by explorers including Bougainville appeared to support this claim because they found uncivilized people who seemed to live good lives in harmony with their environment. Scripture, however, teaches that all humans are born with a sin nature.

2. Answers will vary. Perhaps they found that being governed from far away Britain was inefficient and undesirable.

Freedom is neither right nor wrong. How one uses his freedom distinguishes good from evil.

Living in God's World

1. Answers will vary.

2. Answers will vary but could include details about hostile actions by the explorers, death by diseases, loss of land, new customs, new clothing, and meeting a missionary and hearing the gospel for the first time.

Chapter Goals

Students should be able to

1. Describe the efforts to establish Chinese regional power under the Ming and Manchu dynasties.
2. Explain how Southeast Europe and Southwest Asia became unified under the Ottoman Empire.
3. Discuss the rise and development of the Safavid Empire.
4. Trace the rise and expansion of the Mughal Empire.

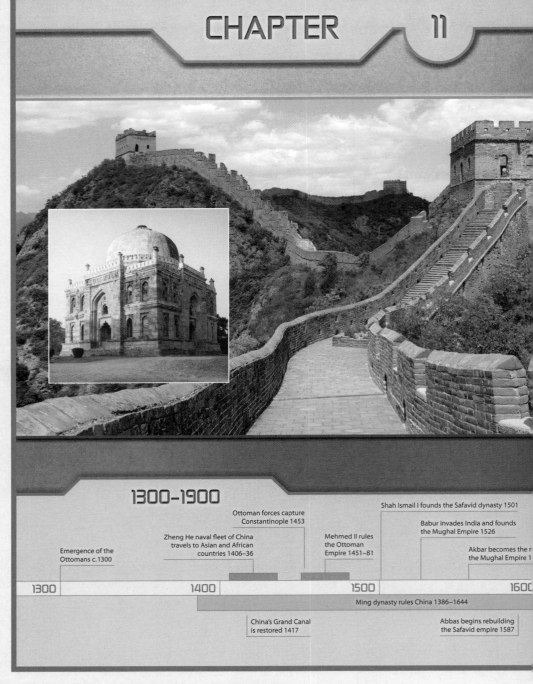

1300–1900

Emergence of the Ottomans c.1300

Zheng He naval fleet of China travels to Asian and African countries 1406–36

Ottoman forces capture Constantinople 1453

Mehmed II rules the Ottoman Empire 1451–81

Shah Ismail I founds the Safavid dynasty 1501

Babur invades India and founds the Mughal Empire 1526

Akbar becomes the r the Mughal Empire 1

1300	1400	1500	1600

Ming dynasty rules China 1386–1644

China's Grand Canal is restored 1417

Abbas begins rebuilding the Safavid empire 1587

Chapter 11 Lesson Plan Chart

	Section Title	Main Activity	Pages	Days
I.	China's Ming and Manchu Dynasties	Activity 1: Map Study: Ming China	190–95	1–2 days
II.	Ottoman Empire	Discussion Activity: Religious Freedom	196–99	1–1½ days
III.	Safavid Empire	Activity 4: Map Study: Asia Minor	200–201	1 day
IV.	Mughal Empire	Activity 5 : Chapter Review	201–2	1–1½ days
TOTAL SUGGESTED DAYS (INCLUDING 1 DAY EACH FOR REVIEW AND TESTING)				6–8 days

Materials List

Section I

- CD: 11A Ming China; 11B Great Wall of China; 11C Grand Canal Map; 11D Grand Canal Photo
- A video showing how locks function in a canal
- Activity 1 from the *Student Activities* manual

Section II

- CD: 11E Anatolia; 11F Falcon Cannon; 11G The Ottoman Empire

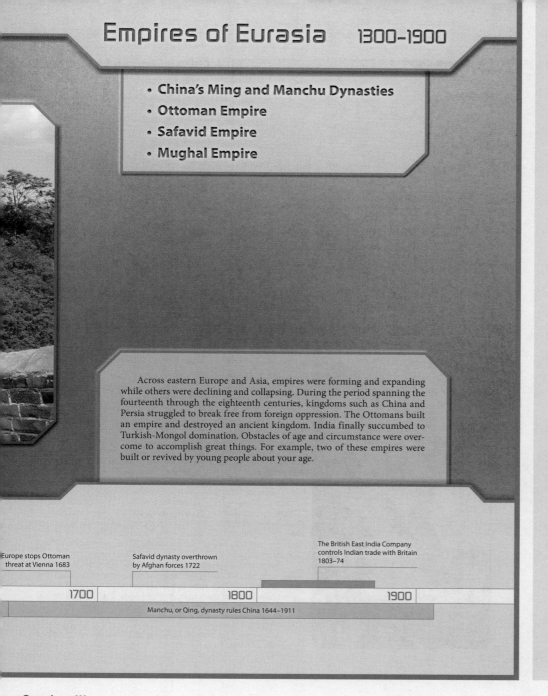

Empires of Eurasia   1300–1900

- **China's Ming and Manchu Dynasties**
- **Ottoman Empire**
- **Safavid Empire**
- **Mughal Empire**

Across eastern Europe and Asia, empires were forming and expanding while others were declining and collapsing. During the period spanning the fourteenth through the eighteenth centuries, kingdoms such as China and Persia struggled to break free from foreign oppression. The Ottomans built an empire and destroyed an ancient kingdom. India finally succumbed to Turkish-Mongol domination. Obstacles of age and circumstance were overcome to accomplish great things. For example, two of these empires were built or revived by young people about your age.

Europe stops Ottoman threat at Vienna 1683

Safavid dynasty overthrown by Afghan forces 1722

The British East India Company controls Indian trade with Britain 1803–74

1700   **1800**   **1900**

Manchu, or Qing, dynasty rules China 1644–1911

Section III

- CD: 11H The Safavid Empire; 11I Safavid Helmet
- Activity 4 from the *Student Activities* manual

Section IV

- CD: 11J Badshahi Mosque; 11K The Mughal Empire
- Activities 2, 3, and 5 from the *Student Activities* manual

Section I

Objectives

Students should be able to

1. Evaluate the exercise of imperial absolutism under the Ming and Manchu dynasties in China.
2. Explain China's self-concept as the "middle kingdom" and its relationship with other Asian countries.
3. Analyze China's exclusion of the outside world after the Zheng He voyages.

Secret Police

Authoritarian regimes often employ a form of secret police to keep the people under their control. Taizu may have developed an early version of this practice, but many have used such methods since then. Examples include the Nazi Gestapo and the Soviet KGB. However, fear and intimidation can repress a people for only so long.

Grand Secretaries

How much government is too much? No doubt the Ming rulers struggled with this question at some point. Their conclusion seems to have been that more government (i.e., greater bureaucracy) is better. This freed the Ming rulers to pursue personal interests. However, it also led to the decline and overthrow of the Ming Dynasty. As the U.S. bureaucracy grows rapidly, the question of how much government is too much becomes increasingly relevant.

Showing Respect

Have the students discuss various ways that people show respect to a person in authority. The Ming Dynasty demanded kneeling to indicate complete submission. In other cultures people make a polite bow or stand when the leader enters the room. In Western society a handshake is used. Believers know that someday "every knee shall bow" in reverence to Christ (Rom. 14:11).

CD: 11A Ming China

This map from the student text is also available on the CD.

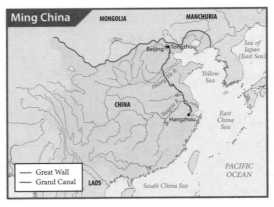

Ming China

MONGOLIA · MANCHURIA · Sea of Japan (East Sea) · Beijing · Tongzhou · Yellow Sea · CHINA · Huang He R. · Yangtze R. · Hangzhou · East China Sea · PACIFIC OCEAN · LAOS · South China Sea

— Great Wall
— Grand Canal

Chinese landscape painting

I. China's Ming and Manchu Dynasties

The Chinese called their land *Chung Kuo*, the **Middle Kingdom**. For two thousand years China existed as the central nation and great power in Asia. Its borders have changed, and one dynasty has overthrown another, but China has remained. Other empires that traded with the Chinese have come and gone. The Babylonians, the Persians, the Greeks, the Romans, all great at one time, have fallen, but China has carried on as a central power among the other Asian nations.

The Ming Dynasty

You learned in Chapter 4 that China was briefly ruled by a foreign power—the Mongols. Their rule was called the Yuan dynasty. After a little more than a hundred years, Chinese forces overthrew the Mongols and established a new dynasty called the **Ming dynasty** (1386–1644).

The Ming dynasty restored native Chinese rule. A renewed national pride caused the Chinese to look down on all foreigners, including European traders. The Ming turned their attention to rebuilding the grandeur of China, and the people enjoyed an era of peace and prosperity under this dynasty. The Ming attempted to maintain a government based on absolutism. In addition, they concentrated on the arts, reconstruction, and exploration.

Imperial Absolutism

Taizu founded the Ming dynasty and established a pattern of absolute rule that his successors followed for the next three centuries. He was a harsh ruler and demanded that his ministers kneel before him. During previous dynasties the ministers had sat or stood in the emperor's presence.

Taizu also labored to manage every aspect of Chinese society, including households. He used a secret police force to discover any who opposed his controls. Officials who dared to ignore or resist imperial control were subjected to public beatings that sometimes resulted in death.

Chengzu became the third emperor after defeating the second emperor, Huizong, in a civil war. He continued Taizu's harsh policies when dealing with his enemies, but he also sponsored many scholarly events. Chengzu collected a vast literary treasury that employed over two thousand scholars. He also reversed Taizu's policy of preventing naval expansion and sent out the Zheng He voyages that will be discussed in more detail later in the chapter.

Succeeding emperors began to entrust more and more authority to government officials known as grand secretaries. In the long term, delegating power led to political corruption and a weakened central government. In the short term, it freed the ruler to explore interests in arts, including porcelain, painting, poetry, and bronze work.

The Arts

Ming craftsmen perfected **porcelain** production, which helped to continue the demand for exports. During different periods of the

Chengzu and State-Supported Literature

What might be some differences between state-controlled literature and privately funded, individually pursued literature? *(Possibilities: The state might emphasize political correctness, man's destruction of the environment, evolution, and other topics. The individual might tend to write about subjects that he or she finds interesting, important, fulfilling, etc.)*

Grand Secretaries

Compare and contrast the "grand secretaries" of the Ming dynasty and modern government officials. What are the advantages and disadvantages of a government bureaucracy? *(Government officials who are appointed due to their skills and desire to serve the people are an advantage. Officials who are appointed as a reward for party loyalty, but do not serve the people, are a disadvantage.)*

Ming and succeeding dynasties, various colors of porcelain were developed. Blue and white porcelain was produced for the royal family alone, but imitations were soon available to sell at home and abroad. Enamel colors were added, and five-colored enamels became highly prized during the fifteenth century.

As in Europe during the Renaissance, increased wealth provided the opportunity for increased literacy and expanded literature. Bookshops sold samples of the examinations that all students had to pass in order to gain government employment. Novels and short stories also became popular. Men who did not pass the rigorous exams for government employment often developed literary careers to support themselves. Many oral stories were written down and sold in collections.

Drama developed into long and complex plays in the Ming dynasty. Language, form, and music combined to produce plays that often lasted for hours and contained more than forty scenes. Over time, plays were reduced by the combining of selected scenes from various plays to shorten the performance.

During the Ming dynasty, painting **landscapes** (nature scenes) became a popular form of expression. Some painters drew the trees and other natural scenes in a way that invited the imagination of the viewer. Poems were written about the paintings that described imaginary creatures such as dragons and giant birds in conflict.

Chinese painting

Exams

The Chinese developed extensive and difficult exams to test prospective government officials. The goal was to enlist only the brightest scholars to serve in government positions. The American government has Civil Service System exams, which are also designed to ensure that the most qualified people are recruited to serve in many government positions.

Enriching Culture

One of the patterns of history seems to be that improved technology and increased wealth often leave more time and opportunity for people to pursue literary and artistic interests. The result is often the enriching of culture.

Porcelain

Porcelain is formed when objects made from materials such as kaolin clay are heated in a kiln to between 1200°C and 1400°C. The finished ceramic product is strong, hard, and translucent (light will pass through it). Artisans make a variety of porcelain products, including vases, plates, cups, tiles, and false teeth.

Artisans during the Ming dynasty perfected the art of making porcelain and exported porcelain products on a massive scale. Ming porcelain was sold literally around the world.

Most people simply refer to porcelain as china.

Example of Ming porcelain

Example of Manchu porcelain

Porcelain

Ask students (with their parents' permission) to bring in examples of porcelain to show the class. An alternative would be to have the students bring in pictures of items made of porcelain.

Ming Dynasty

Visit www.bjupress.com/resources for possible links to articles about the Ming Dynasty.

The Forbidden City

China's Forbidden City is actually located in the heart of Beijing. Chinese workers built this enormous imperial palace during the early fifteenth century; the structure took around fourteen years to build. The palace complex, covering nearly eight million square feet, contains nearly one thousand buildings and over eight thousand rooms. The Forbidden City served as the Chinese imperial palace from the Ming dynasty to the Qing dynasty. The complex was called "forbidden" because no one could enter or leave the palace without the emperor's permission. For nearly five centuries, emperors and their families lived in and ruled from the Forbidden City.

Above, section of the Great Wall; *below,* Forbidden City in Beijing

Great Wall of China

This great line of stone and earth began as a series of isolated fortresses in the fifth century BC. Over the centuries, Chinese leaders linked and rebuilt these structures. The Ming dynasty built most of the portions of the Great Wall that survive today.

Reconstruction

The Ming rebuilt broken portions of the Great Wall and extended it even farther. They repaired roads and bridges and built the **Imperial City** in their capital city, Peking (later called Beijing). Chengzu rebuilt Peking into a magnificent city and completed the restoration of the **Grand Canal**. The construction of a canal had begun about 700 years BC. Over the centuries, various canals were dug and finally connected as one continuous canal. It had fallen into disrepair before Chengzu restored it to a functional canal extending more than eleven hundred miles.

Reconstruction

Have students discuss ways that reconstruction is occurring in their community (e.g., highways being resurfaced or bridges being replaced). These projects are ways of maintaining or improving a community's infrastructure. Good infrastructure is important to a strong, growing society.

CD: 11B Great Wall of China

An additional photo of the Great Wall is available on the CD.

The Forbidden City

Visit www.bjupress.com/resources for possible links to articles about China's Forbidden City.

Top, Temple of Heaven in Beijing; *middle,* Ming Tomb; *bottom right,* Grand Canal; *bottom left,* South gate of the ancient city of Dali, Yunnan

 CD: 11C Grand Canal Map

A map of the Grand Canal is available on the CD.

 CD: 11D Grand Canal Photo

An additional photo of the Grand Canal is available on the CD.

How Locks Function

If possible, find a video of a functioning canal (such as the Panama Canal) to demonstrate how locks allow boats to go to higher or lower elevations while bypassing rapids, waterfalls, and so on.

Dual Diplomacy

Zheng He used diplomacy, a large navy, and troops to accomplish his mission to demonstrate the might and greatness of China. Just as Theodore Roosevelt would do many years later, Zheng spoke softly but "carried a big stick."

Piracy

Piracy has been a problem in many parts of the world for centuries. America had to contend with the Barbary pirates during its early history. Men such as Black Beard became infamous as pirates. Today it is not uncommon for ships to be attacked by pirates based in Somalia, which is on the east coast of Africa.

Model of one of Zheng He's huge ships alongside a model of a ship used by Columbus

Exploration—The Zheng He Voyages

During a thirty-year period in the early fifteenth century, Ming emperors sent out seven naval expeditions. Around sixty large ships and over two hundred smaller ships were sent out to represent a renewed China. The emperor desired to gain control over trade and demonstrate Chinese superiority over countries along the Indian Ocean. This fleet also reduced the ever-present threat of piracy.

Zheng He was made the admiral of this great convoy with an army and crew that may have numbered almost thirty thousand. These ships sailed to many countries, including Arabia, East Africa, India, Indonesia, and Siam (Thailand). Zheng presented gifts of gold, silver, porcelain, and silk to foreign rulers.

The treasures he brought back to China included unusual animals such as ostriches, camels, and giraffes. On these voyages Zheng used diplomacy when possible and his large army when necessary in order to enhance China's reputation and bring countries into submission. On his fourth voyage, Zheng brought envoys from several nations to China. These officials came to honor the Ming court.

Over the course of these journeys, Zheng and his fleet traveled more than 30,000 miles. He extended Chinese influence beyond the Indian Ocean and may have traveled as far as Iran. Zheng died on the seventh voyage and was buried at sea.

The naval voyages ended with the death of Ming emperor Xuanzong in 1436. The restoration of the Grand Canal around 1417 had reduced the need for an ocean navy to transport and protect food supplies to the capital. In addition, a system of locks enabled the Chinese to maintain the water level needed to transport grain by way of the canal to the capital throughout the year.

One of the negative consequences of the reduced navy was the return of piracy and smuggling. Despite attempts to control these problems through regulation, the practices continued. Profits proved to be more powerful than government decrees.

Decline

While the Ming directed their attention to the south and east, foreign invaders from the north slowly gained control. The last four emperors became distracted with matters not related to governing China. One emperor even spent his life building furniture rather than attending to government. As a result, the power of the emperors diminished, and local officials ruled without fear of royal hindrance. Infighting and corruption further weakened the Ming dynasty. Seizing upon this opportunity, Manchurians from a region north of China steadily gained access to and then control of the Imperial City.

The Manchu Dynasty

In 1644 the **Manchu dynasty** seized power from the failing Ming dynasty. They had previously been invited into China to help the Ming government defeat a group of rebels. Once invited into the

Zheng He

Ask the students why the Chinese admiral gave gifts to the rulers of foreign kingdoms, especially since the Chinese viewed themselves as superior to all foreigners. *(Answers may vary, but it might have been a gesture of good will.)*

Activity 1: Map Study: Ming China

This activity is designed to help the students identify some of the key locations mentioned in this chapter and gain perspective on a land about which many have limited knowledge.

Zheng He Voyages

Visit www.bjupress.com/resources for possible links to articles about the Zheng He voyages.

country, however, the Manchus steadily took power from the weak Ming rulers. The Manchus established the second foreign dynasty to rule in Chinese history. The Manchu (Qing) dynasty ruled from 1644 to 1911, when dynasty rule ended in China.

Inclusive Rule

The Manchu rulers worked hard to build a good relationship with the people of their newly conquered empire. They knew that to retain power and succeed in governing, they needed the support of the people. The Manchus tried to become Chinese rather than try to make the Chinese become Manchurian. The Manchus allowed the Chinese to have a part in the government. At the higher levels of government, a Chinese and a Manchu often shared the same office. At the local level, almost all government officials were Chinese.

Imperial Absolutism

The Manchu government differed little from the early Ming government. The emperor still held supreme power and could order any policy to be enforced throughout the empire. Scholars continued to receive positions in government by receiving a high score on civil service exams. Many Chinese scholars held important positions at the imperial court in Peking. In addition, each level of government was responsible to the next higher level so that local governors had little control over their own affairs. This process enabled the Manchus to successfully govern their Chinese subjects for nearly two centuries without major discontent.

Manchuria

The Middle Kingdom

Throughout much of their history, the Chinese have had an attitude of superiority toward all other countries. They called themselves the Central Nation or the Middle Kingdom because they considered themselves to be the center of the world. In many ways China truly was much more advanced than other countries. For example, during the Middle Ages in Europe, China had a period of great achievement. You learned in Chapter 4 that the Chinese invented many technologies, including printing, papermaking, gunpowder, and chemical processing. Before Europe entered the modern age, China was the most technologically advanced region in the world.

The Manchus continued to promote this attitude of superiority. They especially tried to keep China from having any contact with the West through trade. China closed all but one or two ports to Western trade during the eighteenth century.

However, this policy created problems for China. It not only kept the West from receiving quantities of desirable Chinese goods but also prevented the Chinese from receiving the new inventions and learning of the West. While the Western world moved rapidly into the modern age, the Chinese refused to change their traditional culture. Their pride in this culture blinded them to the valuable achievements of other cultures. This isolation caused the Chinese to fall behind in many areas, including technology and the military.

Tradition vs. Change

Discuss the difference between holding onto tradition while rejecting all changes and accepting changes in custom or technology without question. Discuss how both of these positions can be problematic. Both change and tradition are necessary for progress, but each presents a danger when taken to extremes.

Section II

Objectives

Students should be able to

1. Explain how the destruction of the Byzantine Empire contributed to the expansion of the Ottoman Empire.

2. Analyze the reasons for Ottoman military success.

3. Describe the political, institutional, and economic development of the Ottoman Empire.

4. Explain how Muslim, Orthodox, and Jewish populations coexisted under Ottoman rule.

Asia Minor

This area where the Ottoman Empire developed is the same region where the apostle Paul conducted much of his missionary work as described in the book of Acts.

Section Quiz

1. What did the Ming dynasty restore to China?
2. Who founded the Ming dynasty?
3. What clay product did Chinese craftsmen perfect?
4. Who commanded the Chinese fleet during the fifteenth century?
5. The Ming dynasty was overthrown by people from what region?
★ Why was the Chinese concept of the Middle Kingdom contrary to a biblical worldview? Reference Bible verses such as Genesis 1:26–27; Acts 17:26; Daniel 4:17, 30–35; and 1 Cor. 4:7 and explain your answer.

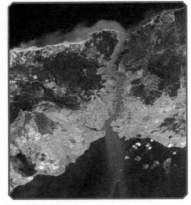

View of the Bosporus from space

II. The Ottoman Empire

The **Ottoman Empire** emerged during the beginning of the fourteenth century in the land east of the Byzantine Empire called **Anatolia**. Its beginnings were small, and most of its population was Turkish and practiced Islam. The Ottomans gained and lost territory over the next century as they wrestled for control of this peninsula with Byzantine forces and endured civil wars. When the Ottoman Empire emerged from internal strife under **Mehmet II** (r. 1451–81), the goal became the conquest of Constantinople.

Destruction of the Byzantine Empire

The Byzantine Empire had survived many wars and assaults over its thousand year history. However, by the fifteenth century, its age was showing. The days of this empire were numbered.

Decline

As is often the case with empires throughout history, weak leadership and internal strife had undermined the strength of the once-

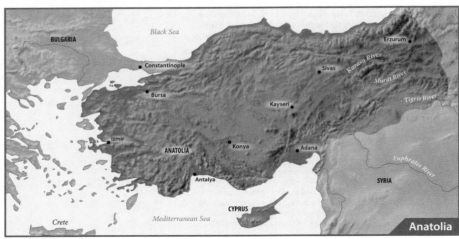

Anatolia

Section Quiz Answers

1. native Chinese rule
2. Taizu
3. porcelain (china)
4. Zheng He
5. Manchuria
★ Answers will vary. It was based on a pride of nationalism. This pride is contrary to the biblical teaching that all humans bear God's image (Gen. 1:26–27; cf. Acts 17:26). It is also contrary to God's rule over the nations. God determines the boundaries and times of empires (Acts 17:26). He decides who will rule and who will be ruled (Dan. 4:17). It is thus sinful and angering to God for people to boast about what they have simply received from God (Dan. 4:30; 1 Cor. 4:7).

CD: 11E Anatolia

This map from the student text is also available on the CD.

mighty Byzantine empire. Crusaders from Europe had attacked Constantinople in 1204 and had severely weakened it with a wound from which it would not recover. Byzantine emperors regained power but concentrated on building defenses west of the city rather than rebuilding aging defenses in the eastern provinces. The Ottomans steadily moved west and captured one Byzantine city after another. Final defeat of the remaining Byzantine forces was imminent.

Defeat

The Ottomans, led by Mehmet II, prepared for the attack by occupying a fort on one side of the Bosporus Strait and building a second fort on the other side of the strait. Using these forts, the Ottomans sought to prevent ships from coming to defend Constantinople. The greatly-outnumbered Byzantine forces repelled many assaults on the ground and prevented siege towers from sending Ottoman forces over the walls. Byzantine defenses also prevented the Ottoman ships from getting close to the city. However, the massive Byzantine walls could not withstand the continual assault of Ottoman cannon. On May 29, **1453**, Ottoman forces breached a section of the wall and poured into the city. They killed the defenders and pillaged (robbed) the city for three days.

Constantinople was rebuilt, and the name was changed to **Istanbul**. This city became the permanent capital of the Ottoman Empire.

Ottoman Military Successes

After the defeat of Constantinople, the Ottomans consolidated territory in eastern Europe and swept south into northern Africa and east across Asia Minor. The Ottoman navy turned the Mediterranean Sea and the Black Sea into Muslim-controlled waters.

The Ottoman army became one of the most advanced fighting forces in the world. They were among the first to use small cannon, called falcons, and muskets on the battlefield. The Ottoman cavalry also developed techniques similar to those used by the Mongols. They used bows and short swords and advanced on fast Arabian horses to attack their enemies. When necessary, the Ottomans also pretended to retreat. Then they surrounded their opponents in a crescent shaped formation and killed the enemy forces when they left the safety of the city walls.

The European nations struggled against repeated Ottoman attacks throughout Europe for the next two centuries. The Ottoman threat finally ended when the European forces were providentially enabled to repel the Ottoman attack on Vienna in 1683. Once again, Europe was delivered from a Muslim invasion. After this defeat, Europe continued to improve militarily while the Ottoman Empire slipped further and further behind.

Ottoman Development

The Ottomans built a strong, powerful, and wealthy empire that endured for six centuries. One might expect to find a complicated system of government and heavy taxing of wealth. However, the Ottoman Empire developed a simple system of rule. They also controlled income flow by limiting taxation of the wealth generated by the working class.

Mehmet II entering Constantinople in 1453

Glimpse of Istanbul with the Hagia Sophia, an Orthodox Church that Ottomans converted into a mosque

CD: 11F Falcon Cannon

A photo of this weapon is available on the CD.

Economic Strategy

The Ottoman rulers were wise to recognize the importance of merchants and artisans to the economic development of the empire. Today it is popular in many circles to advocate taxing the "wealthy" in order to level the economic field. However, the lowering of taxes on the producers of wealth has been shown to improve the economic welfare of all levels of society. This isn't a new concept. The Ottomans built a great empire by taking just enough in taxes to support the government and leaving the rest to be invested by the producers of wealth.

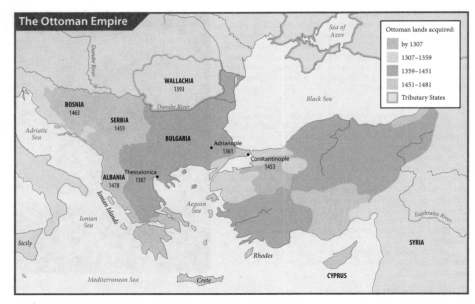

The Ottoman Empire

Ottoman lands acquired:
- by 1307
- 1307–1359
- 1359–1451
- 1451–1481
- Tributary States

Political Organization

The Ottomans developed a two-dimensional form of government: military and civil. The sultan held the highest position and served as both civil and religious leader of this Islamic empire. However, he delegated his authority to advisors and ministers who governed the various areas of the empire. During the period when the Ottoman Empire was quickly expanding, loyal and skilled subjects from many nationalities were appointed to administer the affairs of the empire. Albanians, Hungarians, Greeks, Jews, and others were recruited to manage this vast empire. This preference for qualified and talented officials strengthened the government and resulted in a stable empire during the early years of its development.

Economic Strategies

The leaders of the Ottoman Empire concentrated economic development in key cities like Adrianople and Istanbul. These cities were transformed into important commercial and industrial centers. The Ottomans viewed the merchants and artisans (skilled craftsmen) as essential to the economic success of the empire. These productive classes of society were enabled and encouraged to prosper. As a result, state revenues increased through a controlled taxation that did not hinder the prosperity of those who created the wealth.

In addition, they welcomed Jews who fled other parts of Europe due to persecution. The Jews brought skill and diligent labor in fields such as medicine, trade, and banking to the Ottoman Empire. Their economic success contributed to Ottoman economic success.

Key military conquests had placed the Ottoman Empire between the West and the East. Thus spices, silk, porcelain, and other Eastern treasures had to pass through Ottoman lands. The Otto-

---

CD: 11G The Ottoman Empire

This map from the student text is also available on the CD.

Foreign Workers

Have the students discuss the benefits and problems that result from recruiting foreign workers. (*Benefits might include finding the best qualified workers; problems might include denying work to a qualified citizen who needs to support his or her family.*)

England, France, and other European countries have allowed foreign workers and now find themselves overwhelmed by Muslims, some of whom are determined to bring every country under Muslim control. Similarly, some African countries use Chinese workers to operate mines and supervise development projects. This deprives many Africans of the opportunity to work in these areas.

man merchants made an immense profit by buying these goods and then selling them to the West at a much higher cost. However, this source of wealth had negative consequences for the Ottoman Empire. You learned in Chapter 7 that European nations responded by seeking water routes to India and China in order to bypass the Ottomans. The success of European nations at finding alternate routes to the East resulted in a significant economic decline in the Ottoman Empire.

Diversity

The Ottoman Empire grew into a vast and varied state which ruled over many conquered states. Within this empire a variety of religions, cultures, languages, and nationalities existed. The Ottomans used this diversity to their advantage.

Religious Mixture

Muslims, Christians, and Jews were all allowed to worship in the Ottoman Empire. Only those who practiced polytheism were not tolerated. Since the Ottoman Empire was Islamic (Sunni), the Christians and Jews were required to pay the government an annual tax. In exchange for paying this tax, the Orthodox and Armenian Christians and the Jews were allowed limited and monitored opportunities to worship. For example, Christians were forbidden to share the gospel with Muslims. Consistent with the teaching of Islam, conversion by a Muslim to Christianity was not allowed. In addition, no Orthodox or Armenian church building could be larger than the local mosque. As a result, many large cathedrals were destroyed or converted into mosques. The Muslim authorities even regulated the size and ringing of the bells in Orthodox churches. Christianity was permitted, but Christians were not allowed to practice Christianity in the way God commanded. Religious persecution of Christians and Jews did occur from time to time. As the Ottoman Empire began to disintegrate in the 1800s, persecution increased and intensified.

Cultural Variety

The Ottoman Empire began as a Turkish-dominated state. However, as the empire expanded through conquest, it gained control of territory on three continents. As a result, the Ottoman Empire became a collection of many cultures and languages. The Ottomans made provision for this variety and turned it into a means of strengthening the empire. The careful treatment of the various cultures and minorities enabled the Ottoman Empire to remain strong for several centuries.

Section Quiz

1. Who led the Ottoman forces in the assault on Constantinople?
2. What weapon did the Ottomans use to break through the Byzantine defenses?
3. What did the Ottomans rename Constantinople?
4. What type of religion was not tolerated in the Ottoman Empire?
5. Why is it not accurate to call the Ottoman Empire "Turkish"?
★ What economic strategy did the Ottomans use to strengthen their empire?

Jewish Contribution

The early Ottoman rulers showed remarkable insight when they welcomed Jews who were being persecuted in Europe. The Jews brought with them a wealth of knowledge about medicine, banking, and many other skills that would prove to be an asset to the Ottomans. The Jews were typically hard-working citizens and formed a close-knit community that allowed economic cooperation. Resources were often pooled to enable greater success for the Jewish community. However, eventually the success of the Jews resulted in jealousy and suspicion, which often leads to persecution and suffering. Such has been the experience of the Jews throughout much of history.

Religious Freedom

Have the students discuss the limits of the "religious freedom" allowed by the rulers of the Ottoman Empire. What aspects of Christian living made the Ottomans' "freedom" less than free? *(Suggested answer: they were not free to witness and win others to Christ.)*

Freedom of Worship

What are the pros and cons of a society that allows total freedom of worship? *(On the pro side, Christians retain the freedom to worship according to Scripture even in societies where they are the minority. They also may separate from a state church if it becomes corrupt. On the con side, if a society contains many very different religions, it is difficult for that society to agree on the moral norms that should be protected and encouraged by law. Second, if a non-tolerant religion becomes dominant, the religions that tolerated its rise may in the end not be tolerated.)*

Section Quiz Answers

1. Mehmet II
2. cannon
3. Istanbul
4. polytheism
5. This empire included a number of cultures in addition to the Turks.
★ Answers will vary but should include some of the following: the Ottomans concentrated economic development in key cities, encouraged the merchants and artisans, controlled taxation, welcomed Jews, and bought products from China and then sold them at a much higher price.

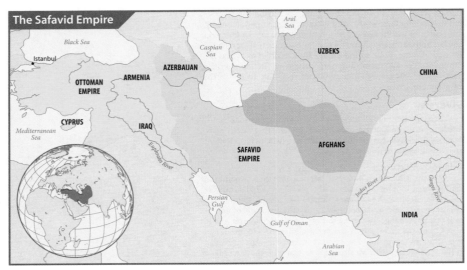

The Safavid Empire

Section III

Objectives

Students should be able to

1. Describe the unification of Persia under the Safavids and Ismail I.
2. Assess Safavid political and cultural achievements under Shah Abbas.

Iran

The Persians were the ancestors of the current nation of Iran. This region has maintained a civilization for thousands of years dating back to shortly after the Flood. Their modern history began around 1921. The ruling dynasty (Qajar) was overthrown, and the new leaders developed industrialism, railroad construction, and a modern education system. Following World War II, Mohammad Reza Pahlavi gained power and continued the modernization of Iran, but he used brutal means to crush all

III. The Safavid Empire

In the region that lay between the Ottoman Empire and India, the Persians reemerged in a new state. Remarkably, this empire grew out of a boy's desire to avenge the murder of some of his family.

Ismail and his family belonged to the Safavid clan. A rival clan killed his father and older brother. This murder resulted in Ismail's becoming the head of his family at the age of seven. To survive, he went into hiding until he was twelve. Then he began his military career by leading forces to take revenge on those who murdered his father.

Once he had exacted his vengeance, Ismail's fame quickly spread and he gathered supporters. Ismail continued to seize territory and began to build a state. With the conquest of the city of Tabriz in 1501, his empire was established. He became **Shah Ismail I** and founded the **Safavid dynasty** (1501–1722). He built this fledgling state into a growing economic and political power. Ismail formed a strong centralized government and brought stability to this region. He also attempted to develop diplomatic relationships with neighboring states. Working with nearby countries was essential to this region because of its location along the trade route between the East and the West.

Whereas the Ottoman Empire was primarily Sunni Muslim, the Safavid Empire became Shia Muslim under Ismail's influence. The Safavids often struggled with the Ottomans, Uzbeks (to the north), and even Portuguese forces for control of disputed territories and to determine which group would dominate this region. Ismail had developed a reputation for being invincible. However, this reputation was shattered in 1514 when the Safavid forces suffered defeat to a much larger Ottoman force. Ismail withdrew from an active role in governing the empire, and it became vulnerable to internal struggles and attack from neighboring states.

CD: 11H The Safavid Empire

This map from the student text is also available on the CD.

CD: 11I Safavid Helmet

A photo of a Safavid helmet is available on the CD.

Activity 4: Map Study: Asia Minor

This activity is designed to reinforce the students' knowledge of a little-known region.

The Safavid Empire

Visit www.bjupress.com/resources for possible links to articles about the Safavid Empire.

During a time of weakness in 1587, a rival family leader replaced the Safavid ruler with his sixteen-year-old son **Abbas**. Abbas proved to be a strong leader and rebuilt centralized authority for the Safavid Empire. Abbas is regarded as the second founder of this empire. He reorganized the army and conquered land that had been taken from the Safavids by the Ottomans and others. Abbas regained control of Baghdad and allied with the British to capture the Strait of Hormuz to enhance trade. Abbas also became a great builder of religious architecture, royal palaces, and public buildings. Under his leadership, a new style of architecture developed.

As with most empires, the Safavid Empire declined due to a lack of qualified successors. Neighboring states, including the Ottomans, invaded and took away territory. Internal strife led to revolts. In 1722 this empire was overthrown by Afghan forces. However, the foundation of the modern state of Iran had been laid.

Masjed-e-shah in Esfahan, an example of Safavid architecture

Section Quiz

1. Where was the Safavid Empire located?
2. Who founded this empire?
3. Who became ruler as a youth in 1587 and proved to be a strong leader?
4. What modern country was founded on the Safavid Empire?
★ Why did the Safavid Empire adopt Shia Islam as its official version of Islam?

IV. The Mughal Empire

The Mongols had attempted to conquer India for centuries. Despite many attempts and the terrible slaughter of Indians by Tamerlane (Chapter 4), the Mongols had only been able to retain control of northern India. During the sixteenth century, a descendant of the Mongols and Turks finally gained control of most of India.

Conquest

The Muslim leader **Babur**, "the Tiger," became the leader of the Turkish-Mongol tribes of modern Afghanistan. In 1526 he invaded northern India with an army of twelve thousand men and overthrew the Muslim government. Babur was a descendant of two great Asian conquerors, Chinggis Khan (Mongol) and Tamerlane (Turk). He established the **Mughal** dynasty (from *Mongol*) and conquered a large region in northern India.

Following the brutal example of his predecessors, Babur directed his forces to practice Muslim jihad by slaughtering their way into control of northern India. When they had destroyed all opposition, the Mughal rulers rebuilt India according to Islamic law and

opposition. When his health failed in the late 1970s, he left the country for medical treatment. During the Shah's extended absence, Ayatollah Khomeini led the Iranian revolution, and to this day Islamist leaders hold the nation in an iron grip.

Section IV

Objectives

Students should be able to

1. Describe the Mughal conquest of central and southern India.
2. Explain the relationship between Muslims and Hindus during Akbar's rule.
3. Describe the decline of the Mughal Empire and the eventual rule of India by Great Britain.

Section Quiz Answers

1. between the Ottoman Empire and India
2. Ismail I
3. Abbas
4. Iran
★ Ismail led the Safavids to adopt this version of Islam.

Babur, "The Tiger"

Many historians have repeated the myth that Babur differed from his Muslim predecessors by conquering regions of India without resorting to slaughter. However, he reported in his journals that he practiced jihad against the Hindus and ordered the erection of pillars of heads from his Hindu captives. (*The Legacy of Jihad: Islamic Holy War and the Fate of Non-Muslims*, 459)

The Taj Mahal, an example of Mughal architecture

acquired great wealth. Over time, the Mughal culture experienced a renewal of the arts, including a distinct type of architecture.

The most effective Mughal ruler came to power at the age of thirteen following the death of his father. **Akbar** (r. 1556–1605), the grandson of Babur, continued the brutal conquest of India begun by his grandfather. Under Akbar's military leadership, the Mughal Empire expanded to the west, east, and south to central India.

Reform

Having conquered central India through military conquest by means of the Muslim practice of jihad against non-Muslims, Akbar gradually began to institute reforms in Indian society. He is said to have abolished the tax on non-Muslims and to have begun including Hindus in government, although he continued to endorse periodic slaughter of non-Muslims as commanded in the Qur'an.

Decline

The last effective Mughal ruler, Aurangzeb, consumed most of the Mughal Empire's resources in conquering lower India. His death in 1707 ended the expansion of the empire and was followed by rapid decline. Succeeding rulers had little power and were dominated by rising warlords. Persian and Afghan forces frequently invaded and carried off treasures from Indian cities, including Delhi.

In 1803 the nominal Mughal ruler Shah Alam II agreed to the offer of protection from the **British East India Company**. The British maintained the appearance of working under the Mughal rulers until 1857, when they exiled the last Mughal Emperor and imposed direct rule.

British East India Company

The East India Company was an early English joint-stock company that was formed to develop trade with the East Indies. The company soon turned its attention to India and China. At first, this company engaged in trading cotton, silk, tea, and other products. Later, with the assistance of British forces, it gained enough power to rule large areas of India and abandoned commercial activity. Company officials proved to be poor governors, and the Indians resisted British efforts to force Western ideas on the natives. Following Indian rebellions, the British government took over direct control of India in 1858, and the East India Company was later dissolved in 1874.

Activity 2: Encounter with a Lion

This excerpt from a diary tells of a Jesuit missionary's experiences on a hunt. The activity is designed to provide students a glimpse into this time period and sharpen their comprehension skills.

Activity 3: Matching Exercise

This activity will help the students distinguish the various dynasties and empires covered in the chapter.

 ## CD: 11J Badshahi Mosque

A photo of the Badshahi Mosque (built by Aurangzeb in what is today Lahore, Pakistan) is available on the CD.

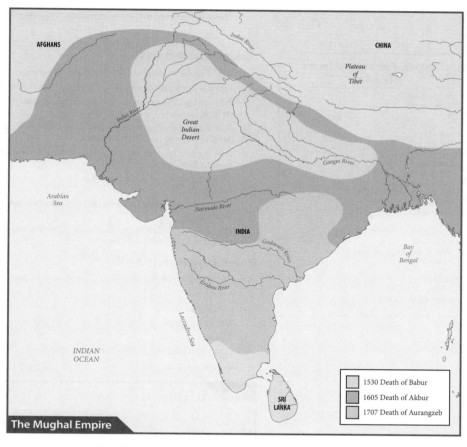

1530 Death of Babur

1605 Death of Akbur

1707 Death of Aurangzeb

The Mughal Empire

Section Quiz

1. When were the Mongols finally able to gain control of most of India?
2. Who founded the Mughal Empire?
3. Who was the most effective Mughal ruler?
4. How did Akbar treat Hindus?
5. What nation gained control of India in 1803?
★ Why was Akbar considered the most effective Mughal ruler?

 CD: 11K The Mughal Empire

This map from the student text is also available on the CD.

Section Quiz Answers

1. during the sixteenth century
2. Babur
3. Akbar
4. He included them in government.
5. Britain
★ Answers will vary. He greatly expanded the Mughal Empire to Central Asia. He is said to have established many reforms, including abolishing taxes on non-Muslims and allowing Hindus to serve in government.

CHAPTER REVIEW

People, Places, and Terms to Know

Middle Kingdom
Ming dynasty
Taizu
Chengzu
porcelain
landscapes
Imperial City
Grand Canal
Zheng He
Manchu dynasty
Ottoman Empire
Anatolia
Mehmet II
1453
Istanbul
Shah Ismail I
Safavid dynasty
Abbas
Babur
Mughal
Akbar
British East India Company

Making Connections

1. Why did China refer to itself as the Middle Kingdom?
2. How did Emperor Taizu exercise absolute power in China?
3. Why did the Chinese government conclude that a navy was no longer essential?
4. How did Ottoman profits on goods from the East result in negative consequences for the empire?
5. How did the Ottomans initially deal with the mixture of religions in their empire?
6. Why did the twelve-year-old Ismail gather an army and begin to conquer?
7. Why is Abbas regarded as the second founder of the Safavid Empire?
8. Why did the two European countries mentioned in this chapter seek to gain influence in Eurasia?

Developing History Skills

1. Match each of the following to its location on the map.
   a. Anatolia
   b. Arabian Sea
   c. Constantinople
   d. India
   e. Mediterranean Sea
   f. Safavid Empire

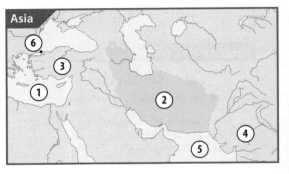

2. Why were the Manchurians able to seize control of China? What history lessons can you draw from this?

Activity 5: Chapter Review

This activity will help the students review the chapter content.

Chapter Review Answers

Making Connections

1. The Chinese considered their civilization to be the center of the world.
2. He regulated every aspect of Chinese society and used secret police to deal with any who opposed him.
3. The restoration of the Great Canal and its lock system enabled grain supplies to be delivered to the capital year round. Thus, ships were no longer needed to deliver and protect these supplies on ocean routes.
4. Europeans sought and found alternate trade routes by sea and bypassed the Ottomans.
5. Muslims, Christians, and Jews were allowed to exist in the Ottoman Empire. Only polytheism was prohibited.
6. to avenge his father's murder
7. He rebuilt a centralized authority, reorganized the army, and conquered land that had been taken by the Ottomans and others.
8. to gain trade advantages

Developing History Skills

1. a. 3
   b. 5
   c. 6
   d. 4
   e. 1
   f. 2

2. Answers will vary. The Ming leaders became distracted and failed to provide strong leadership. Infighting and corruption weakened the central government. Failure to put down a rebellion by the Ming leaders provided an open door for a Manchurian takeover.

Thinking Critically

1. Based on the information in this chapter, describe the devastation of the Mughal invasion of India.

2. What were the long-term consequences of China's exclusion of foreigners during this period?

Living in God's World

1. Imagine that you are a Christian historian analyzing the Ming and Manchurian periods of Chinese history. Write a paragraph analyzing Chinese dislike of foreigners in light of the Christian command to love one's neighbor. Be sure to draw on your answer to the previous question.

2. Imagine that you are a Christian leader in the Ottoman Empire. Write a brief speech to be delivered before the emperor in defense of the Christian duty to evangelize. Address the issue of tolerance. Refer to Acts 4:19.

Thinking Critically

1. Answers will vary. The devastation was drastic. Babur used brutal tactics to gain control and killed many to secure submission. This practice continued under Akbar.

2. Answers will vary. Chinese isolation prevented them from gaining access to new inventions and ideas that developed in the West. Before long, the Chinese had fallen behind in areas such as technology and military.

Living in God's World

1. Answers will vary. Many Chinese failed to love their neighbors through good trade relations when they had something to offer. Likewise, Chinese rulers failed to show love when they deprived their subjects of technological advances of the West.

2. Answers will vary, but the speech should draw on the apostle Peter's response in Acts 4:19, which in the context of evangelism indicates that obedience to God must take precedence over obedience to human government. Students should also note that it is not true tolerance if mandatory aspects of a religion are forbidden. Finally, students should raise the issue of truth. Christianity ought to be free to evangelize because it is the one true religion.

The Revolutionary Age 1750–1900

Following the lead of Britain, European states began to turn the many raw materials from the colonies into finished goods and transformed much of the world during the Industrial Revolution.

Soon the demand for raw materials and the greed of men led to the conquest of regions, including Africa and Asia, in order for Europeans to take full advantage of resources. Rivalries developed as nations competed for control of these resource-rich regions.

Indian servants waiting on British colonial officials.
Getty Images

Chapter Goals

Students should be able to

1. Explain the causes and effects of the French Revolution on the world and especially on Europe.
2. Analyze how the American War for Independence differed significantly from the French Revolution.
3. Explain the rise and fall of Napoleon.
4. Evaluate the nationalistic revolutions in nineteenth-century Europe.
5. Contrast how Germany and Italy achieved unification.

1650–1900

Louis XIV ends religious toleration of Huguenots 1685

Seven Years' War 1754–63

| 1650 | 1700 | 1750 |

Chapter 12 Lesson Plan Chart

Section Title	Main Activity	Pages	Days
I. French Revolution	Activity 1: The Three Estates of France	210–14	1–2 days
II. Rise and Fall of Napoleon	Activity 2: The Battle of Waterloo	214–16	1–1½ days
III. Revolts Across Europe	Activity 3: Map Study: Europe	216–18	1 day
IV. German and Italian Unification	Activity 4: Chapter Review	218–21	1–1½ days
TOTAL SUGGESTED DAYS (INCLUDING 1 DAY EACH FOR REVIEW AND TESTING)			6–8 days

Materials List

Section I

- Activity 1 from the *Student Activities* manual
- CD: 12A Declaration of the Rights of Man
- A copy of *A Tale of Two Cities* or a video of this story

Section II

- CD: 12B Battle Scenes
- A copy of *The Count of Monte Cristo*
- Activity 2 from the *Student Activities* manual

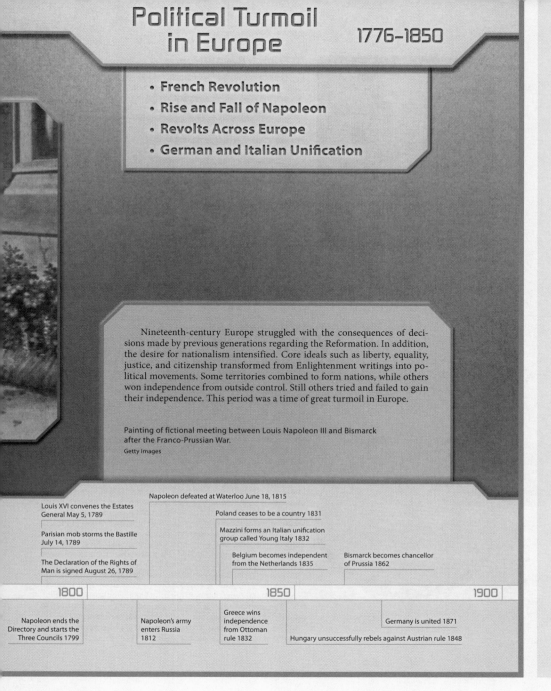

Political Turmoil in Europe

1776–1850

- French Revolution
- Rise and Fall of Napoleon
- Revolts Across Europe
- German and Italian Unification

Nineteenth-century Europe struggled with the consequences of decisions made by previous generations regarding the Reformation. In addition, the desire for nationalism intensified. Core ideals such as liberty, equality, justice, and citizenship transformed from Enlightenment writings into political movements. Some territories combined to form nations, while others won independence from outside control. Still others tried and failed to gain their independence. This period was a time of great turmoil in Europe.

Painting of fictional meeting between Louis Napoleon III and Bismarck after the Franco-Prussian War.
Getty Images

Napoleon defeated at Waterloo June 18, 1815

Louis XVI convenes the Estates General May 5, 1789

Parisian mob storms the Bastille July 14, 1789

The Declaration of the Rights of Man is signed August 26, 1789

Poland ceases to be a country 1831

Mazzini forms an Italian unification group called Young Italy 1832

Belgium becomes independent from the Netherlands 1835

Bismarck becomes chancellor of Prussia 1862

1800 **1850** **1900**

Napoleon ends the Directory and starts the Three Councils 1799

Napoleon's army enters Russia 1812

Greece wins independence from Ottoman rule 1832

Germany is united 1871

Hungary unsuccessfully rebels against Austrian rule 1848

Section III

- Activity 3 from the *Student Activities* manual

Section IV

- CD: 12C Unification of Germany; 12D Unification of Italy
- Activity 4 from the *Student Activities* manual

Section I

Students should be able to

1. Analyze how political incompetence, social problems, and economic troubles prepared France for revolution.
2. Describe the phases of the French Revolution that led to the rise of Napoleon.
3. Explain how the Revolution affected French society.
4. Contrast the French Revolution and the American Revolutionary War.

Voltaire

Some historians have described Voltaire as an atheist, but the term *deist* seems more accurate. He did not deny the existence of God; rather, he rejected Scripture and the concept of a God Who intervenes in the affairs of men. The often-repeated story that his home was later purchased by the Geneva Bible Society cannot be verified.

The Church of Rome and Absolutism

Since the Middle Ages, the Church of Rome had gradually developed the doctrine of the infallibility of the pope and the church councils. Catholics were required to submit to these authorities without question. This mindset was conducive to the development of absolute monarchs, who required citizens to submit to the monarch or his representatives without question. Further, just as Rome rejected the checks and balances that came about through the Reforma-

Voltaire

Population of France

Third Estate
24 million
98.08%

Second Estate
350,000
1.43%

First Estate
120,000
.49%

I. French Revolution

French writers such as François-Marie Arouet (better known as **Voltaire**) wrote volumes of literature to describe and endorse Enlightenment ideals. Voltaire produced over twenty thousand letters, up to two thousand books, and many pamphlets. This flood of literature from Voltaire and other Enlightenment philosophers inspired the French to demand equality, civil liberties, and religious freedom. However, in the eighteenth century, these freedoms were only a dream for the vast majority of the French people.

Enlightenment thought encouraged freedom, but not a freedom tempered by responsibility and accountability to a higher power. Enlightenment philosophers had taken God and His Word out of the equation. Therefore, the freedom that the Enlightenment proclaimed led to certain failure and, finally, to anarchy in France.

You learned in Chapter 6 that France had rejected the Reformation in favor of Roman Catholicism. The Church of Rome taught its followers to submit to papal authority. This submission supported the concept of an absolute monarchy. Yet many people in France embraced the Reformation. These French Protestants became known as Huguenots (HYOO guh NAHTS). The limited toleration of Huguenots ended under Louis XIV in 1685. By royal decree they were required to convert to Catholicism. Many chose instead to flee the country. Their departure removed pressure to retain checks and balances on the king's power.

In addition, the French had retained a corrupt social structure that gave the king absolute power and the elite members of French society immunity from most taxes. As a result, the nation placed a terrible financial burden on the middle and lower classes. Continued mismanagement of the government, refusal to modify the existing system, and the spread of Enlightenment ideals provided an opportunity for violent social turmoil.

Reasons for Revolution

Social Discrimination

On the French social ladder, the leaders of the French church occupied the highest position. The upper tier of the **First Estate**, the archbishops and bishops, numbered about ten thousand. They managed land for the Roman Church that amounted to about ten percent of the country, and they also owned valuable properties in the cities. Under French law, these wealthy churchmen and their properties were exempt from most taxes. Their luxurious lifestyle differed drastically from that of the poor priest or monk who interacted with the French population. These common clergymen struggled to exist and supported the revolution when it finally swept across France.

The **Second Estate** was composed of about three hundred fifty thousand nobles and other aristocrats who owned or controlled about twenty percent of the land. They were also exempt from many taxes. Members of this class gained their wealth by charging rent to the peasants who farmed their land and charging fees for the use of their mills, wine presses, and bakeries. Given their enviable financial and social standing, they opposed any changes to the status quo.

The great majority of French men and women were confined to the **Third Estate**. This group contained a wide variety of citizens, including the middle class, artisans, townsmen, and peasants. At least twenty-four million people occupied the Third Estate. The middle

Activity 1: The Three Estates of France

This matching activity helps the students understand the dramatic differences between the three estates of France.

Tax Inequities

Discuss the great inequities between members of the three estates in eighteenth-century France. Ask students to contrast the great differences in tax burdens in these three estates. Compare this with the fact that about 86% of federal taxes in the United States are paid by 25% of the people. In addition, about half of the American population pays little or nothing in federal taxes. Ask the students if the claims that the wealthy are not paying their fair share in taxes rings true in light of these statistics.

The French Revolution

Visit www.bjupress.com/resources for possible links to articles about the French Revolution.

class accounted for about ten percent of the population and owned between fifteen and twenty percent of the land. Ninety percent of the people were peasants, and they owned or rented up to fifty percent of the land.

In the French society, those who were wealthy produced little or no wealth and were protected from most of the tax burden. Ironically, many of those who produced the nation's wealth were not allowed to benefit from their earned prosperity. Under this imbalanced system, the government oppressively taxed and the nobility charged rents and other fees to groups such as merchants, farmers, and artisans. This system reduced many to poverty, and it limited opportunities for economic growth. At the same time, those who paid the most in taxes, rents, and fees were denied basic freedoms and political representation in the governing of France. Such injustice would not be sustained much longer.

Economic Collapse

French kings had spent the nation's wealth lavishly since the reign of Louis XIV. The cost of frequent wars and the building and maintenance of the Palace of Versailles had drained France of much wealth. Louis XV continued to drain French resources during the Seven Years' War (1754–63) with England. French support of the American War for Independence also placed French finances under a great strain. During the reign of Louis XVI, the French government borrowed its way into near bankruptcy. Payments on the national debt consumed nearly half of the annual income from taxes and other fees. By 1787 the French government faced a major economic crisis. After much delay and hesitancy, Louis XVI convened the **Estates-General** in 1789. This was the only political body with the authority to reform the tax system. The Estates-General had not been convened since 1614 due to the rise of absolute monarchs and the ability of French kings to bypass this assembly. However, France faced a financial crisis, and nothing less than a meeting of representatives of the three estates could save France. Once this meeting occurred, events quickly spiraled out of control.

Political Incompetence

The political and financial collapse in France occurred during the reign of **Louis XVI** and **Marie-Antoinette**. It is only fair to say that they inherited many of the problems from previous monarchs. However, they proved to be totally unqualified to lead the nation and diffuse the mounting crisis.

In 1770 sixteen-year-old Louis married fifteen-year-old Marie-Antoinette, and France celebrated this union as the hope for the future of France. Upon the death of Louis XV in 1774, Louis became the king of France. Initially this royal couple enjoyed great popularity among the French people.

The Estates-General

As the French royal power extended across the territories of France, the king recognized the need for an assembly to represent the people and provide counsel. In 1302 the first assembly was held, and for the next three hundred years it met whenever called by the king. Until the sixteenth century, representatives of the First and Second Estates were selected by the king. The Third Estate was distinct in that its representatives were elected by the people.

At some point prior to and during the Hundred Years' War, this assembly held the power of the purse and retained a measure of control over the French king. However, after this period the assembly surrendered that right and allowed the king greater freedom to tax without restriction.

Following the meeting of the Estates-General in 1614, absolute monarchs, beginning with Louis XIV, avoided calling the assembly into session. The dire economic condition of France in 1789 forced Louis XVI to call this body into session. The rest is history.

Marie-Antoinette by Perin-Salbreux, Lie Louis/Musee des Beaux-Arts, Reims, France/© Scala/Art Resource

Louis XVI

Marie-Antoinette

---

tion, so absolute monarchs opposed limitations of their power.

Huguenots

When Louis XIV required Huguenots to convert to Roman Catholicism, he set off a chain of events that irreparably damaged France. Most of the Huguenots chose to flee to other lands, including Britain and the American colonies. Louis soon realized that his decree would drain France of valuable human resources, but could not prevent the mass exodus. As a result, France suffered the loss of many of its most productive, intelligent, and skilled citizens.

Excessive and Unequal Taxation

In France, most revenue was raised through taxation. Because wealthy churchmen and the nobles were exempted from most taxes, the bulk of the taxes were paid by common citizens, such as peasants. Peasants were required to pay one tenth of their income or crops to the Roman Church. They also had to pay a five percent property tax, as well as a tax on the number of people in their households. In addition, many peasants had to pay rent to landlords as well as give them a portion of their produce. Peasants also had to pay a tax to use a noble's mill, wine press, or bakery. After paying these oppressive taxes, peasants had little left to live on.

Fourth Estate

This term has been used to refer to the press. The literature produced during the Revolution helped to spread revolutionary ideas across France.

Louis XVI

Visit www.bjupress.com/resources for possible links to articles about Louis XVI.

Marie Antoinette

Visit www.bjupress.com/resources for possible links to articles about Marie Antoinette.

Liberal vs. Conservative

During the French Revolution, a *conservative* was one who supported the status quo: the heavy taxation and oppression of the lower classes. A *liberal* was one who favored greater freedom for all citizens. Today the meanings are often reversed. In modern economics, *classical liberals* are those who support conservative politics and the free market economic system.

Royal tennis court where the famous oath was signed

Tennis Court Oath

The members of the Third Estate promised not to disband until a constitution had been approved that guaranteed basic rights to everyone in France. While the goals were admirable and addressed many problems, these efforts were doomed to failure. They made no provision for man's sinful nature. Any document founded on this false assumption is doomed to fail. The U.S. Constitution at least implies man's sinful nature by separation of powers and limitations on the powers of government. The great expectations reflected in this oath were quickly dashed by a rapid decline into anarchy. Sadly, the French constitution became a meaningless document within one year.

However, Louis quickly demonstrated that he was weak and incapable of making difficult choices. Marie-Antoinette convinced Louis to dismiss his father's ministers. The tax reforms that Louis XV had started near the end of his reign to restore financial stability ended with this unfortunate decision. Louis and Marie-Antoinette quickly moved from popular to unpopular. Before long, unpopularity gave way to hatred as the French people saw their hopes vanish under the lavish but ineffective rule of Louis.

Course of the Revolution

On May 5, 1789, Louis XVI convened the Estates-General. From the outset, Louis humiliated the representatives of the Third Estate and gave preference to the members of the First and Second Estates. Traditionally each estate had one vote. However, the representatives of the Third Estate demanded one vote for each representative. This voting method would provide a clear advantage for those representing the large majority of French citizens.

When the First and Second Estates refused to change the rules for voting, the representatives of the Third Estate left the meeting in anger. Members of the Third Estate formed the **National Assembly** of France and signed the famous Tennis Court Oath three days later.

At this point, the members of the National Assembly had no intention of transforming France into a democracy or ending the monarchy. They simply wanted a constitution that would guarantee basic rights to all French citizens and limit the government to a constitutional monarchy. Conditions changed rapidly as the French king continued to aggravate the situation.

Louis made the situation much worse when he ordered troops to assemble outside of Paris. When the citizens learned of this, they began to panic. They responded by searching for weapons to defend themselves. On July 14 a crowd gathered at the Bastille, a fortress-prison formerly used to house political prisoners. When they encountered resistance, possibly even gunfire into the crowd, the mob stormed the building and killed those assigned to guard it. July 14 has since been celebrated as France's day of independence.

Riots and demonstrations continued and grew increasingly violent. Rioters attacked government buildings and destroyed documents that recorded debts and rents due to members of the First and Second Estates. The king remained passive and failed to use troops to end the violence. Louis remained king in name only from this point on.

Destruction of the Old Regime

On August 26, 1789, the National Assembly signed the **Declaration of the Rights of Man**. This document demanded the end of many of the abuses suffered by the French people and advocated ideals that included innocence until guilt is proven and liberty to do anything that does not injure another. The sovereign will of the people became the basis for law, and the false precepts of humanism became the standard for France.

The National Assembly confiscated lands owned by the Roman Church in an effort to pay off the massive national debt. This move resulted in a verbal attack from the pope and great concern among many loyal Catholics in France. Many conservatives and nobles fled France and settled in neighboring countries. They labored to over-

CD: 12A Declaration of the Rights of Man

The text of the Declaration of the Rights of Man is available on the CD.

Change

Discuss the legitimate grievances of the French people. Help students understand how the absence of absolute standards and a strong Christian influence resulted in the desire for change degenerating into violent revolution.

throw the revolutionary government and regain their privileged positions. Even Louis XVI attempted to flee the country on June 20, 1791, but he and his family were captured and held prisoners.

Many of the wealthy French citizens had fled to Austria. The National Assembly demanded that Austria and other countries send these citizens back to France. Austria refused to comply with this demand. In response, the French government declared war on Austria, Marie-Antoinette's homeland, in April 1792. Prussia entered the war as Austria's ally. When the Prussians warned the French not to harm the king, the revolution took a radical turn. Louis was tried and executed.

Reign of Terror

With the mounting problems of dealing with internal and international strife, the French leaders appointed committees to manage the government. The most important of these, the **Committee of Public Safety**, soon gained absolute authority in France.

To maintain control, this group of radicals called for the removal of all opponents and instituted a period of mass execution known as the **Reign of Terror**. At least twenty-five thousand men and women from all levels of society were sent to the guillotine, including Marie-Antoinette. Many members of the Third Estate who had supported the revolution became victims of this violent purge.

Following the rejection of this form of government, a new government was formed that was headed by a five-man committee known as the **Directory**. This government quickly made peace with Prussia and Spain but remained at war with Austria and Britain. The leaders came to rely more and more on the army for support since they lacked the support of most of the French. These circumstances created a rare opportunity for one man to seize power and rule France.

Contrast with the American Revolution

While many attempt to compare the American Revolution with the French Revolution, there are few similarities. France had rejected the Protestant Reformation and persecuted the Huguenots. In stark contrast, the American colonies had been founded and populated to a large degree by Protestants who fled persecution in Europe. Enlightenment ideas influenced both France and the American colonies. However, the French accepted these ideas without the biblical restraints recognized by many American colonists.

The French Revolution also opposed religion and established a secular state. The American colonists, however, were encouraged, supported, and often led by their Protestant religious leaders. In addition, the American colonies experienced a great spiritual awakening prior to the war and an extended period of revival during and following the war. In striking contrast, French revolutionaries exalted the goddess of Reason and elevated Enlightenment philosophy to a religion.

Causes

Britain had spent vast sums of money to win the Seven Years' War against France. The king and Parliament looked to the American colonies to help pay off this debt. However, in the process, the British began to threaten the economic, political, and religious liberties that American colonists had enjoyed for more than a century. The Americans vigorously protested and referred to the writings of

Revolutionary Ideals

While the French Revolution failed to accomplish its many lofty goals, the ideals survived for future generations. Concepts including social equality, human rights, and constitutionalism continue to have an influence on modern society. These concepts are good and noble. However, they can be twisted by the wrong worldview. The foundation upon which they are built will determine whether they bring God's blessing or a curse upon a society. For example, democracy, or majority rule, will result in a thriving and balanced society if the majority is directed by a Christian worldview. However, a majority that is lead by the errors of humanism will produce a society that God cannot and will not bless. Such a society is doomed to ultimate destruction.

Effect on French Society

The French Revolution had a profound effect on French society. Religious institutions such as the Roman Church never regained their former power and wealth. Social relations were drastically altered by the secularization of marriage, and divorce became much easier. The legal and political position of women changed because women often took a leading role in the uprisings and demonstrations. While women did not achieve equality with men during the French Revolution, they did achieve a greater voice in government and society.

With the introduction of state-controlled education, children became the property of the state, and the role of parents was diminished. Although many more students received an education, they were taught to support and serve the state. This child control along with easier divorces had a negative impact on the family in France.

The enormous loss of life during the French Revolution had dreadful consequences for France that defy calculation. From 1798 to the end of the Battle of Waterloo in 1815, an estimated 1.4 million French soldiers died in battle. It would take France generations to recover from these losses. When one adds in the twenty-five to forty thousand people who were executed during the French Revolution, the human cost is staggering.

Decline of Popular Support

The French Revolution began as an unruly mob that attacked symbols of royal authority such as the Bastille. Under these conditions, gaining and retaining popular support was a difficult process for the leaders of the Revolution. Leaders who had the support of the masses one day were often sent to the guillotine the next. By the end of the Reign of Terror, the Directory maintained power only with the support of the military. The prominent role of the military made it possible for Napoleon to stage a *coup d'état* (a sudden and illegal seizure of power).

Role of Religion During the French Revolution

Discuss the campaign to dechristianize French society. Clergy were deported or executed, and churches were closed or destroyed. In 1793 the revolutionaries went so far as to celebrate the goddess Reason in Notre Dame Cathedral.

A Tale of Two Cities

Have some students read and discuss with the class portions of Charles Dickens's *A Tale of Two Cities*. Another option might be to get a video version of this story.

Lack of Qualified Leadership

While France desperately searched for qualified leaders, God blessed the developing American nation with a large number of talented and far-sighted leaders, including many of the early presidents. It seems that God graciously provided an abundance of godly or at least Bible-influenced men to lead the young nation on a path that resulted in great blessing.

The First Shots by William Barnes Wollen/Stringer/Hulton Archive/Getty Images

Minutemen facing British soldiers on Lexington Common, Massachusetts, in the first battle in the War for Independence, 19th April 1775

> ### Reformation Heritage
> In the early days of the Reformation, German nobles protested against attempts to use the government to halt the Reformation. Reformers developed a heritage of holding rulers accountable for the manner in which they ruled. They realized that human depravity affects the actions of leaders. To limit the tendency to abuse power, they developed checks and balances.

men such as John Locke regarding natural rights and the social contract between people and their government. The colonists insisted on the same liberty that had been won by the British in the Glorious Revolution.

In addition, the American colonists founded many arguments on Reformation principles, including the importance of the individual and opposition to oppression. The British government in Canada had recently guaranteed a privileged status for the Roman Church. This decision created genuine concern among the predominately Protestant colonists regarding the possibility that Catholicism would be imposed on them. This combined threat of the loss of economic, political, and religious freedom unified the American colonies for a possible war. The invasion of British forces triggered that war.

The French had suffered under generations of oppression. When the Revolution erupted, the citizens were attempting to overthrow a tradition of tyranny and social, political, and economic inequality. Whereas the Americans followed the local and colonial authorities in repelling an invasion, the French revolted against all authority and attacked government officials. Also, while some in France initially sought religious freedom, the French Revolution soon opposed religion or corrupted it.

Character and Consequences

American colonists were led by local, elected leaders who were guided in many ways by a biblical viewpoint. They balanced liberty with responsibility. Rather than massive rejection of local authority and unrestricted violence, the American colonists limited their resistance to repelling the invaders and defending their freedom. The American Revolution did not lead to mass executions and anarchy. Rather, it led to the birthing of a nation that would be governed by laws and a constitution with a bill of rights to protect its citizens. The American Revolution tempered Enlightenment ideals with scriptural principles.

The French were led by students of the Enlightenment who sought liberty without responsibility. The French leaders were humanists who had rejected the scriptural view of man as fallen. Believing that man was perfectible, the leaders rushed to sweep away the existing government and replace it with one that would ultimately lead to anarchy and massive bloodshed. The cost of these idealistic goals was terrible in terms of loss of life. The result was anarchy and an opportunity for a dictator to seize control.

Section Quiz

1. Briefly describe the members of the three estates in France.
2. What political body had the authority to reform the tax system in France?
3. Who ruled France at the beginning of the Revolution?
4. How long did the first French constitution remain in force?
5. What period in French history began when the Committee of Public Safety gained absolute power?
★ Contrast the American Revolution with the French Revolution in reference to religion.

Section Quiz Answers

1. First Estate—church leaders; Second Estate—aristocrats and nobles; Third Estate—middle class, merchants, artisans, townspeople, farmers, and peasants
2. the Estates-General
3. Louis XVI and Marie Antoinette
4. one year
5. the Reign of Terror
★ Answers will vary but should include the following: Americans were significantly affected by the Reformation; the French rejected the Reformation and later turned humanism into a religion.

CD: 12B Battle Scenes

A couple of paintings of battle scenes, including a painting of Napoleon on the battlefield of Eylau in 1807, are available on the CD.

The Count of Monte Cristo

If you have time, discuss the novel *The Count of Monte Cristo* by Alexandre Dumas. The story revolves around a man who is imprisoned for allegedly conspiring to reinstate the Bonapartists following Napoleon's exile. Warn the students to be aware of the emphasis on revenge in the novel.

Phrases from History

Have the students discuss how certain terms or phrases from history take on extended meanings. Examples could be "He met his Waterloo," "Remember the Alamo," and "Pike's Peak or Bust." For many, the number 9–1–1 will mean much more than a three-digit number to be called in an emergency.

Activity 2: The Battle of Waterloo

This excerpt from a British captain at Waterloo is included to provide the students with insight into the actual conditions of the day and to enhance reading comprehension skills.

II. Rise and Fall of Napoleon

Napoleon Bonaparte took advantage of the chaos in France and used his power to take control of the government. He had risen through the military ranks and became a general in 1793. Napoleon had led French forces to many victories by using unusual battle tactics that included marching his troops all night and launching surprise attacks on unprepared enemy troops. However, his ambitions extended far beyond defeating France's enemies.

Rise

In 1799 Napoleon supported the overthrow of the unpopular Directory. Three consuls led the new government. Napoleon served as one of the three, but he quickly pushed the others aside to become the **First Consul**. He then turned this position into that of dictator of France.

Napoleon Bonaparte

Contribution

Napoleon set about to win the support of the French people. He began by signing peace treaties between Britain and France. In addition, he initiated several public works projects, including the building of roads, bridges, and canals. To stabilize currency and enhance trade, Napoleon founded the Bank of France. He developed an improved tax system and stabilized the national debt—problems that had long plagued France. Napoleon also established a system of public education and placed it under the guidance of the University of France. Finally, he set up a commission to organize the many laws that were passed during the Revolution. The result was a codification of French law that became known as **Code Napoleon.**

Fall

Over the next decade Napoleon conquered several nations in Europe and, initially, played the role of liberator. However, his seizure of each nation's wealth and placement of a relative on each throne revealed his true intentions. French abuses stirred national pride in these conquered nations, and Napoleon faced mounting resistance.

In addition, Napoleon tried to block European trade with Britain in an effort to destroy the British economy. Russia and a few other nations ignored Napoleon's economic blockade. This defiance led to war between France and Russia. Napoleon entered Russia in 1812 with about six hundred thousand troops. The outnumbered Russians withdrew and lured the French deep into Russian territory. When the French finally retreated, the Russian forces and the Russian winter destroyed the French army. Fewer than one hundred thousand French soldiers made it safely out of Russia.

Napoleon suffered another defeat in 1813 at Leipzig, Germany. An alliance of European leaders forced Napoleon to step down as ruler of France and go into exile on an island just off the western coast of Italy. However, while the European leaders met to restore order in Europe, Napoleon escaped and returned to France to raise another army.

On June 18, 1815, the armies of Prussia and Britain confronted Napoleon and his forces in modern Belgium at **Waterloo.** Napoleon launched a surprise attack on the Prussian forces and separated them from the British army. Following thunderstorms and a delay while the ground dried, Napoleon sent his forces directly into the British

Perilous Journey

In 1789 the French revolted against the abuses of an absolute monarchy. However, within ten years France found itself under the control of another absolute dictator. Despite great expectations, the French wandered in spiritual darkness and embraced one form of oppression after another. They exchanged one corrupt ruler for committees of wicked rulers and finally embraced a liberator who turned out to be a ruthless dictator. Napoleon led the country to ruin as he tried to conquer Europe. The French people seemed unaware of the truth that responsible human government cannot be achieved by those who behave in an irresponsible manner.

Section II
Objectives
Students should be able to

1. Explain how Napoleon seized power and became the dictator of France.

2. Evaluate Napoleon's contributions to France.

3. Describe Napoleon's initial military success and later fall at Waterloo.

The Wrong St. Helena?

When residents of St. Helena Island in South Carolina heard that Napoleon was to be exiled to St. Helena, they assumed that he would be coming to their island. The residents made extensive preparations for the arrival of the famous French dictator. However, he never showed up.

Napoleon Bonaparte

Visit www.bjupress.com/resources for possible links to articles about Napoleon Bonaparte.

Napoleon

Ask a student to volunteer to research Napoleon Bonaparte and present a report to the class.

Duke of Wellington at Waterloo

line. However, the British forces held their position, and the Prussians regrouped and trapped the French forces. Napoleon's army collapsed, and he was sent into a final exile on the island of St. Helena in the South Atlantic.

Section Quiz

1. How did Napoleon become the First Consul?
2. What contribution did Napoleon make to French law?
3. What role did Napoleon play in conquering several European states?
4. What nation's trade did Napoleon attempt to block in order to destroy that nation's economy?
5. In what country was Napoleon defeated by winter and a retreating army?
★ How did France respond to the ideas of liberty and equality?

III. Revolts Across Europe

Following the defeat of Napoleon, European leaders met and tried in vain to restore Europe to the state it had been in before the French Revolution. However, a growing sense of **nationalism** (intense devotion and loyalty to one's own people) could not be contained. Revolts soon broke out all over Europe.

The revolts came in three waves. The first wave hit in the 1820s. The second wave arrived in the 1830s. The third wave came in 1848. Many of these revolts failed, but some states succeeded in gaining their independence. Greece and Belgium gained their liberty while Poland and Hungary suffered crushing defeat. Despite many setbacks, the movement toward nationalism could not be stopped.

Greece

Greece came under Ottoman control following the conquest of Constantinople in 1453. The Greeks repeatedly sought to break free

---

Nationalism

The longing of a group of people to form a nation may be a positive desire, depending on the motivation. Some groups pursued nationalism to escape the control of an oppressive power and seek equality for citizens. For example, the Greeks desired independence from the oppressive Ottoman Empire and fought for national independence. Others sought nationhood in order to combine regions with a common language or culture. Nation states can lead to patriotism. If the values shared by people are good, then nation states often reinforce these ideals.

However, nationalism can also be an effective way to justify oppressing others. For example, the Russian government oppressed the citizens of Poland. More modern examples would include Ottoman slaughter of the Armenians and German slaughter of the Jews. In addition, nationalism can provide another way for a corrupt ruler to oppress his own people. Hitler, Mussolini, Stalin, and Mao provide ready examples.

Section III

Objectives

Students should be able to

1. Describe the desire for nationalism that swept across Europe.
2. Analyze why some countries were able to achieve independence while others were not.

Section Quiz Answers

1. Napoleon used his military influence to support the overthrow of the Directory. He became one of the three consuls, then pushed the others aside and became the First Consul.
2. He set up a commission to organize the laws that came out of the French Revolution. The codified law became known as Code Napoleon.
3. liberator
4. Britain
5. Russia
★ Answers will vary but should include some of the following: The French sought liberty without scriptural re-

straints and found only bondage to tyrants. They desired equality, but the only equality they found occurred in the shared fate of aristocrats and common citizens in the executions under the Reign of Terror.

Nationalism

Have the class discuss why nationalistic movements seem so irrepressible. Why might surrounding nations support or oppose a country's attempt to be independent? (Nations that have become independent from the former Soviet Union provide some recent examples of the struggle to be free of foreign domination.)

The Greek Revolution

Visit www.bjupress.com/resources for possible links to articles about the Greek Revolution.

from the Ottomans over the next three centuries. In 1819 the Greeks renewed their struggle. Finally, in 1829 the Greek forces received support from Russia, Britain, and France. The combined naval support of these nations destroyed the Ottoman fleet. French troops then assisted Greek forces in their struggle to drive the Ottoman forces out of Greece. In 1832 Greece gained recognition as an independent state.

Belgium

This small nation formed out of the southern provinces of the United Kingdom of the Netherlands. Due to religious and language differences, this region had little in common with the rest of the Dutch kingdom. The people from this region were Roman Catholic and spoke French, while most in the Netherlands were Protestant and spoke Dutch. This region also suffered from high levels of unemployment and unrest among many in the working class. These differences and the resulting discontent led to uprisings in 1830. Some Belgian leaders took advantage of this strife and supported the idea of secession (becoming independent). Despite intense fighting, the efforts to settle the question of Belgian independence on the battlefield were unsuccessful. The king of the Netherlands appealed to the **Great Powers** (major European nations) for a peaceful resolution. A conference of European powers met in London and recognized Belgian independence in 1831. However, the Dutch continued to resist Belgian independence until 1835.

Romanticized scene of Belgian forces during their successful struggle for independence

Polish countess Emilia Plater leading scythemen in 1831 against Russian forces. She is considered a national hero in Poland.

Poland

This country endured many foreign invasions and partition attempts by neighboring countries. The Poles often rallied against the invaders and tried to expel them in a desperate attempt to regain their independence. This cycle was repeated in the nineteenth century. In 1807 Napoleon invaded a partitioned Poland and established a Polish state. While Napoleon liberated the Poles from other European powers, he also placed Poland under his rule. In 1815, following the defeat of Napoleon, Poland was again invaded. The Allied powers at the Congress of Vienna again partitioned Poland among its neighboring countries. Russia controlled the eastern portion of Poland and soon annexed this region to Russia. The Russians steadily reduced the freedoms of the Poles and installed a brutal regime. In November 1830 some Polish cadets revolted and led an armed rebellion against Russian oppression. As the resistance

Poland

Discuss with the class what it might have been like to live in Poland during the nineteenth and twentieth centuries. Ask students to make a list of countries that controlled areas of Poland. (*The list would include Prussia, Russia, France and Austria.*)

 ## Activity 3: Map Study: Europe

This map activity is designed to help the students visualize the locations of the nations mentioned in this chapter and their proximity to one another.

spread, many Polish citizens joined the uprising. Initially, the Poles succeeded on the battlefield. However, Russia sent a large army and crushed the Polish forces in 1831. Poland did not regain its independence until after World War I.

Hungary

Hungary had been under the control of Austria for centuries. In 1848 the Hungarians carried out mass demonstrations and demanded rights such as freedom of the press, trial by jury, and religious liberty. Initially, the Austrian ruler had to accept these demands due to internal problems. However, a new Austrian ruler rejected Hungary's demands and sent an army to subjugate the Hungarians. Hungarian forces won the first few battles. The Austrian ruler then enlisted the support of Russia, and the combined forces overwhelmed the Hungarians. Many of the Hungarian leaders were executed, and the rest escaped into exile. Like Poland, Hungary gained its independence after World War I.

Section Quiz

1. What movement led to revolts in Europe?
2. What nations came to the aid of Greece in order to help Greece gain its independence?
3. What religious differences contributed to Belgium's revolt against the Netherlands?
4. What powerful nation controlled the eastern portion of Poland?
5. What European nation assisted Austria in subduing the Hungarian revolt?
★ Why were Greece and Belgium able to achieve independence while Poland and Hungary were not?

IV. German and Italian Unification

Unification in Germany and Italy grew out of the surge of nationalism. German intellectuals attempted to revolt against the dominant powers in 1848, but other factors would eventually lead to the formation of the German state. Italy's efforts at unification began with the growth of patriotic societies. In both of these nations, strong leaders used diplomacy and military strategy to work toward unity.

German

Initial progress toward German unification resulted from an economic union called the **Zollverein**, which was formed to enhance trade between the German states. Prior to this agreement, trade was limited between the German territories. This union reduced the cost of selling goods and greatly increased the volume of trade among the member states. Enhanced economic cooperation helped build support for political union.

In 1862, King **Wilhelm I** appointed Count **Otto von Bismarck** as the chancellor of Prussia. Bismarck became the driving force behind political unification of the German states. He used diplomacy, propaganda, and military might to unite the Germans.

Otto von Bismarck

Section IV

Objectives

Students should be able to

1. Describe the unification of Germany and the role of Bismarck.
2. Describe the unification of Italy and the contributions of the movement's key leaders.

Section Quiz Answers

1. nationalism
2. Russia, Britain, and France
3. The area that became Belgium was primarily Roman Catholic, while the Netherlands was primarily Protestant.
4. Russia
5. Russia
★ Answers will vary but should include the following: Greece and Belgium were able to gain European support for their independence. Poland and Hungary were not able to get European support; instead, they were repressed by Russia.

The Age of Bismarck

The Age of Bismarck: Documents and Interpretations contains a revealing document written by Lord Palmerston, the prime minister of Britain at the start of the unification of Germany. He saw the unification as a positive development and assumed that a strong Germany would help to keep France and Russia in check.

Otto von Bismarck

Visit www.bjupress.com/resources for possible links to articles about Otto von Bismarck.

Unification of Germany 1866–71

Prussia before 1866
Annexed to Prussia, 1866
States added to complete the German Empire, 1871
Boundary of the German Empire, 1871

War with Denmark and Austria

Bismarck's first opportunity to promote German unification came in 1864. He provoked a war with Denmark over a dispute regarding the two small territories of Schleswig and Holstein. These regions lay between Denmark and Prussia. Bismarck convinced Austria to side with Prussia against Denmark, and the Danes were easily defeated. Austria took control of Holstein, and Prussia gained control of Schleswig.

Then Bismarck convinced Russia and France to remain neutral while he tricked the Austrians into declaring war on Prussia. This war lasted only seven weeks, with Prussia emerging as the clear victor. As a result, Austria surrendered control of Holstein to Prussia. In addition, Prussia gained a dominant influence over the newly formed North German Confederation.

With Austria and Denmark neutralized, one nation lay between Prussia and a unified German state. Bismarck planned carefully to use France as a tool to complete German unification.

Franco-Prussian War

Though Prussia had gained dominance in northern Germany, the southern German territories remained fragmented and independent of Prussian control. Bismarck believed that a war between the German states and France would convince the southern territories to align with Prussia.

The Franco-Prussian War resulted from a controversy over the next king of Spain. At first, Leopold, a man related to the Prussian ruling family (Hohenzollern), was invited to become the next Spanish king. France felt threatened by this and protested loudly. Even though Leopold declined the offer, the French were not satisfied. The French sent an ambassador to meet with the Prussian king and demand a promise that no member of the Hohenzollern family would ever rule Spain.

The Prussian king refused to make such a promise and sent a dispatch (report) of this meeting to Bismarck. Bismarck carefully changed the wording to imply that the Prussian king and the French ambassador had insulted each other. Then he published

Helmuth von Moltke

While Bismarck formulated strategies and propaganda to gain territory for Prussia, Helmuth von Moltke, the commander of the Prussian army, made the military victories possible. For thirty years, he served as the major strategist of the Prussian army. His battlefield tactics were developed from a study of Napoleon's methods and from the tactics used to defeat Napoleon at Waterloo. Moltke trained his army to be prepared for many strategies, including a cavalry charge, a pincer movement, and a feigned retreat. He also authorized the commanders to make decisions during battle since, as he said, "No plan of operations [is guaranteed to survive] . . . the first contact with the main hostile force." Moltke used modern weapons effectively and transported his troops to the battlefield by railroad, allowing his forces to prepare for battle. His tactics were studied and used with deadly efficiency by both sides during World War I.

🔘 CD: 12C Unification of Germany

This map from the student text is also available on the CD.

the reworded dispatch. Both nations were furious, and the French declared war on Prussia.

Bismarck's plan worked, and the southern German states sided with Prussia in the war against France. The German forces invaded France and trapped the French forces within two months. Ten days before the French surrendered, Kaiser Wilhelm I was declared ruler of the German Reich (empire) in the Palace of Versailles, near Paris. German unification had been accomplished.

Italian

For centuries the Italian peninsula had been divided into many small kingdoms and controlled by foreign powers. However, the drive toward nationalism surged in Italy as it had in other countries. A movement called the **Risorgimento** ("resurgence") contributed to the movement for nationalism.

Crowning of Wilhelm I as emperor of Germany, in Versailles

Mazzini

In 1832 an Italian named **Giuseppe Mazzini** formed a group called **Young Italy** for the purpose of accomplishing Italian unification. The struggle proved to be a slow and frustrating one, but men like Mazzini persisted in their efforts.

Cavour

Count **Camillo di Cavour** proved to be the most successful at uniting Italy. He was the prime minister of the Kingdom of Sardinia (see map on p. 221). Much like Bismarck in Germany, Cavour used whatever means necessary to promote Italian unification. He sent troops to support Britain and France in wars against Russia. While his support was largely symbolic, Cavour used these alliances to build support for unification. On another occasion Cavour supported Napoleon III against Austria in order to remove Austrian control of regions in Italy. Cavour's efforts were frustrated when Napoleon III abruptly made peace with Austria to prevent Cavour from gaining too much power.

Giuseppe Mazzini

Garibaldi

While Cavour unified the regions of northern Italy, a disciple of Mazzini, **Giuseppi Garibaldi**, formed an army known as the "Red

Count Camillo di Cavour

Giuseppe Mazzini

Visit www.bjupress.com/resources for possible links to articles about Giuseppe Mazzini.

Giuseppe Garibaldi

Visit www.bjupress.com/resources for possible links to articles about Giuseppe Garibaldi.

Count Cavour

Discuss how Count Cavour used great diplomatic skill to turn symbolic support into great benefit for Sardinia and the eventual unification of Italy, even though he had little to offer nations such as Britain and France.

Shirts" and conquered the island of Sicily in 1860. Garibaldi and his forces then moved to the Italian Peninsula and captured the city of Naples. Garibaldi planned to capture Rome and gain control of the Papal States, but Cavour traveled south and intervened. Since the French supplied forces to protect Rome, Cavour feared that Garibaldi's assault would draw the French into this conflict. Instead, Cavour convinced Garibaldi to turn his conquered territory over to **Victor Emmanuel II**, the king of Sardinia. In the spring of 1861, an Italian parliament declared the formation of the Kingdom of Italy. They named Victor Emmanuel II as the first king. By 1870 the Papal States and Rome were added to the Italian kingdom despite furious papal opposition. In 1871 the city of Rome became the national capital.

Unification of Italy 1859–71

Giuseppi Garibaldi

Victor Emmanuel II

Section Quiz

1. What economic union enhanced trade between the German states?

2. Who was appointed to be the chancellor of Prussia in 1862?

3. What methods did Bismarck use to unite the German states?

4. Who formed a group of patriots that worked to bring about Italian unification?

5. Who formed an army known as the "Red Shirts" and conquered the island of Sicily?

★ What role did Count Cavour play in accomplishing Italian unification?

 CD: 12D Unification of Italy

This map from the student text is also available on the CD.

Section Quiz Answers

1. Zollverein

2. Count Otto von Bismarck

3. diplomacy, propaganda, and military might

4. Giuseppe Mazzini

5. Giuseppe Garibaldi

★ He used whatever means necessary to unite Italy. Cavour sent Sardinian troops to assist British and French forces, supported French forces against Austria, and convinced Garibaldi to turn his conquered territory over to Victor Emmanuel II, king of Sardinia.

CHAPTER REVIEW

People, Places, and Things to Remember

Voltaire
First Estate
Second Estate
Third Estate
Estates-General
Louis XVI
Marie-Antoinette
National Assembly
Declaration of the Rights of Man
Committee of Public Safety
Reign of Terror
Directory
Napoleon Bonaparte
First Consul
Code Napoleon
Waterloo
nationalism
Great Powers
Zollverein
Wilhelm I
Otto von Bismarck
Risorgimento
Giuseppe Mazzini
Young Italy
Camillo di Cavour
Giuseppi Garibaldi
Victor Emmanuel II

Making Connections

1. Why was the French Revolution unable to build a stable society based on Enlightenment ideals?
2. How did Louis XVI turn his initial popularity into hatred by the French people?
3. How did the National Assembly offend the Roman Catholic Church and cause great concern among loyal Catholics?
4. Why is the name "Committee of Public Safety" ironic?
5. Why was Napoleon successful at defeating one army after another for more than a decade?
6. Why did the Belgians desire independence from the United Kingdom of the Netherlands?
7. Why did Bismarck publish an altered dispatch of a discussion between the king of Prussia and the French ambassador?

Developing History Skills

1. Locate the following on the map:
   a. Austrian Empire   d. Rome
   b. France   e. Sardinia
   c. Papal States   f. Sicily

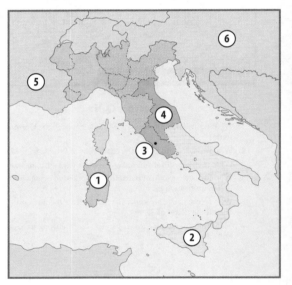

Activity 4: Chapter Review

This activity will help students review the material from the chapter.

Chapter Review Answers

Making Connections

1. The French revolutionaries sought freedom without responsibility and followed Enlightenment ideals instead of Reformation principles.

2. He demonstrated political incompetence, borrowed heavily and increased the national debt, humiliated the representatives of the Third Estate at the meeting of the Estates-General, and secretly summoned troops to Paris.

3. The National Assembly confiscated church-owned lands in an effort to pay off the national debt.

4. Its members instituted a period of mass execution known as the Reign of Terror.

5. He used unusual tactics that included marching his troops all night and launching surprise attacks on the unprepared enemy forces.

6. They had little in common. The Belgians were Catholic, spoke French, and suffered from high unemployment. The Dutch, however, were Protestant, spoke Dutch, and did not suffer from high unemployment.

7. He wanted to trigger a war that would unite southern Germany with Prussia.

Developing History Skills

1. a. (6)
   b. (5)
   c. (4)
   d. (3)
   e. (1)
   f. (2)

2. Answers should include some of the following: The French embraced one government after another. The Directory was unpopular and needed the support of the army. Under these circumstances, Napoleon was able to use his military influence to seize power.

2. Why was Napoleon able to seize control of France?

Thinking Critically

1. Beginning with information in this chapter and adding what you know about American and French history, contrast the impact of the American Revolution and the French Revolution on our world today.

2. What lessons can be learned from the social, political, and economic problems in France prior to the Revolution?

Living in God's World

1. Pretend that you are part of the National Assembly and you have the responsibility of reading and voting on the Declaration of the Rights of Man. If you had the ability to change these rights according to a Christian worldview, how would you do so?

2. You are an editor of a German newspaper watching the events of the Franco-Prussian war unfold. Write an editorial to the German people explaining the pros and cons of nationalism.

represent them. This privilege must be taken seriously: citizens must carefully examine candidates to determine who will best represent the people and do what is best for the country.

Thinking Critically

1. Answers should include some of the following: The American War for Independence produced a free nation that eventually played a leading role in defeating Germany in World War I, the Axis Powers in World War II, and communism in Europe. America has spread wealth, technology, freedom, and other blessings to many nations of the world. The French Revolution set an example for violent overthrow of government, exaltation of humanism, and mass execution of citizens. France has had one government coalition after another and has embraced socialism, becoming a welfare state and a second-rate power with little influence in the world.

2. Answers should include some of the following: Equitable taxation is essential to long-term social stability. Overtaxing the rich and freeing others from paying a portion of their income taxes leads to class envy. All levels of society must have representation in the government. The members of the Third Estate produced most of the wealth but had no voice in the government. Competent leadership is essential to the survival of a nation. While the French could not elect their king, Americans and citizens of other democratic countries have had the great privilege of electing those who

Living in God's World

1. Answers will vary.

2. Student answers should include

Pros:

Nationalism can motivate a nation to gain independence from foreign oppression and seek equality for all.

Nation states can lead to patriotism. If the values shared by citizens are good, then nation states often reinforce these ideals.

Cons:

Nationalism can be used as an excuse to abuse other peoples.

Corrupt leaders are often willing to use nationalism to abuse their own people.

Chapter Goals

Students should be able to

1. Describe early industrialization and the importance of industrial development in England.

2. Explain how industrial economies expanded and societies experienced transformations in Europe.

3. Analyze the causes and consequences of the transatlantic slave trade and slavery in the Americas.

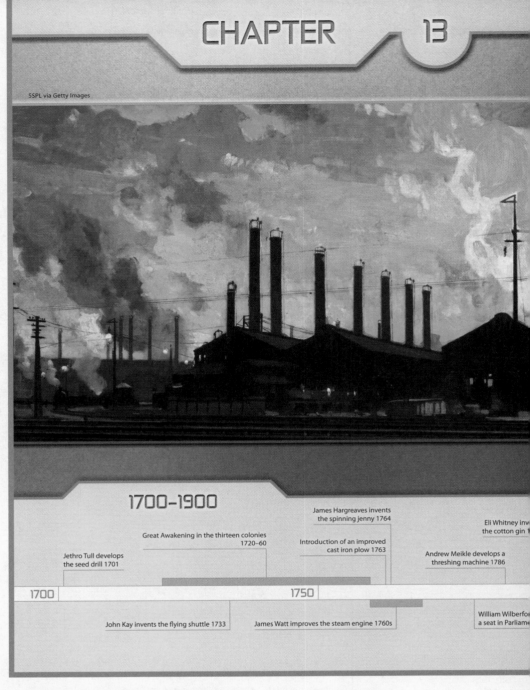

SSPL via Getty Images

1700–1900

Jethro Tull develops the seed drill 1701

Great Awakening in the thirteen colonies 1720–60

Introduction of an improved cast iron plow 1763

James Hargreaves invents the spinning jenny 1764

Andrew Meikle develops a threshing machine 1786

Eli Whitney inv the cotton gin

1700

1750

John Kay invents the flying shuttle 1733

James Watt improves the steam engine 1760s

William Wilberfor a seat in Parliame

Chapter 13 Lesson Plan Chart

Section Title	Main Activity	Pages	Days
I. Laying the Foundation for Industry	Activity 1: Edison, the Inventor	226–32	2–2½ days
II. Expansion of Industry and Rise of Social Reform	Activity 3: "Thoughts upon Slavery"—John Wesley	232–36	2–2½ days
III. End of the Slave Trade	Activity 4: Letter from John Wesley to William Wilberforce	236–40	1–1½ days
TOTAL SUGGESTED DAYS (INCLUDING 1 DAY EACH FOR REVIEW AND TESTING)			7–8½ days

Materials List

Section I

- Special speaker: farmer
- CD: 13A Seed Drill
- CD: 13B Steam Tractor
- Activities 1 and 2 from the *Student Activities* manual

Section II

- Activity 3 from the *Student Activities* manual

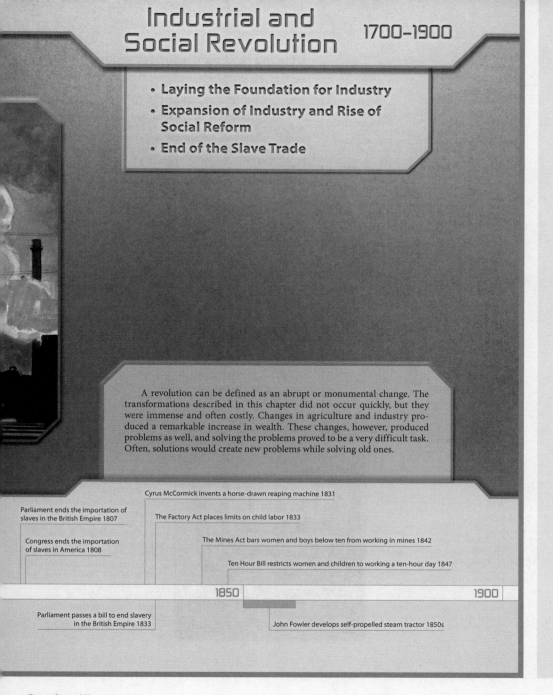

Industrial and Social Revolution

1700–1900

- **Laying the Foundation for Industry**
- **Expansion of Industry and Rise of Social Reform**
- **End of the Slave Trade**

A revolution can be defined as an abrupt or monumental change. The transformations described in this chapter did not occur quickly, but they were immense and often costly. Changes in agriculture and industry produced a remarkable increase in wealth. These changes, however, produced problems as well, and solving the problems proved to be a very difficult task. Often, solutions would create new problems while solving old ones.

Cyrus McCormick invents a horse-drawn reaping machine 1831

Parliament ends the importation of slaves in the British Empire 1807

The Factory Act places limits on child labor 1833

Congress ends the importation of slaves in America 1808

The Mines Act bars women and boys below ten from working in mines 1842

Ten Hour Bill restricts women and children to working a ten-hour day 1847

1850   1900

Parliament passes a bill to end slavery in the British Empire 1833

John Fowler develops self-propelled steam tractor 1850s

Section III

- CD: 13C Slave Ship
- Activities 4–6 from the *Student Activities* manual

Section I

Objectives

Students should be able to

1. Describe the agricultural revolution and analyze its effects on population growth and patterns of land use.

2. Identify the major characteristics of the Industrial Revolution.

3. Assess the various factors that enabled the rise of the Industrial Revolution in Britain.

Population Growth

Thomas Robert Malthus (1766-1834), a British economist, predicted that unchecked population growth would ultimately lead to famine, misery, and poverty. However, Britain's population growth led to increased productivity and a larger work force.

Land Enclosure

When a wealthy landowner enclosed land to increase productivity, not everyone in his family profited. Due to the custom of the oldest son's inheriting the estate, younger siblings in the family had to find other ways of supporting their families when the landowner died. They too had to move to the city and make a living.

Division of Labor

The division of labor that developed in Britain (and in America) was a positive development. It increased the production of a variety of goods that individual workers could not produce alone. The proverbial example is the pencil. Some

Lessons from Farmers

Invite a farmer to your classroom to discuss a number of topics related to farming, such as crop rotation, fertilization, and animal breeding. If some of your students live on farms, they could also present information on these or other related topics.

> **Crop Rotation**
>
> Farmers learned that planting different crops in the same fields each year enriched the soil. For example, wheat would be planted one year and cotton the next. Corn would be followed by soybeans. Each crop adds some nutrients to the soil and takes some from it. The next crop replaces the missing nutrient and consumes another left by the previous plant. Using this method, all farmland could be used each season and none would need to be left untilled as in the past. This greatly increased food production.

Early spinning wheel

Early spinning loom

> **Land Enclosure**
>
> Most English farmland was open, and many could use it for grazing their livestock. Land enclosure, however, prevented common use. The enclosed land could be tilled or otherwise used for the private benefit of the landowner.

I. Laying the Foundation for Industry

In the beginning, Adam and Eve cared for the garden that God had entrusted to them under the Creation Mandate (Genesis 1:28). Succeeding generations continued to farm and carry on basic industry. However, methods remained largely unchanged for centuries. Most farming was done with wooden tools and human or animal power. It involved loosening the soil by pulling a crude device through the ground in order to plant seed. Crops were harvested by hand or with a sharp tool. The labor was intense, and the harvest varied from season to season.

Most industry remained primitive and required a strong back and long hours to produce items required for daily life. Shoes, clothing, tools, and other items were made by hand, and each was slightly different from the rest.

However, with the coming of modern industry and improved farming methods in the eighteenth century, life in Europe entered a period of monumental change. Life would never be quite the same, and the consequences would affect people around the world.

Agricultural Revolution

Over time, farmers developed methods that resulted in an increased food supply. The earliest examples of these improvements appeared in Great Britain. British landowners increased crop production by using four-field **crop rotation**, fertilization, and recently invented machines. A better understanding of animal breeding and care also increased quantities of milk and meat. These changes marked the beginning of modern scientific farming.

Transition to the City

Because of the increased food supply, families were able to provide for more children, who were needed to work on the farm. These changes contributed to a large growth in the British population—from six and one-half million to nine million between 1750 and 1800.

As more land became available, landowners raised more sheep. The sheep's wool provided a cash crop. The landowners sold the wool to weavers who labored in the emerging textile industry in Britain.

The downside was that sheep farmers needed fewer workers than other types of farms. Lack of work opportunities in agriculture led families to develop **cottage industries**, where wool was spun and merged to make cloth. Early spinning wheels and looms could fit in a home or a shop and provided income for the family.

Greater demand also led landowners to enclose the land in order to increase productivity. Many poor farmers were unable to support their families on the small plots of land left to them. They were forced to seek work in the cities.

Inventors and their Machines

Many inventions improved the planting, cultivating, and harvesting of crops. A few of the key inventors and their inventions will be briefly examined.

Jethro Tull developed a **seed drill** in 1701 that efficiently placed seeds in rows across a plot of land. However, farmers were slow to use this tool. For nearly a century, they continued to scatter their seed by hand. When the seed drill gained popularity, it enabled a farmer to grow more crops using much less seed. This invention also paved the way for use of other farming inventions since it produced evenly spaced rows.

Seed drill

Several men worked to develop an iron plow. The first plow to enjoy wide use was developed around 1730. An improved cast iron plow was produced in 1763. This plow turned the soil more easily and enabled the field to be plowed more quickly. Continued improvements to the plow's design made it possible to plow land that formerly could not be farmed due to the composition of the soil.

For centuries wheat and other grains had been harvested and separated from the husk by hand. The process was exhausting and required many laborers. **Andrew Meikle** developed a **threshing machine** in 1786. His machine enabled a few men to separate the wheat from the husks and stalks quickly.

Early threshing machine

workers have to mine, transport, and prepare the materials that make up the "lead" (graphite). Others follow the same procedure to produce the metal band that holds the eraser. Someone collects raw materials to make the eraser. Others harvest and prepare the wood that composes the barrel of the pencil. Someone makes the paint, and another worker applies it to the pencil. Still others make the machines to manufacture pencils from these gathered materials. Together, these people make affordable and functional pencils.

Unemployment

New production methods often result in layoffs. While job loss is often a very stressful experience for the worker, it can allow workers to take new jobs that the market creates. Sometimes, unemployment forces a person to become creative and develop a product or service for which others will pay. Many small businesses have formed because someone turned unemployment into an opportunity.

Inventions' Benefits to Society

The improved threshing machine and the reaping machine lowered the cost of processing grain and allowed more grain to be grown and harvested. This abundance of grain also contributed to the lower cost of grain. Lower grain prices benefited everyone, especially the poor who used flour (ground wheat) or meal (ground corn) in everyday life.

CD: 13A Seed Drill

This illustration from the student text is also available on the CD.

Activity 1: Edison, the Inventor

This activity contains an excerpt from Thomas Edison's writings that gives the student a glimpse into the world of the inventor. Edison experimented thousands of times before developing successful inventions. His story should challenge us all to persist until we succeed.

Jethro Tull

Visit www.bjupress.com/resources for possible links to articles about Jethro Tull.

Activity 2: The Wright Brothers

This activity contains an excerpt from the writings of the Wright brothers.

The Cotton Gin

Before Eli Whitney invented this machine, workers had to remove cotton seeds by hand—a slow and difficult process. Whitney's machine essentially combed the seeds out of the cotton as it passed through the machine. This process was much faster. The cotton gin transformed cotton from an expensive raw material into a resource that brought great profit.

Inventors and Wealth

Some students may assume that greed motivated most inventors. In fact, many inventors made nothing from their inventions. Even if they did profit, their inventions often made work easier, safer, more efficient, and more productive for everyone.

Making a profit is not an evil to avoid. God enables us to work and make a living; our money can support our families and church ministries. On the other hand, greed (the desire to make money at any cost) is wrong. Help your students understand the difference between profit and greed.

Left, Eli Whitney; *right,* cotton gin

Cutaway of a cotton gin

American inventors also contributed to the agricultural revolution. For example, in 1793 **Eli Whitney** invented the **cotton gin**. This device enabled one worker to process fifty pounds of cotton per day. Prior to Whitney's invention, one worker could process only one pound per day by hand. From inventions such as this, raw materials could be processed at a much faster rate. Inventors of textile machines soon had to increase the speed of processing products such as wool and cotton. They did this to keep pace with the speed at which the landowners could provide the raw materials.

Another American, **Cyrus McCormick**, invented a horse-drawn **reaping machine** in 1831 that enabled farmers to cut wheat much more quickly. Prior to his invention, many laborers were needed to

Cyrus McCormick

Early reaping machine

Eli Whitney

Visit www.bjupress.com/resources for possible links to articles about Eli Whitney.

Cyrus McCormick

Visit www.bjupress.com/resources for possible links to articles about Cyrus McCormick.

John Fowler's Steam Tractor

Fowler's engines were far too heavy to pull a plow across fields. Instead, he would place one engine at the edge of the field and place a second engine on the opposite edge. Then, using cables, one engine would pull a two-directional plow across the field, and then the other engine would pull it back. The plow made a furrow back and forth with each pass.

Getty Images

cut the harvest by hand and the process was very slow. Using Mc-Cormick's reaping machine, more acres could be harvested in less time. This device, along with Meikle's threshing machine, led to increased wheat production while reducing the number of farm laborers needed.

Steam power (discussed on p. 230) also assisted the agricultural revolution. During the 1850s and 1860s, an engineer named **John Fowler** developed one of the first known self-propelled steam engines. Fowler designed this **steam tractor** to plow fields and dig drainage channels. His machines lowered the cost of plowing fields. Reducing the number of laborers needed and replacing teams of horses or oxen with steam engines lowered costs. The channels also enabled farmers to till more land by draining water from previously unusable land.

Industrial Revolution

Industry also benefited from new inventions during this time period. The changes in manufacturing were so great that the eighteenth and nineteenth centuries are called the **Industrial Revolution**. As with farming, the industrial changes began in Great Britain.

Transition to the Factory

The development of larger weaving machines led industry to migrate from cottages and shops to large buildings or **factories** that were centrally located. Animals initially provided power for some of the larger machines. Where running water was available, mills and factories used water to turn large wooden wheels and power various machines. However, animals could not produce enough power, and

> ### Why Britain?
>
> By 1815, after Napoleon's defeat, Britain was the most thriving nation in Europe. The British had cottage industries that made many goods. Their large merchant fleet transported those goods abroad.
>
> Britain also had a stable banking system and government. A growing population combined with many natural resources, especially iron ore and coal, made Britain an ideal location for the advance of industry.
>
> Some may conclude that this combination of factors was merely an accident of history. However, Christians can see the hand of God in arranging all of these details and making possible the Industrial Revolution in Britain. We refer to this as divine providence.

Fowler's Steam Tractor

John Fowler's inventions allowed farmers to till land that traditional horse- or oxen-pulled plows could not till. The combination of the steam-powered engines and the two-directional plow turned the most stubborn soil into arable land. By making inventions such as these, man obeys God's command to be "fruitful, and multiply, and replenish the earth, and subdue it" (Gen.1:28).

Factories

The term *factories* is a shortened form of the word *manufactories*. Manufactories were places where items were made by hand (*manu*), or manufactured.

Why Britain?

The development of inventions in Britain was encouraged by minimal government interference. Other than granting patents, the British government did not involve itself in inventors' work.

CD: 13B Steam Tractor

A photo of a steam tractor is available on the CD.

Steam-powered Engines

Mankind has recognized the great energy potential of steam for nearly two thousand years. However, successful harnessing of steam into a stable and powerful form of energy has occurred only within the last three centuries.

Steam engines needed water that could be turned to steam as well as wood or coal to heat the water until it boiled and produced steam. Thus, steam-powered engines were external combustion engines (instead of gasoline or diesel-powered engines where combustion occurs inside the engines).

One of the first successful uses of steam-powered engines was to pump water from mines. Over time, inventive minds found ways to turn linear motion produced by steam into rotational motion. This led to steam engines in factories to power machines and locomotives to pull cars on sets of rails. Soon steam engines powered several types of equipment, including tractors and ships.

Top, James Watt; *bottom,* replica of early portable steam engine; *right,* early steam engine

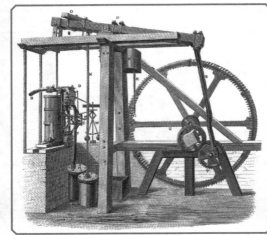

water did not provide a constant source of power. A drought or flood could shut down a mill or factory that depended on flowing water to power its machines. Factories needed a more reliable source of power.

Inventors and their Machines

One of the most important inventions during this period was the **steam engine**. While **James Watt** did not invent this device, he made important improvements in the design during the 1760s that greatly increased its efficiency. Soon steam engines powered machines that had been driven by water or animals. The steam engine also provided the necessary power to pull heavy loads in the form of tractors and locomotives. In addition, steam powered ships and even some early automobiles. Steam engines provided consistent and reliable power for the Industrial Revolution.

Loom with flying shuttle

Inventors developed several machines early in the eighteenth century to support the growing textile industry. Weaving cotton thread into cloth was a slow and tiring process until **John Kay** invented a small device known as the **flying shuttle** in 1733. When added to a weaving machine, this part enabled workers

🕸 James Watt

Visit www.bjupress.com/resources for possible links to articles about James Watt.

🕸 John Kay

Visit www.bjupress.com/resources for possible links to articles about John Kay.

to weave the strands of cotton into cloth much more rapidly. This speed created a growing demand for spools of thread to supply the weavers. To meet this demand, **James Hargreaves** invented the **spinning jenny** around 1764. This machine could quickly spin many strands of cotton into thread.

As demand increased, inventors responded by developing new machines to make cloth more quickly. Another new invention enabled a person to spin the yarn at a faster pace. In addition, production of iron and steel improved and increased to supply the metal needed for many of these inventions. Improvements in one industry often led to growth and job opportunities in many other industries.

Spinning jenny
National Museum of Photography Film & Television/Science and Society Picture Library

Connections Between Industrial and Commercial Relations

Men who developed businesses and sold their inventions were known as **entrepreneurs**. *Entrepreneur* is a French word referring to one who undertakes between two different parties. These businessmen undertook to connect industry to the market. They often risked their personal wealth to develop a market for these laborsaving devices. **Richard Arkwright** became one of the most famous entrepreneurs. While Arkwright is credited with inventing many machines, he also got the government to protect several inventions with a **patent** that prevented others from making a similar device for several years. Then he raised funds to build and sell those inventions.

Men like Arkwright developed contacts with banks and wealthy persons. The bankers and wealthy investors provided the needed **capital**, or money. The entrepreneurs then bought supplies, built factories, and paid wages in order to sell the products. In return, the investors received a share of the profits made by a thriving business. However, they also shared in the losses if the business failed.

Factors that Encouraged the Rise of Industry

Several of the factors already mentioned made the rise of industry possible. A growing population provided the labor force. Abundant raw materials, including wool, iron ore, and coal, fed the growth of industry. Also essential to the rise of industry was a stable government. Patents, among other safeguards, provided inventors with legal protection that ensured an exclusive right to make a product.

As we have already noted, the Industrial Revolution began in Britain. At first, the British tried to prevent knowledge of manufacturing equipment from spreading beyond their borders. However, the British soon realized that they could not prevent this knowledge from going abroad. So they decided to make money by exporting this equipment.

Soon the British exported their inventions to other European countries and North America. British laborers traveled to these countries and helped them set up and operate the machines. British investors also helped to finance industrial growth in European countries such as France. Many nations profited from the spread of industry, and Britain played a leading role in this growth in Europe.

> #### The Patent
>
> Imagine making a new product at great cost. Then you discover that someone has copied your product and is selling it at a lower cost. This action would prevent you from making a profit on your invention.
>
> The modern patent is a set of special rights that a government gives to an inventor for a certain period. During this time no one else can legally copy and sell his invention.
>
> This protection gives the inventor time to recover the cost of developing his invention and to make a profit. In exchange, the inventor must give the government all the needed information to describe his invention.
>
> Once the patent expires, anyone can then make and sell the product without breaking the law.

Patents

Most products today have either a patent number or the words "patent pending" stamped on them. "Patent pending" means that a patent has been applied for but has not yet been granted by the government. An inventor must meet certain conditions to receive a patent.

Capital

Anyone who owns stock or has invested in a mutual fund is investing funds that may be used to provide capital for a business. In this manner, small investors pool their money, which is then invested in companies with the expectation of making a profit. This pooling of money helps the businesses in which the investments are made and eventually helps the investors who make a profit. It also helps society by lowering the cost of finished goods. This is the essence of capitalism.

Patents

Ask volunteers to research and report on the U.S. Patent Office. Some could specifically look for unusual inventions that were patented, such as the self-tipping hat for men.

Section II

Objectives

Students should be able to

1. Explain the connections between population growth, industrialization, and urbanization.

2. Explain how industrialization and urbanization affected class distinctions, family life, and the daily lives of men, women, and children.

3. Analyze and evaluate connections between industrialization and movements for political and social reform in Europe.

Growth of Cities

Some things never seem to change. Cities that experience rapid growth often struggle with housing problems, traffic congestion, and inadequate sanitation systems.

II. Expansion of Industry and Rise of Social Reform

Although society profited from the Industrial Revolution, problems also developed. Cities were unprepared for the tremendous growth in population and the pollution that came with industry. Workers often labored under terrible conditions, and many lived in filthy and crowded housing. In time, conditions improved and government enacted reforms to protect the workers and their families.

Growth of Cities

Villages became towns and towns became cities as the British population increased and industry expanded. Fewer and fewer workers were needed on the farm, and families moved in order to find work. This migration supplied much-needed labor for the factories and other industries that abounded in the urban areas.

Towns and cities tended to grow quickly. However, adequate housing, roads, and sanitation did not keep pace with the rapid growth. As a result, multiple-story tenement buildings that housed many families were quickly built and crowded together. Traffic often congested roads. Water supplies were often impure, and smoke from coal-fired furnaces polluted the air.

Woman and girls in a factory

Effect on Society

In the short term, society struggled to meet the problems and challenges that accompanied the Industrial Revolution. Skilled craftsmen often found themselves out of work as mass-produced and cheaper goods poured out of the factories. Conditions in the factories were dangerous. Wages were low, and everyone (including women and children) had to work long hours to meet financial needs. Family members often had to work different shifts and seldom had time together. Life in crowded cities was difficult, and diseases spread quickly by human contact or impure water.

Industrial Revolution

Have the students discuss how the Industrial Revolution has benefited them. Also discuss some of the negative effects of industrialization, such as pollution, the loss of manual-labor jobs, and the stress on working families.

However, in the long term, the resulting increase of wealth benefited almost everyone. Some complained that the investor reaped most of the wealth. Yet this complaint ignores the fact that the investor also assumed most of the risk. The Industrial Revolution did not bring about a perfect world. However, the size of the middle class dramatically increased, and the wages of the average worker gradually improved. In time, children no longer had to work to help support their families. Wages slowly increased to the point that the parents could provide for the financial needs of the family.

While the need for skilled artisans diminished greatly, the mass-produced goods from mills and factories improved the lives of rich and poor alike. Clothing, shoes, and various household items were available at prices most people could afford.

Boys began to work in factories at an early age.

Class Distinctions

Class distinctions had existed for centuries in Britain and other European countries. The Industrial Revolution tended to break down these barriers. Families that had endured poverty for generations worked, saved, and improved their lives. Men like Cyrus McCormick and James Watt rose from humble beginnings and became very wealthy through their inventions and hard work.

Those who had recently become wealthy also tended to reject the widely accepted view that poverty and ignorance were acceptable. They built libraries and schools to make learning available to everyone. Some wealthy industrialists donated up to half of their annual earnings to improve the standard of living for others. This access to learning continued to break down the distinctions between the classes and provided opportunity for all people.

The Industrial Revolution produced new distinctions as the middle class expanded into the upper and lower middle class. Industrialists and wealthy investors composed the upper middle class. Merchants and small business owners composed the lower middle class. Remaining at the bottom of the social ladder, poor workers composed the lower class.

However, people could move up or down in these classes in one or two generations. For example, in one generation a poor man could work his way up from poverty to the upper middle class by diligence and hard labor. His children or grandchildren could waste the inherited wealth and slide back into poverty. Therefore, carefulness or carelessness in managing family resources tended to determine someone's position in society during the Industrial Revolution.

Family Life

Family life in the industrial cities changed in many ways. At first, several members of the family worked in factories. Industrial labor also required many hours of hard work without the opportunity to take a break between jobs. Parents were unable to spend time with their children.

Class Mobility

Burton W. Folsom, Jr., in *The Myth of the Robber Barons: A New Look at the Rise of Big Business in America*, provides a detailed analysis of the Scrantons and the development of steel production in Pennsylvania under their leadership. Folsom also illustrates upward and downward mobility as he documents how family members often wasted their fortunes or the fortunes inherited from their fathers.

Working Conditions

Without minimizing the bad working and living conditions that characterized the early Industrial Revolution, it is important to help the students understand the context. Without doubt, the workers labored and lived in conditions that were appalling by our modern standards. We have been so blessed by the efforts of past generations that many of us will never have to work or live under such conditions. However, in many countries today, the average worker still works and lives in awful conditions. While this might be repulsive to us, these workers are willing to tolerate poor conditions to receive a wage. For some, it is the only way to support their families, as it was during the Industrial Revolution. Rather than following the popular trend to berate the Industrial Revolution, it might be better to remind the students that God can bring good even from the failures of men.

Each woman had to keep several lines of thread winding on the spindles.

There were differences between working in the city and working on the farm. Laborers performed the same task repeatedly in the factory instead of working a variety of jobs on the farm. However, the long hours of work in a factory at a low wage were similar to the long hours of work required to survive on the farm. While working conditions were terrible, the family, in time, developed greater financial security.

Workers endured dangerous working conditions and health problems due to pollution. Women and children labored in dreadful conditions and endured abuses. However, they labored under these circumstances to provide a better life for their family than was possible in the country.

With the coming of each generation, families found greater opportunities for economic and social advancement. Children had greater access to a free education than their parents had. Higher education became possible for more and more people. The society of an industrialized nation reaped the benefits of an educated people.

Movements for Social Reform

Most modern historians focus on the negative aspects of the Industrial Revolution and minimize the positive contributions. A few may reverse this emphasis. The truth lies somewhere in between.

Problems that Called for Reform

The working class found itself in a desperate situation. Many individuals and families could not survive in the cities unless they labored in a factory. With an abundant work force, some industrialists took advantage of the workers. Inventors tended to make machines that maximized production rather than worker safety. Many employers allowed conditions in the early factories to be dirty and dangerous. Workers often became injured or sick. Many employers would replace their employees when they became ill or injured due to poor working conditions.

Greed may have motivated many who provided housing for the growing numbers of people moving to the cities. They built large buildings with many small apartments that lacked proper sanitation. Safety and comfort were not priorities among many of the owners. The buildings were often built close together to maximize the use of the property. Conditions in these tenement buildings were often terrible.

In addition, some mills and factories dumped their waste into rivers and polluted the water supply. Factories burned coal to fuel the steam engines and created terrible air pollution. People complained to their elected officials about the injuries and diseases that resulted from these conditions.

Growth of Unions

Some workers also sought to improve their wages and working conditions by forming unions. The results were mixed, and opinions differ on the outcome.

Some historians point out that gains made by unions resulted in less money for the factory owner to invest in new machinery. They also argue that unions punished the consumers, who had to pay higher prices for the manufactured goods.

Others believe that it was right for unions to force owners to take a cut in profits and to make consumers pay higher prices in order to provide workers a better wage. This situation provides a good example of the tug-of-war that occurs between men in a fallen world.

England's Struggle

Government Reform

During the 1830s and 1840s, Parliament began to enact laws to protect workers. For example, the **1833 Factory Act** placed limits on child labor. Children under nine years of age could not work in a textile mill. Children from nine to thirteen years old could not work more than eight hours a day. In addition, the children were required to attend school three hours a day. Parliament appointed inspectors to check the mills and enforce mill owner cooperation.

Unfortunately, some mill owners responded by dismissing child workers rather than enduring the government inspections. Children who had to work to survive were reduced to working in old mills where working conditions were much worse. Those who could not find work were forced to live on the streets and survive by any means available.

Other government attempts to improve working conditions included the **Mines Act** (1842), which barred women and boys under the age of ten from working in the mines. In addition, the **Ten Hour Bill** in 1847 restricted women and children to working a ten-hour day in any British industry. While these efforts were well intended, in some cases they restricted the opportunities of women and children to work in order to meet their financial needs. Reform was necessary, but legislation alone could not fix every problem.

Religious Transformation

Social reform could not meet the greatest need of the worker. The mines, mills, and factories were filled with sinners who needed to hear the good news about salvation through Christ. Positive changes to British society came primarily through spiritual conversion rather than through government rules or unions. British pastors and evangelists spent countless hours preaching to assemblies of coal miners and factory workers.

Nathaniel Hone/Bridgeman Art Library/Getty Images

John Wesley

Plant owners, managers, and government officials also heard and responded to the preaching of God's Word. Every level of society changed as individuals were converted. Born-again men and women had a great impact on life at work and at home. Owners and managers learned to take better care of their workers. Laborers worked with a new diligence and sense of purpose. Government officials helped to fashion laws that improved working conditions and abolished many of society's problems.

John Wesley became one of the greatest preachers in Britain during this period. He traveled throughout the country on horseback and preached around 42,000 sermons. He organized his converts into Methodist societies, with laymen serving as leaders.

Thousands from all walks of life were converted under the preaching of Wesley and the witness of many of his followers. Wesley and his followers also supported many reforms, including improved prison conditions and better working conditions. When Wesley died, there were 630 lay preachers and 175,000 members in the Methodist societies.

Activity 3: "Thoughts upon Slavery"—John Wesley

This activity is an excerpt from an abolitionist document written by John Wesley.

John Wesley

Visit www.bjupress.com/resources for possible links to articles about John Wesley.

Charles Wesley

Visit www.bjupress.com/resources for possible links to articles about Charles Wesley.

George Whitefield

George Whitefield, another influential preacher, had an international ministry. He preached throughout Britain, Wales, and the American colonies. Whitefield introduced the Wesleys to the practice of preaching outdoors to masses who did not attend church. It is estimated that Whitefield preached to as many as twenty thousand people at a time. He often preached thirteen times a week to both large and small groups. Many thousands of people trusted Christ during his ministry.

The gospel transformed Britain as large numbers of men, women, and children trusted Christ. Crime rates dropped, and movements for industrial reform remained largely peaceful. The British nation was spared much of the violence that plagued other European nations. The drunkenness that plagued Britain declined as men trusted Christ.

The Struggle in Other European Countries

You learned in Chapter 12 that France endured a terrible revolution as the people sought reform. In the middle of the nineteenth century, Paris again became the scene of several riots over issues including poor working conditions and low wages.

Labor unrest characterized several western European countries in 1848. The desire to achieve freedom also motivated many of these struggles. Workers in France, Hungary, the German territories, and Russia resorted to armed resistance during these disputes. Few if any improvements resulted. Government oppression or indifference continued, and conditions for the laborers did not improve.

> **Whitefield and the Great Awakening**
> Whitefield also played a key role in the **Great Awakening** in the American colonies (1720–1760). This spiritual movement brought many to salvation, started many churches, and prepared the American colonies for independence.

Section Quiz

1. What problems were created by the lack of adequate housing in the city?
2. What were two positive results for society brought about by the Industrial Revolution?
3. Who could afford most of the goods produced in the factories?
4. How did spiritual conversion bring about the greatest changes to British society?
5. Which English preacher played a key role in the Great Awakening in the American colonies?
★ If God made possible the Industrial Revolution, why did many bad things happen in the course of its development?

III. End of the Slave Trade

Although slavery has a long history, the enslaving of Africans became a large and profitable industry during the Age of Exploration. African tribes found a ready market for those captured in war. Muslim, Portuguese, and Dutch traders purchased the African slaves. The Portuguese and Dutch carried the slaves to Europe and the New World to be sold at a profit. Over time, more and more Europeans were confronted with the terrible realities of the slave trade. In response, a growing number found slavery to be a wicked abuse of fellow human beings.

The British were among the first to seek an end to slavery. After decades of debate, the practice of slavery ended peacefully in Britain. Many in America opposed slavery as well. However, Americans were

---

Section III

Objectives

Students should be able to

1. Assess the importance of various influences that brought about the abolition of the slave trade and the emancipation of the slaves.
2. Describe the European movement to suppress the transatlantic slave trade.
3. Assess the degree to which emancipated slaves and their descendants achieved social and economic equality.

George Whitefield

Visit www.bjupress.com/resources for possible links to articles about George Whitefield.

Section Quiz Answers

1. Answers may vary but should include crowded conditions and pollution.
2. two of the following: increase of wealth, increased size of the middle class, improved wages for average workers, gradual ending of child labor, and an abundance of inexpensive goods for the masses
3. most people
4. Conversion transformed lives, which transformed society. Christians became concerned about the needs of others and encouraged various social reforms.
5. George Whitefield

★ Answers should include some of the following: By God's providence, the conditions for the Industrial Revolution were most favorable in Great Britain and America. However, man retains a free will, and he often chooses to place profits over the well-being of his workers. But man's sin does not diminish the goodness of God. He can take even the selfish and covetous desires of men and turn them into that which benefits humanity.

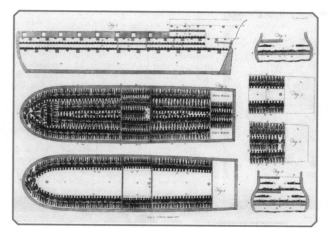

Diagram of a typical slave ship

divided over this issue, and the abolition of slavery did not occur through a peaceful process. During the eighteenth century, slavery thrived in French colonies. The French abolished and then restored slavery for a time in the nineteenth century.

Britain

Quakers were the first known religious group to combat slavery. Initially, Quakers owned slaves and did not oppose this practice. However, some Quakers began to question the right of one person to own another person. By the 1750s, many Quakers rejected slavery and supported abolition.

Around the same time, John and Charles Wesley also promoted the abolition of slavery. Under their influence, many Methodist laymen became involved in a growing abolitionist movement in Britain.

Best known for writing the words to the hymn "Amazing Grace," **John Newton** (1725–1807), a former slave-ship captain, became a Christian in 1748. He had witnessed the horrible conditions of the slave trade and became an outspoken critic of slavery. In addition, Newton played a key role in encouraging a promising young member of Parliament to remain in politics.

William Wilberforce (1759–1833) first won election to a seat in Parliament in 1780. When he became a Christian around 1785, he struggled over whether he should remain in politics. Newton and others convinced Wilberforce to remain in Parliament and serve the Lord and the people of Britain. He worked to improve conditions for many in his country. However, Wilberforce's greatest achievement was leading the effort to abolish slavery in the British Empire.

While the Quakers were the first to oppose slavery, they had no voice in Parliament. Quakers and Anglicans united their efforts with the formation of the **Committee for the Abolition of the Slave Trade** in 1787. Wilberforce supported this committee, but did not officially join until 1791.

From 1791 until 1807, Wilberforce overcame setback after setback in Parliament as he sought to end British involvement in the slave trade. In 1807 Parliament finally passed a bill to end the slave

William Wilberforce

No Easy Solution

Racially based slavery is without a doubt one of the great evils of history. No amount of rationalization can justify one person's owning another. Christians such as William Wilberforce and John Newton demonstrated their Christianity by speaking out against slavery and by supporting its abolition.

However, emancipation became a complicated process. Simply pronouncing someone free did not automatically equip that person to meet his or her needs. Too many who supported emancipation did not shoulder the burden of helping the freed slaves become successful members of society. Freed slaves often could not read and had no way to support themselves. Education, job training, and housing had to be made available to them. This was no small task. Organizations such as the Freedmen's Bureau sought to equip the freed slaves with the tools they needed to succeed.

The Long-term Consequences of Slavery

Nations, including the United States, have paid a price for tolerating slavery. Remedies have often come slowly and reluctantly as racism has lingered. Christians need to be part of the solution by rejecting racism, reaching out to the lost regardless of their ethnicity, and embracing fellow believers without considering the color of their skin.

CD: 13C Slave Ship

This diagram from the student text is also available on the CD.

Activity 4: Letter from John Wesley to William Wilberforce

This activity contains a letter that John Wesley wrote to William Wilberforce. This letter, one of the last letters that Wesley wrote, shows Wesley's burden to encourage Wilberforce's abolitionist work.

John Newton

Visit www.bjupress.com/resources for possible links to articles about John Newton.

William Wilberforce

Visit www.bjupress.com/resources for possible links to articles about William Wilberforce.

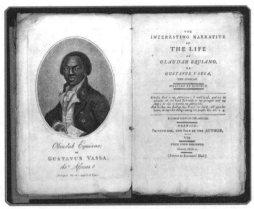

The autobiography of Olaudah Equiano, a former slave, who became a leading British advocate for the abolition of slavery

trade in the British Empire. This did not free slaves throughout the British colonies, but it did lay a foundation for the eventual abolition of slavery.

The struggle to end slavery in the British Empire continued for another twenty-five years. Wilberforce and other abolitionists in Parliament labored against great opposition to end this evil practice. In addition, a growing number of Christian reformers opposed slavery. Pamphlets were published to expose its evils. Abolitionists also refuted the claims that the Africans were inferior. Over time, industrial workers, including women and children, also joined the movement to abolish slavery.

While the struggle in Parliament continued, abolitionists purchased land in West Africa to settle freed British and American slaves. They pressured African chiefs to end the trading of slaves. The British navy played a key role by intercepting ships to search for slaves. The navy's diligence resulted in the rescue of thousands of African slaves.

Wilberforce had spent most of his adult life pressuring a reluctant Parliament to end one of the most shameful practices in modern history. He died in July of 1833 with that goal in sight. One month after his death, Parliament passed a bill that effectively ended slavery in the British Empire.

Meeting of the British and Foreign Anti-Slavery Society in 1840 as the British continued to oppose slavery worldwide

The Influence of Jonathan Edwards

One of Edwards's most prominent students, Samuel Hopkins, published a work in 1776 denouncing slavery. His stated goal was to emancipate, or free, all African slaves.

Jonathan Edwards's son, known as Jonathan Edwards the Younger, also published a work that confronted and condemned slavery in 1791.

Jonathan Edwards had trained both men in theological and biblical studies. Based on Edwards's training, they concluded that slavery was a great evil that had to be abolished.

America

In America, as in Britain, Quakers were among the first to speak out against slavery. Organized as the Society of Friends, the Quakers became a consistent voice in early America in opposition to slavery.

Thomas Paine published the first known article in the American colonies that supported the freeing of slaves. He titled the article "African Slavery in America," and he advocated the abolition of slavery by the emerging nation. Two students of Jonathan Edwards, another important figure in the Great Awakening in the American colonies, also published their support for abolition. Many slave owners shared

Activity 5: "On the Horrors of the Slave Trade"

This activity contains an excerpt of a speech that William Wilberforce delivered in 1789 before the House of Commons. While it may be challenging for your students to read, this excerpt provides a glimpse of Wilberforce's determination to outlaw the practice of slavery in the British Empire.

this desire, and some slaves were freed upon the death of the slave owner.

Even political opponents often agreed to cooperate to abolish slavery. For example, the New York Manumission (to free from bondage) Society was composed of Federalists John Jay and Alexander Hamilton and Democratic-Republican Aaron Burr.

Congress banned the importation of slaves beginning on January 1, 1808. Authorities did not consistently enforce this ban, but slavery seemed to be declining. However, one laborsaving invention changed the course of American history and ended the trend to abolish slavery.

As we noted previously, Eli Whitney invented the cotton gin. Although he did not personally profit from his invention, this machine turned cotton into a highly profitable crop. Slave labor in the cotton fields became the key to southern prosperity. The majority of slaves were owned by about one percent of southern landowners. However, the one percent controlled large plantations and exerted a great influence over government officials. America did not abolish slavery until the end of the Civil War, or the War Between the States, in 1865.

William Lloyd Garrison and **Frederick Douglass** became two of the most famous American abolitionists. Garrison was the editor

Leading American Abolitionists

William Lloyd Garrison
(1805–79)

William Lloyd Garrison became one of the most important and outspoken opponents of slavery in the North. Using his writing skills as a journalist, he relentlessly and zealously assaulted this evil practice. As the editor of the abolitionist newspaper *The Liberator*, he exposed the evils of slavery using fiery language. His writing enraged many in the North and the South. Many in the North took offense at his description of discrimination toward free blacks in the North.

While some in the North preferred the gradual emancipation of slaves, Garrison would have none of it and demanded immediate emancipation. To build support for his position, he also helped found the American Anti-Slavery Society.

Frederick Douglass
(c. 1818–95)

First known as Frederick Augustus Washington Bailey, Frederick Douglass was born a slave in Maryland. Despite laws that prohibited teaching slaves to read, Douglass received basic reading lessons at the age of twelve. His determination to master the skill of reading changed Douglass's world. He read newspapers and every book he could find. Douglass also taught other slaves to read the New Testament on Sundays.

After several failed attempts to escape and brutal beatings by at least one slave owner, Douglass boarded a train dressed as a sailor in the fall of 1838 and escaped to Philadelphia.

Douglass quickly became an active and eloquent spokesman for abolition. Garrison wrote of Douglass's life in *The Liberator* and helped to spread his message of the evils of antebellum slavery.

William Lloyd Garrison

Ask a student volunteer to read about William Lloyd Garrison and present a report to the class.

Frederick Douglass

Ask a student volunteer to prepare a report on Frederick Douglass and share it with the class. Ask this student or another student to make a map showing where Douglass lived as a slave and then later as a free man.

Islam and Slavery

From the beginning of Islam in the seventh century, slavery has been an accepted practice for Muslims. Muhammad captured his enemies, including Jews who refused to convert to Islam, and made them his slaves. He also encouraged his armies to seize slaves during conquest as part of the booty of war. Muslims highly prized women slaves and often used them as musicians or concubines.

With the growth of Muslim slave trade in Africa, slave traders seized millions of native Africans and sent them to Arab countries to serve as slaves. During the 1800s European explorers noted that up to 80 percent of those captured by Muslim traders died during captivity or were murdered before reaching their final destinations. (The slave traders would often slit the throats of those who were too weak or too old to keep up with the slave caravans.) *History of Slavery* by Susanne Everett and *Islam's Black Slaves* by Ronald Segal document Islam's terrible role in slavery.

of the newspaper *The Liberator*. Through his writing, he influenced many to support abolition. Douglass, a former slave, was a persuasive spokesman for abolition.

France

During the French Revolution, the government abolished slavery. However, Napoleon revived this practice when he became the First Consul. He sent troops to put down slave rebellions in various colonies, including Haiti.

For the Haitians, the cost in human lives was immense. However, they would not submit, and thousands of French soldiers died in a failed effort to subdue the Haitians. In 1804 Haiti became one of the first French colonies to gain independence and to end French-imposed slavery.

In the Muslim World

Slavery thrived in the Middle East and Africa before, during, and after the period when Europeans practiced slavery. Some Muslim nations, including the Sudan in East Africa, continue to practice slavery. Estimates vary, but several million people live in slavery in Muslim nations today.

Section Quiz

1. When did slavery become a profitable industry in Europe?
2. What religious group was the first to oppose slavery?
3. What former slave-ship captain became an outspoken opponent of slavery?
4. What invention led to an increased demand for slave labor in America?
5. What island population successfully revolted against French control?
★ What role did William Wilberforce play in the abolition of slavery in the British Empire?

Section Quiz Answers

1. during the Age of Exploration
2. the Quakers
3. John Newton
4. the cotton gin
5. Haiti
★ Answers will vary but should include the following: For many years, he led efforts in Parliament to abolish the slave trade in the British Empire. He also supported and joined the Committee for the Abolition of the Slave Trade.

Activity 6: Chapter Review

This activity helps the students prepare for the chapter test.

Chapter Review Answers

Making Connections

1. Each year, different crops were planted in the same fields to replace depleted nutrients. With this method, all fields could be planted each season.
2. Fewer workers were needed to raise sheep. Suffering from unemployment, families had to find work in town to survive.
3. His invention planted seeds in rows and prevented the farmer from wasting seed. Farmers could grow more crops using much less seed.
4. His machine could process fifty times more cotton per worker in a day than one worker could process by hand.
5. He improved the existing steam engine and greatly increased its efficiency. Steam engines provided power for factory machines, tractors, locomotives, and ships. Steam powered the Industrial Revolution.
6. The Industrial Revolution tended to break down these barriers. People were able to work their way out of poverty and rise to the middle class. The middle class expanded into the upper and lower middle classes.
7. He led the movement to abolish the slave trade in the British Empire and helped lay the groundwork for the eventual abolition of slavery.

CHAPTER REVIEW

Making Connections

1. How did crop rotation increase food production?
2. Why did an increased number of sheep on farms lead people to move to towns?
3. How did Jethro Tull's seed drill lead to a greater food supply?
4. How did Eli Whitney's cotton gin increase the value of cotton as a crop?
5. Why was James Watt's steam engine so important to the Industrial Revolution?
6. What effect did the Industrial Revolution have on class distinctions in Europe?
7. What political and moral victory did Wilberforce win in 1807?
8. Prior to the invention and widespread use of the cotton gin, what seemed to be the direction of slavery in America?

Developing History Skills

1. Based on the information in this chapter, draw a timeline that includes inventions that were developed during the Industrial Revolution.
2. Based on the information in Chapter 9 and this chapter, answer the following question: Why did the Industrial Revolution originate in Britain?

Thinking Critically

1. Identify the positive and negative effects of the Industrial Revolution. Make a list of each on a separate sheet of paper.
2. Evaluate the role of government in regulating industry based on the information in this chapter.

Living in God's World

1. Pretend that you are William Wilberforce. A vicar has recently argued in a newspaper that Christianity is spiritual and thus should not be used to oppose the slave trade. Write a newspaper response defending the role of Christianity and the Bible in the shaping of public policy.
2. You are a Christian historian writing about the period after the Industrial Revolution. As a Christian historian, you know that missions is very significant and should be included in the writing of history. Explain how the Industrial Revolution, in God's providence, opened the way for British and American missionaries to spread the gospel around the world in the nineteenth and twentieth centuries.

People, Places, and Things to Remember

crop rotation
cottage industries
Jethro Tull
seed drill
Andrew Meikle
threshing machine
Eli Whitney
cotton gin
Cyrus McCormick
reaping machine
John Fowler
steam tractor
Industrial Revolution
factories
steam engine
James Watt
John Kay
flying shuttle
James Hargreaves
spinning jenny
entrepreneurs
Richard Arkwright
patent
capital
1833 Factory Act
Mines Act
Ten Hour Bill
John Wesley
George Whitefield
Great Awakening
John Newton
William Wilberforce
Committee for the Abolition of the Slave Trade
William Lloyd Garrison
Frederick Douglass

Positive—multiplied work opportunities; rising wages; availability of low-cost goods; labor-saving devices; increased food supply; increased wealth; improved standard of living; growth of the middle class; removal of class distinctions

Negative—temporary unemployment for some farm laborers; crowded living conditions in the cities; contaminated water in the cities; industrial pollution; unsafe working conditions; abuse by some manufacturers; repetitive work in factories

2. Answers may vary but should include the following: The government sought to alleviate the worst abuses and produced mixed results. For example, legislation limited the working hours of women and children without ensuring that their financial needs would be met afterwards.

Living in God's World

1. Answers will vary.
2. By God's providence, the conditions for the Industrial Revolution were most favorable in Great Britain and America. The benefits of industrialization enabled Great Britain to develop a worldwide empire. Wherever this empire was established, English-speaking missionaries were able to share the gospel. Because Britain and America were primarily Protestant, Protestant Christianity spread around the world.

---

8. It was on the decline.

Developing History Skills

1. Answers should include the following: 1701—Jethro Tull, seed drill; 1733—John Kay, flying shuttle; 1760s—James Watt, improved steam engine; c. 1764—James Hargreaves, spinning jenny; 1786—Andrew Meikle, threshing machine; 1793—Eli Whitney, cotton gin; 1831—Cyrus McCormick, reaping machine; 1850s through the 1860s—John Fowler, steam tractor
2. Answers should include some of the following: **(from Chapter 9)** The English adopted the Dutch banking system, and English economic productivity expanded as a result. The English restricted the rights of their monarch and developed a more representative form of government. **(from Chapter 13)** Britain emerged from the Napoleonic era as the most thriving nation in Europe. Britain had a large merchant fleet to transport goods abroad. Britain's stable banking system and government provided a receptive environment for invention, patent protection, and financing. The British also possessed a large labor force and many natural resources, including iron ore and coal.

Thinking Critically

1. Answers should include some of the following:

Chapter Goals

Students should be able to

1. Explain the impact of new social movements and ideologies on nineteenth-century Europe.

2. Describe cultural, intellectual, and educational trends in nineteenth-century Europe.

3. Evaluate developments in science and technology that occurred in the nineteenth and early twentieth centuries.

4. Analyze the political, economic, and social transformations that occurred in Latin America and Canada in the nineteenth century.

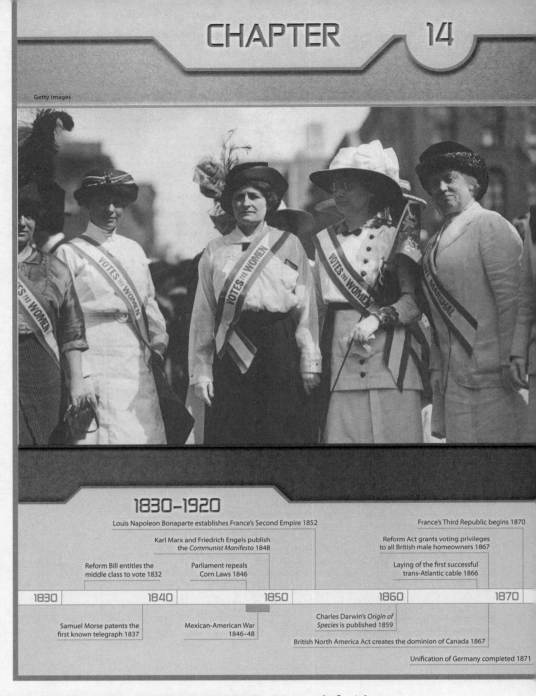

CHAPTER 14

Getty Images

1830–1920

Louis Napoleon Bonaparte establishes France's Second Empire 1852

France's Third Republic begins 1870

Karl Marx and Friedrich Engels publish the *Communist Manifesto* 1848

Reform Act grants voting privileges to all British male homeowners 1867

Reform Bill entitles the middle class to vote 1832

Parliament repeals Corn Laws 1846

Laying of the first successful trans-Atlantic cable 1866

| 1830 | 1840 | 1850 | 1860 | 1870 |

Samuel Morse patents the first known telegraph 1837

Mexican-American War 1846–48

Charles Darwin's *Origin of Species* is published 1859

British North America Act creates the dominion of Canada 1867

Unification of Germany completed 1871

Chapter 14 Lesson Plan Chart

	Section Title	Main Activity	Pages	Days
I.	Reform and Radical Movements	Activity 1: The Dreyfus Affair	244–49	2–2½ days
II.	Changes in Culture and Education	Activity 2: *Hard Times*	249–51	2–2½ days
III.	Progress in Science and Technology	Activity 3: Charles Darwin	251–55	1–1½ days
IV.	Changes in Latin America and Canada	Activity 4 : Chapter Review	255–59	1–1½ days
Total Suggested Days (including 1 day each for review and testing)				8–10 days

Materials List

Section I
- CD: 14A Alfred Dreyfus; 14B Russian Anti-Semitism
- Activity 1 from the *Student Activities* manual
- *Fiddler on the Roof* DVD (optional)

Section II
- A recording of Beethoven's music
- Activity 2 from the *Student Activities* manual

Section III
- Special speaker: someone in the dairy industry

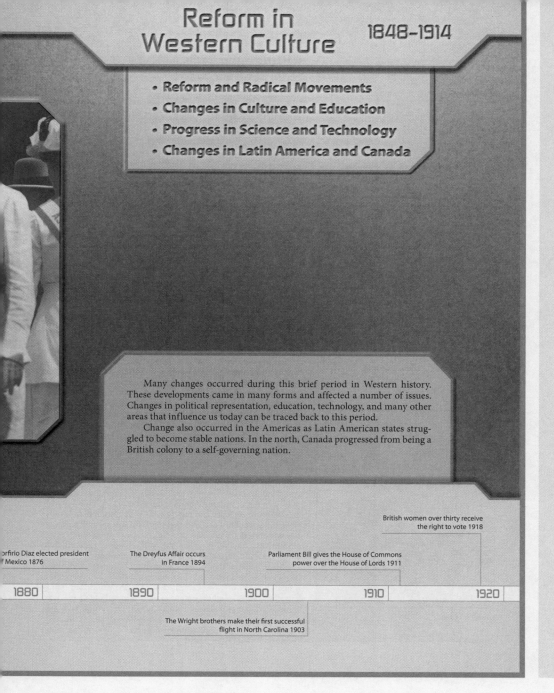

Reform in Western Culture
1848–1914

- Reform and Radical Movements
- Changes in Culture and Education
- Progress in Science and Technology
- Changes in Latin America and Canada

Many changes occurred during this brief period in Western history. These developments came in many forms and affected a number of issues. Changes in political representation, education, technology, and many other areas that influence us today can be traced back to this period.

Change also occurred in the Americas as Latin American states struggled to become stable nations. In the north, Canada progressed from being a British colony to a self-governing nation.

British women over thirty receive the right to vote 1918

orfirio Diaz elected president F Mexico 1876

The Dreyfus Affair occurs in France 1894

Parliament Bill gives the House of Commons power over the House of Lords 1911

| 1880 | 1890 | 1900 | 1910 | 1920 |

The Wright brothers make their first successful flight in North Carolina 1903

- Activity 3 from the *Student Activities* manual

Section IV
- CD: 14C Latin America; 14D Mexico in 1821; 14E Modern Mexico; 14F Canada
- Activity 4 from the *Student Activities* manual

Section I

Students should be able to

1. Explain the main ideas of Marxism and evaluate the movement from a Christian worldview.

2. Describe the course of women's suffrage and other popular movements that arose in Europe and North America.

3. Explain how Britain and France became more liberal and democratic in the nineteenth century.

4. Describe the changing status of European Jews during the second half of the nineteenth century and the rise of new forms of anti-Semitism.

The Delusion of Socialism

Marx insisted that, under socialism, society would continue to progress until government became unnecessary. Contrary to Marx, the Bible never presents a society without government as ideal. The Bible states that government exists to punish evil works and reward good works (Rom. 13:1–7). In the Millennium and throughout eternity, Christ will rule as King over the earth, and the saints will rule with Him (Rev. 20:4; 22:3–5).

Ironically, socialism has consistently led, not to societies without government, but to large totalitarian governments. It is important to explain to the students that there has never been a truly Communist society because all of the so-called Communist societies continue to have strong, centralized governments.

Optional Resources

To learn more about socialism, Marxism, and communism, consult the following resources:

- *Socialism: An Economic and Sociological Analysis* by Ludwig von Mises
- *Planned Chaos* by Ludwig von Mises
- *Marxism Unmasked: From Delusion to Destruction* by Ludwig von Mises
- *The Law* by Frédérick Bastiat
- *Religion: Foundation of the Free Society* by Edmund A. Opitz.

Karl Marx

Friedrich Engels

I. Reform and Radical Movements

The second half of the nineteenth century witnessed many reforms and the development of several radical movements. Socialism developed out of the false belief that man is good, and it manifested itself in many forms. Popular movements, including the universal privilege to vote and the regulation of alcohol, emerged during this period. In response to popular pressure, governments in countries such as Britain and France enabled more citizens to vote and recognized other liberties that tended to provide a more stable society.

Socialism

Socialism has many applications. As an economic term, it refers to government ownership of business. As a philosophy, socialism emphasizes the welfare of the group. Socialism is founded on the error that man is good and that society has corrupted him.

Socialism was a reaction against the capitalistic system. It saw the capitalism that emerged from the Industrial Revolution as unjust because a small number of men controlled the wealth of society. The solution, as socialists saw it, was to press for social equality by restructuring society so that workers controlled the wealth they produced. The socialists also emphasized harmony and cooperation throughout society. Instead of a society developed through competition, they sought a classless society in which everyone cooperated for the common good.

Socialism has developed into several forms, including Utopian socialism, Christian socialism, and Marxist socialism. We will briefly examine the first two before discussing Marxism.

Utopian socialists generally believed that people were the products of their environment. Therefore, education, labor reform, and other improvements to man's cultural environment would improve man's character.

Christian socialists tried to combine a form of Christianity with socialism. Their form of Christianity advocated the good news of achieving justice and equality. Christian socialists denied or distorted the biblical teachings on Creation, the Fall, and Redemption.

Marxism

Karl Marx (1818–83) was a student of philosophy and history. During his years of study, Marx developed radical political views. His support of violent revolution led government officials to expel him from several countries. In Paris, Marx met Friedrich Engels (1820–95), and they became close friends. Together they wrote and published the *Communist Manifesto* in 1848.

In this work, Marx and Engels insisted that history is a series of class struggles. They declared that these struggles would end when the **proletariat** (laborers) united against the **bourgeoisie** (BOOR zhwah ZEE) (capitalists). Then the workers would violently overthrow the middle class and establish a classless society.

Marx believed that private ownership of property and private control of wealth were evil. Like other socialists, he believed that a small number of men controlling most of the wealth was wrong. Therefore, Marx sought to end what he considered unfair practices. He insisted that only violent revolution would end these problems. Marx believed that **communism** (common ownership of property) would result when the proletariat established a dictatorship where the worker would be in power.

Marx and Religion

Marx was a materialist; that is, he believed that only matter was real. Rejecting belief in spiritual things, Marx took a negative view of religion—especially Christianity. He claimed that belief in God, sin, and salvation through Jesus Christ kept the proletariat in bondage, blinding them to their real needs and their power to change society. Marx famously claimed that religion was the "opium of the people." It drugged people and kept them from seeing reality as they needed to see it. As a result, Marx rejected the idea that a sovereign God superintended the course of history. Instead, history moved forward according to a set course determined by social conflicts.

Popular Movements

During the nineteenth century, various groups pressed for reform in society. Two popular movements centered on women's suffrage and the problem of drunkenness.

Women's Suffrage

The privilege to vote, or **suffrage**, became a popular movement in English-speaking countries during the nineteenth and twentieth centuries. Men who had not previously gained the right to vote demanded this privilege. At the same time, women worked to share this freedom. Middle class men in England soon found supporters in Parliament to represent their demands. However, women struggled to overcome decades of resistance and reluctance on the part of British officials. Even when women found a measure of support in Parliament, the majority refused to grant them suffrage. Women in America encountered the same resistance from their elected officials.

Under the leadership of women such as Lydia Becker, British women established suffrage committees beginning in the 1860s. By 1879 these committees united to form the National Union of Women's Suffrage Societies. They presented a united front and relentlessly pressured Parliament. Despite their persistence, British women did not gain the right to vote until after World War I.

While most women sought only to gain suffrage, others developed ambitions that were more radical. They moved beyond petition to heckling political figures and practicing civil disobedience. A minority of radical leaders sought to erase many or all the distinctions between men and women.

Temperance Movement

Britain

Christians and other members of British society became deeply troubled by the increased abuse of alcohol. Various Societies were formed to battle drunkenness by supporting **temperance** (drinking in moderation). They soon realized that **abstinence** (no drinking of alcohol) was the most effective way to prevent drunkenness. Two examples of these groups are the British Association for the Promotion of Temperance, which formed in 1835, and the Band of Hope, which formed in 1847 to protect working class children from becoming victims of alcohol.

A division within the British temperance movement occurred over proposed laws to ban drinking. Some preferred to use moral persuasion rather than making drunkenness a legal matter. Legal efforts lost ground when restricting beer sales led to rioting. Laws that limited or prohibited the sale of alcohol were overturned, and additional efforts met with stiff resistance.

Women's suffrage headquarters in Ohio

American Women's Suffrage

The struggle to win the privilege of women's suffrage also continued in America. With the passage of the Nineteenth Amendment to the Constitution, the law of the land guaranteed women the privilege to vote. Congress ratified this amendment in 1920.

Standard of Living

The general standard of living in countries that have encouraged capitalism has increased dramatically. However, the standard of living in Communist countries has remained consistently low.

The recent growth in China's standard of living was a direct result of the Communist government's allowing its citizens to practice limited capitalism.

People living in Soviet Russia had to wait in long lines just to buy such basic commodities as toilet paper and bread.

Marx and Religion

Marx fell into the trap of rejecting God and His Word. When man rejects the true God, he simply replaces Him with a god of his own making. Marx replaced God with materialism and his own philosophy of history. He rejected the Bible's story of world history in terms of Creation, the Fall, and Redemption for a Hegelian dialectic and the philosophy of class warfare. He replaced the promised coming of Christ's kingdom with the hope that the proletariat's violence would usher in a new world.

Universal Suffrage

Have the class discuss or debate the concept of allowing only homeowners or landowners to vote. Homeowners and landowners have more at stake in government actions and thus are less likely to vote for measures that harm the economy. For example, since those who own homes or land will be adversely affected by property taxes, they will be less likely to vote in favor of increased taxes. Conversely, if those who rent do not realize that increasing property taxes will eventually increase the cost of their rent, they might be more likely to vote for an increase of property taxes.

Negative Effects of Alcohol

Have the class discuss some of the negative consequences of drinking alcohol. There are physical consequences such as alcohol poisoning and liver damage. In addition, Proverbs 21:17 speaks of poverty that arises from drinking. Isaiah 28:7 compares Israel's faulty decision-making to drunkenness.

Perhaps there was a recent incident in your area in which a drunk driver caused an accident and injured himself or others. Help the students learn to avoid drinking alcohol.

Women's temperance march

While legal options proved elusive, efforts to reduce drunkenness continued. In 1873 a Catholic abstinence group formed the League of the Cross. Concerned women also formed the British Women's Temperance Association in 1876 to convince men to stop drinking alcohol.

America

America struggled with drunkenness as early as the late eighteenth century. Temperance societies began to form at this time and continued to multiply through the nineteenth century.

Concerned women in America formed the Women's Christian Temperance Union in 1880 to educate the public regarding the evils of alcohol. They worked with students to warn them before they were tempted to begin drinking.

The goal of many of the American temperance groups was the passage of an amendment to the Constitution (the Eighteenth Amendment) that would make the manufacture, sale, and transportation of alcohol illegal. They sought legal means to protect families from the destructive effects of alcohol.

Reform in Western Europe

Britain and France provide two examples of economic and political reform in Europe during this period. Some of the decisions that preserved Britain from unrest and revolution continued to bless that nation. Likewise, some of the decisions that led the French into revolution and political instability continued to plague them. In the midst of change in Europe, one ugly reality reemerged and continued to become more prominent as the nations rushed toward the twentieth century.

Britain

Economic

Prior to the middle of the nineteenth century, the British government had maintained high tariffs (taxes on imports and exports) on commodities such as imported grain. These taxes protected those who produced these items in Britain. However, the high prices also burdened the British people.

In 1846 Parliament removed one of these tariffs by repealing the **Corn Laws**. This decision allowed merchants to import cheaper grain and lowered the cost of food for everyone. By repealing laws to protect a segment of the market, Britain's foreign policy began to shift toward a free trade economy. This transition resulted in a dramatic increase of trade and brought great prosperity to Britain.

Political

While most of the British population had moved from the country to the cities, representation in Parliament did not reflect this change. The growing middle class began to demand a voice in government. They persisted, and the **Reform Bill of 1832** entitled the middle class to vote. However, members of the working class remained excluded.

Chartism developed among the working class as an effort to accomplish several goals. Members of this movement demanded universal manhood suffrage. In other words, they sought the right for

Developing a Welfare State

While the British insisted on having a greater voice in government, a subtle change began to occur. Many people began to expect the government to develop ways to provide for them. Politicians promised new programs in exchange for votes. Soon Parliament approved programs to provide workers with such guarantees as unemployment insurance, workers' compensation, and old-age pensions. The government increasingly took control of society in order to provide these benefits. It also collected more taxes to pay for them. Seeking security, the people began to lose their freedom.

Tariffs

Ask a volunteer to research the repeal of the Corn Laws and present his findings to the class.

Chartism

Ask a volunteer to read about Chartism and share his work with the class.

every Englishman to vote. They also supported other reforms such as the use of the secret ballot in elections. The secret ballot protected the voter from pressure or bribery. Though this movement failed, many of the issues it raised became law over time.

Following the Reform Bill of 1832, additional reform met with stiff resistance. Finally, in 1867, Prime Minister **Benjamin Disraeli** succeeded in doubling the number of men who could vote. In the **Reform Act of 1867**, Disraeli and Parliament granted voting privileges to all male homeowners. This act increased the number of voters to two million out of a population of around five million men. Later reforms provided more representation to rural communities.

During the many years of demanding the privilege to vote, women were the last to achieve this goal. In 1918 Parliament voted to allow British women who were over thirty to vote. Due to the persistence of reformers, all British women received this privilege in 1928.

Disraeli's political opponent, **William Gladstone**, stressed domestic reform during his terms as prime minister. Among his many accomplishments, Gladstone helped to establish a national court system and voting by secret ballot. In addition, he labored to improve public education. Gladstone believed an educated public would produce informed voters.

Throughout this period in Britain, the House of Lords struggled to retain power over the House of Commons. However, the **Parliament Bill of 1911** changed the balance of power. The House of Lords could no longer veto laws passed by the House of Commons. This bill established the supremacy of the House of Commons over the House of Lords.

France

France suffered devastation because of Napoleon's failed attempts to control Europe. Political instability plagued France. European leaders restored the monarchy, but it did not last. The French overthrew the next government during the Revolution of 1848.

The French then elected **Louis Napoleon Bonaparte** as president of the newly formed Second Republic in 1848. He followed his uncle Napoleon Bonaparte's example and declared himself president for life. In 1852 he gave himself the title of emperor of France, as Napoleon III, and established the **Second Empire**. He remained in power until the people revolted in 1870.

During Louis Napoleon's reign, France experienced growth in several areas. Industry developed, and many French families moved from the country to the cities. The French economy expanded as the Industrial Revolution reaped the benefits of English machinery and British financing.

Louis Napoleon also allowed freedom of the press and the development of labor unions. In addition, suffrage increased to include many more citizens.

However, a disastrous war with Germany led to a humiliating defeat of the French forces. Louis Napoleon lost favor with the people. The forces of the newly formed **Third Republic** (1870–1940) captured and deposed Louis Napoleon. He spent the rest of his life in exile in England.

Jews in Europe

Hostility toward Jews, or **anti-Semitism**, has a long history. You learned in Chapter 5 about violent attacks on the Jews during the Middle Ages. Animosity toward Jews ebbed and flowed in intensity

Time & Life Pictures/Getty Image

Napoleon III

Roger Viollet/Getty Images

France built the Eiffel Tower as the entrance to the World's Fair in 1889. This colossal structure demonstrated that France had become an important industrial power.

Napoleon III

During a time of unrest in France, Louis Napoleon Bonaparte, the nephew of Napoleon I, took advantage of his name and convinced the French to elect him as president of the Second Republic in 1848. Following in the tradition of his uncle, Louis Napoleon staged a coup d'état in 1851 and appointed himself dictator, taking the title of Napoleon III.

For a time, France prospered under Napoleon III as he led it into the Industrial Revolution and strengthened the French economy. Under his direction, Paris was transformed into a modern city.

However, Louis Napoleon also involved France in several wars, including the Crimean War, the Second Opium War, the Franco-Mexican War, and the Franco-Prussian War. This last war in 1870 proved to be Louis Napoleon's downfall. Using this conflict to unite the German states into modern Germany, Bismarck manipulated the French into declaring war. France suffered a humiliating defeat, and Napoleon was forced to flee from France.

Disraeli and Gladstone

Ask two volunteers to read about Benjamin Disraeli or William Gladstone. Have them share the results of their research with the class.

Captain Dreyfus being stripped of his rank

during succeeding centuries. However, it remained like a smoldering ember ready to burst into flame.

Germany

German composer Richard Wagner provided a glimpse into German anti-Semitism in 1850 when he wrote an essay attacking Jewish composers, including Felix Mendelssohn. He opposed the Jewish influence on German culture. Another glimpse surfaced in 1878 when the Lutheran court chaplain to Kaiser Wilhelm I formed the Christian Social Party to resist Jewish influence in Germany.

France

The **Dreyfus Affair** exposed a strong undercurrent of anti-Semitism in France. Alfred Dreyfus, a Jew, served as an artillery captain in the French army. In 1894 the French government accused him of passing military secrets to the Germans. Despite his innocence, the government convicted and sentenced him to life in prison on Devil's Island.

The French government later secretly tried and acquitted (found not guilty) the real spy. The French people became divided over the treatment of Dreyfus and his guilt or innocence. However, a large majority of the French press condemned Dreyfus. Under pressure, the government eventually released Dreyfus from prison and restored his rank in the French army. However, the Dreyfus Affair left an ugly stain on French history.

Russia

Many Jews had migrated to Russia over the centuries. Some fled persecution in western Europe (see chapter 5). The czars welcomed many others because of their skills and strong work ethic.

However, by the nineteenth century, more and more Russians began to view the Jews with jealousy and suspicion. As the level of violence in Russia increased, Russians often blamed the Jews for assassinations and other crimes. Russian authorities and citizens murdered Jews without regard for age or gender. The term *pogrom* (puh GROM) was first used to refer to a sweeping, targeted, and repeated attack on Jews in Russia.

Cartoon showing Russian oppression of the Jewish population. Teddy Roosevelt is seen rebuking the czar.

Devil's Island

During the reign of Louis Napoleon, prisons were built on an island off the coast of French Guiana, located in South America. Convicts imprisoned there varied from political dissenters to violent criminals. Conditions were harsh, and escape was almost impossible. Few ever left the island alive. Dreyfus survived his imprisonment, but suffered ongoing health problems due to his five-year imprisonment.

CD: 14A Alfred Dreyfus; 14B Russian Anti-Semitism

A portrait of Captain Dreyfus and a political cartoon from the student text are available on the CD.

Activity 1: The Dreyfus Affair

This activity is a fictionalized account of the arrest and wrongful imprisonment of Captain Alfred Dreyfus. Use this activity as an opportunity to discuss anti-Semitism.

Anti-Semitism in Russia

You might want to show the students the sections of *Fiddler on the Roof* in which a Jewish wedding is disrupted and in which the Jews are forced to relocate.

Felix Mendelssohn

Visit www.bjupress.com/resources for possible links to articles about Felix Mendelssohn.

Section Quiz

1. According to Marx, what would end the cycle of class struggle?

2. What privilege did the woman's suffrage movement seek?

3. What did the American temperance groups seek in order to make alcohol illegal in the United States?

4. What were the goals of the Chartist movement?

5. How did the Dreyfus Affair expose anti-Semitism in France?

★ Marx claimed that only matter is real and that religion is just a drug. Marx also claimed that oppression of the proletariat is wrong and ought to be opposed. How do these ideas contradict each other?

II. Changes in Culture and Education

Culture in Europe shifted from an idealist view of man to one that emphasized reality. Writers and artists created works that reflected what they saw rather than what they imagined. Leaders also realized that citizens required a basic education in order to become a productive and informed society. Public education became more widely available as a result.

Culture

Romanticism

The nineteenth century was an age of change, and the arts were no exception. Several styles of art appeared during this period. **Romanticism** dominated the first half of the century. Several themes characterize romanticism. It desired to imitate the past, especially the medieval time with its higher call to chivalry. In addition, romanticism placed an emphasis on the mysterious and the supernatural, as well as a love of freedom, nationalism, and nature. These themes also reflect the political ideas of the time.

Romantic paintings are often peaceful scenes of rural life or landscapes. Some artists also painted scenes from the revolutions. In music, composers reacted to the orderly, classical style by changing to the full, emotion-filled romantic style. Ludwig van Beethoven (BAY toh vun) is perhaps the best-known composer of this age. He mixed classical and romantic elements in his works.

Romantic art and literature emphasized emotion rather than reason. Romanticism taught that it was right for a person to do what his heart told him. In other words, it would be better to rise up against impossible odds and do the heroic thing than rationally weigh the possible outcomes.

Realism

By the middle of the nineteenth century, **realism** had replaced romanticism as a new art form. Realism reacted against romanticism's dreamlike quality by emphasizing, as its name suggests, what life is really like. In writing and painting, realists pictured everyday life in realistic detail.

However, realism, like romanticism, failed to portray correctly the sum total of life. Realism tended to show life as pessimistic and hopeless. Realists seemed to be suspicious of redemption, and their literature implied it would be dishonest to have a happy conclusion.

Section II

Objectives

Students should be able to

1. Describe the expanded educational opportunities and increased literacy of nineteenth-century Europe.

2. Evaluate major movements in literature, music, and the visual arts and the ways in which they expressed or shaped social and cultural values.

Section Quiz Answers

1. The workers would overthrow the middle class in a violent revolution and establish a classless society.

2. suffrage (the privilege to vote)

3. an amendment to the Constitution

4. universal manhood suffrage and the secret ballot

5. Dreyfus, a Jew, was sentenced to prison even though he was innocent. The French press largely condemned Dreyfus.

★ In saying that oppression of the proletariat is wrong, Marx made a moral claim even though he denied the existence of a supreme being who makes moral laws. In a world where only matter exists, there is no right and wrong.

Ludwig van Beethoven

Visit www.bjupress.com/resources for possible links to articles about Ludwig van Beethoven.

Romanticism

Have the class listen to some of Beethoven's music and discuss the romantic elements it contains.

Growth of Sunday Schools

Robert Raikes contributed to the development of Sunday schools in Britain. He was a philanthropist and a lay member of the Anglican Church. While working with troubled boys, he decided that it would be preferable to educate them and teach them to read the Bible than to allow them to support themselves with criminal activity. His work had a great impact on the rising generation of British men, some of whom went on to become leaders of British society. In time, girls also attended these schools, and the number of children attending grew to about 1.2 million. This number represented about one-fourth of the British population in 1831.

German Education

Germany developed one of the most structured educational systems in Europe. The results were very impressive. However, the government-run schools viewed the students as tools of the state; training methods taught students to blindly follow a leader without question.

Effects of Education

Have the students debate the proposition that an educated public produces informed voters. (Much depends on what type of education the public receives—accurate transmittal of knowledge or propaganda.)

Activity 2: *Hard Times*

This activity contains an excerpt from Charles Dickens's book *Hard Times*. It has been chosen to help the students understand the plight of many of the poor during the early Industrial Revolution. It is also a fine example of realist writing.

Left, Charles Dickens; *right,* Leo Tolstoy

Rubens Peale with a Geranium. 1801. Rembrandt Peale. Oil on canvas.

Literature

Realist authors did not abandon emotion in their writings. Instead, they sought to describe events that occurred in everyday life. At times, the events they described were sad or unpleasant. For example, **Charles Dickens** wrote about the negative aspects of the Industrial Revolution, including the slums where many workers lived. He vividly described the terrible conditions in the industrial cities and provided the reader a glimpse into the British debtors' prisons. Another realist author, **Leo Tolstoy**, described the difficulties of life in Russia. In his novel *War and Peace*, he emphasized the struggles of all kinds of people rather than focusing on leaders such as Napoleon or the czar.

Visual Arts

Realist painters produced works of art that portrayed everyday life. Scenes included common events such as friends meeting and engaging in conversation. Photography developed during this period, and the reality captured by a photograph may have contributed to the appeal of realism in paintings.

Education

Opportunities for education were very limited in Europe prior to the nineteenth century. The Roman Catholic and Anglican Churches still operated most schools and emphasized religious education. However, in Britain and France public education became a priority during the nineteenth century. The government established and financially supported schools. Literacy and a basic education finally became available to most children in these countries.

Britain

Early private education in Britain began with the Sunday school movement. Though we tend to think of Sunday school as a time for Bible training in church, it began as an effort to teach poor children how to read. The teaching occurred on Sunday, so it became known as Sunday school. By 1831 over one million British children attended these sessions and learned to read. The goal for these students was to be able to read the Bible and learn God's Word.

The public school system began in 1833 when Parliament voted to spend money to build schools for poor children. The government became increasingly involved in education by determining the courses for grammar school in the 1840s. Through succeeding legislation, the government required children to attend school from ages five through ten. In 1893 the government provided educational opportunities for blind and deaf children. By 1918 the British government required education for five- to fourteen-year-old children and part-time education until eighteen years of age.

Germany

During the 18th century Prussia became one of the first European states to provide a free primary education that was required for all children. Improvements included certification for teachers and special schools to train people how to teach.

Shortly after achieving unification in 1871, Germany continued to make great advances in education. For example, the new nation established one of the first separate secondary schools for girls in Eu-

Charles Dickens

Visit www.bjupress.com/resources for possible links to articles about Charles Dickens.

Tolstoy's *War and Peace*

Visit www.bjupress.com/resources for possible links to articles about Tolstoy's *War and Peace*.

rope. Continued improvements led to secondary schools that trained German students in ancient and modern languages. Students also received training in science and math. Those students who did not qualify for a college education could receive technical training in preparation for an industrial job.

By the end of the nineteenth century, Germany had developed one of the finest systems of education in Europe. The state regulated these schools and demanded the right to set educational standards.

France

Modern French education began near the end of the nineteenth century. Jules Ferry, the Minister of Public Instruction, formed the republican school system. He required all children to attend school until the age of fifteen. Ferry made public education required, free, and secular. Prior to these changes, Roman Catholic clergy had played a central role in education. The system established by Ferry has continued with little change.

Section Quiz

1. How did realism differ from romanticism?
2. About what did Charles Dickens write?
3. What new invention possibly influenced realist painters?
4. What was the earliest form of public education in Britain? What was its goal?
5. How did Germany develop one of the finest education systems in Europe?

★ Evaluate romanticism in light of Jeremiah 17:9.

III. Progress in Science and Technology

Science and technology continued to make important discoveries and provide significant contributions to society. However, advances did not always lead to a positive impact on culture. Progress in these fields produced mixed outcomes.

Science

Major scientific discoveries occurred during this period. Physics, chemistry, and microbiology experienced great advances. However, the results from one man's study of nature led to an epic shift in science that caused an ongoing assault on Christianity and the Scripture.

James Clerk Maxwell

James Maxwell (1831–79), a Scottish scientist, made major contributions to the fields of physics and astronomy. Regarded by many as a scientific genius, he predicted the existence of radio waves before their discovery. Perhaps his greatest contribution was combining the sciences of electricity, magnetism, and optics into one model. Other great scientists, including Albert Einstein, built on the foundations laid by Maxwell.

Louis Pasteur

Louis Pasteur (1822–95), a chemist in France, made many important discoveries that prevented several diseases. For example, he developed a method of heating milk and other liquids in order to

James Maxwell

> **Maxwell, Man of God**
> While others recognized Maxwell for his great intellect, he acknowledged himself to be but a humble sinner. His mother trained him at home until her death in 1839. Maxwell experienced a spiritual conversion and matured into a devout man of God.

Louis Pasteur

Section III

Objectives

Students should be able to

1. Evaluate the social significance of the work of such scientists as Maxwell, Pasteur, and Darwin.
2. Evaluate the transformation of global communication and trade caused by inventions such as the railroad, steamship, telegraph, and telephone.

James Maxwell

For more information about Maxwell's work, consult the fourth edition of *Physical Science (BJU Press)*.

Louis Pasteur

For more information about Pasteur and spontaneous generation, consult the fourth edition of *Biology (BJU Press)*.

Section Quiz Answers

1. Realism emphasized everyday reality. Romanticism emphasized idealism and emotion rather than reality.
2. the negative aspects of the Industrial Revolution
3. photography
4. the Sunday school movement; to teach children to read so that they could read the Bible
5. Germany developed free, required primary education; developed special schools to train teachers; and developed extensive secondary education for all types of students.

★ Romanticism embraced several errors, including the ideas of the noble savage and the goodness of man's impulses and emotions. The Bible warns the Christian against trusting his own sinful heart.

🕸 James Maxwell

Visit www.bjupress.com/resources for possible links to articles about James Maxwell.

👤 Dairy

Invite someone who works at a dairy or milk plant to speak to the class about the process of pasteurization.

Charles Darwin

For more information about Darwin, consult the fourth edition of *Biology* (BJU Press).

Technology

Technology can be defined as the practical application of scientific discoveries. Technology is often developed to increase the speed and efficiency of a certain task.

Activity 3: Charles Darwin

This activity is an excerpt from the autobiography of Darwin. It provides some insight into his early life.

Railroads

Have a volunteer research the history of railroads and find some current statistics on modern railroads. This presentation could be followed by a class discussion on the importance of railroads to the U.S. economy. Also consider discussing changes in the technology, power sources, and use of railroads (passenger service, hauling of products traditionally carried by trucks, etc.).

Charles Darwin

Do Christianity and Evolution Mix?

Many Christians have felt compelled by Darwin and scientists who have followed him to fit the biblical Creation narratives into the evolutionary story told by the Darwinists. This attempt is fatally flawed. The evolutionary scheme relies on violence and competition, but the Bible teaches that violence and death are a result of the Fall (Rom. 5:12). Thus there could be no death until Adam sinned. Darwin's theory of evolution also treats man as simply another aspect of the evolutionary process. But the Bible clearly sets man apart as a special creation in the image of God. Because evolution is incompatible with Scripture, the Christian must reject evolution. Christian scientists should work hard to demonstrate the scientific fallacies of evolution and provide scientific explanations that are compatible with Scripture.

slow the development of disease-causing microbes. Today we call this process **pasteurization**.

Pasteur also made an immense contribution to science by proving that spontaneous generation (the idea that life is generated from non-living materials) is a myth. He placed a mixture of sugar and yeast in a special flask and heated it to sterilize the mixture. The design of the flask allowed air to enter, but prevented dust and microbes from coming into contact with the mixture. If the theory of spontaneous generation was correct, some basic life form should have developed from the sugar-yeast mixture. However, no life forms developed. This discovery struck at the very foundation of the emerging theory of evolution.

Charles Darwin

Charles Darwin (1809–82) was born into a Unitarian family that had a history of freethinkers. As a child, he became very interested in nature. At the University of Edinburgh he studied medicine, and in his free time he learned about the study of nature. His classes, however, bored him, and his father then sent him to Cambridge to study to be a pastor. Darwin eventually gave up becoming a pastor as well. In 1831 Darwin sailed on a five-year voyage as a naturalist on the HMS *Beagle*. His discoveries led him to question whether creatures changed over time or not.

Darwin also struggled with the question of how a good God could design and sustain a world filled with pain and suffering. He concluded that God had little or nothing to do with the creation or maintaining of this world. The death of his beloved ten-year-old daughter, Annie, seemed to him to prove his point.

Darwin's observations, combined with this conclusion, provided the foundation for an evolutionary theory to explain the origin and changes of life. His theory assumed a natural explanation for man's origins. His premise also assumed that spontaneous generation was possible. Darwin's observations led him to believe that all living things had developed from a single life form. His works, *Origin of Species* in 1859 and *The Descent of Man* in 1871, led to fundamental changes in the direction of science and its influence on society. As scientists began to apply this theory, they excluded God and the Bible from consideration as a source of reliable information.

Technology

Inventive minds continued to develop improved methods of transportation and communication. Scientists and inventors produced great discoveries. At the same time, society gradually came to replace faith in the God of the Bible with faith in science and human achievement. As a result, improvements in technology tended to increase man's self-confidence and reduce his dependence on God.

Transportation

Railroad

Britain has the distinction of developing the first known railway system in the world. Initially several local railroads operated over short routes. During the 1840s these routes were combined into a national network. The railroad became an important method of transporting goods and people across Britain and, later, across Europe. While canals were frozen and unavailable in the winter, railroads could operate year-round. With continuing improvements, the railroads operated at great speeds and provided transportation

🕸 Charles Darwin

Visit www.bjupress.com/resources for possible links to articles about Charles Darwin.

Getty Images

Promontory Summit in Utah where the Union Pacific and Central Pacific railroads connected to become the Trans-Continental Railroad in 1869

at reduced cost. This provided a variety of benefits to the British economy.

America imported its first steam locomotives and steel rails from Britain and gradually developed rail lines along the east coast. Railroads proved to be strategic during the Civil War as they delivered supplies and troops. The nation quickly recognized the tremendous importance of the railroad, and workers completed the first transcontinental railroad in 1869. The railroad became a vital asset in colonizing the West.

Steamship

With the development of steam-powered engines, several inventors sought to power ships using this new device. For a time, wind-powered ships could travel faster than the early steamships. However, use of Watt's steam engine, combined with improvements by many inventors, led to faster and faster steamships.

With continued improvements, steamships replaced sail-driven ships and traveled across the ocean. Soon ships carrying hundreds of passengers, mail, and other items traveled between Britain and America.

American Entrepreneur

Robert Fulton, an American, quickly saw the potential of the steamship in Britain and built a steamboat using a Watt steam engine. He delivered passengers between New York City and Albany, New York. His idea became a commercial success.

Early steamship

Early gasoline engine

Internal Combustion Engine

While the steam engine received its power from outside the engine, the **internal combustion engine** produced power inside the engine. Powered by gasoline or diesel, this engine revolutionized transportation. Automobiles developed as a combination of many inventions after years of trial and error. While Europeans probably developed the first working automobiles, American entrepreneurs like Henry Ford took the automobile and made it an essential part of mobility in America and around the world.

Flight

Man has dreamed of flying for centuries. Sketches by Leonardo da Vinci reveal his interest in human flight. However, the first successful flight did not occur in Europe. Wilbur and Orville Wright, two brothers who owned a bicycle shop in Ohio, built the first successful airplane. On the sandy beach of Kitty Hawk in North Carolina, the **Wright brothers** made their first successful flight on December 17, 1903.

First flight by the Wright brothers

Communication

Inventions such as the telegraph and the telephone laid the foundation for global communication. Messages that took days or weeks to be delivered could now be transmitted and received in a matter of minutes or seconds. While instant communication was convenient, it also enabled a rapid response. Demands could be made and responses could be sent in the heat of the moment. Not all the consequences were positive.

Telegraph

The word **telegraph** combines two Greek words *tele* ("far") and *graphein* ("to write"). The telegraph enabled people to write messages to others who lived far away. Operators sent the first messages over wire lines using a code developed by **Samuel Morse** and his assistant. In

Samuel Morse

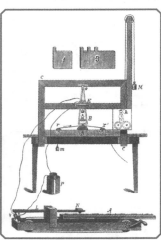
Early telegraph

Class Project 1

Have part of the class produce diagrams and an oral presentation to show how the internal combustion engine works.

Class Project 2

Have another section of the class produce diagrams, photos, and an oral presentation to show man's progress in flight.

1837 Morse patented the first known machine to send these coded messages. By 1861 telegraph lines stretched across the country to the west coast. Continued developments enabled operators to transmit many messages at the same time through existing wire.

In 1866 the first successful telegraph cable was laid across the Atlantic Ocean. This cable enabled operators to send messages directly to Europe. By 1870 Britain had laid a submarine cable to India. Within a few years, operators could literally send messages around the world.

Telephone

Similar to the word telegraph, the word **telephone** combines the Greek word *tele* with another Greek word *phone* ("voice"). While many men worked to develop the technology that resulted in the telephone, **Alexander Graham Bell** was the first to patent it. The great inventor Thomas Edison also worked to improve Bell's invention. Edison had lost most of his hearing as a child. When he first tried to use a telephone, he could not understand what he heard. As a result, Edison made improvements to Bell's phone that enabled Edison (and many others) to hear the caller clearly.

Alexander Graham Bell

Section Quiz

1. What did James Clerk Maxwell combine into one model?
2. What theory did Louis Pasteur prove to be a myth?
3. Over what issue did Darwin struggle?
4. What two modes of transportation developed because of the invention of the steam engine?
5. Why couldn't Edison use Bell's early version of the telephone?
★ Evaluate some of the improvements in technology. How might they have increased man's self-confidence and decreased his dependence on God?

IV. Changes in Latin America and Canada

While most of Europe and the United States benefited from stable governments and growing economies, Latin and Central America searched for stability. Far to the north, Canada slowly advanced toward its goal of becoming a self-governing nation.

Latin America

Latin and Central America struggled for stability following independence from Spanish and Portuguese control. Although this region is rich in natural resources, many of the people lacked opportunity to develop those resources. The vast percentage of the wealth and power resided in a tiny portion of the population. A large majority of the people remained in poverty and had no voice in the governing of their nation.

In the Region as a Whole

Successes

Latin American states, including Uruguay, Chile, Costa Rica, and Columbia, developed some form of democracy. These countries

Section IV

Objectives

Students should be able to

1. Assess the successes and failures of democracy in Latin American countries that gained their independence in the nineteenth and early twentieth centuries.

2. Explain the steps that led to nation-building and self-government in Canada.

The Telephone

Visit www.bjupress.com/resources for possible links to articles about the telephone.

Section Quiz Answers

1. the sciences of electricity, magnetism, and optics

2. spontaneous generation

3. how a good God could design and sustain a world filled with suffering

4. the railroad and the steamship

5. He had lost most of his hearing as a child.

★ Answers will vary but should include some of the following: Steamships and railroads enabled many to sell more goods and transport them to distant locations. As man accumulated wealth and gained power, he tended to develop a false sense of security and blind himself to his need for God. Improvements in technology led some men to embrace the error that man can overcome any obstacle with his own intelligence and hard work.

CD: 14C Latin America

This map from the student text is also available on the CD.

avoided some of the political instability that much of Latin and Central America suffered.

Some of the dictators ruled in a responsible manner and gained the support of a majority of citizens in the country. They tended to share more of the wealth generated by the natural resources sold to Europe and America.

Failures

Most of the countries in Latin America tried for many years without success to develop a sense of nationality. Often the states warred with one another over territorial disputes and access to natural resources.

For example, in one war (1864–70) Argentina, Brazil, and Uruguay defeated Paraguay. Due to the war and other factors, Paraguay's population dropped from over five hundred thousand to two hundred thousand. In a later war, Chile defeated the combined armies of Bolivia and Peru (1879–84) to gain control of mineral-rich areas.

The gap between the rich and poor also remained great in Latin America. By 1910 about one percent of the population controlled eighty-five percent of the land. Wealthy landowners controlled gold mining and food production. Wages for the average worker remained very low, and opportunities for improvement were rare.

In Mexico

Mexico's struggle resembled that of other countries in Latin America. This young country tried in vain to overcome economic and political instability. In addition, the Mexican-American War

Mexico

Spanish control and adopted the Spanish language. Even after gaining independence from Spain in 1821, Mexico endured foreign rule under Maximilian and dictatorships under leaders such as Porfirio Diaz.

Located in the southwest region of North America, Mexico has been inhabited for thousands of years. Ancient Indian civilizations built empires in this area, although many had disappeared or suffered great decline prior to the arrival of the Spanish in 1519.

For the next three centuries, the Indian population of Mexico endured

Left, *Mexico City;* center, *Ferdinand Maximilian;* right, *Porfirio Diaz*

Maximilian

Ask a volunteer to read about the French-imposed dictator Maximilian and present a report to the class.

Porfirio Diaz

Ask a volunteer to prepare a report about Mexican dictator Porfirio Diaz and present his work to the class.

(1846–48) resulted in Mexico losing a large section of its territory to the victorious United States.

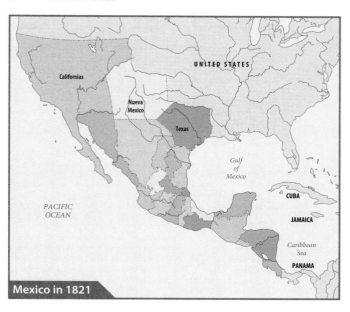

Mexico in 1821

Modern Mexico

CD: 14D Mexico in 1821
This map from the student text is also available on the CD.

CD: 14E Modern Mexico
This map from the student text is also available on the CD.

Under the leadership of Louis Napoleon Bonaparte, France forced Mexico to submit to a foreign ruler during the 1860s. Archduke Ferdinand Maximilian of Austria served as the puppet ruler for Bonaparte. However, this foreign rule ended in 1867 when the Mexican government regained power and then tried and executed Maximilian.

Mexicans elected **Porfirio Diaz** in 1876 based on his promises of a constitutional democracy and prosperity. Once elected, Diaz maintained order and welcomed investments from foreign businesses. Under his leadership, Mexico became one of the most prosperous nations in the region.

However, Diaz transformed his government into a dictatorship and ruled for another thirty-one years. Over time, the people saw him as a pawn of the foreign businesses. Many of these companies took advantage of Mexico's financial weakness. As a result, Mexicans developed a hatred for foreign influences.

Following a rigged election in 1910 where Diaz was declared the winner, the people overthrew the dictator. The people of Mexico elected Francisco Madero in 1911, but an assassin killed him two years later. Civil war followed, and an estimated nine hundred thousand people died in the fighting. Assassinations and revolutions continued to prolong Mexico's struggle for democracy.

Canada

Canada began as a French colony. The British won this vast territory because of their victory in the Seven Years' War (1756–63). To maintain the loyalty of the French Canadians, the British passed the Quebec Act in 1774 and granted them many rights, including the freedom to practice Roman Catholicism. While this pleased the

Canada

French Canadians, it played a role in the eventual War for Independence by the American colonies.

Nation Building

The pacifying of colonists in Canada proved to be short-lived. In 1837 rebellions against the British government occurred throughout Canada. The British forces defeated the rebels and arrested hundreds of Canadians.

In order to establish a long-term solution, the British government sent Lord Durham to investigate. He examined the situation in Canada and returned to Britain with a report. Durham recommended that Parliament grant the Canadians the right to govern themselves in domestic matters while Britain would control foreign dealings. He also recommended that Parliament unite the Canadian provinces. Parliament accepted the second recommendation and made this formal with the Act of Union in 1840.

The **British North America Act** in 1867 created the dominion of Canada with four provinces: Ontario, Quebec, New Brunswick, and Nova Scotia. The government established the province of Manitoba in 1870. British Columbia and Prince Edward Island became provinces in the 1870s. In 1905, Alberta and Saskatchewan also became provinces. Newfoundland and Labrador became the tenth province to join the Canadian Confederation in 1949.

Self-Government

In theory, a constitutional monarchy governs Canada. In fact, the British Crown serves as a symbolic head of government. The federal and provincial governments wield the actual power to govern. An elected House of Commons and an appointed Senate provide the Canadians with representation.

The party with a majority of seats in the House of Commons retains the legislative power to govern. To strengthen its influence, the party in power nominates its supporters as senators. The influence of the Senate becomes more noticeable when a new party wins a majority of seats. Then the ruling party nominates new senators to replace those appointed by the previous administration.

Interior and exterior Canadian Parliament building in Ottawa

Section Quiz

1. List Latin American countries that developed some form of democracy.

2. Why did many Latin American countries fail to develop stable governments?

3. What country invaded Mexico in the 1860s and set up a puppet ruler?

4. What act initially secured French Canadian loyalty to Britain?

5. What role does the British monarch play in Canadian government?

★ Contrast the treatment of Canada and the American colonies by the British government.

Government of Canada

Visit www.bjupress.com/resources for possible links to articles about the government of Canada.

Section Quiz Answers

1. Answers may vary but should include Uruguay, Chile, Costa Rica, Colombia, and Mexico.

2. They could not develop a sense of nationality.

3. France

4. the Quebec Act

5. The British monarch is Canada's symbolic head of government.

★ Answers should include some of the following: The British invaded the American colonies and stripped them of their right to protection by the Crown. The American colonies were forced to seek independence through war. However, the British granted the Canadian colonies many freedoms and gradually allowed them to become independent and self-governing.

Activity 4: Chapter Review

This activity will help the students review the material in the chapter.

CHAPTER REVIEW

<table>
<tr><td>

People, Places, and Terms to Know

socialism
Karl Marx
proletariat
bourgeoisie
communism
suffrage
temperance
abstinence
Corn Laws
Reform Bill of 1832
Chartism
Benjamin Disraeli
Reform Act of 1867
William Gladstone
Parliament Bill of 1911
Louis Napoleon Bonaparte
Second Empire
Third Republic
anti-Semitism
Dreyfus Affair
pogrom
romanticism
realism
Charles Dickens
Leo Tolstoy
James Maxwell
Louis Pasteur
pasteurization
Charles Darwin
internal combustion engine
Wright brothers
telegraph
Samuel Morse
telephone
Alexander Graham Bell
Porfirio Diaz
British North America Act

</td></tr>
</table>

Making Connections

1. Why did several European countries expel Karl Marx?
2. Why did the British temperance movement divide over supporting regulation to ban drinking alcohol?
3. What was the result of Britain's shifting toward a free trade economy?
4. Why did the British seek the right to use a secret ballot for elections?
5. How did German composer Richard Wagner demonstrate an anti-Semitic attitude?
6. Which type of painting would probably be more bright and colorful, Romantic or Realist? Why?
7. Describe Louis Pasteur's immense contribution to science.
8. What impact did Darwin's work have on the direction of science?

Developing History Skills

1. Based on the information in this chapter, draw a timeline that shows the development of Canada from British colony to self-governing nation. Provide the significance of each date.
2. Based on the information in previous chapters and this chapter, explain why Britain consistently enjoyed greater prosperity and political stability than France did.

Thinking Critically

1. Darwin struggled with the question of how a good God could design and sustain a world filled with pain and suffering. He resolved the question by proposing that God had little or nothing to do with the creation and maintaining of this world. How would you resolve this question according to the Bible?
2. The following is a famous quotation from Karl Marx. Evaluate this statement from a Christian worldview: "Religion is the sigh of the oppressed creature, the heart of a heartless world, and the soul of soulless conditions. It is the opium of the people. The abolition of religion . . . is the demand for their [the people's] real happiness. To call on them to give up their illusions about their condition is to call on them to give up a condition that requires illusions."

Living in God's World

1. Divide into two groups. One group should create a story or piece of artwork according to the description of romanticism in this chapter. The second group should do the same according to the description of realism in this chapter. Share your creation with the class. Explain to the class the elements of

Chapter Review Answers

Making Connections

1. He supported violent revolution.
2. Some preferred to use moral persuasion to end the drinking of alcohol while others supported making drunkenness a legal matter.
3. The cost of food and goods dropped, and the increase of trade brought great prosperity to Britain.
4. The secret ballot protected the voter from pressure and bribery.
5. He wrote an essay attacking Jewish composers, including Felix Mendelssohn.
6. Romantic painting would likely be more colorful. Romantic painters portrayed the ideal, while realists portrayed daily life, which is often not bright and colorful.
7. He developed pasteurization to prevent the spread of many disease-causing microbes and proved that spontaneous generation is a myth.
8. He attempted to prove that evolution could explain the origin of life and the assumed change from one species to another. His conclusions contradicted

the clear teaching of Scripture. As scientists applied Darwin's theory, they excluded God and the Bible from consideration as sources of reliable information.

Developing History Skills

1. Answers should include the following: 1763—became a British colony following the Seven Years' War; 1774—was granted many rights, including the freedom to practice Roman Catholicism; 1837—rebelled against British authority; 1840—Act of Union; 1867—British North America Act; 1870—Manitoba became a province; 1870s—British Columbia and Prince Edward Island became provinces; 1905—Alberta and

Saskatchewan became provinces; 1949—Newfoundland and Labrador became the tenth province in Canada.

2. Answers should include some of the following: Britain accepted the Reformation; France rejected the Reformation. Britain developed a limited monarchy; France developed an absolute monarchy. Britain avoided revolution; France maintained the status quo until its government was overthrown by revolution. Britain had a stable economy and stable government that provided ideal conditions for the Industrial Revolution; France retained a medieval economy and was weakened by unstable governments. Britain de-

romanticism and realism. Note ways in which romanticism and realism may be used contrary to the Christian worldview and ways in which they may be compatible.

2. Sometimes Christians are attracted to socialism because of its emphasis on righting injustices. Imagine that you are an author for a Christian magazine tasked with explaining why socialism is not compatible with Scripture. Use the following Scripture passages as the basis for your article: Exodus 20:15; 21:33-15; Numbers 36; Acts 5:4; Proverbs 10:4; 12:24; 13:11, 18, 22; James 1:27; 2:14-16; Galatians 6:10.

veloped a free trade economy; France continued to struggle with social and economic problems and could not develop a stable government.

Thinking Critically

1. Darwin was inattentive to the Bible's teaching regarding the origin of death and suffering. The Bible explains that death and suffering are results of human sinfulness. No human deserves anything better than death and suffering. Nevertheless, through Christ's death, regeneration and resurrection are offered to all humans.

2. The Bible insists that the material world is not the whole of reality. Those who insist on ignoring the invisible, spiritual part of creation end up with a truncated view of reality. Not only do they fail to understand true reality, but they also misunderstand a great deal of what they do acknowledge to exist.

Furthermore, though Marx claimed to be concerned about oppression, his rejection of Christianity and embracing of materialism removed any basis for a morality that could identify or oppose evils such as oppression. As a result, nations that embraced Marxism became some of the most oppressive nations in the world.

Living in God's World

1. Answers should include some of the following: Romantic art forms emphasize the goodness of man and man's impulses. Nevertheless, romanticism's emphasis on the beautiful can be compatible with the Christian worldview. Realist art may emphasize the Fall without emphasizing Redemption. However, realism can highlight problems in our fallen world, possibly causing man to seek biblical solutions.

2. The student's answers should note that these passages defend the goodness of private ownership (Exod. 20:15; 21:33–35; Num. 36; Acts 5:4). The loss of private ownership is viewed as an evil, not as a good (Num. 36). Even when helping others, individuals have the right to decide how to use their own property (Acts 5:4). These passages also teach that humans bear responsibility for their actions. Laziness and other sins bring poverty (Prov. 10:4; 12:24; 13:11, 18, 22). Owning private property does not mean that Christians should fail to show real compassion. Christians should show compassion in tangible ways (James 1:27; 2:14–16; Gal. 6:10), especially toward the needy who become so through no fault of their own (e.g., widows and orphans).

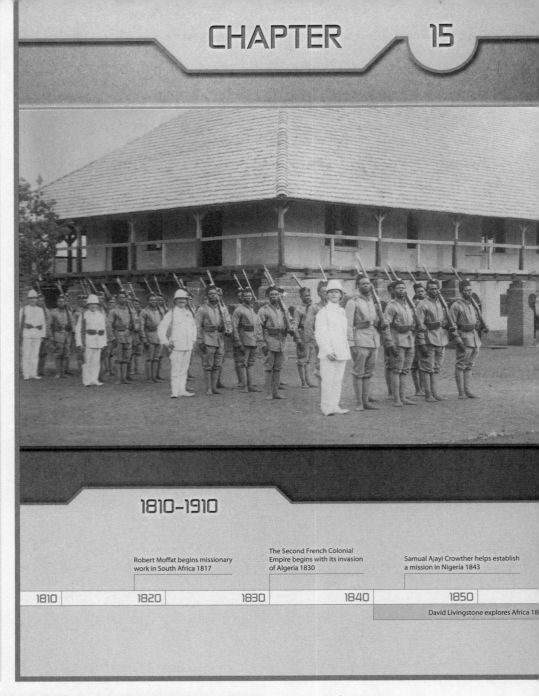

1810–1910

Robert Moffat begins missionary work in South Africa 1817

The Second French Colonial Empire begins with its invasion of Algeria 1830

Samual Ajayi Crowther helps establish a mission in Nigeria 1843

| 1810 | 1820 | 1830 | 1840 | 1850 |

David Livingstone explores Africa 18

Chapter Goals

Students should be able to

1. Explain the impact of slavery in Africa.
2. Describe Africa's transition to modern states.
3. Evaluate the motives and methods of the European partitioning of Africa.
4. Analyze the consequences of European imperialism in Africa.

Chapter 15 Lesson Plan Chart

Section Title	Main Activity	Pages	Days
I. Transition from Trading Partner to Possession	Activity 1: David Livingston	264–70	2–2½ days
II. Partitioning of Africa for Imperialism	Activity 2: *Through the Dark Continent*	270–75	2–2½ days
III. Consequences of Imperialism	Activity 3: Abuses of Colonialism	276–79	1–2½ days
TOTAL SUGGESTED DAYS (INCLUDING 1 DAY EACH FOR REVIEW AND TESTING)			7–9½ days

Materials List

Section I

- CD: 15A Early Colonial Holdings; 15B Rubber Tree; 15C Oil Palm Trees; 15D Samori Ture; 15E The Spread of Islam and Christianity in Africa; 15F Samuel Ajayi Crowther

- Activity 1 from the *Student Activities* manual

Section II

- CD: 15G Imperialism in Africa; 15H John Africanus Horton; 15I Maxim Gun

- Activity 2 from the *Student Activities* manual

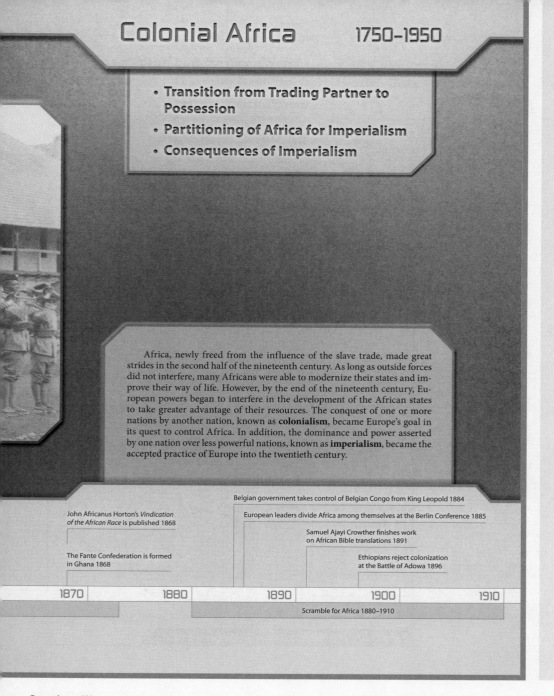

Colonial Africa   1750–1950

- **Transition from Trading Partner to Possession**
- **Partitioning of Africa for Imperialism**
- **Consequences of Imperialism**

Africa, newly freed from the influence of the slave trade, made great strides in the second half of the nineteenth century. As long as outside forces did not interfere, many Africans were able to modernize their states and improve their way of life. However, by the end of the nineteenth century, European powers began to interfere in the development of the African states to take greater advantage of their resources. The conquest of one or more nations by another nation, known as **colonialism**, became Europe's goal in its quest to control Africa. In addition, the dominance and power asserted by one nation over less powerful nations, known as **imperialism**, became the accepted practice of Europe into the twentieth century.

Belgian government takes control of Belgian Congo from King Leopold 1884

European leaders divide Africa among themselves at the Berlin Conference 1885

John Africanus Horton's *Vindication of the African Race* is published 1868

Samuel Ajayi Crowther finishes work on African Bible translations 1891

The Fante Confederation is formed in Ghana 1868

Ethiopians reject colonization at the Battle of Adowa 1896

| 1870 | 1880 | 1890 | 1900 | 1910 |

Scramble for Africa 1880–1910

Section III

- Activities 3 and 4 from the *Student Activities* manual
- Special speaker: missionary to Africa

Section I

Objectives

Students should be able to

1. Explain the tremendous growth of African slavery that occurred between 1600 and 1800.
2. Analyze the progress of African states that abandoned the slave trade.
3. Explain the factors that led to the opening of the African interior.
4. Describe early Christian outreach in Africa.
5. Explain the early colonization of Africa.

I. Transition from Trading Partner to Possession

Growth of the Slave Trade

Before 1600 about two thousand slaves were captured and taken from Africa each year. One hundred eighty years later this wicked trade had expanded to over seventy thousand slaves per year. The settlement of the Americas became the major reason for this growth. European landowners developed large plantations throughout South America, the Caribbean, and North America, and they needed laborers to work the land.

Rather than farm the land themselves, the landowners enslaved Indians and forced them to work the land. When most of the Indians died or fled, Europeans turned to Africa for slave labor. They reasoned that the Africans were used to the hot climate and hard work. Most of the Europeans were motivated by greed and a false sense of superiority. As a result, they convinced themselves that the slave trade served as a respectable way to farm the land.

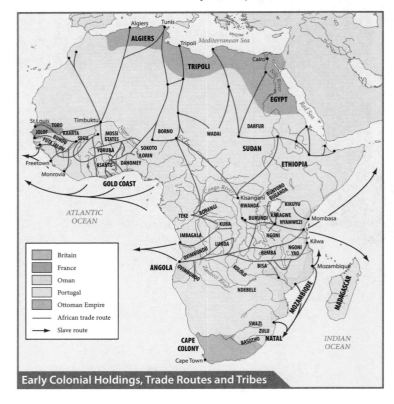

Early Colonial Holdings, Trade Routes and Tribes

CD: 15A Early Colonial Holdings

This map from the student text is also available on the CD.

Slave Trade

Ask a volunteer to research the numbers of Africans sold into slavery and the regions where slaves were sent. Have him prepare a chart or a map and show it to the class.

European slave traders (mostly from Britain, France, and Portugal) anchored their ships off the western coast of Africa to pick up their human cargoes. African raiders brought slaves from the interior to the coast. Held captive in chains, ropes, or yokes, the slaves were forced by the raiders to walk many miles to the coast.

After the harsh treatment received during the land journey, the slaves' sea voyage proved to be even worse. The traders crammed the slaves into their ships, which had decks too low to stand between and were often too crowded to move in. Sailors chained each slave to the ship to prevent his escape. For two months they lived—or died—in these hot, filthy quarters. At times they were allowed fresh air and exercise above deck, but in poor weather they were kept below with no fresh air. As much as twenty-five percent of these men, women, and children died before reaching the New World.

Africa had entered the nineteenth century with a few powerful leaders engaged in supplying slaves to European and Muslim nations. As this evil practice ended, African states found positive and productive ways to produce wealth.

Tapping a rubber tree

Progress in Africa after the Slave Trade

As they had for centuries, several states in Africa maintained their independence during most of the nineteenth century. Kings and chiefs continued to rule over expanding states, and a modern Africa began to emerge.

Oil palm tree fruit

Trade in slaves had ended, thanks in large part to efforts of the British and their navy. The African economy changed from selling slaves to providing raw materials needed by industrial countries. These materials included ivory, beeswax, honey, cotton, and rubber. Palm oil remained the leading export because industrial nations used it to lubricate their machines.

Oil palm tree

Transition in Africa

The transition of the African economy brought many benefits. We will briefly examine a few of them.

Warfare and raiding of enemy tribes did not begin with the advent of slavery. However, the growing demand for slaves in the New World led to a great increase of both. When the British navy effectively ended the slave trade around 1850, the warfare and raids declined significantly.

Powerful leaders of African tribes had controlled the slave trade and the wealth it generated. Once slavery had ended, most Africans enjoyed an improved distribution of wealth. Since anyone could harvest the natural resources, many Africans took advantage of this opportunity. Known as a **gathering-based economy**, this change allowed more Africans access to the wealth that poured into Africa. Crops that could quickly be sold for cash included cocoa and peanuts (in addition to those mentioned above).

With the decline in warfare and the end of the slave trade, Africa experienced a steady increase in population.

Cocoa beans from the cocoa fruit

Natural Rubber

Rubber was first processed from the latex sap of certain trees growing in South America. The sap was collected as it dripped from incisions made in the bark and was then refined into rubber.

In the eighteenth century rubber received its name when an English educator, Joseph Priestley, observed that this substance effectively removed "rubbed" pencil marks from paper.

Although the French appear to have been the first Europeans to discover the many properties of rubber, the British were the first to develop rubber on a commercial basis. British explorer Henry Wickham collected thousands of para rubber tree seeds from Brazil and sent them to several British colonies, including Ceylon, Indonesia, and Singapore. In these colonies, British planters cultivated the rubber trees. Under British influence, India also developed a significant rubber industry.

CD: 15B Rubber Tree; 15C Oil Palm Trees

A photo of a rubber tree and a photo of oil palm trees are available on the CD.

Menelik and Samori Ture

These two African leaders are fascinating characters in the struggle to resist European imperialism. More information about their lives is included later in the chapter.

Winning Representation

It is difficult to say why some African states granted representation to their citizens peacefully while other states resisted. An examination of the peaceful states provides a possible answer. Movements such as the Fante Confederation displayed a willingness to embrace new concepts. Also, some African leaders educated in Europe brought ideas about representative government to Africa. The influence of European missionaries such as Robert Moffat may have also contributed to the peaceful adoption of representative government in some African states.

Tribes also gained a measure of stability. Peaceful conditions allowed the African tribes to settle rather than continue to migrate. One exception to this reduction in warfare occurred in areas such as West Africa because of the great spread of Islam through jihad. Muslim rulers conquered their weaker neighbors and enforced the practice of Sharia (Muslim law).

In addition to the long history of trade and economic prosperity along the coasts of Africa, the internal or rural economy of Africa began to develop. As a result, more and more Africans experienced the benefits of trade.

Most important of all, according to noted African historian A. Adu Boahen, was the changed status of the African himself. After centuries of being treated as an object for sale, he claimed his place as a fellow human being and became a producer of merchandise to sell to others.

Unification of Africa

African commerce had been regional for centuries. For example, the coast bordering the Atlantic Ocean served as one market. The Mediterranean Sea formed another commercial region. Yet another centered on the coast bordering the Indian Ocean. However, during the nineteenth century these commercial routes merged and unified. This unification resulted in a large expansion of trade and brought great wealth to Africa and its people.

The old African empires were crumbling, but new ones were growing. As previously mentioned, some African states grew because of Islamic conquest. The Sokoto (in modern Nigeria) and Tukulor (in modern Mali) empires are two examples of Islamic expansion. In addition, nations such as Ethiopia and Egypt expanded by conquering neighboring states. However, even through conquest, Africa migrated toward unification as these conquering states imposed a common language and culture on subject states.

Modernization of Africa

Industry

African states began to modernize by setting up factories. For example, Egypt developed textile and cotton mills. This nation also developed mills to process wood, make glass, and produce paper. Some African states also began to experiment with constitutional forms of government.

Military

Some African states in North and West Africa, including Morocco, Tunisia, and Ethiopia, began to modernize their armies in anticipation of possible threats from European nations. For example, **Menelik** of Ethiopia replaced his poorly trained volunteer army with well-equipped and well-trained soldiers. He also built factories to build modern military equipment. West African general **Samori Ture** also developed a modern army with current weapons to defend the **Wassoulou** Empire.

Education and Representation in Africa

Many Africans gained access to education and insisted on a voice in their governments. Some struggles led to violence, while others transitioned without bloodshed. For example, states on the West Coast of Africa won representation without violence.

The **Fante Confederation** formed in Ghana in 1868. This African organization, led by African pastors and teachers, provides

Samori Ture

British Intrusion

While the Fante Confederation developed, the British steadily gained control over portions of the Gold Coast in West Africa. To solidify these gains, they purchased a Dutch fort along the coast. However, the Asante African state had worked in cooperation with the Dutch and used this region to gain access to the sea. The British purchase threatened to cut off Asante trade. The Asante responded by invading this region to preserve their trade route. The British responded with well-trained soldiers and forced the Africans to retreat. To secure their investment, the British invaded Asante territory and seized control of this region in Ghana in 1873. This seizure by Britain effectively ended the Fante Confederation.

CD: 15D Samori Ture

This portrait from the student text is also available on the CD.

Menelik of Ethiopia

Visit www.bjupress.com/resources for possible links to articles about Menelik of Ethiopia.

an excellent example of Africans working to maintain self-rule and improve the lives of their people. The confederation produced a constitution that reflected a spirit of cooperation, promoted male and female education, and advocated the development of African resources to benefit Africans.

The goals of this organization were progressive. For example, its educational objectives included technical training in addition to a basic education for all African children. Members of this confederation also promoted the development of self-reliant citizens. Finally, this organization supported cooperation between educated Africans, who tended to abandon traditions, and those who retained African traditions. Sadly, political forces destroyed the possible attainment of these lofty goals.

Opening the Interior

The interior of Africa, or the regions inland from the coasts, became more accessible to the world during the second half of the nineteenth century because of at least two factors. First, tribes from the interior increased trade with other African states. Second, European exploration dramatically increased knowledge of and interest in the African interior.

Increased Trade

As previously stated, cash crops provided a growing income for many Africans. As a result, African states that had not previously engaged in trade began to do so. Natural resources increased in value as demand increased. Increased trade and economic opportunity spread into the heart of the African continent.

European Exploration

Many Europeans explored Africa in search of answers to a number of questions. For example, Sir Richard Burton searched for the answer to a mystery that began in ancient Egypt: the elusive source of the Nile. He and another explorer concluded that the Nile originated in a lake called *Ukerewe* or *Nalubaale* by the Africans. Burton's former associate later named the lake Victoria in honor of Queen Victoria.

The most famous European explorer in Africa during the nineteenth century was **David Livingstone** (1813–1873). Born in Scotland, he arrived in South Africa in 1840 and traveled throughout Africa until his death in 1873. His few trips to Great Britain allowed him to set before Europe the need for missionaries in Africa.

Livingstone ventured inland to places no known European had ever visited. He followed the Zambezi River and discovered the falls that the Africans called *Mosi-oa-Tunya* (the Smoke that Thunders). Other Europeans named these falls **Victoria Falls**.

Livingstone also traveled to Lake Tanganyika, and it was there in 1871 that **Henry Stanley**, a Welsh reporter, found him. The *New York Herald* newspaper had sent Stanley to find Livingstone after he had been out of contact for several months. Livingstone later died near this lake. Livingstone's African companions buried his heart in Africa. Then they took Livingstone's preserved body to the coast. The British returned it to England for burial in Westminster Abbey.

Getty Images

Getty Images

Top, Livingstone; *middle,* Livingstone's casket; *bottom,* Victoria Falls

Livingstone's Heart

Because Livingstone dedicated much of his life to exploring Africa, it seemed logical to the Africans to bury his heart in Africa at the base of a mvula tree. His body was sent to Britain, but his heart literally remained in Africa, where it had been during the majority of his life.

Travel Writing

The work *Travel Writing, 1700–1830: An Anthology* contains a fascinating account by William J. Burchell about his travels in the interior of southern Africa in 1811.

Activity 1: David Livingstone

This activity is an excerpt from David Livingstone's report on an expedition to the Zambezi. The account provides the students with a rare glimpse into nineteenth-century Africa and reveals Livingstone's opposition to the slave trade.

David Livingstone

Visit www.bjupress.com/resources for possible links to articles about David Livingstone.

Henry Stanley

Visit www.bjupress.com/resources for possible links to articles about Henry Stanley.

Robert Moffat

Robert Moffat was born in Scotland in 1795. His parents were diligent, thrifty, and religious. His mother would gather the children together on winter evenings to teach them to sew and knit. (This skill would prove very helpful to Moffat on the mission field.)

In 1816, Moffat took a job as a gardener in London. Just as his parents had taught him, he continued to read his Bible faithfully. It was at this time that the Lord brought Moffat into contact with a group of Methodists who had been saved under the preaching of John Wesley. After he attended several Methodist meetings, Moffat began to wonder whether he was truly converted. This question burned in Moffat's heart and sent him back to the Scriptures for an answer. Reading in the book of Romans, he came to realize what God had done for sinners. He recognized his own need and trusted Christ for salvation.

A few months later, Moffat was crossing a bridge and saw a sign that advertised a missionary meeting. As he read the sign, he resolved to go to a foreign land and give his life as a missionary. Within one year Moffat landed in South Africa to begin a lifetime of service to God.

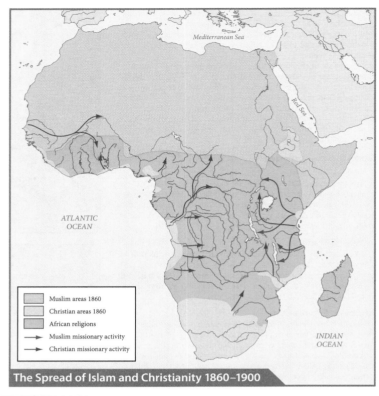

Muslim areas 1860
Christian areas 1860
African religions
Muslim missionary activity
Christian missionary activity

The Spread of Islam and Christianity 1860–1900

Getty Images

Robert Moffat

Early Christian Outreach

Europe's initial missionary outreaches did not include Africa. Instead, early mission societies focused on recruiting missionaries for India and China. However, despite a slow beginning, British Christians played a great role in evangelizing Africa.

British Missionaries

Scottish-born **Robert Moffat** became one of the earliest missionaries from the British Empire to serve in Africa. At the age of eighteen, Moffat came into contact with Methodist laymen. After weeks of searching the Bible for answers, he trusted Christ for salvation in 1816. Shortly after his conversion, Moffat decided to serve abroad as a missionary. In 1817 Moffat landed in South Africa and began a ministry that spanned fifty-three years. His fiancée joined him in South Africa two years later. They were married in December 1819.

Moffat took the gospel to many tribes and established a mission that became a way station for later missionaries. He established friendships with several tribal leaders and worked to bring peace to the area. Moffat also translated the Bible and other works into one

---

 CD: 15E The Spread of Islam and Christianity

This map from the student text is also available on the CD.

Missionary Biographies

Ask some volunteers to bring in biographies of some of the missionaries mentioned in this chapter and to share some accounts from these works. Plan these presentations to correspond with the class periods in which you will discuss these missionaries.

Robert Moffat and Bible Translation

Discuss with the students why it is vital for missionaries to translate the Bible into the language of the people to whom they are ministering. *(Bible translation enables the people to read and study the Word of God for themselves, even when the missionary is not there to teach them. Bible translation multiplies the effectiveness of the missionary's witness.)* Missionaries often establish schools, provide medical care, and train the nationals in a variety of occupations; discuss how this would further the missionaries' ministry. *(Education enables people to read the Bible and Bible-study materials. Providing medical care and job training helps the missionaries to*

gain the nationals' trust and to demonstrate concern for their physical needs and economic well-being.)

Robert Moffat

Visit www.bjupress.com/resources for possible links to articles about Robert Moffat.

of the African languages. His work continued to the next generation when his daughter, Mary, married David Livingstone.

In response to the plea for workers from men like Moffat and Livingstone, many missionaries took up the work in Africa. In addition, new missionary societies formed with the specific goal of recruiting missionaries for Africa. These men and women trusted God to deliver them from the many dangers in Africa while they worked among the various African tribes. In addition to sharing the gospel, many missionaries established schools, provided medical care, and trained Africans in a variety of occupations.

Samuel Ajayi Crowther

Africa produced a long and distinguished list of scholars during the nineteenth century. Some became pastors, while others became medical doctors, lawyers, or one of many other careers. One of the most fascinating biographies is that of a Nigerian boy named Ajayi (c. 1809–1891).

When he was only twelve, Ajayi and his whole village were captured by Muslim slave raiders. The Muslims then sold them to Portuguese slave traders. Providentially, a British navy ship intercepted the Portuguese ship containing these captives and rescued them. The British took them to Freetown, Sierra Leone. There Ajayi received care from the Anglican Church Missionary Society and learned English. He converted to Christianity and, upon baptism, took the name **Samuel Ajayi Crowther**. Crowther traveled to England and received an education. Years later, he became the first African bishop in the Anglican Church.

He returned to Freetown in 1827 and continued his education at an Anglican missionary school. During this period, Crowther developed a great interest in linguistics and mastered several languages. He soon advanced from student to teacher. In 1843 he helped establish a mission in Nigeria.

In addition to his missionary work, Crowther labored for many years to translate the Bible into the **Yoruba** language. He concentrated on this language because many of the Africans at Freetown were members of the Yoruba tribe. When they returned home, they took the gospel and education back to their people. Crowther also promoted an African-led outreach to the Yoruba and, eventually, to all of Africa. While he made great progress in his endeavors, the Anglican Church eventually decided to replace him with a European bishop.

In 1864 Oxford University recognized Crowther's great contribution to Africa by giving him a Doctor of Divinity degree. He continued to serve in various roles, including overseeing the production and refining of African translations of the Bible, until shortly before his death in 1891.

Early Colonization of Africa

Initial European colonization of Africa involved setting up colonies on uninhabited islands to establish trade with mainland Africa. Over time, European nations began to lay claim to more coastal territory in Africa. Portugal, Britain, and France established some of the earliest coastal settlements in Africa.

Portugal

In Chapter 7 you learned that Portugal was one of the first European states to explore the coasts of Africa and establish trade

Samuel Ajayi Crowther

Yoruba

Students may wonder why Crowther chose to translate the Bible into Yoruba. Part of the answer is that he encountered many Africans at Freetown who spoke this language. In addition, he was probably aware that the Yoruban people forms one of the largest native populations in West Africa. Therefore, his translating the Bible into Yoruba would enable several million people to read God's Word in their own language. Knowing these factors helps us to understand why Crowther poured many years of his life into the Yoruban translation.

 ### CD: 15F Samuel Ajayi Crowther

This portrait from the student text is also available on the CD.

African Perspectives on Colonialism

The work *African Perspectives on Colonialism* by A. Adu Boahen provides an excellent and balanced evaluation of the European colonial period in Africa. The work is brief and engaging and includes extensive documentation.

Samuel Ajayi Crowther

Visit www.bjupress.com/resources for possible links to articles about Samuel Ajayi Crowther.

French Algeria

In 1830, French leaders determined to seize foreign territory to demonstrate France's status as a world power. They chose a region in North Africa from which the French had purchased grain during the Napoleonic Wars. While maintaining independence from Ottoman rule, this region enjoyed protection by the declining Ottoman Empire. Despite this protection, the French saw this province as territory that could be easily captured. The initial assault involved six hundred French ships and thirty-four thousand soldiers. Despite initial French success, some of the region's native population resisted, and achieving victory proved to be more difficult than the French had anticipated. What the French had initially perceived as an easy conquest turned into an eighteen-year struggle. Following the French conquest, thousands of Europeans migrated to this territory, which the French named "Algeria," and it became one of France's longest-held foreign territories.

Still, even after pacification, various Muslim leaders continued to oppose French control, and unrest lay close to the surface. Popular uprisings resumed in the 1950s, and the French finally gave up their claims on Algeria in 1962.

Section II

Objectives

Students should be able to

1. Evaluate the European motives for imperialism.
2. Describe the three phases of the Scramble for Africa.
3. Analyze the African reaction to the forced colonization of Africa.

Section Quiz Answers

1. gathering-based economy
2. Peaceful conditions led to added stability.
3. trade
4. He explored places Europeans had never visited and made trips to Britain, where he set before Europe the need for missionaries to Africa.
5. Yoruba
★ Answers will vary but might include some of the following:

Samuel Ajayi Crowther knew the languages and customs of the people to whom he ministered. He evangelized the nationals and trained them to be

settlements. While Portugal lacked the ability to develop into a major power, the Portuguese retained control of these coastal settlements and profited from the ongoing trade. Portugal claimed territory in the southern regions of West Africa and East Africa.

Britain

In Chapter 10 you learned that Britain expanded its exploration following the loss of the American colonies in the eighteenth century. In addition to major discoveries in the South Pacific, British explorers established trade colonies in West Africa. Early British trade with Africa primarily involved slaves. British ships transported about three and one-half million African slaves to the Americas and the British Caribbean. When the British ended this terrible practice, African raw materials grew into a large and profitable industry for British merchants. The expanding Industrial Revolution provided a growing demand for several of these raw materials.

France

In the eighteenth century, the British frustrated and ultimately ended early attempts by the French to establish their first colonial empire. However, the French viewed themselves as a world power, and a world power must have colonies. As a result, the **Second French Colonial Empire** began in 1830 with the invasion of Algeria in North Africa. However, the Algerians resisted for several years before French forces triumphed. Another fifty years passed before France acquired additional territory in Africa. France's renewed efforts to colonize had a catastrophic effect on Africa.

Section Quiz

1. What did Africans transition to for income following the abolition of the slave trade?
2. Why were African tribes able to settle in one place rather than be forced to migrate?
3. What unified Africa prior to European colonization?
4. How did David Livingstone contribute to the growth of missions in Africa?
5. What African language did many of the Africans in Freetown speak?
★ Who do you think was more effective in evangelizing Africans: Samuel Ajayi Crowther or David Livingstone? Explain your answer.

II. Partitioning of Africa for Imperialism

Between 1880 and 1910 Africa went from a continent filled with many independent, sovereign states to forty artificially created colonies subject to European control. In a brief span of time, the Africans lost their freedom to govern and make independent decisions.

In 1879 several events occurred in rapid succession, triggering a rapid conquest and partitioning of Africa. The French made the first move by sending three French groups to determine routes for a trans-Saharan railway. Then the French appointed a commander in North Africa to expand French interests farther inland. King Leopold of Belgium and the French made the next move by sending diplomats to secure treaties with the African tribes in the Congo basin.

missionaries. His Yoruba translation of the Bible was an invaluable asset to African evangelism and discipleship.

David Livingstone saw the need for evangelism in Africa and challenged Europeans to send missionaries there. He spent more than thirty years in Africa and became very familiar with African customs.

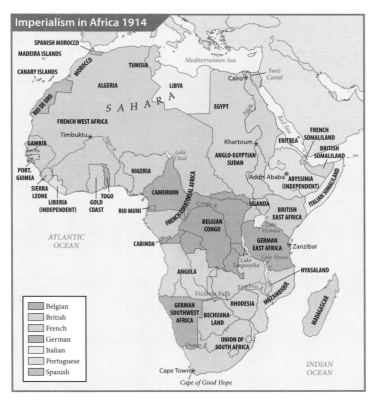

Imperialism in Africa 1914

SPANISH MOROCCO
MADEIRA ISLANDS
CANARY ISLANDS
RIO DE ORO
MOROCCO
TUNISIA
ALGERIA
LIBYA
Mediterranean Sea
Cairo
Suez Canal
S A H A R A
EGYPT
Niger R.
Red Sea
FRENCH WEST AFRICA
Timbuktu
Niger R.
GAMBIA
Lake Chad
KHARTOUM
ANGLO-EGYPTIAN SUDAN
ERITREA
FRENCH SOMALILAND
BRITISH SOMALILAND
PORT. GUINEA
NIGERIA
Addis Ababa
ABYSSINIA (INDEPENDENT)
ITALIAN SOMALILAND
SIERRA LEONE
LIBERIA (INDEPENDENT)
GOLD COAST
TOGO
CAMEROON
FRENCH EQUATORIAL AFRICA
Congo R.
UGANDA
BRITISH EAST AFRICA
RIO MUNI
BELGIAN CONGO
Lake Victoria
ATLANTIC OCEAN
CABINDA
GERMAN EAST AFRICA
Zanzibar
Lake Tanganyika
Lake Nyasa
ANGOLA
NYASALAND
Victoria Falls
Zambezi R.
MOZAMBIQUE
GERMAN SOUTHWEST AFRICA
BECHUANA- LAND
RHODESIA
MADAGASCAR
Orange R.
UNION OF SOUTH AFRICA
INDIAN OCEAN
Cape Town
Cape of Good Hope

	Belgian
	British
	French
	German
	Italian
	Portuguese
	Spanish

Since Britain and Portugal had previously laid claim to this region, these moves created great alarm. Continued expansion by the French and King Leopold resulted in claims by Britain and other European states. Soon, almost all of Africa came under European domination.

European Motives

Today it is difficult to understand why the Europeans would treat Africans in such a harsh way. However, the Europeans did not see themselves as behaving cruelly or unjustly. Their motives conditioned them to see the colonization of Africa as good. Understanding these motives enables the Christian to evaluate the false reasoning that led to this behavior.

Economic

Because of the Industrial Revolution and free trade policies, international trade grew rapidly. As more European nations fostered a growth in industry, competition for foreign markets increased.

Nations reacted to the increased competition by abandoning free trade. To protect their markets from lower priced foreign goods,

European Motives

Many Europeans sought economic advancement by colonizing Africa. The goal of economic advancement is not an unbiblical goal (Deut. 28:1–14). However, it must be sought in ways that are consistent with the command to love one's neighbor as oneself (Matt. 22:39). Europeans should have sought mutually beneficial trade partnerships with the Africans.

Some European states colonized for nationalistic purposes. Nations are completely legitimate forms of political organization, as is demonstrated by the Lord's formation of the nation of Israel. However, the international nature of the church demonstrates that no one nation is more important than the others.

The advance of the gospel is far more important than the growth of nations. Some Europeans saw colonization as an opportunity for evangelism. This is a good motive, but it is possible for people to do right things in wrong ways. Furthermore, it is easy to use good motives as a cover for wrong actions.

The racist motivation for colonialism flatly contradicts the Bible's teaching that all humans were created in God's image (Gen. 1:26–27). God intends to include people from every ethnic group in His church (Rev. 5:9). Ethnic distinctions should not be used to exalt some or denigrate others (Col. 3:11).

CD: 15G Imperialism in Africa

This map from the student text is also available on the CD.

Activity 2: *Through the Dark Continent*

This activity contains an excerpt from Henry Stanley's account of his explorations. This source material is intended to help the student visualize the exploration of Africa through the eyes of an actual explorer.

European Motives

Using the Bible, help your class evaluate the European motives for subjugating Africa. You might want to use the information in the side margin above.

Phase One

You might want to compare the African chiefs' signing treaties without knowing the consequences to the American Indians' signing treaties that gave away their tribal lands. They both did so without understanding the European concept of private property.

they raised tariffs. This increased the price of foreign goods, but it also hindered trade between nations. These shortsighted responses to competition created a demand for colonies that European states could force to buy European products and support the European economies.

The increasing need for raw materials also made control of resources in Africa appealing to the European states. Africa already supplied a growing quantity of raw materials to industrialized Europe. However, European powers decided that Europeans could better manage Africa's resources and increase their profits by taking direct control.

In addition, industrialists and investors in Europe enjoyed a quickly rising amount of profit (capital). As the Industrial Revolution produced greater wealth, investors sought new places to invest these funds in order to continue to increase their profits. Africa appeared to present a vast potential for great economic profit. Whether the Africans had a say in this seemed to be unimportant to government officials and entrepreneurs.

Missionary Advocacy

Though missionary activity served as a justification for colonialism, and though colonialism helped the spread of missionaries around the world, the missionaries in fact were often in conflict with the colonial rulers. Because the missionaries lived among the Africans, they often developed close relationships with them, and some missionaries began to understand life from the Africans' point of view. As a result, some missionaries protested the ill treatment of the Africans by the colonial rulers.

Nationalistic

Nineteenth century Europe displayed an exaggerated spirit of nationalism. This extreme sentiment was especially dominant in the recently unified states of Germany and Italy. These nations were barely a decade old when they set out to prove themselves worthy of being world powers. Colonization of regions in Africa provided them an excellent opportunity to compete with the established European powers.

You may remember from previous chapters that France had suffered from internal and international defeats. The latest humiliating defeat by Germany in 1870 left France desperate for a victory. French pride was at stake, and the conquest of African states provided France with a way to regain its standing in the world.

Religious

Some people, especially in Britain, viewed colonialism as a way to open Africa for expanded evangelistic outreach. For some people, evangelization simply provided religious cover for sinful treatment of the Africans. Others genuinely saw colonialism as a way to spread the gospel but were blinded to the negative aspects of colonialism. In fact, the colonial era was a time of great missionary advance. By the end of the nineteenth century, almost six thousand British missionaries traveled to foreign lands under British control. Many of these missionaries were in Africa.

Racist

Tragically, many Europeans used the lie that Europeans were superior to the African race to justify colonialism and imperialism. As Darwin's theory of evolution became more popular, it offered support for the idea that some people groups were more advanced than others. Using Darwin's theory of the survival of the fittest, Europeans assumed they were part of a superior race. This attitude of superiority was reflected in some of the literature of the day, such as Rudyard Kipling's poem "The White Man's Burden," which asserted the white man's obligation to civilize the "heathen."

Many African scholars sought to challenge this prejudice against Africans. For example, **John Africanus Horton** disproved the claims that the black man was racially inferior. His work *West African Countries and Peoples: A Vindication of the African Race*, published

John Africanus Horton

"The White Man's Burden"

Discuss this work with your students. To keep Kipling's poem in context, it is important to note that he lived and worked in India. Thus, although this poem has been used to justify various instances of European imperialism, including the European colonization of Africa, Kipling's comments were specifically directed toward European efforts to improve the lives of Indians.

 ## CD: 15H John Africanus Horton

This portrait from the student text is also available on the CD.

in 1868, argued that different stages of civilization had nothing to do with race.

The Scramble

As previously stated, the French and Belgians began to lay claim to African territory. They also pressured African states to sign treaties giving the Europeans exclusive rights to trade and mining. In response, the rush for European conquest of Africa was set in motion. In what is known as the **Scramble for Africa**, or the Race for Africa, European nations advanced in three phases to control the continent. By the end of the third phase, all but two African states (Liberia and Ethiopia) had lost their independence and had become the possessions of European powers.

Phase One

This phase began when Europeans convinced African rulers to sign treaties with a particular European state. On the surface, these treaties reserved trade and natural resources for that European power. In exchange, many of the contracts promised protection by the European power. The Europeans often resorted to empty promises and deception in order to gain exclusive access to an African state. Lord Lugard, an enthusiastic British agent of the British East African Company, made an incriminating note in his diary about these treaties.

> No man if he understood would sign it, and to say that a savage chief has been told that he cedes all rights to the company in exchange for nothing is an obvious untruth. If he had been told that the [British East African] Company will protect him against his enemies, and share in his wars as an ally, he has been told a lie, for the Company have no idea of doing any such things and no force to do it with if they wished.

Often the African rulers signed documents they could not read and surrendered control of their states without realizing it. Some were willing to sign because they faced great threats on their borders and believed the European state would provide them with a valuable ally.

However, some African rulers refused to sign treaties. For example, African king **Macemba** of the Yao tribe wrote to the German authorities who pressured him to submit to a treaty. Macemba eloquently explained that he saw no need to submit to their pressure. He expressed a desire for friendship with Germany but rejected any thought of subjection. Macemba even cautioned that he was prepared to fight to protect the freedom of his people rather than meekly bow to German demands.

Phase Two

To make sure the jostling for territory in Africa did not lead to war, representatives of European nations met to work out agreements. Imperial powers signed treaties that defined their regions of interest and agreed on boundaries to avoid conflict. They signed these treaties in Europe with no Africans present. Therefore, Africans remained unaware of the existence of these treaties and their dreadful consequences.

Several European powers established key agreements by 1885 at the **Berlin Conference**. For example, the Europeans agreed to allow unrestricted access to the Niger and Congo rivers for the free flow of

---

King Leopold of Belgium

Leopold had tried using his family fortune to purchase existing, undeveloped colonies in Africa from other European countries. However, his efforts failed.

Leopold then took advantage of pleas by men like Livingstone "to heal the open sore of Africa" from its slave trade and spiritual darkness. He played the role of a humanitarian (one concerned for human welfare). However, his motives were anything but noble.

Leopold hosted a convention of explorers in 1876 and offered to help pay for the cost of exploration. He also encouraged investments by other countries in an organization called the **International African Association (IAA)**, but he retained control of the organization as president.

Europeans initially saw Leopold as the leader of the crusade against slavery. The fact that he used his own money led others to call him a great humanitarian. Leopold had finally gotten access to Africa. By 1882 Leopold owned the company that resulted from the IAA. His questionable actions made the other European nations nervous.

The investors in the IAA later found that, far from humanitarian work, Leopold encouraged the harsh treatment and torture of African workers (slaves) on his plantations. Leopold's detestable actions caused an outcry that persuaded the Belgian government to take control of the territory itself in 1884. The territory in the interior of Africa along the Congo River was called the **Belgian Congo**.

Sources

Lord Lugard's writings are available in *The Diaries of Lord Lugard*. The quotation in the student text is taken from Volume II.

Basil Davidson's work *The African Past: Chronicles from Antiquity to Modern Times* contains Macemba's letter to the German authorities.

Both Lord Lugard's writings and Macemba's letter are quoted in A. Adu Boahen's work *African Perspectives on Colonialism*.

Berlin Conference

Mary Evans Picture Library/Alamy

trade. On a more ominous note, the European powers also carved up the continent of Africa with no regard to the wishes of Africans.

African Reaction

Phase three began with the arrival of ships and troops off the coast of African states. The Europeans had carefully planned this phase. However, the Africans received little or no advance warning of this invasion and conquest by European powers. We will examine three broad responses by the Africans, understanding that they varied over time, depending on a number of circumstances.

Submission

Some African leaders immediately recognized they could not protect their people through armed resistance. They chose to protect their people by submitting. Given the modern weapons of the Europeans, most Africans would have been slaughtered had they chosen to fight. Some submitted with no thought of eventual resistance, while others did so either to buy time and seek a peaceful resolution or to prepare for an armed resistance.

Alliance

Other African leaders accepted European forces and saw them as a means of protection from hostile neighbors or internal forces that threatened their rule. Often the Europeans would allow a ruler to maintain a semblance of power in order to gain the cooperation of the people. Some African leaders embraced an alliance with Europeans with the hope that their place on the throne would remain secure.

Often the Africans discovered that these alliances offered them no protection at all. Some European powers made promises to the ruler of an African state while supporting his enemies at the same time. This treachery left some African leaders no option but to submit or confront the European forces. Some even committed suicide rather than embrace either of these choices.

Samori Ture's Resistance

Samori Ture had established a Muslim empire in West Africa. When the French attempted to take control of his land, he resisted and defeated them in many battles. However, he realized that he could not overcome the French completely, so he signed a treaty with them in 1886. Despite signing the treaty, the French continued to undermine Ture's rule. Ture spent two years preparing for one major battle to defeat the French. Despite heroic efforts, Ture's men could not defeat the well-armed French forces. Following a move to establish a new empire on the Ivory Coast and Ghana, Ture set out to form an alliance with other African states. British and French forces responded by moving against Ture, capturing him in 1898. He died in captivity two years later.

African Reaction to Colonialism

You might want to compare the Africans' reaction with the reaction of various American Indian tribes. (Both Africans and American Indians responded to colonialism with submission, alliance, or armed resistance.) To increase class participation, have some students research various American Indian tribes ahead of time.

Confrontation

Many African states chose to confront the European forces who demanded control of their land and resources. This confrontation took two forms, and African leaders frequently used one form or the other depending on the situation at hand.

Diplomacy became the more restrained form of confrontation. African leaders negotiated with the Europeans to try to maintain as much control over their land as possible. Some sent diplomats to Britain or one of the other European nations to seek a solution that would preserve African independence. The European powers often refused to meet with these diplomats or proceeded to invade the African nation even as they met with the African diplomats. Diplomacy only worked to the extent that Africans were able to slow down the process of colonization.

Other African tribes resorted to armed resistance as soon as they realized the Europeans' true intentions. Muslim rulers were determined not to submit to rule by the infidel Europeans. They offered stiff resistance and died in large numbers because of the advanced weapons used by the Europeans. With few exceptions, even the most advanced African forces still used flintlock weapons, while the Europeans returned fire with rapid-firing guns like the **Maxim gun.** Often, a small European force could defeat a much larger African force because of their technological advantage in weapons.

Technological Advantages

Transportation, including railroads and roads, could be used to enhance trade or to move troops and supplies where they were needed to suppress rebellion. Communication included telegraph and telephone lines to rapidly issue instructions for a purchase or sale. However, they could also quickly transmit battle plans and alarms when resistance was discovered. The Africans were effectively suppressed by superior European technology.

Flintlock musket

Early Maxim gun

Section Quiz

1. Why did European investors see Africa as a desirable way to increase their wealth?

2. What two recently unified nations quickly joined the race to colonize Africa?

3. Which European leader used the pretense of humanitarianism to gain access to territory in Africa?

4. In phase one, what did the European states use to establish claims in Africa?

5. Why didn't the Africans object to the treaties signed between the European states in phase two?

★ How did Europeans use technology to subjugate Africa?

CD: 15l Maxim Gun

This photo from the student text is also available on the CD.

Section Quiz Answers

1. Africa contains many valuable raw materials and other resources. Europeans believed Africa had a vast potential to produce great returns on their investments.

2. Germany and Italy

3. King Leopold of Belgium

4. treaties

5. They were not aware of these secret treaties.

★ Trains and roads enabled the Europeans to quickly move military forces. Telegraph and telephone lines provided instant communication, allowing Europeans to maintain control over the Africans. Advances in weaponry gave the Europeans a tremendous and lethal advantage over the Africans.

Section III

Objectives

Students should be able to

1. Evaluate the political consequences of European imperialism in Africa.
2. Analyze the economic consequences of European imperialism in Africa.
3. Analyze the social consequences of European imperialism in Africa.

III. Consequences of Imperialism

While it is easy to condemn European imperialism, evaluating the actual results is a bit more complicated. Europeans can take little or no credit for any positive results of imperialism. It would not be an exaggeration to state that most of the positive results of European imperialism were accidental rather than intentional. However, there were positive results mixed in with many negative results. The Christian should not be surprised to find that God can bring good things out of the worst actions of fallen man.

Political

Evaluating the political consequences is like unwinding the many strands that compose a cable. Some strands were positive, while others brought terrible long-term consequences. Together, they form the political consequences that resulted from colonialism and imperialism.

Peace and Stability — At a Price

Over time, European forces captured or killed the leaders of rebellions. Weapons were confiscated and armed resistance declined. New African leaders emerged who had no choice but to work within the system to benefit their people. As long as the African leaders submitted to European control, African states experienced a temporary peace and stability. However, Africans paid a great price for this artificial tranquility: the loss of their freedom.

Formation of New African States

Gradually, over fifty new African states emerged from colonial rule. While this appeared to be an improvement over the hundreds of tribes that existed before, these divisions were artificial states. Europeans often drew boundaries on maps in Europe with little regard for the actual location of tribes. As a result, they divided tribes or

Two States that Withstood European Conquest

Joseph Jenkins Roberts

Joseph Jenkins Roberts served as president of Liberia from 1848 to 1856 and again from 1872 to 1876. He combined protection afforded by the United States with wise diplomacy to preserve Liberian independence.

Menelik, king of Ethiopia, refused to submit to Italian demands. When he had exhausted efforts to negotiate with the Italians, he prepared for battle by importing thousands of rifles and several cannon. At the battle of Adowa, 100,000 well-trained and well-armed Ethiopians easily defeated the 17,000-man Italian force. The Ethiopians killed or wounded nearly forty percent of the Italian army in this decisive battle in January 1896.

Menelik

RIA Novosti/Alamy

Activity 3: Abuses of Colonialism

This activity is an excerpt from a missionary's account of the negative aspects of European imperialism.

Joseph Jenkins Roberts

Ask a volunteer to read about Joseph J. Roberts and his role as president of Liberia during the nineteenth century. Have him present a report to the class.

Menelik

Ask a volunteer to study the life of Menelik, king of Ethiopia, and present a report to the class.

combined segments of various tribes at the stroke of a pen and without African input. Europeans often thrust together groups that had little in common and even spoke different languages. These differences led to unrest in several of these states, especially as they gained their independence in the twentieth century.

Development of Political Organization

European powers did succeed in establishing bureaucracies of civil servants needed to manage and govern the African states. The British system produced well-trained and effective civil servants. The French proved to be much less successful in developing civil servants. However, the Portuguese had the dubious distinction of producing the worst-trained civil servants of any European colonial power. A bureaucratic structure proved beneficial to African states as they later gained their independence.

Another positive development for African states was the formation of modern judicial systems. These have undergone very little change since their formation and have been very successful.

Development of Professional Armies

Prior to the colonial period, few African states had armies; those they had were often poorly trained volunteers. However, that situation changed dramatically when Europeans took control of African states. They trained professional armies to control the population and put down armed resistance. Tragically, these armies became a chronic source of instability, confusion, and anarchy that continues in some African states today.

Delayed Development

When Africa became a victim of European colonization and imperialism, many African states were developing into modern countries. Some had made much progress, and others were just beginning to develop. However, European conquest effectively ended the natural development of modern states in Africa.

In addition, the loss of sovereignty and independence had a long-term negative effect on the African states. At least two generations of Africans grew up under the control of Europeans and had no experience in self-government. Much of the progress made by their parents and grandparents had been lost and forgotten.

Under European control, the Africans became isolated from the rest of the world. European nations limited all economic and political activity with other countries. These restrictions prevented the normal development of African states for many years.

Economic

The economic consequences of European control of African states produced mixed results. Clearly, there were positive results, but even these often had negative aspects. Other results had no redeeming qualities.

Positive

The Europeans built a modern **infrastructure** in Africa. They laid thousands of miles of track for railroads and built many miles of roads. In addition, the Europeans strung miles of wire for telegraph and, later, telephone communication.

In addition, while the Africans were already harvesting natural resources, the Europeans introduced improved farming methods and greatly increased production of many natural products. The railroads and roads enabled much larger harvests to be delivered to markets.

The Europeans also brought with them an understanding of the value of land. The Africans learned that the vast lands of Africa served as a great asset. As a result, the value of land in Africa increased dramatically.

Africans were already developing cash crops. European management techniques simply improved and elevated this agriculture to a new level. European control also hastened the decline of the traditional barter-based economy. It was quickly replaced with a money-based economy.

Finally, along with a money-based economy, the Europeans introduced Africans to modern concepts of banking. This system, along with other contributions, became a great asset to the African states as they regained their freedom from European control.

Negative

Even though the Europeans brought a modern infrastructure to Africa, they established it to benefit themselves rather than the Africans. As a result, the Europeans distributed transportation and communication improvements unevenly. Some areas experienced great improvements in their infrastructure while areas that were of no interest to the Europeans received no improvements.

In addition, when the Europeans carved Africa into manageable regions, the result was an uneven development of regional economies. Some regions had access to the coast, rich mineral deposits, and other natural resources. Others were land-locked and had access to few natural resources. These arbitrary decisions left some African states with little opportunity to prosper.

Even though the Europeans brought industry and technology to Africa, they denied Africans the opportunity to develop industry and technology on their own. This had a long-term effect of hindering natural African development in these areas.

Another problem developed as the Europeans forced the people to concentrate on growing cash crops rather than food to feed their people. The Europeans imported food from other areas to supply the Africans' dietary needs. Unfortunately, Africans have found it difficult to change their agricultural practices. Many African nations continue to depend on other nations to provide food for their people.

Furthermore, as we learned earlier in the chapter, the African states had developed a maturing inter-African trade before the colonization of Africa. The European colonization effectively ended this trade, and African states have yet to restore it.

Finally, European colonization resulted in great wealth for European investors. However, the investors often took this wealth back to Europe rather than reinvesting it in Africa. As a result, Europeans left Africa with an underdeveloped and underfunded economic system.

Social

European colonization and imperialism also brought social consequences. As with other aspects of European control, some results were positive. Others created long-term problems for Africans.

Positive

After an initial decline, Africa began to experience a significant population growth. The initial decline was due to contact with European diseases and armed conflict with European forces. But as violent resistance subsided, African population growth rebounded.

In addition, villages grew into towns, and towns expanded into cities. Under European control, Africa experienced significant urbanization. This development proved to be an important long-term contribution to Africa.

In some African states, especially those controlled by the British, Europeans encouraged the spread of religion and education. In addition to proclaiming the gospel, missionaries also provided most of the education for the Africans. The British encouraged the expansion of Islam as well as Christianity. They may have found that allowing the spread of Islam resulted in less resistance by the African Muslims.

Finally, African historian Adu Boahen notes that European colonization created a new social order based on merit and achievement. Prior to European control, many Africans based their social order on birth. Under European management, Africans who worked hard and cooperated with the system could advance and gain promotion.

Negative

Although the Europeans urbanized Africa, they also created a large gap between the urban and the rural areas. The urban areas had access to most of the modern infrastructure, while the rural areas remained undeveloped. African cities also had most of the medical facilities and schools. The Europeans constructed few of these facilities outside the urban areas.

In addition, Europeans tended to downgrade the status of African women. Europeans built more educational facilities for boys than for girls. Lacking equal educational opportunities, women could not gain access to many professions, including medicine, law, and civil service. The colonial world favored men, and women were restricted to menial tasks.

Finally, Europeans, including many missionaries, condemned everything African. They opposed African names, music, art, and anything else that originated in Africa. Europeans also forced Africans to wear European-style clothing. These measures disrupted the cultural development of Africa.

African wildlife

Section Quiz

1. What was the price of African peace and stability during the colonial period?

2. Why did European formation of new African states create many problems?

3. Which European nation produced the most well-trained civil servants?

4. Why did the development of African professional armies produce long-term problems for African states?

5. What new social order did the Europeans establish in Africa?

★ Evaluate the results of the modern infrastructure established in Africa by European states.

 ## Missionary Speaker

Invite a missionary who serves in Africa to speak to your class if you have the opportunity to do so.

Section Quiz Answers

1. submission to European dominance

2. The states were formed without any consideration for the Africans. Tribes were divided, and segments of tribes were combined with other tribes. Often members of these new African states had little in common and spoke different languages.

3. Britain

4. They became a source of instability, confusion, and anarchy.

5. a social order based on merit and achievement

★ Answers will vary but should include some of the following:

Positive: The Europeans built railroads and roads to improve transportation and built telegraph and telephone systems to improve communication.

Negative: The infrastructure was unevenly distributed. Africans were denied the liberty to develop an infrastructure on their own.

Activity 4: Chapter Review

This activity helps the students prepare for the chapter test.

CHAPTER REVIEW

People, Places, and Terms to Know

colonialism
imperialism
gathering-based economy
Menelik
Samori Ture
Wassoulou
Fante Confederation
David Livingstone
Victoria Falls
Henry Stanley
Robert Moffat
Samuel Ajayi Crowther
Yoruba
Second French Colonial Empire
John Africanus Horton
Scramble for Africa
International African Association
Belgian Congo
Macemba
Berlin Conference
Maxim gun
infrastructure

Making Connections

1. Distinguish colonialism from imperialism.
2. Why did Menelik of Ethiopia establish a modern army?
3. Why did the efforts of the Fante Confederation abruptly end?
4. Why did Samuel Ajayi Crowther labor for years to translate the Bible into the Yoruba language?
5. How did the abandoning of free trade contribute to the pressure to colonize Africa?
6. How did France's struggle to regain national glory play a role in the colonization of Africa?
7. What impact did Darwin's work have on the justification of colonialism and imperialism?
8. How did King Leopold of Belgium take advantage of calls "to heal the open sore of Africa"?

Developing History Skills

1. Based on the information in this chapter, draw a timeline that shows important events outlined in this chapter. Provide the significance of each date.
2. Evaluate this excerpt from a letter to the British by a king of an African state in northern Ghana. What did he desire to gain by signing this treaty?

> Tell my friend, the Governor of Accra, I like his friendship, I like a man who is not a foolish man. I like a man who is truthful. Tell my friend I like my country to be quiet and secure; I want to keep off all my enemies and none be able to stand before me. . . . Let plenty guns, flint, powder and cloth, and every kind of cost goods be sent here for sale. I want a rare magnificent cloth myself to put on. Tell him also to send for sale here those short small guns firing many times [revolvers].

Thinking Critically

1. Evaluate European colonialism in light of the Ten Commandments in Exodus 20. Link each of your points to the relevant commandment and give the Bible reference.
2. Given the European rejection of everything African, evaluate how the biography of Samuel Ajayi Crowther may have reflected this bias.

Living in God's World

1. Imagine that you are a modern missionary to an African country. Do a research report that investigates the culture of

---

Chapter Review Answers

Making Connections

1. (Note: This information is found in the chapter opener spread.) Colonialism involves the conquest of one or more nations by another nation; imperialism is the dominance and power asserted by one nation over less powerful nations.

2. to defend against possible threats by European nations

3. The British annexed a portion of Ghana.

4. Most of the Africans at Freetown spoke this language. When they returned home, they would take the gospel back to their people in their own language.

5. The abandoning of free trade led to high tariffs on foreign goods and resulted in less foreign trade. The Europeans sought colonies that could supply raw materials and be forced to buy European products and support the European economies.

6. France invaded Algeria in 1830 to gain a colony and thus prove that it was a world power. In 1879 France planned to construct a trans-Saharan railway and appointed a commander to expand French interests in North Africa.

7. His writings supported the false theory that some species are more developed than others. Assuming they were part of a superior race, Europeans used the theory of the survival of the fittest to justify their racism and exploitation of Africans.

8. He built a reputation as a humanitarian while encouraging the harsh treatment and torture of African workers in the Belgian Congo.

Developing History Skills

1. Answers should include: 1817—Robert Moffat begins his fifty-three-year ministry in South Africa; 1840—Livingstone arrives in Africa; 1850—The British navy effectively ends the slave trade; 1864—Samuel Crowther receives

that country. Discuss aspects of that culture that need to be challenged by the Bible. What aspects of the culture are perhaps more in line with Scripture than Western culture?

2. Imagine that you were a Christian journalist from Europe who was covering the Congo during the Scramble. Write a report of what you observed.

a Doctor of Divinity degree from Oxford; 1879—France and Leopold of Belgium trigger European movement toward colonization; 1880—The European colonization of Africa begins; 1885—Europe divides Africa at the Berlin Conference; 1896—The Ethiopians defeat Italian forces and secure their independence; 1910—By this date, most African states are under complete European control.

2. Answers may vary but should include some of the following: He desired peace and security. He wanted access to many European goods, including guns.

Thinking Critically

1. Answers will vary but should include some of the following: The Europeans worshiped wealth and power (20:3); they were willing to take African states by force and murder those who resisted (20:13); they stole the resources and wealth of the Africans (20:15); they lied to the Africans to convince them to sign away their lands (20:16); they coveted the wealth and resources of Africa (20:17).

2. Answers will vary but should include the fact that his African name (Ajayi) was lengthened to Samuel Ajayi Crowther. In addition, he was replaced as bishop by a European.

Living in God's World

1. Answers will vary, but students should construct something similar to the following example: Africans tend to respect elders. Negatively, this could lead Africans, out of deference to elders, to be slow in adopting biblical lifestyles. However, the Bible commands people to respect their elders, and the respect that Africans accord their elders is more aligned with the teaching of the Bible than is the Western trend toward rebellion.

2. Answers will vary.

CHAPTER 16

Chapter Goals

Students should be able to

1. Evaluate how the Ottoman Empire responded to the challenges of territorial loss and imperialism.
2. Analyze Russian reform, expansion, and internal unrest.
3. Evaluate the consequences of European imperialism in India.
4. Describe how China's Qing dynasty responded to economic and political crises.
5. Describe how Japan transformed into a modern nation-state.

1750–1914

Seven Years' War between England and France 1756–63

Charter Act gives the British crown control of all British East India Company possessions 1814

Alexander I becomes the czar of Russia 1801

Napoleon invades Russia 1812

Decembrist Revolt in Russia 1825

Nicholas I becomes the czar of Russia 1825

| 1750 | 1775 | 1800 | 1825 |

Battle of Plassey breaks France's strength in India 1757

Napoleon invades Egypt 1798

Mahmud II rules the Ottoman Empire and lays the foundation for modern Turkey 1808–39

Chapter 16 Lesson Plan Chart

Section Title	Main Activity	Pages	Days
I. Decline of the Ottoman Empire	Activity 1: Slaughter of the Armenians	284–86	1–1½ days
II. Changes in Russia	Discussion Activity: Anarchy	286–90	1–1½ days
III. Domination of India by Britain	Activity 2: The Sepoy Mutiny	290–93	1–1½ days
IV. Domination of Asia	Activity 3: The Goforths and the Boxer Rebellion	293–300	1–1½ days
V. Modernization in Meiji Japan	Activity 4: Perry's Expedition to Japan	300–301	1–1½ days
TOTAL SUGGESTED DAYS (INCLUDING 1 DAY EACH FOR REVIEW AND TESTING)			7–9½ days

Materials List

Section I
- CD: 16A Black Sea Region
- Activity 1 from the *Student Activities* manual

Section II
- No materials needed

Section III
- CD: 16B British India, 1860; 16C Ganges Canal
- Activity 2 from the *Student Activities* manual

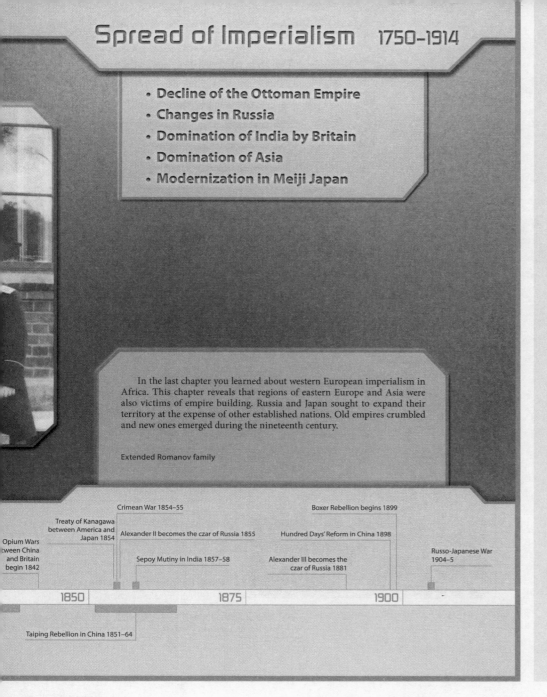

Spread of Imperialism 1750–1914

- Decline of the Ottoman Empire
- Changes in Russia
- Domination of India by Britain
- Domination of Asia
- Modernization in Meiji Japan

In the last chapter you learned about western European imperialism in Africa. This chapter reveals that regions of eastern Europe and Asia were also victims of empire building. Russia and Japan sought to expand their territory at the expense of other established nations. Old empires crumbled and new ones emerged during the nineteenth century.

Extended Romanov family

Opium Wars between China and Britain begin 1842

Treaty of Kanagawa between America and Japan 1854

Crimean War 1854–55

Alexander II becomes the czar of Russia 1855

Sepoy Mutiny in India 1857–58

Taiping Rebellion in China 1851–64

Boxer Rebellion begins 1899

Hundred Days' Reform in China 1898

Alexander III becomes the czar of Russia 1881

Russo-Japanese War 1904–5

1850   1875   1900

Section IV

- Activity 3 from the *Student Activities* manual
- CD: 16D Taiping Rebellion; 16E Empress Dowager Cixi; 16F Foreign Influences in China, 19th Century; 16G Imperialism in the Far East, 1914

Section V

- Activities 4–6 from the *Student Activities* manual

Section I

284   Chapter 16

Objectives

Students should be able to

1. Explain why the Ottoman Empire was forced to retreat from the Balkans and the Black Sea region.

2. Evaluate the impact of the French invasion of Egypt in 1798.

3. Analyze the efforts of Mahmud II to establish a modern state and economy.

I. Decline of the Ottoman Empire

At its height, the Ottoman Empire had ruled a vast kingdom that spanned three continents. The Ottomans controlled large regions of southeastern Europe, western Asia, and areas in North Africa. However, by the beginning of the nineteenth century, the empire began to show definite signs of decline. Political corruption, failure to modernize the military, and other common ailments of aging empires plagued the Ottomans. Neighboring states began to seize Ottoman land. A weak response resulted in an increasing loss of the empire's territory. During this decline, the central Ottoman government proved to be unable to respond to external as well as internal threats.

Loss of Territory

In Chapter 12 you learned that Greece gained its independence from the Ottoman Empire. Later in the nineteenth century, other subject states declared their independence. Assisted by Russia, several eastern European states won their freedom from Ottoman control. As a result, the Ottoman Empire steadily decreased in size and strength.

The Balkans

The **Balkans**, a large region in southeastern Europe, received its name from the Balkan Mountains. The Ottoman Empire had ruled this territory for centuries. However, during the nineteenth century, several of the Balkan states declared their independence. Russia extended its influence by supporting these struggling states and helping them to break away from Ottoman control. For example, Serbia, Montenegro, and Romania led the way in gaining their freedom.

Other states, including Bulgaria, gained their independence from the Ottoman Empire following the Russo-Turkish War in 1877. The Ottoman Empire continued to lose large portions of its empire.

The Black Sea Region

The Ottoman Empire had maintained control of territory around the **Black Sea** for centuries. However, during the nineteenth century the Ottomans lost control of most of this land. As previously stated, some states gained their independence, but others, such as Moldova, came under the control of an expanding Russian Empire. In addition, Russia seized control of Ottoman lands along the eastern shore of the Black Sea. This region transformed from one of Ottoman control to one of Russian dominance.

External and Internal Pressures

In addition to revolts by subject states, the Ottoman Empire suffered assaults from foreign powers including France and Russia. Internal instability further weakened the aging empire. Weak rulers invited uprisings and plots to seize power.

Crimean War (1854–55)

Russian expansion threatened the balance of power in Europe. European nations, including Britain, sided with the Ottoman Empire in the Crimean War in 1854 to stop the increase of Russian influence in this region.

The Black Sea Region

CD: 16A The Black Sea Region

This map from the student text is also available on the CD.

Activity 1: Slaughter of the Armenians

This activity contains several accounts of the massacres of minorities in the Ottoman Empire. Reading these accounts will help students understand the extent of the brutal persecution that non-Muslims endured under Muslim rule.

Napoleon in Egypt

French Invasion of Egypt

Napoleon I attempted to conquer Egypt, an Ottoman territory, in 1798. The French forces easily defeated the Ottoman forces in Egypt. However, Lord Nelson and the British fleet destroyed the French ships anchored off the Egyptian coast. This attack greatly hampered the French forces.

The Ottomans tried to defeat Napoleon by sending two armies to Egypt. He responded by attacking one of the Ottoman armies in Syria before it could travel to Egypt. This tactic failed, and Napoleon was forced to retreat to Egypt. He initially held off the second Ottoman force in Egypt but soon decided to abandon his army and return to France rather than risk loss of popular support at home.

Napoleon's forces in Egypt continued to suffer from attacks and disease. They finally surrendered to the British in 1801. While the Ottoman Empire regained control of Egypt, this invasion had demonstrated how vulnerable the empire had become.

Mahmud II

Mahmud II (r. 1808–1839) came to power in the Ottoman Empire during a period of decline and political instability. His half-brother staged a coup, murdered the sultan, and then ordered Mahmud's execution. Mahmud barely escaped this attempt on his life. A palace rebellion ended the coup and placed Mahmud on the throne.

Mahmud ruled the Ottoman Empire during the period when Greece, the Balkans, and other regions gained their independence. In addition, Mahmud found himself powerless to stop the French from seizing Algeria, an Ottoman province, in 1830.

However, in the midst of decline, Mahmud laid the foundation for a modern Turkey. For example, he abolished the military organization developed in the fourteenth century and replaced it with a modern Ottoman army. In addition, Mahmud enacted reforms that resulted in social and legal changes. As a result, the Turks began to embrace European clothing, European laws, and land reform.

Getty Images

Mahmud II

Napoleon in Egypt

Ask a volunteer to research Napoleon's invasion of Egypt and share his research with the class.

Mahmud II

Ask a volunteer to read about Mahmud II and prepare a report to share with the class.

Section Quiz

1. Where are the Balkan states located?
2. What empire had maintained control of the Black Sea region for centuries?
3. What Ottoman territory did Napoleon attempt to conquer in 1798?
4. Who came to power in the Ottoman Empire during its period of decline?
5. How did the Ottomans respond to the emperor's reforms?
★ Why did the Ottoman Empire experience decline during the nineteenth century?

II. Changes in Russia

In Chapter 4 you learned that Russians gained their independence from Mongol control around 1480. By the eighteenth century, Russia had grown to become the largest state in the world. Under leaders such as Peter the Great, Russia controlled an immense territory from the Baltic Sea to the Pacific Ocean.

However, much of Russia suffered from a harsh climate, and limited growing conditions restricted the food supply. As a result, this vast state had a population of only about fourteen million people. Succeeding rulers moved west and south to seize new lands, gain access to warm-water ports, and increase Russian influence.

While Russia expanded its control over neighboring states, much of the Russian population remained in virtual slavery as **serfs**. Uprisings increased as Russian citizens grew increasingly impatient with the status quo. In order to survive, Russia would have to make major reforms to benefit its people. Failure to do so would provide fertile ground for the growth of violent revolution.

Russian serfs being used like animals to tow a boat on the Volga River.

Territorial Expansion

Russian imperialism continued during the reign of **Catherine the Great**. Catherine was a German princess who married a German

Section II

Objectives

Students should be able to

1. Describe the effects of the Napoleonic invasion on Russia.
2. Assess the significance of Russian imperial reforms.
3. Analyze the reasons for the popularity of opposition movements in nineteenth-century Russia.

Section Quiz Answers

1. in southeastern Europe
2. the Ottoman Empire
3. Egypt
4. Mahmud II
5. They embraced European clothing, European laws, and land reform.
★ Political corruption, an outdated military, and other common ailments of aging empires plagued the Ottomans. The central Ottoman government also proved unable to respond to external or internal threats.

Serfs

Have some students gather information about the living conditions of the Russian serfs. After hearing their findings, have the class discuss what it must have been like to live as a Russian serf.

heir to the Russian throne. Her husband proved to be a weak leader. He soon died under mysterious circumstances, and Catherine became the ruler of Russia.

Under her aggressive leadership, Russia continued to move west. During her reign, Russia seized Ottoman land that lay between Russia and the Black Sea. Catherine also joined with other nations in partitioning Poland in order to continue the expansion of Russian political control westward.

Alexander I became the czar of Russia following Catherine's death in 1796. He continued Russia's expansion by seizing control of Finland from Sweden in 1809. Alexander also took control of additional Ottoman territory in 1812.

Reform

While Russian rulers succeeded in gaining territory, they continued to tolerate the oppression of nearly one third of the Russian population. Millions of Russians lived on land owned by nobles and spent most of their time working to support the nobility. As a result, they were little more than slaves and lived in terrible, impoverished conditions.

Internal Influences

In 1773 Catherine made life for the serfs even worse by making it legal to sell serfs separate from selling the land. In response, the peasants revolted and nearly entered Moscow before royal forces brutally defeated them. Succeeding Russian rulers tended either to work for reform or to react to violence and suppress the people in order to prevent reform.

Popular Opposition Movements

Nicholas I (r. 1825–1855) came to power in the midst of a revolt. Several well-educated Russian officers had traveled to Europe on various military assignments. They learned of representative government in western Europe and brought this idea back to Russia. As a result, a small group of nobles and army officers sought to replace Nicholas with his brother in order to establish a constitutional monarchy. This rebellion occurred in December 1825 and became known as the **Decembrist Revolt**.

Decembrist Revolt

The Decembrist Revolt

The seeds for the Decembrist Revolt were sown when Russian officers formed the Union of Salvation in 1816. A moderate wing of this group, known as the Northern Society, sought political goals that included a British-style constitutional monarchy, the abolition of serfdom, and equality of all citizens before the law.

The death of Czar Alexander I provided the spark that ignited the Decembrist Revolt. When Constantine, the czar's eldest son, declined to become czar, Constantine's younger brother Nicholas stepped forward to claim the throne. During this brief time of confusion, the Northern Society tried to seize power. Officers commanding a force of three thousand men gathered in Senate Square and refused to pledge their allegiance to Nicholas. They believed that many other troops stationed nearby would join the rebellion, but this support did not materialize. In addition, the top two leaders of the planned revolt either defected or disappeared.

Nicholas's forces routed the rebels within three weeks. The surviving leaders were sentenced to be hanged. However, during the hanging of five Decembrists, the ropes broke and the condemned men survived. Contrary to Russian tradition, Nicholas ordered new ropes and hanged these men a second time.

Nicholas I

Ask a volunteer to read about Nicholas I and share a report with the class.

Orthodoxy, Autocracy, and Nationality

Nicholas and other czars used the Russian Orthodox Church, absolute rule of the czar, and exaggerated nationalism to suppress the growing discontent of many Russian citizens. For example, the church encouraged submission to the state. In addition, the czar assumed the right to rule without question, and no criticism could be tolerated. Leaders also emphasized the importance of individual sacrifice for the good of the nation.

However, God gave the church the responsibility to win the lost and grow believers into Christlikeness (Matt. 28:19–20). He established government to protect the innocent and enable us to live quiet and peaceful lives (I Tim. 2:1–2). Finally, Proverbs 14:34 reminds us that righteousness, rather than exaggerated nationalism, exalts a nation.

Nicholas's strategy was unsuccessful and contrary to Scripture.

Anarchy

In simple terms, *anarchy* means "without law" or "the absence of law." We often use this term to describe a state of lawlessness and political disorder. The French Revolution provides a clear example of the anarchy that follows the overthrow of government.

However, Tolstoy imagined a theoretical state where there is simply no law or government and where man has the liberty of governing himself. Tolstoy dreamed of achieving this state without resorting to violence and disorder.

Property and Success

The emancipation of the serfs meant little because the freed peasants did not receive free land to farm. In the Old Testament, when a slave was released, the master was required to provide the newly freed slave with the economic means to establish himself (Deut. 15:12–18). By failing to acknowledge this biblical principle for loving one's neighbor, the Russians hurt not only the serfs but also the entire nation of Russia. An examination of prosperous nations shows that they place a high value on private property. Private ownership of property is essential for the development of agriculture and the raising of capital for investment.

Nicholas and his forces quickly defeated this revolt. However, such a threat led Nicholas to reject the westernization begun by Peter the Great and embrace "Orthodoxy, Autocracy, and Nationality." As a result, opposition groups became more popular, and more people began to accept radical proposals to solve Russia's problems.

Michael Bakunin became one of the Russian radicals to emerge during this period. Known as the Father of Anarchism, Bakunin supported **anarchy**, or the concept of society without government. To escape imprisonment, Bakunin fled to western Europe. However, his participation in an uprising in Dresden, Germany, led to his imprisonment and deportation to Siberia. Bakunin managed to escape and return to Europe, where he worked with Karl Marx.

Fyodore Dostoevsky

In addition, Russian authors, including Fyodore **Dostoevsky** and Leo Tolstoy (refer to Chapter 14), provided their readers with a glimpse into Russian society during this period. Their conclusions, however, were polar opposites. For example, Dostoevsky embraced Eastern Orthodoxy and opposed the anarchists and atheists who were becoming popular in Russia during this period.

Tolstoy, on the other hand, rejected Eastern Orthodoxy and emphasized the Sermon on the Mount. However, his interpretations of the Sermon conflicted with the rest of Scripture. He interpreted the command to "turn the other cheek" to teach pacifism (refusal to fight), denial of sexual desires, and the abolition of private property. In fact, Tolstoy played a key role in developing anarchist reasoning. In works such as *The Kingdom of God Is Within You*, he attacked the church, the state, and the principle of law in Russian society.

Imperial Reforms

Following the failed invasion by Napoleon, Alexander I discussed possible constitutional reforms and introduced a few minor changes. However, the fundamental problems remained, and pressure continued to mount for reform.

Alexander II (r. 1855–81) sensed the growing demand for reform in Russia. Rather than wait for reform to occur through violent revolution, he made a bold move in 1861. Alexander II abolished serfdom and freed twenty-three million people out of a total Russian population of sixty-seven million. This emancipation created a great supply of free laborers to move to the cities and fill jobs created by developing industries.

However, freed peasants did not receive free land along with their new status. Instead, the government required them to pay a huge tax in order to continue to farm the land. The government then used this money to pay the nobles large sums for the land the government had taken. The peasants often ended up with the least produc-

---

Anarchy

Discuss Tolstoy's concept that Russia (or any other nation) could establish a stable nation without law or government. Students need to understand that no country can prosper under anarchy. Point the students to Bible verses such as Romans 3:23 to remind them that all people are sinners and thus do not make good citizens without laws to limit their actions. In addition, Romans 13:1–4 reminds us that God has instituted government to reward good and restrain evil.

Dostoevsky

Visit www.bjupress.com/resources for possible links to articles about Dostoevsky.

tive land, and this land belonged to the village community rather than to individual farmers.

In the end, simply abolishing serfdom did little to improve the lives of millions of Russians. Russia needed fundamental reforms to correct centuries of repression. Because the Russian government did not implement these reforms, conditions did not improve. The support for revolution continued to grow.

Imperial Reactions

Despite Alexander II's attempts to bring reform to Russia, his efforts proved to be in vain. In 1881, he died at the hands of assassins. His successor, Alexander III (r. 1881–94), suppressed all real and imagined threats to the monarchy. He censored the press and persecuted many groups, including the Poles and Finns. Under Alexander, pogroms (mentioned in Chapter 14) became a brutal tool of the government to terrorize those considered a threat. These vicious policies continued under Alexander's son Nicholas II (r. 1894–1917).

External Influences

Napoleonic Invasion

Napoleon had allied France with Russia in order to prevent the British from trading with countries in Europe. However, by 1811 this alliance began to collapse. When Napoleon learned that Russia was preparing for war, he ignored all warnings and invaded Russia in June 1812.

The Russians refused to engage Napoleon's forces and drew them deep into the heart of Russia. When the Russians did stand and fight, they suffered defeat. Russian retreats pulled the French into Russia but denied the French any significant victories.

Despite Napoleon's capture of Moscow, the Russians would not surrender. Concern over unstable conditions back in France and the approaching Russian winter led Napoleon to retreat, and the Russian people rallied to destroy the French forces as they tried to flee. Ninety percent of Napoleon's army died in battle, from the harsh Russian winter, or from Russian attacks.

> #### Free and Self-sufficient
> Freeing the serfs without giving them land or other resources to support themselves was doomed to fail. In Deuteronomy 15:12–18, God established a principle for freeing a servant. God commanded His people to generously provide for the needs of a freed servant. This practice provided the servant with the resources he needed to survive and become a productive citizen.

Napoleon and his forces retreating from Russia

Popperfoto/Getty Images

Napoleon's Invasion

It is interesting to compare Napoleon's failed invasion of Russia in 1798 to Hitler's failed invasion in 1941. During both invasions the Russians used the "scorched earth" policy and drew the invaders deeper and deeper into Russia. The Russians then cut off the enemy supply lines and destroyed the retreating enemy forces.

Napoleon's Invasion

Have the students discuss why Napoleon invaded Russia despite repeated warnings not to do so. Ask them to suggest motives behind such leaders' takeovers of other countries.

Ingredients for Success

Countries that have stable governments and educational systems and allow their citizens freedom tend to enjoy greater economic success.

Russia lacked these key ingredients and also failed to use its abundant resources.

Section III

Objectives

Students should be able to

1. Explain the advance of British power up to 1850.
2. Describe patterns of British trade that linked India and China with Europe.
3. Describe the consequences of British control of India.

A War by Any Other Name

In this chapter we refer to the Seven Years' War, better known to many students as the French and Indian War. The first is the European name for the war, and the second is its American name.

Napoleon's invasion had disrupted much of Russian society and led those who suffered most to expect reform. The serfs had played a major role in defeating Napoleon. In return, they demanded major reforms that would free them from their virtual slavery. However, as we have seen, Alexander I offered only minor changes. No significant reform followed Napoleon's invasion.

European Economic Growth

In Chapter 13 you learned about the tremendous changes that occurred in western Europe because of the Industrial Revolution. Economic growth from this revolution propelled western Europe far ahead of countries such as Russia. While Russia had the necessary natural resources, it lacked the free and mobile laborers, stable government, and other ingredients needed to develop industry on a large scale.

While Russia continued to expand its empire by seizing land from weaker states, it lagged further and further behind economically. Western Europe became wealthy through industry, expanding sea trade, and the exploitation of African colonies. Russia could not compete or catch up. Western success exposed the great weaknesses of the Russian Empire. Radical groups used these weaknesses to attract increasing support for their efforts to overthrow the existing system in Russia.

Section Quiz

1. By the eighteenth century, which country had grown into the largest state in the world?
2. How did Catherine become ruler of Russia?
3. What group led the Decembrist Revolt?
4. Who became known as the Father of Anarchism? Briefly define anarchy.
5. What did Czar Alexander II decree in 1861? Did it accomplish his intended goal?
★ Briefly contrast Dostoevsky's and Tolstoy's interpretations of Scripture and their views on anarchy.

III. Domination of India by Britain

As you learned in Chapter 11, the English initially came to India for trade. However, as the Mughal Empire declined, England gradually took control of most of the country. Britain was not the only European country to seek influence in India. France also labored to establish and maintain trade with this vast country.

Advance of British Power to 1850

The East India Company developed extensive trade relations with states in India. Over time, the British government became more involved and eventually took control of British affairs in India. However, Britain had to deal with its main competitor before extensive trade could continue.

Conflict with France

Britain soon ended the threat of French competition by winning the Seven Years' War (1756–63). At the **Battle of Plassey** in 1757,

---

Section Quiz Answers

1. Russia
2. She married a German heir to the Russian throne. He died under mysterious circumstances, and Catherine became the ruler of Russia.
3. a small group of nobles and army officers
4. Michael Bakunin; society without government
5. He abolished serfdom. No.
★ Dostoevsky adopted a traditional Eastern Orthodox approach to Scripture. Despite governmental abuses, he saw a legitimate role for government. Tolstoy rejected Eastern Orthodoxy. He emphasized the Sermon on the Mount but failed to interpret it in light of the rest of the Bible. He advocated the abolition of government.

Consequences of British Rule

The British faced many problems in ruling India. The country had over one hundred million inhabitants who spoke over a hundred different languages. In addition, they followed several religions.

British officials in India often misunderstood the Indians and had little desire to learn about Indian culture. The British rulers also tended to isolate themselves from the Indian population and assumed the role of master over their Indian subjects. Indians found employment as servants and performed other menial tasks the British would not lower themselves to do.

Many British officials also hindered missionary efforts to evangelize the Indians. They feared that this evangelism would lead to unrest and instability as the missionaries revealed the error of Indian religions and idolatry. For example, British officials compelled William Carey to carry out his translating and printing work from the Danish settlement of Serampore.

To reduce the strife in India, Queen Victoria proclaimed a policy of noninterference. This policy, though proclaimed with good intentions, hindered missionary efforts to spread the gospel and to bring about reforms to protect women, children, and the outcastes of Indian society.

Despite these negative aspects of British rule, there were positive results for India as well. These results included improvements in agriculture, industry, transportation, and education. In addition, British and American missionaries were able to evangelize much of India. When the British government restricted direct evangelization, missionaries often used the meeting of medical and educational needs to provide opportunities to witness.

To improve agriculture, the British brought in better equipment, introduced fertilizers, and taught the Indians improved methods of farming. To increase production, they also built many miles of irrigation canals.

The British also developed raw materials such as tea, cotton, and jute into products for export. India soon exported more tea than China.

British officials planted the first rubber trees on the island of Ceylon (Sri Lanka). These plants thrived, and Ceylon became a major exporter of rubber.

In addition, Britain laid thousands of miles of track to construct a massive railroad system. They also set up a telegraph system and reorganized the postal system.

Woman harvesting tea

Irrigation canal in India

British commander **Robert Clive** defeated a much larger Indian force whose leader supported the French. With only three thousand men, Clive routed a disorganized Indian force of eighty thousand. This battle broke France's strength in India. Within three years the French were defeated in India.

Conquest of India

Following the end of French influence, British trade with India grew over the next hundred years. The British government began to exercise greater control over the East India Company in 1773 due to the company's financial mismanagement. As the British government became more involved, officials quickly realized the importance of

Robert Clive

Visit www.bjupress.com/resources for possible links to articles about Robert Clive.

Battle of Plassey

In this decisive battle that ended French influence in India, British forces representing the British East India Company opposed Siraj-ud-Dawlah. Siraj stood as the last independent ruler in the Bengal province of India. To defeat him the British employed various tactics, including bribing several of Siraj's military leaders. When many of the Indian soldiers failed to join the battle, Siraj's fate was sealed. He was later captured and executed by the British. His death signaled the end of Indian independence and led to British control of much of India.

Lord Cornwallis

You will note the statement about Lord Cornwallis's putting down rebellions in India. This is the same Lord Cornwallis who surrendered to George Washington at Yorktown, effectively ending the American War for Independence.

stabilizing India to enhance British trade. British commanders such as Lord Cornwallis put down rebellions and enforced stability.

During the late 1700s and early 1800s, the British government continued to exert more control over the activities of the East India Company. In 1814 the **Charter Act** gave the British crown control over all that the company possessed. The final incident that led to the British government taking complete control occurred when Indian soldiers called **sepoys** (SEE poyz) revolted.

The **Sepoy Mutiny** (1857–58) began because of a rumor that the cartridges for a newly issued rifle had been greased with either pork or beef fat. In order to use the cartridges, the soldiers had to open them, usually by biting them. The Hindu soldiers were offended because the cow was sacred to them. The Muslim soldiers were offended because they considered pork unclean.

When the British commanded the sepoys to load the new rifles, they refused and the British stripped them of their uniforms and pensions. British forces arrested and imprisoned other sepoys when they also refused to obey this command. As news spread of the British actions, a mutiny arose. Before the British could restore order, both sides had massacred many innocent people.

The British suppressed this mutiny within a year. Queen Victoria responded by proclaiming India under control of the British crown and by declaring that the Indian people had the right to a voice in their own government. Yet at the same time, with no input from the Indian people, Britain absorbed India into its empire.

Patterns of British Trade with India and China

British merchants, with the support of the British government, developed extensive trade between India and China. The British be-

Ganges Canal

 ## CD: 16B British India, 1860; 16C Ganges Canal

This map from the student text and a photo of the Ganges Canal are available on the CD.

Activity 2: The Sepoy Mutiny

This is an excerpt from a missionary's account of the causes and results of the Sepoy Mutiny.

 ## The Sepoy Mutiny

Visit www.bjupress.com/resources for possible links to articles about the Sepoy Mutiny.

came very wealthy in the process. The massive flow of wealth tended to blur the lines between legitimate trade and the growing trade in a destructive drug.

The British developed cotton production and weaving in India. British ships transported goods, including cotton cloth and raw cotton, to Chinese ports. In exchange, the Chinese traded rhubarb, tea, and silk. However, the goods brought from India were worth less than those offered by the Chinese merchants. As a result, British merchants had to pay the difference in silver. This situation created a negative balance of trade for British merchants.

However, the British also produced **opium** from poppy plants in India and exported it to China. Soon, the Chinese demand for the addicting and destructive opium reversed the balance of trade. Now silver flowed from China to Britain. In addition to the terrible damage inflicted on the Chinese due to opium addiction, this reversal became a great financial drain on China.

Section Quiz

1. Why did the English originally travel to India?

2. What other European state sought to compete with Britain for control of India?

3. What act in 1814 gave the British crown control over all the East India Company's holdings?

4. What rumor led to the Sepoy Mutiny?

5. What drug did British merchants sell to the Chinese in order to gain a favorable balance of trade?

★ In light of Exodus 20:13 and 17, evaluate the British motives for selling addictive opium to the Chinese.

IV. Domination of Asia

You learned in Chapter 15 that Europe dominated Africa during the second half of the nineteenth century. During this same period, European nations and one Asian state also dominated Asia. China came under domination as the Manchu or **Qing** dynasty weakened. In addition, most of Southeast Asia became subject to European imperialism.

Weakening of the Middle Kingdom

The Manchus seized control of China in 1644. Although their formal rule did not end until 1911, the Qing dynasty experienced serious decline in the nineteenth century. Growth of trade with the West and the imperialism of European nations played a role in this decline. However, China had remained isolated from the rest of the world for centuries. China's continued resistance to change ultimately led to the collapse of its central government.

Opium Wars

For many years Chinese officials took bribes from British merchants in order to bring chests of opium into China. When the Chinese government finally tried to end this destructive trade, the British strongly objected. The British government intervened on behalf of the merchants and became directly involved in the opium trade. Mounting tensions resulted in the **Opium Wars**. Following

Top, immature growing poppy; *bottom,* mature poppy flower

Indian Cotton and the Confederacy

The increased production of cotton in India may have contributed to Britain's failure to recognize the Confederate States of America during the American Civil War. The Confederate government assumed that the British needed Southern cotton. However, the expansion of Indian cotton production made Southern cotton unnecessary in Britain.

Section IV

Objectives

Students should be able to

1. Analyze the causes of governmental breakdown and social collapse in China.

2. Explain why China resisted political contact and trade with Europeans.

3. Describe how the opium trade forced China to allow Europeans access to more Chinese markets.

4. Analyze the causes and consequences of the Taiping Rebellion.

5. Describe missionary efforts in India and the rest of Asia.

Section Quiz Answers

1. for trade

2. France

3. Charter Act

4. that rifle cartridges had been greased with pork or beef fat

5. opium

★ The British sold a destructive drug that eventually led to death. They were willing to go to war and kill Chinese soldiers to protect their market. They coveted the wealth of the Chinese.

✸ The Opium Wars

Visit www.bjupress.com/resources for possible links to articles about the Opium Wars.

British Mercantilism

One of the principles of mercantilism is that colonial wealth in the form of silver or gold should be sent to the mother country. Note how the British used opium sales to protect their mercantile practice and to ensure a positive trade balance for themselves.

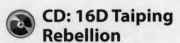

CD: 16D Taiping Rebellion

This map from the student text is also available on the CD.

Hong Xiuquan and Christianity

Hong was a gifted student who tried repeatedly to pass the government exam for civil service. Whether it was true or not, he believed his failures to pass resulted from corrupt officials. His frustration led to a serious illness. During his illness, he believed that he had visited Heaven and received a calling to rid China of demon forces.

After his illness, Hong met Chinese Christians who gave him a Bible. He read the Old Testament and concluded that he had indeed met with God and that God had chosen him as a son. When Chinese Christians pointed out his errors, he rejected their counsel and formed his own cult, known as the God Worshippers Society. In this cult, God was the Father, Christ was the Son and Elder Brother, and Hong was the Younger Brother.

the first Opium War in 1842, Britain forced China to open more ports to British merchants. During the second Opium War (1856–60), France joined Britain to gain even more trade concessions from the Chinese. These wars and the increased influence of European countries continued to weaken the Qing dynasty.

Rebellions

Throughout China, more and more people rebelled to express their rejection of the Qing government. The heavy taxation and government corruption especially angered the people. Famine became another serious problem for China. The Chinese population had rapidly increased, but the people had no additional farmland on which to grow more food. During some years, the farmers could not produce enough food to pay taxes and feed their families. Hungry and angry peasants often joined in rebellions against the government.

A frustrated Chinese student named Hong Renkun became the leader of one of the worst rebellions in Chinese history. Hong channeled his frustration into the development of a cultic political movement that attracted a huge number of the roaming peasants. As his movement grew, he changed his name to **Hong Xiuquan** ("Heavenly

Jonathan and Rosalind Goforth

Canadian missionary Jonathan Goforth and his family, along with other missionaries, began their escape on June 28, 1900. They faced a journey of about twenty-four days through territory overrun with Boxers.

The Chinese Christians at their mission urged them to go. They knew that the Boxers had a special hatred for Chinese converts to Christianity. (They believed these Christians had denied traditional Chinese culture and heritage.) However, the Chinese Chris-tians could blend into their villages or hide in the countryside, while the foreigners could not.

On July 8 Boxers attacked Goforth and his group but failed to kill Jonathan, despite several blows with swords and a club. The Boxers soon became more interested in the goods in the missionary's carts, and the missionaries slipped into the crowd to safety. Two years later the Goforths returned to China and their mission.

King") to reflect his claims that he was the younger brother of Jesus Christ.

The weakness demonstrated by the Qing government during the Opium Wars caused more people to join Hong's movement. By 1851 he had a ten-thousand-man army with which he could attack the Manchurian forces.

The resulting **Taiping Rebellion** lasted from 1851 to 1864. Hong's movement quickly grew to over one million peasants who joined him in rebellion. At first, the rebels were difficult to suppress because they remained mobile. However, once they established a capital in Nanking, the British and Chinese forces were able to mount an attack and end this serious threat. During the many battles required to suppress this rebellion, between twenty and thirty million people died.

However, the unrest continued. In 1899 the **Boxer Rebellion** broke out. The Boxers were members of a secret society officially named the *Society of Righteous and Harmonious Fists.* The Europeans nicknamed the group Boxers because the martial arts they practiced looked like shadowboxing. Initially, this society opposed the Chinese government. However, they concluded that an alliance with the Imperial government against European imperialists would better represent Chinese interests. The Empress Dowager Tz'u-Hsi (or Cixi) (see p. 298) discouraged the Imperial government from restraining this movement.

In the early months of 1900, the Boxers began by killing missionaries and other foreigners in northern China. About two hundred and fifty foreigners died in the attacks. The Boxers also slaughtered thousands of Chinese Christians.

Foreign navies from eight countries began to expand their presence on the northern China coast by the end of April 1900. Initially, European commanders dispatched 435 troops to help put down the rebellion. However, the crisis deepened, and marine and army forces numbering over 49,000 were required to crush this violent and deadly rebellion.

In addition to Britain, France, and the United States, Japan and Russia sent large numbers of warships and troops. Germany, Italy,

Members of the Boxer Rebellion

Cooperative Imperialism

Although the British practiced imperialism toward China during this period, they also cooperated with the Chinese government when it served Britain's interests to do so. The Taiping Rebellion proved to be such an occasion. Realizing that British economic interests were at stake and that many British citizens were at risk, Britain sent its troops to join Chinese forces in crushing this violent rebellion in China.

Boxer Rebellion

Ask a volunteer to read about the Boxer Rebellion and share his findings with the class.

Missions in the Far East

William Carey
1761–1834

William Carey was an English Baptist preacher and linguist who translated the Bible into many languages, including Bengali and Sanskrit. His motto ("Expect great things from God; attempt great things for God") and book, *An Enquiry into the Obligations of Christians to use Means for the Conversion of the Heathens*, published in 1792, show his passion for missions. Carey is considered the Father of Modern Missions.

The Granger Collection, New York

Robert Morrison
1782–1834

Robert Morrison became the first Protestant missionary to China, arriving there in 1807. He learned Mandarin and Cantonese in order to translate the Bible into Chinese. Morrison also produced an English-Chinese dictionary. He had to contend with Catholic missionaries who opposed his ministry.

Adoniram Judson
1788–1850

Adoniram Judson became America's first foreign missionary, arriving in Burma in 1813. In spite of various afflictions, including imprisonment and the deaths of his first and second wives, he completed a Burmese Bible translation so precise that it is still used today.

Missionary Biographies

Have some students prepare and present to the class grade-appropriate biographies of some of the missionaries mentioned in this section.

Activity 3: The Goforths and the Boxer Rebellion

This activity is an excerpt from the first-hand account of Rosalind Goforth, a missionary to China who fled the country with her family during the Boxer Rebellion.

William Carey

Visit www.bjupress.com/resources for possible links to articles about William Carey.

Adoniram Judson

Visit www.bjupress.com/resources for possible links to articles about Adoniram Judson.

Samuel R. Brown
1810–1880

Samuel R. Brown, a New Englander who attended Yale in 1832, founded China's first Protestant school at Canton. After a visit to America in 1847, he left for Yokahama, Japan, in 1859. Brown became one of the first Christian teachers in this city. During his years of ministry in Japan, he translated the Bible into Japanese and wrote a grammar entitled *Colloquial Japanese*.

James Hudson Taylor
1832–1905

James Hudson Taylor established the China Inland Mission (CIM) in 1865. Over time, this mission agency guided hundreds of missionaries to China. Taylor adopted Chinese customs and dress, a practice uncommon among most Western missionaries.

J. C. Hepburn
1815–1911

J. C. Hepburn served as a missionary-doctor in Japan. He spent many years producing an English-Japanese dictionary. Hepburn started a school that later became Meiji Gakuin University. The Japanese government recognized his contribution by awarding him the Order of the Rising Sun.

Pandita Ramabai (1858–1922)

Born into an educated Brahman family, Pandita Ramabai became a leader in relieving the plight of women in India. Prior to her conversion to Christianity, Ramabai traveled across India, witnessing the hopeless existence and suffering of most Hindu women. Stirred by what she saw, she later wrote books exposing the mistreatment of women in India, including the marriage of child brides, the abandonment of widows, and the practice of suttee.

In 1883 Ramabai visited England and began to study the Bible. Over time she forsook her Hindu upbringing and turned to Christ. Her conversion created a controversy in India. Ramabi returned to her homeland and renewed her work in behalf of Indian women. She founded a center for unwed mothers, developed a program to provide famine relief, and established schools for poor girls. In 1889 she organized the Mukti ("liberation") Mission to serve as a place of refuge for young, abused widows. This mission has since expanded to care for orphans and the blind.

James Hudson Taylor

Visit www.bjupress.com/resources for possible links to articles about James Hudson Taylor.

Pandita Ramabai

Visit www.bjupress.com/resources for possible links to articles about Pandita Ramabai.

Hundred Days' Reform

The goal of this ambitious reform was to transform China from an outmoded empire into a modern nation. The young emperor Guangxu and a small group of reformers in the Qing court supported several key goals that were intended to revive the declining Chinese empire. These goals included

- Reforming the traditional exam system.
- Eliminating redundant government positions.
- Developing a modern education system.
- Transforming the government from an absolute monarchy to a constitutional monarchy.
- Applying principles of capitalism to strengthen the economy and modernize manufacturing.

Ruling elites opposed these reforms and quickly supported Empress Dowager Cixi's coup d'etat that occurred just 104 days into the reform movement. Cixi forced the young emperor into seclusion and placed him under house arrest until his death in 1908. Six of the reform's chief advocates, known as the "Six Gentlemen," were executed, and the reforms were rescinded.

Member of the Boxer Rebellion

and Austria-Hungary also provided a token force to complete the Eight-Nation Alliance.

Continued Opposition to Contact with the Outside World

A child born with the name Zaitian became the tenth emperor of the Qing dynasty in 1875. He became token ruler at the age of four and received the name of **Guangxu**. The **Empress Dowager Cixi** adopted Guangxu as her son and served as the actual ruler of China for the first fourteen years of his reign. She used her considerable power to oppose reform and change in China.

Once Emperor Guangxu began to rule, he worked to modernize China and develop a constitutional monarchy similar to the one developed by Japan. In June 1898 the young emperor began the **Hundred Days' Reform** with the goal of implementing sweeping political, legal, and social changes in China. By September the Empress Dowager had staged a coup and imprisoned Guangxu. She issued an edict stating that Guangxu was not fit to be emperor and quickly reversed his efforts to reform China.

Guangxu remained under house arrest until his mysterious death at the age of thirty-seven. The next day Empress Dowager Cixi died. Theories about the possible murder of Guangxu abound.

Empress Dowager Cixi

![CD icon] **CD: 16E Empress Dowager Cixi**

An artist's rendering of Empress Dowager Cixi is available on the CD.

Empress Dowager Cixi

Ask a volunteer to prepare a report on Empress Dowager Cixi and share it with the class.

Foreign Intervention

As foreign nations saw the Qing dynasty continue to weaken, they began to take advantage of China. The emerging state of Japan made the first move. Europeans nations quickly moved to limit Japan's access to Chinese territory.

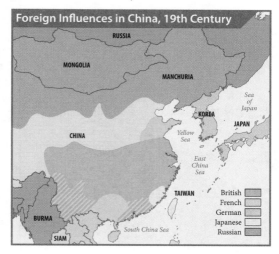

Foreign Influences in China, 19th Century

	British
	French
	German
	Japanese
	Russian

China

For many years Korea had been under token Chinese control. In 1876 Japan forced the Koreans to sign a treaty declaring their independence from China. China immediately began to maneuver to recover control of Korea. When a Korean secret society rebelled, the pro-Chinese king of Korea requested military assistance from China. The Japanese also sent troops. In 1894 the **Sino-Japanese War** began. The Japanese easily defeated China and humiliated the Manchu government. The Japanese took possession of Korea and received Taiwan along with other Chinese territories.

Fearing that Japan would gain control of more Chinese territory, several European nations sought ways to claim territory for themselves and establish **spheres of influence** in China. Like children eyeing a huge pie, each nation demanded a "slice" of China. Britain, France, Germany, and other European countries all chose areas they wished to control. The weak Chinese government had little say in these decisions except to give away land.

Southeast Asia

This area lies east of India and south of China. Several regions of this area had come under European control prior to 1800. However, the nineteenth century witnessed European assimilation of the entire region, with the exception of Siam (Thailand). Siam escaped European control by serving as a buffer between French and British territories. Europeans seized control of many states and islands in the area for strategic and economic reasons. For example, the

Spheres of Influence

Japan's victory over China in 1894 in the Sino-Japanese War demonstrated China's weakness. Between 1897 and 1899, European nations quickly demanded and received control of strategic territories in China, especially ports. Germany gained exclusive mining and railroad rights in the Shandong province, located on the upper east coast of China. Russia received control of Dairen and Port Arthur in northeastern China. The Russians also demanded the right to build a railroad across Manchuria; this railroad enabled them to control much of northwestern China. The British controlled Weihaiwei and the Yangtze Valley. The French controlled Guangzhou Bay and other provinces in southern China.

By 1899 the United States became concerned that American businesses would be excluded from Chinese markets. Secretary of State John Hay pressed the European powers to adopt a policy that ensured equal trading privileges. An agreement that came to be known as the Open Door policy assured equal trading opportunities and prevented the annexation of Chinese territory. To protect their economic interests, Europeans sought to keep the Chinese government weak but independent. No one appeared concerned about the long-term damage these policies would inflict on China.

CD: 16F Foreign Influences in China, 19th Century

This map from the student text is also available on the CD.

Imperialism in the Far East, 1914

Great Britain
France
Germany
Portugal
Holland
Russia
Japan
United States

Europeans exported many natural resources from this area, including rubber, tea, and food not grown in Europe.

Section Quiz

1. What led to the collapse of the Qing dynasty?
2. What motivated more and more Chinese peasants to rebel?
3. Whom did Hong Xiuquan claim to be? What rebellion did he lead?
4. What rebellion resulted in the deaths of many missionaries?
5. Why was Emperor Guangxu imprisoned while in office?
★ Evaluate Japan's actions toward a weakened China.

V. Modernization in Meiji Japan

Over two hundred years of Japanese isolation ended in 1853. In that year **Commodore Matthew Perry** of the United States visited Japan with his fleet and pressured the Japanese to open to trade. In 1854 Japan and the United States signed the **Treaty of Kanagawa**. This treaty opened Japan to trade with other nations.

In a later visit, Perry brought with him several inventions that amazed the Japanese people. One was a telegraph system, which

> ### Decision to Modernize Japan
> Once Perry and his fleet had ended Japanese isolation, the Japanese had to decide how to respond to the West. Would they follow China's example of resisting change? The Japanese fought a civil war to decide this issue. In the process, the victorious forces overthrew the shogun and recognized the Japanese emperor as the leader of Japan. The emperor embraced contact with the West and led Japan to become a great power in Asia.

Section V

Objectives

Students should be able to

1. Analyze the causes of the Meiji Restoration and assess the impact of the Meiji state on Japan's modernization.

2. Assess how Western ideas and reformed Shintoism impacted Japan in the Meiji period.

3. Explain the changes in Japan's relations with China and Western powers from the 1850s to the early 1900s.

CD: 16G Imperialism in the Far East, 1914

This map from the student text is also available on the CD.

Section Quiz Answers

1. trade with the West, foreign imperialism, and China's policy of isolation

2. heavy taxation, government corruption, and famine

3. the younger brother of Christ; the Taiping Rebellion

4. the Boxer Rebellion

5. Because Guangxu sought to modernize and reform China, Empress Dowager Cixi had him arrested and imprisoned.

★ The Japanese demonstrated imperialism and aggression toward China. Coveting China's territory, the Japanese used their recently acquired technology and skills to ruthlessly seize the land they wanted from China.

Activity 4: Perry's Expedition to Japan

This activity contains a partial account of Commodore Perry's visit to the Japanese court and a letter written to the emperor of Japan by President Millard Fillmore.

Commodore Matthew Perry

Visit www.bjupress.com/resources for possible links to articles about Commodore Matthew Perry.

could send messages from one town to another. Another was a miniature train and railroad track. The Japanese realized that they had much to learn if they were to catch up with the rest of the world.

Impact of Western Ideas

The Japanese began to trade with the United States and many other countries. Soon the Japanese adopted the Western way of life. They built factories to make new products. The Japanese also sent some of their young men to the United States and Europe to learn more about Western ideas and new developments in industry. In addition, Japanese commissions studied Western governments, schools, and militaries.

The Meiji Restoration

In 1868 the emperor used the title **Meiji** (MAY jee) ("enlightened rule") to describe his reign. He led the transformation of Japan from a feudal society (refer to Chapter 4) to a modern state. Japan became the first nation in Asia to become industrialized. In addition, the Japanese developed a constitutional form of government. They also developed modern educational and judicial systems modeled after the West.

Japan transformed their feudal military forces into a modern, well-trained army and navy. Despite a lack of raw materials including coal and iron ore, the manufacture of modern weapons and a modern naval fleet quickly made Japan a powerful nation in Asia. We noted earlier that Japan supplied warships and thousands of well-armed troops to help suppress the Boxer Rebellion in China. Japan soon demonstrated imperialist desires toward its weaker neighbors.

Expansion of Japan

As we mentioned in the section on China, Japan began to expand its territory at the expense of China in 1894. A few years later, Japan astonished the European states by quickly and decisively defeating the Russian army and navy during the **Russo-Japanese War** (1904–5). This war forced the world to notice that Japan had developed into a world power.

Emperor Meiji

Russo-Japanese War

U.S. President Teddy Roosevelt mediated the peace agreement that ended this war. For his work, he received the Nobel Peace Prize.

Section Quiz

1. What treaty opened Japan to foreign trade?
2. What European developments did Japan study?
3. What does the term *Meiji* mean?
4. What did Japan manufacture to become a powerful nation?
5. What major power did Japan defeat in 1905?
★ How did Japan's transformation into an industrial nation differ from Britain's (refer to Chapter 13)?

Japan and Shintoism

In Chapter 4 you learned about this ancient Japanese religion. During the Meiji Restoration, political leaders transformed Shintoism into a tool of the Japanese government. They sought to unify Japan under the rule of the emperor.

Shinto priests taught the young people Shinto theology that supported the divinity of Japan's national origins and the emperor. Shintoism also became a tool to motivate improvements such as industrial growth in a way that would enhance extreme nationalism and promote militarism.

Activity 5: Map Study: Spread of Imperialism

This map activity provides the students with a general overview of where the events in this chapter occurred.

Section Quiz Answers

1. the Treaty of Kanagawa
2. industry, government, education, and military
3. enlightened rule
4. modern weapons and a modern naval fleet
5. Russia

★ Answers will vary but should include some of the following: Britain had abundant natural resources, including coal and iron ore; Japan did not. A strong Christian influence tempered Britain's industrial development; Shintoism influenced Japan's industrial development.

Activity 6: Chapter Review

This activity helps the students prepare for the chapter test.

CHAPTER REVIEW

People, Places, and Terms to Know

Balkans
Black Sea
Mahmud II
serfs
Catherine the Great
Nicholas I
Decembrist Revolt
Michael Bakunin
anarchy
Dostoevsky
Alexander II
Battle of Plassey
Robert Clive
Charter Act
sepoys
Sepoy Mutiny
opium
Qing
Opium Wars
Hong Xiuquan
Jonathan Goforth
Taiping Rebellion
Boxer Rebellion
Guangxu
Empress Dowager Cixi
Hundred Days' Reform
Sino-Japanese War
spheres of influence
Commodore Matthew Perry
Treaty of Kanagawa
Meiji
Russo-Japanese War

Making Connections

1. Why did Europe side with the Ottoman Empire in the Crimean War?
2. Why did Napoleon abandon his army in Egypt?
3. Why was Russia able to support only a meager population?
4. Why were serfs unable to escape terrible poverty?
5. Why did a small group of nobles and army officers seek to replace Czar Nicholas I?
6. Why did the Chinese effort to end the sale of opium lead to war with Britain?
7. Why did several European nations seek ways to claim Chinese territory for themselves?
8. What did the Meiji Restoration in Japan quickly lead to?

Developing History Skills

1. Locate the following on the map. Then match each area with the corresponding number on the map.

   a. Burma   d. Japan
   b. China   e. Russia
   c. Indian Ocean   f. South China Sea

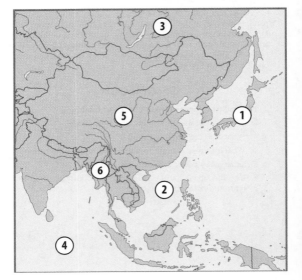

Chapter Review Answers

Making Connections

1. to stop the increase of Russian influence in eastern Europe
2. to return to France and maintain his popular support
3. Much of Russia suffered from a harsh climate, and growing conditions were limited.
4. They lived on land owned by nobles and spent most of their time working to support the nobility.
5. They sought to establish a constitutional monarchy.
6. When the British merchants complained to the British government, the British government intervened in behalf of the merchants and became directly involved in the opium trade. War ensued.
7. They feared that Japan would gain control of additional Chinese territory.
8. It quickly led to imperialism and war to seize additional territory.

Developing History Skills

1. a. 6
   b. 5
   c. 4
   d. 1
   e. 3
   f. 2
2. Answers will vary but should include some of the following: Africa was invaded, partitioned, and colonized. China lost control of many valuable ports and endured European domination but was not partitioned or colonized. Europeans developed an extensive infrastructure in Africa but did little to develop an infrastructure in China.

Thinking Critically

1. Answers will vary but might include some of the following: The British rulers tended to isolate themselves from

2. Contrast the imperialism of Europe in China with that in Africa (refer to Chapter 15).

Thinking Critically

1. Evaluate British rule of India.
2. Contrast the British rule of India with the European and Japanese imperialism in China.

Living in God's World

1. Dostoevsky wrote short stories and novels that confronted people with human sinfulness and the importance of the Christian religion. His works were very influential and are still read today. Write a short story dealing with problems in modern culture. Throughout your story, suggest that the Bible and a right relationship with God can solve these problems.

the Indian population and assumed the role of master over their unfortunate Indian subjects. Many British officials opposed missionary efforts and were insensitive to Indian culture.

However, there were positive results for India as well. These included improvements in agriculture, industry, transportation, and education. In addition, British and American missionaries found creative ways to evangelize much of India.

2. Answers will vary but should include the following: Britain improved industry, transportation, agriculture, and education in India. European nations that dominated China concentrated on accumulating wealth rather than on making infrastructural improvements in China. Japan seized Chinese territory and plundered China's natural resources to fuel their own industrial development.

Living in God's World

1. Answers will vary.

UNIT 5

The 20th Century and Beyond

1900–Present

Rivalries and small wars led to alliances designed to ensure victory in future conflicts. Improved technology produced weapons that were more lethal, and men became confident that their nation would prevail over others. Two world wars would result from several causes, including extreme nationalism, real and perceived injustice, and failure to respond to aggressive actions by dictators.

Following these wars, much of the world aligned with either the democracies or the Communist-dominated states. Years of regional conflicts tested the resolve of the two superpowers during the Cold War. Following the Cold War, the world has remained unstable and new enemies have surfaced. At the same time, the global community has struggled to build an economy that knows no national boundaries and offers financial prosperity to more of the world's growing population.

Christianity and Islam have continued to expand. Areas of the world that have historically been mission fields for Christians are now developing mission-sending churches. Regions that have a history of Christian influence are coming under the increasing influence of Islam. The last chapter revealing how these transitions will develop has yet to be written.

Left, Attack on Pearl Harbor
Top right, Tiananmen Square in China
Bottom right, Chinese house church

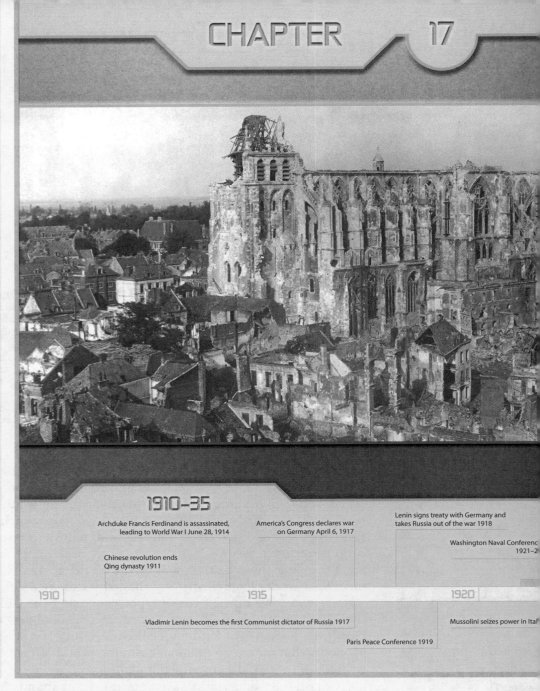

CHAPTER 17

Chapter Goals

Students should be able to

1. Explain the causes of World War I.
2. Describe the key events of World War I.
3. Analyze the instability following the war and the rise of dictatorships.
4. Evaluate developments in science and art during this period.
5. Outline the causes of the Great Depression.

1910–35

Archduke Francis Ferdinand is assassinated, leading to World War I June 28, 1914

Chinese revolution ends Qing dynasty 1911

America's Congress declares war on Germany April 6, 1917

Lenin signs treaty with Germany and takes Russia out of the war 1918

Washington Naval Conference 1921–2

1910 1915 1920

Vladimir Lenin becomes the first Communist dictator of Russia 1917

Mussolini seizes power in Ital

Paris Peace Conference 1919

Chapter 17 Lesson Plan Chart

Section Title	Main Activity	Pages	Days
I. Prelude to World War I	Activity 1: Alvin York and His Struggle with War	308–10	1–1½ days
II. Course of the War	Activity 3: World War I Review	311–16	1–1½ days
III. Instability Following the War	Discussion Activity: Dictators	316–21	1–1½ days
IV. Developments in Science and Art	Discussion Activity: Media	322–24	1–1½ days
V. The Great Depression	Activity 4: "The Only Thing We Have to Fear . . ."	325–26	1–1½ days
Total Suggested Days (including 1 day each for review and testing)			7–9½ days

Materials List

Section I
- Activities 1 and 2 from the *Student Activities* manual

Section II
- CD:17A Sides in World War I; 17B German Submarine
- Activity 3 from the *Student Activities* manual

Section III
- CD: 17C Lenin; 17D Lenin and Stalin; 17E Stalin; 17F Hitler; 17G Mussolini

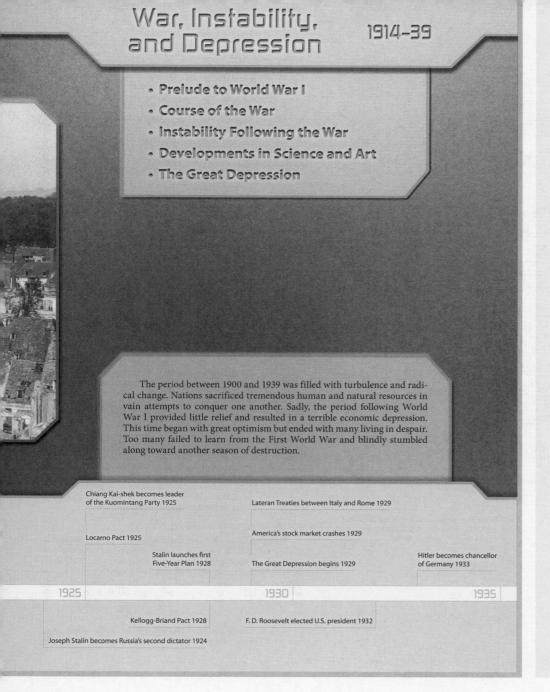

War, Instability, and Depression   1914–39

- Prelude to World War I
- Course of the War
- Instability Following the War
- Developments in Science and Art
- The Great Depression

The period between 1900 and 1939 was filled with turbulence and radical change. Nations sacrificed tremendous human and natural resources in vain attempts to conquer one another. Sadly, the period following World War I provided little relief and resulted in a terrible economic depression. This time began with great optimism but ended with many living in despair. Too many failed to learn from the First World War and blindly stumbled along toward another season of destruction.

Chiang Kai-shek becomes leader of the Kuomintang Party 1925

Lateran Treaties between Italy and Rome 1929

Locarno Pact 1925

America's stock market crashes 1929

Stalin launches first Five-Year Plan 1928

The Great Depression begins 1929

Hitler becomes chancellor of Germany 1933

1925

1930

1935

Kellogg-Briand Pact 1928

F. D. Roosevelt elected U.S. president 1932

Joseph Stalin becomes Russia's second dictator 1924

Section IV
No materials

Section V
- Activities 4 and 5 from the *Student Activities* manual

Section I

Students should be able to

1. Analyze the role of European alliances in contributing to war.
2. Explain how science and technology contributed to a more lethal war.
3. Explain the role of the Balkans in triggering the war.

Science and Technology

When God created humans in His image, He gave them the skills needed for solving problems and developing technology. Because of the Fall, these skills are often used with improper motivations. Those with a secular worldview often develop and use technology to foster self-reliance—as if technology could solve all the problems created by the Fall. Fallen men can also use their technological prowess to commit evil deeds. Christians, on the other hand, ought to develop technology in obedience to God's command to subdue the earth and with the goal of demonstrating love to their neighbors. God has given humans the ability to mitigate some of the effects of the Fall, and He is pleased when man uses those abilities in such efforts as disease prevention. All human effort ought to be guided by proper respect for and fear of God.

I. Prelude to World War I

Competition between nations continued during this period. However, the struggle for additional territory or disputed territory often became heated. Nations continued to have an exaggerated sense of nationalism, and in Europe war remained a popular way to demonstrate a nation's importance. In addition, states that had been absorbed in the last century struggled to regain their freedom. Alliances formed and dissolved as nations played a dangerous game of checking and blocking their opponents. In addition, old opponents became new allies as European powers sought to gain an advantage against a neighboring state or potential foe in battle.

Rivalries

England, France, and Spain had traditionally regarded each other as rivals. However, during this period newly formed nations, such as Germany, surged forward and turned former rivals into allies. In addition, former allies changed priorities and often became rivals.

Economic

Recently unified Germany quickly industrialized. By the beginning of the twentieth century, Germany came close to its goal of replacing Great Britain as Europe's primary industrial nation. Other European countries lagged behind and struggled to modernize their industries.

Political

You learned in Chapter 12 that Germany humiliated France in 1870. France remained hostile, and Bismarck, Germany's chancellor, made alliances with other European powers to isolate the French diplomatically. Later in the chapter we will briefly examine some of these alliances.

The English worked to maintain their isolation from the political strife that plagued western Europe. However, Britain could not remain neutral forever. Soon the British would have to give their support to one of these feuding countries.

Russia, always looking for more Ottoman territory, encouraged Balkan states to drive the Ottoman Turks out of the Balkans. Russia sought to influence and later dominate the Balkan region.

THE DOGS OF WAR.

British cartoon showing Russia and the Balkan countries trailing the aging Ottoman Empire while Britain looks on with concern

Faith in Science and Technology

Faith in science, technology, and progress became prominent at the beginning of the twentieth century. Men began to believe that they could solve any problem and cure all of society's ills. Ultimately, this confidence led nations to stumble into a war that could not be resolved quickly. This war would exhaust the greatest military and scientific minds as they desperately attempted to overcome their enemies.

Science

Scientists made a number of discoveries about the atom and its structure. For the first time in history, scientists leaped from using

Scientific Discoveries

The fourth edition of *Biology* and the third edition of *Chemistry* from BJU Press contain additional information about scientific discoveries during this period.

Scientific Advances

Ask a volunteer to compile a list of significant scientific advances prior to World War I and share this with the class.

the term *atom* as a philosophical term to using it as a scientific term. Additional experiments led to the discovery that the atom had negatively charged particles called electrons. Continued research greatly expanded understanding of the nature of the atom and its enormous potential.

In addition, physicians developed a process to reveal and confirm the causes of certain diseases. For example, in the 1870s German physician Robert Koch discovered the cause of a disease called anthrax. This disease spreads from animals such as cattle to humans and can be deadly. Koch's discovery helped others learn how to understand the spread of other diseases.

Ongoing research led to a number of other scientific discoveries by the end of the nineteenth century. These findings opened new fields of experimentation and study. Such revelations encouraged men to believe they could ultimately unlock the secrets of the universe.

Technology

Improvements in processing steel and the production of electricity and chemicals led to a tremendous growth of technology during this period. European countries used these advances to build infrastructures, modernize their militaries, and multiply wealth as new products became available.

In addition, developments in chemicals resulted in mass production of paper, soaps, and fertilizer. Germany became the largest producer of chemicals. Among other achievements, German scientists developed synthetic dyes and improved ways to refine oil.

Causes of the War

There are many theories about the causes of World War I. We will look at some of the basic causes that led to this destructive period of warfare between nations.

Militarism

Several European nations built militaries with capacity far beyond the need for defense. A large army and navy became an expression of national glory and a symbol of power. In addition, the military dominated the government of some nations. Sadly, during the early twentieth century, citizens often glorified war without regard for its justification.

Imperialism

You learned about imperialism in Chapters 15 and 16. The competition for colonies continued into the twentieth century. Nations such as Germany and Italy still sought to gain access to foreign lands in order to compete with Britain and France. This increasing rivalry led to tension and suspicion among the European states.

Rival Alliances

Bismarck made an alliance with Russia and Austria-Hungary that protected Germany against an attack by France. When this agreement fell apart, he allied Germany with Austria-Hungary and Italy. In addition, Bismarck arranged a secret treaty with Russia known as the **Reinsurance Treaty**. He considered this treaty crucial to protecting German interests.

However, when **Wilhelm II** became the ruler of Germany in 1888, he dismissed Bismarck and allowed the Reinsurance Treaty to expire. France took advantage of this blunder and convinced Russia

Arm & Hammer advertisement from circa 1900

Anthrax

Some scientists have developed anthrax, a naturally occurring disease, into a deadly biological weapon that is capable of killing large numbers of people. This is an example of fallen man's using technology to commit evil. However, man's attempts to develop protection against the spread of anthrax illustrate the use of technology to mitigate some effects of the Fall.

Anthrax caused widespread concern shortly after the 9/11 attacks when several envelopes containing a white powder thought to be anthrax were mailed to various people, including some involved in the government and the media.

The disease's spores are spread through physical contact or inhalation, and anthrax is often lethal if the victim does not receive an antidote soon after being exposed to the spores.

German Technology

The same technology that German scientists used to make fertilizer prior to World War I proved useful in making explosives during the war. In addition, the Germans produced poison gas for artillery shells using technology that was originally developed to produce synthetic dyes for industry.

Entangling Alliances

Rival alliances contributed to the outbreak of World War I. Several of the Founding Fathers of the United States warned against such entangling alliances. Time has demonstrated the wisdom of their cautions.

Wilhelm II

Ask a volunteer to read about Wilhelm II and present a report to the class.

The Balkans

This region remains a powder keg in the present day. During President Clinton's administration, America intervened in a war between Bosnia and Serbia in this region. United Nations forces remain in the area to maintain a fragile peace.

to sign an alliance with the French. Wilhelm then proceeded to provoke Britain by ordering the construction of a massive naval fleet. Continued German miscalculations convinced England to end its isolation. To defend against German aggression, Britain and France developed an *Entente Cordiale* (friendly understanding).

In 1907 Russia joined this loose confederation, and these three nations formed the **Triple Entente**. Germany and other European states would soon test this system of alliances, which would ultimately lead to a world war.

The Balkans

The Balkan region, located in southeastern Europe, has a long history of conflict, whether it was between ethnic groups or from invading forces. In addition, several states, including Russia, the Ottoman Empire, and Austria-Hungary, had overlapping claims to land in this region. These overlapping claims, combined with a growing sense of nationalism in the Balkans, made this area the "powder keg" of Europe. In other words, any spark of war in this region could ignite a major war throughout Europe.

De Agostini/Getty Images

In 1912 several Balkan states united to drive out the Ottoman forces. Following a brief war, the Balkan states decisively defeated the Ottomans. However, they fought among themselves over remaining Balkan territory.

The spark that ignited the crisis that became World War I began on **June 28, 1914**. On that date, a Bosnian radical (based in Serbia) assassinated Archduke **Francis Ferdinand**, heir to the throne of Austria-Hungary. The Austrian government then made demands that the Serbian government could not meet. Germany responded by pledging its support to the Austrians, while Russia mobilized in order to defend Serbia.

Francis Ferdinand and his wife moments before their assassinations

Germany demanded that Russia stop mobilizing its forces within twelve hours. When Russia failed to comply, Germany declared war on Russia. This decision led to a rapid series of declarations of war. Germany, Austria-Hungary, and the Ottoman Empire formed the **Central Powers**. On the other side, Russia, Serbia, and France formed the **Allies**.

Section Quiz

1. What nation did Germany strive to replace as the industrial power of Europe?
2. How did advances in science and technology change the way people thought about the world?
3. What country became the largest producer of chemicals during this period?
4. Why did European nations develop large militaries?
5. What country took advantage of Germany's failure to renew the Reinsurance Treaty with Russia?
★ Why were the Balkans known as the "powder keg" of Europe?

Activity 1: Alvin York and His Struggle with War

This is an excerpt from the writings of Alvin York, the great American hero. It provides a glimpse of the struggle he endured about going to war and possibly having to kill enemy soldiers.

Activity 2: Sergeant York

This is an excerpt from the diary of Alvin York. It helps students understand the intense fighting that American soldiers encountered in World War I. York's understated account also reveals how he risked his life to save many American soldiers and convince many Germans to surrender.

Section Quiz Answers

1. Britain
2. People thought science and technology could unlock the secrets of the universe and solve all man's problems.
3. Germany
4. national glory; symbol of national power; the military domination of some governments; civilian glorification of war
5. France
★ The Balkan region had a history of conflict; several European countries had overlapping claims in this region; the Balkan states had a growing sense of nationalism. Any spark of war in the Balkans could quickly ignite a major war throughout Europe.

Archduke Francis Ferdinand

Ask a volunteer to study the life of Archduke Francis Ferdinand and share his research with the class.

II. Course of the War

As Europe rushed to war, both sides were confident that they would win and that the war would be over quickly. German forces made the first move, and the French quickly responded. However, the war dragged on, and casualties swiftly climbed into the millions with little to show for the massive loss of life. After four brutal years, the war finally ended, but its conclusion laid the groundwork for another war in less than twenty-five years.

Initial Movements

Germany had the initial advantage and sought to make short work of the French by quickly attacking Paris. The French did not initiate the conflict, but they responded with surprising speed. The Russians surprised everyone and disrupted Germany's carefully planned strategy.

Sides in World War I

Germany

With France on the west front and Russia on the east front, Germany found itself fighting a two-front war. However, this did not take the Germans by surprise. Several years earlier a German general named Schlieffen prepared a strategy that would enable Germany to win a two-front war. The **Schlieffen Plan** called for the Germans to send most of their forces west through neutral Belgium and quickly surround Paris. Once France surrendered, the German forces would rush to meet the advancing Russian forces on the eastern front.

When the Germans demanded the right to travel through Belgium, the Belgians refused. However, the Germans broke their treaty with Belgium and forced their way through. This violation brought Britain into the war on the side of the Allies.

Section II

Objectives

Students should be able to

1. Define the major turning points of the war.

2. Assess the significance of nationalism and propaganda in the promotion of a total war.

3. Analyze how industrial production and innovations affected the tactics, scale, and duration of the war.

Rapid Reaction

European nations reacted quickly once officials made the decision to declare war. Armies can respond quickly when military leaders plan strategies for reacting to hypothetical incidents ("What if country X attacks us? What if country X attacks allies Y and Z?"). These strategies are often rehearsed in the military exercises that nations use to train their military forces for actual combat.

CD: 17A Sides in World War I

This map from the student text is also available on the CD.

The Great War

Visit www.bjupress.com/resources for possible links to articles about World War I.

France

The French stopped the German advance outside of Paris and re-inforced their troops at the Marne River. Taxicabs from Paris helped to deliver troops to the front. Despite the German push into France, the French held their position. British forces soon joined the French and helped to prevent German forces from advancing.

Russia

The Russian army surprised the Germans by mobilizing more quickly than anticipated in the Schlieffen Plan. Russian forces enjoyed initial success against German and Austrian forces. However, under the command of General Paul von Hindenburg, German troops defeated the Russians and seized more than two hundred thousand Russian prisoners. German victories demoralized the Russian troops, driving them back to Russia. Although the Germans ended the Russian threat, they had to keep troops on the border to prevent another attack.

Stalemate

While the Germans were able to end the Russian threat from the east, armies on the western front sacrificed large numbers of troops without major gains on either side. This condition is known as a **stalemate**. As the two sides established battle lines, the troops dug a long series of trenches that extended from the English Channel to the border of Switzerland.

Over-running these entrenched forces proved to be nearly impossible. For example, the British carried out a series of battles along the Somme River in 1916. Four months of fighting cost the British six hundred thousand men with only a slight gain of territory. When German forces attacked French positions, they suffered the same tremendous loss of life with similar results.

Industrialism and Innovation

Industrial production of modern weapons made possible such horrific loss of life. Inventors designed machines that could fire hundreds of bullets per minute. Thus, a small, well-armed force could slaughter thousands of enemy troops. In addition to machine guns, flamethrowers could spray a deadly stream of burning liquid into trenches and foxholes.

Early British tank

Designers of artillery invented shells filled with poisonous gas. Many on both sides suffered terrible burns and agonizing deaths from the deadly contents of these shells. Once fired, the deadly gas was blown by the wind. No one was safe, not even civilians.

The British gained a temporary advantage by secretly developing the tank. Tanks finally enabled the Allies to overrun the German trenches. However, the Central Powers quickly developed measures to

Comparing Casualties

During the Battle of the Somme, the British lost about 600,000 men in four months. In contrast, the total loss of life in the American Civil War totaled just over 650,000 men in four years. Twentieth-century inventions and innovations that enabled men to kill more rapidly and efficiently resulted in horrific loss of life in a much shorter period of time.

Tanks

Ask a volunteer to research the development of tanks and present a report that includes photos of tanks from the First World War to the present.

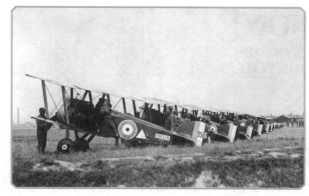

American planes used during WWI

Getty Images

German zeppelin

Captured German submarine

stop the tanks. Adapting rapidly, the Germans also developed tanks. By the end of the war, both sides had produced more than eight thousand of these offensive weapons.

In addition, aircraft changed the dynamic of war. Both sides initially used airplanes to monitor the troop activities of their enemies. However, they were soon equipped with bombs and machine guns to enable them to kill enemy troops and pilots. The Germans also used zeppelins (aircraft similar to blimps) to bomb civilian areas of England.

While the British enjoyed naval supremacy, the Germans introduced a lethal weapon to neutralize Britain's advantage. German submarines sank over six thousand Allied ships. The British started using blimps to spot German submarines, and they developed depth charges to destroy them.

Propaganda and Total War

Governments on both sides used every available form of media to maintain support for their side while demonizing the enemy. Propaganda emphasized national pride and

CD: 17B German Submarine

This photo from the student text is also available on the CD.

Balance of Power

One of the reasons the United States entered the war was to maintain a balance of power in Europe. In other words, U.S. leaders sought to prevent any one group from gaining too much power since this leads to a monopoly of power by that group. As in the business world, competition is healthy. Since a German victory would severely alter the balance of power in Europe, the United States sought to offset the German threat by supporting those who were in danger of defeat.

Propaganda posters

the atrocities (real and exaggerated) committed by the enemy to mobilize civilian support for **total war**. A total war is a war in which all the resources of a country are devoted to destroying the enemy.

In addition, total war brought the war to civilians, who became targets during the war. As previously mentioned, Germans bombed civilian areas with zeppelins. They also fired artillery from great distances, and exploding shells often struck civilian targets. As the war took its terrible toll, food became scarce and strikes became common among those who were suffering. Civilian deaths from attack, disease, and famine climbed into the millions.

Major Turning Points

Russia's disastrous defeats at the hands of the Germans resulted in the collapse of central government in Russia. Czar Nicholas II stepped down on March 15, 1917. In 1918 the new Communist Russian leader, **Vladimir Lenin**, signed a treaty with the Germans and took Russia out of the war. This freed the German forces to concentrate on the western front and possibly defeat the Allied forces.

The Germans had angered the United States on several occasions, including their sinking of two American vessels. Also, the United States sought to maintain a balance of power in Europe. Therefore, at the request of President Woodrow Wilson, Congress declared war on Germany on April 6, 1917. At first the American forces had little influence on the war. However, during the war's final months, America sent over two hundred and fifty thousand troops to France every month. The American forces provided the Allies with a much-needed advantage and helped defeat the German forces.

Propaganda

Ask a volunteer to research the use of propaganda and have him present examples in a report to the class.

Aftermath of the War

The war had led to the deaths of millions and resulted in immense destruction of property. Representatives from major nations met and worked out treaties. However, World War I did not end with a decisive defeat. The Germans agreed to sign an armistice (truce or ceasefire) because they believed that the Allies would treat them fairly. The outcome proved to be very different.

The Paris Peace Conference

Delegates from thirty-two nations attended the **Paris Peace Conference** in January 1919. The Allies excluded countries that had supported the Central Powers. They also excluded Russia because of its early withdrawal from the war.

Representatives formulated five treaties, with the **Treaty of Versailles** being the most important. This treaty between the Allies and Germany contained harsh demands and blamed Germany for the war. Germany lost territory and its colonies and was ordered to pay massive reparations (payment for war damages). In addition, Germany would have to reduce its military capability dramatically.

Armenian Genocide

Most of the Armenians came under control of the Ottoman Empire in the 1400s. When the empire began to decay in the 1800s, the Ottomans began to view the Armenians as a threat. The Armenians were Orthodox Christian, whereas the Ottoman Turks were Muslim.

In addition, many Armenians lived in nearby Russia. The Russians hoped to use the Armenians in the Ottoman Empire in their ongoing attempt to seize more Ottoman territory. When the Armenian people began asking for more self-rule, the Ottomans responded violently.

Over one hundred thousand Armenians died in the first round of killing in the 1890s. Another round of repression in 1909 saw the deaths of over thirty thousand more. The Ottomans resorted to genocide (the planned killing of a race of people) during World War I.

When the war broke out, some Ottoman leaders feared the Armenians might side with the enemy. Others saw an opportunity to settle "the Armenian question" permanently. At first there was the harassment, tor-

Armenians on deportation march

ture (such as nailing horseshoes to the feet of victims and making them dance), and killing of individuals.

In 1915 the violence dramatically escalated. Ottoman officials decided to eliminate all the Armenians living in the Ottoman Empire without regard for women, children, and the disabled. The Ottomans had determined that Armenian existence must come to an end.

Soldiers killed Armenians without restraint. They shot them, bayoneted them, or burned them to death in their houses. Then the Ottomans decided to march the survivors over two hundred miles to detention camps in Syria and Palestine. Guards killed some on the march, and a vast majority of the others died of hunger, abuse, or disease. For example, one group began the journey with eighteen thousand Armenians. When they arrived at the detention camp, only one hundred and fifty had survived.

Estimates vary, but approximately 1.5 million Armenians died between 1915 and 1923. This attempted genocide forced another half-million Armenians to live in exile.

Only a small population of Armenians remains in Turkey today. Despite a large body of evidence supporting the attempted genocide, the nation of Turkey denies that the slaughter ever took place and refuses to use the term *genocide*.

Armenian Massacres

Turkish authorities and others continue to deny that Armenian civilians were brutally slaughtered prior to and during World War I. However, Adolf Hitler is reported to have referred to the "annihilation of the Armenians" in a speech to members of the Wehrmacht at his home one week before the German invasion of Poland (Sept. 1, 1939). In his speech Hitler boldly proclaimed that the imminent war had as its goal the "physical destruction of the enemy" and explained that such destruction included "men, women, and children of Polish derivation and language." Hitler justified this slaughter as the necessary means to "gain the living space" that he claimed the German people needed. He concluded by saying, "Who, after all, speaks today of the annihilation of the Armenians?" Hitler counted on the short memory of the world to enable him to massacre the Poles just as the Turks slaughtered nearly two million Armenians. Hitler's gamble led to World War II and ended Germany's dream of conquest.

(Hitler's words are inscribed on a plaque at the United States Holocaust Memorial Museum in Washington, D.C. to prevent viewers from forgetting either the slaughter of the Armenians or the atrocities of the Third Reich.)

Activity 3: World War I Review

This activity reviews the course of World War I. It is designed to help your students improve retention and test for comprehension before they proceed to the events following World War I.

Treaty of Versailles

Compare and contrast the Allies' severe demands for reparations after World War I with the United States' policy toward its enemies following World War II. For example, after World War II, the U.S. provided Germany, Italy, and Japan with the resources to rebuild their countries and restore their economic and political structures. Following World War I, France and Britain punished Germany with financially crippling war reparations and stripped Germany of mineral-rich regions that the country needed to rebuild its economy.

Treaty of Versailles

Visit www.bjupress.com/resources for possible links to articles about the Treaty of Versailles.

The War to End All Wars

President Wilson and others sought to build support for the Allied cause by assuring the world that this war would be the last war fought on the planet. However, in Matthew 24:6–7, Christ declares that war and its deadly consequences will remain a part of human experience until His return. Any claims to the contrary will always be proved false.

Section III

Objectives

Students should be able to

1. Explain the rise of dictatorships following the war.

2. Describe the struggle for a lasting peace through organizations and agreements.

3. Analyze the changes in Asia, Africa, and the Middle East following World War I.

Nicholas II

What's in a Name?

The violent wing of the Social Democratic Party represented a minority of the party. Yet, for propaganda purposes, they took the name Bolshevik, which means "majority". The moderate wing of this party comprised a solid majority of the Social Democrats, yet their opponents called them the Mensheviks or minority wing of the party. The fact is that the Communists never had anything like a majority in the Soviet Union. It is remarkable that less than ten percent of the population could control the Soviet Union for nearly seventy years.

The Cost

It is almost impossible to comprehend the losses that both sides sustained in this terrible war. Ten million men died in battle, and twenty-six million more were wounded or missing in action. Civilian deaths may have equaled the number of those killed in battle. About fifteen thousand people died for each day of the war.

In addition to the tremendous cost in human lives, the direct and indirect costs of the war exceeded three hundred and fifty billion dollars. Some believed that the cost had been so great that no nation would ever go to war again. They would tragically be proven wrong within a few years.

Section Quiz

1. Who made the first military move in World War I?

2. How did the Russians upset the Schlieffen Plan?

3. How did industrialism and innovation increase the death toll in World War I?

4. What weapon did the Germans use to reduce the impact of British naval superiority?

5. Briefly define "total war."

6. What were two major turning points in World War I?

★ After tens of millions of dead and wounded, many thought that World War I was the war to end all wars. But roughly two decades later a second world war broke out. Why would such devastation not actually cause war to cease, as many thought? Reference James 4:1–3 in your answer.

III. Instability Following the War

The world following the war proved to be much different than it had been before the war. Democracies struggled to survive, and nations turned to dictators who promised them security and stability. The United States and several European powers labored to secure a long-term peace, but their reasoning excluded the reality of man's fallen nature.

In addition, major changes occurred in Asia and other areas as European imperialism began to lose its influence. The world proved to be very unstable, and no amount of precaution could overcome the human drive to seek power and dominate weaker nations.

Rise of Dictators

Russia—The Rise of the Soviet Union

In Chapter 16 you learned about the conflict in Russia. Despite brutal suppression by the czar and the central government, unrest continued to grow. During the reign of Czar Nicholas II, many radical parties formed in Russia. One of the most radical, the Social Democratic Party, soon split. The more radical faction took the name **Bolsheviks**, and the more moderate faction became known as the **Mensheviks**. The Bolsheviks supported violence, while the Mensheviks sought change through peaceful methods.

While many events contributed to the overthrow of the Russian monarchy, violent strikes and riots beginning on March 8, 1917, quickly led to Nicholas's abdication on March 15. Initially, a tem-

Section Quiz Answers

1. Germany

2. They mobilized faster than the Schlieffen Plan had anticipated.

3. New weapons such as machine guns and flamethrowers enabled horrific loss of life. Airplanes and zeppelins were used to drop bombs on the enemy.

4. the submarine

5. A total war is a war in which all the resources of a country are devoted to destroying the enemy.

6. Russia made peace and left the war; the U.S. declared war on Germany and began sending troops to France.

★ The devastation of war occurs because peoples and nations are willing to murder to obtain what they covet.

Dictators

Have students discuss why dictators such as Lenin and Stalin fear religion in general and Christianity in particular. They consistently strive to eliminate and defame Christianity by teaching their people that religion is bad.

porary government led by Menshevik Alexander Kerensky tried to stabilize the chaotic conditions in Russia. However, the Bolsheviks sabotaged these efforts and stirred up Russian workers to prevent the possibility of Menshevik success.

While exiled in Switzerland, Vladimir Lenin led the Bolshevik party. In a strategic move, the German government enabled Lenin to return to Russia from exile. As we learned earlier, Lenin signed the peace treaty that removed Russia from the war and aided the German cause in World War I. On November 7, 1917, Lenin's forces took over the government offices in St. Petersburg. With little effort, Lenin became the virtual dictator of Russia.

While Lenin embraced Marxist teaching, he disagreed with Marx on several issues. First, Lenin rejected the possibility of peaceful change in favor of violent revolution. Lenin also believed that revolution would only occur under the direction of strong leadership, instead of the spontaneous revolts by the working class taught by Marx. Third, Lenin limited power to a small elite group who would exercise great authority, rather than Marx's dream of a dictatorship by the masses.

Lenin also became a strong opponent of religion. He declared that atheism was a vital and inseparable part of Marxist teaching. Agreeing with Marx, Lenin declared religion to be "the opium of the people." He viewed religion and churches as tools used to take advantage of the working class.

Lenin's hatred of religion quickly transformed from rhetoric to bloodshed. For example, in 1918 when pastors and priests dared to oppose Lenin's violent tactics and his orders to empty the churches of valuables, he ordered the military to put down their resistance with great brutality. In addition, Lenin instructed his forces to execute large numbers of religious leaders.

When Lenin died in 1924, two of his followers, Leon Trotsky and **Joseph Stalin** (1879–1953), struggled for control of the Communist Party in Russia. However, Stalin quickly outmaneuvered Trotsky and became the second dictator of the Soviet Union.

In 1928 Stalin launched the first of several Five-Year Plans. Using these plans, Stalin tried to build up industrial production and brought agriculture under central government control. However, many peasants opposed Stalin's plan to control agriculture. Stalin used the secret police and army to burn the homes of offending peasants. Authorities also deported or executed those who resisted. Stalin's forces crushed the resistance and, in the process, destroyed over half of the homes in Russia.

Stalin also continued and intensified oppression of religion. The Soviet government systematically closed thousands of churches and religious schools. Stalin also ordered the execution of an unknown number of pastors and priests. Many Christians suffered terrible persecution during the vicious assault on Christianity under Communist rulers like Stalin.

Germany—The Rise of the Nazi Party

At the end of World War I, German delegates formed the **Weimar** (VEYE mar) **Republic** (named after the town in Germany where the republic was organized). Despite early optimism, this German government had little opportunity to succeed. Most Germans did not support it. In addition, the large number of political parties in Germany made it very difficult for one party to win a majority in elections.

Vladimir Lenin

Joseph Stalin

Roger Viollet/Getty Images

Lenin and Stalin

Vladimir Lenin grew concerned about the growing power and ruthlessness of one of his assistants—Joseph Vissarionovich Stalin. In 1923, one year before his own death, Lenin wrote a document that became known as Lenin's Testament. In this document he suggested changes to the Soviet system and commented on the leading Soviet officials. Despite Lenin's request that this document be read at the Twelfth Party Congress in the spring of 1923, his wife retained his work and kept it a secret. Following his death on January 21, 1924, she presented Lenin's Testament to the Communist Party Central Committee Secretariat and asked that it be read to the delegates at the next party congress.

In the document, Lenin criticized the three men who ruled the party—Joseph Stalin, Grigory Zinoviev, and Lev Kamenev—as well as others, including Leon Trotsky. However, he advised the removal of only one Soviet leader from power—Joseph Stalin. Lenin described Stalin as a man who had unlimited authority, without the ability to use that authority "with sufficient caution." Lenin realized that the struggle for power between Stalin and Trotsky would inevitably split the party, and he counseled the removal of Stalin to prevent such a schism.

However, Stalin controlled the people's access to Lenin's Testament to preserve his own position and later declared mention of Lenin's work to be "anti-Soviet agitation." The Soviets finally published Lenin's Testament in 1956, three years after Stalin's death.

CD: 17C Lenin; 17D Lenin and Stalin; 17E Stalin

Additional portraits of Lenin and Stalin are available on the CD.

Animal Farm

Have one or more of your students read George Orwell's *Animal Farm* and present an overview of the book to the class. Through this work, Orwell cleverly exposes the hypocrisy of absolutist regimes.

Lenin

The Unknown Lenin: From the Secret Archive by Yale University Press provides an excellent look into Lenin's documents and real intentions, including his animosity toward religion.

Chronology of Russian History

Visit www.bjupress.com/resources for possible links to articles about Russian history.

Russian Baptists

Visit www.bjupress.com/resources for possible links to articles about Baptists in Russia.

Weimar Republic

Visit www.bjupress.com/resources for possible links to articles about the Weimar Republic.

Hitler's Rise to Power

It is a tragic irony that Adolf Hitler came to power using legal means. The Weimar Republic had a constitution and guaranteed free elections, but those political restraints alone do not prevent the rise of evil men to power. The United States is not guaranteed continued freedom just because it has a constitution and free elections. Americans' failure to exercise diligence could easily lead to a tragedy in America, like the one that befell Germany. The price of freedom is constant vigilance to ensure that elected officials do not strip citizens of guaranteed freedoms through legislation or by fiat from unelected bureaucrats.

Adolf Hitler

Basic Principles of Fascism

1. Businesses are privately owned but tightly controlled by the government.

2. Fascists place an extreme emphasis on nationalism and glorify the state.

3. Dictators supported by the military often govern in a fascist state.

Benito Mussolini

With the growing unpopularity of the Weimar Republic and continued political instability, radical groups became more popular. One group, the National Socialist German Workers' Party (commonly known as the **Nazi** Party), became a contender for power. Led by **Adolf Hitler**, the Nazis used the political process to gain control of the German government in 1933.

However, once in power, Hitler suspended the republic and declared himself the dictator of Germany. Using the principles of fascism, the Nazis controlled industry and used it to rebuild Germany for future military conquest. One example is the modern highway system throughout Germany. This road system would enable German troops to move rapidly from one front to another in the event of another two-front war. Hitler also worked to make Germany self-sufficient (able to produce everything needed by the country). Self-sufficiency would limit the ability of enemy forces to cut off supplies in a time of war.

Italy—The Rise of Fascism

Italy had supported the Allies during the war and had suffered the loss of five hundred thousand men. However, Italy received no territory or colonies. Instead, the Italian economy suffered from a large war debt and strikes by discontented workers. The wealthy looked for protection from a possible Communist revolution, and the masses wanted a strong leader to restore Italy's national pride.

Benito Mussolini had been a member of the Socialist Party in Italy, but he proved to be too violent for the Socialists. As a result, he formed the Fascist Party and quickly gained popularity. In his writings and speeches, Mussolini promised order and stability. Sensing that the government was vulnerable, Mussolini led thousands of followers in a march on Rome in October 1922. King Victor Emmanuel III agreed to the Fascists' demand that he appoint Mussolini the leader of Italy.

Mussolini gradually transformed Italy into a dictatorship. While he maintained the image of a representative government, Mussolini and the Fascists sought to gain total control over the government. Within three years, the transition was complete, and Mussolini became the absolute ruler of Italy.

Like Hitler, Mussolini set about to make Italy economically self-sufficient. In order to accomplish this goal, he organized Italy's work force into thirteen groups. The Fascists carefully monitored and controlled all economic activity. They also determined wages, prices, and other policies that affected the economy.

In order to add the appearance of legitimacy to his rule, Mussolini ended the long-standing dispute with the Roman Catholic Church. In 1929 Mussolini and Catholic representatives signed the **Lateran Treaties**. These agreements ended Rome's opposition to the unification of Italy that had continued since 1870. Until 1929 the papacy had refused to cooperate with succeeding Italian governments. However, in exchange for money and a small independent region known as Vatican City, the pope recognized Mussolini's government and ended the papacy's prior claims to additional territory.

Struggle for a Long-Term Peace

Led by men like President Wilson, many nations sought a way to ensure that the world would never again experience a major conflict like World War I. Leaders formed organizations to promote peace and enable non-violent resolution of conflicts. Others embraced

 ## CD: 17F Hitler; 17G Mussolini

Additional portraits of Hitler and Mussolini are available on the CD.

...armament (doing away with weapons) as a way to prevent future ...nflicts.

...ague of Nations

Following World War I, U.S. President Woodrow Wilson led in ... formation of the **League of Nations**. Wilson and other founders ...ieved such an organization could bring about international co-...eration. They hoped to achieve peace by preventing future wars.

However, the United States Senate refused to ratify the treaty ...t formed this League. The League only had power to recommend ...ion. It had no power to enforce its recommendations. The League ...n proved to be weak and ineffective, especially when dealing with ...werful nations.

...sarmament and Nonaggression Pacts

In a continuing effort to prevent future wars, nations signed ...ee pacts or agreements. These agreements were doomed to fail ...ause they did not take into account man's fallen nature.

Several nations met in 1921–22 for the **Washington Naval Con-...ence** and agreed to limit the number of war ships each could build. ...e participants assumed that nations could avoid war by simply ...ucing or eliminating the weapons. However, Japan's participation ...he conference did not prevent it from continuing to build a large ...al fleet.

In 1925 European nations met in Locarno, Switzerland. At this ...eting, Germany signed an agreement with France and Belgium ...ognizing her present borders with those two nations as perma-...t. In theory, this would have prevented World War II. The **Lo-...no Pact** briefly offered the promise of peace in Europe.

In 1928 the American secretary of state, Frank Kellogg, decided ...t the best way to prevent war was to get nations to agree to re-...nce offensive war. Those who signed the **Kellogg-Briand Pact** ...eed to settle their disputes by negotiation rather than force. Kel-...g naively believed that this agreement could prevent wars from ...ng started. However, three years after signing this pact, Japan in-...ed Manchuria.

...ifts in the Post-War World

European imperialism, described in Chapters 15 and 16, changed ...r World War I. Sadly, colonies did not gain their freedom, al-...ugh many demanded it. However, China entered into a struggle ...reform and independence that continued after the end of World ...r II. Japan made a radical shift from being a European ally in the ...st World War to being a major threat heading into the Second ...rld War. African nations that had been governed by Germany ...w came under French and British rule. Finally, the Middle East ...nsferred from Ottoman rule to French and British rule.

...ina—The Struggle for Power

In Chapter 16 you learned about the decline of the Qing dynasty ... its continued resistance to change. By 1911 young Chinese of-...als, along with military officers and students, staged a revolution ...replace the Qing dynasty with a republic. Led by **Sun Yat-Sen**, ...Chinese worked to bring reform to China. However, others pres-...ed Sun Yat-Sen to postpone reform and allow the last Qing mon-...n to abdicate. He soon regretted agreeing to this compromise. ...fortunately, Chinese prime minister Yuan Shikai took advantage

Sun Yat-Sen

Nonaggression Pacts

Discuss with the class what it takes to make nonaggression pacts work. *(mutual trust and honesty on the part of all signatories)* What do these agreements overlook? *(man's tendency to break promises to benefit himself)*

 ## Washington Naval Conference

Visit www.bjupress.com/resources for possible links to articles about the Washington Naval Conference.

Chiang Kai-shek (1887–1975)

Born to a merchant family in the Cheki-ang province of China, Chiang Kai-shek became one of China's most important soldiers and political leaders. At the age of nineteen, Chiang initiated his military career at the Paoting Military Academy in northern China. He gained military experience by serving in the Japanese army (1909–11) and made friends with fellow Chinese soldiers living in Tokyo. While there, he joined with others who plotted to free China from the Qing (Manchu) Dynasty. In 1911, after hear-ing of the rebellion in China, Chiang returned home and participated in the fighting. In 1918 he joined Sun Yat-Sen and the Nationalist or Kuomintang par-ty. Sun sent Chiang to Russia in 1923 to learn the Soviet system of rule; however, Chiang quickly decided that the Soviet system would not work in China.

The Chinese Communist Party, un-der the leadership of Mao Zedong, increased in power and struggled for control of China. Chiang led his armies against this Communist threat. How-ever, by 1936, Chiang was forced to develop a temporary alliance with the Chinese Communists and turned his military attention to the growing Japa-nese threat.

Following World War II, the Soviet Union supported the Chinese Communists and ensured their victory against Chiang and his forces. Chiang and his followers had little choice but to relocate to the island of Taiwan. Generous American aid, free enterprise, and hard-working Taiwanese people soon turned Taiwan

Left, Chiang Kai-shek; *right,* Mao Zedong

of Sun Yat Sen's restraint and used his influence to dismantle the new republic before he was forced to step down in 1916. As a result, a power vacuum developed and Sun Yat-Sen struggled to bring unity to China through the **Kuomintang** (KWO min TAHNG) or Nation-alist Party.

Following the death of Sun Yat-Sen in 1925, **Chiang Kai-shek** (CHANG KYE-shek) (1887–1975) became the leader of the Kuom-intang. In 1927, a radical element of this party split off into what became the **Chinese Communist Party**. Led by **Mao Zedong** (1893–1976), the Communists stirred up peasant revolts in order to under-mine the conservative government of Chiang Kai-shek. These two forces fought a civil war gain control of China. The Japanese inva-sion in 1931 postponed this struggle until the conclusion of World War II.

Japan—The Rise of Militarism

The military developed a strong influence in Japan during the Meiji Restoration. As Japan became more aggressive toward China and other countries, this influence grew into control. Japanese lead-ers viewed a strong military as essential for expanding and control-ing Japan's overseas empire.

Japan developed a form of fascism to manage the growing econ-omy. Fascism combined with the growth of monopolies (when a per-son or company has control over a product or service) enabled Japan to quickly grow into a major financial power. A strong economy and a strong military combined to form a military state with a growing appetite for foreign territories.

Mandate System and Colonial Rule

The League of Nations established a procedure that enabled France and Britain, primarily, to take possession of colonies previ-ously ruled by the Central Powers. Some American observers com-plained that Britain and France merely divided the colonies to suit their interests. The map indicates which regions in Africa and the

Mao Zedong

Visit www.bjupress.com/resources for possible links to articles about Mao Zedong.

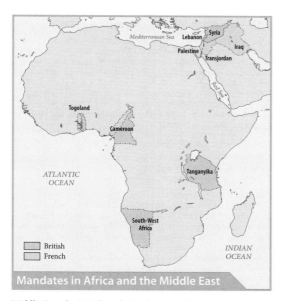

Mandates in Africa and the Middle East

Middle East the British and French governed under the mandate system.

Middle East

During World War I, Arabs began to seek a united state of Arabia and an Arab League that would spread from the west coast of northern Africa to Saudi Arabia. This secular movement, known as **Pan-Arabism**, suffered several setbacks, including the Balfour Declaration in 1917, which authorized the British to administer Palestine. Later, the creation of the nation of Israel provided a major obstacle that resulted in many failed attempts to destroy this tiny country. The destruction of Israel has remained the goal of Arab nations, in part because of the dream of Pan-Arabism. More recently, this has transformed into a religious movement with the growing influence of what many refer to as militant Islam.

Section Quiz

1. Into what two groups did the Social Democratic Party (Russia) split? What do their names mean?

2. Who became the first two dictators of Russia?

3. What German republic fell to the Nazis?

4. What nation supported the Allies during the First World War but turned to a dictatorship after the war?

5. What was the goal of the Kellogg-Briand Pact?

6. Name the first two leaders of the Kuomintang Party.

★ Respond to the new atheist claim that religion is the root of wars, conflicts, and mass killing around the world.

into an economically powerful force in Asia.

Pan-Arabism

The desire for Arab unity can be traced back to the time of Muhammad in the seventh century. However, its modern revival began near the end of the nineteenth century and continues to this day. At the beginning of the twentieth century as the Ottoman Empire disintegrated, Arab states won their independence. The formation of the Ba'th Party in 1943 provided united leadership for many Arabs in Middle Eastern countries including Syria and Iraq. The founding of the Arab League in 1945 resulted in increased Arab unity. However, no significant leader appeared to lead the movement until 1952 when Gamal Abdel Nasser seized power in Egypt. In 1956 he became president of Egypt through an election in which his was the only name on the ballot. Nasser ruled from 1956 to 1970 and used his substantial influence to promote Pan-Arabism.

Since Nasser's death in 1970, other Arab leaders have endeavored to maintain Arab unity. These leaders have included Hafiz al-Assad of Syria, Saddam Hussein of Iraq, and Muammar al-Qaddafi of Libya.

Section Quiz Answers

1. Bolsheviks and Mensheviks; "majority" and "minority," respectively

2. Lenin; Stalin

3. Weimar

4. Italy

5. to prevent nations from starting wars to settle disputes

6. Sun Yat-Sen; Chiang Kai-shek

★ Most of the killing done during the twentieth century was the work of atheistic dictators. Many of those they killed were Christians.

Section IV

Students should be able to

1. Describe some of the great scientific advances that occurred between the wars.
2. Analyze how the art produced during this period reflected the pessimism of the age.
3. Explain how the media communicated Western ideas and culture around the world.

Albert Einstein

Einstein was a Jewish physicist who fled Nazi Germany in the 1930s to take refuge in the United States. He wrote a letter to President Roosevelt warning the United States that German scientists were working fervently to develop an atomic bomb. Roosevelt then authorized the development of the Manhattan Project, enabling the United States to become the first nation to produce such a weapon.

Albert Einstein

Visit www.bjupress.com/resources for possible links to articles about Albert Einstein.

IV. Developments in Science and Art

Scientists continued to make progress in many fields and made many important discoveries. During this period scientific discoveries and inventions transformed transportation. In addition, scientists helped to develop products that eventually became affordable to most people.

Postwar literature and art reveal the emptiness and disillusionment that characterized many in this generation. Their expectations were dashed when they discovered that material wealth and possessions did not lead to happiness.

Great Scientific Leaps

We will briefly examine how physicists made major contributions to scientific theory. In addition, we will examine the influence of science on transportation and products for the common man.

Scientific Experiments and Theories

French physicists **Pierre and Marie Curie** pioneered work in radioactive matter. They also discovered that radioactive elements could be reduced to simpler elements. The Curies contributed to the growing body of knowledge about the building blocks of the universe.

Albert Einstein made tremendous contributions to science with his theories on the relationship between matter and energy ($E=mc^2$) and relativity. His work led others to refer to Einstein as the father of modern physics. In addition, he theorized about the existence of black holes in space and other celestial concepts that helped man realize the vastness of our universe.

Albert Einstein

Science Transforming Transportation

Scientific research used discoveries in fields such as math, physics, and chemistry to develop many improved modes of transportation, including the airplane. Between the first flight and the end of World War I, the airplane changed dramatically. World War II would elevate the airplane to an essential tool for war.

In addition, many scientific discoveries combined to produce a vehicle that was self-propelled. We refer to this scientific marvel as the automobile. Scientists continued to play a role as larger and more powerful engines powered cars, trucks, and weapons such as tanks.

Another invention that underwent tremendous change because of science was the railway. From slower wood-powered steam locomotives to faster coal and then diesel-powered engines, the railway continued to progress. Important during times of peace, it became essential during the next war.

These various modes of travel affected commerce positively. Industry relied on these forms of transportation to get goods to the market quickly. In addition, these vehicles enhanced migration within and between nations. For example, laborers could more easily travel to locations where they could find work. The middle and upper classes could also travel in comfort for work or vacation.

Mass Consumption

Additional products became mass produced and available to an eager public. Products such as bicycles, refrigerators, and radios became very popular in many nations. Continued scientific discoveries and improvements made these products less expensive to produce and thus affordable to more people. Credit enabled the eager customer to buy the latest product immediately and make payments later on the balance.

Chemists continued to experiment with natural materials and chemical combinations. Artificial fibers made from wood included rayon and acetate. Scientists developed the first synthetic fiber, nylon, in 1939 as a substitute for silk. Gradually artificial and synthetic fibers became the raw materials for products used around the world.

Postwar Art

The Allies had triumphed over the Central Powers, and many experienced financial wealth after the war. However, much of American and European society found life to be empty and ultimately futile. To them, feelings became more important than facts. These feelings found expression in literature and art. Even architecture changed during this period.

Literature

Literature following World War I often reflected the despair and emptiness of modern life. For example, T. S. Eliot (1888-1965) wrote an intricate poem entitled "The Waste Land" that attempted to describe this emptiness. German writer Thomas Mann (1875–1955) wrote works whose main characters were passive victims of forces beyond their control. Much of the literature from this period expressed misery and gloom.

Painting

Two schools of art emerged during this period, **Expressionism** and **Cubism**. Expressionist painters created art that reflected how the artist felt about his subject, rather than what he saw as he painted his subject. Cubist painters reduced their subjects to geometric shapes (often cubes). This school of painting attempted to depict

Left, The Scream by Edvard Munch, example of Expressionism; *right, Le guitariste* by Pablo Picasso (1910), example of Cubism

AFP/Getty Images

T. S. Eliot

Visit www.bjupress.com/resources for possible links to articles about T. S. Eliot.

Thomas Mann

Visit www.bjupress.com/resources for possible links to articles about Thomas Mann.

Walter Gropius

(1883–1969)

Walter Adolph Georg Gropius, a German architect and founder of the Bauhaus School of architecture, is considered one of the pioneers of modern architecture. Gropius, a third-generation architect, had a serious drawback—he could not draw. Therefore, Gropius depended on others to put his ideas on paper. Nevertheless, he placed an indelible mark on modern architecture.

Gropius suffered a near-fatal setback when German authorities drafted him to serve in the German army during World War I. He fought on the western front and almost died from a severe battle wound.

In 1919 Gropius became the master of the Grand Ducal Saxon School of Arts and Crafts in Weimar. Under his leadership, this school was transformed into the world-famous Bauhaus—the birthplace for much of modern architecture.

By 1934 the Nazis had taken control of Germany, and Gropius, taking a temporary visit to Britain, used this opportunity to flee Germany. Following a brief stay in Britain, he moved to the United States and continued to influence modern architecture through his teaching at the Harvard Graduate School of Design.

the subject from several perspectives at once. Cubist painters often designed their works to astonish the observer and confront his view of the world.

Architecture

Using concrete, glass, and steel, architects designed buildings with a sense of openness and functionality. American architect Louis Sullivan (1856–1924) developed the concept of skyscrapers. Walter Gropius (1883–1969) developed the concept of functional architecture in Europe. Frank Lloyd Wright (1868–1959), an American architect, added his own personal touch by designing buildings that blended in with their surroundings.

Left, building designed by Walter Gropius; *right,* home deisgned by Frank Lloyd Wright

Getty Images

Louis Sullivan's Prudential Building, Buffalo, New York

Media

Improved printing machines and mass production of paper from wood pulp lowered the cost of producing various forms of print, including newspapers and magazines. Commercial advertising also multiplied as companies paid to get the public to notice and buy their products.

During this period, moving pictures developed, and scientists soon found a way to add sound. Movies became a popular and inexpensive form of entertainment. Continued improvements to the radio led to mass production, and soon no home was complete without one. Through print, picture, and sound, these forms of media became effective means of communicating ideas and aspects of culture around the world.

Section Quiz

1. With what type of matter did the Curies make discoveries?
2. What sciences contributed to improved modes of transportation?
3. What did Expressionist painting reflect?
4. What characterized architecture during this period?
5. How were ideas and culture spread around the world during this period?
★ Why did materialism fail to result in happiness?

Media

Discuss the impact that media such as advertising, radio, and movies have had on our culture. Help the students understand how these could be used to unite nations in the next world war.

Section Quiz Answers

1. radioactive
2. math, physics, and chemistry
3. how the artist felt about his subject
4. openness, functionality, and blending into one's surroundings
5. newspapers, magazines, advertising, films, and radio
★ Humans are not merely material beings. Therefore, an abundance of material goods can never meet people's deepest longings.

V. The Great Depression

Following World War I, some nations seemed to recover and prosper financially. Others struggled and found themselves awash in national debt. The United States appeared to be able to absorb massive war debt and yet prosper. However, that apparent prosperity faded and economic fractures began to appear. Many blame the stock market crash in 1929, but that was only a symptom of underlying problems. The costs of the Depression created a great burden for the world to bear, and the consequences endure to this day.

Causes of the Depression

The causes for the **Great Depression** are many, and historians continue to debate this subject. However, we will briefly look at three basic problems that the United States experienced leading up to the Depression. By this period, America had grown into one of the most prosperous nations in the world. Therefore, when America experienced an economic downturn, many other nations also suffered.

Financial Devastation of World War I

The United States had loaned the Allies over ten billion dollars during the war. This increased the national debt from about one billion dollars to twenty-four billion dollars in three years. While most of the Allies promised to pay back their debt, only Finland actually repaid the United States. When European nations experienced financial problems, they simply refused to pay their war debt to America. This placed immense stress on the American economy.

Failure of the Federal Reserve

In 1913, the U.S. Congress created the **Federal Reserve** to control the money supply and help protect the American banking system. To accomplish these goals, the Federal Reserve had the power to set interest rates and loan money to banks.

However, the Federal Reserve raised interest rates four times during 1928 and 1929, from three and one-half to six percent. This doubling of the interest rate had a negative impact on the U.S. economy. Increased rates made it very hard for businesses to borrow money and invest. This hindered economic growth and contributed to the stock market crash in October 1929.

Protectionism

As the U.S. economy weakened in the late 1920s, American companies began to pressure presidential candidate Hoover and members of Congress to pass tariff legislation that would raise the prices on foreign goods and protect American-made products. In response, Congress debated and passed the highest tariff (duty or tax on foreign products) in U.S. history. In 1930 President Hoover signed the **Smoot-Hawley Tariff Act**, and many European states quickly responded with restrictive tariffs of their own.

This tariff resulted in American exports dropping from seven billion dollars in 1929 to two and one-half billion dollars in 1932. The loss of trade devastated the American economy, and the damage spread throughout many nations as one government after another imposed tariffs on imported goods.

Costs of the Depression

The United States and other nations had experienced financial panics and brief depressions many times prior to 1929. However, this

The Danger of Tariffs

The Smoot-Hawley Tariff made many foreign products much more expensive. For example, this tariff increased the price of Swiss watches. The Swiss responded by placing a high tariff on automobiles and other products made in America. However, the Swiss bought more American cars than Americans bought Swiss watches. Therefore, the American automobile and other industries suffered more than did the Swiss watch industry. This shortsighted tariff cost many American jobs.

Section V

Objectives

Students should be able to

1. Analyze causes of the Great Depression.
2. Explain the costs of the Great Depression.

The Great Depression

Visit www.bjupress.com/resources for possible links to articles about the Great Depression.

Federal Reserve

Ask a volunteer to read about the history of the Federal Reserve and present a report to the class.

Consequences of the Depression

During the 1930s, several leaders, including President Roosevelt, abandoned capitalism and led their nations far down the road toward socialism.

Socialism also gained ground in European countries, including Britain. In 1900, several British socialist groups combined and formed the Labour Representation Committee. In 1906, members changed the organization's name to the Labour Party and gained strong influence through the electoral process. The growth of labor unions increased the power and size of the Labour Party in Britain. As a result, socialism spread through this dominant political party.

Activity 4: "The Only Thing We Have to Fear . . ."

This is the famous inaugural address made by Franklin D. Roosevelt in 1933. Students should compare his claims to the realities of his administration.

The New Deal

Burton Folsom Jr.'s work *New Deal or Raw Deal* is an excellent and well-documented resource for understanding the Great Depression.

Section Quiz Answers

1. The U.S. loaned over ten billion dollars to the Allies during the war.
2. a high tariff
3. four interest-rate hikes that eventually doubled the interest rate
4. Governments intervened and prevented natural economic corrections from occurring.
5. to create jobs and bring the U.S. out of the Depression; no
★ Answers will vary but should include some of the following: We know that God judges nations for their sins. The Great Depression was an unprecedented national disaster following a decade of materialism.

Activity 5: Chapter Review

This activity helps the students prepare for the chapter test.

Chapter Review Answers

Making Connections

1. Germany invaded Belgium.
2. to defend Serbia

time, the federal government in America and national governments throughout Europe took a much more active role in trying to revive their economies. Consequently, natural economic corrections did not occur. The Great Depression endured for many years with little improvement, despite massive spending of the taxpayers' money.

Unemployment

Massive unemployment became one of the immediate effects of the Depression. Up to one-third of the work force lost their jobs, and many people looked to government to meet their needs. Since the Depression began during the administration of Herbert Hoover, many blamed him for this economic downturn and pressured him to do something to help those in need.

Contrary to popular opinion, President Hoover did spend large amounts of taxpayer dollars to assist various areas of the American economy. However, despite his spending over two billion dollars, the unemployment rate remained high and recovery proved elusive.

Growth of Government

President Hoover began to increase the size of the federal government by supporting the Federal Farm Board to shore up the price of farm products. In addition, he endorsed the Reconstruction Finance Corporation and its efforts to help failing businesses.

Franklin D. Roosevelt, the Democratic candidate for president, repeatedly attacked Hoover's efforts as an unwarranted growth of federal government and wasteful spending of the nation's wealth. Ironically, following his election in 1932, Roosevelt set about to substantially grow and transform the federal government.

For example, Roosevelt established a growing number of federal agencies that were supposed to create jobs and bring America out of the Depression. His administration spent billions of dollars and created thousands of temporary make-work jobs. Yet the unemployment rate never dropped below fourteen percent, and the Depression continued.

Section Quiz

1. Why did the U.S. national debt grow from one to twenty-one billion dollars in just three years?
2. What did American companies demand from Congress to protect the competitiveness of American products?
3. How did the Federal Reserve make it difficult for businesses to borrow and invest?
4. Why did the Great Depression last longer than previous depressions?
5. Why did President Roosevelt establish a growing number of federal agencies? Did they help to end the Depression?
★ What may have been the divine purpose for the Great Depression?

3. The Germans believed that they could quickly defeat the French before Russian forces could mobilize.
4. They both had modern weapons and quickly adapted to fight new weaponry introduced by their enemies.
5. Both sides sought to maintain support for themselves by demonizing the enemy. They also needed to boost national pride and mobilize civilian support for total war.
6. He rebuilt the German infrastructure to prepare for future military conquest. The highway would enable German troops to respond quickly to a two-front war.

7. The Japanese invaded Manchuria in 1931.
8. Other nations retaliated with restrictive tariffs of their own. The U.S. lost much more than it gained by enacting this tariff.

Developing History Skills

1. Answers will vary but should include some of the following: Bismarck tricked others into going to war with Prussia; Prussia then quickly conquered these countries to gain land. Bismarck later used alliances to protect Germany from opponents such as France. Wilhelm II threatened German security by carelessly allowing vital treaties to expire. Under Bismarck, Germany achieved

CHAPTER REVIEW

Making Connections

1. Why did England side with the Allies in World War I?

2. Why did Russia mobilize its troops at the beginning of the war?

3. Why did the Germans send most of their forces against France at the beginning of the war?

4. Why were the Central Powers and the Allies unable to attain a quick victory?

5. Why did both sides resort to propaganda?

6. Why did Hitler rebuild the German infrastructure, including a modern highway system?

7. Why did the Kuomintang and the Chinese Communist Party temporarily stop fighting for control of China?

8. Why did the Smoot-Hawley Tariff lead to a drastic decline in American exports?

Developing History Skills

1. Compare and contrast German methods for acquiring land and using war to bring about German unity in Chapter 12 and this chapter.

2. Respond to the following statement: "The isolation of the Unites States following World War I contributed to the conditions that led to World War II."

Thinking Critically

1. Evaluate President Roosevelt's expansion of the federal government during the Great Depression.

2. Evaluate conditions leading to World War I in light of Bible passages such as Exodus 20; 2 Chronicles 16, 18; Psalm 20:7; and James 4:1.

Living in God's World

1. Write an essay for a technology magazine presenting a Christian view of a recent communications technology. The essay should discuss how Christians can wisely use the technology.

2. Read Amos 1:3–2:8 and 5:18–20. Imagine that you are a pastor who lived during World War I. Write a brief essay addressing Europe in light of Amos 1–2.

People, Places, and Terms to Know

Reinsurance Treaty
Wilhelm II
Triple Entente
June 28, 1914
Francis Ferdinand
Central Powers
Allies
Schlieffen Plan
stalemate
total war
Vladimir Lenin
Paris Peace Conference
Treaty of Versailles
Bolsheviks
Mensheviks
Joseph Stalin
Weimar Republic
Nazi
Adolf Hitler
Benito Mussolini
Lateran Treaties
League of Nations
Washington Naval Conference
Locarno Pact
Kellogg-Briand Pact
Sun Yat-Sen
Kuomintang
Chiang Kai-shek
Chinese Communist Party
Mao Zedong
Pan-Arabism
Pierre and Marie Curie
Albert Einstein
Expressionism
Cubism
Great Depression
Federal Reserve
Smoot-Hawley Tariff Act

---

unification. Under Wilhelm II, Germany endured a terrible war and was essentially destroyed.

2. Answers will vary but should include some of the following: The United States' isolation after the war emboldened aggressive nations to seize weaker nations without fear of U.S. intervention. But Americans played a leading role in seeking to prevent future wars, however naive these attempts may have been. In addition, Americans volunteered to fight in China against Japanese aggression, and President Roosevelt secretly aided the British prior to an American declaration of war. It is impossible to prove that American isolation contributed to World War II.

Thinking Critically

1. Answers will vary but might include some of the following: Every dollar that President Roosevelt spent on federal programs meant one less dollar for a natural recovery in the private sector. When the president created temporary jobs, he made it very difficult for companies to produce permanent jobs. Federal programs such as Social Security lived on long after the president had died, and many have had disastrous consequences for the long-term economy of the United States.

2. Answers will vary but should include the following: Militarism—European nations trusted in large armies and powerful weapons to protect themselves. However, Psalm 20:7 encourages people to trust in God, not in military might. Imperialism—European states seized and conquered weaker nations. However, Exodus 20:17 prohibits coveting, and imperialism violates that command from the Lord. Rival alliances—Germany, France, and other nations trusted in alliances for security. However, we see examples in 2 Chronicles 16 and 18 that demonstrate the futility of alliances if God does not bless them. Political instability in the Balkans—This region has a history of ethnic violence and has often been invaded. James 4:1 reminds us that wars and fighting come from man's lusts, or strong desires. The solution is not found in war, but in submitting to God (James 4:7).

Living in God's World

1. Answers will vary but should include benefits such as businesses' and missionaries' being able to communicate quickly across long distances. Answers should also include detriments such as the fostering of distracted, non-contemplative lives. Students should also note practical steps that can be taken to minimize the detriments.

2. Answers will vary but may include the following: In light of all that Europe had been doing in turning away from the Lord, some believe that this was a "day of the Lord" for Europe. There was a permanent change for Europe in world history. In the years after World War I and World War II, Europe was no longer a center for the spread of Christianity as it had been since the time of the late Roman Empire.

Roger Viollet/Getty Images

Chapter Goals

Students should be able to

1. Explain the causes of World War II.
2. Outline the course, outcome, and human costs of the war.
3. Analyze the philosophical and religious consequences of the two decades following the First World War.

1935–46

Anti-Comintern Pact is signed
November 1936

Nonaggression Pact between Germany and the Soviet Union
August 1939

Rome-Berlin Axis is formed
October 1936

Japan invades China
July 1937

Munich Conference is held
September 1938

Germany invades Po
September

| 1935 | 1936 | 1937 | 1938 | 1939 | 1940 |

Italy's army conquers Ethiopia
October 1935–May 1936

Francisco Franco becomes fascist dictator in Spain
July 1936–April 1939

Pact of Steel is formed
May 1939

Chapter 18 Lesson Plan Chart

Section Title	Main Activity	Pages	Days
I. Causes of the War	Activity 1: The Bombing of Rotterdam	330–35	1½–2 days
II. Course of the War	Activity 2: Churchill's Inspiring Words	335–41	2–2½ days
III. Consequences of the War	Activity 4: Chapter Review	341–45	1–1½ days
TOTAL SUGGESTED DAYS (INCLUDING 1 DAY EACH FOR REVIEW AND TESTING)			6½–8 days

Materials List

Section I

- CD: 18A Emperor Hirohito; 18B German and Italian Expansion; 18C Soviet-Japanese Nonaggression Pact
- Map of Asia
- Activity 1 from the *Student Activities* manual

Section II

- CD 18D WWII European Theater of Operations; 18E WWII Pacific Theater of Operations; 18F Model of the "Fat Man" Atomic Bomb
- Activities 2 and 3 from the *Student Activities* manual

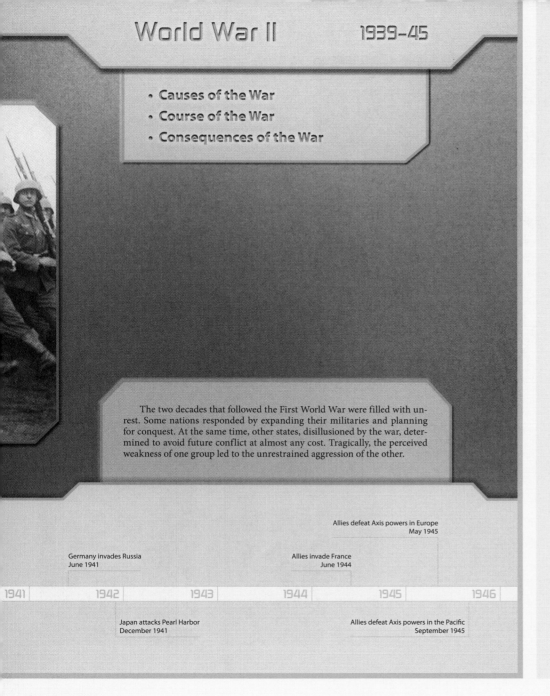

World War II　1939–45

- Causes of the War
- Course of the War
- Consequences of the War

The two decades that followed the First World War were filled with unrest. Some nations responded by expanding their militaries and planning for conquest. At the same time, other states, disillusioned by the war, determined to avoid future conflict at almost any cost. Tragically, the perceived weakness of one group led to the unrestrained aggression of the other.

Allies defeat Axis powers in Europe
May 1945

Germany invades Russia
June 1941

Allies invade France
June 1944

| 1941 | 1942 | 1943 | 1944 | 1945 | 1946 |

Japan attacks Pearl Harbor
December 1941

Allies defeat Axis powers in the Pacific
September 1945

Section III
- Activity 4 from the *Student Activities* manual

Section I

Objectives

Students should be able to

1. Explain how authoritarian regimes seized power in Spain and Japan.
2. Analyze the underlying causes of World War II.
3. Describe Japanese, Italian, and German military conquests and empire-building in the 1930s.
4. Evaluate the failure of Western democracies to effectively oppose fascist aggression.
5. Analyze the causes of the war and the reasons for early Axis victories.

Francisco Franco

I. Causes of the War

Fascism multiplied and spread in Europe and Asia. In addition, old wounds created by the harsh treaties signed following World War I refused to heal. Land-hungry states began to seize territory from weaker neighbors. The democratic states hesitated to respond with the threat of force. This situation became a recipe for another world war.

Spread of Dictatorships

In addition to Italy and Germany, Spain came under the leadership of a dictator. Furthermore, Japan's military continued to gain power even as the civilian government steadily lost influence. This military growth enabled the figurehead emperor to gain real power because he supported the Japanese military.

Europe

In the last chapter you learned about the rise of fascism in Italy and Germany. In 1936 **Francisco Franco**, a general in Spain, overthrew the republican government and imposed a fascist dictatorship in Spain. Mussolini and Hitler supported Franco and used the Spanish Civil War to test their new weapons and tactics in preparation for future conquest. This war became a practice run for World War II.

Japan

In addition to adopting fascism, Japan transformed into a society where the representative civilian government declined in influence as the military steadily gained more power. As a result, the power of the emperor also increased since Emperor **Hirohito** played an active role in military decisions. General Hideki **Tojo** also played a central role in expanding the power of the military in Japan and supporting Japanese conquest. However, rather than dominating the emperor, General Tojo maintained a strong loyalty to Emperor Hirohito. He faithfully carried out the emperor's wishes, including the decision to attack the U.S. naval fleet.

Left, Hirohito, 1919; *right,* Hideki Tojo, 1940s

Emperor Hirohito

Hirohito and the Making of Modern Japan by Herbert P. Bix is a good resource for anyone who would like to learn more about the active role this Japanese emperor played in events leading up to and during the war.

 ### CD: 18A Emperor Hirohito

An additional photo of Emperor Hirohito is available on the CD.

Legacy of World War I

In the last chapter you learned that the Allies treated the Central Powers harshly following their agreement to stop fighting. For example, the war guilt clause in the Treaty of Versailles placed all of the blame for World War I on the Germans and their allies.

In addition, the Central Powers lost territory at home and abroad. Germany especially suffered great hardship in this loss of land and colonies. A revived and well-armed Germany under Hitler would quickly address this German grievance.

Furthermore, the demand that Germany pay the Allied nations huge sums in the form of war reparations destroyed the German economy and led to the chaos that enabled the rise of the Nazi party. Germany would not be satisfied until these injustices had been corrected.

Aggression in the 1930s

The fascist countries took advantage of their growing military power and expanded their borders at the expense of their neighbors. When the democracies failed to challenge this aggression, the facist states continued their expansion.

Japanese

The Japanese had taken a progressively more dominant role in Manchuria. In 1931 someone destroyed a section of railroad in Manchuria controlled by the Japanese. The Japanese used this event as justification to invade Manchuria and seize additional land. China protested, but no European powers intervened to stop the Japanese aggression.

Japan became increasingly bold and staged a major assault on China beginning in 1937. This attack forced the Nationalist Party and the Chinese Communists to suspend their struggle for control of China in order to resist the Japanese invasion.

When the League of Nations protested this invasion in 1937, the Japanese simply ended participation in the league. Japan brutalized China and seized its many natural resources to build its military.

When war erupted in 1939 with the German invasion of Poland, Japan expanded into Southeast Asia. Japanese forces seized several islands and heavily fortified them. The United States and Great Britain objected to this expansion and blocked shipments of oil to Japan. This move threatened to cripple Japan's fleet and end Japanese imperialism.

Italian

In Chapter 15 you learned that Italy suffered a humiliating defeat when it tried to conquer Ethiopia in 1896. In 1935 Mussolini sent a well-equipped, modern army into Ethiopia and quickly conquered this poor African country. Despite pleas by the Ethiopian leader to the League of Nations, Europe made no serious attempt to stop or punish Italian aggression.

The League of Nations proved unable or unwilling to respond to aggression. Mussolini took advantage of this weak response and seized Albania in 1939. The Italians had been increasing their influence in this strategic country for several years.

Haile Selassie I, Emperor of Ethiopia, before the League of Nations after Mussolini's invasion of Ethiopia

Nanking Massacre

Mass murder and indescribable physical violence followed the 1937 Japanese capture of Nanking, the Republic of China's capital, during the Second Sino-Japanese War. For six weeks, Japanese soldiers went on a rampage, murdering hundreds of thousands of Chinese civilians and unarmed Chinese soldiers. In addition, thousands of Chinese women endured brutal assaults. Exact numbers cannot be determined because the Japanese authorities systematically destroyed evidence of such crimes at the end of the war. However, the International Tribunal of the Far East refers to over 200,000 victims. Chinese officials estimate that 300,000 people perished at the hand of the Japanese military during this massacre. Officially sanctioned Japanese brutality occurred many times during World War II. These types of vicious assaults on the Chinese, Koreans, and other East Asian peoples have had long-term repercussions and periodically strain relationships between Japan and other East Asian nations.

Early Japanese Aggression

To provide the students with context for the early Japanese invasion of mainland China, consider using a map of Asia to point out the location of Manchuria.

League of Nations

Ask a volunteer to read about the League of Nations and present a report to the class. Have the student include strengths and weaknesses of the League.

Haile Selassie

Ask a volunteer to read about Ethiopian emperor Haile Selassie and present a report to the class.

Third Reich

The nations should have known what Hitler was planning. He had written about many of his ambitions in his autobiography *Mein Kampf* ("My Struggle"). It was translated into English, and many Americans bought this work. In addition, many films of Hitler's speeches were translated and shown in theaters in many countries, including the United States.

"Legitimate Claims"

Hitler concealed his boundless ambition for conquest with the seemingly legitimate claims that he desired only to unite all German-speaking peoples and that the Germans needed more living space (*Lebensraum*).

German and Italian Expansion 1935–39

- Rhineland
- Sudetenland
- Axis Powers
- Axis-controlled lands, Sept. 1, 1939

When the Albanian king refused to submit to Italian domination, Italian forces seized control of Albania.

German

As soon as Hitler came to power in 1933, he began to carry out his goals to make Germany a world power and a nation free of "defective" and "undesirable" citizens. Later in the chapter we will examine this second goal in detail.

Hitler centralized his nation's resources to construct a new German empire. To defend this **Third Reich**, Hitler needed to establish a military presence in the neutral territory west of the Rhine River. He made a bold move and sent German troops into the Rhineland on March 7, 1936. The French responded with angry words, but no European nation moved to stop German expansion. Germany fortified this region to protect against future attack from France.

According to the Treaty of Versailles, Germany and Austria could not form a political alliance. Despite this restriction, Hitler secretly planned to gain control of this state. In 1938 he arranged to have an Austrian Nazi selected as the chancellor. The Austrian chancellor then invited Germany to send troops and stabilize Austria. Thus Germany and Austria defied the treaty. Germany became the dominant partner in this alliance.

Hitler's previous success emboldened him to demand that an area of Czechoslovakia, called **Sudetenland**, come under German control. To resolve this issue, British and French leaders met with Hitler at the **Munich Conference** in September 1938. Without even consulting the Czech government, the British and French leaders agreed to meet Hitler's demands.

Despite Hitler's promise not to invade Czechoslovakia, German troops marched into the Czech capital six months later and took control of most of the country. The weak response of Britain and France had led Hitler to conclude that he could continue to seize neighboring countries without fear of European interference.

Neville Chamberlain, Édouard Daladier, prime minister of France, Hitler, Mussolini, and Count Ciano, foreign minister of Italy, at the Munich Conference

---

CD: 18B German and Italian Expansion

This map from the student text is also available on the CD.

Suggested Reading

Some of your students may be interested in reading additional books about the Second World War. Suggestions include the following:

- *The Rise and Fall of Adolf Hitler*, a juvenile nonfiction work by William L. Shirer
- Books on the Jews' efforts to escape the Holocaust, such as *The Diary of Anne Frank*; *The Last Jew of Rotterdam* by Ernest

Cassutto; and *The Hiding Place* by Corrie ten Boom

Kristallnacht

Visit www.bjupress.com/resources for possible links to articles about *Kristallnacht*, the German assault on Jews in Nazi Germany.

Failure of Democracies to Oppose Aggression

As we have seen, Japan, Italy, and Germany learned that they could attack and conquer weaker states without fear of serious consequences. Much of Europe had not recovered from the destruction of World War I. As a result, leaders remained reluctant to resort to conflict. The empire-building fascist states took full advantage of this paralyzing fear and rushed toward another world war. For a time, the democratic nations failed to intervene and resist these acts of aggression.

Neville Chamberlain served as the prime minister of England. He led the European nations in a policy to avoid war by means of **appeasement** (avoiding conflict by making concessions). Chamberlain used Britain's influence to pressure weaker nations to submit to Hitler's demand for territory. European leaders, including French Prime Minister Édouard Daladier, followed Britain's lead and sought to appease Hitler and Mussolini.

The United States, under President Roosevelt, maintained a policy of isolation. Most Americans wanted to leave European conflict to the Europeans and supported Roosevelt's neutrality. In addition, many Americans continued to suffer under the Great Depression and had little interest in foreign affairs.

Events that Triggered the War

The aggressive nations gambled on the assumption that they could continue to seize land without war and that European leaders would continue to appease. However, the Europeans finally realized that these aggressive states would not stop until forced to do so by threat of war. To prepare for the coming war, or to try to prevent war, nations formed alliances to strengthen their position. Then lines were drawn, and the crossing of those lines would lead to war.

Alliances

Initially, Germany had no allies in Europe after World War I. Even Mussolini had opposed some of Hitler's early attempts at conquest. However, in 1936 Mussolini and Hitler formed an alliance called the **Rome-Berlin Axis**. Later that same year, Germany and Japan formed an agreement known as the **Anti-Comintern Pact**. This pact allied Germany and Japan against Communist Russia. In 1937 Italy and Japan signed a similar agreement. The three nations that would become the **Axis powers** were now connected.

The alliances against the spread of communism provided Europe with a false sense of security. Many European leaders feared communism more than they feared fascism. However, Hitler and Mussolini shattered the illusion of security when they signed a military alliance in May 1939 called the **Pact of Steel**.

The final shock came in August 1939 when Germany and the Soviet Union signed an agreement to refrain from attacking one another for the next ten years. This accord protected Germany from a two-front war and encouraged German conquest. Japan signed a similar agreement with the Soviets and helped to pave the way for continued aggression.

German Invasion of Poland

Over 1.5 million German troops rushed across the border into Poland on **September 1, 1939**. Despite Hitler's confidence that Britain and France would continue to appease, these countries demanded an immediate end to the invasion.

Soviet Foreign Minister Molotov signs the German-Soviet nonaggression pact; Joachim von Ribbentrop and Joseph Stalin stand behind him, Moscow, August 23, 1939.

American Isolation

Americans did not sense any great danger from events that occurred in Europe. They felt safe because America is separated from Europe by a vast ocean.

Comintern

Because of communism's stated goal to spread its ideology around the world by any means necessary, many nations opposed it. The fascist powers hated communism. They rallied around this common hatred and allied with each other as the Axis powers. *Comintern* is an abbreviation for Communist International, a Communist organization formed in Russia in 1919. During the 1930s, Germany and Italy lulled other European nations into a false sense of security by signing the Anti-Comintern Pact, thereby promising to oppose the spread of communism. However, the fascists were willing to make a "deal with the devil" and made empty promises not to attack Communist Russia. In exchange, Russia promised not to resist Axis plans to seize more territory.

 ## CD: 18C Soviet-Japanese Nonaggression Pact

A photo of the signing of this pact is available on the CD.

Appeasement

Have the class discuss reasons why appeasement does not work. Appeasement of dictators always seems to fail.

Japan

The United States became an obstacle that threatened to halt Japanese expansion. Japanese officials came to the conclusion that war with America was inevitable, given Japan's plans for conquest. Although there were differing viewpoints, supporters of an attack on the United States prevailed. These Japanese military leaders hoped to destroy the American naval fleet and remove any American military threat in the Pacific. Others saw the United States as a "sleeping giant" and feared that war would awaken the Americans and have disastrous results for Japan. The latter position proved to be correct.

Polish Resistance

The Polish forces fought bravely against the much larger German force from the west and the invasion of the Soviet Union from the east. Polish soldiers destroyed many German vehicles and nearly three hundred aircraft during the brief conflict. Although Poland became Hitler's victim of conquest, Polish forces continued to oppose German and Soviet occupation through a large resistance movement.

When Germany refused to comply with Allied demands regarding Poland, Britain and France declared war. Although the determination of the **Allies** surprised Hitler, he resolved to fight and take control of Europe. The Allies had declared war, but they were in no position to provide Poland with any military assistance.

Japanese Bombing of Pearl Harbor

The Japanese developed a two-track policy for dealing with the United States. Japanese diplomats continued to negotiate in an effort to get the United States to end economic restraints such as the oil embargo. However, the Japanese military, with the consent of the emperor, also prepared for war against the United States. When the Japanese concluded that war presented their best option for conquest of Pacific islands, they planned a major assault to end the American threat.

On **December 7, 1941**, the Japanese launched a surprise attack on the American naval base at **Pearl Harbor**, Hawaii. During this unprovoked assault, the Japanese forces killed more than two thousand Americans, destroyed most of the aircraft, and sank several battleships. Providentially, the American aircraft carriers were away on maneuvers and escaped destruction in the Japanese assault. This brutal attack quickly turned the previously neutral United States into a key Allied power.

Top left, Japanese Zeros preparing for takeoff;
top right, aerial view from a Japanese plane;
bottom left, a burned B-17C;
bottom right, USS *West Virginia* in flames

Pearl Harbor

Visit www.bjupress.com/resources for possible links to articles about the Japanese attack on Pearl Harbor.

"A Date Which Will Live in Infamy"

Visit www.bjupress.com/resources for possible links to articles or audio files about President Roosevelt's speech following the Pearl Harbor attack.

God's Samurai

God's Samurai: Lead Pilot at Pearl Harbor by Katherine V. Dillon, Donald M. Goldstein, and Gordon W. Prange is a fascinating biography of Mitsuo Fuchida, the lead pilot of the Japanese aerial assault on Pearl Harbor. The work includes accounts of Fuchida's many experiences during the war. Fuchida eventually trusted Christ as his Savior and was greatly used of God as an evangelist.

Activity 1: The Bombing of Rotterdam

This is a fictionalized account of the German bombing of Rotterdam at the beginning of Germany's unannounced attack on Holland (the Netherlands).

Section Quiz

1. Who rose to power in Japan as the military replaced the weak civilian government?

2. What country did Italy invade to avenge a previous defeat?

3. With what country was Germany forbidden to form a political alliance?

4. With what country did Germany and Japan sign an agreement to refrain from war?

5. At what military base did Japan attack American forces and trigger the United States' entry into World War II?

★ Why were the fascist powers able to seize territory without fearing serious opposition?

II. Course of the War

The Axis powers had prepared extensively for war and enjoyed the initial advantage. Using brutal tactics, they threatened to destroy the Allied forces. However, they made serious miscalculations and found the Allies to be a formidable force, especially when the U.S. entered the fight.

Principal Theaters of Conflict

This conflict was truly a world war. Battles occurred on several continents, and soldiers from many nations engaged in this deadly struggle. To varying degrees, nearly sixty countries participated in the Second World War.

Western Europe

In the spring of 1940, Germany invaded Denmark and Norway. Hitler especially wanted to prevent the Allies from developing military bases in Norway. Then the Germans attacked the Netherlands and Belgium. The British and French responded by rushing troops into Belgium to stop the Germans.

However, German forces anticipated this maneuver and slipped past French defenses south of Belgium. Then the German army swept into France, behind the Allied lines. Within one month, the Allied army found itself trapped near the English Channel on the beaches of Dunkirk. The German military could have easily destroyed this force and eliminated all possibility of future Allied military threats.

Nevertheless, Hitler decided to allow the German air force (**Luftwaffe**) (LOOFT vahf uh) to wipe out the Allied force composed of more than three hundred and fifty thousand troops. However, Hitler could not control the weather. While fog and clouds made it impossible for the *Luftwaffe* to launch air attacks, British citizens ferried the trapped Allies across the English Channel to safety in Britain.

With the defeat of the Allies, France quickly fell to the German conquerors. Germany occupied more than half of France and

WWII European Theater of Operations
- Major Axis Powers
- Maximum Areas of Axis Control
- Neutral Nations
- Maginot Line

Evacuation at Dunkirk
It is difficult to understand the evacuation of Allied forces from the beach at Dunkirk as anything less than an act of God. Fog, rain, and low cloud cover prevented the *Luftwaffe* from bombing this area for nine days. In addition, the channel was unusually calm, and mild winds blew from the east instead of the north as they often do. These conditions made it possible for more than eight hundred ships to carry the soldiers to safety.

Section II

Objectives
Students should be able to

1. Describe the principal theaters of conflict in World War II.

2. Define the major turning points of the war.

3. Analyze the events that led to the conclusion of the war.

Section Quiz Answers

1. Emperor Hirohito
2. Ethiopia
3. Austria
4. the Soviet Union
5. Pearl Harbor
★ European leaders sought to avoid war at any cost and tried to appease the aggressors by making concessions.

 ### CD: 18D WWII European Theater of Operations

This map from the student text is also available on the CD.

Silence over Dunkirk

Silence over Dunkirk by John R. Tunis is a juvenile novel about the successful evacuation of Dunkirk. Consider reading portions of the book to the students or recommending it as a good book to read outside of class. The book is written on a level that will enable your students to better understand this event in the history of World War II.

Winston Churchill

Visit www.bjupress.com/resources for possible links to articles about Winston Churchill.

Activity 2: Churchill's Inspiring Words

This is an excerpt from a speech given by Winston Churchill shortly after Germany conquered France. Churchill's optimism and defiance helped sustain the British during the Battle of Britain.

Invasion of Russia

Just as they had done when Napoleon invaded Russia, the Russians destroyed everything that could be used by the Nazis, employing a "scorched earth policy." This proved to be very effective against the Germans because the Germans had calculated on feeding and supplying their troops with Russian resources. However, this tactic also led to the starvation of many Russians as food became very scarce.

allowed a puppet French government to represent German interests in the unoccupied regions of France. However, many French citizens rejected the puppet regime and maintained an active resistance movement to hinder German occupation.

Hitler then began a bombing campaign against Britain to prepare for a land invasion. After destroying many military targets, the *Luftwaffe* began to bomb London and other British cities in order to kill civilians and destroy British morale. However, the bombing of civilian targets strengthened British resolve. In addition, the Royal Air Force (RAF) destroyed many German bombers and fighter planes. Hitler grew impatient with the resistance of the British and made a change in strategy that doomed the Third Reich to ultimate failure.

Russian soldier on his horse

Eastern Europe

Russia took advantage of the fighting in Western Europe. As previously mentioned, Russia invaded eastern Poland a few days after the Germans had begun their invasion. In addition, the Russians seized the small countries of Latvia, Lithuania, and Estonia. These conquests provided Russia with control of territory from the Baltic to the Black Sea.

Soviet Union

In 1940 German forces began to prepare for an invasion of Russia. Despite a peace treaty with Russia, Hitler determined to overrun this vast country and take advantage of Russia's many natural resources, including great oil reserves. The attack began on June 22, 1941, with three million Nazi troops rushing into Russia along an eighteen hundred mile front.

German forces quickly captured thousands of Russian prisoners and seized one-half million square miles of Russian territory. Despite the fact that the Russians suffered up to five million casualties, the Germans could not achieve victory. The severe winter saw temperatures that fell to forty degrees below zero. German forces could not advance, and most German equipment would not function in these extreme conditions.

Even after several more months of fighting in the spring, the Russians continued to resist and victory eluded the Germans. Gradually the Russian forces wore down the German army. In February 1943 the surviving German army surrendered.

North Africa

Italy had observed Germany's rapid conquest of Europe and decided to conquer North Africa. Since Britain was enduring German bombing and preparing against a possible Nazi invasion, Italy assumed it would have a free hand in Africa. However, the British troops in Africa proved to be more than a match for Mussolini's forces. The British expelled the Italians from Egypt and captured over one hundred thousand Italian troops.

Hitler responded by sending General **Erwin Rommel** in the spring of 1941 with highly trained German troops to rescue the Italians. Despite a lack of supplies and adequate forces, General Rommel advanced into Egypt and nearly defeated the British. In 1942 British

General Erwin Rommel

Weapons of World War II

Have volunteers build and bring to class models of some of the ships, planes, tanks, or other military weaponry used during World War II. As an alternative, have the volunteers find photographs of these weapons and write brief descriptions explaining how these weapons were used and by whom.

commander General **Bernard L. Montgomery** finally defeated the German forces that threatened British control of Egypt.

Pacific

Following the attack on Pearl Harbor, the Japanese military staged attacks on many islands throughout the Pacific. The Philippines became one of the victims of Japanese aggression. American soldiers on these islands concentrated their defenses on the island of Luzon and withstood Japanese attacks for several months. Finally, President Roosevelt ordered the American commander, General **Douglas MacArthur**, to leave the Philippines in order to escape capture. The Japanese treated captured American forces with great brutality, and hundreds died.

Japan also conquered several Dutch and British colonies with little resistance. However, Japan had conquered more than it could defend. General MacArthur became the supreme Allied commander in the Pacific, and the Allies gradually began to win key victories over Japan.

Two major naval battles in 1942 ended Japanese expansion and preserved Australia from a major Japanese invasion. The first battle occurred in the Coral Sea, northeast of Australia. American planes destroyed many Japanese ships. One month later, American forces discovered that the Japanese planned to attack **Midway Island**. The Americans had an important naval base on this island. Although the Japanese forces far outnumbered American naval forces, the Americans attacked first. American pilots sank several Japanese aircraft carriers and forced the Japanese to retreat.

American forces advanced toward Japan by capturing important islands that the Allies could use for air bases. They bypassed other islands and left the Japanese troops there stranded to await the end of the war.

General Bernard L. Montgomery

WWII Pacific Theater of Operations

Operation Torch

General Montgomery benefited greatly from the American amphibious landing in North Africa. The combined forces of Montgomery and Eisenhower made Rommel's defeat possible.

Doolittle's Raiders

On April 18, 1942, Lieutenant Colonel James Doolittle led a force of sixteen B-25B bombers to attack Japanese cities. Doolittle's planes launched from the USS *Hornet* in the western Pacific and flew east toward Japan's main islands. All sixteen planes were lost on this mission, and the bombs did little physical damage, but the psychological damage inflicted on the Japanese was immense. Following this attack, the Japanese military leaders made a series of decisions that contributed to their defeat.

The Doolittle Raid

Visit www.bjupress.com/resources for possible links to articles about the Doolittle Raid on Japan.

CD: 18E WWII Pacific Theater of Operations

This map from the student text is also available on the CD.

Missionary Account

Darlene Deibler Rose served as an American missionary in Papua New Guinea during World War II. Her work *Evidence Not Seen: A Woman's Miraculous Faith in the Jungles of World War II* provides a glimpse into her harsh treatment by the Japanese and her experience of the sustaining hand of God even when the Japanese imprisoned her.

D-day

June 6, 1944 was the day chosen by General Eisenhower to begin the invasion of Normandy on the northwestern shore of France. This invasion was also known as *Operation Overlord* and *Operation Neptune*. The air assault involved nearly 24,000 Allied troops entering at night by glider or parachute. The amphibious assault covered a fifty-mile region of Normandy's coast and involved about 160,000 troops. Over 5,000 ships were used to transport troops across the English Channel on the first day.

The Allies also staged decoy operations in other areas to conceal the actual invasion site.

General Dwight D. Eisenhower

Left, An American landing party lends helping hands to others whose landing craft was sunk by enemy action off the coast of France; *right,* Landing ships putting cargo ashore on Omaha Beach at low tide during the first days of the operation

Major Turning Points

Hundreds of battles occurred during the Second World War. While many important events took place, we will briefly consider several key decisions as turning points in the war. We have already examined Germany's invasion of Russia and Japan's attack on Pearl Harbor. The first event proved disastrous for Germany and resulted in the Nazis facing a two-front war. From this point on, Germany sought to defend against an Allied invasion. Additional conquest was no longer an option. The second event brought the sleeping giant of the United States into the war. As previously mentioned, American forces pushed toward Japan by island hopping, or seizing strategic islands while bypassing others. By the end of 1944, General MacArthur returned to the Philippines and American forces destroyed forty Japanese ships as the Allies regained control of these islands. By 1945 American forces captured Iwo Jima and Okinawa with terrible loss of life on both sides. From these islands, American bombers could strike Japan.

To make matters worse for Germany and Italy, when the U.S. declared war on Japan, Germany and Italy declared war on the U.S. This brought America into the European theater of the war. Soon American troops poured into Britain, bringing much-needed supplies and equipment. In 1942, under General **Dwight D. Eisenhower**, U.S. troops landed in North Africa and defeated Axis troops there within a year. Then, in 1943, Eisenhower led a force of 160,000 during an invasion of Sicily, an island off the coast of Italy. As the Allies advanced to Italy, the Italian government surrendered. However, large numbers of German troops continued to resist the Allied advance north through Italy.

The next important decision for the Allies was where next to invade Europe. After lengthy discussions between Churchill, Roosevelt, and Stalin, they decided to invade France. After much planning, on **June 6, 1944**, the Allies launched a massive invasion of France along a fifty-mile front on five beaches. One hundred and seventy-five thousand men landed and established a beachhead on that first day, which was known as **D-day**. Within three weeks, one million Allied soldiers, five hundred thousand tons of supplies, and nearly two hundred thousand vehicles had landed in France. The fighting in

D-day

Have a volunteer research and share with the class information about the invasion of France on D-day. Researched material could include photos of the naval landing, information about the gliders that landed behind enemy lines, and reasons why this risky invasion succeeded. It is also important to note how many Allied soldiers died to make this invasion a success.

Battle of the Bulge

Have a volunteer in your class research the details of this final German offensive and share his findings with the class.

Veterans

Have your class organize a special recognition ceremony for local veterans of World War II. This could be a wonderful outreach opportunity. As an alternative, have a World War II veteran speak to the class about his or her experiences during the war. (World War II veterans are dying at the rate of nine hundred to one thousand per day. Help the students realize the urgency of getting first-hand accounts from the rapidly diminishing number of survivors.)

Destruction of Nürnberg

Visit www.bjupress.com/resources for possible links to articles about the destruction of Nürnberg by the Allies in WWII.

Activity 3: The Iron Curtain

This is an excerpt from the speech made by Winston Churchill in 1946 about the spread of communism in Eastern Europe and the formation of the Iron Curtain.

Europe would continue for another year, but this successful landing sealed the fate of Germany.

The dropping of two atomic bombs on cities in Japan became one of the final turning points in the war. We will examine this in more detail in the next section.

Conclusion of the War

With the massive infusion of troops and military equipment from the United States, the Allies steadily regained territory from the Axis powers. British, French, and American forces pushed German forces out of one country after another. Soon the Allies had expelled the German army from almost every conquered territory. Continued Allied movements from the west and the east would ultimately compel Germany to surrender.

The Japanese fought with a fierce determination, and few lived to become prisoners of war. Most died in battle or committed suicide rather than allow themselves to be captured. However, their zeal proved to be no match for superior air and naval power. At great cost of life for the Allies and the Japanese, the Americans continued to close in on the Japanese islands. When the Allies demanded the surrender of Japan in 1945, Japanese resistance forced the Allies to use more and more destructive weapons to end the war.

Europe

American and British troops attacked German forces from the west while Soviet troops seized territory in the east that Germany had previously conquered. Allies liberated France and carried out intense bombing of German cities. By December 1944 the Allies in the west had reached the border of Germany. Hitler ordered a final push in order to break through a lightly protected section of the Allied line. This failed attempt became known as the **Battle of the Bulge**.

Germany had consumed much of its remaining military strength, but the Allies held the line and continued to advance into Germany. In the spring of 1945, the Allies waited west of Berlin and allowed the Russians to fight their way into Germany's capital from the east. On May 7 the Germans unconditionally surrendered. The Allies declared **May 8, 1945**, V-E Day for the victory in Europe.

Winston Churchill, Harry Truman, and Joseph Stalin at the Potsdam Conference

Popperfoto/Getty Images

Hitler's Suicide

Facing certain defeat and the invasion of Russian forces, Hitler committed suicide in his underground bunker on April 30, 1945. Instead of telling German troops the truth about Hitler's suicide, German authorities told them that Hitler died in the line of duty while fighting the Russian forces. German generals surrendered a few days later and ended the war in Europe.

Why Did Japan Resist Surrender?

Ask your students this question and have them offer some suggestions.

On several occasions, the Allies demanded that Japan surrender. As they edged closer to Japan, the Allied forces dislodged Japanese forces from the Philippines and several other Pacific islands. Defeat was inevitable, yet the Japanese government refused to surrender even after Allied bombers began to destroy Japanese cities. Why did Japanese leaders continue to send thousands of young men to their deaths in the face of superior Allied firepower?

Help your students understand that the Japanese considered themselves superior to other people. They had been indoctrinated with the myth that they were invincible and that their emperor was divine. This blind prejudice and national pride made the Japanese leaders unwilling to consider surrender until the emperor commanded them to do so.

Out of the Loop

When President Roosevelt died on April 12, 1945, his vice president, Harry S. Truman, became president. Until this time Truman had been kept virtually in the dark about the secret American project to build an atomic bomb. He quickly took charge of the war effort and used this weapon to America's advantage. At a meeting in Potsdam, Germany, Truman led the Allies to demand that Japan surrender and warned Japan that failure to comply would lead to its "prompt and utter destruction." Despite this warning, Japan refused to surrender. The first atomic bomb was dropped less than two weeks later.

Manhattan Project

The Manhattan Project was the code name assigned to the development and construction of the first atomic bombs. The project was initiated following a letter sent to President Roosevelt in 1939 that was signed by scientists, including Albert Einstein. This letter warned that the Germans were possibly working to develop nuclear weapons. At its peak, the project employed over 130,000 people and cost nearly 2 billion dollars.

Morality of the Atomic Bomb

The atomic bombing of Japan remains one of the most controversial events in human history. Detractors describe the decision to drop the bombs as unnecessary, immoral, and inhumane. Supporters point to the rapid end of a horribly destructive war.

Rather than accept Allied demands for surrender after Japanese cities had been

CD: 18F Model of the "Fat Man" Atomic Bomb

A photo of a model of this atomic bomb is available on the CD.

The Atomic Bomb

Visit www.bjupress.com/resources for possible links to articles about the atomic bomb.

Japan

In April 1945 President Roosevelt died, and his vice president, Harry Truman, became the president of the United States. To him fell the great responsibility of deciding whether to use the secret weapon that American scientists had developed during Roosevelt's administration.

Emperor Hirohito walking by a destroyed section of Tokyo in October 1943

Below, mushroom cloud from the bomb dropped on Nagasaki; *bottom left,* the "fat man" atomic bomb; *bottom right,* close-up of the plane that dropped the bomb on Nagasaki

Despite massive bombing of Japanese cities with explosives and incendiary bombs (designed to start fires), the Japanese emperor and his military council refused to surrender. While the death toll continued to rise, the leaders assembled thousands of planes and other war supplies to attack the Americans when they invaded the Japanese islands.

In July 1945 the Allied leaders insisted that Japan surrender or suffer terrible consequences. Japanese officials rejected this demand. President Truman responded by ordering that an atomic bomb be dropped on the Japanese city of Hiroshima on August 6. The blast destroyed nearly five square miles of the city and immediately killed an estimated seventy thousand people. In addition, another seventy thousand people suffered terrible injuries from the blast.

Truman again demanded the surrender of Japan and threatened additional destruction if they failed to do so. However, the Japanese leaders refused to surrender. In response, on August 9 an American bomber dropped a second atomic bomb on the Japanese city of Nagasaki. This blast immediately killed about forty thousand people, with another forty thousand injured who died soon after the blast.

On August 14, the Japanese government finally surrendered. Their only request was that Emperor Hirohito be allowed to retain his position. On **September 2, 1945** (V-J Day), the Japanese and Allied representatives signed the documents that formally ended Japanese involvement in World War II.

Section Quiz

1. In what European country in 1940 did the Allies find themselves surrounded by German forces?
2. What prevented a German victory over the Soviet Union?
3. What general traveled to North Africa to rescue Italian forces and push back the British?
4. What American general had to flee the Philippines in order to avoid capture by the Japanese?
5. What battle became Germany's final attempt to break through the Allied lines?
★ Evaluate the morality of dropping atomic bombs on Hiroshima and Nagasaki.

III. Consequences of the War

World War II resulted in loss of human life and destruction of property on a scale not previously witnessed in human history. The consequences are even difficult to quantify. Statistics alone fail to provide an adequate description of the horrific losses.

It is unlikely that anyone could have imagined a more destructive war than World War I, with about twenty million deaths. However, World War II resulted in more than fifty million deaths. Populations of nations in Europe suffered significant decline as millions of their citizens died in battle or as helpless victims of brutal conquest. For example, the Russians lost over twenty million people during the war. Between eight and ten million Russian soldiers died while fighting the Germans. Over twelve million Russian civilians died as a result of the fighting, disease, or famine.

Communism spread rapidly after the war as the Communists under Joseph Stalin seized most of Eastern Europe. Soviet forces had invaded Poland and virtually every other country east of Germany during the war. Despite promises of free elections, these states quickly became subject to the Soviet Union, and Stalin installed Communist regimes in these countries.

Long-term Consequences for Society

For centuries European culture was the dominant culture in the world. England, France, and Germany had boasted the strongest armies, the wealthiest economies, and the most advanced centers of learning. However, for generations Europe had been forsaking the Christian worldview that had positively influenced it. Leading Europeans had produced the Enlightenment, had scorned biblical religion, and had emphasized nationalism above allegiance to God and His Word. By the war's end, Europe was crushed. Now the United States and the Soviet Union would dominate the world.

General MacArthur and Emperor Hirohito

fire-bombed, Japanese leaders prepared their people to resist an Allied invasion. There is little doubt that kamikaze attacks would have inflicted great damage on Allied shipping during such an invasion, and many thousands would have died in these attacks. In addition, an invasion of Japan's main islands of Kyushu and Honshu would probably have resulted in the deaths of at least one million Allied troops and millions of Japanese who would have fought to the death to protect their homeland. While the loss of life from the two bombings was tragic, the preservation of life enabled by Japan's surrender is undeniable.

Section III

Objectives

Students should be able to

1. Describe the long-term consequences of this war's unprecedented violence and destruction.
2. Assess the long-term philosophical and religious consequences of the trauma of this period.
3. Assess the consequences of World War II as a total war.
4. Analyze how and why the Nazis sought to eliminate the "weak and unfit" members of German society.

Section Quiz Answers

1. France
2. continued Russian resistance and the Russian winter
3. General Erwin Rommel
4. General Douglas MacArthur
5. Battle of the Bulge
★ Pro: The dropping of the bombs was designed to prevent the additional deaths of millions of people who would have been killed in an invasion of Japan. This bombing was believed to be the quickest way to end the war.

Con: The bombs resulted in extensive civilian casualties.

✷ World War II in Documents

Visit www.bjupress.com/resources for possible links to World War II documents.

Stalin Already Knew

When President Truman hinted to Stalin that the United States had developed a new destructive weapon, Stalin was not surprised. Later, American officials discovered that Russian spies had infiltrated the Manhattan Project and that American Communists had sent plans and technical information to the Russians about the first atomic bomb. American officials tried many of those involved, and many of the offenders served time in prison. However, Ethel and Julius Rosenberg were executed in 1953, becoming the only Americans to be executed for their involvement in this affair.

Cold War

Ask a volunteer to read about the Cold War and present a report to the class. Another volunteer could find or make a map showing the nations who supported America and its allies. A third volunteer could find or make a map showing the Soviet Union and its allies.

Beginning of the Atomic Age

The United States initially had the advantage regarding the development of atomic weapons. However, the Germans had also been working to develop these weapons. When the Russians invaded Germany, they seized German scientists and information about this new technology. In addition, the Russians used American spies in the atomic industry to obtain valuable American research. As a result, the Russians soon became an atomic power and developed their own crude atomic weapons.

Development of atomic weapons affected the strategy of future wars. The destructive power of these weapons also caused people to realize that scientific and technological developments are not always good. This knowledge played a role in the rejection of Enlightenment ideas that had influenced human reasoning for two hundred years.

Beginning of the Cold War

While Churchill had been one of the first to warn of Soviet intentions toward Eastern Europe, many soon became aware of Russia's intention to dominate world affairs. As a result, a period known as the **Cold War** (political rivalry that stops short of actual war) developed, with America and its allies aligned against continued aggression by the Soviet Union and its allies. We will examine this period in detail in the next chapter.

Disillusionment

The sense of hopelessness and despair that you learned about in the last chapter continued and heightened following the Second World War. Post-war literature and art reflected the view that life has no meaning or purpose. For example, American painter Jackson Pollock developed a form of painting known as **abstract expressionism**. He created many of his paintings by randomly splashing wet paint on the canvas with brushes.

Other artists expressed their hopelessness by writing stories or plays that demonstrated the meaninglessness of life. For example, Albert Camus, a French philosopher, wrote stories dealing with absurdity. He reasoned that people value what is meaningless, since all people value their life even though all die.

Economic Changes

World War II led to dramatic economic changes for countries such as France and Britain. They lost most of their colonies and much of their overseas empires. The few colonies still under their control demanded freedom. Within a few years, the Europeans granted freedom to these remaining colonies. The loss of income and inexpensive resources from these colonies greatly reduced the prestige and influence of European countries, including France and Britain. They could no longer lay claim to world power status.

Political Changes

World War II ended Europe's domination of the world. Both wars had resulted, in part, from exaggerated nationalism and the illusion that one nationality enjoyed superiority over other nationalities. These errors had been disproved at an incredible cost. Political change emerged as one of the consequences of these wars. Rather than many strong political powers, only two remained. Following the war, power shifted to the United States and the Communist powers. Europe would merely side with one or the other of these political camps.

The Granger Collection, New York

Jackson Pollock

The Holocaust Slaughter of the "Weak" and "Unfit"

Violence against civilians struck a new low under men like Adolf Hitler. Shortly after coming to power in 1933, Hitler began a program to rid Germany of those he considered weak and unfit. While many have heard of the German attempts to destroy all of the Jews in Europe (commonly called the **Holocaust**), his

Left, *crematorium in a concentration camp at Weimar, Germany; above, A German girl walks past the bodies of 800 slave workers murdered by SS guards near Namering, Germany*

systematic murder of other groups has received less attention. For example, Hitler planned and carried out the destruction of thousands of Gypsies, the disabled, and the chronically ill. German forces also treated Poles, Russians, Ukrainians, Czechs, and others as inferior and murdered them in large numbers.

Euthanasia

Deceptively calling it "mercy killing," Hitler and others used starvation, lethal injection, and poison gas to purge the German nation of the weak. Hitler's definition of the weak included the mentally ill, the disabled, and those suffering from long-term illnesses.

The Nazis assigned the codename **Operation T-4** to this terrible program. By 1940 they had constructed six centers to kill thousands of these victims. The killing continued until American troops liberated these centers in the spring of 1945. An estimated 200,000 people died in the name of euthanasia, or mercy killing.

The Hunger Plan

Nazi leaders developed this plan to ensure adequate food supplies for the German forces and German civilians. To accomplish this, they limited the amount of food available to Poles and Russians under German control. The Jews in the ghettos of these countries suffered the most, but millions of civilians died of starvation. This horrific plan continued until the Russians drove German forces out of these countries.

Shoah

Many use the word "holocaust" to refer to the mass murder of the Jews. However, many Jews prefer the Hebrew term **Shoah** which means "calamity." Whichever term you use, the Nazi attempt to destroy the Jewish population in Europe has proven to be one of the worst atrocities in history.

Jewish persecution began shortly after Hitler became the ruler of Germany. The Nazis began by pressuring Jews to leave Germany. Of course, they had to leave their wealth behind to fill Nazi coffers. Then German authorities boycotted Jewish busi-

nesses and forced them to sell their businesses. Soon the Nazis forced the Jews to relocate to the ghettos (slums). Relocation to concentration camps followed soon after.

As German armies marched into Russia, the Nazis sent along special mobile killing units to hunt down and kill Jews, Gypsies, and Communists.

Later the Germans developed centralized killing locations in Poland and Germany. The German camp at Auschwitz gained the terrible distinction of killing more people than the other five concentration camps. At least one million two hundred thousand Jews died at this camp. The officials at Auschwitz also murdered one hundred thousand Poles, Gypsies, and Russians.

Rows of bodies of dead inmates at the Gestapo concentration camp at Lager Nordhausen

Lager Nordhausen

American forces discovered this concentration camp during their push toward Berlin in 1944. When they arrived at the camp, they found over six thousand emaciated bodies of prisoners the Gestapo had used as slave laborers. Some had died from starvation, and others had been shot or beaten to death. German forces had taken these "enemies of the state" from several countries including Belgium, Czechoslovakia, Romania, and France.

American forces were given the gruesome task of burying the victims. An American soldier bulldozed long trenches, about three feet deep, into which the bodies would be laid for burial. German civilians, rounded up by American military policemen, were ordered to move the bodies from the streets to the trenches—using doors, boards, blankets, or stretchers to transport the bodies to the shallow graves. SS troops who had fled the camp just before the arrival of the American forces were captured and executed.

Death by Design

Death by Design: Science, Technology, and Engineering in Nazi Germany by Eric Katz is a useful teacher resource but should **not** be recommended for students to read. It contains graphic material about Nazi medical experiments.

Return to Materialism

Following the war, many turned back to the emphasis on acquiring material goods that had been prevalent prior to the onset of the Great Depression. With the ever-present danger of atomic warfare and the loss of confidence in government to prevent war, people sought to find temporary comfort by seeking and enjoying the benefits of material wealth.

Philosophical and Religious Consequences

The world wars devastated the illusions upon which most philosophies have been founded. The wars smashed the fantasy that man is born without a sin nature. Philosophies and religions could not explain the outpouring of animosity and hatred that led to the deaths of multiplied millions. They found themselves unable to provide answers for the past or hope for the future.

Philosophical

The horrors of World War I followed by the intensified horrors of World War II altered the thinking of most Europeans. They abandoned the idealism that prevailed in the nineteenth century. This collapse of idealism led to relativism, the idea that truth and moral values are not absolute but rather vary with each person or group.

The philosophy known as **existentialism** became popular during this period. This philosophy stresses a person's uniqueness while encouraging free choice and accepting the consequences of that choice. Existentialists deny that an all-powerful God rules over the affairs of humans. In fact, many leading existentialists were atheists. They also denied the existence of a moral code defining what a human being is or should be. Instead, they believed that humans are free to determine their own values and their own meaning in life. Humans are not obligated to obey the dictates of a government or a church. They are to choose a course of action that seems right to them and then strive to be faithful to that selection.

The most famous existentialist was Jean Paul Sartre, who wrote the famous book *Being and Nothingness* in which he encouraged people to reject the illusions that deceive them. His philosophy should have led him to oppose every political ideology as mere illusion, but Sartre was inconsistent and supported Marxism.

Beyond the failure of human philosophies to explain the atrocities of these wars lay the reality that they did not predict the devastation of the twentieth century. This level of destruction contradicted man's high view of himself and left men without hope or answers.

Religious

The world wars discredited religious teaching that assumed humans are basically good. Gone were the dreams of a perfect society. As a result, the churches of Europe began to empty. Atheism grew more popular, and eventually even some prominent theologians concluded that God was dead. Many Jewish people struggled with the idea of God after the Holocaust.

Nevertheless, Christianity also grew during this period. In the United States, many men returned home from war and used the G. I. Bill to attend Christian colleges. These men had seen the world and had seen death. They were prepared to sacrifice to spread the gospel around the world. Many of them returned to minister in places they had been during the war.

> ### G. I. Bill
>
> In 1944 President Roosevelt signed the Serviceman's Readjustment Act of 1944. This became known as the G. I. (government issue) Bill of Rights. In this legislation, the federal government helped pay for college or vocational education for returning veterans. When the program ended in 1956, nearly eight million veterans had taken advantage of this benefit. Another provision in this bill offered veterans low interest loans to buy homes. This provision enabled over two million veterans to move to the suburbs and purchase their own homes.

Total War and Its Consequences

You learned about the terrible realities of total war in the last chapter. Sadly, improved technology and weapons that were more powerful increased the suffering and death of civilians during the Second World War. In addition, few escaped the consequences of a rigidly controlled national economy. Total war resulted in widespread affliction due to a rationing of food, medicine, and anything else that would contribute to the military effort.

Massive Loss of Human Life

In addition to government control of a nation's economy, total war resulted in the deaths of millions of civilians. Although estimates vary widely, as many as thirty-five million civilians may have died from a variety of causes, including bombing of cities, disease, murder by invading troops, and famine.

Massive Destruction of Property

Entire cities were bombed into rubble or firebombed into ashes. Europe lay in ruins. Her industries and infrastructure suffered almost complete destruction. While the cost of the war had been an incredible one at one-half trillion dollars, the cost of rebuilding would tax the resources of the free world.

Section Quiz

1. What political system spread rapidly over Eastern Europe by the end of World War II?
2. How did the Soviet Union acquire the knowledge to become an atomic power?
3. List five groups that the Nazis systematically murdered prior to and during World War II.
4. Given the failure of philosophy and religion, how did many respond after the end of the Second World War?
5. Why did philosophy fail to predict the devastation of these two world wars?
★ Why did Bible-based Christianity not suffer the same disillusionment common among unbelievers after the war?

Section Quiz Answers

1. communism
2. by capturing German scientists and using American spies
3. any five of the following: Jews, communists, Gypsies, the mentally ill, the disabled, the chronically ill, Poles, Russians, Ukrainians, and Czechs
4. with disillusionment
5. Human wisdom, the basis of philosophy, tends to exalt man. Thus, fallen man believes he is basically good. However, the level of devastation that occurred during these two world wars contradicted man's high view of himself.

★ Christianity expects such devastation and offers hope through Christ. Though man was originally placed in an ideal world, Genesis 3 records that mankind fell through Adam's sin. The devastation of the twentieth century is a part of the consequences of that sin, and it is not surprising to a Christian. The Christian also has the hope of personal salvation though Christ (Titus 3:5–7) and the expectation of a restored order when Christ returns to rule the world (1 Cor. 15:24–28).

Activity 4: Chapter Review

This activity helps students prepare for the test.

People, Places, and Terms to Know

Francisco Franco
Hirohito
Tojo
Third Reich
Sudetenland
Munich Conference
Neville Chamberlain
appeasement
Rome-Berlin Axis
Anti-Comintern Pact
Axis powers
Pact of Steel
September 1, 1939
Allies
December 7, 1941
Pearl Harbor
Luftwaffe
Erwin Rommel
Bernard L. Montgomery
Douglas MacArthur
Midway Island
Dwight D. Eisenhower
June 6, 1944
D-day
Battle of the Bulge
May 8, 1945
September 2, 1945
Cold War
abstract expressionism
Holocaust
Operation T-4
Shoah
existentialism

Making Connections

1. How did Germany and Italy's support of General Franco in Spain prepare their forces for war?
2. Why did Japan become increasingly confident that no nation would come to China's defense?
3. How did seizure of the Rhineland provide a military advantage for Germany?
4. Why did the French and British declaration of war not deter Germany from invading Poland?
5. Why did Hitler invade Russia in 1941?
6. Why was it a mistake for Germany and Italy to declare war on the U.S.?
7. Why did European nations decline in importance and influence following the Second World War?
8. Why did the Nazis murder Jews, the disabled, and many other groups?

Developing History Skills

1. Compare and contrast total war in Chapter 17 and this chapter.
2. Respond to the following statement: "The refusal of the United States to lift the oil embargo against the Japanese forced Japan to attack American naval forces."

Thinking Critically

1. Respond to this quotation by a survivor of the Holocaust: "A suffering so great leaves nothing to be redeemed, and precious little to forgive or be forgiven. It is not that God died after Auschwitz; it is that He is no longer needed. The covenant has been broken, not by the people but by their Lord." Use passages such as Hosea 4:6 and Romans 3:10-23 as points of reference.
2. Evaluate conditions leading to World War II in light of Bible passages including Exodus 20; 2 Chronicles 16, 18; Psalm 20:7; and James 4:1.

Living in God's World

1. Suppose that you are a Christian historian responding to the denials of an unbeliever regarding God's providence at Dunkirk. Specifically respond to the charge that the events at Dunkirk cannot demonstrate the providence of God because the Germans' conquest of France has its own equally remarkable series of events. Use Genesis 50:20 and Daniel 4:34-35 to prepare your answer.

Chapter Review Answers

Making Connections

1. They tested their new weapons and tactics to prepare for a possible war.
2. European powers demonstrated a reluctance to become involved in defending China.
3. The Germans quickly fortified this region to protect themselves against a possible attack by France.
4. Hitler realized that the Allies would not be able to provide Poland with military assistance.
5. He wanted to seize Russian resources, including Russia's oil reserves.
6. This declaration of war brought the Americans into the European theater of the war.
7. They lost their colonies and much of their overseas empires. The loss of this wealth-producing territory resulted in a decline of European prestige and influence.
8. They considered these people weak or unfit to be a part of the German Empire. They also withheld food from many of these groups to ensure an adequate food supply for the German people and the German military.

Developing History Skills

1. Answers will vary but should include some of the following: In both wars, national governments exercised a rigid control over the national economies. In both wars, civilian populations suffered from bombing and bombardment by the German forces. Casualties were much greater during the Second World War due to improved technology, but technology played a key role in civilian casualties in both wars.
2. Answers will vary but should include some of the following: Such reasoning is problematic because it assumes that Japan had a right to continue its aggressive actions toward China and many other nations in Southeast Asia. While America's actions certainly forced the Japanese to make a critical choice, attacking American naval forces was not Japan's only option. In fact, the attack on Pearl Harbor proved to be a fatal decision for Japan because it brought a united America into the war with a zeal that it would not otherwise have had. The American cry became "Remember Pearl Harbor!"

Thinking Critically

1. Answers will vary but should include some of the following: In reality, God's people repeatedly broke the covenant in the Old Testament and again when they rejected the Messiah (Hosea 4:6).

2. Suppose you are a member of a small church in Germany. It is the summer of 1945, and other members are in despair. In an attempt to explain God's ways, you decide to present a lesson on the topic of the Day of the Lord from the Old Testament prophets. Develop a Bible lesson on this topic from the following verses: Isaiah 2:12-3:3; 3:8-10; 4:2-6.

Furthermore, God often works in ways that we cannot understand, but all humans are obligated to trust God even when they cannot understand. Finally, because of the universal depravity of humans, we should not marvel when God permits the depravity of humanity to explode on the stage of human history (Rom. 3). We should marvel that He so regularly restrains it.

2. Answers may vary but should include the following: Militarism—European nations trusted in large armies and powerful weapons to protect themselves. However, Psalm 20:7 encourages men to trust in God, not in military might. Imperialism—During this period, Fascist states and other dictator-ships seized and conquered weaker neighboring states. However, Exodus 20:17 prohibits coveting, and imperialism violates that command from the Lord. Alliances—The Axis powers and the Allies trusted in alliances for security. However, we can find examples in 2 Chronicles 16 and 18 that demonstrate the futility of alliances if God does not bless them.

Living in God's World

1. Answers will vary but should include the concession that the historian should be humble about the purpose of God in what He providentially orchestrates. God's providence extends over all that happens, both good and bad (Gen. 50:20; Dan. 4:34–35). God's providentially permitting the conquest of France does not negate the providential rescue of the Allies from Dunkirk. When God does something for good in such a way that His special providence is notable, it is only right for historians to take note and praise Him for it.

2. Answers will vary but may include some of the following points: These verses describe God's judgment on Judah and Jerusalem. This judgment is similar to what Germany (and all of Europe) has just experienced. Judah and Europe both enjoyed the blessing of God's Word and His care, but Judah and Europe turned away from devotion to God and became puffed up with pride. In pride they began to trust in men rather than trusting in God. So God took away from Judah and Europe all the objects of their trust. But just as God offered hope to Judah, so He offers hope to Europe. First, people need to heed God's command in Isaiah 2:22 and refuse to depend on humans, whose lives continually hang in the balance. Second, people need to put their trust in the Messiah—Jesus, God's own Son. Finally, they need to ask God to cleanse them of their sin and restore them to a right relationship with Him (Isa. 4:3–4). Those who submit to God may focus on the hopeful words given in Isaiah 3:10.

Getty Images

CHAPTER 19

Chapter Goals

Students should be able to

1. Describe major political and economic changes that accompanied postwar recovery.
2. Explain why global power shifts took place and why the Cold War broke out in the aftermath of World War II.
3. Delineate how colonies achieved independence from European colonial rule and describe the subsequent development of their cultures.
4. Analyze the causes and consequences of the collapse of the Soviet Union.

1940-95

- Cold War begins 1945
- India gains independence from Britain 1947
- Israel becomes a modern nation 1948
- Berlin Blockade 1948–49
- Arab-Israeli War 1948–49
- Chiang Kai-shek establishes the Republic of China in Taiwan 1949
- Sputnik launched into outer space 1957
- China's Great Leap Forward 1958
- Cuban Missile Crisis

1940 | 1945 | 1950 | 1955 | 1960 | 1965

- Greece endures civil war 1944–49
- Korean War 1950–53
- Battle of Dien Bien Phu 1954
- Ghana becomes first African colony to gain independence 1957

Chapter 19 Lesson Plan Chart

Section Title	Main Activity	Pages	Days
I. Postwar Reconstruction	Activity 1: UN Charter	350–52	1½–2 days
II. Development of the Cold War	Activity 2: "Ich Bin Ein Berliner . . ."	353–59	2–2½ days
III. Transition in the Third World and Middle East	Discussion Activity: African Struggle for Independence	359–63	1–1½ days
IV. Collapse of the Soviet Union	Activity 4: "Tear Down This Wall!"	363–67	1½–2 days
TOTAL SUGGESTED DAYS (INCLUDING 1 DAY EACH FOR REVIEW AND TESTING)			8–10 days

Materials List

Section I
- Activity 1 from the *Student Activities* manual

Section II
- CD: 19A China and Taiwan; 19B Berlin Blockade
- Activities 2 and 3 from the *Student Activities* manual
- Special speaker: Vietnam veteran

Section III
- CD: 19C Decolonization of Africa since WWII; 19D Decolonization of Southeast Asia since WWII

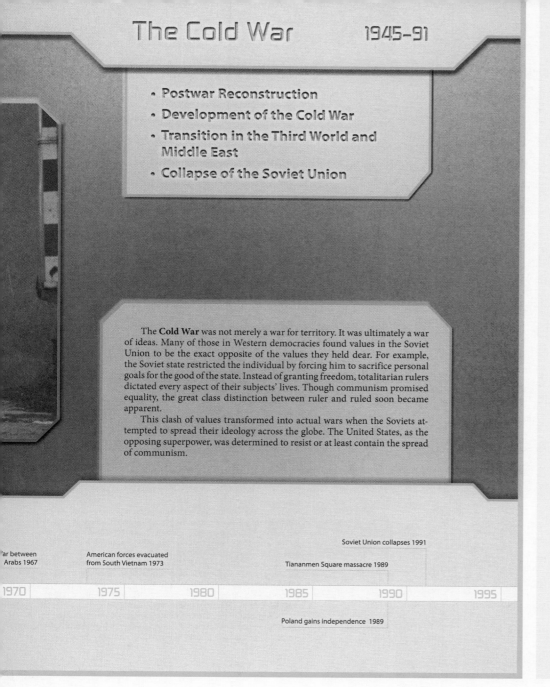

The Cold War 1945–91

- Postwar Reconstruction
- Development of the Cold War
- Transition in the Third World and Middle East
- Collapse of the Soviet Union

The **Cold War** was not merely a war for territory. It was ultimately a war of ideas. Many of those in Western democracies found values in the Soviet Union to be the exact opposite of the values they held dear. For example, the Soviet state restricted the individual by forcing him to sacrifice personal goals for the good of the state. Instead of granting freedom, totalitarian rulers dictated every aspect of their subjects' lives. Though communism promised equality, the great class distinction between ruler and ruled soon became apparent.

This clash of values transformed into actual wars when the Soviets attempted to spread their ideology across the globe. The United States, as the opposing superpower, was determined to resist or at least contain the spread of communism.

'ar between Arabs 1967

American forces evacuated from South Vietnam 1973

Soviet Union collapses 1991

Tiananmen Square massacre 1989

| 1970 | 1975 | 1980 | 1985 | 1990 | 1995 |

Poland gains independence 1989

Section IV

- CD: 19E Six-Day War; 19F States Formed from the Former Soviet Union
- Activities 4 and 5 from the *Student Activities* manual

Section I

French Governments

France has endured frequent shifts in government, beginning with the formation of the First Republic in 1792 during the French Revolution. The French formed the Second Republic in 1848 during unrest in Paris when Louis Napoleon Bonaparte came to power. Following France's defeat by the Prussians in 1870, the French established the Third Republic. After World War II the French established the Fourth Republic; however, this weak government lasted only eleven years. In 1958 Charles de Gaulle established the Fifth Republic, which governs France to this day.

Made in Japan

During the early years of Japanese recovery, many Japanese products were inexpensive and viewed as inferior. However, improvements to Japanese manufacturing and technology gradually transformed Japanese-made products

Konrad Adenauer

Visit www.bjupress.com/resources for possible links to articles about Konrad Adenauer.

Japanese Recovery

Discuss with the students how Japan rapidly recovered from the terrible devastation of the war and became a world leader in manufacturing goods such as cars and electronics. Help them to understand that the United States played a key role in making this possible.

I. Postwar Reconstruction

World War II had left most of Europe and Japan in ruins. Extensive bombing and shelling had destroyed whole cities. Europe and Japan would have to be completely rebuilt and infrastructure replaced. The cost would be immense, and the United States would have to provide most of the materials and financing.

Recovery after World War II

Recovery needed to occur quickly. The Soviet Union actively sought to destabilize European countries in order to bring them under Communist domination. A prosperous and stable Europe would be a great deterrent to the spread of communism.

Konrad Adenauer

Western Europe

Under the leadership of German Chancellor **Konrad Adenauer**, West Germany experienced an incredible recovery. Known as the *Wirtschaftswunder* (economic miracle), Adenauer tripled national income and led the small nation to produce more goods by 1955 than a larger Germany had produced prior to the war. He also rejected socialism and embraced the principles of the free market. Germany quickly became a major economic force in Europe.

France struggled with instability following the formation of the Fourth Republic in 1946. In addition, France tried to demonstrate that it was still a world power by regaining possession of its colonial empire. However, French forces suffered a catastrophic defeat by the Vietnamese Communist forces in 1954. France gained a measure of stability when **Charles de Gaulle** became the president of France and established the **Fifth Republic** in 1958. This government provided the French with a constitution and strengthened the office of president.

Britain emerged from the war as a nation in decline. The British Empire began to crumble as vast territories, including India and Burma, gained their independence. Rather than continue to have a leading role on the world scene, Britain could only play a supporting role with the United States and European powers.

Japan

Under the initial leadership of General MacArthur, Japan made an astonishing economic and political recovery. MacArthur gave Japan a constitution and helped to establish a stable democratic government.

When the occupation government turned power over to the Japanese, they made a successful transition to a democratic government. In 1955 the Japanese voted the **Liberal Democratic Party** into power. This party ruled Japan until political scandals led the Japanese to replace it with a coalition government in 1993.

Japan took advantage of American financial and technological aid and developed a formidable industrial base. Since the West provided military protection, Japan's financial resources were devoted to creating a competitive heavy industry. Japanese automakers gradually became world leaders in auto manufacturing.

In addition, Japan created new technologies in electronics. By the 1980s, Japan had developed a world market in high-quality electronic equipment such as televisions, radios, and computers.

Stabilization and Growth in Western Europe

To help Europe recover from the devastation of World War II, the United States sent billions of dollars in aid. As a result, Britain, France, West Germany, and others quickly rebuilt their infrastructure. These countries recovered economically at different rates depending on their embracing of capitalism or socialism. This recovery accomplished a key American goal of strengthening Western Europe against Soviet aggression.

Stabilization

Beginning in 1948, under the Economic Recovery Act, the United States poured billions of dollars into Western European countries. Commonly called the **Marshall Plan**, this distribution of funds enabled Europe to rapidly rebuild and retool for a strong economic recovery. As Western Europe recovered economically, communism became less attractive and Communist parties in various countries declined in influence.

Growth

European leaders realized the need for some form of unity to prevent future wars between European countries. While political unity proved to be elusive, economic unity became a reality through at least two organizations.

In 1951 six European states agreed to establish the European Coal and Steel Community (ECSC). France, West Germany, Italy, Belgium, the Netherlands, and Luxembourg coordinated these industries. One of the goals was to prevent future wars, since steel would be essential for any future military buildup. In addition, the ECSC sought to eliminate waste and inefficiency. The resulting industrial products could be produced at a lower cost.

Encouraged by the success of the ECSC, these six nations established the European Economic Community in 1957. Known as the **Common Market**, the member states expanded cooperation to include many other products. Removing trade barriers led to lower prices and increased sales. Over the next forty years, the Common Market grew to include nearly thirty countries.

Welfare States and Stagnation

Most developed countries have instituted some form of welfare or government provision of economic and social benefits for their citizens. Some countries are able to pay for limited welfare by taxing a thriving economy. We will briefly examine two European nations that have suffered from the effects of welfare.

After the Second World War, the British government, under the Labour Party, created the National Health Service and took control of key industries, including coal and railroads. By the late 1970s, unemployment and inflation had crippled the British economy. The British responded by voting out the Labour Party and electing the Conservative Party in 1979. In a later section, we will examine the results of that election.

France has developed into a classic welfare state since World War II. For example, France has a universal national health care system and a generous, tax-subsidized retirement plan. In addition, the French have a minimum wage that is nearly double that of the United States. The costs for these policies are high taxes, high unemployment, and regulations that hinder the competitiveness of French companies.

George Marshall

Time & Life Pictures/Getty Image

George C. Marshall served as secretary of state from 1947 to 1951, and President Truman placed him in charge of the European Recovery Program. The United States offered financial aid to relieve Europe and help it recover after World War II. By the end of the program, America had either given or loaned Europe almost thirteen billion dollars for rebuilding. Britain and France were the two largest recipients, followed by Germany. The Korean War played a role in ending the program and diverted America's attention from Europe to Asia.

into high-quality goods that became greatly sought after.

Postwar Recovery

Few countries in history have defeated their enemies in war and then helped them to rebuild their infrastructures and economies. The United States has proved to be a gracious conqueror on several occasions, especially following World War II. In the process, several of America's former enemies became some of its strongest allies.

France and Socialism

The French welfare system developed at an economy-crushing cost. French companies are burdened with government regulations that increase the cost of doing business. These businesses are often reluctant to hire because the government makes it very difficult to suspend or terminate employees. French unemployment ranges from ten to over sixty percent depending on the region and neighborhood. In addition, workers pay an average of forty-four percent of their income in some form of tax.

Western Europe and Welfare States

Discuss with the students how Western European nations developed into welfare states following the war. Britain transformed into a welfare state following the First World War. Following World War II, the British continued to embrace this failed system, and France followed suit. Help the students understand why welfare states experience political and economic decline and eventually become economically unstable.

NATO

The North Atlantic Treaty Organization (NATO) is an international league that was founded in 1949. The league's original intent was to protect its member nations from Soviet aggression. Its original members included the United States and the nations of Western Europe. The organization proved to be effective during the Korean War and on other occasions. Challenges to NATO included the Soviet Union's formation of the Warsaw Pact in 1955 and the withdrawal of France from NATO in 1966. Following the collapse of the Soviet Union in 1991, several Eastern European states also joined NATO.

Spread of Democracy

Nations including Germany, Italy, India, and Portugal embraced democracy after the Second World War. Some of these nations quickly stabilized and thrived economically as well as politically. Others experienced struggles along the way and endured conflict as various groups tried to destroy these young democracies.

Greece became one of those nations that struggled to establish a successful democracy. This nation endured a civil war between 1944 and 1949 because Greek Communists attempted to seize control of the country. British and American support enabled the anti-Communist forces to prevail. Once the Communist forces had been defeated, Greece quickly joined **NATO** and sought to maintain close ties with the United States and Western Europe.

The struggle with communism became more than a conflict between nations. Communist parties took root in many nations, including the United States. Few countries had to resort to an armed conflict as did Greece, but many countries experienced an internal struggle between democracy and communism.

Role of the United Nations

As the American, British, and Soviet leaders met to discuss strategy during World War II, they also agreed to form an international peacekeeping organization after the war. In 1945 diplomats representing fifty nations organized the **United Nations** (UN).

These nations founded the UN to ensure international peace. The role of this organization soon expanded to include seeking solutions to social, economic, and humanitarian problems around the world.

However, because the United Nations includes almost all the nations of the world, nations that cause problems also hold positions of status in the UN. For instance, during the Cold War the Soviet Union caused major problems in the world while at the same time possessing the power of veto in the UN Security Council.

Unfortunately, the UN recognizes no biblical moral standard by which to judge and respond to the conduct of nations. As a result, while the UN condemns atrocities like genocide, it also supports immoral actions like abortion.

United Nations Headquarters, New York City

Section Quiz

1. Who led West Germany during the 1950s and played a key role in its "economic miracle" following the war?
2. Who became the president of France in 1958 and established the Fifth Republic?
3. What U.S. economic plan helped to stabilize Western Europe?
4. Why do French companies find it difficult to be competitive?
5. What western nation fought a civil war in the 1940s to determine the success or failure of democracy?
★ From a biblical perspective, what is a key reason for the United Nations' inability to work toward solutions to the world's problems?

Spread of Democracy

Discuss with the students the struggle between democracy and communism following the war. If possible, have students locate the following countries: Germany, Italy, India, Portugal, and Greece. These countries embraced democracy after World War II. Discuss why these countries escaped communism when so many others did not.

Activity 1: UN Charter

This is an excerpt from the United Nations Charter. This activity is designed to demonstrate the high goals of the UN and its confidence in human ability to bring about peace.

NATO

Visit www.bjupress.com/resources for possible links to articles about NATO.

Section Quiz Answers

1. Konrad Adenauer
2. Charles de Gaulle
3. the Marshall Plan
4. government regulations
5. Greece
★ Answers should include some of the following: The United Nations rejects any biblical moral standard. Rejecting the Bible as the standard by which all actions are judged, the member states, having their own religions and ideologies, are often unable to agree on the morality of actions. Therefore they are unable to determine what ought to be done about the world's problems.

II. Development of the Cold War

By the end of the Second World War, a different sort of war had begun. The United States and the Soviet Union emerged from the conflict as the clear world leaders. Although they had been allies in fighting against Hitler, their differences were so deep that both quickly realized they could not remain allies. Over the next four decades, Americans and Soviets fought what has been called the Cold War. The relationship between these nations was not outright war, but neither was it peaceful. Each side tried to dominate the other through the development of new weapons or through involvement in conflicts between other nations.

Differences Between Democracy and Communism

In order to understand the events that unfolded during the Cold War, one must first understand why the Soviet Union and the United States were rivals. Each nation was driven by different worldviews. These worldviews differed, most obviously, in the following ways.

The United States and the Soviet Union were opposed economically. The United States promoted a capitalistic approach to the economy that allowed privately owned businesses to serve customers and pursue profits. The Soviet Union attempted to impose a central plan on its national economy. The state owned the industries and controlled all decisions for items produced. Since the Soviets placed a great emphasis on building a strong military, little was manufactured to meet the needs of most people.

Politically, the United States practiced a democratic form of government that stressed the role of the individual in the political process. The Communist Party controlled the Soviet Union, and the citizens had little say in their government.

Differences in economic and political systems alone are not enough to lead nations into war, however. The United States and the Soviet Union also differed religiously. Marxist-Leninists believed that capitalism was immoral and that it must be overthrown in a revolution that would establish socialist states. They taught that religion is itself evil because it drugs people into submission when they actually need to be stirred into revolutionary fervor. Americans, on the other hand, believed they were a Christian nation that needed to stand up to the atheistic Soviet Union. This was true of Fundamentalist preachers as well as politicians like presidents Truman and Eisenhower.

Though Americans agreed that America was a nation under God (something Congress added to the pledge of allegiance under Eisenhower), it was not always clear who the American god was. The civic religion of Cold War America was empty of theological content. Americans were expected to have faith, but in whom was unclear. The key dogmas were the continuation of the American way of life, the free market system, and personal peace.

Fall of China to Communism

In Chapter 17 you learned about the struggle for power in China. After the Second World War, this struggle resumed. Communist leader Mao Zedong received support from the Soviet Union, and Chiang Kai-shek received aid from the United States. Mao Zedong and the Communists made empty promises to the peasants and

Section II

Objectives

Students should be able to

1. Contrast Western democracies and Communist regimes.
2. Explain the rise of the Communist Party in China and analyze the Great Leap Forward and the Cultural Revolution.
3. Analyze the causes and consequences of some of the Cold War crises including the Berlin Blockade, the Korean War, the Cuban Missile Crisis, and the Vietnam War.
4. Examine the superpower rivalries of the Cold War and the development of new military, nuclear, and space technology.

Western Civilization

Francis A. Schaeffer (1912–84) was an American pastor who ministered for many years in Switzerland. Attempting to become a more effective minister, he gave himself to studying the history of Western civilization. He eventually became a prophet of sorts, crying out against the twisted affections that had corrupted the civilization of the West.

In his book *How Should We Then Live?* Schaeffer presents his understanding of the history of the West from the Roman Empire to the late twentieth century. He argues that the greatness of the West was found in its embrace of Christianity. When the West was most consistently Christian, it was at its greatest. When, however, it was not true to its Christian beliefs, it declined. Toward the end of this book, Schaeffer observes that the

Projects

There are several fascinating people and events in this section. Perhaps some of your students would enjoy researching them or reading a book about them and presenting their findings in class. For example, students might provide a more detailed account of the events at Tiananmen Square.

 ## Documents of the Cold War

Visit www.bjupress.com/resources for possible links to articles about documents of the Cold War.

West at the end of the twentieth century was unraveling. It was discarding the Christian beliefs that held Western civilization together. Rejecting these beliefs, people had begun to idolize personal peace and affluence.

Can anything be done for a civilization so given over to pursuing the inward effects of the Fall? Schaeffer insists that, to remedy the situation, the West must return to the worldview that made it great—the Christian worldview. But, for this to happen, Schaeffer warns, Christians must be the first ones to renounce their idolization of personal peace and affluence.

Great Leap Forward?

Chairman Mao demanded that steel production be doubled. In response, the Communist bureaucrats enlisted laborers who were unskilled in steel production to produce the required steel. History lessons like this demonstrate the folly of placing unqualified officials in power and expecting their demands to translate into economic or political success.

Cultural Revolution

Many of those targeted during this violent purge of Chinese society were intellectuals. Any person in China who openly opposed the folly of collectivization and socialism found himself facing imprisonment or execution. The radicals who carried out this purge also demanded that all art promote the Communist Party rather than enhance Chinese culture. Any art that did not conform was subject to destruction.

Communist Chinese banner

progressively gained enough popular support to drive Chiang's forces to an island off the coast of China in 1949. On the island of Taiwan, Chiang established the **Republic of China**, which has governed this island to the present.

China under Mao

Mao's forces had seized the major cities in China by 1949 and had placed loyal Communists in key leadership positions. Despite receiving support from the Soviet Union in the 1940s, under Mao's leadership, Communist China developed animosity toward the Soviets. During the 1960s this hostility deepened and resulted in a diplomatic war of words, with each denouncing the other. In 1969 the tensions escalated into a border conflict, with the Russian and Chinese forces engaging in a limited war.

To revive the struggling Chinese economy, Mao developed a Soviet-style Five Year Plan in 1949. The Communist leaders sought to increase agricultural and industrial production. To accomplish these goals, they combined the farming regions into large collective units and controlled industrial development through a centralized economic plan. At best, the results were mixed.

In 1958 Mao announced a new economic plan known as the **Great Leap Forward**. Mao intended to double the production of steel and agricultural products from that of the previous year. To meet these ambitious goals, the Communist authorities compelled peasants to produce steel without proper equipment or training. The steel they manufactured often proved to be impure and useless.

The farm collectives also proved to be inefficient. Their ineffectiveness, combined with poor growing conditions, resulted in reduced harvests. As a result, famine swept across China.

Despite the famine, Mao continued to export grain to convince other nations that communism in China had produced a great bounty. The devastation caused by the famine and Mao's exportation of much-needed grain led to the deaths of twenty to thirty million Chinese people during the Great Leap Forward.

By the mid 1960s, Mao became convinced that the Chinese people had been influenced by ideas that would lead to the spread of capitalism. In order to remove these influences from Chinese society, Mao unleashed a social and political purge in 1966 known as the **Cultural Revolution**. This purge resulted in political chaos and economic upheaval for a decade.

Mao's young Chinese followers formed Red Guard groups. These gangs of extremists threatened all elements of Chinese society through their violent attacks on anything considered a threat to the Communist revolution. By 1969 Mao had to withdraw his support for these zealous followers and allow authorities to suppress them. However, the Cultural Revolution did not end until Mao's death in 1976.

CD: 19A China and Taiwan

This map from the student text is also available on the CD.

China after Mao

Chinese leaders who succeeded Mao appeared to take a more practical approach to governing China. They allowed limited reform of the economy and reduced or eliminated some of Mao's repressive controls. Because of these economic reforms, many foreign companies built factories in China and created millions of jobs for the Chinese people.

However, economic reform did not lead to significant political reform. China remained a Communist country, and political freedoms remained very limited. In the spring of 1989, student protestors filled **Tiananmen Square** in the Chinese capital of Beijing. For several days the world watched broadcasts of peaceful protests for political reform. After initial hesitation by the Communist leaders, tanks arrived in the square, and the military violently ended the demonstrations. Troops killed more than two thousand people in the process of smashing this student movement.

Cold War Crises

At various times, the United States and Soviet Union came dangerously close to a major war. However, each time the two major powers averted direct conflict by compromise or limited war that could be contained in a particular region. We will briefly look at several of these crises.

Berlin Blockade

At the end of the war, the Allies divided Germany into four zones. The British, French, and American forces occupied three of these zones. The Russians occupied the eastern zone. The German capital of Berlin lay in the Russian zone, and the Allies divided this city into four zones. The British, French, and American forces combined their zones to form the Federal Republic of Germany. The Russians established the German Democratic Republic from East German territory they controlled.

In 1948 the Soviets tested the resolve of the Allies by blocking all traffic through East Germany into West Berlin. This **Berlin Blockade** forced the Allies to make a difficult decision. In order to deliver much-needed supplies to West Berlin by road or rail, they would have to use military force. If they allowed the Soviet blockade to succeed, all of Berlin would face starvation or fall into Soviet control. However, the Allies devised an alternative plan that avoided both war and concession.

For eleven months, the United States and Britain delivered everything from coal to milk in a massive airlift. Unarmed cargo planes loaded with supplies landed in West Berlin every ninety seconds, twenty-four hours a day. The Soviets finally backed down and lifted the blockade to the German city. This struggle between the Allies and the Soviets ended without a shot being fired.

Korean War

The Allies also divided the Korean Peninsula between the Soviet Union and the United States following the war. The Soviets quickly built a strong Communist government and military and prepared to conquer all of Korea. In June 1950 the North Korean army invaded South Korea and quickly overran most of the country.

In September General Douglas MacArthur made a daring attack at **Inchon** (see map) with a UN force composed of a limited number of American and South Korean troops. MacArthur's forces drove

Popperfoto/Getty Images

Time & Life Pictures/Getty Image

Getty Images

Berlin airlift: *top*, planes lining up for supplies; *middle*, planes being loaded; *bottom*, children waiting as planes fly into West Berlin

In addition, many high-level Communists were imprisoned or executed during this purge. Mao did not even trust his friends. His last wife and three other associates were removed from positions of power within the Communist Party and charged with treason.

China after Mao

It is interesting to note that the Communist leaders allowed limited capitalism in China following the death of Mao. Lenin and Stalin also used this technique to restore the Russian economy after the disastrous experiments of collectivization. However, the Soviets soon returned to socialism, whereas China continued to allow its people a measure of capitalism. This temporary adoption of capitalism indicates Communists' knowledge that capitalism works and that communism does not work. However, the Communist Party prefers power and control to individual economic success. China continues to balance limited capitalism with Communist control but cannot maintain this shaky stance indefinitely.

CD: 19B Berlin Blockade

These photos from the student text are also available on the CD.

Memories of World War II

Memories of World War II and Its Aftermath by Inge E. Stanneck Gross gives an excellent first-person account of the suffering of the German people during and after the war. This work also includes an account of the Berlin Blockade.

Berlin Airlift

Visit www.bjupress.com/resources for possible links to articles about the Berlin airlift.

Activity 2: "Ich Bin Ein Berliner . . ."

This is the text of President John F. Kennedy's speech in support of the people of Berlin. This speech indicates President Kennedy's, and therefore America's, support for the German people in the face of the Soviet threat.

Korean War

Visit www.bjupress.com/resources for possible links to articles about the Korean War.

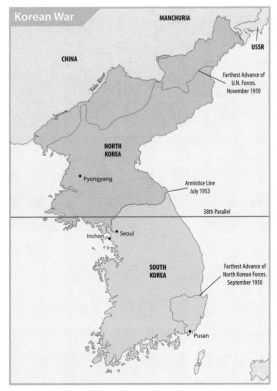

Korean War

MANCHURIA

USSR

CHINA

Yalu River

Farthest Advance of
U.N. Forces.
November 1950

NORTH
KOREA

• Pyongyang

Armistice Line
July 1953

38th Parallel

Inchon • Seoul

SOUTH
KOREA

Farthest Advance of
North Korean Forces.
September 1950

Pusan •

the Communists deep into North Korea. The entry of over one hundred thousand Chinese Communist troops preserved North Korea from total defeat. This massive infusion of troops surprised the UN troops and forced them back across the **38th parallel** (see map) into South Korea.

Fighting continued until July 1953, when both sides signed an agreement to stop fighting. Neither side had won or lost. At best, communism in Korea had been contained. The Korean Peninsula remains divided to this day.

Cuban Missile Crisis

During the fall of 1962, the United States discovered that the Soviets had placed nuclear missiles in Cuba. Reconnaissance planes had photographed construction of several missile bases. These missiles posed a serious threat to American security. The United States promptly demanded the removal of these missiles and imposed a naval blockade to prevent access to Cuba.

America and the Soviet Union came dangerously close to engaging in a nuclear war during this two-week period in October. Complicating an already tense situation, a local Soviet commander launched a missile and shot down a U-2 spy plane flying over Cuba. The crash killed the American pilot, and tensions peaked on October 28. Following secret negotiations, the Soviets agreed to remove the missiles. However, American forces did not inspect the Soviet ships to verify the actual removal of the missiles. In exchange, the United States removed recently installed missiles from Turkey and promised not to invade Cuba.

Vietnam War

Following World War II, the French tried to regain control of their colonies in Indochina, including Vietnam. However, a Communist leader named **Ho Chi Minh** resisted French efforts and declared Vietnam independent.

Vietnamese Communists ended French efforts to regain this colony at the Battle of **Dien Bien Phu** in 1954. Communist forces destroyed the French army. At the peace conference, diplomats divided Vietnam into the Communist north and the non-Communist south. However, Communists in the north began to coordinate with Communist agents in the south (known as the **Viet Cong**) in order to seize control of the whole country.

The United States and several other countries soon began to provide financial support to South Vietnam in order to prevent its fall to communism. Presidents Eisenhower and Kennedy also sent military advisors to train the Vietnamese forces.

U.S. presence increased dramatically under President Johnson beginning in 1964. Soon the government deployed over five hundred thousand American troops to Vietnam. Although U.S. forces won

Getty Images

U-2 spy plane

Soviet Invasion of Hungary

The Bridge at Andau by James A. Michener is a good teacher resource that describes the Soviet invasion of Hungary in 1956.

Model Planes

Ask volunteers to make a model of a U-2 spy plane or to obtain photos of this plane and give reports on its features and uses during the Cold War.

Vietnam War

Visit www.bjupress.com/resources for possible links to articles about the Vietnam War.

Vietnam Veterans

Some of the students' grandparents or other family members might have been involved in the Vietnam War. Invite veterans to speak about their experiences.

every battle against the enemy, many troops died and many Americans grew tired of the war. Critics questioned the morality of the American presence and the growing price of fighting communism. They also complained about real and perceived corruption in the South Vietnamese government. In addition, the media convinced many Americans that the United States was losing, and the war became very unpopular.

Richard Nixon became the president in 1968 and began to withdraw American forces from Vietnam and train the Vietnamese to defend themselves. Following the evacuation of American forces in 1973, the South Vietnamese forces slowed the Communist advance until 1975. However, Congress voted to reduce aid to the South Vietnamese during this critical period. Soon the well-supplied Communists conquered South Vietnam.

The cost to America had been high with the deaths of more than fifty thousand soldiers. In addition, the United States had spent one hundred and forty-six billion dollars to pay for this war. Following the failure to contain communism in Vietnam, America returned to a policy of isolation, and communism rapidly spread to many nations.

Rivalry for Technological Supremacy

By the end of World War II, the rush for technological supremacy increased in intensity. The development of atomic weapons, jet engines, and rockets created great potential for good or for evil. The free world and the Soviet Union worked to get ahead of one another. Many assumed the winner of the technology race would become the dominant world power. However, the winning power turned out to be the nation with the stronger and more vibrant economy.

During the course of this race for technological supremacy, some people began to question the scientific achievements that resulted. Science and technology appeared to be working toward the destruction of mankind. For example, the development of germ warfare and a growing stockpile of nuclear weapons led many to despair of the future.

Military

Both the United States and the Soviet Union developed improved versions of military weapons, including tanks, planes, submarines, and ships. In addition, radar system technology advanced and became able to detect enemy vessels much farther away.

Since the United States and Britain developed a technological edge on the Soviets, they had to constantly guard against spies who worked for the Soviet Union. Soviet military advances often looked suspiciously like those developed in the free world.

Getty Images

Ho Chi Minh

Loss of American Confidence

The United States of America had rescued the Allies in World War I. Its role in World War II was even more dramatic and led to the defeat of the Axis powers in multiple areas of the world. In 1950 America also rushed to rescue South Korea from a Communist invasion from the North.

Vietnam proved to be the war that resulted in a temporary loss of American confidence. Political decisions denied American soldiers the opportunity to win the war, and the American public questioned the role of the United States in fighting communism in distant lands.

The resulting lack of confidence led American leaders to appease the Soviets. For example, America began to sell grain to the Soviet Union as a gesture of good will. In addition, American leaders met with the Soviets and signed treaties in an attempt to end the arms race and lower the level of tension between the two superpowers.

Left, Russian Tupolev Tu-22M3, "Backfire" bomber; *right,* B-2 Spirit stealth bomber

Southeast Asia

Following the conquest of South Vietnam by the Communists, neighboring countries such as Laos and Cambodia also fell to communism. However, the Communist victory did not result in peace or stability. Cambodia endured terrible loss of life when a Communist group known as the Khmer Rouge seized power in 1975. This group emptied the cities and forced all the people to work the land. Some estimate that up to twenty-five percent of the Cambodian population died from execution, starvation, and disease during the reign of the Khmer Rouge.

In 1975, Vietnam invaded Cambodia to protect Vietnamese security interests. The Vietnamese invasion weakened the Khmer Rouge; internal Cambodian opposition took advantage of this invasion and drove the Khmer Rouge from power. In response to Vietnam's invasion of Cambodia, China invaded Vietnam in 1979. The ensuing war was brief but bloody. Both sides claimed victory.

Activity 3: *Children of the Storm*

This is an excerpt from the autobiography of Natasha Vins. Her father was a leader of the underground church in the Soviet Union. Vins's account of suffering under communism is compelling and enlightening for the reader.

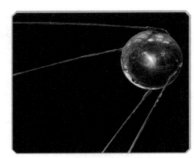

Replica of *Sputnik 1*

Apollo 15's Command/Service Module *Endeavour* as seen from the Lunar Module *Falcon*, during rendezvous

Nuclear

The United States became the first nation to harness the power of the atom, but Russia and other nations quickly developed their own nuclear weapons. During the Cold War, governments developed missiles with single and then multiple nuclear warheads. In addition, improved atomic bombs increased the amount of damage that one nation could inflict on an enemy target.

An early example of nuclear rivalry appeared when the Soviet Union exploded its first atomic bomb in 1949. The United States responded by working to develop the much more powerful hydrogen bomb. However, the Soviets soon developed their own hydrogen bomb.

This ongoing struggle to match or exceed one another led to the arms race. Over the course of the Cold War, the United States and the Soviet Union developed the technology and stockpiled more than enough weapons to destroy one another. Known as mutually assured destruction (**MAD**), this strategy contributed to American and European appeasement. It also led to the signing of treaties designed to reduce the number of nuclear weapons. The Soviets took advantage of this perceived weakness and continued to seize territory.

Space

The Soviets took the lead in the race to place machines in space. In 1957 Soviet scientists launched ***Sputnik***, the first man-made satellite. While the American government hurried to catch up in this race, the Soviets made another leap forward by launching the first man into space. From this point on, Americans determined to win the race to send a mission to the moon.

While the Soviet Union had initially led in the space race, the United States quickly outpaced Soviet efforts, rapidly developed the necessary technology, and launched the first of several successful trips to the moon by the end of the 1960s. The Soviets soon abandoned their efforts to travel to the moon and concentrated on building a space station.

In addition to manned flights into space, the United States and other countries developed satellites for communication. Satellites also enabled nations to spy on their enemies without the risk of being

Astronaut Eugene A. Cernan driving a lunar roving vehicle on the moon

Astronaut Alan Bean taking soil samples on the moon

shot down. This technology developed many civilian uses, including satellites designed to record weather conditions.

Early satellite

Section Quiz

1. How do Communist values differ from those of Western democracies?
2. Briefly describe the results of Mao Zedong's Great Leap Forward.
3. Why did Chinese Communists kill students in Tiananmen Square in 1989?
4. Who won the Korean War?
5. At what battle did the Vietnamese destroy the French Army?
★ In what ways was the American civil religion better than Soviet suppression of Christianity? In what ways was it worse?

III. Transition in the Third World and Middle East

As the Cold War progressed, Western nations continued to stress freedom and democracy. Men and women in the third world increasingly adopted this emphasis. If nations like Great Britain and France were so pleased with democracy and freedom, they asked, why could the colonies not have the freedom to become independent democracies?

Indian Nationalism

Indians had pressed the British government for independence over many years. Britain gradually granted India a measure of self-rule through provincial councils. However, the people wanted to achieve independence at a faster pace than the British were willing to concede. Several Indian revolutionaries resorted to violent confrontations with the British. However, one man rejected violence and played an important role in India's independence through methods that were more peaceful.

Mohandas Gandhi (1869–1948) led a movement known as **passive resistance** to achieve Indian independence. Rather than fight against British rule, Gandhi encouraged his many followers to resist

> **The Third World**
> During the Cold War, the regions that remained neutral and did not ally themselves with the free world or the Communist powers became known as the **third world**. These regions included Latin America, South America, Africa, the Middle East, and Southern Asia.

Time & Life Pictures/Getty Image

Mohandas Gandhi

Section III

Objectives

Students should be able to

1. Assess the impact of Indian nationalism and explain why the British partitioned the subcontinent into India and Pakistan.
2. Assess the impact of World War II on the rise of nationalist movements in Africa and Southeast Asia.
3. Analyze why some African and Asian countries achieved independence through constitutional means, while others did so through armed revolution.
4. Explain how international conditions influenced the creation of Israel and analyze the reasons for the persistent conflict between Israel and its Arab neighbors.

Gandhi

Martin Luther King Jr. and other American civil rights leaders followed Gandhi's teaching on passive resistance. They staged sit-ins, strikes, and marches to highlight their demand for justice and equality.

Third World Countries

While not all countries in the third world were poor, many of them were. Often, these countries lacked freely elected governments or capitalist economies. Without freely elected governments, the people could not place checks on the unbridled power of government officials. Eventually, the people had no voice in political decisions and could not elect those who would represent

The Third World

Help students understand the meaning of this term. Some use this term to refer to the very poor countries of the world. However, students should know that this term originally signified nations that did not formally take sides with the free world or the Communist world during the Cold War.

Section Quiz Answers

1. Answers may vary but should include the following: Communists emphasize the state, while Western democracies emphasize the role of the individual. Communists have consistently carried out religious persecution, while Western democracies value religious freedom.

2. Communist officials forced poorly trained peasants to manufacture steel; the steel they produced was often impure and worthless. Inadequate harvests combined with exportation of Chinese grain led to over twenty million deaths.

3. The Communists sought to crush a student movement that was seeking political freedom.

4. no one

5. Dien Bien Phu

★ Answers will vary but should include some of the following: The acceptance of a generically Christian civil religion in mid-twentieth-century America meant that Christians were not persecuted and that they had broad opportunities to function in society and government. However, accepting this nominal Christianity, many unsaved people deceived themselves into thinking that they were true Christians.

their interests. Without the presence of free-market economies, the wealthy retained their wealth, and the poor often remained poor, with little opportunity to advance to the middle class. A capitalist economy enables the development of a growing middle class and provides a balance to the extremes of abject poverty and excessive wealth.

Lingering Effects of Colonization

Beginning in the late 1940s, African colonies began to gain their independence from European countries. Some colonies quickly transitioned into nations. Others struggled and endured years of political instability. To some extent, the forced colonization of the previous century created many of the problems. Europeans developed African economies and infrastructures to advance European interests rather than to benefit the Africans. After the Second World War, most of the European nations were struggling with their own staggering problems and could do little to prepare African colonies for successful independence. European greed in the nineteenth century followed by twentieth-century European impotence created many problems for the emerging African nations.

the British through strikes, refusal to pay taxes, and other non-violent means.

After years of Indian resistance, the British finally granted India full independence in 1947. However, independence did not end the turmoil. For example, a supporter of Hindu nationalism assassinated Gandhi in 1948. India contiued to struggle with internal violence and occasional wars with its neighbors.

To minimize the growing hostility between Hindus and Muslims in India, the British partitioned India into two nations, India for the Hindu population and Pakistan for the Muslim population. Despite the efforts to avoid violence, rioting broke out between Sikhs, Hindus, and Muslims and about one half million people died.

In addition to the violence, nearly twelve million Sikhs, Hindus, and Muslims moved between these newly created nations. Violent clashes have continued, and these countries have endured many deadly struggles between various ethnic and religious groups.

Rise of Nationalist Movements

World War II led many colonial powers to realize that the citizens of their foreign empires had the right to be free just as they had fought to remain free of fascist control. In addition, the African colonies had contributed men and materials in support of the Allied cause. Following the war, these colonies expected to receive their freedom. The European nations gradually granted independence to their colonies. As a result, over the next thirty-five years, nearly one hundred and twenty nations emerged from Africa, Asia, and the Middle East.

Africa

Ghana became the first African nation to achieve independence. The British government had already recognized that the colonies needed to be developed and that the Africans needed to have a greater voice in the functioning of the colonies. Ghana had an educated population and appeared to be an ideal colony to start this process.

In preparation for Ghana's independence, the British announced a general election in which Africans could vote and run for offices in a national assembly. In 1951 Kwame Nkrumah and his Convention People's Party captured the national assembly in a landslide victory. On March 6, 1957, Ghana became the first African colony to develop into an independent African nation. Within a few years, the majority of African nations had gained their independence.

However, not all colonies gained independence peacefully. In colonies that had large populations of European settlers, the transition to independence often involved armed conflict. For example, the European population in Southern Rhodesia declared independence from Great Britain in 1965, fearing that Britain would force them to accept majority rule. In the early 1970s, a guerilla war began. Finally, in 1979 the Africans gained the right of self-government, and Southern Rhodesia became Zimbabwe.

At first, gains made by independence were remarkable, and many of the young African nations seemed to prosper. The governments set up schools and health-care clinics. However, over time, conditions began to deteriorate. Europeans had designed the economic structures to function in a mercantilist rather than a free market economy.

In addition, many of the early African leaders became convinced that socialism held great promise for bringing their people out of

India's Struggles for Stability

Ask one or more volunteers to research the struggles between Hindus and Muslims in India and to present the results of their research to the class. For example, one student could examine the formation of Pakistan as a homeland for Muslims, and another student could examine the British efforts to prevent violence as India became independent.

African Struggles for Independence

Ask volunteers to research the struggles that occurred in African colonies as these regions gained their independence. Have the volunteers select countries from the map on page 361 and present the results of their research to the class.

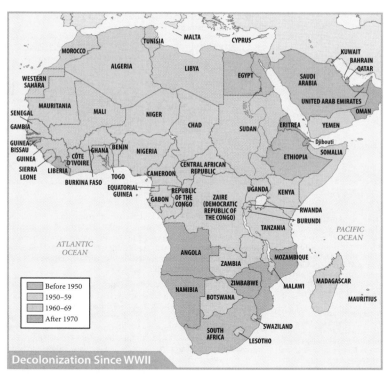

Decolonization Since WWII

poverty. Thus, even well-intentioned leaders often set up policies that hampered their countries' growth. Sadly, not all leaders cared for the welfare of their people. Corrupt leaders often channeled a great deal of wealth into their personal bank accounts rather than using it to benefit their people.

African nations also found themselves caught between the United States and the Soviet Union. Soviets often took advantage of the weakness of these young nations and tried to spread communism across Africa. America responded by trying to prevent the spread of communism.

Often the United States government supported African dictatorships if they aligned with the West against the Soviet Union. As a result, many dictators received supplies of cash and arms that enabled them to maintain a firm grip on their people. However, following the Cold War, many of these dictatorships collapsed as aid to African countries became subject to humanitarian treatment of the people.

Southeast Asia

We have already examined developments in India, Pakistan, and Vietnam. In addition, several mainland and island nations gained independence during this period. The United States had prepared the Philippines for eventual independence, and this independence

CD: 19C Decolonization of Africa since WWII

This map from the student text is also available on the CD.

occurred in 1946. European colonies in this region gained their independence over the next twenty years (see map).

Decolonization Since WWII

Clashes Between Islam and the West

Muslims viewed the creation of modern Israel as intolerable. Muslim leaders claim Palestine as Muslim land and have repeatedly vowed to exterminate the Jews. In addition, Muslims recognize the Dome of the Rock in Jerusalem and the Al Aqsa Mosque on the Temple Mount in Jerusalem as sacred Muslim sites. Thus, Muslim leaders see the Jewish presence in Israel as defiling their land and their holy sites.

The West's support for Israel has led to violent clashes between Islam and the West. The Iranian hostage crisis in Iran, between 1979 and 1981, demonstrated this violent hostility toward the West. During this crisis, Muslim militants invaded the American embassy in Iran and held fifty-three Americans hostage for over a year. Following the election and inauguration of President Reagan, the militants freed these hostages. However, this proved to be only the first of many Muslim attacks on Americans.

Rebirth of Israel

Since the Roman legions had destroyed Jerusalem in AD 70, the Jews had no homeland and spent centuries scattered throughout many nations. However, during the late nineteenth century, Jewish leaders began to work toward establishing a homeland. At the beginning of the twentieth century, Jews returned to Palestine in small numbers and purchased land.

Creation of Israel as a Modern State

In 1917 British Foreign Secretary Arthur Balfour issued a policy statement declaring that the British government favored the idea of a homeland for the Jewish people in Palestine. Known as the **Balfour Declaration**, it became the first official recognition by a world power that the Jews needed a land to call their own.

The British had governed Palestine as a mandate following World War I. However, by 1947 British forces realized they could no longer restrain the Jewish immigration and the growing Arab resentment. The British decided to partition Palestine into a Jewish state and an Arab state.

The British Mandate expired on May 14, 1948. On May 13 Jewish leaders proclaimed independence and named their new country Israel. The United States immediately recognized Israel as a country

May 16, 1948, edition of Jewish newspaper *The Palestine Post*, soon renamed *The Jerusalem Post*

 CD: 19D Decolonization of Southeast Asia since WWII

This map from the student text is also available on the CD.

The Rebirth of Israel

Ask a volunteer to research the Jewish people's efforts to bring about the rebirth of their nation. Another volunteer could research the Arab response to Israel's reformation as a nation in the Middle East. Have the students present their findings to the class.

 Conflict Between Israel and Arab Nations

Visit www.bjupress.com/resources for possible links to articles about conflict between Israel and Arab nations.

and provided military aid. Surprisingly, Stalin and the Soviet Union also recognized the nation of Israel.

Arab Response

Arab forces from Egypt, Syria, Jordan, Lebanon, and Iraq attacked Israel on May 14 and started the **1948 Arab-Israeli War**. After a year of fighting, both sides signed a ceasefire. Arab nations continued to support attacks on Israel and planned another major assault in June 1967. Egypt, Jordan, and Syria prepared to invade Israel with the assistance of several other Arab countries. However, the Jewish forces struck first and quickly destroyed most of the tanks, planes, and other weapons that were waiting to invade from Egypt and Syria. Known as the **Six-Day War**, Israel smashed the imminent Arab threat and seized control of several key areas that greatly enhanced Israel's security.

Section Quiz

1. What method did Mohandas Gandhi use to pressure the British to grant India independence?

2. Why did Britain partition India into India and Pakistan?

3. What problems did African states encounter upon independence?

4. What nation governed Palestine from the end of World War I until 1948?

5. What was the Arab response to the creation of Israel as a nation in 1948?

★ What religious reasons cause Muslim leaders to reject Israel's right to exist as a nation in the land often referred to as Palestine?

IV. Collapse of the Soviet Union

In hindsight, it seems that the Soviet Union was destined to fall. Like other empires from the past, the Russians and their allies had seized more territory than they could successfully govern. In addition, the Soviet Union was composed of many nationalities and ethnic groups with little in common. Considering the fact that only five to ten percent of the people became members of the Communist party, it is astonishing that the Soviet Union survived until 1991. However, almost no one predicted the rapid demise of the Soviet Union during the 1970s and into the 1980s.

Soviet Aggression

By the end of the 1960s and on into the 1970s, freedom appeared to be on the decline, and communism appeared to be winning the Cold War. However, the election of strong leaders, including Margaret Thatcher and Ronald Reagan, resulted in a dramatic reversal during the 1980s.

The 1970s

The invasion of Czechoslovakia in 1968 provides a clear example of Soviet aggression. Alexander Dubček (DOOB chek) became the leader of Czechoslovakia in January 1968 and began to restore rights to the Czech people. He loosened control of the media, allowing free

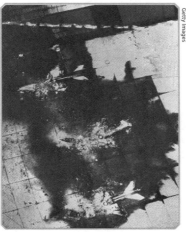

Six-Day War in 1967: *top,* Soviet-made tanks used by Egypt during the Six-Day War; *above,* Egyptian planes destroyed by Israel's Air Force

Students resisting Soviet invasion of Czechoslovakia

Section IV

Objectives

Students should be able to

1. Trace the development of the Cold War through the 1970s and 1980s, giving special attention to the strong leaders who helped dissolve the Soviet Union.

2. Explain why the Soviet and other Communist governments collapsed in the 1990s.

3. Describe how the Soviet Union splintered into various states by the early 1990s.

4. Analyze the impact of the Soviet Union's collapse on the growth of Christianity in these areas.

Hungary, 1956

When the Soviets invaded Czechoslovakia in 1968, they opposed the Hungarians with the same aggressive tactics that they used to squelch a Hungarian revolt in 1956. The Hungarians hoped that the Americans and others would come to their aid when they revolted in 1956, but the West allowed Soviet forces to crush the Hungarian revolution.

CD: 19E Six-Day War

A photo of the Six-Day War is available on the CD.

Section Quiz Answers

1. passive resistance

2. to provide separate nations for Hindus (India) and Muslims (Pakistan)

3. Answers may vary but should include some of the following: They struggled with civil war, declining conditions, leaders who embraced socialism, and pressure to align with the Soviet Union or the United States.

4. Britain

5. a year-long war that ended in an armistice

★ The Muslims believe that Palestine is a holy land belonging to the Muslims. The Dome of the Rock and the Al Aqsa Mosque are holy sites for Muslims. They believe that the Jewish presence in Israel defiles the land and Muslim holy sites.

Expansion of the Soviet Union

Ask a volunteer to research the expansion of the Soviet Union that occurred during the 1960s and 1970s. Have this student share the report with the class.

American Isolationism

American political leaders restrained American military forces and denied them the opportunity to attain a victory during the conflict in Vietnam. Following the demoralization of the military and American society, the nation withdrew from international involvement in the mid-1970s. The next seventeen years saw the rapid expansion of communism and the rise of Muslim radicalism. During this time the United States and its leaders proved unwilling to become involved in any foreign affairs. Leaders of both U.S. political parties sought to maintain a peaceful existence with the Soviet Union, Communist China, and other nations, including Iran. However, American isolationism ended following the defeat of President Jimmy Carter and the election of President Ronald Reagan. The United States again assumed its position as a superpower.

speech, and began to privatize the economy. This reform angered the Soviets, and they demanded that these changes cease.

When the Czech government refused to submit to the Soviet threats, the Russians and their allies sent a large armed force to crush resistance in Czechoslovakia in August 1968. Despite protests by Czechs and Western governments, no serious attempt was made to liberate Czechoslovakia. The Soviet troops remained until 1990.

The Soviet Union also supported North Vietnam's attempt to defeat the U.S.-supported government in South Vietnam. With the departure of American forces in 1973, communism gained an immense victory and succeeded in humiliating the United States. As America turned to isolationism, the Soviets became more bold in their spread of communism throughout Africa and Latin America.

Left, Afghan soldier aiming an American-made stinger missile at enemy aircraft; *right,* Afghan guerilla soldiers known as the mujahideen

The 1980s

The Soviets engaged in aggression again when a large Russian force invaded Afghanistan in 1979. On the pretense of bringing stability to this country, the Soviet Union sent over one hundred thousand troops to seize control of this region. However, the Afghans vigorously resisted the Soviet occupation. With the U.S. providing weapons and financial support, the Afghans fought the Soviet troops to a stalemate. Although several hundred thousand Afghan fighters and civilians died because of the Soviet invasion, the Russians found victory to be elusive. Facing growing losses with no prospect of victory, the Soviet forces withdrew in 1989.

Strong Leadership in the West

In 1979 **Margaret Thatcher** led the Conservative Party in Great Britain to victory. She returned many nationalized industries to the private sector and tried to reverse many of the socialist programs that had weakened the British nation. In addition, she supported the anti-Communist strategy of a newly elected American president and forged a strong alliance with the United States during her eleven years as prime minister of Great Britain.

Ronald Reagan became the fortieth president of the United States in 1980. His strong leadership turned a struggling America into a political, social, and economic force that influenced the world. Reagan rejected the commonly accepted concession that the free world must peacefully coexist with communism. Instead, he focused the resources of the United States in an effort to overthrow this oppressive system of government. Through alliances with other

Margaret Thatcher

Strong Leaders in the West

Ask a volunteer to research the life of Margaret Thatcher. Have another volunteer examine the life of Ronald Reagan. Encourage the volunteers to emphasize these leaders' strong conservative standpoints and have them share their findings with the class.

Margaret Thatcher

Visit www.bjupress.com/resources for possible links to articles about Margaret Thatcher.

Ronald Reagan

Visit www.bjupress.com/resources for possible links to articles about Ronald Reagan.

Left, woman looking through a hole in the Berlin Wall; *below left,* President Reagan speaking at the Brandenburg Gate in West Berlin; *below right,* President Reagan (center), Vice President Bush, and Gorbachev, ca. 1988

conservative leaders such as Margaret Thatcher, he led an effective campaign to plant or restore democracy in many countries.

In addition, his policy of peace through strength led to the re-building of America's military might. In a speech made in 1983, President Reagan called for a space-based defensive system that would protect the United States from foreign missile attacks. Critics called Reagan's **SDI** (Space Defense Initiative) program Star Wars, but programs such as this convinced the Soviets that they could not compete with America. This realization contributed to the unraveling of the Soviet Union and led to its rapid disintegration.

While the Soviet Union supported the spread of communism in other countries, dissatisfaction and unrest continued to build in Soviet-dominated countries of Eastern Europe. Poland and the growth of the Solidarity Free Trade Union clearly demonstrated this unrest. Led by an electrical technician, **Lech Wałęsa**, Polish work-ers formed an anti-Communist movement that combined labor, the Roman Catholic Church, and Polish nationalism to oppose Soviet domination. Wałęsa endured job loss and imprisonment to lead the **Solidarity** movement and help achieve Polish independence by 1989. Pope John Paul II also lent his support to this movement in 1987.

Lech Wałęsa

The Reagan Era

In the late 1970s many viewed Ronald Reagan as a has-been actor and a man too conservative to be elected presi-dent of the United States. However, he proved to be one of the greatest presi-dents in American history. Ignoring polls in 1979 that predicted the re-election of Jimmy Carter, Reagan persevered and became the fortieth president of the United States. Despite the liberal me-dia's portraying him as a man of limited intelligence, he proved to be a wise and principled leader. Surviving a near-fatal gunshot wound early in his first term, Reagan labored with renewed determi-nation to bring down the Soviet empire and stop the spread of communism. Al-lied with other strong leaders, including his close friend Margaret Thatcher, he pressured the enemies of freedom and sent aid to those who opposed tyranny. Shortly after Reagan's second term, the Soviet Union collapsed, and much of Eastern Europe gained its freedom. While some pretend that this was due to the efforts of Russian leader Mikhail Gorbachev, history will show that the collapse of the Soviet empire was ac-complished because of the consistent leadership of President Reagan.

Activity 4: "Tear Down This Wall!"

This is the text of President Reagan's speech given before the Brandenburg Gate at the Berlin Wall where Reagan called upon Gor-bachev to "tear down this wall!" Although many scoffed at Reagan's demand, the Soviet Union soon collapsed, and the East Germans began to dismantle the Berlin Wall less than two years later.

SDI

Ask a volunteer to research President Rea-gan's plan to create a space-based missile defense system called SDI. Have the student share the report with the class.

Poland's Struggle for Independence

Discuss the struggle in Poland to gain in-dependence and the role that Lech Wałęsa played in that struggle. Also, explain the growth of the Solidarity movement as the Poles united to gain Polish independence.

Glasnost

Glasnost is the Russian word for publicity or openness to the public. Corruption was rampant in the Soviet Union when Mikhail Gorbachev came to power. To reduce this corruption and revive the stagnant Soviet economy, Gorbachev instituted the policy of glasnost. He hoped to weaken political corruption by making the government more transparent. Gorbachev also allowed Russians freedom of speech to openly discuss problems, with the goal of reforming Soviet society. However, he remained a Leninist and had no intention of ending communism. Gorbachev merely wanted to try new ways of reforming the Communist system while preserving the Soviet Union. However, freedom is difficult to control, and glasnost played an important role in the final unraveling of the artificially created Soviet Union.

Perestroika

Perestroika is the Russian word for restructuring or rebuilding. Mikhail Gorbachev instituted this political movement as a way to reform the Soviet systems and revitalize the Communist Party. He reformed the political system by giving Russians more Communist candidates for local elections. Despite conservative opposition, Gorbachev was also able to reduce the power of some members of the Politburo. He was less successful at reforming the economic system. However, perestroika did play a key role in the collapse of the Soviet Union as the Communist government lost control of economic conditions. The Soviet economy essentially

Fall of the Soviet Union and Division along National Lines

The Soviet Union used force and military threats to enslave millions and hold an artificial empire together. However, the Soviet Union had to accept grain shipments from the United States and steal military technology from America and other countries in order to survive. Socialism and communism are not self-sustaining, and nations that embrace these forms of government cannot survive without the aid and support of others.

Collapse of the Soviet System

Following Stalin's death in 1953, **Nikita Khrushchev** ruled the Soviet Union until 1964. His policies became unpopular, and Kremlin leaders voted him out of office while he was out of the country on vacation. Khrushchev was succeeded by several aging Russian leaders. Meanwhile, a younger leader rose through the ranks of the Kremlin. Upon the death of the Soviet leader in 1985, **Mikhail Gorbachev** emerged as the leader of the Soviet Union. He assumed power without violence or opposition.

For decades the Soviet government had emphasized building a strong military. During these years the people had endured rationing of food, clothing, and other material goods. Gorbachev tried to revive the Soviet Union by ushering in a period of political and economic restructuring. He allowed private ownership of businesses and released thousands of political prisoners. In 1987 Gorbachev moved the Soviet Union closer to democracy by calling for multi-candidate elections. In 1990 the people elected him as the first president of the Soviet Union.

Because of these dramatic changes, the Communist Party lost control of the Soviet Union and additional changes could not be prevented. As the people realized that their government had been lying to them for years, they revolted against the Communist system and demanded freedom from Soviet domination.

Division into Many States

The people of Romania violently opposed their Communist rulers and overthrew them. Other nations, including Bulgaria, Czechoslovakia, East Germany, Hungary, and Poland, broke away from their Soviet masters and declared their independence. By 1991 the Soviet Union had quickly divided into fifteen independent states.

Mikhail Gorbachev

States Formed from the Former Soviet Union

CD: 19F States Formed from the Former Soviet Union

This map from the student text is also available on the CD.

New Opportunities for Christians

With the fall of the Soviet Union, many changes occurred in Eastern Europe. Some of those changes included religious freedoms that the Communists had denied millions of people for over seventy years.

Freedom to Worship

While religious persecution became more intense at some times than at others, Communists consistently discouraged or prohibited Christians from publicly assembling to worship. Often believers had to meet in barns, forests, or fields in order to hold a church service. Yet, despite the discomfort and danger associated with public worship, Christians continued to meet whenever possible to worship and to encourage one another.

With the collapse of the Soviet Union, Christians could now meet in public and worship without fear of arrest or harassment. Believers in Eastern Europe thronged to churches to take advantage of this new freedom.

Freedom to Evangelize

In addition to the freedom to worship, Christians could now witness to their neighbors and family members without fear of arrest and possible imprisonment. Many Christians had faithfully witnessed under the Communist regime, but they did so at great personal risk. This new freedom enabled Christians in many Eastern European countries to spread the good news of the gospel without government interference.

Missionary Outreach

Missionaries from the West could now obtain visas and minister in former Communist nations. This new freedom allowed Christians, primarily from the United States, to take the gospel to remote regions of the former Soviet Union and shine the light of God's Word across this vast region.

Section Quiz

1. How did the Soviet Union respond to the Czech attempt to restore basic rights to its people?

2. What country did the Soviets invade and try without success to conquer over a ten-year period?

3. What program did President Reagan propose that convinced the Soviet Union that it could no longer compete with the United States?

4. What Soviet leader came to power in 1985?

5. What impact did the Soviet emphasis on a strong military have on the civilian population?

★ Why did the reforms supported by Gorbachev lead to the collapse of the Soviet Union?

collapsed, and Communist leaders lost credibility with the people. Under these conditions, Communist loss of power was inevitable.

Christianity in the Former Soviet Union

Christian pastors and missionaries are often invited to present the gospel in public schools located in these formerly Communist nations. In some ways, there is now more religious freedom in these countries than in many parts of the United States. However, recent crackdowns in these nations may indicate the return of repression.

Section Quiz Answers

1. They invaded Czechoslovakia and occupied the nation until the fall of the Soviet Union.

2. Afghanistan

3. Space Defense Initiative (SDI)

4. Mikhail Gorbachev

5. They had to endure rationing of food, clothing, and almost everything else.

★ Gorbachev's reforms gave the people a taste of freedom. As a result, the Communist Party lost control. The people revolted and demanded their freedom.

Activity 5: Chapter Review

This activity helps the students prepare for the chapter test.

CHAPTER REVIEW

People, Places, and Terms to Know

Cold War
Konrad Adenauer
Charles de Gaulle
Fifth Republic
Liberal Democratic Party
Marshall Plan
Common Market
NATO
United Nations
Republic of China
Great Leap Forward
Cultural Revolution
Tiananmen Square
Berlin Blockade
Inchon
38th parallel
Ho Chi Minh
Dien Bien Phu
Viet Cong
MAD
Sputnik
third world
Mohandas Gandhi
passive resistance
Balfour Declaration
1948 Arab-Israeli War
Six-Day War
Margaret Thatcher
Ronald Reagan
SDI
Lech Wałęsa
Solidarity
Nikita Krushchev
Mikhail Gorbachev

Making Connections

1. Why was the economic recovery of Europe urgent following World War II?
2. How did Japan recover rapidly from the devastation of the World War II?
3. Why did Britain and France resort to high tax rates?
4. How do Communist states and Western democracies differ regarding ownership of property?
5. Why did Mao Zedong instigate the political purge known as the Cultural Revolution? What happened as a result of this purge?
6. Why did the United States retreat from the war in Vietnam?
7. Why are spy satellites more effective and safer than spy planes?
8. How successful was Britain's attempt to separate Hindus and Muslims in order to minimize hostility between these two religious groups?
9. How did Ronald Reagan and Margaret Thatcher play a leading role in the collapse of the Soviet Union?

Developing History Skills

1. On the map on the facing page, locate the following countries that received aid from or came under the domination of the Soviet Union.
   a. China
   b. Czechoslovakia
   c. East Germany
   d. North Korea
   e. North Vietnam
2. How did President Reagan's SDI proposals play a role in ending the Cold War?

Thinking Critically

1. How is the Islamic threat that emerged toward the end of the Cold War similar to the Soviet threat? How is it different?
2. A growing number of historians credit Mikhail Gorbachev with dismantling the Soviet Union. Evaluate this view in the light of what you have learned in this chapter.

Living in God's World

1. During the Cold War, many liberal theologians spoke out against the arms race as un-Christian and immoral. Write a brief newspaper editorial taking the opposite position on biblical grounds.

Chapter Review Answers

Making Connections

1. The Soviet Union actively sought to destabilize European countries to bring them under Communist domination.
2. Japan received financial and technological aid from the U.S. With the Americans providing military protection, Japan could pour its resources into heavy industry and the development of electronics technology.
3. to support government-run programs and expensive social-security systems
4. Communist states reject private ownership and replace it with government ownership of property. Western democracies recognize the need for and the value of private ownership of property.
5. to remove any capitalist influences on China; political chaos, economic upheaval, and violent attacks on those viewed as threats to the Communist revolution
6. growing casualties, negative media reports, and many Americans' criticism of the war
7. Nations can spy on one another from space with little or no risk. Spy planes can be shot down.
8. It was unsuccessful. They continued to fight and kill one another in large numbers.
9. They provided strong leadership and actively supported democratic movements in many countries. Thatcher supported Reagan's anti-Communist strategies and formed an alliance with the United States. Reagan rebuilt America's military might to a level that the Soviets could not match. His call for the destruction of the Berlin Wall helped to inspire Germans to demand the restoration of their divided country.

Developing History Skills

1. a. 3
   b. 2
   c. 1
   d. 5
   e. 4

2. Imagine that you are a newly elected president from a recently independent colony. Write a report detailing how you plan to learn from the mistakes of colonies liberated in the twentieth century.

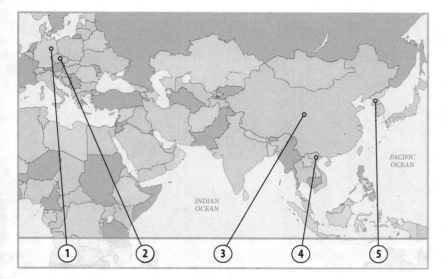

2. Answers will vary but should include some of the following: Many of the concepts for the development of the SDI proposed by President Reagan proved to be viable, and the accuracy of these defensive weapons continues to improve. President Reagan's proposals led the Soviets to realize they could not compete with American technology. This contributed to the collapse of the Soviet Union and the ending of the Cold War.

Thinking Critically

1. Answers will vary but should include some of the following: The Islamic threat is similar to the Soviet threat in its hatred toward Western civilization and in its determination to destroy it. However, with the exception of Iran, most of the Islamic groups opposing the West are not states. Furthermore, religious fervor motivates the Islamic groups. Soviet motivations varied, but religious fervor was not one of them.

2. Answers may vary but should include some of the following: Gorbachev attempted to revive the Soviet Union with reforms. His goal was not the dissolution of the Soviet Union but its survival. Much of the credit for the collapse of the Soviet Union should go to strong leaders in the West, including Margaret Thatcher and Ronald Reagan.

Living in God's World

1. Answers will vary but could include the following: The Bible permits countries to maintain self-defense; thus wars of self-defense are not immoral. Nations have the obligation to protect their citizens from harm; nations that do not prepare to protect their citizens violate that trust. Developing military strength serves as a deterrent against attacks. Thus, military buildup can actually avert war rather than cause it.

2. Answers will vary but may include the following: Having learned from the mistakes of others, the new president may advocate the establishment of rule of law, an independent judiciary, a free press, strong penalties for corruption, rejection of socialist approaches to economics, and a forgiving attitude toward the colonial power.

Getty Images/photosindia

CHAPTER 20

Chapter Goals

Students should be able to

1. Describe major environmental trends.
2. Explain the development of the global economy.
3. Evaluate trends in technology and technology's impact on culture.
4. Analyze political and religious trends.

1960–2010

Central American Common Market is formed 1960s

Saddam Hussein attacks Iran 1980

Iran is taken over by radical Muslim forces 1979

| 1960 | 1970 | 1980 |

Development of the Internet for military use 1960s

Iran holds fifty-two Americans hostage 1979–80

Materials List

Section I
- Activity 1 from the *Student Activities* manual
- CD: 20A Nuclear-Powered Ship; 20B Solar Power Plant; 20C NASA Solar-Powered Plane

Section II
- CD: 20D Member States of the European Union; 20E Formation of the European Union

Section III
- Activity 2 from the *Student Activities* manual

Chapter 20 Lesson Plan Chart			
Section Title	**Main Activity**	**Pages**	**Days**
I. Environmental Trends	Activity 1: European Union	372–75	1–2 days
II. Global Economy	Discussion Activity: Product Safety	376–78	1 day
III. Technology and Culture	Activity 2: Stem Cell Research	378–80	1 day
IV. Political and Religious Trends	Activity 3: Chapter Review	380–84	1½–2 days
TOTAL SUGGESTED DAYS (INCLUDING 1 DAY EACH FOR REVIEW AND TESTING)			6½–8 days

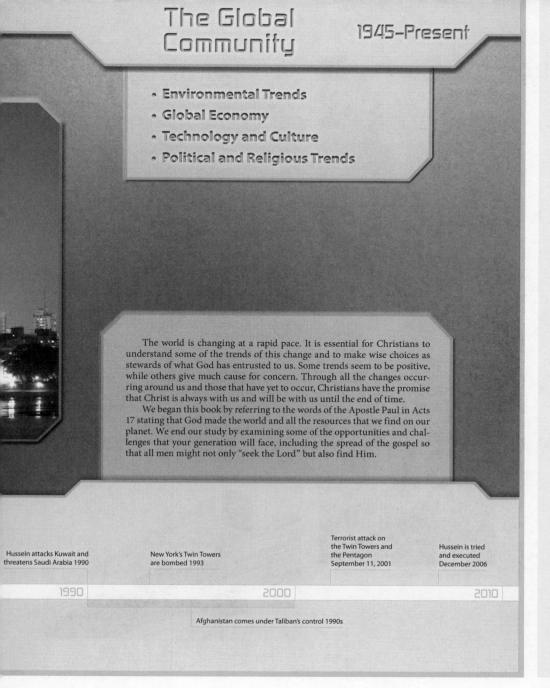

The Global Community

1945–Present

- Environmental Trends
- Global Economy
- Technology and Culture
- Political and Religious Trends

The world is changing at a rapid pace. It is essential for Christians to understand some of the trends of this change and to make wise choices as stewards of what God has entrusted to us. Some trends seem to be positive, while others give much cause for concern. Through all the changes occurring around us and those that have yet to occur, Christians have the promise that Christ is always with us and will be with us until the end of time.

We began this book by referring to the words of the Apostle Paul in Acts 17 stating that God made the world and all the resources that we find on our planet. We end our study by examining some of the opportunities and challenges that your generation will face, including the spread of the gospel so that all men might not only "seek the Lord" but also find Him.

Hussein attacks Kuwait and threatens Saudi Arabia 1990

New York's Twin Towers are bombed 1993

Terrorist attack on the Twin Towers and the Pentagon September 11, 2001

Hussein is tried and executed December 2006

1990

2000

2010

Afghanistan comes under Taliban's control 1990s

Section IV

- CD: 20F Fallujah
- Activity 3 from the *Student Activities* manual

Section I

Objectives

Students should be able to

1. Describe population shifts.
2. Explain the growth of urban life.
3. Describe the theories of climate change.
4. Evaluate the issues related to energy resources.
5. Explain man's role in the environment.

I. Environmental Trends

The earth with its billions of human inhabitants and varied species of animal life continues to experience changes in its environment. These alterations are reflected in shifting population numbers, continued movement to cities, ongoing climate change, and the growing need for energy sources.

Population Shifts

Recently the human population passed six billion, and it may reach nine billion by 2050. Some areas of the world maintain a stable or gradually declining population, while others have a rapidly increasing population.

Stable or Declining

Most nations in Europe are experiencing a decline in population due to low birth rates. Large numbers of immigrants have slowed this decline, but many European states continue to experience a reduction of population. North America also has a lower birth rate. However, the migration of foreign-born individuals to the United States has enabled this nation to maintain a stable population.

In our study of history, we can see that population growth or decline and movement to urban areas has resulted in significant changes. Eventually, a society's culture alters because of these changes. For example, the shrinking of Western culture in relation to the world's population is gradually resulting in post-Western culture, which is influenced more and more by emerging cultures from Latin America and Africa.

Nations that are maintaining a stable population are learning to manage environmental problems that accompany an industrial society, including various forms of pollution. Even though these states maintain a stable population, their influence in the world tends to diminish because of the growth of other regions.

Nations that experience a declining population tend to have significant problems. For example, they do not produce enough children to maintain the needed population to provide a future labor force and solve environmental issues. Over time, immigrants used to meet labor needs will dominate these states. Declining states will cease to play any significant role in the international arena. They may even be absorbed by other countries.

Scenes from modern Tokyo, Japan

Activity 1: European Union

This map exercise helps the students understand the geographic makeup of the European Union and sharpens their geography skills.

Growing at Varying Rates

A growing percentage of the world's population will live outside of the countries traditionally considered advanced. While the long-term effects of this population shift are impossible to determine, significant change is to be expected.

Regions such as Latin America and Asia, especially India and China, have produced the largest and fastest growing populations. In addition, the populations of many states in Africa are rapidly growing despite regional wars and diseases.

A growing urban population and increasing industrialization are forcing these countries to deal with the environmental problems that result. For example, improved sanitation and increasing supplies of safe drinking water are essential to prevent the spread of disease. Increased use of coal and oil has also created significantly more pollution. Many of these emerging nations struggle to balance growing industry with protecting the environment.

Growth of Urban Life

The growing human population is continuing its movement to urban centers in order to find employment. Therefore, the world's largest cities will need to provide an infrastructure to handle tens of millions of people in each city. The task will be daunting.

In 1900 the world's largest cities were located in Europe or North America. Currently, eight out of ten of the largest cities are in Asia or Latin America. The emerging mega cities are located in India, Brazil, China, Mexico, and Africa.

Today, around forty-five percent of the world's population lives in cities. Scholars predict that by 2025 sixty percent of people will dwell in urban areas. Not only is the world population growing, it is also migrating.

Climate Change

You may remember that Chapter 5 referred to the Medieval Warm Period that began in the eleventh century. This period resulted in increased farming and a multiplied food supply. Later in that chapter, you learned about a cooling period in the early fourteenth century that led to famine and great loss of life.

One lesson we can learn from these periods and others like them is that the earth's climate experiences cycles of change. Some periods are warmer and allow greater food production, while others are cooler and reduce food production. These cycles occur naturally.

Top, Beijing, China; *bottom*, Mumbai, India

Fastest-Growing Cities

Accurately predicting the ten fastest-growing cities that will arise in the next twenty-five years is a difficult if not impossible task. However, current trends suggest certain regions in which these cities will be located. For example, hundreds of cities in China, India, and Latin America are currently growing at rates that vary widely—from 16 percent to well over 100 percent. Whether such growth is sustainable is impossible to predict. However, China has several cities that should continue to grow steadily as the rural population moves to the cities for reasons such as better living conditions and improved job opportunities. The potential growth of China's cities is demonstrated by the fact that between 2000 and 2010, 84 of the world's 300 rapidly growing cities were located in China. Africa is currently the least urbanized continent, but African cities are beginning to grow at a modestly accelerated rate of 3 percent. Most of Latin America's cities are growing at nearly 19 percent, but this growth does not represent all Latin American countries. For example, Argentina's urban growth was just over 11 percent, while Guatemala's growth topped 40 percent.

The growth of cities presents many problems, including housing, sanitation, and transportation. However, the growth of cities also provides new opportunities for the spread of the gospel through national believers and missionaries.

Fastest-Growing Cities

Visit www.bjupress.com/resources for possible links to articles about the world's fastest-growing cities.

Al Gore

Recently, the topic of climate change has intensified because some insist that man is causing climate change and that dire consequences are just over the horizon. **Al Gore** has become an outspoken advocate of this position in his books *Earth in the Balance, An Inconvenient Truth,* and *Our Choice.* Those who embrace the view that man is causing **global warming** tend to insist on a consensus among scientists.

In order to develop answers regarding the issue of climate change, we need to ask several questions. First, is the earth warming beyond normal cycles? Second, if the earth is warming, is that a bad thing? Third, if the earth is warming, has man done anything to cause it? Finally, are the proposed measures to curb global warming sensible? In other words, do the benefits outweigh the costs? What will be the world economic impact of these measures? The answers to these questions will help us determine support for or opposition to many of the proposals that some scientists and governments are currently advocating.

Energy Resources

While man has discovered many energy sources, oil remains one of the main sources of energy for transportation, heat, and production of electricity. Even though oil is available in many regions of the world, most nations import much of their oil from the volatile Middle East. These imports grant significant importance to an area dominated by Islam. Since oil continues to produce most of the energy consumed in many countries, those who provide this resource will continue to exercise a great influence over the nations that import it.

The rapidly growing economies in China and India have also increased the demand for oil. This increased demand has resulted in an increasing cost of imported oil. This trend is likely to continue for the next several years.

Many nations have expressed the goal of energy independence, or the ability of a nation to produce energy without importing resources. Opposition to domestic drilling and to increased use of nuclear energy in some countries makes the goal of energy independence difficult if not impossible to achieve. However, other countries, such as France, meet many of their energy needs by producing most of their electricity with nuclear power plants.

Man's Role in the Environment

With all the debates about man's role in the climate and in the change that man may or may not be causing, the Christian should remember at least two things. First, we find the Creation Mandate in Genesis 1. God gave man the earth to use wisely as stewards. This authorizes man to maximize the usefulness of God's creation.

Second, the Lord commands the Christian in Matthew 22:39 to love his neighbor. Christians can demonstrate love by carefully developing resources to provide the greatest number of people with such basic needs as affordable food and clean water.

Men should also use resources to conserve human life. Scientists accomplish this task by developing improved medicines and medical care as well as removing pollutants from the air and water. Careless destruction does not accomplish these goals, but careful management of the environment for the good of mankind does.

Václav Klaus, scientist and political leader in the Czech Republic, has stridently rejected the claims of global warming. He compares environmentalism to a leftist ideology and a religion.

Stewardship

Ask the students to think of ways to conserve energy and wisely use the resources in their own households.

Energy

When God created the earth, He filled it with resources that could be used to meet many needs, such as production of energy. Whether the resource is coal, oil, the sun, or nuclear materials, man has the responsibility of using these fuels wisely for the betterment of mankind and man's dominion over the earth.

Coal

Coal is often used to produce electricity. The coal is crushed and burned in a furnace under a boiler. Water is turned into steam, and the steam spins large turbines that turn generators and produce electricity.

Currently about forty percent of the world's electricity is produced by burning coal. Power plants in the U.S. produce about half of the nation's electricity by burning coal. Coal also provides the least expensive energy.

Wind

Wind power is converted into electricity by the use of wind turbines. Wind has also been used to power mills and pump water in the past.

Nuclear

Nuclear energy is used to heat water and produce steam for the production of electricity. Currently the U.S. produces about twenty percent of its electricity in nuclear power plants.

Nuclear power is also used to power submarines and some ships, such as aircraft carriers.

Solar

Light and heat from the sun are used to produce electricity through heat engines and solar panels. Solar heat engines use the sun's heat to turn water into steam and produce electricity. Solar panels turn the sun's light directly into electricity.

Water

People can use water to produce electricity by channeling the water restrained by dams through tubes. The rushing water turns turbines that are connected to generators.

At this time, about twenty percent of the world's electricity is produced by water-powered turbines.

Oil

Oil can be processed into many products, including gasoline or heating oil. Gasoline is most often used for automobiles. Diesel is used to power cars, trucks, and locomotives. Oil is used to heat homes or produce heat in power plants to turn water into steam and produce electricity.

What Forms of Energy Should We Use?

The short answer is—all of them. As Christians we should realize that God, the Creator, placed all of these resources at man's disposal, commanding him to subdue the earth and have dominion over it. Turning fossil fuels, nuclear energy, wind, water, and sunlight into fuel is a very practical fulfillment of the Creation Mandate. God also gave man an intellect to use these resources responsibly. Therefore, man is to develop these resources in a manner that does not endanger the health of his fellow men. Although coal and oil, for example, produce pollution as they are burned, man is finding ways to limit this pollution and minimize any other negative effects of creating energy through these resources. The solution is not to choose one form of energy over another. Rather, man needs to use all God-provided resources responsibly.

CD: 20A Nuclear-Powered Ship; 20B Solar Power Plant; 20C NASA Solar-Powered Plane

Additional photos are available on the CD.

Section II

Objectives

Students should be able to

1. Briefly describe the causes of the development of the global economy.
2. Provide some examples of regional trade zones.
3. Evaluate the global economy.

Coca-Cola Museum

The Coca-Cola Museum in Atlanta, Georgia, has a tasting section where visitors can taste Coke that is sold in foreign countries. In many foreign countries, Coke is blended in different flavors to suit the tastes of the population.

A McDonald's restaurant in Shanghai, China, illustrates the global economy.

Section Quiz

1. Most nations in Europe are experiencing a(n) _____ in population.
2. In the coming years, a growing percentage of the world's population will live outside of _____.
3. Name an outspoken supporter of the man-made global warming theory.

4–5. List two energy sources and briefly describe how they are used to produce energy.

★ Briefly describe man's role in the environment based on Genesis 1:28 and Matthew 22:39.

II. Global Economy

Today a person can go almost anywhere in the world and find his favorite soft drink or fast food. In addition, products previously available only in a distant market can be purchased locally because of our global economy.

Causes

While the global economy began to develop following World War II, its growth has accelerated in the last two decades. Many recent events have made possible a truly global economy. In Chapter 19 you learned about the fall of communism in Eastern Europe. This political change dramatically increased opportunities for trade. Improvements in transportation and trade agreements have also made it possible to ship products across many national boundaries. In addition, technology has contributed to the efficiency of trade on a global level. Finally, sustained peace among many nations of the world allows global trade to flourish.

Examples

Organizing regions into large trade zones has taken several forms. We will look at two examples.

Free Trade Areas

Many nations have established economic trade zones in order to increase trade. Members of these trade blocs agree to remove tariffs and quotas (amounts of products that other countries can sell to the members of these trade zones). **Free trade areas** exist in many regions, including parts of Africa, Latin America, Southeast Asia, and the South Pacific.

Single Market

Several regions have developed economic and monetary zones that cross national boundaries and include multiple states. This **single market** enables states to trade with one another without restriction. The single market has resulted in greater wealth for the member states. We will briefly examine three examples of this system.

The **European Union** (EU) is an economic and political alliance of nearly thirty nations across Europe. This organization built upon the European Economic Community described in Chapter 19. The

Section Quiz Answers

1. decline
2. countries traditionally considered advanced
3. Al Gore

4–5. Accept any two of the following: Coal is burned to generate steam and produce electricity. Oil is used to produce gasoline and diesel fuel or to provide heat and generate electricity. Solar energy is used to produce electricity and to heat water. Wind is used to turn turbines and produce electricity; in the past, it was also used to pump water. Nuclear energy is used to heat water and produce steam for the production of electricity. Water is used to turn turbines and produce electricity.

★ Answers will vary but should include some of the following: In Genesis 1, God gave man the Creation Mandate to multiply and to have dominion over the earth. Because man was created in God's image, he possesses the ability to make decisions that will result in wise stewardship. In Matthew 22, Christ commanded Christians to love their neighbors. Supplying food and clean water and improving medical care are several ways in which Christians can demonstrate love for others.

Member States of the European Union

EU has developed a single market using standardized laws that enable free movement of people, products, and funds throughout the member states. At least sixteen member states have also made the **euro** their common currency.

Several Central American states formed the **Central American Common Market** in the early 1960s. This organization has sought to increase trade between member states. However, conflict between El Salvador and Honduras, two of the member states, erupted in 1969. In addition, ongoing political turmoil in this region has diminished the effectiveness of this economic effort.

Eight West African states currently form the **West African Economic and Monetary Union**. Their organization strives to promote economic cooperation and the use of a common currency, the **CFA franc**. This union also works to develop products that are competitively priced for the global economy.

Evaluating the Global Economy

There are many aspects to developing a global economy. Many of these aspects have positive results. However, the global economy also creates challenges that affect job opportunities as competition increases.

Advantages

In the global economy, companies build factories in countries where the cost of labor, capital, and technology is lower. This strategy enables corporations to produce goods at a lower cost and remain competitive. In addition, small companies have almost unlimited potential for growth because they can offer their products to customers around the world. Increased sales can quickly build small industries into large corporations. Furthermore, mass production for a global customer base can lead to more products available at lower costs.

Euro bills and coins

CD: 20D Member States of the European Union

This map from the student text is also available on the CD.

CD: 20E Formation of the European Union

A map showing the formation of the EU is available on the CD.

European Union

Visit www.bjupress.com/resources for possible links to articles about the European Union.

Tentmaking Ministries

Those who use their talents to work for companies in other countries and carry the gospel to these foreign lands follow in the steps of the apostle Paul. He often raised his own support by making tents. Modern tentmakers include those who teach English or nursing in countries like China. Christians who serve in this way often have opportunities to share their faith and win nationals to Christ.

Section III

Objectives

Students should be able to

1. Assess the potential benefits of technology.
2. Discern the perils of technology and its impact on culture.

Dangers in Using Technology

Technology is beneficial for mankind because it simplifies the tasks that must be done from day to day. Instead of driving to a bookstore, browsing through stacks of books, buying a book, and driving home, a person can access a website and buy a book from the comfort of his own home. If he has an e-reader, the text of the book can be instantly delivered to his device. But such conveniences are only good if they are used for good purposes. Technology facilitates evil as well as good. A person can now access pornography in the privacy of his own home without being seen by others. Our hearts are bent to lust after evil things; technology can make it easier to nourish those lusts. Christians need to

The global economy also provides another means to carry out the Creation Mandate of maximizing the use of God's creation. Free trade enables utilization of resources and allows the creativity of man to have greater expression as he develops products to meet needs.

In addition, trade has historically provided an opportunity for Christians to work in foreign lands and to evangelize. Many nations will allow Christians to work in businesses located in their countries. In this setting, Christians have the opportunity to witness to fellow workers and others with whom they come into contact, thus fulfilling the Great Commission.

Disadvantages

We will briefly examine two significant disadvantages for some regions in a global economy. First, when companies in developed countries manufacture in less-developed countries, domestic manufacturing jobs in developed countries decline and unemployment becomes a serious problem. There are long-term solutions, such as retraining workers and continuing education, but the transition is often difficult for older workers. Many look to their government to protect their jobs or to provide income when they lose their jobs.

Second, producing goods in a less-developed country can result in a variety of problems. For example, it is difficult to develop standard regulations and legislation in the foreign country that ensure the production of safe products. In addition, concerns about the working conditions of foreign laborers can become an issue.

Often the disadvantages of the global economy are unavoidable results of living in a fallen world that is constantly changing. Christians can help to minimize some of these disadvantages by reaching out to help those in need and thus fulfill Christ's commandment to love our neighbor.

Section Quiz

1. Briefly describe a free trade area and the desired economic benefit.
2. In what ways has the West African Economic and Monetary Union sought to improve economic conditions in West Africa?
3–4. List two advantages of the global economy.
5. What is a long-term solution for domestic job loss?
★ Why has the Central American Common Market enjoyed less success than the EU?

III. Technology and Culture

Technological advances seem to occur on a daily basis in the modern world. No sooner has a consumer purchased a computer or cell phone than a newer version becomes available on the market. However, it is important for us to examine the revolution in technology and observe how it affects our culture.

Promise

The list of technological advances is long and growing longer by the day. The possibilities of technology seem to be endless. We will

> **The Internet**
> Of the many inventions that have influenced our lives, perhaps no system has had more of an impact than the Internet. The Internet began in the 1960s as a U.S. government-funded project to enable the military to continue to communicate following a nuclear attack. The military believed that as long as the computer networks remained operational, communication would be possible. It is doubtful that anyone envisioned the incredible influence this technology would have on the modern world.

Negative Aspects of the Global Economy

Have the students respond to the statement that "many look to their government to protect their jobs or to provide income when they lose their jobs." Is this the proper role of government? What are the alternatives to governments' protecting jobs or providing income for unemployed workers?

Product Safety

Have the students respond to the statement in the text about developing "standard regulations and legislation . . . that ensure the production of safe products in foreign countries." Discuss products from other countries, such as baby cribs or toys painted with lead-based paint, that do not meet U.S. safety standards. How might the use of forced labor result in dangerous or poor-quality goods?

Section Quiz Answers

1. A free trade area is an economic trade zone that is established to increase trade. The removal of tariffs and quotas is intended to increase business between members of the free trade area.

2. Its members have sought to promote economic cooperation and have developed a common currency. In addition, they work to produce competitively priced goods.

3–4. two of the following: increased individual wealth, increased corporate and national wealth, lower cost for labor and goods, great potential for the growth of small companies

5. retraining; continuing education

★ Unlike the European Union, the Central American Common Market has suffered from regional conflicts and

briefly examine four areas where technology has improved the quality of life.

Medical Advances

DNA studies have enabled scientists to better understand diseases and to develop drugs to overcome several diseases. In addition, researchers have developed vaccinations to cure or prevent diseases such as polio and smallpox. Advances in medical technology include laser surgeries and other procedures to destroy tumors or repair injured organs through tiny incisions. These procedures protect the patient from many surgery-related infections and enable more rapid recovery.

Time-saving Devices

Household appliances, including washing machines, dishwashers, and vacuum cleaners, have enabled people to quickly do jobs that previously consumed many hours. Automobiles make it possible for people to travel great distances in less time. These time-saving devices have provided people with more leisure time. Some would argue that they have also improved our quality of life.

Communication Advances

Telephones, cell phones, e-mail, and social networking sites form a partial list of modern communication tools. Many people are able to communicate almost instantly because of these advances. Businesses can communicate in real time in all parts of the globe. This rapid communication cuts costs and enables a global reach for businesses. Missionaries can communicate with their supporting churches in real time and rapidly share their needs, prayer requests, and answers to prayer. Families also find it easy and inexpensive to converse over long distances.

Information Explosion

Many Internet sites provide free access to a wealth of material that was previously available only in print at specific libraries. Now you can view a newspaper from another part of the world or read a book from your computer. Information becomes available much more rapidly than a person can examine it. We are literally experiencing an explosion of information.

Peril

While technology holds great promise, it also generates concerns that Christians should address. We will look at a few of these concerns.

Medical Advances

Medical technology tends to obscure a sense of our own mortality. For example, people living in 1900 were more aware of death and were tempered by its reality. Technology also affects the doctor-patient relationship because the doctor tends to rely more on technology than on the patient's description of symptoms. Medical personnel also use technology for sinful purposes, including abortion and embryonic stem cell research.

Timesaving Devices

While technology has provided many timesaving devices, many people tend to consume their time using these devices. As a result, little time remains for thinking about important matters. We often

Illustration of a stent entering an artery and being expanded to open the artery

Getty Images

Stem Cell Research

Technology has enabled scientists to produce human embryos. Some scientists want to experiment with the embryonic stem cells to find cures for many diseases. It is important to note that during this process the scientist destroys the embryo. Many Christians oppose this practice because life begins at conception and an embryo is a developing person. This would mean that the destruction of the embryo is essentially murder.

Supporters of research on **embryonic stem cells** argue that this research is vital to curing a variety of crippling diseases. However, opponents point out that research on **adult stem cells** does not present the same moral dilemma. In addition, they note that this research is actually being used to treat a growing number of diseases. Currently, embryonic stem cell research is not being used to treat any diseases.

think carefully about both the benefits and the dangers of various technologies as they consider using them

political turmoil that have reduced its effectiveness.

Activity 2: Stem Cell Research

This excerpt from the fourth edition of the *Biology* student text by BJU Press deals with stem cell research. The wording of the excerpt may be challenging for your students, but it will be well worth their time to read and answer the questions following the excerpt.

fill our leisure time with things that add little or nothing to our lives. One of the keys to a proper use of technology is to control the technology rather than allowing technology to control the user.

Communication Advances

Constant communication interrupts work and lowers productivity. It also robs us of time for deliberation and quietness. Excessive communication often results in less thoughtful, reflective, and substantive communication.

Information Explosion

Christians should be concerned about the deluge of information with which the Internet bombards them. It is often difficult to filter out what is important and what is unimportant. In addition, it can be challenging to determine the accuracy of this information. Another result of this information explosion is easy access to harmful and sinful materials.

Mass communication—most notably TV—tries to grab the largest market and thus reduces the quality of public discourse. Since careful evaluation of important issues does not "sell," public discourse often degenerates into sound bites and sensational reporting.

Section Quiz

1–2. List two areas where technological advances have improved human life.

3–4. List two perils of technology.

5. What role does TV play in the quality of public discourse?

★ Briefly evaluate the perils of stem cell research.

IV. Political and Religious Trends

Political and religious trends can affect one another. For example, democracies tend to tolerate or embrace religious freedom. Communist or Islamic governments often deny religious freedom. However, Christianity continues to grow in many societies that persecute Christians. This trend has been true throughout the history of the church, and it remains true in many oppressed nations today.

Political

Muslim terrorists have been at war with the West, especially with the United States, for at least three decades. The war began with the taking of American diplomats as hostages in Iran during the Carter presidency. It continued with attacks on American forces in Lebanon, Saudi Arabia, and other countries.

The war dramatically accelerated with the attack on the Twin Towers in New York City and the Pentagon in Washington, D.C. American leaders tended to ignore the growing threat, but the attack on September 11, 2001, (9/11) forced the United States and other countries to respond with military action and take the battle to the enemies of the free world.

In addition, Communist China has quickly developed into a wealthy and powerful force in Asia. We will briefly examine the economic restructuring of China following the death of Mao Zedong that resulted in this transformation.

Section IV

Objectives

Students should be able to

1. Evaluate the different forms of political trends.

2. Explain why Islam is spreading around the world.

3. Analyze the spread of Christianity in the global south and Christians' response to persecution.

Technology and Time

Challenge your students to keep track of how much time they spend during a week in such activities as watching television, chatting with friends on their cell phones, playing computer games, texting, and blogging. Then have them evaluate whether their use of technology helped them or simply diverted them from wisely using their time. Have them list several ways in which they can make better use of the technology in their lives.

Section Quiz Answers

1–2. Accept any two of the following: advances in medicine, time-saving devices, improved means of communication, the explosion of information.

3–4. Accept any two of the following: Medical technology tends to obscure a sense of our mortality; technology can negatively affect doctor-patient relationships when doctors trust machines to establish diagnoses rather than listening to their patients; time-saving devices can consume our time and control us; communication devices can interrupt work and lower productivity; excessive use of communication devices often results in less substantive communication.

5. Television works to gain the largest market and reduces the quality of public discourse to secure this market. Television is characterized by sound bites and sensational reporting.

★ Answers will vary but should include some of the following: Embryonic stem cell research results in the destruction of an embryo and the ending of a developing life. Supporters of this practice argue for its potential benefits while disregarding the destruction of the embryos.

The Rise of Terrorist States

Following years of rule by a pro-Western, brutal dictatorship, Iran came under the control of radical Muslim forces in 1979. To demonstrate their hatred of the United States, they held fifty-two American diplomats and their staff hostage for over four hundred days during 1979 and 1980. Iran has become a major supporter of terrorism throughout the Middle East and other countries. In addition, its outspoken hatred of Israel combined with a growing nuclear threat continues to have a destabilizing influence on this region.

Iraq, under the dictatorship of **Saddam Hussein**, also became an important state in the Middle East. Initially, Hussein allied himself with the West against the common enemy of Iran. He attacked Iran in 1980 and engaged in a war that led to over three hundred thousand deaths but ended in a stalemate.

Hussein abandoned any pretense of support for the West in 1990 and invaded his neighbor Kuwait. He seized Kuwait's vast oil reserves and threatened to march on into Saudi Arabia. After American and allied forces halted his advance, Hussein's military was quickly routed and sent back to Iraq in 1991. Despite economic sanctions, U.N. resolutions, and warnings by the U.S., Hussein continued to develop offensive weapons, to provide financial support for suicide bombers, and to refuse to allow inspections of sensitive nuclear facilities. To end Iraq's growing threat, a U.S.-led military coalition invaded Iraq in 2003. U.S. troops captured Hussein in December 2003. After a lengthy trial in an Iraqi court, the new Iraqi government executed him in December 2006.

Afghanistan is a rugged, landlocked country that lies east of Iran. During the 1990s, this region came under the control of a radical Muslim group called the **Taliban**. This regime provided a safe haven and base of operations for the Saudi extremist **Osama bin Laden**. He built a terrorist network known as **al Qaeda** that operated out of Afghanistan. Bin Laden has aggressively supported attacks on the United States, including the bombing of the Twin Towers in New York City in 1993.

Scenes from Manhattan following the terrorist attack on September 11, 2001

The Taliban

Taliban is the Pashto word for students. The Taliban is an Islamic political group that controlled Afghanistan from 1996 until American forces removed it from power at the end of 2001.

Under the repressive rule of the Taliban, Afghani citizens were forced to abide by a strict interpretation of Sharia law. Anything connected to the West was strictly forbidden. Violators were subjected to beatings, mutilation, or brutal execution. However, Afghani women suffered the most. Women were forbidden to work outside the home, and girls were denied an education beyond the age of eight. What little education they received was limited to the study of the Qur'an. Afghani women were also required to wear the burqa in public—a garment that covered them from head to toe. They were often flogged in public for minor infractions or for daring to speak out against abuses.

Although the Taliban was removed from power in Afghanistan, it remains a dangerous force in many parts of Afghanistan and continues to wage a guerilla war against U.S., Afghani, and Pakistani forces.

CD: 20F Fallujah
A photo of Marines engaging enemy targets at Camp Fallujah, Iraq, is available on the CD.

Saddam Hussein
Visit www.bjupress.com/resources for possible links to articles about Saddam Hussein.

Gulf War
Visit www.bjupress.com/resources for possible links to articles about the Gulf War.

However, Osama bin Laden became infamous for his role in the destruction of the Twin Towers and an attack on the Pentagon on September 11, 2001. President George W. Bush quickly rallied support for an invasion of Afghanistan when the Taliban refused to turn bin Laden over to international authorities. Despite dire predictions by some, U.S. and allied forces promptly routed Taliban and al Qaeda forces, removing them from power. However, time has revealed that al Qaeda and the Taliban remain a grave threat. Efforts to establish a free and stable Afghanistan have proven elusive, and the outcome is still uncertain.

The Rising Influence of China

China has transformed from an isolated nation with a predominately agricultural economy to a rapidly growing economic world power. From 1952 until 1978 China's GDP (gross domestic product) remained stagnant. At that time, Communist leaders began to adopt economic reforms that encouraged a measure of free enterprise.

As a result, China's GDP has risen dramatically from around nine billion U.S. dollars in the 1970s to nearly three trillion dollars in 2005. China's GDP continues to rise despite major economic downturns in the world economy. This phenomenal financial growth, combined with a large military force, has made China a key player in all economic and political decisions. China is poised to become a superpower.

Religious

In Chapter 1 we examined the foundations upon which Christ built His church. In Chapter 2 we studied the formation and growth of Islam. While other religious movements have appeared in history, these two have ebbed and flowed throughout history and our study in this book.

Growth of Islam

During several periods of world history since the seventh century AD, Islam resurfaced following its advance across Saudi Arabia into Africa and beyond. However, Islam seemed to have lost its fervor until the rise of a zealous Sunni Muslim in Saudi Arabia during the eighteenth century. Muhammad ibn Abd-al-Wahhab was a Muslim scholar who utterly opposed changes to historic Islam. He advocated the violent suppression of these changes.

> **GDP**
> Gross Domestic Production is a measure of a country's total economic output for a given year.

Rally of militant Muslims in Pakistan

AFP/Getty Images

September 11, 2001
Visit www.bjupress.com/resources for possible links to articles about September 11, 2001.

Typical madrassa where Muslim boys memorize the Qu'ran

The **Wahhabist** movement (so-called by its enemies) gained control of Saudi Arabia. This movement has used the vast wealth generated by oil sales to spread the literal application of Islam to many parts of the world. Wahhabists attack Muslims who reject their violent teachings with as much hatred as they do non-Muslims. As a result, many Muslims fear and quietly oppose the Wahhabist interpretation of Islam.

In addition, Wahhabist-controlled Saudi Arabia has exported terrorism and hatred to many countries in the Middle East, Southeast Asia, and Africa. Saudi money has also paid for the construction of mosques in many of these regions. The leaders of these mosques are required to promote Wahhabism. Furthermore, many Muslim religious schools, called **madrassas**, use educational material produced in Saudi Arabia that teaches Wahhabist intolerance and hatred for anything that is not purely Islamic.

Islam also continues to grow through large families and conversions. Since Muslim couples are encouraged to have many children, their influence grows in every nation where Muslims have settled. Many people have also voluntarily converted to Islam for various reasons, including an attraction to a religion that provides a regulated religious life and many rituals, such as the Five Pillars discussed in Chapter 2.

Spread of Christianity

Earlier you learned that the largest population growth is occurring in Latin America, India, China, and Africa. At the same time, Christianity is growing at an accelerated rate in these regions known as the **global south**.

Accurate numbers are difficult to obtain, and the numbers available often combine Roman Catholics, Pentecostals, and Mormons along with mainline Protestants and Evangelicals. However, the exciting news is that biblical Christianity continues to grow. One significant development is that missionaries may soon be coming from the global south to evangelize the traditionally Christian-influenced nations of the West.

Christianity is spreading throughout Latin America. Distinct from the Roman Catholic Church and traditional Protestant churches, Evangelical and Charismatic congregations are growing and multiplying in many Latin American countries.

The expansion of Christianity in Africa also provides a clear example of growth. For instance, there were an estimated ten million

Wahhabism
Visit www.bjupress.com/resources for possible links to articles about Wahhabism.

Voice of the Martyrs
Visit www.bjupress.com/resources for possible links to articles about Voice of the Martyrs, an organization that seeks to help persecuted Christians around the world.

Persecution
Have some students research and share information about countries that persecute Christians. Voice of the Martyrs has much information on this subject.

Jesus in Beijing

The book *Jesus in Beijing: How Christianity Is Transforming China and Changing the Global Balance of Power* contains helpful information about Christianity in China, including details about several leaders who have endured years of persecution because of their Christian testimonies.

Section Quiz Answers

1. New York City and Washington, D.C.
2. Saddam Hussein; a stalemate
3. Saudi Arabia
4. madrassa
5. Latin America, India, China, and Africa
★ Wahhabism and financial support from Saudi Arabia, construction of mosques that support Wahhabism, Muslim schools (madrassas) that promote Islam, large Islamic families, voluntary and forced Islamic conversions

Activity 3: Chapter Review

This activity helps the students prepare for the chapter test.

Chapter Review Answers

Making Connections

1. to find employment
2. The earth naturally experiences cycles of climate change.
3. If a nation has a declining population, its culture and way of life will decrease in influence and may be swallowed up by the cultures and lifestyles of nations with increasing populations. For example, nations with declining population do not produce enough children to ensure a future labor force and to solve environmental problems.
4. They should be used to maximize the usefulness of God's creation. They should also be used to meet the needs of humans; for example, man can use earth's resources to develop medicines and find ways to clean the air and water.

A Chinese Soldier of the Cross

Wang Mingdao (1900–1991) is one of many Chinese Christians whose life is worthy of study. Wang's ministry started with a Bible study in a tiny hut, and he soon became a popular speaker in many Chinese cities. Wang established the Chinese Tabernacle in Peking on August 1, 1937. One week later the Japanese marched into this city. He refused to join a puppet Japanese religious organization and gained the respect of the Japanese invaders by his consistent stand.

In 1949, when the Communists gained control of China, they tried unsuccessfully to get Wang to join their Three Self Reform Movement that referred to Christianity as a tool of imperialism. Despite a growing threat of imprisonment, he continued to hold evangelistic meetings in Beijing. The authorities finally arrested Wang and his wife in 1955.

For two months, carefully coached cellmates terrified Wang about methods of persecution he might endure. He finally broke and confessed his "guilt."

The Chinese released Wang, but he felt that he, like Peter, had betrayed his Lord. Wang refused to follow through with the Communists' demands. As a result, authorities arrested Wang and his wife again in 1958. However, this time Wang withdrew all of his earlier confessions. The Communists responded by brutalizing Wang over the next twenty-two years. However, he remained true to his faith in Christ. Authorities released his wife in 1975 and Wang in 1980. His testimony has encouraged many other Chinese to boldly stand for Christ in Communist China.

Christians in Africa in 1900. By the year 2000, the number had increased to around three hundred and sixty million.

China provides another example of the phenomenal growth of Christianity. Some estimate the number of Christians in China in 1949 to have been between three and five million. Current estimates reveal that the Christian population in China may have reached one hundred million.

Persecution of Christianity

Christianity in the global south is growing in spite of and during a period of intense persecution in many regions, including Southeast Asia, China, and some states in Africa. Many political leaders view the spread of Christianity as undesirable and a threat to their humanist goals.

Believers in African countries such as Nigeria, Egypt, and the Sudan live in constant danger of persecution or forced conversion by Muslim groups. Many have been required to renounce their faith or suffer imprisonment or death. These believers can readily identify with the Apostle Paul's words in several of his letters, including Ephesians, Colossians, and Philippians.

As Christianity spreads throughout Southeast Asia, believers have encountered violent opposition and execution in regions like the island nation of Indonesia. For example, Christians on the Malaku islands of Indonesia have endured massacres and forced expulsions by Muslim forces. Some of their leaders have described this as a means of the Lord purifying His church, and they bravely continue to witness.

Christians in China have also learned to thrive despite ongoing persecution by the Chinese Communists. As the Chinese church continues to grow, the Communists fear the potential influence of Christians. Communist officials have responded with brutal tactics in an effort to disrupt services and drive people away from local congregations.

As the Chinese church matures, many of its leaders have demonstrated a determination to serve no matter what the cost. Despite ongoing persecution, they continue to witness. In addition, they demonstrate evangelistic zeal by preparing to send missionaries to foreign countries where Western missionaries cannot go.

Section Quiz

1. What two American cities were attacked on September 11, 2001?
2. What dictator invaded Iran in 1980? What was the outcome of that war?
3. Wahhabism first appeared in what country?
4. What is the name for a Muslim religious school?
5. In what areas is Christianity growing at an accelerated rate?
★ Why is Islam growing rapidly?

5. Business relationships provide opportunities for international cooperation. These relationships could contribute to peace.
6. Answers will vary but may include some of the following: Medical technology is used for abortion and embryonic stem cell research. There are many useful resources on the Internet, but there is also much information that contains error and has a morally corrupting influence.
7. in Latin America, India, China, and Africa
8. violent opposition, massacres, forced expulsions, arrests, forced conversions
9. The number of Chinese Christians is estimated to have increased from three

million to around one hundred million since 1949. Communist officials employ brutal tactics to suppress Christianity in China.

Developing History Skills

1. Answers will vary.
2. Answers will vary.

Thinking Critically

1. Answers will vary but might include the following: Many cannot afford to pay a doubled or tripled cost of energy to heat and light their homes. In addition, increased fuel costs will result in greater job loss. However, cheap fuel sources such as coal do pollute the

CHAPTER REVIEW

Making Connections

1. Why are people continuing to migrate to the cities?
2. What lesson can we learn from studying the history of climate change?
3. How is a declining population a disadvantage?
4. How should the earth's resources be used?
5. How could a global economy contribute to peace between nations?
6. How is technology used for sinful purposes?
7. Where is Christianity spreading most rapidly?
8. What is the Muslim response to the growth of Christianity in many areas of the global south?
9. How has Christianity in China been affected by the Communist takeover in 1949?

Developing History Skills

1. Using the information in this chapter and any additional research you may wish to do, write a one- or two-page paper on the uses of water, wind, or solar energy in human history.
2. Using the information in this chapter and in previous chapters (2–5, 11, 15), trace the history and expansion of Islam.

Thinking Critically

1. In light of Christ's command to love one's neighbor, evaluate the demands of many environmentalists that more expensive sources of fuel be developed in order to reduce pollution.
2. How might you take advantage of the global economy in the coming years to help spread the gospel?

Living in God's World

1. Write a brief essay titled "Technology: My Generation's Blessing and Burden."
2. Suppose you are a historian who has been asked to address a conference of professional historians. You have titled your address "Has the Human Race Outgrown the Christian Religion?" Write a brief speech that seeks to answer this question.

People, Places, and Terms to Know

Al Gore
global warming
free trade areas
single market
European Union
euro
Central American Common Market
West African Economic and Monetary Union
CFA franc
embryonic stem cells
adult stem cells
Saddam Hussein
Taliban
Osama bin Laden
al Qaeda
Wahhabist
madrassas
global south
Wang Mingdao

---

environment, and man should develop processes to reduce that pollution since it is a legitimate health threat. Loving our neighbors means providing resources at the lowest possible cost while also reducing or eliminating pollution.

2. Answers will vary but might include some of the following: Students could get an education in international business or some other area that would enable them to work in countries where missionaries might not be allowed. The students could then hold Bible studies with co-workers in these foreign lands and win nationals to Christ.

Living in God's World

1. Answers will vary but should include some of the following:

Blessing: Technological advances have greatly increased man's ability to live out the Creation Mandate. Medical technology saves lives and enriches human existence. Time-saving devices provide us with more leisure time than previous generations have enjoyed. Communication advances have broken down the walls of communication in remarkable ways. An explosion of information gives us access to amounts of data that previous generations could not have imagined.

Burden: With each of these blessings come dangers. Our medical advances may keep us from acknowledging the reality of death. Our time-saving devices expose us to the temptation of wasting our leisure time on selfish and sinful activities. Our communication advances interrupt our work and times of thoughtful reflection. Our much-praised information explosion floods us with information that is often useless and degrading.

2. Answers will vary but might include some of the following:

Thesis: The human race has not outgrown the Christian religion because Christianity is alive and growing in the global south.

Latin America: Roman Catholics have had a large influence in Latin America for centuries. Now, however, Evangelical and Charismatic congregations are multiplying.

Africa: In the last hundred years, the number of Christians in Africa has grown from ten million to about three hundred sixty million. This has happened despite much Islamic persecution in many African countries.

China: The most remarkable growth of Christianity has taken place in China. Despite fierce persecution by this nation's Communist government, the Christian church in China has exploded. The Christian population in China is estimated to be about one hundred million. In other words, ten percent of the world's largest nation is Christian—an especially amazing fact when you consider that China is officially atheistic.

Standards for World Studies, Third Edition

GLOSSARY

A

Abbas: Second founder of the Safavid Empire

Abbassid: Muslim caliphate under which Islam experienced a renaissance

Aborigines: European name for natives of Australia

Akbar: Most effective ruler of the Mughal emperors in India

Alexander II: Russian ruler who abolished serfdom

anarchy: Radical concept of society without government

ancestor worship: The practice of praying to dead family members

animism: Belief that spirits live in physical objects

anti-Semitism: Animosity toward Jews

appeasement: Avoiding conflict by making concessions

Atahualpa: Emperor of the Incan Empire

B

Babur: Founder of the Mughal Empire in India

Balkans: A large region in southeastern Europe

barbarian: A culture or civilization that was neither Roman nor Greek

barrios: Neighborhoods of poor people in the center of cities in Latin America

Batu Khan: A grandson of Chinggis Khan who led an invasion into eastern Europe

Black Death: A plague during the Middle Ages

Bolsheviks: Radical Russian political group led by Lenin that supported violence

Bushido: Japanese unwritten military code of the samurai

C

caliph: Islamic leader

caravel: A ship used for European exploration

caudillos: South American leaders who established dictatorships

Charter Act: Parliamentary decree that gave the British crown control over the British East India Company

Chartism: Movement in England in the 1800s that called for universal manhood suffrage and elections by secret ballot

Chinggis Khan: A Mongol title meaning "Great Ruler," and the title given to the Mongol Empire's founder

chivalry: A code or strict set of rules for a knight

Cold War: Political rivalry and conflict of ideas that stopped short of actual war between the U.S. and the U.S.S.R. (1945–1991)

colonialism: Conquest of one or more nations by another nation

communism: Economic system in which property is commonly and not privately owned

Corn Laws: British parliamentary law that made food in England expensive

Creoles: People of pure Spanish or Portuguese descent born in the Americas

crop rotation: Farming practice in which different crops are grown in the same field to maintain the soil's fertility

Cubism: Art style after World War I that showed subjects in geometric shapes and from several perspectives at once

culture: The physical and mental environment developed through human thought and labor

Cuzco: The capital of the Incan Empire

D

didgeridoo: Musical instrument played by Australian Aborigines

Dien Bien Phu: Battle in 1954 in which Vietnamese Communists defeated French forces

divine sovereignty: God's complete and permanent control over this world

E

effigy mound: Earthen mounds in North America that were made in the shape of an animal or object

empiricism: Belief that man can find knowledge only through experience

entrepreneurs: Businessmen who sell inventions for financial gain and accept risk of personal loss

Estates General: An assembly in pre-Revolutionary French government that authorized royal spending

excommunication: A dismissal from the Roman Church denying any opportunity for salvation

existentialism: Philosophy that stressed a person's uniqueness, free choice, and the consequences of those choices

Expressionism: Art style after World War I that showed how the artist felt about his subject

F

Fante Confederation: African organization formed in 1868 by African pastors and teachers to maintain self-rule

Federal Reserve: American agency that controls the U.S. money supply and works to protect the American banking system

feudalism: A system whereby European land was subdivided from king to nobles and then to serfs in exchange for loyalty and allegiance

Five Civilized Tribes: A group of Indian tribes who formed an alliance in the American Southeast

Five Pillars: Islamic practices of affirming Islam, daily prayers, almsgiving, fasting, and pilgrimage to Mecca

flying buttress: External support of a Gothic cathedral

flying shuttle: Invention that enabled weavers to combine strands of cotton into cloth more quickly

G

gathering-based economy: Economic system that allowed more Africans to access wealth coming into Africa by harvesting the continent's natural resources

gauchos: Cowboys in Argentina

global warming: The theory that the earth is warming and that this is due to man-made emissions

Gold Coast: A name for Western Africa that derives from the gold trade that occurred at its coasts

Golden Horde: A Mongol empire based in western Asia and founded by Batu Khan

Greek fire: A chemical weapon used by the Byzantines against their enemies

H

hacienda: A large country estate in Latin America

hara-kiri: Ritual suicide practiced by Japanese warriors

Hegira: Muhammad's flight from Mecca to Medina

high islands: Pacific islands whose height enables agriculture to grow and humans to reside on them

Huguenots: French Protestants during the Reformation

I

imam: Leader of the Shiite faction of Islam

Index of Prohibited Books: List of books that were declared heretical by the Roman Catholic Church

indulgence: A document issued by the Church of Rome granting pardon from the punishment of certain sins

infrastructure: Network of travel and communication

Inquisition: A Roman Church court set up to find and punish heretics

J

Jesuit: A Catholic monastic order formed during the Reformation to stop the spread of Protestantism

Judaism: The religion of the Jews that developed during the five centuries BC

jury: Legal process developed in the Middle Ages whereby a group of local citizens made lists of accusations before a circuit judge arrived to hear them

K

Ka'bah: A stone building in Mecca toward which all Muslims pray

kamikaze: The Japanese name for a sudden storm; means "divine wind"

Kuomintang: Nationalist Chinese Party in the early 1900s

L

Lalibela: A Coptic holy city in Ethiopia that contains churches carved in rock below ground level

landscapes: Paintings that feature nature scenes

Lateran Treaties: Agreements between Mussolini and the Vatican City that ended the pope's opposition to Italy's unified government

liberal arts: Studies taught in medieval universities for the nobility

low islands: Pacific islands that have little fresh water and few places where humans can live

Luftwaffe: Germany's air force in World War II

M

madrassa: Muslim school

Marn Grook: Game developed by Aborigines that has elements of football or soccer

Melanesia: Group of Pacific islands that includes Papua New Guinea, the Solomon Islands, and Fiji

Mensheviks: Moderate Russian political group who sought change through peaceful methods

Micronesia: Pacific Islands that are small and low; means "tiny islands"

mestizos: Children with Indian and Spanish parents

monotheism: The belief in and worship of one God

N

National Assembly: Members of the Third Estate in the French Revolution who convened and signed the Tennis Court Oath and the Declaration of the Rights of Man

nationalism: Intense devotion and loyalty to one's own people and country

NATO: North Atlantic Treaty Organization; formed in 1949 to oppose Soviet aggression

Era 7 An Age of Revolutions

1750–1914

O

Old World: A term for Europe

opium: An addictive drug that British merchants brought to China in order to gain a favorable balance of trade

P

Pact of Steel: Military alliance between Hitler and Mussolini

passive resistance: Resisting foreign rule by nonviolent means (e.g. strikes, not paying taxes)

pasteurization: A process developed by Louis Pasteur in which milk and other liquids are heated in order to slow the development of disease-causing microbes

patent: Set of government-issued rights granted to an inventor to prevent others from copying and selling his invention for a certain amount of time

Peace of God: A church decree making church property off limits for fighting among knights

Polynesia: Pacific islands located between the Hawaiian Islands, Easter Island, and New Zealand; means "many islands"

polytheism: The belief in and worship of many gods

porcelain: Product developed by the Chinese through the process of shaping kaolin clay into objects and then hardening them by heat

proletariat: Communist term for laborers who rebel against the middle class and bourgeoisie to make a classless society

Protectorate: Government founded by Oliver Cromwell after the English Civil War

Q

Quetzalcoatl: An Aztec god whom the Aztecs were expecting to return to them

Qur'an: Sacred Islamic book that records Muhammad's visions

R

Ramadan: The holy month of Islam

rationalism: Belief that the path to truth is through human reason

Reconquista: Roman Catholic seizure of Spain and Portugal from the Muslims

Romanesque: An architectural style used in the early Middle Ages that used elements of Roman styles of architecture

romanticism: Western style of art, music, and literature characterized by an emphasis on the mysterious and supernatural, a longing for the Medieval Age, and a love for freedom, nationalism, personal emotion, and nature

S

Sahara: A desert that covers most of Northern Africa

Sahel: A narrow strip of land in Africa between the Sahara Desert and the rain forests

saltpeter: A mixture of chemicals that produces an explosion when ignited; also called gunpowder

samurai: A Japanese warrior

savannah: Flat grasslands in Africa

Schlieffen Plan: Germany's two-front war strategy in which Germany would quickly conquer France and then fight Russia

scurvy: Disease that many sailors contracted because of a lack of vitamin C in their diet

SDI: "Strategic Defense Initiative"; system that protected America from missile attacks

Second Estate: Second-highest level of French society before the French Revolution; it contained the aristocracy

secularism: Concept that biblical Christianity should be excluded from education and society

sepoys: Indian soldiers hired by the British

shaman: A man in Mongol religion who is believed to have power over spirits

Sharia: Islamic law

Shintoism: A Japanese religion that taught nature worship, the deity of the emperor, and patriotism

shogun: The title of a Japanese clan's leader; means "great general"

spinning jenny: Invention that could rapidly spin spools of cotton thread into yarn

Sputnik: First man-made satellite; launched by the Soviets in 1957

stalemate: Wartime condition in which two opposing forces have no major gains on either side

suffrage: The privilege to vote in elections

T

Taoism: A passive Chinese religion centered on living in peace and harmony with nature

Tartars: The European name for the Mongol forces that invaded eastern Europe

Third Estate: Lowest level of French society before the French Revolution; it contained the middle class, artisans, and peasants

third world: Regions that remained neutral during the Cold War

total war: War in which all of a country's resources are devoted to destroying the enemy

town charter: A legal document issued by the king that lists privileges of the town's inhabitants and frees them from most feudal duties

trade winds: Winds that blow from east to west and brought European explorers across the Atlantic Ocean

transubstantiation: Roman Catholic doctrine that the bread and wine of the Lord's Supper change into the very body and blood of Christ

tribe: Two or more African clans living together and sharing a common language, beliefs, and customs

Triple Entente: Loose confederation between Russia, England, and France prior to World War I

Truce of God: A church decree restricting fighting among knights to certain days of the week

V

vaccine: Weakened form of a disease exposed to a person on purpose to prevent his getting a serious form of the disease

Vernacular: National language such as French or German

viceroy: A ruler of a Spanish colony who represented the king of Spain

Viet Cong: Vietnamese Communist agents who tried to take over South Vietnam

W

Wars of Apostasy: Abu Bakr's conquest against Arabs who sought independence after Muhammad's death

Washington Naval Conference: Meeting of several nations that agreed to limit the number of warships each could build

Wassoulou: Empire in Africa led by Samori Ture that resisted European colonization

Weimar Republic: German government after World War I organized at Weimar

Y

Yoruba: African language into which Samuel Ajayi Crowther helped translate the Bible

Young Italy: Italian nationalist group founded by Giuseppe Mazzini

yurt: A movable house used by the Mongols

Z

Zen Buddhism: Version of Buddhism that teaches intense mental concentration and self-control

Zollverein: Economic union of German states in the nineteenth century that resulted in German unification

Era 8   A Half-Century of Crisis and Achievement
1900–1945

- Reform, revolution, and social change in the world economy of the early twentieth century . . . . pp. 300–301, 308–10

- The causes and global consequences of World War I . . . . pp. 309–10, 315–18

- The search for peace and stability in the 1920s and 1930s . . . . pp. 318–26

- The causes and global consequences of World War II . . . . pp. 330–34, 341–45

- Major global trends from 1900 to the end of World War II . . . . pp. 308–45

Era 9   The Twentieth Century and Beyond
1945–Present

- The reconstruction of nations, transformation of international relationships, and dissolution of colonial empires after World War II . . . . pp. 350–52, 360–62

- The search for community, stability, and peace in an interdependent world . . . . pp. 351–52

- Major global trends since World War II . . . . pp. 350–67

- The Cold War . . . . pp. 350–67

- Globalization . . . . pp. 372–84

INDEX

Photo Credits

The following agencies and individuals have furnished materials to meet the photographic needs of this textbook. We wish to express our gratitude to them for their important contribution.

Alamy
Art Resource
Associated Press
Australian Tourist Commission
Beedell, Mike
Berger II, Daniel
BigStockPhoto
Bob Jones University Museum & Gallery
Bolen, Todd
Bollinger, Dennis
The Bridgeman Art Library
COREL Corporation
Dover Publications
Fotolia

Fotosearch
Getty Images
The Granger Collection
iStockphoto
JupiterImages Corporation
Kansas Department of Economic
 Development
Landis, Joyce
lemur.com
Library of Congress
www.marketoracle.co.uk
National Aeronautics and Space
 Administration (NASA)
National Archives

National Maritime Museum
National Portrait Gallery
Naval Historical Foundation
Photodisc
Ronald Reagan Library
Science and Society Picture Library
University of London School of Oriental
 & African Studies
University of Michigan
Wikimedia Commons
Wikipedia
World of Stock

Unit 1

DEA/W. BUSS/De Agostini/Getty Images x

Chapter 1

NASA 2–3; Photography: Mike Beedell 5 (top right); © 2009 JupiterImages Corporation 4 (bottom left and right), 5 (top left), 12, 13, 18, 19; kertis © Fotolia.com 4 (center); Jessica Blanc © Fotolia.com 5 (bottom); Wen–Yan King/Wikimedia Commons/Creative Commons Attribution 2.0 License 4 (top); 2009 © Chris Jewiss. Image from BigStockPhoto.com 7; 2009 © Radist. Image from BigStockPhoto.com 9; © Daniel Berger II 15 (both); Todd Bolen/BiblePlaces.com 16

Chapter 2

© 2009 JupiterImages Corporation 24–25, 28 (top), 30 (top), 32 (top); © Jumrah Al–Aqabah/Wikimedia Commons/Creative Commons Attribution 2.0 28 (28–bottom); Fotosearch 30 (center); ZAKIA NUGRAHENI/AFP/Getty Images 30 (bottom); KHALED DESOUKI/AFP/Getty Images 31 (top); © Trammell Hudson/Wikimedia Commons/GNU Free Documentation License/Creative Commons Attribution ShareAlike 3.0 31 (bottom); © Heretiq/Wikimedia Commons/GNU Free Documentation License/Creative Commons Attribution ShareAlike 3.0 33 (top); © Dennis Bollinger 33 (center)

Unit 2

© 2009 JupiterImages Corporation 40 (top right); © iStockphoto.com/Nico Smit 40–41 (bottom right); Library of Congress 40 (left)

Chapter 3

© iStockphoto.com/Nico Smit 42–43; © 2009 JupiterImages Corporation 44 (bottom), 45 (center left and right), 47, 52 (top); © Naseem Abi Shaheen/Wikimedia Commons/GNU Free Documentation License/Creative Commons Attribution ShareAlike 3.0 45 (top); 2009 © Derrick Neill. Image from BigStockPhoto .com 45 (bottom); © iStockphoto.com/Klaas Lingbeek–van Kranen 49 (all); © Dominique Dumont – Fotolia.com 51; © iStockphoto.com/salem 52 (bottom); COREL Corporation 55 (top); © Jan Derk/Wikimedia Commons/Public Domain 55 (inset)

Chapter 4

© iStockphoto.com/Bart Parren 58 (top left); © iStockphoto.com/Joe Brandt 58–59; © iStockphoto.com/Alexander Podshivalov 58 (bottom left); © iStockphoto.com/Clayton Hansen 60 (left); © iStockphoto.com/Melanie Cowell 60 (right); © iStockphoto.com/Steve Goodwin 61 (left); www.marketoracle.co.uk 61 (right); © 2009 JupiterImages Corporation 62 (center), 67, 71; Christelle © Fotolia.com 62 (right); © Gerd A.T. Müller/Wikimedia Commons/GNU Free Documentation License/Creative Commons Attribution ShareAlike 3.0 62 (left)

Chapter 5

Berthold Werner/Wikimedia Commons/Public Domain 76–77; © Tobias Helfrich/Wikimedia Commons/GNU Free Documentation License/Creative Commons Attribution ShareAlike 3.0 79 (left); © Aleph/Wikimedia Commons/Creative Commons Attribution ShareAlike 2.5 79 (right); Wikimedia Commons/Public Domain 80 (bottom); © 2009 JupiterImages Corporation 85 (all); © Dennis Bollinger 86 (all); © iStock-

photo.com/Andrew Dernie 90; Duccio di Buoninsegna/Wikimedia Commons/Public Domain 91; 2009 © Mohamed Farouk. Image from BigStockPhoto.com 92

Chapter 6

© iStockphoto.com/Dario Rota 96–97; Portrait Bust of Lorenzo de' Medici, probably after a model by Andrea del Verrocchio and Orsini Benintendi/The Bridgeman Art Library 98; Madonna and Child with Saints, Niccolò de Pietro Gerini, Bob Jones University Collection 99 (top left); Madonna and Child with St. John the Baptist and Angels, Ansano di Michele Ciampanti, called the Master of San Filippo, Bob Jones University Collection 99 (top right); Leonardo da Vinci/Wikimedia Commons/Public Domain 99 (center); The Last Supper, by Leonardo da Vinci/The Bridgeman Art Library 99 (bottom); 2009 © Bobby Dockery. Image from BigStockPhoto .com 100 (top); © 2009 JupiterImages Corporation 100 (bottom), 102, 107, 108 (top), 110; © iStockphoto.com/Sabrina Dei Nobili 101 (top right); © iStockphoto.com/Pierre Chouinard 101 (top left); © Bernard Gagnon/Wikimedia Commons/GNU Free Documentation License/Creative Commons Attribution ShareAlike 3.0 101 (bottom); Angelo Bronzino/Wikimedia Commons/Public Domain 104 (top); Hans Holbein the Younger/Wikimedia Commons/Public Domain 104 (bottom); © Jean–Marc Rosier/Wikimedia Commons/Creative Commons Attribution ShareAlike 3.0 106 (top); Raffaello Sanzio/Wikimedia Commons/Public Domain 106 (bottom); © R. Kukačka /Wikimedia Commons/Public Domain 108 (bottom left); Diebold Schilling the Older/Wikimedia Commons/Public Domain 108 (bottom right); Martin Luther Discovering

Images 376; AFP/Getty Images 381 (top), 382, 383

Maps

Wikimedia Commons/Public Domain: 123; Map Resources: all others

Acknowledgments

Careful effort has been made to trace the copyright ownership of selections included in this textbook. Errors or omissions are inadvertent and will be corrected in subsequent editions, provided written notification is made. The publisher gratefully acknowledges the following individuals and publishers for copyrighted material.

Robert O. Collins, *East African History* (Princeton: Markus Wiener Publishing, 1990), 65. (p. 55)

Frederick Lugard, *The Diaries of Lord Lugard*, Volume 2, Margery Perham and Mary Bull, eds. (Evanston, IL: Northwestern University Press, 1959). (p. 273)

Ghana National Archives, Ferguson's Report 1892. (p. 280)

How to Use the Teacher's Toolkit CD

Contents:

The Teacher's Toolkit CD contains the following materials:

- Maps
- Photos and Illustrations
- Historical Documents

Getting Started

Viewing the Teacher's Toolkit materials requires Adobe Reader® 9.0 or higher. The most recent version of Adobe Reader may be downloaded at no charge from the Adobe website at www.adobe.com. An Internet connection is required to download Reader.

Windows

Insert the CD. If it does not start automatically, open the CD's file listing and launch the file Startup. exe." Read and accept the license agreement to begin using the Teacher's Toolkit materials. Navigate within the CD using the bookmarks on the left side of the screen.

Mac

Insert the CD, click on the CD icon, and open the file "main.pdf." to begin using the Teacher's Toolkit materials.

Minimum System Requirements

Processor: Pentium IV

Operating System: Windows XP or Mac OS Leopard (version 10.5)

RAM: 256 MB

Display: 1024 x 768

Adobe Reader: version 9.0

Additional Help

Additional usage information can be found on the CD on the Usage/Printing pages. For further assistance, call BJU Press Customer Service at 1-800-845-5731.